W9-AVM-024

Richard Wiley

A
SATISFIED
MIND

West Plains, Missouri, 1951 [COURTESY DON RUSSELL].

A Satisfied Mind

THE COUNTRY MUSIC LIFE OF

Porter Wagoner

STEVE ENG

Rutledge Hill Press
Nashville, Tennessee

Copyright © 1992 Steve Eng

All rights reserved. Written permission must be secured from the publisher to use or reproduce any part of this book, except for brief quotations in critical reviews or articles.

Published in Nashville, Tennessee, by Rutledge Hill Press, 513 Third Avenue South, Nashville, Tennessee 37210.

Typography by D&T/Bailey, Inc., Nashville, Tennessee
Design by Harriette Bateman

Library of Congress Cataloging-in-Publication Data

Eng, Steve, 1940-
    A satisfied mind : the country music life of Porter Wagoner /
Steve Eng.
        p.   cm.
    Includes bibliographical references and index.
    ISBN 1-55853-133-5
    1. Wagoner, Porter.   2. Country musicians—United States—
Biography.   I. Title.
ML420.W12E5   1992
782.42'1642'092—dc20
    [B]   92-6889
                                                                 CIP MN

Printed in the United States of America
1 2 3 4 5 6 7 8 — 98 97 96 95 94 93 92

"There's something
No matter how wore
out you are, you never
feel a bit tired when
those spotlights hit you
and you see all those
smiling faces out
there."

—Porter Wagoner,
in Caleb Pirtle III's
The Grandest Day

FOR

MOTHER & FATHER

and

ANNE & OUR CHILDREN

PREFACE

In the spring of 1986 I happened to visit Porter Wagoner's office and met his office manager, Ruth B. White. I was enthusiastic over a manuscript she had written with her husband, and she quietly suggested *I* ought to write her boss's biography. Rather flippantly, by way of an answer, I sang a couple of bars of "A Satisfied Mind" and told her how flattered I was by the proposal. To clear the air, I said I had read a few things in the press I wished Porter had *not* said, back in the late seventies.

Mostly, though, I wondered if I were up to such a task. I asked my first writing friend in Nashville, *The Romantist* editor John C. Moran, Jr., and he said I had *better* do it. I called my oldest friend in music (since 1969), Bob Lind, and he said, "make sure you get into the man's music." Already I had begun listening to secondhand Porter Wagoner albums down at the Great Escape, a nostalgia nirvana off Music Row, over their generously provided headphones.

At some point my wife observed, "This isn't the usual country music story of triumph over personal problems or redemption from sin. It sounds more like an American story of hard, hard work." Yes, and I was also impressed by a recurring theme in Porter's career. Repeatedly he had seemed down, almost out—or at least left behind by a music business whose only constant is its fickle unpredictability. However, each time he had rebounded stronger than before, outshining some once-brighter stars who had long since dimmed or even fizzled. Porter appeared to have the knack for redoubling his energies at the right time and for digging in his ornate cowboy boot heels and staying put until his turn came once again.

By the late 1980s, he was more visible to millions via cable TV on The Nashville Network (TNN) than many singers of number one records. Porter Wagoner possessed a name familiarity and visual recognition that even a national politician might envy.

As I began delving, dozens of people opened their memories, personal files, and priceless scrapbooks, with consideration that was touching. In my interviews I tried to obtain anecdotes that were firsthand. The considerable dialogue comes from interviews or from documentary sources; there are no reconstructed scenes, no hypothetical conversations.

Porter and his management encouraged my research in countless charitable ways, from supplying free record albums and singles and opening Porter's professional files (other than financial, which I made no effort to see), to unlocking some important doors with a crucial phone call or letter.

Porter himself has been most of the places that country music has been these past four and one-half decades. There are few twists in the trail that the Wagoner wheels have not taken and few obstacles they have not encountered. To try to tell Porter's story has been an honor, but one with the implied obligation to portray vividly, with empathy, those situations an entertainer of his magnitude was destined to confront and endure. Not to relive the story of the Springfield–Nashville rivalries, the mid-seventies "crossover" controversies, the RCA purge of older acts, and the tragicomic imbroglio of Porter's business interests with those of Dolly Parton would be to trivialize Porter's career as well as the industry to which he has devoted his life.

I have tried to present these conflicts dispassionately, not always taking Porter's side. In many, many instances I could find no side to take, as nobody seemed to be in the right in traumatic episodes where sincere and serious professionals fought as best they could to gain or hold ground. Porter's first manager, Si Siman, believes that in show business everyone wins in the end.

So this chronicle is not an "authorized" biography, but only one author's attempt to capture an immensely complex life and career. Mistakes of fact or judgment are mine and no one else's. Those who have helped are acknowledged at the end of the book, especially the 161 persons who consented to formal interviews, plus all those who shared records, photos, clippings, documents, or just good advice. My publishers, Larry Stone and Ron Pitkin at Rutledge Hill Press, deserve special thanks for their faith and determination. Porter's sister, Lorraine Hall, has earned a whole page of gratitude, and if Roger Bishop (Booktalk/Bookpage) hadn't connected me with Howard White, this book wouldn't have happened.

Thanks, too, to Porter Wagoner for having treated me with princely regard for more years than we anticipated and for having lived a life true to himself, an audacious, creative life that, I believe, is very much worth the telling.

—Steve Eng
Nashville

CONTENTS

PART THREE
The Years of Dolly Parton

PART FOUR
The Last Great Hillbilly

Introduction
RHINESTONE REUNION
1988

When they ask who's in the picture with me,
I say, "Just someone I used to know . . ."

—Jack Clement, "Just Someone I Used to Know,"
number five hit for Porter and Dolly, 1969

Well, I'll be damned.
Here comes your ghost again . . .

—Joan Baez, "Diamonds and Rust," 1975

*P*orter Wagoner. The name rolls across the memory and into the present like one of those rhinestone-spangled wagon wheels stitched onto his famous stage costumes. With the name comes a bewildering whirl of images, facts, statistics, and snatches of gossip, all blurring together like sequins in a kaleidoscope.

Porter himself would probably shrug and matter of factly sum himself up in two plain words: country music. That's all he's ever wanted, been, or stood for. As E. W. ("Bud") Wendell, longtime manager of the Grand Ole Opry, once remarked, "Porter doesn't come to life just in front of a microphone. He's living country music when he's eating a hamburger. He's just so darned genuine. It's Porter and 'here I am.' What you see is what you get."

His career has been country-simple since the 1940s, but still you sense that Porter's personal life has grown pretty complex at times. Songs like "The Rubber Room" (about going insane) reveal his self-doubting side. His boyish grin is said to mask a temper held mostly under control. Nevertheless, whatever tensions Porter may have known, he's kept them out of the limelight, unlike some entertainers whose torments are practically part of their act. Porter Wagoner, you suspect, would sooner give up fishing for life than break his faith with audiences who expect him not only to show, but to put on a good show. As he told television news reporter Patricia Nolan in 1988, "Retirement scares me. I love working so much that I could never give it up."

Virtually anyone on this planet with the mildest interest in country music knows who you mean by "Porter." Partly it's because in that industry the more money that's made, the more everyone insists they're like a family. The bigger stars are on a first-name basis with America, whether the "late" Hank (as if he'd died recently and not in 1953), or Johnny, Merle, Loretta, Waylon, Reba, or Garth. "Jones" for George Jones and "Mister" Acuff are the exceptions that confirm the rule. "Porter" has been a country music brand name for more than thirty years. It's hard to think of anyone else who has kept at it so hard and long, on both the Opry and on television, as well as down the numbing trail of fair and concert dates.

Always the journalists have emphasized the *visual* Porter Wagoner, at times slighting the music itself, for even in a profession that rewards exhibitionists, Porter has stood out like a peacock in a parade of penguins. First, there's that once-notorious peroxide pompadour, now matured to fluffy grey. Next there's the tall, bony frame that makes the perfect clothes tree for the most written-about stage apparel in country music. Then there's the expressive, unforgettable Porter Wagoner face, making him look like a character from a country song ("long-jowled, companionable face" wrote Jack Hurst in his history of the Opry).

More than anything, though, it's the rhinestone outfits that up-stage their proud possessor. They seem divinely hand tailored for color film, whether that of the television cameraman, the magazine photographer, or the Opryland tourist. They weigh around forty pounds each, and Porter owns more than fifty of them. He wears them in such colors as red, lime green, lavender, and, especially, purple. In the mid 1950s they cost around $350 apiece (from Hollywood, where else?). Today he pays around $10,000. Porter jokes that rhinestones have climbed in cost— "Maybe Michael Jackson drove the price up." Anyway, they're a good investment, never going out of style and, as Hollywood reporter Nancy Anderson wrote in 1983, "Luckily his dimensions never change any more than rhinestones do." It's not uncommon for fans to approach Porter and say that, in part, they like his show because *he* looks like a show.

It was Porter Wagoner's syndicated television program that etched this folksy yet flamboyant persona indelibly upon country music's consciousness. It ran an unbeatable twenty years, with at least five million viewers (forty million subscribers) via eighty stations at its zenith. This, plus three and one-half decades on the Grand Ole Opry (since 1957) as one of its loyal but restless members, has made him one of the most visible presences in show business history.

All of which somewhat obscures the inevitably lengthy string of records and awards. At best count there've been more than eighty albums and numberless singles, of which eighty-one were *Billboard* chart hits. Forty-nine of them were in the Top 20, twenty-nine were Top 10, and fifteen were in the Top 5. Songs like "Green, Green Grass of Home," "The Carroll County Accident," and "The Cold, Hard Facts of Life" are unflinchingly honest country standards. Porter netted three Grammys for gospel albums, and he and Dolly Parton won three Country Music Association (CMA) awards for their duets.

As a singer, Porter has mostly avoided the pop-oriented "positive love song," preferring the grittier, harder-hitting story song. His voice has not been a crooner's but a country boy's, sounding swimming-hole happy on the fast songs and devastated and wounded on the sad ones.

Having produced his first number one hit, "A Satisfied Mind" (1955), Porter eventually began producing most of his own sessions, including the Dolly duets and her solo recordings. Often this went unacknowledged on the record labels and album cover information. As he said in 1975, "I'm really not interested in paper-credit. I just want to get them [the sessions] right. It's hard to get a live feel from a studio recording, but that's what I want." In a day when other producers would have hidden Dolly's original-sounding voice under layers of backup singers and violinists (not fiddlers), Porter as producer usually kept out of the way and let the world hear Dolly's naked vocals in all their piercing beauty.

Strangely, his least recognized activity must surely be his songwriting. His golf, his fishing, even his golden retrievers get more publicity. You might expect an artist of his stature to have written a dozen or two self-indulgent songs, and perhaps to have claimed cowriting on a few others that he touched up in the studio. In fact, about 175 Porter Wagoner songs have been recorded, many of them written with Dolly.

Thus had Porter Wagoner been increasingly occupying my mind, and his records my turntable, starting in the summer of 1986. Simultaneously, country music had been making the latest of its cyclical lurches back toward traditional material.

Porter, too, seemed to be receiving renewed mention in the trade and fan press. In the fall of 1987 he also began popping up on the newsstands, linked once again to Dolly Parton. The occasion was, naturally, the ABC-TV series "Dolly," with its projected forty-million-dollar budget. "Dolly" was a more or less weekly, hour-long variety program, showcasing many, many styles of music.

There was no particular reason to think Porter would be a guest on the show. He certainly wasn't going to call up and *ask*. They hadn't spoken person to person in years, communicating only through lawyers, national headlines, and speculations in the supermarket tabloids. However, in January 1988 *The Tennessean* announced that Dolly would be taping an entire show in Nashville, featuring various Opry stars including Porter Wagoner. There was no official word on the scope of Porter's role.

Dolly's taping was to begin February 15 in Nashville. Even a few days beforehand, Ruth White and his accountant Nancy Hurt had heard nothing. Was Porter to be used simply as one more Opry cast member, as a backup and colorful backdrop for Dolly? If so, he would walk—flatly refuse to show up. Neither of them needed *that*.

At the very last moment, word came down that Porter and Dolly would have a respectably long portion of the program on screen together.

The week of February fifteenth, as the local press reported it, was a study in contrasts, some of them surrealistic. Besides the "Dolly" show rolling through town, methodically scooping up old friends and memories, Roy Acuff would be celebrating his fiftieth anniversary on the Grand Ole Opry the following Saturday. But on Tuesday the eighteenth a letter writer to the *Nashville Banner* editorial page felt obliged to defend Nashville as *not* being a "hick hillbilly town" where "too many people" love country music. (Nashville had just lost its symphony after forty-two years, although later it was resurrected.) National print and electronic media were also noticing Nashville since on Tuesday night the Metro Council was to vote on an ordinance that would prohibit "sex" in Metro-owned buildings. They voted it down in a fit of embarrassed irritation.

At the Monday morning, February 15, Dolly Parton press conference, I decided that here was one entertainer whose personal publicity was not propaganda. Dolly Parton is as gorgeous as anyone you'll see or meet. Her face has a porcelain finish to it, recalling her own matter-of-fact statement that she spends an hour prettying-up before confronting the public.

The questions were the expected ones. What did she think of her show's ratings? What are her latest, postdiet measurements?

The most pointed exchange of the hour occurred when someone said, "A lot of people are surprised that you are going to do something with Porter Wagoner. Because the last we heard there was not a friendship there . . . "

Tactfully conceding the pains of severing their eight-year relationship, Dolly got in a thrust or two of her own. But she said that singing together again "was the thing to do. I felt that it was bigger than me and Porter. I figured we could be small if we chose to be, but the fans would like to see us be bigger than that, and they would like to see us do something together . . . this will be like a healing for both of us . . . So I got with Porter yesterday. It was wonderful, I was a bit nervous, I have to admit, because I hadn't seen Porter in a long time." She then dismissed various magazine interviews with Porter, saying that he apparently had the need to "release himself" now and then. As to whether or not the stories were accurate, Dolly neatly said that would be "beside the point."

She added, "When we were singing the duets—we were doing the pre-records—it just brought back old memories, and it just made me real emotional. It gave me chill bumps. And I just realized how great those things were." I asked her what her favorite duet with Porter Wagoner was. She named the "funny fight" songs and of their serious numbers, "Holding On to Nothin'."

The following week on Ralph Emery's "Nashville Now" television show, Porter gave his version of their poignant first meeting at the studio after so many years' pained estrangement. Dolly had been stuck in traffic and had arrived late, blurting out, "I know how punctual you are and how cranky you are when someone don't show up on time!"

"So that just sort of lightened the air between us," Porter explained to the host, "and we went to the studio and started running down the tracks. Well, the first one that we sang, I looked at Dolly and she had big goose pimples come out on her neck. And she said, 'Whooo, I'd forgotten we were *this* good.' It was like a magical moment. I told her, 'You know what, we act like a couple of kids that's gotten together that hadn't seen each other in a long time.' She told me later, 'That was the most exciting thing I've had happen to me in the last several years.'"

I attended the taping at the Ryman Auditorium.

The Ryman is a massive, red brick barn opposite the Nashville Convention Center. Nashville wouldn't be the tourist and convention magnet it is today, had not the radio (and later, TV) station WSM beamed the Grand Ole Opry from the Ryman stage from 1943 to 1974. In the 1982 Clint Eastwood film *Honkytonk Man*, Porter Wagoner, playing the character Dusty, auditioned from the Ryman stage. A bronze tablet proclaims the Ryman as being on the U.S. Department of Interior's Register of Historic Places. The building's medieval, Gothic-arched windows remind one of its beginnings in the 1890s as the Union Gospel Tabernacle, a sort of Protestant cathedral for revival and temperance meetings. The fabled Carry Nation, the hatchet-swinging smasher of saloons, once appeared onstage. Its founder, steamboat magnate Capt. Tom Ryman, had been converted in a tent meeting in 1885. He later lived on Rutledge Hill, which afforded a clear view of his massive tabernacle. And with hardly any exaggeration, Jack E. Custer wrote of Captain Ryman in 1979, "Had that not happened, it is possible Dolly Parton would never have become a superstar and subsequently appear on the cover of *Playboy* . . ."

At the Ryman you sit in venerable oaken pews dating from the 1890s. Overhead hangs the balcony with the legend "1897. Confederate Gallery." It was built for the Confederate veterans' reunion by Thomas H. Yeaman, and today's cameras and lights seemed incongruously modern. Everyone from Caruso to Bela Lugosi to Gene Autry and Champion has played the Ryman. Occasionally America gets to see the auditorium on the movie screen; extras were paid around twenty-five dollars a day to sit in period clothes and clap during such films as *Coal Miner's Daughter*, the Loretta Lynn story, and *Sweet Dreams*, Patsy Cline's story.

Before the filming started, Dolly came out, followed by Porter. They began working on us, the audience, almost as if they were someone else's warmup act. Both of them were "on" the second they were visible.

Dolly wore a ruffled, ankle-length, silver lamé dress, cut characteristically low, and Porter was as pretty as Dolly in his lavender suit agleam with sparklers and his rose-colored shirt with a white, Roy Rogers-style tie.

In a passage that was spliced in later, Dolly said, "When I think about my memories of Nashville, one man stands out in my mind more than anybody else. He's the one who actually introduced me to big-time television." Then followed footage of her 1967 début on "The Porter Wagoner Show." Porter, in a red rhinestone outfit, was seen presenting the twenty-one-year-old Dolly. She was to sing her hit "Dumb Blonde," and he added, "She ain't no dumb blonde."

Now, two decades later, they were joking again for us and the television audience about the sure-fire products of their erstwhile sponsors, the Chattanooga Medicine Company, makers of Wine of Cardui for a woman's time of the month and Black Draught. Said Dolly, "We were *awful*." They jumped into the Black Draught jingle—"Smile from the inside out"—and Dolly reminded everyone that it was a laxative. "And a *good* one, too," put in Porter, ever the consummate pitchman.

Then Dolly volunteered, "I just wanted to thank you right here on network television for all the years that you spent trying to help me build my career. I know we've had our problems . . . "

Next they moved to the television set onstage to watch another vintage re-run. "Remember, I look old in this," Porter warned. It was one of their classic Breeze commercials, in the words of Lola Scobey "unlike any other sixty seconds of broadcasting on the American TV screen." Dolly, onscreen, asked, "Why, Porter! Flowers for me?" Porter was holding one of those cheap "two-way towels" alive with gaudy orange flowers printed on both sides, part of the Breeze "collection," he revealed, available only inside boxes of Breeze detergent. This soap-plus-towel bargain was "the right combination," Porter insisted, reinforcing the title of the famous song he wrote and they recorded.

They moved to center stage for a medley of their hits. Behind them was Porter's original band, the Wagonmasters.

When Porter hit his opening lyric, "It's a lesson too late for the learning," there was a current of excitement. Then they plunged into their first duet record, "The Last Thing on My Mind," from 1967, a song in which nearly every line evokes the passions of their 1974 breakup. "Fight and Scratch," which followed, was one of their humorous marital combat specials written by Dolly, which helped convince many that they were married to each other. Next, "Holding On to Nothin'," had Dolly sing, "So turn me *loose!*" After that "farewell" vibration, they closed with a song Dolly wrote with her preacher–aunt, Dorothy Jo Hope, "Daddy Was an Old-Time Preacher Man."

On the first take of the medley, Porter missed a line and laughed,

"You sing so good on the solo, I'm listening and I mess up." There'd been other mistakes, so the whole had to be redone. Some more lines were garbled, but they sang right through these new blunders, Dolly saying, "Come on, let's finish it . . . we made a career out of screwin' up." This final gaffe was left in, a document of their legendary looseness that still had that unforgettable brother–sister closeness that always made Porter and Dolly seem tighter than a mere duet.

Thursday, February 19, was the night of Dolly's taping at the Grand Ole Opry House, opulent successor to the Ryman. Onstage, Porter was tuning up the audience. Since all the tickets had been free, he was saying, "This is great proof that if you make the ticket price right you'll get a crowd."

Dolly appeared and joked about her old days on Porter's TV show, especially the size and solidity of both their hair-dos ("if we'd have run into each other, we'd have *broken* our hair . . . ").

All in all, the "Dolly" tapings (aired March 19) created as honest a country music show as anyone could have put together, in spite of and because of the hundreds of thousands of dollars the package must have cost.

For Roy Acuff's fiftieth anniversary on the Opry, Saturday, February 20, Porter, as usual, hosted two half-hour segments, as he had the night before. He opened with his 1955 number one hit, "A Satisfied Mind," the song that persuaded the Opry to offer him permanent membership.

In 1957 Porter had become the twenty-fourth regular member of the Grand Ole Opry. In 1969 Dolly Parton had become its fifty-fourth, being already a member of Porter's road and TV show, and, thanks to him, on RCA records.

On February 20, Dolly was Porter's guest in both of his segments. They did their duet medley, including one snipped from the final television version, "Just Someone I Used to Know," a Grammy nominee for them. Roy Acuff said he hoped they'd record again. At some point, though, entwining Porter's career with Dolly's distorts and distracts. But show business fanfare is never balanced. Of all celebrities, The Man in Purple understands this.

Even by the early eighties, the overworked label *legend* had begun to attach itself to Porter Wagoner. He probably deserved it more than most, and the list of legends to which he probably belongs is shorter than some might suppose. Such a list might include Woody Guthrie, certainly Jimmie Rodgers, Hank, Marty, Patsy. Of the living, Roy Acuff, Bill Monroe, Hank Snow, Johnny, Willie, George Jones, Loretta, Waylon. Such lists should reflect much more than musical talent. They should signify such intangibles as presence, influence, stamina, and the ability to jam five or ten careers into one lifetime. Another ingredient is enough character to surmount various personal or even professional shortcomings. Such restrictions shorten the list, and short lists are easier to carry around.

In 1985 George Jones asked rhetorically in the Max D. Barnes/ Troy Seals song, "Who's Going to Fill Their Shoes?" At the time, the answer was the New Traditionalists like Ricky Skaggs or mavericks like Steve Earle, whose vehement traveling songs recalled tunes like Porter's "Highway Headin' South." In a few more years the ranks of traditional-sounding acts had expanded, with stars like Patty Loveless and Randy Travis aggressively recapturing country music's lost ground.

Today, however, the hit charts are determined by computerized listener surveys; yet during most of Porter's recording career, folks were still going into stores to buy single records. His first record was available on 78 rpm only. Changed also, mercifully, is that condition of poverty, the threat or memory of which formed a bond between performers and audiences. "Back in the Good Old Days When Times Were Bad" Dolly titled one of her songs. Johnny Cash picked cotton and later sold vacuum cleaners door-to-door in Memphis. Hank Snow ran away to work on ships in the North Atlantic off Nova Scotia at the age of twelve to escape his child-battering stepfather. Young George Jones sang for tips on the streets of Beaumont, Texas. Merle Haggard was born in a converted boxcar in California and was reborn in a solitary cell in San Quentin prison.

Porter Wagoner knows the posterior of a mule, the inside of a shoe factory, the sulphur fumes of a foundry, and the relative charm of a butcher shop. He never dropped *into* high school. Entertainers like him learned all too many things the hard way, not so much because they knew that experience is the best teacher but because they couldn't find or afford any other.

In 1975 Jack Hurst in his book, *Nashville's Grand Ole Opry*, called Porter "a latter-day Hank Williams." Hank Williams, still alive when Porter signed with RCA, was not yet four years old when Porter Wayne Wagoner was born.

The year was 1927. The place was Howell County in southeastern Missouri, down near the Arkansas border.

In the Ozarks.

A
SATISFIED
MIND

PART ONE

TAKE ME FAR ACROSS THE WIDE MISSOURI

The state has always harbored doubts
about anything associated with a large city.
Citizens believed that the good
in mankind—such as there was—
flourished in a rural setting.

—Paul C. Nagel,
Missouri: A Bicentennial History (1977)

One of the kids was different,
He looked beyond the hills,
Over the corn, over the cows,
Over the sorghum mills . . . "

—from "The Boy from Lanton,"
by Anita Jones Caldwell
of Thayer, Missouri

1

HOWELL COUNTY

With his horse, gun and violin,
the wanderer had come into the heart
of the Ozark wilderness . . .

—Harold Bell Wright,
The Shepherd of the Hills (1907)

The immigration consisted mostly of farmers and
mechanics . . . some of the settlements being 15 miles
apart—yet the early settlers thought nothing of
neighboring and assisting each other for a distance of
15 miles . . . No place at that time was thought worth
settling unless it had a spring on it . . . The
people then had many advantages that they are
deprived of now, in the way of wild meat, abundance of
honey and fine range.

—William Monks,
Howell County pioneer of 1844,
A *History of Southern Missouri and Arkansas* (1907)

Missouri's license plates proclaim it to be the Show Me State, as in "I'm from Missouri . . . you'll have to *show* me." Strong personalities like Mark Twain and President Harry Truman seem to embody this supposed local trait of hard-headed skepticism, salted down with worldly humor.

The first permanent settler in Howell County was Josiah Howell, who led a wagon train crowded with his large family out of Smith County, Tennessee, in 1839. They stopped at a spring, the same spring that one of Porter's grandfathers would stop at more than forty years later, and here they settled. The spring became known as the Town Spring, as the village of West Plains grew up around it. A glimpse of it may be seen today in, of all places, the basement of the public library, burbling from a rusty pipe under a plate of clear plastic. West Plains is on the edge of what is called the Big Springs country of Missouri.

Sometime before the Civil War, Porter's colorful great-grandfather,

Lark Allen, arrived in Howell County. Larkin Allen was born in 1833 and married a local girl, Sarah, from nearby Koshkonong. They built their cabin about six miles from where Porter was born. Lark Allen was a dashing horseman, and he wore two "pearl-handled" (probably ivory-gripped) pistols. He was to become a marked man, in the bull's-eye sense of the term.

Lark Allen was a pie supper fiddler. Holding pie suppers was a rural tradition to raise funds for the school. Girls would prepare pies or boxed meals to be auctioned off to the "right" boy, or so they hoped. Several relatives told Porter's late cousin, Dixon Wagoner, that when Lark fiddled, "tears would run down his cheeks and he seemed to be suffering great loneliness and sorrow." (Dixon tape-recorded his recollections in the 1970s.) And Porter's namesake, Uncle Porter Bratcher, used to say that his own grandfather, as a small boy, would sit in the back of the schoolhouse while Lark performed, proudly holding both of Lark's ivory-handled revolvers.

Lark Allen needed both of his six-guns. A horse-breeder, once he surprised four of his neighbors trying to rustle one of his prized Morgan horses (or maybe steal it back, since there are differing judgments of Lark's character). The thieves opened fire—missed!—and took off, with Lark in pursuit. Suddenly he halted, wheeled about, and whistled. His stolen steed responded, rearing up under its surprised rider and giving Lark the split second he was maneuvering for. He needed no more. He dropped the rider dead, then charged the others, scattering them.

West Plains had been founded in 1848, Howell County in 1857. By 1860 the town had 150 residents and the county, 3,169, 1 percent being slaves. Ozark pioneers didn't need slaves on their hilly little farms. They couldn't have afforded them anyway.

No state had less need to take sides in the approaching disunion than Missouri, and no state tried harder to stay neutral. Ultimately, no state gave more troops to both sides proportionate to its population.

Slavery was less an issue with the average soldier, North or South, than is generally supposed. Many fought for the Union, not out of a desire to end slavery but to preserve a nation that had already won three wars. Many fought for the Confederacy to defend their homeland, which was being invaded, and because they believed in their legal right to secede. In Howell County, as in neighboring Kentucky and Tennessee, the populace had divided loyalties, with Confederate sympathy predominating. Lark Allen supported the Union, thus becoming a pariah to his neighbors.

Fighting in Missouri broke out in 1861. Late in 1861, Union troops attacked the West Plains courthouse on the square, the same square where Porter and Jan Howard would hold jobs in the 1940s. In the skirmish, six Confederates were killed and sixty taken prisoner. Down along South Fork Creek, Porter's boyhood haunt near the Allen farm, armed guerrillas—or bushwhackers—fought a pitched battle. With Union sympathizers usually away fighting—or fleeing—their Confederate partisan neighbors might fall upon the defenseless families. Porter's sister, Lorraine Hall of Springfield, Missouri, recalls hearing that women would hide their food under the floorboards of their homes because the bushwhackers "would ride in to a farm home, if the man was away, and shoot a fat hog or beef, then order the woman of the house to cook it for them."*

Such a band of saddle trash descended on the Allen farm. Lark was off in the Union army—he was of the hated German extraction that usually sided with the Union. His wife, Sarah, was alone, pregnant, and sick in bed. She had hidden her baby clothes under the mattress, but the bushwhackers, between five and seven of them, burned her bed clothes and her mattress. One of them commandeered her baby clothes for his wife. Primarily after Lark's money, which he had buried, they pistol-whipped Sarah across the breast, but she wouldn't talk.

During the assault, the marauders' masks had slipped down, and Sarah knew who they were. When Lark came home on furlough, he forced her to reveal their names. Lorraine recalls hearing that Lark went to one neighbor's home—called him to his porch—and shot him dead across his threshold. Dixon Wagoner recounted how, one by one, the offenders' bodies began turning up, shot to death.

While settling these accounts, Lark had been absent without leave from the Union army. His captain showed up and offered him leniency if he would return, but he refused. Sarah was unguarded and now in even direr peril because of Lark's methodical retribution against her abusers. So the army placed a $200 bounty on the head of Larkin Allen, deserter.

Sarah, whom Aunt Nova remembered had defended her home with pistols and knives, escaped north by wagon.

Only a dozen families stayed in Howell County. By 1863 West Plains was deserted. A few months later the Confederate guerrillas burned West Plains to the ground, lest it become a Union outpost.

Families, including the Allens, gradually moved back after the war. Lark and Sarah had two daughters, Martha, Porter's great-aunt (born 1867), who lived till 1955, and Susan Ellen, Porter's grandmother (born 1866), who lived till 1945. Both these children told Porter's sisters, Lola and Lorraine, of the bushwhackers' outrages against their mother. And their memories of April 13, 1872.

They were in the house when they heard shots.

*See also Michael Fellman, "Women as Victims and Participants" in *Inside War: The Guerrilla Conflict in Missouri During the American Civil War* (1989).

Larkin Allen, Porter's great-grandfather, Howell County horse breeder and pie supper fiddler. Born in 1833 and murdered in 1872, Lark lived near the site of the Myatt schoolhouse. Not shown are his two revolvers [Courtesy Jean Wagoner].

Lark had been riding up the lane toward the cabin when seven neighbors firing from cover had laid a fusillade across the road. Lark was pitched from the saddle, his Morgan stallion slain, too. Staging their ambuscade from behind trees and brush, they well deserved the cowardly designation of bushwhackers.

Drawn by the sound of the volley, Lark's wife and his sister rushed down to the site. His sister picked up her fallen brother's rifle and squeezed off a shot, but her aim was off. Sarah had lunged at her, deflecting her fire.

Fortunately.

The killing-time was now over for the Allens. All the murderers were known to Lark's wife. Lorraine says the Wagoners have always shunned certain families whose forebears had murdered her great-grandfather.

One of Porter's grandfathers, John G. Wagoner, was twenty when he arrived in West Plains around 1883. Most suitably, he was riding a magnificent black stallion, which he paused to water at the town spring. So impressed were the townsfolk that one of them offered him fifteen acres of land around the spring for his horse. In 1933, on the occasion of his golden wedding anniversary, John Wagoner laughed to a reporter, "Why, I wouldn't trade that horse for the whole damned town!"

He had been born in Illinois as John Wagner; but, unable to read or write, he had permitted his name to become Wagoner. In May 1883 he married Susan Ellen Allen, daughter of Sarah and the martyred Lark Allen. Grandpa John, Porter's sister Lorraine remembers, was an outspoken, "full-blooded Irishman, red-headed, mustached, high-tempered . . . everything was 'dad-gummed' or 'doggone.'" His wife, Ellen, was sweet and placid, habitually calming down her husband with "Now John, now John."

Porter's other grandfather, Isaac W. Bridges, sounds like a composite of a couple of Dolly Parton songs: "Daddy Was an Old Time Preacher Man" and "Travelin' Man," about the roving, rural peddler. He was an itinerant preacher for the Christian Church, a Church of Christ offshoot. Traveling by buggy, he dispensed the gospel and sold spectacles along the way. He was also an itinerant photographer. In stature and build, Porter always reminded his family of his grandfather Bridges.

The preacher had a daughter named Bertha May, born in 1891. In 1908 she married Charles E. Wagoner, son of John and Susan Ellen Wagoner. Charley and Bertha were Porter's parents.

Charley never progressed past third grade. By 1917 the family had moved to Kansas where Charley took a railroad section gang job. He cleared brush, tamped in new ties, and spiked them down.

The children included Oscar (born 1909), Lola (born 1912), and Lorraine (born 1917). The Wagoners lived in a railroad section house in the little one-street town of Redfield, Kansas.

Bertha Wagoner did laundry and sewed for people, thus saving for her own sewing machine. On his day off from the railroad, Charley worked in the local restaurant. Charley never took vacations, but Bertha and the children did, riding by his free railroad pass back to Howell County, 200 miles away. They'd stay a month, visiting grandparents, aunts, and uncles, such as great-uncle Dow Cannon and his wife, Martha, a daughter of Lark Allen. The Cannons reportedly owned seventeen farms in Howell County.

A son, Glenn Lee, was born to the Wagoners in 1924. With this extra mouth to feed, the family pondered seriously an offer made by Uncle Dow. He'd offered them a 180-acre farm near Lanton to live on if they pleased. The year was 1925. The farm they moved to is still in operation about eighteen miles south of West Plains, run by Porter's boyhood chum, Kenneth Chapin.

South Fork Creek circles the farm on the west side, enriching the moist bottom land so good for planting. On the west side is a large bluff. A cedar-lined lane runs up from the road to the top of the hill, where the Wagoners' large white house stood among the sheltering oaks. I'd been

The family of John Wagoner, circa. 1909. Back row, left to right: sons Grover, Clarence, and Charles (Porter's father), Charles's wife Bertha (Bridges) Wagoner, and son Othel. Seated: daughter Dora and her son, John Wagoner, daughter Nova, and wife Ellen Wagoner (Susan Ellen Allen, daughter of Larkin Allen) [COURTESY LORRAINE HALL].

told it had been torn down, that it all was gone. Yet Porter's birthplace still stands, the bedroom in which he was born being all that is left of the house. It's a storeroom today, jammed full of old furniture. A few feet away stands a newer house.

Down below sits the old barn, still in use.

The year was 1927, and television was a-stirring. On February 3, John L. Baird told the world about his television system at Glasgow, Scotland, and on April 7 television was demonstrated to President Herbert Hoover.

Some would say that the first week of August 1927 was the most important week in country music history. In an empty hat warehouse on State Street in Bristol, a town that straddles the Virginia–Tennessee border, Ralph Peer was conducting auditions. An executive for the Victor Talking Machine Company, Peer was a dilettante who raised camellias and was a bit embarrassed at how he earned his living. Earlier he had recorded what was called "nigger music," which he tactfully had renamed "race music"; and now he was deep in that twin musical ghetto of "hillbilly music," a term he claimed to have first employed commercially. *

That week in Bristol, Peer's unerring ear was harkening to the sounds of two immortal music acts. The first was the Carter Family, whose impeccable harmonies would influence, at least indirectly, every white southern singing group for generations. The second act was Jimmie Rodgers, the Yodeling Brakeman, who became the first superstar of country music. Rodgers set the stereotype of lavish living and tragic early death.

During that week, both the Carters and Jimmie Rodgers recorded their first sides for Victor.

On August 12, Dr. H. A. Thompson from Lanton, Missouri, visited the Charley Wagoner farm three miles away in the South Fork township. Charley and Bertha were, respectively, forty-one and thirty-five years old. With the assistance of Kenneth Chapin's mother, Dr. Thompson delivered their fifth child and third son, Porter Wayne Wagoner, at eleven o'clock in the morning.

---

*Mitford M. Mathews' *Dictionary of Americanisms* (1951) records the earliest known use of *hillbilly*, in the New York *Journal*, April 23, 1900: "In short, a Hill-Billie is a free and untrammelled white citizen of Alabama, who lives in the hills, has no means to speak of, dresses as he can, talks as he pleases, drinks whiskey when he gets it, and fires off his revolver as the fancy takes him."

2

WAGONER'S LAD

Take me far across the wide Missouri,
To a ridge where white oak trees grow tall and slim,
To a little hillside farm in Hopewell County,
Let me see my childhood playground once again.

—Porter, "Childhood Playground" (1973)

My daddy was not known outside of
Howell County.
But there his name held the highest regard.

—Porter, unpublished recitation

A good sense of the times and the place can be gleaned from the pages of the *Howell County Gazette*.

On August 18, 1927, six days after Porter's birth, the *Gazette* reported the "thirty-third bank failure in Missouri since January." There were headlines like "A Resident Held for Selling Home Brew" and "Stole Chickens in the Night," the latter about two thieves who earned two years in jail for stealing forty Rhode Island Reds. And there was an advertisement for the women's remedy that would be a mainstay sponsor of Porter's television show: "Nurse Advises Weak, Run-Down Women to Take Cardui."

On January 5, 1928, a family reunion was reported at Lanton, at the home of Mr. and Mrs. John Wagoner. Mrs. Wagoner, daughter of the bushwhacked Lark Allen, boasted of having five sons, two daughters, and seventeen grandchildren, "all living." Baby Porter was in attendance, no doubt.

The Depression was on its way. Down in the Wagoners' neighborhood of South Fork, petty thieves were hitting the corncribs. "Auto tramps" were a new problem, vagabonds who would bum a tank of gasoline then move on. All the bank failures were being blamed on the Republicans. Some Missourians were being forced to form their own "anti-chicken thief association."

Then in the week of October 24, 1929, it finally happened: the stock market toppled. At least the Charley Wagoner household had a solid farmouse roof over their heads, food enough to eat, and even a surplus of cream and eggs they could sell on the side.

Young Porter was brought up in large part by his teenaged sister Lola, who acted as his second mother. Once, though, when he was three years old, "Porter wouldn't even be alive if Mother hadn't been hard-headed like she was." The girls and Mother were washing dishes and Porter was eating a stick of peppermint candy. Suddenly Lola cried, "Mama, this baby's choked!" A piece of candy was jammed crossways down his throat. "Pound him in the back!" his mother cried.

"Mama, that don't work," Lola shouted.

"Shake him by the heels."

"That don't work—"

Bertha grabbed Porter, sat him down by the back door and jammed her fingers down his throat. But she couldn't get it. Lola screamed. Lorraine ran into the fields for her father, crying, "He's dyin'." Porter was turning blue. Finally his mother "shoved it on through," Porter retells the story. There was blood on her fingers and on Porter's mouth.

Porter remembers seeing his father hurrying up from South Fork Creek in his iron-wheeled wagon, hay falling out, whipping his mules, till he finally reined in, telling one of the mules, "Whoa-a-a-a, Pete."

In the years 1930–34, in Missouri alone 18,000 farms were fore-closed. Still, one-fourth of all Americans were trying to live off the land. In the summer of 1932 disgruntled World War I veterans, the Bonus Marchers, were tear-gassed into retreat in Washington, D.C. Men sold apples on street corners. In St. Louis, Missouri, men, women, even children, were visibly scrounging for food scraps in the city dumps. That fall, one bank in four across the country failed. By then close to half the nation's workers were out of a job.

In 1932 Bing Crosby and Rudy Vallee each had a number one hit with the same song, "Brother, Can You Spare a Dime?" Down in Nash-ville, Grand Ole Opry regulars were getting five dollars for a Saturday night's work. Yet the Blue Yodeler, Jimmie Rodgers, was earning $2,000 a week. Record sales were down, however, with only six million sold in 1932, compared with 104 million in 1927.

Deep in Howell County, Lorraine and her older siblings could only ask themselves whether they had voted right in electing to leave Kansas. Sure, they had one of the finest farmhouses in the area—four rooms, big front porch, a screened back porch, a deep well—and they boasted one of the biggest barns around. Back in Kansas, though, they could afford coal—the railroad used plenty—but here they had to chop wood. They were always having to go down to the wood lot for more.

Older brother Oscar worked for other farmers when he could, leaving more work on the shoulders of Lola and Lorraine. Glenn Lee and especially little Porter were mostly too young to help.

As anyone who knows Porter can attest, he's never on time for appointments. He's early. Charley Wagoner got his family up at four every morning. If a visitor made the mistake of staying as late as 8:30 in the evening, Charley would make a show of taking out his watch and emphatically winding it.

The Wagoners had twenty cows, Jerseys mostly, which had to be milked by hand, then the cream extracted by a hand-cranked separator. They gathered the eggs from the Rhode Island Reds and white Leghorns, hens that had been hatched in the 300-egg incubator warmed by a kerosene light. Bertha raised little chicks on a brooder stove, also lit by a kerosene lamp and shielded by a metal canopy. The year-old hens were sold and replaced by young pullets.

There were hogs to be fed corn and later butchered and hickory smoked, then salted down in barrels because of no electricity and no refrigeration. The Wagoners raised sweet and Irish potatoes, which had to be dug in the fall. In the spring the family would pick wild greens, and in summer Bertha would put up blackberries, peaches, and apples.

To the north spread a one-thousand-acre forest. Lorraine especially felt isolated in spite of all the relatives in the area. The family had no telephone, even though phone service had reached West Plains in the 1890s; and they had no electricity (it didn't come to the South Fork area until around 1956). They had no church and no Sunday school. Once a year, maybe, a Pentecostal preacher might arrive and drive out the devils and work some healings in open-air revival meetings. These would go on for days, held in brush arbors made of poles and tentlike canopies crafted from overhanging pieces of brush.

Charley Wagoner may have stood six-foot-three, but he was not strong. In time, arthritis would fell him completely. In her manuscript memoir, "That Was Yesterday," Lorraine writes:

> Our father worked on the farm from sun-up to sun-down. He was deep in debt, even owed for the cows that we milked, and there was no hope in sight. The droughts came and fields burned up; sometimes the floods came and washed the crops away! I've seen my father cry in despair. There were no government programs back then. I have seen patch upon patch on his clothes. Still our father and mother carried on. How it must have grieved them, trying so hard and not being able to succeed.

Historian Duane Myer says that the Missouri droughts of 1930, 1934, and 1936 "withered the crops, dried up ponds, creeks, and wells,

Above: *Earliest known picture of Porter (front row, center) being held up by his dad* [COURTESY LORRAINE HALL]. *Below: Class of 1937, Hopewell School, Howell County. Front row, left to right: Zela Lawhorn, Lola Holloway (Mrs. J. D. Harris), Sybil Lawhorn, Billy Lawhorn, Burl Holloway, Oline Holloway, Clarence Cole; second row, left to right: Berniece Holloway, Nellie Mae Stephens, Billy Stephens, Porter (note bare feet); back row: Euel Holloway, J. D. Love, Norman Holloway, Glenn Lee Wagoner, Roy Holloway and (teacher) Elsie Eldringhoff (Elsie Bohrer). One-room school in the background* [COURTESY MRS. LOLA HARRIS, RESTORATION BY DOUG BRACHEY].

and crazed the parched land like an old plate left too long in the oven."
Also in 1936, grasshoppers ruined a million acres of Missouri crops.

One morning when he was around four years old, Porter woke up
crying. Startled, his mother told Charley to light the lamp. They heard
something smack into the wall, then noticed *blood* on Porter's pillow. A
rat had chewed off part of his right ear and left a wound over his eyebrow.
The scars are visible yet.

Until then, his mother hadn't let any cats into the house, but her
policy changed immediately. The cats made straight for the leather divan
where they rousted and killed two rats. The granary, filled with wheat and
shelled corn, had been too close to the house and had attracted the rats,
and with doors and windows open for ventilation, they'd gotten in.

Once a week from then on, the cats had their day indoors.

The Lee Chapin family lived less than half a mile from the
Wagoners. Their son Kenneth remembers, "We had plenty to eat and
enough to wear . . . but we didn't have no money." Even nearer lived
the Harv Holloways, several of whose numerous children Bertha Wagoner helped to deliver. Often the Wagoners shared flour and sugar with
the Holloways, who were painfully poor. Ruth Lawhorn, a Holloway
relative, recalls four-year-old Porter fetching her a pail of milk for her two
small children. Burl Holloway says at times he went to bed hungry and
points up a contrast between the two families: at school Porter had mustard on his biscuit and bacon sandwich, and Burl didn't. Burl, who
"hunted, fished, trapped and fought with Porter," says Porter "was raised
to do without a lot of things, so he understands how the next fellow feels."

Porter wrote a song, "Harold Dee," about Harold Dee Holloway.
Harold remembers he and Porter would climb up red sapling trees and
"ride" the boughs down until they touched the ground. Porter remembers
having a crush at age nine on Bernice Holloway, who doesn't remember
Porter doing other than "normal things boys do, like teasing girls with
lizards."

All the neighbors would get together once a season when the big
threshing machines came through to thresh their wheat. Then the
women would cook big dinners out of everything they had on hand. In
the winter the farmers would go up to the Pease Moore mill at West
Plains and have their wheat ground into flour and their corn into meal.

Porter's closest friend was his brother Glenn Lee. The family
called him "Bud" and Porter "Pug." Both of them had whitish blond hair
when they were young and some people thought they were twins. They
were the staunchest allies of their sister Lorraine, or "Rain" as they called
her. They went to school with her, arriving early as she earned four

dollars a month for janitorial duties. They'd help her start the fire in the wintertime.

After she married Ed Hall, Glenn and Porter would visit Lorraine on weekends. All three young men would fish at night with a lantern, "gig fishing" it was called. *

At dinner the boys sat along the wall on a bench. Overhead hung a shotgun on a rack, which they would eye with silent longing. One year there was a turkey shoot—shooting at stationary targets with a turkey as the prize and Charley said to Porter, "Son, if you're big enough to plow, I think you can handle the old shotgun." Porter was trusted with the shotgun; he scored high and won a turkey.

When they hunted, Glenn and Porter and neighbor friends used .22 rifles for possum, squirrels, and rabbits. Once, recalls Norman Holloway, Glenn was starting to unload his .22 and it went off, the slug passing through Porter's trouser leg between the ankle and the knee.

In the wintertime they set steel traps by the creeks for possums and "civy cats" (polecats or skunks). The skunk smells permeated their clothes and were especially noticeable when they got near the stove in the house. Porter wrote a song about such an experience, "Wake Up, Jacob": "As I waited there for Jacob to unlock the door, the polecat's perfume filled the morning air, And the odor was so strong that my eyes burned, and as the smell began to curl my hair . . ." Porter and Glenn would trap rabbits in wooden boxes about two and one-half feet long, with a door propped open by a forked stick and baited with corn, a turnip, or an apple core. They sold the rabbit pelts for ten cents apiece to the mailman who came to the school; he'd string the pelts across his car.

Despite his third-grade education, Charley Wagoner served on the Hopewell school district board. The one-room Hopewell school, serving grades one through eight, was heated by a wood stove but had no water supply; finally, in 1941, someone dug a well. The Hopewell school was used for church services when a preacher could be found—and for the inevitable pie suppers.

Since Porter lived only a quarter-mile from school, he was the one sent to fetch water from the Chapins' pump. Porter had the intelligence to make this task last hours longer than necessary, and once when assigned to cut a Christmas tree—about an hour's work—stretched it out all day. Sometimes he argued with the teacher or teased the teacher in

---

*Porter designed the Nighthawk fishing boat for the Winner Company of Dickson, Tennessee. This 17.5-foot boat is equipped with black lights that magnify the fishing line so you can tell if it even quivers with a nibble. Porter told Robert K. Oermann of *The Tennessean* that it was "the first of its kind in the world." The lights are under the seats, to shine down under the water.

Above: *Left to right: Glenn Lee Wagoner, Charley Wagoner, Bertha Wagoner, and Porter in front of their farmhouse* [COURTESY LOLA BRANT]. Below left: *Young Porter* [COURTESY LOLA BRANT]. Below right: *Glenn Lee Wagoner, Porter's older brother and musical mentor* [COURTESY LORRAINE HALL].

class, remembers Lola (Holloway) Harris. Porter admits, "Maybe I was a mischievous kid . . . but the teachers could make you more that way." Burl Holloway recalls Porter bringing a cap pistol to class and Norman Holloway adds they would use red berries from wild bushes to shoot the teacher in the rear when she was writing on the blackboard.

His teacher in 1937 was Elsie Eldringhoff. She remembers going ice-skating with her class at noon on South Fork Branch. However, this had to be discontinued, "because the boys were a wee bit reckless." In a letter in 1989, Elsie wrote:

> Had it not been for a boy named Porter, school might not have been so interesting. He did, indeed, keep things lively. Porter's big, broad grin kept his *rear* out of trouble several times.

A few years later a lax male teacher let the boys leave the classroom to hunt squirrels with their slingshots. The school board found out, and that ended that.

Porter did at least average work. He had several above average marks in reading, some in writing; he and Glenn got "excellent" in music.

By 1939 there were 849,300 radios in Missouri. In the 1930s the radio was like a member of the family. Like television a decade later, it brought people together. The house that contained a radio attracted all the neighbors.

At the Charley Wagoner farmhouse, Saturday night was Opry night. Neighbors like the Holloways would gather around the Wagoners' radio, which was powered by a car battery brought into the house and hooked up with cables. A ground wire was run outside to a metal rod stuck in the earth. Porter remembers improving the reception by going outside and pouring water on the wire. Kenneth Chapin, whose parents also had a radio, says, "You couldn't hear nothing . . . you could hear a *word* once in a while."

The origins of the Grand Ole Opry lie, in part, in the Ozarks. Around 1918 a reporter from the Memphis *Commercial Appeal*, George D. Hay, was covering a funeral at Mammoth Springs, Arkansas. Someone invited Hay, later known as the Solemn Old Judge, to an all night hoedown in a lantern-lit log cabin. The night of music enchanted him, and he determined to bring that sound to the airwaves.

Hay became a Memphis radio announcer, rated most popular among 120,000 readers of *Radio Digest* magazine. By 1924 he had started the "National Barn Dance" show in Chicago, a fact always minimized by Nashville-slanted country music histories, such as those written by Hay himself. By 1925 he had started what became the Grand Ole Opry over WSM at Nashville, and the Opry's first star was Uncle Dave

Macon, who had played his banjo and sung for tourists in the Ozarks in 1920.

The Wagoners no doubt listened to the "National Barn Dance" show since, for a time, it was more popular than the Opry. During the forties, Porter remembers also liking "Suppertime Frolic" (WJJD–Chicago), a pioneer country disc jockey show.

Porter's parents owned a Victrola, and Porter was a big fan of Bill and Charlie Monroe's bluegrass records, purchased by mail from Montgomery Ward on the RCA Bluebird label, their budget line. Bill Monroe had evolved his old-time hillbilly into what was called "bluegrass," featuring his high tenor voice and violent, fast mandolin picking. Bill Monroe was Porter's first musical idol, and the music store in West Plains always laid aside its latest Bill Monroe product for Porter. After playing a Bill Monroe record for his sister Lola, he would ask, "Isn't that the purtiest thing you ever heard?" Remarks Lola, "It *was* pretty, but he was obviously getting something out of it I was not."

At church, Charley Wagoner sang with immense feeling and considerable volume, tears welling in his eyes on numbers like "City on the Hill" and "When the Roll Is Called Up Yonder." He would plunge from tenor on one line to bass on the next, unmindful of the change. He simply gave his singing all he had. Charley and two neighbors were in demand for the Christmas sing at the Hopewell school. At the pie suppers held there, the Wagoners were noted for singing "Beautiful Gleanings."

Porter was ten when he made his public singing debut at Lorraine's urging. Porter was real bashful, and Lorraine would blackmail him into singing. She would say, "Young man, I'll tell Mama on you for smokin' them cigarettes." Lorraine used to clean up Porter's grammar to help him sing better.

Lorraine married at sixteen, but the marriage didn't last. She miscarried her first baby on a cattle drive. Next she married Ed Hall of the singing Hall Brothers. This marriage lasted, although at the outset they were so poor Lorraine sold her wristwatch and even her guitar. Lola married Ed's brother Earl, later a noted auctioneer.

The Halls were gospel singers. The Wagoners were already Baptists, Charley having been converted by a preacher. Aunt Martha Cannon was a Methodist. And Grandmother Ellen was a Pentecostal, a source of strength in her marriage to the red-faced, red-haired Irishman John Wagoner. Grandma Wagoner was prone to shouting her praise of the Lord and to telling Aunt Martha about her communion with the Holy Ghost. And grandfather Bridges was, of course, a Church of Christ preacher.

Porter was baptized in South Fork Creek by the Reverend Mr. Endicott.

All that's left of the Wagoner farmhouse. The room in which Porter was born is now converted into a storage shed [PHOTO BY AUTHOR].

Porter, Glenn, Lorraine, and some Hall brothers were present at one of the great social events of the season, probably in 1940. Actually it was more an antisocial event that we might call The Great Square Dance Brawl. A wooden platform had been constructed alongside a country road. Memories differ as to who built it—certainly Bud and Pug (Glenn and Porter) had driven some of the nails, and they also had made around a dozen posters. The dance floor was lit romantically by three lanterns hung from trees. The plan was to charge ten cents a couple for each dance, which lasted six to eight minutes. "That was big chips," recalls Porter, "lots of money." Glenn did the fiddling, and Ed Hall, Lorraine's husband, did the calling. He was also the right person to collect the dimes, being stocky and "tough as a briar" from cutting hundred-pound slabs of timber used for barrel staves and heaving them into a truck. But the dance only lasted three numbers.

Some fellows from Hocomo, Missouri, showed up, drunk, and announced to everyone, "We're here from Hocomo, we don't pay to dance anywhere we go."

Replied Ed Hall, "You pay here, or you don't dance."

One responded, "I guess you misunderstood me. We're from Hocomo, and we don't pay."

Ed punched him and, says Porter, "His hat went in the air and so did his feet."

With little delay a pair of Hocomo hands began tightening around Ed Hall's throat, until the spunky Lorraine interceded with a chunk of wood called a "tie juggle," which was hewn by a broad ax and one to two feet long, with the bark still on it. "He had my husband down, so I tapped him on the head," she recalls. Also getting into the melée were other members of the Hall Brothers singing quartet, Riley and Lloyd Hall. Berneice Holloway was at the dance, though she emphasizes that she left before fists and rocks began flying: "I didn't go back. I kept going."

Porter adds, "It was the awfulest thing you ever seen in your life." Rocks hummed through the air; people scattered about in the dark. The Hall brothers "just whipped these guys" until they tried to leave. But their car struck a log and their radiator sprang a leak. So the interlopers from Hocomo got back out of their car—or were pulled out—for another round.

Glenn and Porter counted their earnings: $1.20 from three dances. Next day they returned with a wagon to salvage some of their lumber. Someone else remembers that certain civic-minded neighbors hitched mules to the dance floor and dragged it away as a public nuisance. *

Porter likes to tell the story of Old Man Hall's first driving lesson. There had been three Wagoner–Hall marriages in the 1930s, and the father was around seventy years old. The episode happened at the Hall farm; the car was a Model–T Ford. Mr. Hall let the clutch out too fast, and the car lurched into high gear. Faster and faster it went, around the barn and the nearby pond. Then, out of control, Mr. Hall and the car sped straight into the pond amid a spectacular shower of water! But two-thirds of the way across the pond, the car simply stopped. No one dared laugh; Mr. Hall had quite a temper. Even at supper that night, no one mentioned the afternoon's mishap. Late that night the boys dragged the car out of the pond with ropes.

Norm Holloway remembers that Porter had his own mishap in a buggy. It had cultivator wheels installed upon it, and the two boys were heading downhill, out of control, in the direction of Charley Wagoner, who was driving the mule with a load of hay. "Dad-blast you boys! *Whoa,*

---

*Such a disturbance was unusual as local dances had apparently tamed down by the 1930s. Notes Robert K. Gilmore of an earlier period (1885–1910), in his *Ozark Baptizings, Hangings and Other Diversions* (1985), "More drunken disturbances occurred at dances than at any other Ozark entertainment." He reports more than twenty revolvers observed among the guests at a Douglas County dance in 1898.

The Wagoner farmhouse in Howell County, Missouri, as it looked in 1959 (with Mrs. Kenneth Chapin in the foreground). No longer standing [COURTESY MR. AND MRS. KENNETH CHAPIN].

Pete! Dad-blast you boys! *Whoa*, Pete!" cried Charley. The buggy left the road, hit a fence post, and capsized. The youthful operators were flung into the barbed wire fence.

In another bucolic story, Porter was conducted on his rite of passage to manhood by a helpful neighbor lady. He was doing some chores for her when she invited him indoors and into her bedroom slipping him out of his coveralls and out of his inhibitions. Milk and cookies afterwards. (Porter's mother had taught him how to kiss by having him suck an orange till it turned white.)

Meanwhile, Charley Wagoner was sinking into ever-deepening poverty and failing health. And the saddest of luck was beclouding the days of Porter's musical hero and elder brother, Glenn Lee Wagoner.

But through it all beamed the wavering signal of WSM radio out of Nashville on Saturday nights.

A DREAM IS BORN

The dominant popular music
of the U.S. today is hillbilly.

—"Bull Market in Corn,"
Time (October 4, 1943)

O
ne day Porter asked his sister Lola, "What would you rather
do, of anything in the world?"
"I don't know. What would *you* rather do?"
"Play on the Grand Ole Opry."
As Porter has so often told, he used to get up on a stump and
entertain his sisters putting on "shows." He would pretend he was on the
Grand Ole Opry, introducing Roy Acuff. Then he would introduce himself as Roy and sing one of his songs. Then introduce someone else, and
so on.

Once when he was ploughing corn, he was still carrying on,
introducing imaginary "special guests" out loud and singing their songs,
believing that no one was around. But his friend Kenneth Chapin over-
heard it all. Porter says, "I had to tell him what I was doing 'cause I didn't
want anyone to think I was crazy! He told me, 'You're probably as close to
the Grand Ole Opry as you'll ever be. You'll be looking that mule in the
rear end when you're sixty-five!'"

Possibly the most important day in Porter's life was when Roy
Acuff came to West Plains, in about the summer of 1942. It had a double
impact on Porter. He got to meet Roy personally—and he saw up close,
for the first time, how a full-scale show differed from mere performing, or
from just getting up and singing.

Roy Acuff had been an Opry regular since 1938, the first real
singer on the show to impose his own vocal style. As Maurice Zolotow
wrote for the *Saturday Evening Post* in 1944, "Like the pure hillbilly
singer, Acuff hardly moves a muscle in his face when he sings. He sings
mainly with his eyes closed, and now and then as he feels a note deeply,
tears will roll down his face."

Porter didn't know Roy had been turned down by the Opry for years, riding buses and sometimes hitch-hiking back and forth from Knoxville, where his wife worked in a drugstore. Porter didn't know that even Opry regulars had to hold other jobs, that Roy was probably the first Opry member to even wrest a living from his music.

"Did you know they weren't making any money?" I asked Porter.

"Oh, no. It shocked me later when I heard. But I wasn't interested in money . . ."

Already Roy had been in one movie, with several more to come. By 1944 he was earning $150,000 a year. The tent shows, starting in 1941, had become really popular.

With Roy Acuff coming to town in two weeks, Porter began counting the days. The day of the show, his dad took him to town early. He began ambling around the square, reconnoitering, on the lookout for Roy's car. Then, right in front of the restaurant, he spotted a long "stretch" automobile of the kind preferred by entertainers: chopped in half at the middle and artificially lengthened, with extra seats installed at the midsection.

Porter sauntered over to the restaurant, though he hadn't money even for a Coke. He pretended he was looking for the restroom, but the manager came over and Porter told the truth. "Why don't you just sit down here at the counter," said the manager. "When he finishes eating, you can meet him."

So he did. Roy was wearing a string tie with colored checks, and his shoes were black and white wingtips. Porter told him he wanted to be a singer, and Roy spent at least five minutes chatting. "If you want to be a singer, if you work at it hard, practice a lot, and make it a top priority with you, you probably *will* be one day." Roy added, "I hope you do become a singer one day. Good luck."

Porter says, "The fact that he took time out to just stop and visit with me—*me*, just a little nobody kid there—really stuck with me all through the years."

Later, watching Roy's tent show, Porter realized that a star like Acuff didn't just sing his hits supported by docile side musicians. Roy gave Bashful Brother Oswald (Pete Kirby), in his goofy bib overalls, his featured moment. Kirby played dobro, the metal, Hawaiian-style guitar that was the forerunner of the steel guitar. Oswald's Sister Rachel (Rachel Veach) played a five-string banjo. They sang duets and joked a lot, no doubt the distant inspiration of the Porter–Dolly duets. According to Roy's biographer, Elizabeth Schlappi, "The two would tell jokes, sing duets—and when Os would laugh, Rachel would follow right away with her laugh."

Porter grasped the biggest secret of all: the show was the star. It didn't matter so much which star's name was painted on the tent, a lesson all too few country singers know, especially today. Porter believed that one day he would have a show of his own, and not merely as a vehicle for his own performing. Maybe learning how to put a show together was the biggest talent of all.

One day Oswald and Rachel would be guests on Porter's television show.

In February 1989 Porter, wearing a cap and gown, addressed twenty-one graduates of the GED (high school equivalency) program. "One of the things I touched on was how important it was for people to keep their minds active," he said of the occasion. And a song he wrote in 1974 about his daughter Denise, "Graduation Day," underscores his troubling self-consciousness about his inability to attend, let alone finish, high school.

The one-room school at Hopewell no doubt blurred the grades together—Porter repeated one year—and by the spring of 1942, for reasons poignant and personal, his education was drawing to a close. On Saturday, May 2, at 2:00 P.M., at First Christian Church in West Plains, Porter Wayne Wagoner was graduated from the eighth grade. Present at the graduation was his girlfriend, Velma Johnson, watching with pride.

Porter hung on at Hopewell school as a "postgraduate," no doubt an embarrassment, being stuck with the younger kids and unable to progress. The Wagoners had not the means to get him to West Plains for high school, and anyway he was needed more and more on the farm. His teacher didn't like Porter, and a look at his record of absenteeism shows why. He was treading water, going to school (when he went at all) with no reachable goal in sight.

Porter's depression in school had a more profound cause, however: his brother Glenn Lee.

A foreshadowing of storm clouds ahead came when Glenn was still in school. One day the teacher thought Glenn was not studying, so he slapped the ruler on his desk. *Whap!* Glenn fainted. Another time he stumbled over a loose board in front of the henhouse and fainted again. Once in the wintertime a mule got loose, and Glenn chased it down, commenting, "I couldn't even hear my heart beat," an odd observation. Then when he was working on a produce truck in Willow Springs, he fainted by the side of the truck.

Brother Oscar had moved to Iowa. He, too, had married one of the Halls, Eva Hall. So in the spring of 1942, Glenn headed out to join him and to find work. Then in the Omaha bus station, he fainted again. Oscar took him to three doctors who found nothing wrong, but a fourth diagnosed him as having an enlarged heart.

The month before Porter's graduation, Oscar brought Glenn back to West Plains for a four-month stay at the West Plains Hospital. Porter

Porter and his brother, Glenn Lee Wagoner [COURTESY LORRAINE HALL].

and his dad were now stranded down on the farm alone, the work growing more and more difficult with Charley's arthritis progressing. Mrs. Wagoner had moved to West Plains to work at the hospital as a cook so she could watch over Glenn.

On August 12, 1942, Porter turned fifteen. On August 25, Glenn turned eighteen. Two days later, on the night of August 27, brother-in-law Lloyd Hall sat up with Glenn.

Glenn would wake up and say in a dreamy voice, "*I was dead . . .*" and then sink back into slumber.

On the morning of August 28, at 7:30, Glenn Lee Wagoner died of myocarditis, inflammation of the heart. Down below the Wagoner farm at the State Line Cemetery adjoining Arkansas, Glenn was buried in the family burial plot.

Charley and Porter struggled on the farm over the summer of 1942, but arthritis was felling Charley fast. On *The Farmer* album (1973) Porter speaks eloquently of his father in the recitation "My Dad":

> The first thing I remember learning from my Dad was the meaning of honesty. He said, "If you're honest, son, it means a whole lot more than you just won't lie and cheat. If you're honest you'll do unto others like you'd have them do unto you. And you'll always give more than just your share in everything you do. Honesty stands like a giant oak tree with roots strong and deep in the ground. And if you're always honest with yourself, son, it covers many of the Commandments of God."
>
> *Pride* was another word that my Dad lived by. He took pride in each thing and one day he told me why. He said, "Always take pride in each thing you do, boy, no matter how small it may be, for God gave you the mind that you did it with. And take pride in each new thing that you see. And don't ever think that you're better than anyone but always remember—you're just as good as anybody, son. And just because you're wearing overalls with patches to cover each hole, why, it's not what's on the outside that makes a man, boy, it's what's hidden deep in his soul. So always be honest and proud, son, in each thing that you do. And when you're in doubt about something, ask God about it, 'cause He's always honest with you."

In the same recitation Porter says that when his dad needed money at the bank, "the banker said, 'How much do you need, Charley? Your word is like a bond on a check'"—and "I've seen him baling hay . . . his back would get so tired he'd have tears in his eyes . . . Mom would tell him to rest. He'd say, 'I'll have plenty of time to rest when the kids get their education and have left.'"

But in the fall of 1942, Porter was missing as many days of class as he was attending in his nebulous status at the Hopewell school. He dropped out in December to work on a neighbor's farm, according to the records.

In the spring of 1943 Lola's husband Earl ("Red") Hall, the auctioneer, presided over the funeral of the Wagoner farm. All the animals were sold off, including Porter's pinto pony, Foxy, and their beloved mule, Pete. Even the cows and chickens had names, and they were more than livestock; they were personal friends to Porter. "Selling them was such a heartbreak for me. I thought they didn't bring what they were worth." Porter kept his dog.

Whipped by the Depression, like so many families, the Wagoners were moving to West Plains, where, with men away at war, there was the promise of jobs in the factories, plants, and shops.

Porter was taking with him an eight-dollar National guitar that his mother had ordered from Montgomery Ward, paying for it with money he'd earned by trapping rabbits. He still has the guitar. Glenn had picked it out; he said a National was better than Sears' Gene Autry models. Glenn was going to teach Porter to play; now maybe Lorraine could.

Many people have wondered, whimsically, what might Glenn and Porter have accomplished if Glenn had lived. Porter had been outstripped by his older brother, and perhaps his death inspired him like the death of Joe Kennedy inspired his younger brothers to achieve in his place. Or like the death of Jack Cash, Johnny Cash's older brother, a preacher who fell into a spinning table saw in 1944—or the passing of Tom T. Hall's musician hero, Clayton Delaney, memorialized in "I Remember the Year That Clayton Delaney Died," with Tom musing, "I'd give a hundred dollars if he could only see me now."

Porter says, "I felt like after he died, that I should carry on his music . . . because it meant so much to him."

4

WEST PLAINS

He works for his living
and his money's his own,
And if they don't like him
they can leave him alone.

—"Wagoner's Lad," old folk song

Small towns like West Plains are the sort which Norman Rockwell sentimentalized in his *Saturday Evening Post* cover art and which the Statler Brothers and Tom T. Hall have sung about romantically in country music. West Plains is proud of locals who made good, like Brooklyn Dodgers pitcher Preacher Roe, country comic Speck Rhodes, and Opry stars Jan Howard and Porter.

And small towns like West Plains pick up the tab for America's defense. Howell County donated around eighty lives to World War II.

In 1940 the population of West Plains was 4,026. As county seat of Howell County, it drew in the farm families on Saturday to sell their grain and cream and to buy staples like sugar, coffee, and salt. Sometimes they'd linger on the square to hear live music.

Since anyone can remember, the most prosperous store was Aid's Hardware. In his enterprising early years, Charles T. Aid had set up a full-length mirror in his store window to catch the eye of women on Sunday hurrying to the church next door, causing them to pause and check out their Sunday finery. A national magazine once named Charlie Aid as one of the nation's top twelve country merchants.

In 1943 the Wagoners were settling into West Plains. They rented a house on Johnson Street, close to Christa Hogan Hospital, where sister Lola was training to be a nurse. Porter, fifteen years old, worked his first in-town job, helping at Charlie Phelps's service station for a few months.

Next, he delivered groceries for the Hull–Thornburg Market on the square. Lorraine's husband, Ed Hall, was a meat cutter there, and he trained Porter. There were no electric saws in those days, so he learned to cut meat on a great chopping block with a large knife while the customer watched. Sometimes Ed would sneak Porter a slab of bologna to eat on his delivery run.

Ed Hall also tried to teach Porter how to drink. After a training session with peach brandy while driving with Ed in the Wagoner family car, a 1930 Chevrolet, Porter threw up all over the interior. Later, Doris Hardin remembers driving Porter and some friends to a pie supper. When they arrived too late to play music, everyone but Porter wanted to head for a tavern. "I do what my mama says," Porter said, "and I don't go to no bars."

Interviewing Velma Holzkamper in 1989, I learned that she and her husband were running a hardwood floor business in Rogers, Arkansas.

People sometimes ask her whether she was in West Plains in the forties. Yes, she was. She was Velma Johnson in those days. Did she know Porter Wagoner? Oh, everyone knew Porter. West Plains is a pretty small town.

She'd met Porter at a country dance. He began taking her places, like over to Ed and Lorraine's for a fish fry. Or to the movies. Of all things, Velma and Porter talked whimsically about starting a shelter for battered women, since Velma's mother had been slammed around. And then there was Lorraine, terrorized by Ed when he was drunk.

They were in love. "We were both crazy," says Velma. "We wanted to do something."

They sure did.

They were married on April 29, 1944. The marriage license lists Porter as sixteen and Velma as eighteen, which is false as she was *younger* than him and would have me know she was "not the aggressor." Velma is listed as being from Koshkonong, Missouri, which was the home of Lark Allen's wife, Sarah. The civil ceremony was conducted at Hardy, Arkansas, whose other claim to country music fame is that of birthplace of the Wilburn Brothers.

Velma says the union lasted maybe months, others say weeks, and she remembers visiting Porter's brother Oscar in Iowa. "We were two teenagers that could not make a go of marriage," states Velma. "We should have been home with Mama, getting dried behind the ears." Porter's sisters always believed that their mother had the marriage annulled at the West Plains courthouse. However, circuit clerk and recorder of deeds Fern Freeman Welker, having been supplied with a copy of the marriage license, responded in writing, "Checking our records up to

1954, I do not find a divorce record for these people. I am assuming an annulment or divorce would have occurred immediately."

Velma Holzkamper and her husband hope she is not still married to Porter Wagoner. She has nine sons and a daughter, grandchildren, even great-grandchildren.

In later years, she would drop in on Charley and Bertha Wagoner when visiting West Plains. Charley always called her his "Dot" for "daughter." She would push him in his wheelchair to his car; and, wrote Velma in a 1989 letter, "he was always telling me how great his son was. He had two prized possessions: Porter and his car."

Velma's children knew, vaguely, that some country singer was "Mama's friend." Since Velma's favorite country singer is black singer Charley Pride, they thought that was the one. Velma wrote me that she told them "Mama's friend" had curly hair and a big mouth. And, "I very quietly added, 'And wagon wheels on his pant legs.'"

For many years, "The Porter Wagoner Show" featured comedian Speck Rhodes, who played a stand-up bass, wore a loud, yellow-checked suit, and had two of his front teeth blacked out. Dolly gave Speck a part in her 1984 film *Rhinestone*.

Gilbert ("Speck") Rhodes came from West Plains although his family had moved out in 1918. The Rhodeses were well-known entertainers, hustling nickels and dimes on many a town square in Missouri. Speck Rhodes made his first banjo out of an old banjo hoop, using for the banjo head an opossum skin complete with pocket.

The Rhodeses were favorites of Charley Wagoner. After leaving the farm, Charley got a job at the Dr. Pepper soft drink bottling plant. He used to have handbills printed up, advertising "Slim Rhodes and the Log Cabin Mountaineers," along with Dr. Pepper.

Ed Hall and Porter had gravitated to the Dr. Pepper plant. Porter drove a truck, delivering cases of the soft drink.

Porter especially admired a couple of black musicians from Memphis named Doc and Shorty who came in by train for two or three days about once a month. They didn't hop freights, at least not often; Doc and Shorty could afford tickets. As soon as they started working the public square, a crowd would gather. Doc would fiddle, and Shorty would strum guitar with his thumb. Sometimes, while Doc fiddled "You Can't Put That Monkey on My Back," Shorty would omit the guitar and slap his face, slap his legs (ham bone), slap his forehead, never missing a lick.

The apprentice white entertainer looked up to the Negro, with the awe of the amateur for the professional. The white boy played for a slice of pie, coffee, maybe a kiss, maybe half a tank of gas. The black man

Above: *Porter at sixteen* [Photo by Miller Studio, West Plains Gazette, Winter 1979]. Below: *Porter at Dr. Pepper plant, circa 1944* [West Plains Gazette, Winter 1979].

Right: *Velma Johnson: Mrs. Porter Wagoner, 1944– ; Velma Holzkamper today* [COURTESY VELMA HOLZKAMPER].

Ruth Olive Williams, 1943: Mrs. Porter Wagoner, 1946–86 [COURTESY LORRAINE HALL].

worked for cash, in the whorehouses, the juke joints, or on the levees and the sidewalks. If the white boy wanted to escape the homespun circuit of schoolhouses and church socials, he needed role models. The itinerant black musician had gambled his life on a song, and, if he died violently over a woman or slowly from too much gin, or wasted in prison, at least he had lived his music full-time.

To Porter, the nickels and dimes collected by Doc and Shorty looked like big money.

Meanwhile, country music had been going to town.

Rural workers were migrating toward city jobs, especially in defense plants. Country boys in uniform were spreading the music abroad as well; among the G.I.s in Europe there were at least twenty-five hillbilly bands. As Bill Malone notes in his 1968 edition of *Country Music, U.S.A.*, Roy Acuff even beat out Frank Sinatra in a popularity poll of servicemen. Elton Britt's "There's a Star-Spangled Banner Waving Somewhere" was a country song analogous to "Over There" from World War I. If the Japanese at Okinawa didn't screech "To hell with Roosevelt, to hell with Babe Ruth, to hell with Roy Acuff" as is often reported, well, they should have. In 1943 *Billboard* counted 198 hillbilly recording artists out of a total of 608, and by 1944 it had started to list folk music jukebox hits.

Lorraine was working at Christa Hogan Hospital as a cook; Ed was there recovering from eye surgery; and Porter was there checking things out one day in 1945.

"Rain, who's that pretty nurse?"

The comely face belonged to Ruth Olive Williams, born February 27, 1924, a farm girl from Winona. They began dating, going to movies or for drives in the Wagoner family car. Porter was not one for parties or drinking, and they do not seem to have frequented the popular Echo Club or George's Round-Up that Jan Howard mentions in her *Sunshine and Shadow* memoir.

At Ed and Lorraine's house on January 25, 1946, Porter and Ruth were married, with the Reverend Frank Hall, Ed's brother (later Judge Hall), officiating. In 1946 their son Richard was born.

The 300 block of Oak Street still lacks sidewalks, and the modest frame house at number 318 was a tawdry rental in 1989; but Porter's parents kept it nice in the 1940s when they were buying it. Still it was so cramped. Porter and Ruth lived on the left side, in rooms sealed off to make an apartment for the young couple and their baby. They shared the bath, the kitchen, the livingroom. Charley slept in the livingroom in a special bed built low to accommodate his worsening arthritis. His daughter-in-law's nursing came in handy.

Here lived Porter, Ruth, and Richard for a frustrating five and one-half years.

＊　　　＊　　　＊

Though Porter's days at Vaughan's Market as a meat cutter are central to the Porter Wagoner legend, in fact he worked at other markets first. In spring 1946 Ted Pernick, just home from the war, opened a meat market at 301 Washington Avenue at the corner of Cass Avenue and hired Porter full time. "I made a butcher out of him," says Ted. "He was young and hunting any kind of job he could get to eat on, like so many of them." Pay was around twenty-five dollars a week. In front of Pernick's Market on Saturday nights there might be Speck and Dusty and the rest of the Rhodeses, scrambling for pass-the-hat tips on the sidewalk.

Porter left Ted for a better job, one that paid thirty-five dollars a week, at the V & Y Market on Washington Street. It was owned by Virgil and Bessie Yadon, and Bessie's brother, Sid Vaughan, hence the V in the name V & Y Market. (Later Sid Vaughan would give Porter his "big" radio break). Virgil Yadon played fiddle, and Porter was now trying to flat-pick his guitar and sing. Porter might join the Hall Brothers up on the square on a flatbed truck to perform.

Fresh meat draws flies. Overhead at the V & Y Market was a huge electric exhaust fan. One day it wobbled itself loose and came crashing down onto the meat block. Providentially, Porter was out singing at a funeral. "Thank the Lord he wasn't there," says Bessie. "If it'd hit him there wouldn't be no Porter Wagoner!"

Porter switched jobs and had an even closer brush with danger. He had started working for the local Jeep dealership, probably motivated by the access to a company vehicle. He was driving Ruth and Richard over to Winona to see his in-laws when another vehicle slammed into them. The Jeep turned over and crashed right into a tree. Baby Richard, only a few months old, was unconscious for three days. "Mother was banged up from head to toe," Richard says. Miraculously, he recovered only to get kicked in the head by a horse not long after at the farm of his Williams grandparents. From whichever accident, Richard became deaf in one ear.

From the Jeep wreck Porter bore a scar over his right eye. He also lost six front teeth. The West Plains dentist was no specialist, and he did mediocre bridgework. Already shy and tending to look down while he talked, like the young Elvis Presley, now he adopted a second, awkward habit of putting his hand over his mouth. This pathetic mannerism was conspicuous even in his days on the "Ozark Jubilee" TV show. Porter, the aspiring singer, now had become self-conscious over the very act of smiling. He developed an uneasy way of laughing to conceal his teeth, and in early promotional pictures the future Porter Wagoner grin is an uptight grimace.

＊　　　＊　　　＊

Above: *The public square, West Plains, Missouri. Vaughan's Market was on the corner, where the automobile at the left is parked, at 47 Court Square* [PHOTO BY AUTHOR]. Below left: *Porter in West Plains, early 1940s* [COURTESY LORRAINE HALL]. Below right: *Porter in West Plains with unidentified girl* [COURTESY PORTER WAGONER ENTERPRISES].

When he finally got to Nashville in 1956, a trip to a good dentist was high on the list. Finally he was at ease with himself. He was proud of himself and was no longer afraid to laugh.

When Porter was first delivering groceries for Hull & Thornburg's on the square in 1944, at the nearby Model Drugstore worked a twelve-year-old girl named Grace Johnson. Porter didn't know her then. She'd been born in West Plains and later would marry then divorce Harlan Howard, one of Nashville's greatest songwriters. As singer Jan Howard, she had thirty hits, some of them duets with Bill Anderson.

Over in Willow Springs, twenty-one miles away, lived Bob Ferguson. Porter didn't know him either, but he remembers his parents, who ran Ferguson's Market. Bob Ferguson ended up in Nashville by way of Washington State and was Porter's RCA producer and writer of his unforgettable hit, "The Carroll County Accident."

The town of Thayer lies about twenty miles south of West Plains, adjacent to Koshkonong. The Wilburn Family entertainers were playing music for coins on the sidewalks of Thayer in 1938. By 1941 they had made it to the Opry.

Once Bill Monroe came through West Plains with his tent show. "Porter followed my show around Missouri for three days once," Bill remembers.

And Smiley Burnette appeared at the Davis Theater. Comic actor and sometime Gene Autry sidekick, Smiley brought along his horse Ringeye to delight the kids. Porter was playing enough guitar to persuade Smiley to take him along for a few weeks. Smiley taught Porter to travel light with a single wash-and-wear outfit because "You can only wear one thing at a time." They worked small theaters and audiences of thirty to forty children. Smiley played accordion, sang, and imparted to Porter his famous axiom, "Make 'em laugh, make 'em cry . . . and *scare hell out of 'em!*" To demonstrate this last piece of advice, Porter remembers how Smiley would give the children a lesson in "gun safety." Piously he would tell them, "I always check my pistol twice to make sure." Decisively, he would snap the hammer down on an empty cylinder. Then, pausing dramatically, with children on the edge of their seats, he would squeeze the trigger a second time, this time with a live blank in the chamber! "Those kids would just die when that gun went off!" says Porter.

Some news stories from the West Plains *Quill* in the late forties suggest how different times were when Porter was getting his start as a family man and working man. In 1947 a man was charged with "disturbing religious worship" (being drunk) and fined fifty dollars, and a couple was caught living together unmarried and given a year's imprisonment on a morals charge.

The composite Ozark story, though, has to be from December 1949 when a man was arrested for entering the Farmer's Exchange with a .22 rifle, a jug of whiskey, and a Bible.

The world's largest shoe manufacturer in the forties was International Shoe Company. In 1946 it began constructing a plant at West Plains, on Missouri Avenue, north of the square by the railroad tracks. Ed and Lorraine got jobs there, and so did sister Lola's husband. The pay was fifty-seven and one-half cents an hour.

Porter worked there from February 17, 1947, till August 2, 1950, taking three months off in the summer of 1949. He worked in the lasting department, shaping metal shoes on a metal form. One of his co-workers was Roy Hardin, another refugee from farming. Ruth also worked at the shoe factory, from August 4, 1947, until April 16, 1952, in the fitting department with Lorraine. Once she got her hand caught in one of the stamping machines—fortunately the one with cold ink, not hot—and couldn't get her hand loose! Ruth fainted, with her hand still stuck in the machine. Someone extricated her, and two mechanics carried her—unconscious—into the First Aid room. When Ruth revived, her first words to Lorraine were, "Was my dress down as they carried me here . . . ?"

The Wagoners were Democrats, like many rural Southerners, whether on the farm or in the factory. Yet three of their children had married Halls, a primarily business-professional clan active in the Republican party. In the presidential election of 1948, the Republicans gambled that big business candidate Thomas E. Dewey would win even the small businessman's vote. But Missourian Harry S. Truman pulled enough votes from people like Charley and Bertha Wagoner to whip the effete Dewey. The plain-spoken Truman hit the little towns and turned the derisive term *whistle stopping* into a victory cry. Years later he would tell Merle Miller that "The most peaceful thing in the world is riding behind a mule, plowing a field . . . I've always thought farmers are the smartest people in the world." Truman believed farmers had more time for *thinking* while they plowed.

In an unpublished recitation, Porter says, "my dad never had an education, but he was the smartest man I have ever known." Says Judge/Reverend Frank Hall of Charley Wagoner, "You hear of the Ozark hillbillies. He was 'Mister Hillbilly.' When you refer to a hillbilly, that's *not* disrespectful."

Lorraine owned a Gibson flattop guitar. She taught Porter the standard, Carter Family lick with a flat-pick, strumming chords, striking the bass strings alternately. Porter just had to have a Gibson to show other people, and himself, that he was serious.

Lorraine's husband, Ed, was a singer in a quartet with his brothers. Frank Hall played guitar, Lloyd the violin, while Ed and Earl ("Red") just sang. Lorraine would sing when there was a gap in the ranks, becoming almost an honorary Hall Brother herself. Sometimes Porter sang with the Halls on radio.

Porter's first group all his own was the Oak Street Pals, a duo. Both lived on Oak Street, Tom Moore across from Porter. Tom played guitar, and Lorraine says he taught her brother more guitar than she did. On local radio Tom played and they both sang. Soon Porter's shoe factory colleague, Don Hoglen, was dropping by with his mandolin. This nucleus soon expanded into the Blue Ridge Boys band. Porter bought all of them hats so they might more resemble Bill Monroe.

There were other subtle but distinct clues that Porter took his musical career more seriously than his level of success thus far indicated. He treated himself to almost-unheard-of barbershop shaves. He even sent his clothes to the dry cleaner, which he could ill afford. At the slightest provocation, he would have pictures of his band printed and mailed around, a repetitive process, with the faces changing.

One of Porter's band members, Urel Albert, remembers how they drove through a storm to reach an Arkansas schoolhouse for a show. "The creeks were up terrible," says Urel, and the crowd had left. There was only one man left. He told them he had a little store. "I can't pay you money but I got some of the best cheese you ever tasted." So they played for the customers in the store and wolfed down cheese and crackers.

Harry L. Palmer grew up on a farm near Thomasville, about twenty-two miles east of West Plains, and in 1988 he wrote his recollections in a letter:

> On Saturday nights the big thing for the young people was attending a movie in the little dirt floor theater, owned by Mrs. Cecil Williams, who also owned the only cafe and gas station in the small town. One Saturday Porter was to play and sing at this theater. Porter and his band ran out of gas, just before he got to Thomasville. He walked across the bridge, over the Eleven Point River, and got a gallon of gas from Mrs. Williams and made it on to the theater. I am sure there wasn't over two dozen people at Porter's performance but all had a good time and after the show, we all gathered at the cafe and had a good time visiting and talking with Porter. I have always thought he was the best from that night.

On Saturday nights all the pickers rallied for the Howell County Jamboree, held sometimes at a furniture store up on the square, more often at the Avenue Theater about a block north. These were paying dates, with the musicians getting a cut of the gate, sometimes as many as 250 to 300 people. Orbie Goodin, another musician from the shoe

LOOK WHO'S COMIN'!
TO THE EMINENCE THEATRE
Eminence, Mo.
THURSDAY, AUGUST 2, 1951

PORTER WAGONER
And
The Blue Ridge Boys
K.W.P.M. Radio Stars

Featuring
Don Russell and his Magic Fiddle
Urel Albert, the Heart Song Singer
Don Hoglen and his red hot mandolin
Nic Nichols, the laugh a minute boy
The Blue Ridge Quartet, singing your
Favorite Gospel Hymns

Don't Miss A Big Hour and A Half
Show of Fun, Music and Comedy!

Doors open at 7:30 Show starts at 8 P.M.
Admission: Regular Prices, Adults 30c,
Children Under 12 10c, All Taxes
Paid

[COURTESY DON RUSSELL]

Above: *Porter with his siblings and parents in 1952. Lola and Lorraine (standing); Charley, Bertha, and Oscar (seated)* [West Plains Gazette, Winter 1979]. *Right: Tom Moore (left) and Porter, 1947, The Oak Street Pals* [West Plains Gazette, Winter 1979].

factory, says sometimes Porter and others were cheated out of their money by the powers that were.

Other times, they'd play in each other's homes, "musicals" they called them. The intrepid Halls, with any available Wagoner, sang at every possible gathering.

The columns of the *Quill* in the late forties were full of singing announcements. They advertised group "sings," or singing contests, or even the opening of a singing school down at the courthouse.

Clearly, Americans used to sing together more than they ever will again.

5

KWPM AND VAUGHAN'S MARKET

When you shop at our meat department
we assure you less waste and more quality.

—ad for Vaughan's Market,
West Plains *Quill*, July 14, 1950

Porter's rise from Vaughan's meat market owes much to Bob Neathery, who started West Plains station KWPM in 1947.

Bob had been mesmerized by things electrical all his life. In the 1920s he had been enchanted by *Electrical Experimenter* magazine and built his own radio with "an inverted cake pan for a receiver." Over the years he dreamed of having his own radio station.

Bob gambled on his dream when station KWPM went on the air on July 15, 1947. The call letters signified "Keep West Plains Moving."

Bob noticed that the dairy trucks were rolling by four in the morning, that the cafés had customers by six. So each day at five, KWPM went on the air. They faced near-stifling competition from Springfield's KWTO, which reached four states. KWTO had live music, airing many acts like the Goodwill Family, a polished family show with more than a decade's experience, featuring Aunt Martha, charismatic Slim Wilson, and guitar whiz Herschel ("Junior") Haworth. So Bob Neathery began letting anyone sing for free who wanted to, and sometimes KWPM got what it paid for, which was nothing. Remembers Urel Albert, "Some of 'em was so bad it was pathetic. *Anyone* could get on. But we were the best!"

At Porter's début on KWPM in 1947, he was accompanied by Lorraine, and they sang "Leaf of Love." Other times Porter stood in with the ubiquitous Hall Brothers; sometimes he sang on Red Hall's auctioneer show.

West Plains even had its own recording studio, if the chaotic world of Austin R. ("Happy Hop") Hopper can be so dignified. Some called him an eccentric. "Like a mad scientist," says Porter with awe in his voice. Hopper lived in the back of his radio shop with his wife and

63

son, at 721 Washington Avenue. Porter says going into the store was like cutting your way into a thicket, so jumbled up was it with loose wires. The innovative Hopper had rescued the arm off an old jukebox and fashioned himself a direct-to-disc recording machine. Such machines carved their grooves into soft acetate discs called dubs that wear down with each playing, the phonograph needle cutting deeper, like a lathe. In the forties, record companies used acetates as their masters before they had tape recording.

These sessions cost Porter a dollar each, and the discs were 78 rpm. Porter's first recording was "Just a Closer Walk with Thee" with Ed, Lorraine, and Don Hoglen. Usually they cut gospel, like "Decoration Day in Heaven." But they sang secular songs, too, like "Poison Love."

And Porter recorded "Lovesick Blues."

The song was a number one hit for Hank Williams in 1949; it stayed on the charts forty-two weeks. Portentously, it reached number twenty-four in pop as well. Its lyrics had been written by a Russian-born swing band leader, Irving Mills, its melody by Cliff Friend. Copyrighted in 1922, "Lovesick Blues" saw various versions and only gradually became a country song.* Hank gave the one word *blues* three syllables, anticipating, slightly, rockabilly, as well as Buddy Holly. The melody is lengthy and complicated, with many bluesy chord shifts, finally starting over when you least expect it. It's hard to do, and by all accounts, Porter did it better than anyone else in town.

Porter's mastery of the song (his old static-filled acetate is still astounding) dramatizes his prudent move from homey bluegrass to moan-and-sob, honky-tonk country. Hank was his new hero, his new vocal model.

"Lovesick Blues" had been Hank's début number at the Opry, June 11, 1949. Porter probably was in the audience that night (Hank was on several times that summer) with Ruth, Ed, Lorraine, and Granville Nichols, his bass player, having driven from West Plains so Porter could see Bill Monroe. These West Plains tourists stayed at the Merchant's Hotel at 401 Broadway, in the same block as the Ernest Tubb Record Shop. On the front steps of the Ryman they cavorted for a touristy snapshot or two. Exhausted, Porter slept for most of the drive back to West Plains. Little did he realize that one day Hank's widow, Audrey, would give him a spot in a movie she produced. Little did Ruth realize that someday she would live across the street from Audrey.

Hank's presence onstage was by now compelling, and on the night of his début he'd done seven encores of "Lovesick Blues." He had learned

*The song's circuitous travels have been charted by Nick Tosches in *Country: Living Legends and Dying Metaphors in America's Biggest Music* (1977; rev. ed. 1985).

to sing on key and his cutting-edge voice was born for the jukebox. He was an antidote to the staid, homey, family-group style of country music from the mountains. It was time to rip country music out of its strict confines. When Williams sang, poverty ached in every crack in his voice, and sexuality radiated from his bony body that swayed as he sang. The driving, dance hall beat had not a little Negro juke joint in it, a reminder that Hank played for money, not for sentiment. It was a stark foreboding of rock 'n' roll to come. His son, Hank, Jr., would finish the job, singing borderline black blues in a white man's cowboy hat.

If the music of Bill Monroe had gotten Porter into the pie suppers and onto KWPM occasionally, maybe the music of Hank Williams could take him further. Meanwhile, Porter was an assembly line cobbler in a union-shop shoe factory, where even his wife had to work. If he found this an embarrassing comedown from his Opry dreams, Ruth must have found it embarassing to have a husband who left home whenever there was music to be played. The Hank Williams influence must have been even more disquieting to Ruth. It was becoming clearer and clearer that Porter would have preferred to sleep scrunched up in the back of a car than at home with his family, *if* the car were headed toward a gig, however far away it might be.

Dale Bradford remembers that Porter made a commercial-quality record of "Lovesick Blues." He was with him when they went to St. Louis to record it, along with L. C. Bell and Floyd Hoglen, Don Hoglen's brother. It cost more than $100 for the session and to get a few singles pressed, which they placed in some West Plains jukeboxes. Dale also remembers when they had a gig at the Echo Club on the highway into West Plains; the *Quill* for April 2, 1950, ran an ad billing "Porter Wagner" and his band.

Another Hank Williams song with a melancholy resonance, at least for Porter's father, was "Lost Highway" by the Blind Troubadour, Leon Payne. Its lyrics really fit Hank. The narrator, once "a kid like you," has been propelled down that lost highway by the sure-fire formula of a woman's lies, a deck of cards, and a jug of wine. The narrator himself is beyond redemption ("too late to save"), but at least he can warn other young men not to follow in his wretchedly wayward footsteps. Lorraine says she's never told Porter, but tears used to come to his father's eyes when he'd hear that song. Charley would say, "I'm so afraid Porter's going to end up the same way."

But Porter says his mother never worried about his well-being. "There is one thing your daddy don't even know, honey," Bertha would say. "You are the kind of person who can sense danger. You won't be driving too fast, and put yourself in a vulnerable position where you can be hurt or killed." Even as a kid, his mother remembered, unlike other boys, Porter wouldn't dive out of a tree into shallow water. Other boys

Above: *The Avenue Theater, 307 Washington Avenue, West Plains, site of the "Howell Country Jamboree," a show on which Porter often performed.* Below: *Porter Wagoner Boulevard (left) and Jan Howard Expressway (right), West Plains, Missouri* [PHOTOS BY AUTHOR].

Right: *Ruth and Porter, late forties* [Courtesy Denise Kelton]. Below: *From the West Plains* Daily Quill, *April 28, 1950* [Courtesy The State Historical Society of Missouri].

DANCE

at

ECHO CLUB

WEST PLAINS, MO.

— DATE —

TONIGHT—FRIDAY, APRIL 28

Music by

PORTER WAGNER AND HIS
OZARK MELODY BOYS

— Square and Round —

might, and maybe split their heads open.

Another song that hit close to home was "Old Log Cabin for Sale." Lorraine taught it to Porter. It's a Stamps–Baxter number from 1939, written by Mrs. J. W. Payte, and it tells how an old couple pines for a missing son "whose last promise did fail." Finally the prodigal son returns. He finds his parents' old cabin up for sale. He's too late. They're dead.

In the 1986 Wagoner divorce trial, Ruth admitted she had "never" approved of Porter's musical career. But how could she have? She was married to a shoemaker and sometime butcher's apprentice who was always out singing somewhere.

"I know it was unbelievable for her," Porter says. "She told me that so many times. She couldn't believe that I would keep on, with no money in it. I did love Ruth, and I never met a woman that was better quality than she was. But I could not bring myself to be a regular eight-to-five person, which would have made her an excellent husband. That's what she talked to all the neighbors about. I felt bad about it, but when you have an inner longing for something, there's no way you can stop it. Had I never made any money and just gone under, I would still have pursued it. I really felt if I couldn't play music, I would die. I would be no good to her or anyone else."

Porter's band members testify to Ruth's hospitality. Ruth was no doubt intimidated by it all at times, for the horde of musical Halls must have been overpowering. Lorraine tells of a particularly uncomfortable episode when a group of them were sitting around making music. Ruth was perched warily on a bed while Porter pathetically abased himself, pleading, "Babe, won't you come on and sing with us?" Ruth remained shy, withdrawn, refusing.

In 1949, probably in the summer when Porter was off from the shoe factory, the Blue Ridge Boys made it to Omaha. Porter told Jack Hurst of *The* (Nashville) *Tennessean* in 1971 that they slept in a cheap room that they hadn't paid for, even running out of food money. He went to a grocery store and told the butcher he needed some soup bones for his dog. He got a bagful. "I took them back to the boys and put them in some water, and we made us some stew. We borrowed some crackers from the lady who ran the place where we were staying."

Then he tried to scare up some work. Taverns weren't interested in bluegrass music, at least not from out-of-towners. Finally the woman who owned the Top Hat Club said Porter had an honest face and booked the band for Friday and Saturday nights at forty dollars a night. On the strength of this, they borrowed money from the landlady.

Then to their shock, the club owner ran an ad in the paper for

"Porter Wagoner and His Blue Ridge Orchestra." He hastened to tell her that his "orchestra" possessed only a guitar, a banjo, and a steel guitar. Naively she replied, "Music's music."

That night as they were setting up, Porter remembers that "the people started comin' in, in Cadillacs and Lincolns, and I knew right then that we were in for a hell of a night." About one hundred patrons showed up, well dressed, to eat dinner. "Well, we got up there on the stage and lit into this first breakdown [high-speed banjo solo], and that banjo sounded like it had four amplifiers on it."

"It was so loud that you just couldn't believe it," he continued. "And them people that was sittin' there eatin', they couldn't believe it, either. They just kind of raised up in their chairs, lookin' around like they were askin', 'Where in hell is it comin' from?'"

As for the banjo player, "He just stood there with his head down, watchin' his feet while he played." But the people were pretty nice. As soon as they ate, they left, but they didn't throw anything or say anything about it."

The club owner tried hard to put it nicely. "Honey, it wasn't that they didn't like your music. It was just that they were expectin' somethin' else. Uh, why don't you just let me pay you for tomorrow night now, and you all can just go on ahead?"

Feeling bad about getting paid without playing, they still decided to keep the eighty dollars, pay the landlady, and head back home.

Porter also had a fling at working in a foundry in Peoria, Illinois, in 1949. In vain he wrote letters to radio stations, seeking auditions. Then he hitchhiked back to West Plains.

Bessie Yadon's brother, Sid Vaughan, had opened his own meat market at number 47 on the public square. In late 1950 Porter went to work at Vaughan's Market. On September 4 President Truman talked to America all at once, via the first coast-to-coast television hookup. On September 30, the Opry took a hesitant step and was first televised.

In his 1988 letter, Harry L. Palmer remembered Porter at the market.

> When I was a sophomore in high school, we moved to West Plains. Each day I would walk by the little grocery store where Porter was employed in the meat department. Some days, when no one was in the store, Porter would be picking on his guitar behind the meat cooler.

Even in West Plains, Porter was probably the only white kid in town to venture up "the hill," as the black ghetto was called. He liked to

Left: *West Plains Tourists on the steps of the Ryman Auditorium, Nashville, Summer 1949. Left to right: Granville Nichols, Lorraine Hall, Porter, Ruth* [PHOTO BY ED HALL, COURTESY GRANVILLE NICHOLS]. Below: *Late forties picture of The Blue Ridge Boys. Left to right: Porter, Dale Bradford (guitar), Tommy Bassham (guitar), Don Shepard (fiddle), Archie Bassham (mandolin), Al Blackburn (fiddle), L. C. Bell (bass).*

visit a Negro dive in a mere shack ("I coulda probably gotten killed") to listen to a saxophone player, Good Jelly Jones, and his trio. "He had a lot of country feeling to his playing," says Porter.

Sid Vaughan grew more and more exasperated with Porter's wavering ambition for meat-cutting.

"Now Porter, are you going to sing, or are you going to cut meat?"

"This time I'm really going to stay."

"Well, I'm going to try you . . . one more time."

Sid liked to hear Porter sing "Jimmy Brown the Newsboy" and "The Birmingham Jail," so he decided perhaps he could put his singing to work selling meat. He bought a fifteen-minute early spot on KWPM, about three times a week, and set up a microphone in the store. Porter asked who was going to do the commercials. Sid replied he would write them out, prices and everything, for Porter to read.

The night before the first show, Porter couldn't sleep. He lay awake, rehearsing, planning what he was going to say. Next morning, he rushed through maybe ten songs in fifteen minutes, without saying anything. For a kind of monitor, they kept the radio going, turned down low, and Sid's son Leroy would listen for the words "We take you now to Vaughan's Market," then turn and point to Porter. Somehow they stumbled through the first few shows. Porter figures he was so scared that listeners began writing in out of pity. Letters even arrived from adjoining counties. At last he had something he could talk about, if only his mail.

After two or three months, he accidentally laughed at something over the air. People began writing in saying they liked to hear him laugh. For the first time, he began to gain confidence and began devising little things to talk about. He pretended he was speaking to someone right there in the store, even if his only audience was the store's cat.

Sid's daughter Eula was married to Joe Fite, the local Trailways bus driver, and sometimes Joe would play cards with Porter at the market. Joe got himself a seven-day-a-week run from Springfield, passing through West Plains. Joe Fite became friendly with the KWTO staff up at Springfield, playing with their company baseball team. He began telling program director Lou Black that Porter sounded just like Hank Williams.

One day a large black Lincoln appeared outside the Vaughan Market. Inside was Lou Black, and he sat there listening to Porter on the radio. Porter says he thought the car looked like a gangster's, which isn't so farfetched considering that in the thirties the Ozarks were Bonnie and Clyde territory.

Lou Black waited until Porter went off the air, then talked to him about coming to Springfield to work for KWTO. E. E. ("Si") Siman had also heard Porter on his car radio while driving home from a convention in Memphis. Si was a KWTO executive, and he also thought Porter had the Hank Williams sound. So Si called Bob Neathery at KWPM and said, "I'd like to hire your boy, but I'd hate to hurt you and take your paid show away." Bob said, "That's all right. We can't do very much for him here."

Yet Porter lacked the confidence to decide. Sid Vaughan's sister Bessie fairly hammered on him to go. Bessie says Porter was very shy and "He'd blush easily, especially if you bragged on him." She pressed him, "You've got to try, Porter."

There was an audition, and Porter took along Granville Nichols and Don Russell, although both of them knew the only spot open at KWTO was for a single. They backed Porter on "Lovesick Blues."

He burst back into the market with the news. KWTO had offered him thirty-five dollars a week, a reduction from his current fifty dollars with Sid Vaughan. But if the listeners liked him, he might get a raise. He gave Sid two weeks' notice, but Sid quickly said, "You can leave anytime you want to. I'll take care of the store. Tell 'em you'll be down next Monday."

On Sunday, September 29, 1951, Porter headed for Springfield in his 1940 Chevrolet "with slick tires." He rented a sleeping room in Springfield, but got no sleep whatever. Show time was 5:30 A.M. the next day.

Ruth Wagoner hung in at the shoe factory until the next April. Presumably Sid Vaughan made sure his next butcher trainee didn't own a guitar.

6

SPRINGFIELD, KWTO, AND SI SIMAN

Among KWTO's new air personnel is the fellow
you seem to have already taken to your heart,
Porter Wagoner. You're right—he does sound
a little like Hank Snow, Eddy Arnold, Hank
Williams and Roy Acuff all rolled into one.

—Chuck Hessington, "Inside the Studio,"
KWTO Dial (October 1951)

Porter Wagoner is, without question,
the most successful native entertainer or
musician to come out of the Ozarks of
Missouri and Arkansas.

—Wayne Glenn, host of "Remember When"
syndicated radio show (KXTR Springfield),
letter, April 25, 1989

Porter was up at 4:00 A.M. on Monday morning, September 30, 1951. He was waiting outside the KWTO studio when Lou Black arrived. Porter was touched that the musicians had learned his repertoire so well that it sounded like a phonograph record.

Porter, who had learned to talk to listeners by now, made his strong pitch for mail. Days went by, and his spirits fell when—each day—his mail box out by the receptionist's desk was empty. He was very worried by Thursday and was near panic by Friday. Going in to do his 11:30 A.M. show, he was stopped by the switchboard operator. She wondered when he was going to get his mail. Mail? She directed him to the basement.

There sat three large cardboard boxes full of mail!

Porter's co-worker from the shoe factory, Lucile Goodin, says, "Everyone in West Plains wrote cards and supported him all they could."

Porter says he just sat down and cried. He was astounded that people who didn't even know him cared that much to see him get a break. For weeks he couldn't talk about it. As he told Paul Soelberg in 1971, "That changed my whole personality, my whole soul. I began to get some confidence."

When he went back upstairs, Lou Black summoned him into his office, raised him to seventy dollars a week even though he hadn't yet picked up his first paycheck. With three shows a day, Porter would earn it. The first two were called "The Porter Wagoner Show" (5:30–6:00 A.M. and 7:45–8:00 A.M.), plus "The Ozark Home Hour" (11:30 A.M.–12:00 noon). He was again working in a factory, only this one was a music factory. Incredibly, KWTO employed around forty entertainers, generating 150 live quarter-hour shows a week.

Ruth quit the shoe factory in April 1952. Never again would she have to work "out" since, against all the odds, her husband was now a professional entertainer, and even a salaried one.

Porter had been living at Mrs. Robert Bell's rooming house at 933 East St. Louis Street. KWTO was relatively near, at number 600, across the street from the Shrine Mosque, where many country acts would play over the years. When Ruth arrived, she was pregnant. She had German measles, but the baby, Debra Jean, was unaffected. They lived in rental quarters at 441 South Grant.

The KWTO story had begun in a St. Joseph, Missouri, tire shop in 1926. Ralph D. Foster and Jerry Hall (no relation to the Howell County clan) had set up a fifteen-watt station, KGBX, in a four-by-twelve-foot room. The noise from the tire shop added humor to their broadcasts, and when a customer came in with an innertube needing a patch, they'd leave the air and attend to their real business.

In Springfield in 1933 they started a parallel station, KWTO (Keep Watching The Ozarks), which Foster eventually took over completely. Their stated goal was to reach "every deer lick, rabbit warren, and hawg waller" in those hills. By the midfifties, Springfield was boasting of being the "Crossroads of Country Music," and the owner of KWTO, Ralph D. Foster, had become a millionaire.

His loyal assistant, Ely E. ("Si") Siman, also craved to earn a million. The first songs Si published were Porter Wagoner compositions, and the first hit he published was Porter's first hit. Si got Chet Atkins his first record deal, having already turned "Chester" into "Chet"; he got Porter his first record deal; and he invented the Ozark Jubilee, which made fools out of the Grand Ole Opry management for having spurned the opportunity of network TV exposure, twisting the knife by using the Opry's former star host, Red Foley. The Jubilee also launched Red's discovery, Brenda Lee.

Si was twelve years old when he blundered into KWTO in 1933 selling Popsicles. He hauled them around in an orange crate with two wagon wheels attached and a broomstick for the handle. Dry ice kept the merchandise cool, and Si kept his feet cool on the hot sidewalks, by lining his shoes with chilly Milky Way wrappers.

Ralph Foster admired Si's sales pitch so much that he bought everyone in the studio a Popsicle. Soon after, Foster hired him to wipe ashtrays and lug equipment. By the time he was in high school, Si was booking big-name bands like the Dorseys and Glenn Miller into the Shrine Mosque.

After World War II and college, Si hit up Ralph Foster for a real job. Si said, "What I'm really looking for is not a job but a chance to become somebody in business. If I ever made you any money, would you let me have any of it?" Foster had never heard that pitch before, but it sounded reasonable.

By the war years KWTO had become a venerable institution, once spreading the news that some Italian prisoners of war had escaped, so the highway patrol could nab them. KWTO had a country music show spiced with bumpkin comedy they sold to Mutual Broadcasting for two years called "Korn's-a-Krackin'." They also specialized in making live "open-end transcriptions"—mini-shows with space left for a local station's messages. They cut these by the hundreds on acetates and sometimes sold them to competing stations or even competing networks, since KWTO could always come up with something for everybody.

Si Siman never exactly worked for KWTO, but for the various corporations Foster was always starting with his other partners, Lester E. Cox, John Mehaffey, and Si. Foster fired Si five different times, twice in one day, even though Si was a surrogate son for Foster, who had no children. Si became something of a father figure for Porter and served as his first manager, although there was precious little to manage at first.

Porter studied the music business under Si, who was vice president of RadiOzark Enterprises, Inc.; of Earl Barton Music, Inc.; and of Top Talent, Inc., to name but three. He and his partners usually cut things four ways; and they used assorted wives and other kin to staff their plentiful corporate boards, a practice that gave the IRS fewer people to interview later. Si told me he was "basically a farmer," and he told John W. Rumble of the Country Music Foundation's library, "I originally wanted to be a comedian, but didn't know how."

Probably Si's Big Band phase had instilled in him the concept of the star, as opposed to that of the group like KWTO's venerable Goodwill Family. Si didn't want Porter to fade into the landscape of a group act such as the Foggy River Boys.

If Porter were going to become a Hank Williams, though, a couple of details had to be attended to. Porter would have to write some songs—Si could help him here— and he would have to get on a major record label. Si wanted Porter on RCA since his Nashville role model, Fred Rose, had Hank on MGM, and Red Foley, whom Si had his eye on, was on Decca.

Left: E. E. ("Si") Siman, Porter's first
manager and originator of the "Ozark Jubilee" ABC television show [KWTO DIAL,
COURTESY WAYNE GLENN]. Below: *The
Wagoners' rental home in Springfield at
422 South Ferguson, 1953–55* [PHOTO BY
AUTHOR].

For Si, it was getting Porter on RCA or nothing. He had already landed Chet Atkins an RCA deal. Chet had been fired from KWTO for no good reason—Si was out of the office and couldn't save his job—but he had a great consolation prize. Steve Sholes offered Chet an RCA contract, having liked the demo of "Canned Heat" Si had gotten to him. Si couldn't very well manage Chet long-distance, however. That was in 1948.

But Chet boomeranged back, playing with the Carter Family. KWTO was on the site of a funeral parlor, and they'd record commercials down in the embalming room where the echo was good. Si told Chet his playing was getting too good, and Chet wondered, too good for *what*? Too good for Springfield, Si admitted.

Martha White flour lured the Carters to the Opry, where Chet could earn three to five dollars a night. Chet laughs, "I was never really hired by the Opry. They fired me once, but they never did hire me," which he suspects was due to their aversion to paying benefits.

In 1952 Si was sitting on the front porch of the Kentwood Arms Hotel in Springfield with Steve Sholes, the New York-based head of RCA's country and western division. They were in wooden rocking chairs listening to Porter Wagoner acetates. "I'd like to meet this Wagoner boy," said Steve.

Si bought Porter a white suit, white shoes, and a plane ticket for New York.

It was Porter's first plane trip. For Steve he played "Jimmy Brown the Newsboy" and "Lovesick Blues" and was starting "Old Log Cabin for Sale" when Steve interrupted. "I don't need to hear any more. I like how you sound."

"I'm very nervous," answered Porter. "I'm just a long ways from home, in such a big city."

Steve said, "We'll sign you to a contract, and we'll record a hit sooner or later. We won't set a specific date. We'll just keep recording till we make a hit. I know you can sing a hit if we get you the right song."

The contract was dated June 5, 1952, and RCA obligated itself to a mere four sides.

Porter's first session at KWTO was held on September 19, 1952, with Steve Sholes present. They cut ten songs in two three-hour stints. Almost certainly they used tape recorders, although a disc copy was made simultaneously, since no one knew how long a tape, or a signal on a tape, might last. The jazzy piano player Paul Mitchell was on the session—he'd been with Tommy Dorsey—and of course Speedy Haworth was playing his hollow-body (F-hole) electric guitar, good for those shuffling barred chords up the neck. Audie ("Buster") Fellows played fiddle; Claude Jackson, steel guitar; George Rhodes, acoustic guitar; Robert White, bass.

The first number was a play-it-safe cover version of a song Hank Williams had just released, "Settin' the Woods on Fire." Written by Fred Rose and Ed G. Nelson, it would be the A–side of Porter's first single. Flip-side was "Headin' for a Wedding," written by Porter and Dave Estes, a KWTO staff announcer. Publisher was Earl Barton at the KWTO address.

One of RCA's white-label advance copies of Porter's first single floated into Roy Queen's record shop in St. Louis. And one of Porter's old West Plains picking pals, Uiel Albeil, just happened in. He knew Roy, and he got himself a free Porter Wagoner record. There was no charge because, Roy said, "That boy's not going to make it."

RCA sent out a sales letter dated September 29, 1952, gushing, "With this record we figure to cash in big in the Country-Western market." The record was released October 4, and next day the Springfield *News-Leader* announced: "Springfield Folksinger Hits Big Time," adding that "at least one Ozarks jukebox operator is putting Wagoner's record on all of his music machines" and that it was starting to get airplay in Chicago, Cincinnati, Omaha, Louisville, St. Louis, Kansas City, and even on "one 50,000 watter in Mexico."

Hank Williams's version entered *Billboard* on October 11 and went to number two on the charts for twelve weeks. On October 18, Frankie Laine's cut of the song, mistitled "Tonight We're Settin' the Woods on Fire," went on the pop charts and up to number twenty-one. Porter's version set no one's woods or heart, let alone the world, on fire. Porter, ostensibly the "next Hank Williams," and Si Siman would eventually learn that no one is ever really the "next" anybody else.

In November Porter and Si went to Nashville to hawk their new single to the disc jockeys. Si was going to Nashville almost monthly in those days, and when Porter would accompany him, they would write songs as they drove. The Opry had decided it needed to celebrate its twenty-seventh anniversary, and about ninety-two disc jockeys signed in at the Commodore Room of the Andrew Jackson Hotel on November 21, 1952. In a 1976 article in *Independent Songwriter*, Jimmie Helms recalled driving down with Porter and Si in Si's station wagon. Down in Printer's Alley Jimmie claimed to have spotted Hank Williams in his familiar suit with musical notes up and down his pant legs working on a fifth of whiskey.

Meanwhile, Porter was little more than another KWTO staff singer. That he was "on RCA" sounded good when booking schoolhouses, but it didn't buy the gasoline. The next single, "I Can't Live Without You/Takin' Chances," recorded December 5, 1952, didn't sell either. None of them would for a long while.

Entertainer Harold Morrison recalls the first time he saw Porter, driving a 1946 Chevrolet with four antennas, each with a fox tail, and Porter wearing his Bill Monroe hat. Vic Willis, of the Willis Brothers, recalls his Acme boots and drape-style western suit, the Hank Williams style. He remembers seeing Porter once, patiently waiting outside Si's office, holding in his hand three or four cheap bolo ties, the kind with the metal tips and the slide that tightens under the neck. "He was hungry then, he wasn't making any money. It kinda touched me. Here he wanted to impress the man who was trying to do something for him. Just to improve his appearance a little."

Porter's hand-over-the-mouth shyness was noticed by many, as was his habit of looking down while he talked. The late Bill Ring, a KWTO announcer, said that as a talent Porter was "unbeatable," but he remembered having to do his commercials for him. Speedy Haworth, who backed him on his show with guitar, says, "He had courage and guts, he'd get right in there and try. He might pronounce things wrong or didn't know what he was reading . . . he might get kinda scared. But he did pretty good at it."

Windy Luttrell and Lloyd Presley—later well-known performers in Branson, Missouri—used to have an "Ozarks Playboys" nighttime show over local KGBX radio in Springfield. Remembers Windy, "Porter would come by and just slap that ole guitar and just *sing*. He has a much higher pitched voice than people really realize. He just couldn't stand still, either. He'd tell jokes and fish stories and get to laughing where he couldn't stop. I've seen him laughing till he couldn't sing."

He also haunted the Reverend Fred Lynn's "Hillbilly Heaven" evening show on KWTO. It was a call-in, audience rapport show. Even after midnight, coming back from a live date, Porter would drop by and loyally field his quota of listener calls. Some of these were heard over the air, others, not. In its tireless efforts to bring the public closer, KWTO had provided private phone lines. This service was especially popular with female connoisseurs of Ozark music. "Hillbilly Heaven" had its public, as well as its private, definition.

In February 1953 Porter and Si headed for Nashville for Porter's first recording session there. They were going to Thomas Productions, a television and photography studio in a large industrial garage with a makeshift recording studio and a loading dock outside. In 1953 Hank Snow would cut thirty-seven sides at Thomas, and here the Davis Sisters cut "I Forgot More Than You'll Ever Know," also for RCA. It went to number one; but by the time it entered *Billboard*, the lead singer, Betty Jack Davis, was dead from a car wreck. Her partner, Mary Frances Penick, survived and made an independent career with her stage name of Skeeter Davis.

The reason for recording in this gloomy garage was RCA's union

Above: Porter and Rev. Fred Lynn open the listener mail on Fred's "Hillbilly Heaven" show on KWTO, Springfield [COURTESY REV. FRED LYNN]. Below: "Busy Bee Jamboree," broadcast 6:45–7:00 A.M. every morning over KWTO, Springfield. Buster Fellows played on, and helped pay for, the recording of "A Satisfied Mind."

contract. RCA could not use local personnel or equipment, so they almost never recorded at Castle studio in the Tulane Hotel where Hank Williams recorded. As Chet Atkins remembers, "RCA would bring their home-made tape machine and microphone down to Nashville. Jeff Miller, the engineer, would bring a Hammond reverb unit." Earlier RCA had used Brown Radio Productions, a commercials studio, until it had closed up. The Brown brothers who ran it were from Springfield; Charlie Brown had worked at KWTO and had gone to school with Si.

In 1989 Porter deplored these primitive recording conditions to Debi Moen in *Performance* magazine:

> At one time when country music was recorded they used the cheapest equipment available; they didn't go to New York or L.A. where all the big studios were to make records. Those were for the Sinatras and people in more pop-oriented music. Roy Acuff and others recorded on the cheap stuff in Nashville. All that's turned around. We have the finest recording facilities here in the world. So country music really *has* come a long way—fans don't like the whiney or muddy sound we used to have. Hell, they have good ears, too!

The walls at Thomas Productions were hung with baffles, the portable walls that keep sound in, if not out. Nearby was the newspaper printing plant that served both Nashville daily papers; and when a newspaper truck went by, it could ruin a take and they'd have to start again. When the lady next door would make too much noise raking leaves and gravel, they'd ask her to stop until they finished recording.

The studio belonged to Cliff Thomas and was located at 109 Thirteenth Avenue North. It's gone today, torn down to make room for Interstate 265.

The date of the session was February 14, 1953. Chet Atkins was on guitar and among other personnel was "Papa" John Gordy on piano. Papa John was a Dixieland, rinky-tink piano player who'd performed on Nashville's first number one hit, the pop record of "Near You" in 1947.

Porter recorded again in Nashville on September 19, 1953, one year to the day after his inaugural RCA session at Springfield. It was a historic session according to Bob Tubert, since Porter cut a song he had written with Bob and Si back in Springfield, the inane "Dig That Crazy Moon." Bob says solemnly, "It was the turning point of Porter's career . . . it took him as low as he could get."

Meanwhile, Hank Williams was doing even better dead than alive. He had departed on January 1, 1953, with a hit on his cold, cold hands, "I'll Never Get Out of This World Alive," which had gone to number one posthumously. He had more number ones in 1953 than he

Thomas Productions, 109 13th Avenue North, Nashville, 1953. Cliff Thomas (in checked shirt toward far left) ran this makeshift studio used by RCA. (Thomas had written "Portia Faces Life" radio soap opera scripts before coming to Nashville.) Porter, Hank Snow, Chet Atkins, and Skeeter Davis are among those who recorded here. Band leader (and later country producer) Owen Bradley is standing fourth from left [COURTESY MORT THOMASSON].

had had in any previous year—three of them. Of some small consolation to Steve Sholes was the fact that each year RCA was beating Hank's label, MGM, in number of Top 10 hits. But how long Steve was going to wait for Porter to have that first hit was not clear.

However, there were other media than records; there was television. Nashville and WSM had television, of course, in a local, humdrum way. So did Springfield. Si knew nothing about television, but his friend Eddy Arnold had been on network TV, and so had Hank Williams once. Did it all have to come out of New York or Chicago or L.A.? It certainly wasn't going to come out of Nashville, not with its current state of mind (mindlessness) concerning network TV.

Si's role model, Fred Rose, died in 1954. Fred had tried and succeeded at everything but one thing: television. Though Porter didn't exactly ooze self-confidence, his shyness might have a certain convincing quality on the TV screen if he had some coaching. Porter was always game for anything.

7

RED FOLEY AND THE "OZARK JUBILEE"

Springfield is nipping at the heels of
Nashville, Tennessee, home of the Grand Ole Opry
and the long-established home of country music.
More cowboy-booted players breeze around in
Cadillacs in Springfield than in
any other place its size.

—Phil Dessauer, "Springfield, MO.—Radio City
of Country Music," *Coronet* (April 1957)

Not one of us really
knew anything about television;
in fact, we had barely seen a camera.
We didn't know that we *couldn't* produce
a TV country music show, so why not try it?

—Si Siman to Sherlu Walpole,
Springfield! magazine (June 1986)

Porter has been a familiar television face for thirty years. Someone once called him "Country Music's King of the Small Screen." The twenty-year run of his syndicated TV show, plus all his appearances on cable TV, would seem to offer persuasive evidence.

Whatever Porter has accomplished on TV owes greatly to Red Foley and the program he hosted: the "Ozark Jubilee." The Jubilee's success laid the groundwork for Porter's TV show and for all the syndicated shows subsequently to come out of Nashville, chiefly from Porter's producers at Show–Biz, Inc. Certainly the Jubilee is the distant ancestor of the cable-TV "Nashville Now" on which Porter so frequently appears. Its omnipresent host is Ralph Emery.

Today, with Nashville vying with Branson, Missouri, for the country music tourist dollar, the story of the "Ozark Jubilee" takes on an uncanny sense of *déjà-vu*. For Nashville it might serve as a reminder and a warning.

The gradual shift back to Nashville from Springfield in 1957 may be traced to Porter's "A Satisfied Mind," which he recorded in Springfield and which went to number one in 1955. Porter's exit, followed by that of Brenda Lee, signaled the breaking of Springfield's hold and of Nashville's retaking of lost ground.

Though everyone soon adjusted and smoothed over the wide rifts, as show business people tend to do, there is something of Wordsworth's phrase in the whole story: *"old unhappy far-off things, and battles long ago . . ."*

The birth of the Jubilee stems directly from Si Siman's desire to make a million dollars, and that goal was moving farther and farther out of reach, because of what the increasing popularity of television was doing to his RadiOzark business. Fewer and fewer people wanted all those open-end transcriptions; sponsors and therefore radio stations were canceling.

In April 1949 *Look* magazine ran an article titled "Radio Is Doomed," written by a former president of NBC. In 1948 fewer than two households in a hundred owned a TV set, but that number had jumped to sixty-eight in a hundred by 1953.

If Si detected a trend in there somewhere, the Opry did not. With embarrassment, Minnie Pearl says that the WSM management had been afraid TV might hurt Opry ticket sales. With general admission tickets costing thirty cents, obviously hundreds of dollars were at stake.

WSM had been started in 1925 by Edwin W. Craig, vice president of National Life and Accident Insurance Company, as a kind of hobby that his father, the company president, let him indulge. By 1933 "clear channel" WSM with its 50,000 watts was reaching maybe two-thirds of the United States.

Edwin W. Craig may have been a radio pioneer, but he wanted to freeze the Opry in its folk song, Elizabethan mode of, say, 1935 because it was easier to control that way. When it came to television, he emulated the ostrich and the mouse. In 1947 he told Pee Wee King not to go to Louisville and try to start a television station: "Pee Wee, it's a fad. It'll never make it."

When WSM finally started its TV station in 1950, Craig promised the "very highest in public entertainment"—but that didn't mean a regular Opry show. The National Life insurance sales motto, "We Shield Millions," insured that millions would be shielded from any kind of regular network country music show emanating from Nashville. A record promotions man, Murray Nash, tried in vain to interest WSM in televising an Opry show. Nash suggested they convert the Gem Theater at 1003 First Avenue South into a sound stage, but no one wanted to. Nash says Opry manager Jim Denny "didn't want it to change any from what it was. He didn't want it to get out of hand." The still-standing empty theater is a mute monument to the Opry's myopia.

✳   ✳   ✳

A television show required a star at its center and, preferably, a new face, not one that was already familiar through films. Si's three partners had told him not to come back from Nashville without Red Foley. It took Si four trips to bag Red, and Porter was riding shotgun on two of the forays.

Actually, Red was running out of enthusiasm for Nashville, and the feeling was mighty mutual. Si but offered Red a ticket out.

Red was already a hovering presence, from his long-time appearance on WLS on the "National Barn Dance" out of Chicago beginning in 1931 to the "Renfro Valley Barn Dance," to, finally, his hosting of the Opry starting in 1946 on the Prince Albert Tobacco portion. This was the network radio segment, with Red replacing Roy Acuff, who was touring the nation with his tent. Red would chart dozens of country hits, plus numerous pop hits.

Porter has often called Red his own greatest influence in the area of showmanship, of handling audiences and hosting shows, not in singing style. Says Sally Foley, Red's widow, "Porter has no jealousy, same as Red. Red would go out first, introduce everybody, do his own songs last. Porter reminds me of Red more than anybody."

In November 1951 Red's second wife, Eva, died of a heart condition, according to the press. But Hank Snow's son, Reverend Jimmy Snow, in his *I Cannot Go Back* autobiography, says she committed suicide over Red's philandering. In December of 1952, thirteen months to the day of Eva's death, Red secretly wed entertainer Sally Sweet after publicly denying he was going to marry her. Sally's ex-husband, music publisher Frank Kelton, had sued Red for alienation of affections. Sally was a singer-comedienne, a protégée of Eddie Cantor and an old friend of Jimmy Durante. Red's domestic profile belied, somewhat, the hearth 'n' home sentimentality of *Red Foley's Keepsake Album*, a booklet of pious and rustic recitations that WSM sold by mail order.

By 1952, it was starting to look as if Red had more in common with Hank Williams than mere charisma, namely "problems," which is Music City terminology for you-name-it. Most written contracts provide for unforeseen "acts of God," to which Si Siman laughingly adds, "self-inflicted acts of God," speaking of Red. Si told me Red had "political problems" at the Opry, and Chet Hagan writes that Edwin Craig disliked Red, probably because he was too much the star. Then again, Red may have chafed under the Opry requirement for a minimum twenty-six appearances a year. Red needed to move up, not down. Si says, "I think Red at this point had outgrown the Opry. When you've gone to the top of the bottle, like cream does, there isn't anyplace else to go."

By April 1953, Opry manager Jim Denny was protesting to the

Clyde Julian ("Red") Foley

press that "there is no feud between Red and WSM." In the next breath Jim admitted that Red was not renewing his Opry contract but would have guest spots when he was in town and not touring. Red said he was selling his house: "I'm going to let someone else worry with that swimming pool."

That July around 20,000 people in Nashville's Centennial Park watched Red and Sally cavort in a comedy act in a package show. "The old master of folk music," *Tennessean* reporter John Seigenthaler called him. Pat Boone was on the bill, his first hit record almost two years away (Pat would marry Red's daughter by the late Eva, Shirley Foley).

Si kept the sales pressure on, and when he closed the deal with Red, it was thanks, in part, to a baseball accident. Si had been a batboy for the Springfield Cardinals and, more lately, sliding into second base with the KWTO company team, he had broken his leg. He had to be helped onto the airplane to Nashville. He and Red met at the Andrew Jackson Hotel. Red had had a number of teeth pulled, so Si and Red required the soothing solace of three or four bottles of Jack Daniel's whiskey. When the weekend was over and the bottles emptied, Red had become enchanted with the prospect of greener grass, maybe greener bucks, up in Springfield.

Sally Foley remembers hearing the spiel, too: "Honey, when Si talks, he could sell you the Brooklyn Bridge. We sat talking for hours and by the time he walked out the door, I said, 'Honey, what a wonderful person he is. As long as the Opry is going to just pay [union] scale, let's gamble, if you think you can better yourself.' Si is a go-getter. We started out small, but it outgrew us all."

Si Siman was talking up television—about which he at present knew nothing. So on February 20, 1954, Red signed two contracts: one with Top Talent, for exclusive bookings, the other with RadiOzark to do fifteen-minute open-end transcriptions for syndication. Considering how little Springfield could offer Red tangibly, he let them tie him up for five years. However, no one in Nashville was even talking about television. As it turned out, both parties certainly got a good deal.

On April 23, the national tabloid *Pickin' and Singin'* headlined "Red Foley Goes to Springfield" in boldface across the front page. An advertisement placed by RCA announced "Special Guest in Little Rock: Porter Wagoner," along with details of the RCA "Country-Western Caravan" package tour of fourteen cities. Porter had been tacked onto the end of the tour by Si, who was handling the Little Rock date. The tour itself was run by "Colonel" Tom Parker, who a year or two earlier had been bumming free long-distance phone calls in the WSM lobby. Parker was a pseudo-Southerner—he claimed to be from West Virginia but really was from Holland—who ran Jamboree Attractions out of his grey stone house in Madison, north of Nashville.

Digging through Si's boxes of memorabilia in his storage shed in Springfield, I came across what looked like a photo of Smiley Burnette. "No," said Si, "that's Colonel Parker, dressed up like Smiley. He used to play poker with us and clean us out. Then he'd come back next day and give us our money back."

The "Ozark Jubilee" had already started on local television (KYTV) back in December 1953. Red Foley was on hand to host its network radio (ABC) inauguration on July 17, 1954.

But the question on everybody's mind was how to get it on ABC television.

Flying to New York to make their pitch to the ABC executives were Si, Ralph Foster, John Mahaffey, and KWTO vice president Les Kennon. This was the first year ABC–TV had enjoyed much success. They had lent Walt Disney half a million dollars and acquired 35 percent interest in Disneyland and Disney's TV programs. Now here came Si Siman the poker player, with Red Foley as his trump card. Red already had thirty-nine country hits, nearly all Top 10, plus thirteen pop hits. He was also a radio star. ABC went for it. Si says, "We sold 'em a pig in a poke. We didn't even own a camera. We didn't know what we were getting into." Si told the Country Music Foundation Library's Oral History Project in 1989, "We had so much faith in what we were doing that failure was not even in our minds. If you don't bet on your own talents, whose talents *are* you going to bet on?"

Si has ridiculed the ABC executives' grasp of geography: "They thought to reach Springfield you went to Times Square and turned left." However, they called on the phone and improved his education as well. It seemed that Springfield could receive but couldn't transmit a television signal because of the earth's curvature. Across the country were microwave relay stations, every twenty-five miles, bouncing the signals along, but Springfield was not in the path.

So, for the first three months they drove twenty-four hours a week by bus, every week. There was a microwave tower at Columbia, Missouri, where the University of Missouri had a station. They could rehearse on Friday night, get up at four in the morning, drive to Columbia, rehearse some more, and do the Saturday night show.

But when the little red lights went on in the studio in Columbia that first time, Si says he felt the thrill of a lifetime. Red Foley asked for mail, and he pulled 25,000 letters from that first show. Si told Sherlu Walpole, writing for *Springfield!* magazine, that "Red always had a lump in his throat for about thirty seconds at the start of the program. It was the idea that more people were seeing him in one instant than would ever see him in person in his entire lifetime."

As the "Ozark Jubilee" flourished, Si gradually began nudging Porter into position as a kind of understudy of Red Foley. He recalled:

> Porter's a clutch hitter. He likes to come from behind. When that red light comes on, it takes that first thirty seconds just to get your breath straightened out. You're going to have to make it happen—they're not going to back the tape up and start over. At first, Porter came across like he was very insecure. We talked about that. If there was any one thing we did, it was put him in key positions when maybe he wasn't ready to play shortshop. 'Cause he got into the ballgame, and became almost the second star only to Red Foley on the Jubilee. All those guys who left here with that experience, the emcee experience—Leroy Van Dyke, Bobby Lord—they got their own television shows later. We were involving Porter in the scripts, even. Originally he had trouble tuning his guitar. It was all part of our farm club training program, getting him ready for the major leagues.

Sally Foley says, "Red used to adopt people. He adopted Porter. Did you know that Porter was bashful? He would talk to Red for hours. I remember seeing him standing in the stage entrance, his big blue eyes popping out of his head, listening to Red so attentively."

Red trained Porter how to emcee. "Never try to talk *over* anyone, don't try to talk loud enough where you'll be heard in the back row. Talk directly to one person. If the P.A. [public address system] is correct, they'll hear you and it's all on a one-to-one basis. Because it becomes offensive if you start talking to everybody overall. Just talk to one person, and it comes across on a far more personal level." Porter had thought you should speak louder if the audience were noisy, but Red said speak lower and they'll listen more intently.

Porter was captivated by Red's recitations, like "The Funeral," where a black preacher consoles the parents of a dead boy. The audience would grow deathly still, no movement at all. Still Porter decided he would do his own recitations in his own style.

Bobby Lord, later an Opry member, says Red was the father figure who taught them all. "He was the authority, greatest country singer who ever lived, in my opinion." Bobby asked Red how he drew such emotion out of his gospel songs, and Red said he just imagined his mama and papa sitting on the couch in their livingroom. "That's a little hokey," laughs Bobby, "but he said it really works." And Red coached Bobby in how to control an audience, what to say and what not to say. When Bobby was about to pounce on someone's line, or say the punch line or the straight line too fast, Red would hiss under his breath, "Hold it, hold it!" Porter's masterly sense of timing on stage is straight from Red.

Red lived in the alcoholic's glass house, so he didn't throw rocks at others. Slim Wilson says that in seven years he never heard Red criticize anyone's intonation or say they were singing too fast or too slow. "Everything was just beautiful with Red," Slim told Jim Ellison for *Springfield!* magazine, "It was really a joy to work with him."

Television director Gene Hudson adds a note of dissonance to the chorus of praise Red inspired. "Foley was an asshole," Gene told me. "Everyone laid on the floor and wanted to be walked on, so star struck were they. Foley was weak, just trying to pay off his booze bill. All those young entertainers, snapping at his ass!"

The "girl singer" on Porter's later television show for seven years was Norma Jean, actually Norma Jean Beasler. Red got her to drop her last name for the Jubilee. Like all the other performers, Norma Jean loved Red. Unlike some of the flame-keepers, she remembers him realistically. She says he had praise for everyone, always. "He was so emotional in his performances. He was a deep, emotional person, he would cry when he'd sing. He was capable of taking an audience into the palm of his hand, he'd get them involved, like hand-clapping on 'He's Got the Whole World in His Hands.' I doubt if his abilities were even tapped as an entertainer because of his drinking problem."

Norma Jean says Red went on binges for days, days when they couldn't find him. She's seen Red so bad they couldn't straighten him up. "By show time he might have been drinking several days," she regretfully remembers.

Porter contrasted sharply with Red—and with most other musicians—offstage. "After a show, you never saw Porter go out with the boys and have a drink," says Sally Foley. "He was a loner when it came to people."

Porter's mentor Red was an alcoholic, and so was his own brother, Oscar, and his brother-in-law, Ed Hall. If Porter ever made it to the Grand Ole Opry, he had decided they wouldn't be kicking him off or coaxing him off due to any "problems," that was for damn sure.

After thirteen weeks of trekking to Columbia, the Jubilee troupe settled into Springfield, the necessary communication links successfully completed.

The old Jewell Theater at 216 South Jefferson Street and McDaniel had been darkened first by the Depression and then by World War II. It had reopened in 1948, then closed down again because of television. Yet it was television that turned its lights back on. Ralph Foster's latest subsidiary, Crossroads TV, Inc., began remodeling it.

The show was one-half hour at first, then one hour, then longer when ABC could work it in. And it was drawing some two thousand visitors a week to Springfield. Many bought advance tickets at a dollar each. Hotels and motels would buy up advance tickets too, and so would tour buses. A crowd would line up an hour or so before the show, like at the Ryman in Nashville. Visitors were counted from as many as thirty states, as well as from Canada, Mexico, Hawaii (not yet a state), and Nova Scotia. Some would stay a week and catch two shows. A million dollars a year now rolled into Springfield.

The show was carried by 105 stations, reaching eight million viewers. In a couple of weeks in 1957, it came in third after "Gunsmoke" and either "Encore Theater" or "George Gobel." For its ratings, it had the lowest cost per thousand dollars of any show on the air.

The straggling Opry brought up the rear. Every fourth week in the 1955–56 season ABC deigned to run an hour of the Opry. But it was shot as-is, not specially created like the Jubilee. In 1955 ABC ran another show shot in Springfield, "Talent Variety" starring Slim Wilson. From spring to fall 1956, it also ran "The Eddy Arnold Show," with Chester, now Chet, Atkins thrown in. Springfield became the third biggest television origination point after New York and Hollywood. "That's unbelievable," sighs Si.

The Jubilee tourist traffic spilled over into the Fantastic Caverns near Branson, Missouri, which gradually evolved into today's Branson music scene.

One evening at the Jewell Theater, Ruth Wagoner was watching the Jubilee with daughter Debra. A little girl in a ruffled dress and shining patent leather shoes was entertaining onstage. Debra asked, "Who's that, Mother?"

Ruth answered, "That's Brenda Lee."

Though Brenda does not remember the political struggle—she was only twelve in 1957—it was Porter's departure for Nashville that precipitated her own. She had been born in a charity ward in Georgia in 1944. Her father had died in a construction accident, and her mother remarried. Little Brenda's big-voiced singing was her family's ticket out of oblivion.

Red Foley discovered Brenda, got her on Decca records and onto the Jubilee. Ralph Foster's group moved Brenda's family to Springfield; they even bought her clothes. Soon "Little Miss Dynamite" was on "The Perry Como Show," a national sensation.

Red cautioned Brenda's mother not to sign with anybody hastily but to get herself a good manager such as Dub Albritten who managed him. Sally Foley says even Red could have managed Brenda, though stars managing other stars is the supreme show business folly. Sally continues, "She [Mrs. Rainwater, Brenda's mother] would sign anything. But they [Lou Black of Top Talent, Inc.] signed her before we heard about it. We were *shocked!*"

Red told Sally, "There must be something in the contract so we can break it. After all, this child is too *good* to be here in Springfield."

THE PORTER WAGONER TRIO

Don came into my world when I had first begun.
He stuck with me in the hard old days—
I love him as I do my own son;
He built me up when I was down
and the way was hard to find,
He was on my side in all I tried
when we didn't have a dime.

—Porter, from the recitation
"My Boys" (1971)

Bandleader Lawrence Welk said many times that he looked for character in a musician, even above playing ability. He said you could improve a man's playing, but not his character. Porter's choice of musicians has always reflected the same thinking, especially in the early days when the money was so meagre.

Don Warden began playing steel guitar for Porter in 1953, becoming his road manager almost immediately, and eventually his business manager once they had some actual business to manage (such as their publishing company). Don left Porter in 1975 to work for Dolly Parton, and he is her Nashville manager today.

Don was born in 1929, the son of a Pentecostal preacher. After finishing high school in West Plains, he began playing steel guitar with his Rhythm Rangers band, sometimes getting on Bob Neathery's KWPM. He worked as an electrician's helper at an appliance shop four doors down from Vaughan's Market and vaguely knew that Porter "sang a little."

By 1953 he was in Springfield, singing high-tenor with Porter and playing steel. Speedy Haworth sang along with Don, developing the trademark Porter Wagoner sound: mournful backup singing, with an audible gospel tone. Sometimes Buster Fellows played fiddle.

Don also handled the bookings, extending the Porter Wagoner Trio, as it was now called, over an ever-widening circle in about a hundred-mile radius of Springfield. Don drew a small salary from KWTO, but there was all too much free time. Occasionally he located a good date, but nine out of ten of the gigs were for a percentage of the gate.

The band might take 75 percent, and the Future Farmers of America or the high school senior class get 25 percent. Porter could have demanded more, but he was more interested in just playing and in being invited back next time. Since Porter could guarantee his band nothing, he promised them shares, assuming there was anything to share. Next morning at the radio station, Don would tally up the take and deduct expenses, say four or five cents a mile, and give Porter 50 percent of what was left. Then the "band," meaning two or three sidemen, would split the other half among themselves. Sometimes this meant two or three dollars each. "We felt three dollars was better than nothing at all, and we needed the money," said Don. "I can think of a few of those people—and some were fairly established stars—who refused those dates. Now they're starved out. They didn't make it or last."

Don believes Porter was the first country entertainer to systematically pay shares; certainly he has been the most committed to the process over the years.

In a 1988 interview, Don reminisced about his early road days with Porter. They played small clubs, including one particularly rough joint in Sedalia, Missouri, that was owned by some musicians. The fiddler was the bouncer. He kept a string hanging down over the bandstand, so that when a fight erupted, he could hang up his fragile fiddle quickly and jump into the brawl. Don explained, "The secret to stopping a fight is to get to it early, before it spreads over the whole club." Once at a rodeo in Camdentown, Montana, the announcer said they were going to do the national anthem. "I went into it," Don recalled, "and it was probably the worst rendition of the national anthem that ever was. So I went home and learned it in case that would ever happen again. Of course it never did."

Porter wrote an unpublished song that is obviously about Don, called "A Most Unusual Man":

> *He stands only 5 feet and 4 inches*
> *But much taller in the eyes of other men.*
> *I never knew a brother quite like him,*
> *A most unusual man . . .*

Gary Walker lives in Nashville today, but he was born in Ozark County, Missouri. He owns and manages The Great Escape, a used record store and memorabilia bazaar. Gary grew up listening to KWTO. Attending college in Springfield, he delivered newspapers on the side. One of his customers, he discovered, was Ralph D. Foster, "patriarch of KWTO," Gary calls him fondly. When he told Mr. Foster his greatest dream was to work at KWTO, Foster hired Gary, and soon he was writing songs with Porter.

The best of these songs was "Trademark," whose lyric extols the virtue of being a committed ladies' man. Pitching woo is this fellow's "trademark." Complicated rhymes like "exciting/igniting" may reflect Gary's education. Recorded in Springfield, Porter's version shows off his best blues-moaning voice, capitalizing on all those times he'd performed "Lovesick Blues." The instrumentation, too, is right from Hank's Drifting Cowboys band. There's even the "dead string" effect, of muffling the bass string on the electric guitar to give it a covert drumbeat sound without actually using a drum (drums being still taboo), but posting fair warning that rock was just around the bend.

Opry star Carl Smith liked "Trademark" and recorded it in February 1953 on Columbia. It entered *Billboard* in July, going to number two in sales; it was on the charts for ten weeks. He sent for Porter and gave him a couple of guest spots in the Opry. Roy Acuff slipped Porter his personal phone number, telling him he could call him any time he needed. "Although I never had to call, I always knew I could," Porter says.

Meanwhile single after single came out from RCA, none of them doing anything.

Steve Sholes's patience with Porter Wagoner was not infinite. The first RCA contract ran from June 1952 to March 1953. They'd then issued a more encouraging, full-year contract, until March 1954. But then their faith faltered, and they extended Porter only until September 9, 1954. One of Porter's luckless singles was "Bringing Home the Bacon," which is what his records were not doing for Ruth Wagoner or for Steve Sholes.

Back in 1954 Johnny Mullins had been a milk truck driver when he came up with Porter's first hit. While delivering milk in Springfield, he used to make up songs in his head. But he despaired of getting anything recorded. He didn't know anybody at KWTO.

Then one evening, walking home from a western movie, he spotted Porter in a drugstore having coffee and a doughnut at the counter. Johnny introduced himself, and they experienced instant rapport. They both needed a hit. Porter drove Johnny home to his tiny apartment in a woman's garage.

One day Johnny was driving his milk truck down a hill, when some children came running out and waved. This triggered a childhood memory: the old-timey phrase, *company's comin'*. Pretty good chorus for a song!

Back at his apartment, Johnny began groping for the verses to his song. Since it wasn't going to open with the chorus, this would mean he would have to work backwards, never easy in songwriting. As his biographer Heno Head, Jr., writes in *America's Favorite Janitor*, "Like a bloodhound on the trail of a lost child, he began searching out the verses."

Oddly, they began coming in reverse order, third verse first, then the second; but the first one just wouldn't come. Finally he went outside and stared at the stars. Then he found the opening verse of the song:

> Oh, Mama, I'm excited, I'm almost out of breath,
> What I saw like to make me run myself to death.
> I was on the mountain when I looked down below,
> And glory be, I thought I'd better come and let you know,
>
> Oh, we've got company comin' . . .

With his song in hand, Johnny rushed out to a pay phone to set up a session at a friend's small studio on Walnut Street.

Next day Johnny headed down to KWTO and hunted up Porter, who took him to Si's office, which had "Earl Barton Music—Si Siman, President," on the door. The mythical Barton had never had a hit. Si liked the song so much he summoned Red Foley. Part way through the demo, Red told Johnny to stop. Johnny thought Red didn't like it, but Red just stepped out to grab some more people to hear it.

In the summer of 1954 no one at KWTO was going to invest any money in a Porter Wagoner session, and, although Porter was still on RCA, Steve Sholes was hardly going to fly down to cut another record by him. Johnny recalls that they came up with their own money to rent the equipment from KWTO, even though RadiOzark, Inc., managed Porter. Since the number one rule in songwriting is Don't pay anyone to record your song, Johnny says apologetically, "I needed a break. Porter didn't have much money, and I didn't either. We were both so anxious to get this done. When you write a song, you're afraid if you don't get it out right away, you'll wake up some morning and turn the radio on and hear somebody singing a song called 'Company's Comin'.'"

Sometime in spring or early summer they cut "Company's Comin'" at KWTO. A guitar player from Harrison, Arkansas, named Red Gale was on the session. Porter's "trio" sometimes was three people including himself, sometimes four, and increasingly Red was taking Speedy's place. For the exciting introduction they almost certainly used a blind man named Bill Mount from Harrison, Arkansas. Bill had two wooden blocks lashed to his knees, which were padded with leather patches. He held two other wooden blocks in his hands and popped them against his knees in vigorous syncopation. This provides "Company's Comin'" with that "signature" intro that gives the listener instant identification. Since there's no music behind it, just a monotonic *clackety-clack*, it grabs the ear like those shuffling blocks at the start of Johnny Cash's 1956 hit "I Walk the Line."

Porter's singing on "Company's Comin'" was just as arresting as the introduction. In the very first line, after singing that he's "almost out

PORTER WAGONER
OZARK JUBILEE ABC-TV
Springfield, Missouri

The Porter Wagoner Trio [COURTESY LONNIE LYNNE LACOUR, RHINESTONE ROOSTER RECORDS].

JUNIOR "Speedy" HAWORTH
OZARK JUBILEE ABC-TV
Springfield, Missouri

DON WARDEN
OZARK JUBILEE ABC-TV
Springfield, Missouri

of breath," he lapses into a superb *gasp*, as though he'd come running into the recording studio late. It's easy to imagine Porter running up hill to the Wagoner home place, bounding across the porch and into the parlor, blurting out the lyric. The song fits him like his boyhood coveralls.

It was probably in June or July that Si Siman called Steve Sholes and said, "We've cut a hit." Steve replied, "We've gone as far as we can go with Porter. We've put out some records, and nothing's happened." (It had been eight records, in fact.) Si countered, "We'll foot the bill, we've already got it done."

So the master of "Company's Comin'" was shipped to New York. But nothing was done with it right away.

With "Company's Comin'" now in Steve Sholes's hands, an even bigger song came along for Porter. Probably in August 1954 "A Satisfied Mind" floated onto the third floor at KWTO. It was on the independent label Starday and probably had been recorded in the livingroom of Starday's legendary founder, Pappy Dailey, in Houston, Texas. It was performed by Red Hayes, who had written it with Jack Rhodes.

Certainly the song was an unlikely hit, and it's easy to imagine a publisher or artist and repertoire (A & R) man, as producers were called, rejecting it as uncommercial. It's not about love, and despite its three-quarter (waltz) time, it's scarcely a dance number. Like any timeless song, it would have been easy to call it dated even for 1954—especially for 1954—with rock noises rumbling on Sam Phillips's Sun Records out of Memphis. By the time "A Satisfied Mind" was finally released on a major label (on three of them in fact), after an excruciating delay of nearly a year, the market for such a tranquil yet thoughtful song must have seemed even more unpromising. And as any jaded music publisher could say smugly, the lyric really doesn't "go anywhere." Its lulling, almost abstract, message would become even more halting in the hesitant cadence that Porter and his band eventually stumbled onto, the formula that outsold all the others.

"A Satisfied Mind" has the same whimsically enduring qualities of Red Foley's million-seller "Peace in the Valley." (The Reverend Thomas A. Dorsey had written that song in the late thirties, after viewing from the window of a train cows and sheep grazing side by side in a valley. He wondered why people couldn't live together at peace.) Similarly, Red Hayes packed "A Satisfied Mind" full of wistful wisdom absorbed over the years from his mother. But he lacked a title. One day his father-in-law asked him who he thought was the richest man in the world. Hayes began ticking off the names of millionaires. "You're wrong," his father-in-law said. "It's the man with the satisfied mind."

Si Siman jumped on the Starday single right away, but he says he couldn't interest Porter in the song. Or Red Foley. Or Jean Shepard, although her recollection is different. "You can take this to the bank and put it in, honey. I was up listening to records at the old KWTO studio and ran across this record by Red Hayes. I thought, 'That was a great song; it says so much.' So a couple or three weeks later I copied the words down."

Gradually the song began taking hold, first with Jean and then with Porter and Red Foley. As Si told John W. Rumble of the Country Music Foundation in 1989, "A good song doesn't know or care who sings it."

Porter, Don, and Speedy began singing "A Satisfied Mind" wherever they appeared, to especially strong applause. One day as they drove en route to Harrison, Arkansas, to play a dance, they experimented with the harmony, apparently discontented with how it came out. The problem lay with the opening lines, "How many times have you heard someone say 'If I had his money I would do things my way?'" Don remembers them groping around, not knowing quite where to come in. Finally, by default, they let Porter start out *a cappella*, with "How many . . ." while they held back. Then after a split second pause Don and Speedy came in with "ti–i–mes . . . have you heard someone . . . sa–ay," getting two syllables out of *say*. That brief pause helps hook the listener's ear, and this—along with pulling two syllables out of one word—established the recognizable Porter Wagoner sound for years to come.

They were playing at the American Legion Hut that night at Harrison, a log cabin, "strictly an Ozark antique-type building," says Hugh Ashley, a local songwriter who was there.

On September 3, 1954, RCA released "Company's Comin'."

On September 9, Steve Sholes failed to re-sign Porter to RCA. Porter was now off the label, with "Company's Comin'" out there in orbit.

Then on September 11, Porter, Don, Speedy, and Buster Fellows recorded "A Satisfied Mind" at the KWTO studio. Don thinks the session may have been intended only as a demo to impress RCA, and no one thought it would be released as-is.

The studio costs were around forty dollars, and the musicians themselves were paid by Porter. Thus Porter had to cover the costs on his first two hits, one of them his most famous song. As Porter told Paul Soelberg in 1971 (*Country Song Roundup*):

> No one from RCA was there, and I guess we knew this was going to be our last chance. After all, RCA was a business, and no matter what Steve Sholes thought of me, we knew we'd *have* to sell some records and soon.
>
> I played open-string guitar [flat-top acoustic in the first position]. We recorded the trio vocal, then we went back and put on the bass fiddle. I played bass, Don played steel guitar, and Speedy played rhythm guitar [hollow-body, playing barred chords up the neck].

From the RadiOzark point of view, the pocketbook concerns of the Porter Wagoner Trio were beneath notice. Everyone should merely pull together and keep all eyes focused on the big picture, that is, the small ten-inch screen that was becoming their crystal ball of the future. Springfield had sold ABC on the "Ozark Jubilee" concept, even if they had no idea how to get the show transmitted out of Missouri. Soon, with all the network TV exposure, Porter and his fellow entertainers in the KWTO orbit would all have a satisfied mind.

Still, it's ironic that the recording artist had to fund the session of such an idealistic song. Three of its four stanzas preach against placing too much faith in worldly goods: "It's so hard to find one rich man in ten with a satisfied mind . . . The wealthiest person is a pauper at times compared to the man with a satisfied mind."

Porter now had two potential hits recorded, one released but not yet charting, and the other in the can. Yet he was off RCA. So those strident noises of rock 'n' roll must have made him nervous. If he happened to catch the Opry the night of September 25, he would have heard Elvis Presley, whose "Good Rockin' Tonight" was just out on Sun Records.

On October 30, 1954, "Company's Comin'" entered *Billboard*, where it was on the charts twelve weeks but didn't sell many records. It was a disc jockey hit, number seven eventually. To even hear a Porter Wagoner record on the radio consistently was certainly astonishing.

Si says Steve Sholes called him in disbelief.

"You and Porter can have my job. This has never happened at Victor before. We've got an artist whose contract has expired who's got a hit on the charts."

"Hey, that's not so bad."

"You don't understand. You don't *do* that at RCA Victor!"

And Si adds, "Well, if it hadn't been for that, there wouldn't have been any 'Satisfied Mind.'"

As Porter climbed aboard the "Ozark Jubilee" that January, he had a hit record to flaunt over network TV. One of the people who saw him do "Company's Comin'" on the Jubilee from the Jewell Theater was an Air Force enlisted man named Mel Tillis. Mel was stationed in Newport, Nebraska, and with his buddies drove down to Springfield on a weekend pass. They miscalculated the mileage, and all they caught of the Jubilee was the final act. Porter was doing his song, and the black group, the Philharmonics, was supplying the clappety-clap by doing the hand jive. "I liked the way he handled an audience," says Mel. "And he was a young man. He did a recitation which knocked us all out. Then he did 'Setting the Woods on Fire.'" After the show they went over to the Wagoner home.

❊   ❊   ❊

Porter, Ruth, and their two children were now renting a house at 722 South Ferguson Street, a meagre frame house built in the late nineteenth century. They were living there when Denise was born in 1955.

Ruth entertained the pickers who dropped by and is remembered fondly for her cooking. Otherwise, she maintained a polite distance from all connected with the music business, a distance that lengthened in proportion to Porter's success. Few of the KWTO personnel recall Ruth distinctly. *Shy* is the word everyone uses to describe her. Don Richardson, Sr., KWTO publicist, remembers spotting Ruth in the crowd at a small show in Springfield and trying to invite her onstage with Porter for some routine applause. She headed off in the other direction, making herself invisible. And Si told me, "They were separated for all practical purposes, all the time he was in Springfield, always on the road . . ."

Once I called Ruth up on impulse, despite having been told she would never be interviewed. She confirmed this supposition instantly. A second time I called her to check some facts, and the conversation lasted, surprisingly, half an hour. "Now don't you go interviewing me," she said. However leery she may be of what lies outside her sphere, she is not shy; she is witty, outspoken, tough-minded, and very subtle.

Not unlike the man she married.

I decided my first question to Porter about his marriage had better be my last. He cannot discuss Ruth without choking up and becoming troubled. Except for his remarks in court during the divorce trial of 1986, when a large amount of money was on the line, Porter cannot be made to say a single word against his ex-wife. I told this to Ruth and she said, "Well, I've always heard that he never ran me down to other people. But it's nice to hear it from you."

In March 1955 yet another corporation was started in Springfield by Foster, Cox, Mahaffey, and Siman. This one was called Top Talent, Inc., and it would begin booking music dates for the various country acts that the Jubilee was now attracting. Porter, managed by RadiOzark, was booked by Top Talent and thereby was obligated to Crossroads TV, which operated the Jubilee. So was Brenda Lee.

Don Richardson wrote Porter's first bio sheet, stressing his Jubilee exposure and calling him "one of the top singers of folk music on RCA records." To satisfy the fans' curiosity, Porter listed his favorite recording artists as being Hank Snow and Eddy Arnold (both on RCA). He revealed that his favorite actor was Robert Mitchum. He said his favorite actress was Jane Russell. (Jane's twin talents required a brassiere engineered by Howard Hughes).

In February or March, Jean Shepard performed "A Satisfied Mind" on the Jubilee. It was a "mail pull" idea of Si's, and it drew a lot of letters. Jean says she asked Porter and Red Foley not to record or release it until she could cut it also, on her once-a-year trip to Los Angeles, where she recorded for Ken Nelson at Capitol Records. Jean cut the song on April 11, after Red had cut it in Nashville on April 6, for Decca, as a duet with his daughter Betty. Betty's husband, Bentley Cummings, thinks Red held back on the song to give Porter his shot.

Anyway, Porter, then Red, then Jean, had versions in the can and none in release. With Red Hayes's original Starday record still circulating, it would be just their luck if some Opry singer also recorded it and got it out first on a major label.

Steve Sholes's idea for a follow-up of "Company's Comin'" had been "Hey, Maw," backed with "How Quick," another classic forgettable Porter Wagoner single. In April "A Satisfied Mind" was finally released, with "Itchin' for My Baby" on the flip side, a song with a beat. *Country and Western Jamboree* for June 1955 banked on "Itchin' for My Baby" being the hit and ran a picture of Porter leaping off the ground, Elvis-style, his legs splayed out in a split.

Red Foley's and Jean Shepherd's "A Satisfied Mind" both came out in May.

On May 1 Elvis began a tour for Jamboree Attractions, managed by Colonel Parker and Hank Snow.

On May 28 "A Satisfied Mind" by Porter entered *Billboard*. Porter told Craig Baguley in a 1989 story in *Country Music People* that Steve Sholes called and said, "This is the one we've been looking for! I just heard from Houston, Texas. The record has finally broken wide open there. It sold 20,000 there this week." By July 9 it was number one with the disc jockeys. Porter's "A Satisfied Mind" was number two on jukeboxes, and finally—after ten previous releases—he was in the retail record business. "A Satisfied Mind" was number two in sales, too.

All in all, Porter's rendition was in *Billboard* for thirty-three weeks. Speedy Haworth remembers hearing it sold 200,000 copies.

Then on June 29, two more versions entered the charts, Red's duet with Betty, and Jean Shepard's. As Si says, "All three got on the Top 10, but Porter was out first, Porter had the best record, Porter won the race."

Since all three acts were on the Jubilee, Si Siman had knocked three runs in across the plate. There were precedents, as Red himself had scored one of the five Top 10 versions of "Candy Kisses" in 1949. But seemingly nothing like it has happened since, with cover versions becoming virtually obsolete.

Although Porter's rendition is definitive, "A Satisfied Mind" has been a country hit three more times, twice in the 1970s (Roy Drusky and Bob Luman) and once in the eighties (Con Hunley with Porter as guest vocalist). Black singer Bobby Hebb had a pop hit of the song in 1966. The

Nitty Gritty Dirt Band put it out the following year, and Glen Campbell even did the song in 4/4 time as the title cut of an album in 1968.

The pathmaker of country music scholars, Bill C. Malone, calls "A Satisfied Mind" one of the "most finely crafted songs in country music." Red Hayes says one night he came out of the Opry and heard his song wafting out from a church across the street. He fell down on his knees.

Four years earlier Porter had been cutting meat for Sid Vaughan. Now, on the strength of his number one record, the Grand Ole Opry had invited him to join!

But his contract with RadiOzark tied him up and, of course, he was sold back through Crossroads TV, to the Jubilee. Si reasoned that the Grand Ole Opry would be a step down for Porter, from network TV to mere network radio. So Porter would have to try to put the vision he had harbored since his boyhood out of his head. Si Siman had his own dreams for Porter. As someone once said, a star is a figment of a manager's imagination!

The Springfield *News–Leader*, on the "Home Page," reported that Porter had bought a "seven-room ranch-type home at 1912 Valley Road, with electric kitchen and double garage, for an indicated $21,000." A picture of the little house on Oak Street in West Plains, next to a photo of the Valley Road home, would make good "before" and "after" pictures of what Si Siman and his friends had done for Porter Wagoner. The paper also reported that Porter had "just purchased his first four-door Cadillac Fleetwood to jockey around on his personal appearance tours. Color of the Caddy: charcoal and lavender."

And when Porter stepped out of his Cadillac, he just might have been wearing a peach-colored western suit, all covered with flashy embroidered wagon wheels and cactuses.

9

CALL ME "NUDIE"

I've never worn exactly
what everyone else has worn.

—Porter to Vernell Hackett,
Country News (April 1984)

S omeone described Nudie Cohn as looking "like the caricature of an American cowboy drawn by an enraged Russian cartoonist." Nudie told S. J. Diamond for *People* magazine in 1976, "If Tom Mix got out of his grave and saw my clothes, he'd get back in again." That particular issue of *People* ran a picture of Porter and Dolly in their famous Nudie costumes.

Nudie was a Russian-born tailor from Brooklyn who ran a shop in North Hollywood. He created clothing that illuminated the Opry stage for decades and decorated the musicians on such television programs as "The Porter Wagoner Show" and "The Bill Anderson Show." Nudie outfitted Hank Williams, Johnny Cash, and Elvis and designed the most ostentatious western-style automobile anyone ever saw.

Nudie approached Porter after a concert in Greenville, Missouri, proposing to brighten up Porter's act with some flashier clothes. But Porter was only making fifty dollars a night, and the suit Nudie wanted to hang on Porter's fence-post frame would cost $350. So Nudie made one of his best investments since his first purchase of a sewing machine: he offered Porter a free, custom-fitted suit. A few weeks later the package arrived.

According to Porter, "It was the darndest-looking thing I'd ever seen. It was a peach-colored suit with rhinestones, wagon wheels, cactus, all kinds of different embroidery. It was breathtaking! People would just go *aaah* when I'd come on stage at times. When the lights hit 'em it would be really exciting." That first free suit can be seen on the cover of Porter's second album, A *Slice of Life–Songs Happy 'n' Sad* (1962).

Porter was not the only customer Nudie sought out, just the most identifiable in the long run. His widow, Bobbie, remembers her husband went looking for someone with the guts to wear rhinestones, and she believes he settled on Lefty Frizzell. "You shouldn't be wearing sports jackets like they do in the audience," he told Lefty. Another early rhinestone patron was Little Jimmy Dickens, who visited Nudie's shop in Hollywood, as did Cowboy Copas. Jimmy is a fishing partner of Porter's, and Porter has told him repeatedly how impressed he was the first time he saw Jimmy's show. "He'd never in his life seen a show like mine," Jimmy says. "With everyone dressed alike in the Western costumes."

But Porter outlasted many of the others who wore the rhinestones. In time, the Wagoner wagon wheel-and-cactus opulence (duplicated on his Wagonmasters' uniforms) came to be the longest-running advertisement for Nudie and his suits.

A reporter in 1972, in the South Bend, Indiana, *Tribune*, captured Porter's onstage impact:

> When Porter Wagoner leans into the microphone to deliver a plaintive lyric, his audience is greeted by a flash reminiscent of an old-fashioned 4th of July celebration.
> No, it's not a footlight reflection from his pulsating guitar. It's the blinding glare from hundreds of tiny sequins [rhinestones actually] that pattern his performing costume. They sparkle and glitter almost in time with the driving sound of the music.

Nudie put the western into country. And though Porter has recorded fewer western songs than most country singers have, it was his last name that gave Nudie the ideal opportunity to indelibly evoke the Southwest, via Conestoga wagons and cactus, in the public consciousness.

Nudie Cohn was born in 1902 in Kiev. His father was a bootmaker to the Russian army, and the boy trained as a tailor. Anti-Jewish purges (*pogroms*) caused him to emigrate with an older brother to America in 1911, and they settled in Brooklyn. He became a Hollywood tailor, fashioning western costumes for the cowboy film clientèle. Nudie designed Hank Williams's "drape" style western suit. He was buried in one.

The real inspiration for the fancy cowboy clothes of entertainers was the Buffalo Bill Wild West Show. Bill's sharpshooter heroine, Annie Oakley, wore a fringed western dress and big hat with a silver star. Annie Oakley, in that Buffalo Bill troupe, was in some ways a rôle model for the country music shows' "girl singers" later.

"The biggest thing that helped me was the rhinestones," Nudie once said. Just for the record, Nudie used rhinestones but not sequins.

His widow, Bobbie, remembers her and Nudie coming to Nashville and staying at the Dickerson Road Trailer Park, where so many entertainers lived, such as Hawkshaw Hawkins, whose jacket had a big hawk on the back. Bobbie remembers that Porter introduced Nudie at least twice from the stage of the Opry.

Eventually Nudie upstaged his own rhinestones by creating the "Man in Black" garb for Johnny Cash, as well as Elvis's blinding gold lamé suit. Porter also had a gold lamé, which he is wearing on the cover of his 1965 album, *The Thin Man from West Plains*.

Bill Anderson and his Po' Boys band wore kaleidoscopically hued Nudie suits for their road and TV shows. Bill's pickers wore pink, green, yellow, or blue suits, and Bill wore white with gold trim, or black with silver, or purple with snowflakes, or red with flowers. Concerning these costumes, Bill writes in his autobiography, *Whisperin' Bill*, that "anything worth doing is worth overdoing."

Nudie himself was something of a San Fernando Valley landmark, sometimes wearing $25,000 worth of jewelry. He posed for *Fashion Week* in 1969 in a suit with coiling coral snakes up and down the pant legs, boasting, "I'm an old man, but when I go to a party I get all the girls around me. Why? Because I've always worn something that's different. Something that says Nudie is here." Nudie remarked in 1971, "My wife says I'm taking a chance, wearing all this gold. So, you gotta die sooner or later. And if I die tomorrow, I'll say I had a good time."

Even more conspicuous than Nudie himself was his white western-style Pontiac convertible that so many reporters mistook for a Cadillac. In 1973 it was valued at $20,000, certainly an underestimate. The car had for a hood ornament two giant horns from a Texas longhorn. The interior was of intricately patterned tooled leather, of the sort seldom used on anything larger than a belt. Brakes and gas pedal were covered with the same leather. Situated throughout the car were at least fourteen guns, such as three rifles mounted on the rear deck, derringers to operate the emergency brake and the directional light, as well as a number of Colt single-action pistols as arm rests, door handles, and gear shift levers—you had to pull the trigger—and one to sound the horn, which played Dale Evans's "Happy Trails." Between the back seats was a silver saddle decorated with around 150 silver dollars; the dashboard was encrusted with close to 200 silver dollars; and hundreds of others were embedded elsewhere, 15 on the steering wheel alone. On each front fender was mounted a chrome quarter-horse. The car's tape deck played a recording of a cattle stampede, and redundantly, the spare tire rack was emblazoned "Nudie."

Nudie's wife, Bobbie, would suggest they take *her* car when they went anywhere together. Once the western car was stolen but quickly

Nudie circa 1974.

found since the thieves were hardly difficult to spot. There were eighteen of these Nudie-mobiles, driven by such folks as Elvis, Webb Pierce, and Hank Williams, Jr. They tended to change hands over the years.

At least one person I've interviewed believes Ruth Wagoner threw one or more of Porter's Nudie suits out onto the lawn, in a righteous rage. The source of this most plausible rumor is the Porter-Dolly duet, "Her and the Car and the Mobile Home," written by Dave Kirby and Don Stock. In this song, the wife has taken the car and everything but his clothes. "I found little consolation in my wardrobe / That you left scattered on the patio . . ." Since the husband has been "carrying on," he has it coming, and she has stomped his Nudie suits into the mud. She even "stepped on them wagon wheels, busted the spokes out . . ." Across his prized lavender outfit she has written in chalk, "Have a good time, darling, when you're hot, you're hot." She had tossed the suit up in a tree, while the neighbors watched with the expected interest.

By the 1970s Nudie was grossing a million dollars a year. Displayed in his shop was a photograph of that distinguished American stripper, Lili St. Cyr, stepping from a bathtub, inscribed, "If I ever wear clothes, they'll be yours." Nudie died in 1984. At the funeral one of his famous automobiles was on display. Dale Evans delivered the eulogy. Nudie's store still operates, managed by his widow, Bobbie.

Nudie had a talented apprentice named Manuel, who in time came to work on Porter's clothes. In 1974 he left Nudie's employ, and he crafts Porter's outfits today. "You don't need my last name. Manuel is enough," he said. For the record, it's Manuel Cuevas. Dolly Parton, Emmylou Harris, and Linda Ronstadt are wearing Manuel creations on the cover of their *Trio* album. Manuel says some customers become frustrated when he refuses to make them a suit they have seen on someone else. Every garment has to be unique and must reflect the wearer's personality. Manuel's clients have included Loretta Lynn, Bob Dylan, Sylvester Stallone, Kenny Rogers, Waylon Jennings, and Dwight Yoakam.

When I glibly suggested that Porter, at least, had probably enough rhinestone suits for the time being, supposedly around fifty-five, Manuel sounded terror-struck. "Don't tell *him* he doesn't need them! He has one on order for ten thousand dollars! He'll cancel it, and I'll starve to death!" Manuel says the movie studios will call him requesting a stock "Nudie" suit. "Manuel, we want . . . like a . . . Porter Wagoner type . . ." In summation, Manuel says, "Porter Wagoner is the status quo of flash."

In 1989, a new boutique opened at 1922 Broadway in Nashville: Manuel's Exclusive Clothier.

10

STUCK IN SPRINGFIELD WITH THE NASHVILLE BLUES

Our little "Ozark Jubilee" now has an audience
of twelve million people . . . It's a pretty big thrill
for a boy who, only about four years ago, thought
he had a big audience when he climbed up on a
stage made out of a stake-body truck
to sing for the "Dollar Days" shoppers
on the Public Square in my
hometown of West Plains, Missouri.

—Porter, *Country Song Roundup* (July 1955)

Folk music fans are becoming
more "Wagoner-conscious" every day.

—*Hillbilly and Cowboy Hit Parade*
(Winter 1955–1956)

The first two big country hits to be recorded in the Ozarks—
"Company's Comin'" and "A Satisfied Mind"—would be the
last. An even bigger song would come out of the Ozarks of northern
Arkansas in 1959, but how that was published by Don Warden and Porter
and how it became a monster hit is another story.

In 1955 the first Japanese Sony transistor radios were being mass-
marketed. The Germans had already introduced their tape recorders, and
almost imperceptibly, Nashville moved ahead of Springfield in the crucial area of recording. In 1954 RCA moved out of the noisy warehouse on
Thirteenth Avenue South, and Cliff Thomas helped set up their new
equipment at 1525 McGavock Street. They shared quarters with the
Methodist Television, Radio and Film Commission, which has its special
irony. Since before the Civil War, Nashville had been known as a "publishing town," specializing in hymnals, Sunday school literature, religious tracts, and Bibles. However, Nashville would soon become
famous also for publishing music.

McGavock Street was a couple of blocks from Sixteenth Avenue South, where Owen Bradley had built a studio in 1954 and by 1955 would be installing a three-track machine from New York and toying with echo chambers. Porter had recorded at McGavock back in January. Then on August 7, he cut "Eat, Drink and Be Merry (Tomorrow You'll Cry)," written by two Missouri girls, Celia and Sandra Ferguson. There would be no more Springfield sessions.

The following week Colonel Tom Parker and Hank Snow signed Elvis to an ambiguous contract where they assisted in managing Elvis, while acting as his booking agents as well, a bold conflict-of-interest arrangement typical of those flamboyant times. Springfield held Porter and Brenda Lee in similar straitjackets.

In July, Elvis—still on Sun Records—had scored a number five on the country disc jockey charts with "Baby, Let's Play House," and by September had his first number one on the jukeboxes and in record sales with "I Forgot to Remember to Forget." What was happening to country music? Paul Ackerman at *Billboard* in New York had to fend off complints from Nashville, no doubt peppered with racial accusations because of Elvis's black sound.

That year "A Satisfied Mind" probably sold more copies for Porter than Elvis had sold on Sun Records. "A Satisfied Mind" stayed on the charts until February 1956. Elvis was simply on the wrong label. Hank Snow was on RCA, and Hank helped woo Elvis away from his parents. Hank possessed some residual value still for the Colonel—he introduced Parker to Steve Sholes.

Parker set up his battlefield outpost at the Warwick Hotel in New York, laying siege to Steve. Porter and Si were doubtless at the disc jockeys' convention that November—so was Steve Sholes, and so probably was Elvis since he was voted Most Promising New C&W Artist.

Colonel Parker had by now priced Elvis above all expectations. By asking at least $35,000 for him, partly to buy him out from Sun Records, Parker imbued Elvis with immense charisma. Steve Sholes fell for it. Elvis now went with RCA in an industry-rocking deal. Elvis gave the Colonel a promotion and began calling him The Admiral.

Porter's "Eat, Drink and Be Merry" went on the charts on December 3, reaching number three in sales and jukebox play and making it even more frustrating that he couldn't join the Opry with this kind of momentum. The flip side reflected the desperation of those times, a pathetic Ozark attempt at having a teenage dance hit, called "Let's Squiggle."

Elvis's "Heartbreak Hotel" entered the country and pop charts in March 1956. That same month Porter's version of "What Would You Do (If Jesus Came to Your House)?" charted, and it beat two other renditions: Tex Ritter's, which didn't chart, and Red Sovine's, which lasted but a week. Porter's went to number eight in sales and number fourteen with the disc jockeys. The song rhetorically asks, If Jesus came to your house, would you hide some of your favorite magazines and substitute the Bible in their place? A reporter for *Time* magazine had heard the song on a tavern jukebox "through the clink and tinkle of the bottles and glasses," and decried its "embarassing chant . . . [and] corn pone accompaniment."

In another article that same year, *Time* declared that Springfield "could lay claim to being the hillbilly capital of the world." And in an article on the Jubilee, *Business Week* ran a picture of Porter with the Ferguson girls, who had written his "Eat, Drink and Be Merry" hit.

Porter was now at the top of his profession, which is to say that Hap Peebles could get the Porter Wagoner Trio fifty-dollar-a-night dates, often in taverns. Porter calls them "skull orchards," which *Country Music Who's Who* for 1972 defines in its Glossary of Terms as "a nightclub having a reputation for rough-housing." Porter said, "I hate to play beer joints, 'cause there's so much noise, there's so much going on. It's like you become part of the noise in order to make people want to drink more. I played beer joints as a matter of survival. Elvis was really hot, and country music had really made a dip, the biggest I've *ever* seen."

Porter was seldom home, for, as he told *Cowboy Songs* in 1956, "Of late I've really had to move around. I've hit as many as eighty-two counties in a four-state area on personals." Since KWTO covered four states, at least it reinforced Porter's touring career, and he never missed a split second's air exposure when he was in town.

Ruth Wagoner had a satisfied mind of sorts, with her new house. There was a double garage and a fenced yard for the children. There were no houses yet across the street, just mud everywhere. They literally put down roots, planting grass, Ruth putting shrubs all around, not realizing how soon their lives would be uprooted. When Porter was home, they adopted the fad of backyard cooking, and Ed and Lorraine were frequent guests, as well as both sets of parents.

Porter would regularly send money home to his mother, Lorraine remembers, maybe two hundred-dollar bills and a fifty, with a note: "Mother, for your utilities." Bertha still used an oil-burning stove until Porter convinced her to change to electric heat out of fear of fires. "He never failed to send money, more than enough."

Ruth didn't drive, and since they lived in a suburb in southeast Springfield, Porter figured she'd better learn. Mysteriously he went to Michigan; then one evening when Ruth returned home, she was confronted with a blue and white sporty Chevrolet in the garage. Keys were in the ignition, Lorraine says, and a note was attached: "This is your car, Dear. You will learn to drive it? If you don't learn to drive it, I'll sell it."

Ruth and Porter entertained the inevitable friends from the Jubilee. Their son Richard remembers Red Foley lived in the next subdivi-

Above: *The Wagoners' home at 1912 Valley Road, 1955–56. Thanks to "A Satisfied Mind," they were buying this home at the same time the Opry was beckoning Porter to Nashville* [PHOTO BY AUTHOR]. Right: *Porter circa 1954* [COURTESY PORTER WAGONER ENTERPRISES].

sion (Brentwood) and would drive by in his Thunderbird. Sometimes Opry stars would come by, since the Jubilee was always featuring them. Their talk of Nashville tugged at Porter, confusing him. Ruth was happy in her house. Porter wanted to be in Nashville. It cut him in half sometimes.

In April 1957, the mass market digest magazine *Coronet* ran an article by Phillip Dessauer on "Springfield, Mo.—Radio City of Country Music," emphasizing Springfield's ascendancy over Nashville. Porter, and especially Red Foley, figured prominently in the piece.

Dessauer called Red a "barnyard Bing Crosby" who indulged "in such homely expressions as *Well, bless yore heart* or *That just shows to go ya*. He introduces acts with the air of a man who hopes he hasn't forgotten what comes next, and you never know when a number will be interrupted to let the audience help with the singing."

Dessauer claimed that "more than a dozen other recording stars" had followed Red to Springfield. While probably not that many, Nashville was definitely losing blood. Webb Pierce, the jukebox operators' Number One Singer of 1953, had scored three number one country hits in 1955 and in that year had hosted the Jubilee once a month. Some other Jubilee regulars were Jean Shepard (1955), Hawkshaw Hawkins (1955), Bobby Lord (1957–60), Marvin Rainwater (1957), Billy Walker (1957), Leroy Van Dyke (1958), and Porter (1955–56).

The *Coronet* article also reported that "Porter Wagoner, who was working in a butcher shop in West Plains, Missouri, for $35 a week in 1950, hit the limousine level last year on the crest of successive smash records. After working his way through two medium-size cars, he bought a lavender Cadillac, explaining, 'Well, you gotta have a Cadillac some time.' Expensive cars are not entirely a luxury for stars on the stage-show circuit, however. Wagoner reports he traveled 126,000 miles by automobile in 1956."

By the time the *Coronet* article appeared, Porter had slammed the door, hard, on the Ozark Jubilee. Nor did the article report that in September the police had intervened in a Foley family domestic dispute at four in the morning. Sally pressed no charges, but the Associated Press put the story out on the wire: "Hospital Releases Hillbilly Star's Wife," was the headline in *The* (Nashville) *Tennessean*.

Speedy Haworth remembers riding with the Porter Wagoner Trio. They would take turns every two hours, driving a hundred miles apiece. Porter owned a "stretch" type vehicle so popular with musicians, with the fifth seat in the middle. It was pink with a white interior, although colors and descriptions of Porter's vehicles in the mid fifties vary with the teller. Speedy says the longest trip he recalls making was with Porter and Don

Warden from Baltimore to Calgary, Canada.

Guitarist Red Gale remembers them rigging a hammock for Porter to sleep in lengthwise in their Fleetwood Cadillac. They called it their stretcher. Once at a gas station the attendant said, "What's *that?*" Don Warden replied, "That's a corpse. We're from the mortuary, we're taking the body back to bury it." As the attendant peered close, an awakening Porter poked his head out and yawned. The attendant dropped his hose and started running.

Jubilee star Bobby Lord often traveled with Porter. He says most entertainers merely tolerated the road but that Porter thrived on it. "I think he probably liked the business more than anyone I've known," says Bobby.

Jubilee acts were already appearing at the Medical Center for Federal Prisoners in Springfield (Chuck Berry would sojourn there in the sixties). Porter's performances at the prison-mental institution anticipate his hit "Green, Green Grass of Home," his *Soul of a Convict* album, and his cycle of insanity songs like "The Rubber Room." Lorraine remembers her husband, Ed, accompanied Porter, and they did Jimmie Rodgers's "In the Jailhouse Now." Speedy Haworth remembers doing a Christmas show there with Red Foley, and Red yelled, "What'd you all like for Christmas?" Someone shouted, "A helicopter!" After the show a riot ensued, and that was the last outside music for the prisoners for years to come.

The Ferguson girls had pitched "Eat, Drink and Be Merry (Tomorrow You'll Cry)" to Porter in the dressing room of the American Legion hall at Sedalia, Missouri. With them was a former artist for the Hallmark Card company, Ann Bybee, who'd ridden up with them by Greyhound. "My parents had listened to his early morning radio show; I was in awe when I first met him," remembers Ann. But while Porter listened to the song, Ann and Don Warden were noticing each other.

Soon Ann was staying up all night, stapling together black-and-white shots of the Porter Wagoner Trio. With money earned from picture sales, Don mailed Ann bus fare ("I'd never been out of Missouri in my life") and she connected with the trio in Winston-Salem, North Carolina, where they got married. Best man Porter managed to drop the ring at the crucial moment and would kid them later, "Maybe I was trying to tell you something."

In 1956 Don and Ann Warden lived in a modest house trailer, and the center of their livingroom was decorated with a gray metal file cabinet with pull-down desktop for Don's portable typewriter. Don and Porter had started their own Warden Music, perhaps to upstage Earl Barton, the fictional name of Si's company.

✻ ✻ ✻

The Jubilee only paid around fifty dollars a night to top acts, but that was better than the Opry. By mid 1957 it was reaching eighteen million viewers and selling records and attracting bookings for anyone lucky enough to be on the show.

Lou Black probably managed Top Talent, Inc., and since his death coincided with Porter's abrupt exit, Porter probably did not have much experience with his successor at Top Talent, the late Jim McConnell. But Leroy Van Dyke's account of Jim's tactics suggests what Porter was leaving behind.

Leroy says that when a buyer called asking for an act, perhaps one seen on the Jubilee, Jim would automatically say *yes*, whether or not the performer were actually available. Then as the show date drew near, Jim would say, "Kid . . . [he called everyone Kid] we're going to have to do a little switching here. Bobby Lord can't make it, but Leroy Van Dyke will take his place." Laughs Leroy, "I don't know how many times I was Bobby—or Billy Walker—or they were me."

They would also resell acts for more than they told the artists themselves. Leroy says there's nothing wrong with reselling. "The only objection is in the magnification of the contract. Most of us want to be entertainers so badly, we would sign our death certificate to get it." Leroy says Top Talent would sell a show for $1,000 to $1,500, with the star getting one hundred dollars and the sidemen thirty-five dollars apiece.

Bobby Lord waxes philosophical about it. He says he won't defend their ethics because they were wrong, but as businessmen they saw and seized their opportunities. "No one starved to death in Springfield," says Bobby. "Their deviousness didn't help them that much or hurt us that much."

There are several stories of entertainers "picking up the wrong check." That is, being handed a check made out to them by a promoter while on the road—but a check much larger than they thought they were getting. In other words, a slip-up. Strictly, cat out-of-the-bag! They might cash such a check, just to eat and get home on, but later they'd have to surrender the excess to Top Talent, then pay their 10 percent commission and try to forget what they'd seen. At least it was flattering to learn how much they were really worth behind their backs! Red Foley—and Jean Shepard—once picked up the "wrong check."

Thanks to "A Satisfied Mind," Ruth Wagoner now had her first dishwasher. But if Springfield was so great, why did Porter now have to go to Nashville to record? And how long was the Jubilee going to last on TV? And besides recording, Nashville had publishing. Was Earl Barton going to come up with more hits for Porter? Down in Nashville, Chet knew where all the songs were.

✻   ✻   ✻

Porter will no more knock his Springfield employers than he will criticize his ex-wife. He puts the nicest face on his departure from Springfield, saying that he and Si and Red Foley talked it out together. Red said Porter should go to Nashville for the good of his career, if the Opry wanted him. Red was himself an expert on how to hit the road, having cleared out of Nashville himself. The Jubilee had built around him, so he felt a personal concern for Porter and Brenda Lee now that their Ozark contractual yokes were starting to chafe a mite.

On a trip to Mexico, Missouri, Speedy Haworth remembers that here Porter *picked up the wrong check*. It was supposed to be for $150 for the Trio. It was for around $300, however.

Speedy's wife's sister had married William Bland, an attorney. Porter's sister Lorraine remembers Porter paid Bland a painful $1,800 to help him break his Jubilee contract. He also represented Brenda Lee.

Brian Bisney, director of the Jubilee, says that Porter and Don Warden "had a falling out [with Springfield]. I was in my office when Don Warden came in and wanted to use my phone. He wanted to call Nashville and he was really riled up. He made arrangements right then, there in the office. And I think that was the last time I ever saw Porter." Don was probably talking to Jack Stapp at WSM or to Red Foley's manager, Dub Allbritten, now in Nashville.

Sometime in November 1956 the Porter Wagoner Trio hit the highway headin' south, with Warden Music no doubt tucked in a shoebox or folded into a guitar case.

Speedy Haworth stayed behind, and Red Gale was now the rhythm guitar player. Soon Porter and Red Gale had rented a trailer in the Dickerson Road Trailer Park at 1508 Dickerson Road. Don lived there, too, having left Ann in Springfield, pregnant.

The move down may have been timed to coincide with the disc jockey convention. Si was there, but the days of driving down with Porter, writing songs as they rode, were finished. On November 12, 1957, Si found Lou Black lying dead on the floor of his room at the Andrew Jackson Hotel. He had had a heart attack. It had been Lou Black who'd gotten Porter out of the meat cutting trade, and it was Lou Black who'd been all agog lately about his prize catch, little Brenda Lee. Lou had just signed Brenda—or rather, her mother—to a new five-year contract.

Now with Lou Black dead, Dub Allbritten (with nudges from Red Foley) had room to maneuver. Dub and Don Warden did their share of talking at the WSM offices up on Seventh Avenue. Once they cinched the deal, Porter could begin looking for a house for his family.

On Saturday, February 23, 1957, Porter signed with the Grand Ole Opry. He appeared that same night, backed by the Opry staff band, including Jerry Byrd, the role model for a generation of steel guitar players. Finally Porter had fulfilled his cornfield fantasies, where he would get up on a stump and pretend to introduce Roy Acuff. Less than eight years previously he had watched Hank Williams perform on the same spot where he was now standing.

The day of Porter's performance, Ann Warden was taken to the hospital. Immediately after the show, Porter, Don, and Red drove to Indiana, then Don caught a plane. Springfield was so fogged in he had to drive a car to get there. Ruth Wagoner was in the delivery room immediately after the baby was born and told Ann, "It's a boy." Three weeks later, Don and Ann moved their trailer to Nashville and into the Dickerson Road encampment, an enclave of musicians.

Then on March 2, Charlie Lamb's *Country Music Reporter*, headlined: "Porter Wagoner Quits Jubilee to Join Opry." Porter said, "I definitely resigned from the Jubilee, and I have no intention of going back, even for guest appearances." Actually, he had to make a guest spot or two to finish his contract, remembers Ann Warden. The *Reporter* also said that Porter had logged 120,000 miles in the past year and had appeared personally in forty-six states, as well as Canada and Mexico. His new manager was Don Warden, and his latest single, "I'm Daydreaming Tonight," which had been released three weeks earlier, was getting good airplay.

The *Reporter* summarized the backstairs politics that had sprung Porter from the Ozarks:

> Jack Stapp, WSM program manager and supervisor of Opry network talent, had been in conference with Steve Sholes, RCA-Victor manager of specialty artists and repertoire, and with Dub Allbritten, well known talent manager, about a year ago relative to bringing Wagoner to the Opry.

Yet Goober Buchanan, a disc jockey and comedian from Mexico, Missouri, remembers Porter still fulfilling some dates for his former handlers in Springfield:

> He had trouble getting loose from Springfield. He was supposed to go back and play the Jubilee every so often. He still had to give them 10 percent of everything he made. We played some dates in Montana with the Red Foley show, and were working our way back home when the fellow collecting the money wouldn't pay Porter. He said he'd been ordered to keep the money because Porter owed it. Porter wanted to pay us boys and needed it to get home on. So he blew his stack and got on the phone. When we got back to Springfield, Don wouldn't let Porter out of the car, he was so mad. Then about a week later they went back and made some kind of big settlement. Don's a smart little booger, you know that.

The "Ozark Jubilee" loses Brenda Lee, August 15, 1957, in Chancery Court, Nashville, as Judge Ned Lentz refuses to enjoin Brenda from singing. Left to right: Buell Rainwater (stepfather), Mrs. Rainwater (mother), Brenda Lee, Dub Albritten (manager), and Charles E. Mosley of the Ernest Tubb Record Shop (legal guardian) [THE MUSIC REPORTER].

Nor had Dub Allbritten finished pillaging Top Talent, Inc., of its top talent.

In June 1957 he returned to Springfield, supposedly to help Red Foley with his "tax problems," a quixotic mission if ever there was one. Coincidentally, very soon after, Jubilee star Brenda Lee and her mother and stepfather evacuated Springfield. In Nashville, they moved in with Dub.

The Ozark millionaires saddled up and lit out after them, their legal guns blazing. In Chancery Court at Nashville they sued Mr. and Mrs. Rainwater, Brenda's stepfather and mother, as well as Dub Allbritten, and tried to get an injunction to stop Brenda from singing until they got her back or were paid off. Since Mrs. Rainwater, as legal guardian of Brenda, was herself under contract to deliver Brenda, she decided to make Charles E. Mosely, who was part-owner of the Ernest Tubb Record Shop, Brenda's new legal guardian. Mosely immediately appointed Dub Allbritten as Brenda's manager, while discovering one of his own first duties as guardian was to get sued by the Ozark bunch.

As in the case of Porter, the conflict of interest was blatant. Top Talent had managed Brenda, then sold her back to the "Ozark Jubilee" via Crossroads TV. Like Porter, Brenda's mother owed much to the Springfielders' largesse: they had bought her daughter's clothes, paid the rent, and had upped Brenda's earnings from thirty-five dollars a night to a total of $34,000 over the previous six months.

On August 16 the combatants went to court over twelve-year-old Brenda Lee. She wore a pink polka-dot dress with a white lace collar. Upon hearing it might take hours, Brenda said, "My goodness, I've got to eat sometime today."

Don Warden was in the audience, furthering his music business education; so was country comedian Pete Stamper. Si was there too, although his name does not appear in the pages of depositions, insults, and counter-insults. They said they'd lost $40,000 in bookings, that Allbritten had meddled with their client. Mrs. Rainwater recalled that back when she was still her daughter's legal guardian, she had been given only "two minutes" to decide to sign Brenda's contract.

Witnesses had been rounded up to testify by affidavit whether charging a management fee of 25 percent was "reasonable" or not. The opinions tended to coincide with where the witnesses lived, Springfield or Nashville.

At all this, Judge Ned Lentz finally threw up his hands and threw out the contract.

> The principal thing going through my mind is this little girl. She is at the height of her career—the flashing star. She might fall as quickly as she rose. If I grant this temporary injunction, I may hurt this little girl. I am not interested in the dollar and cents angle but in what is best for the little girl.

Si Siman gave me his own summation of the case: "We put our tail between our legs and got on our chartered airplane with three attorneys, and headed our ass back to the hills of the Ozarks. It just shows you a contract ain't worth the paper it's written on sometimes. I have a marriage contract with Rosanne [his wife] but that doesn't make our marriage *work!*"

Back in Springfield, a show-biz mother type accosted Si with a singing daughter who sang "twice as good as Brenda Lee."

"*Drown her!*" Si recommended.

The Jubilee finally gained a sponsor. But *The Tennessean* exulted in a two-page feature in its Sunday magazine section, "Grand Slam for Brenda Lee." Her stepfather boasted that if it weren't for her school obligations, she could earn $100,000 that year. Brenda attended Maplewood High School in Nashville, even edited the school paper, but she ended up using private tutors when her hit records started happening (twenty-nine pop hits, thirty-four country), and her worldwide traveling began. A country singer with a blues voice, who claimed Edith Piaff and Judy Garland as influences, Brenda would never fit any category for long, except that of star.

In recent years, Brenda has headlined musical production shows at Opryland. Of Porter, she says, "I've known him through the years, and he's always been so kind. I know he's always been prone to help fledgling writers and artists. He's helped out so many artists by his TV shows."

A *typical Jubilee audience with spectators on a single night representing as many as thirty different states* [OZARK JUBILEE SOUVENIR ALBUM, SECOND EDITION].

Jubilee veteran Bob Tubert believes that "A Satisfied Mind" was the turning point for Springfield. Among the entertainers leaving were Pete Stamper and Harold Morrison, who says he left because Porter did.

As for Red Foley, ABC executives and Jubilee sponsors could hardly have been entertained by Red's off-camera road show with the Internal Revenue Service. As Si says, "Red thrived on crises. If he didn't have a crisis, he'd invent one."

The IRS contended he owed more than $300,000 for 1948–55. Both sides accused the other of not having any substantiating records. Red's attorney said, "He's the worst businessman I've ever been in contact with." Retorted a judge, "It's difficult for me to believe Mr. Foley is quite the idiot in financial matters his attorneys seek to indicate." Red's way with an uncashed check took on an almost folkloric quality in the many tales told. Once, when forced to empty his pockets, he yielded five thousand dollars in very old checks. Dub Allbritten said, "When a stranger asked Red for a few bucks, he always got it. If Red didn't know him, he always figured he should have."

Gradually, the Jubilee subsided. Masochistic name changes hurt it, such as "Country Music Jubilee" and "Jubilee USA". Its final telecast was September 24, 1960, the month of Red's first trial for criminal tax evasion. The unions had dealt perhaps the death blow, trying to keep any show from emanating out of anywhere but New York, Los Angeles, or

Chicago. Si's autopsy cannot be surpassed: "The Jubilee died due to illness. ABC got sick of us."

Red's first trial ended in a hung jury. He was acquitted after his second. Indiscreetly, Si had remarked of the IRS, "We'll beat their ass." So they audited him for the next ten years straight.

As for the stars Si Siman worked with, often discovered, and watched escape, Si says, "I didn't keep the Browns [Jim Ed, Maxine, and Bonnie, whom he got onto RCA], I didn't keep Sonny James, I didn't keep Porter, I didn't keep Brenda Lee. Nobody wants to lose their top acts. We invested time and money we never got back."

Si wrote me a follow-up note in 1990:

> We only got $5,000 per show—my salary was $250 per week—not much for an executive producer of a weekly network TV show. Lots of talent I helped live, out of my pocket, to get started. I managed anyone who couldn't afford a manager—free. Whatever success I had was due to their friendship and I hope respect— I wound up with lots of talented artists in important positions in show-biz.

With Chet Atkins and so many others in Nashville, Si had plenty of people to pitch songs to. "I've been to Porter's office dozens of times, we've played golf, had dinner. The good part is, nobody ever loses. Their lives have touched mine," he says.

Speaking about the squabbles that enlivened Nashville's Chancery Court in 1957, Bobby Lord says, "People in show business have a way of forgiving each other for anything. I've seen people have bitter arguments and end up being better friends. We're a very forgiving group." In 1986 Brenda Lee did a benefit for a Springfield hospital and dedicated a song to Si, posing with him onstage cheek-to-cheek.

Porter feels Si Siman ought to be in the Country Music Hall of Fame. After all, he shortened Chester Atkins's name to Chet Atkins.

PART TWO

RHINESTONE-STUDDED STARDOM

This is the man who once walked behind a plow,
and now owns a $60,000 luxury liner bus,
complete with color television, stereo, and
—believe it or not—a golf putting green.

—*Country Song Roundup* (February 1967)

The wandering life was common to minstrels,
for varying reasons. Those who were lucky enough
to be patronized by a noble were only required
at his court at certain times. For the rest
of the year, they were left to increase
their income as best they could by
travelling in search of audiences.

—David Cohen and Ben Greenwood, *The Buskers:
A History of Street Entertainment* (1981)

I remember one summer they did not have one day off.
They'd come in and they're tired and they're sick
and they're dragging suitcases with dirty clothes.

—Ann Warden, interview, August 30, 1989

11

"DON'T THIS ROAD LOOK ROUGH AND ROCKY"

You've risked your life on dangerous highways,
And gone without sleep and rest for days and days,
Many times you've been out in snow, sleet and rain,
And for what? she asked me.
Seems to me all in vain.

—James ("Goober") Buchanan,
recitation, "My Way of Life,"
Shameless Poetry by a Dirty Old Man (1989)

In June 1957 the Porter Wagoner family moved to Nashville. Porter's son, Richard, remembers riding down with Red Gale, with a big potted plant in the back seat and their large boxer dog jumping from back seat to front seat over and over, slobbering up the window. The Wagoners rented a house in the Berry Hill suburb of Nashville at 2717 Greystone Road. The house no longer stands, usurped by Interstate 440. They lived a few blocks east of Franklin Road and Acuff–Rose music publishing company, a couple of miles from the home of Audrey Williams, Hank Williams's widow.

Richard didn't like Nashville at first. "Everybody made fun of how we talked. They thought we were from some other country, not just some other state. But we were close to all the neighbors."

Porter's daughter Debra felt set apart from other little girls, and she wanted very much to be accepted. A constant, rather rude question was, "Does your daddy sing?" Debra says that at first, all she seemed to do was explain what Porter did. "When I was growing up, there was a kind of hush-hush air about who Daddy was. Perhaps out of a fear of something happening to us if we told the wrong person."

They would go to the Grand Ole Opry. "I can remember Patsy Cline because of her ruby-red lipstick. She had a gold dress, and she looked absolutely gorgeous. And Jim Reeves in a businesslike suit. Dad would say, 'Deb, that's so-and-so, they used to be on the "Ozark Jubilee."' I remember him saying that about Jim Ed Brown, Carl Smith, Jean Shepard."

Debra was ten when she first went to Tootsie's with her father. He told her not to talk.

Once Debra spotted Audrey Williams and her son, Randall Hank Williams, billed already as "Hank Williams, Jr." Porter said to Debra, "That boy's got a good voice, but she's pushing him too much." Lorraine remembers that Audrey gave Porter one or two of Hank's shirts and talked briefly about him playing Hank in her projected film-biography project, a faint echo of Jimmie Rodgers's widow passing on sacred relics to Ernest Tubb.

Debra says her daddy didn't sing Porter Wagoner songs around the house, he sang Hank Williams songs. Once, in the back yard, Porter lit their outdoor grill, sprayed on the fuel, threw on a lighted match, and began dancing around the fire singing "Kaw-Liga," Hank's song about the wooden Indian. Debra says, "I remember thinking the neighbors will think the Wagoners are crazy."

Porter was playing "The Louisiana Hayride" when the family dog was run over. Debra remembers him calling home, and all he heard was tears. So Porter announced the dog's death over the radio, and soon the Wagoner home was being surfeited with crate after crate, each with a dog. They picked the best and dispatched the rest to the animal shelter.

Debra remembers a birthday party at which Porter's band performed. The comedian-bass player Curly Harris was there. "I remember just looking at him and laughing. The way he held his face and made those buggy eyes."

Once Debra went into her father's closet and found a hunting jacket. She asked her mother, "When does he *ever* wear this?" When Porter would leave, Debra would try to carry his suitcase to the car and would cling to him. "I didn't want him to leave. Other children's fathers go to the office. I knew this was his job from the very beginning." Porter's long absences took their toll, and once when Porter came home Debra was so excited she couldn't calm down. "He'd been gone so long. So he'd say, 'Just breathe *deep* and just control yourself.' Daddy does that himself when he's excited."

Always, the question in the air and in Debra's heart, was *I wonder where Daddy is playing tonight?* So she would put on one of his records. "That's something the average child who has a traveling father doesn't have . . ."

In Springfield Porter had charted two more hits, both Top 20 in 1956: "Uncle Pen," the old bluegrass standard and "Tryin' to Forget the Blues" by Boudleaux and Felice Bryant. Boudleaux once brought Chet Atkins a song, "Bye Bye Love," which Chet thought would be good for Porter if Boudleaux would make some changes. *No changes!* It became the Everly Brothers' most famous song, going to number two in pop.

Porter had one more Top 20 hit in 1957, "I Thought I Heard You Call My Name," a song he still sings. Then he went hitless till 1959, when "Me and Fred and Joe and Bill" (by Bill Hale and Paul Gilley) reached number 29, on the chart but for one week.* It's a light-hearted number about four fellows in a tavern watching a girl walk in with her latest boyfriend; in the past few months they've all dated her.

By keeping him in Springfield, Porter's employers had cost him years in career progress. He had lost the momentum of "A Satisfied Mind," and it was hard even finding gigs because of the onslaught of rock 'n' roll. Opry membership didn't directly mean much money, and it carried only so much weight with the bookers.

One of the witnesses on behalf of Brenda Lee had been Herb Shucher, who had briefly managed Porter in 1957. Shucher also managed Jim Reeves, who was Nashville's answer to Red Foley, a country singer whose smooth delivery could sell pop records. Porter had elected to call his band the Wagonmasters, only to discover that was what Jim was calling his. "I understand you and I have a band named the same," said Jim to Porter. "'The Wagonmasters' doesn't fit me, but it's a perfect name for your band. So I'll change the name of my band."

"Did you know that Porter attracted women?" Sally Foley asked me. "Of all the people I've known, he was the biggest attractor of women. They just loved him. He didn't have to run after women. It was his shy, country ways, that 'Yes, ma'am' and 'No, ma'am,' and that *gets* women, you know."

Comic Goober Buchanan began traveling with Porter in the late fifties and remembers Porter and Red Gale lived in a trailer when they first moved down "Now Red brought this old gal out to the trailer, but she wouldn't have nothing to do with Red. She wanted Porter; he was the star." Goober says after a show, a particularly aggressive fan wanted to meet Porter, but Don Warden fended her off. She wanted to give Porter a present, a matchbox with a plastic baby inside. "This is Porter Junior. You can change his diaper." The fan persisted, writing Porter letters and hanging around Linebaugh's, the musicians' restaurant at 405 Broadway. She sent Porter letters in care of WSM, which went undelivered. Goober says she took these spurned missives and presented them to Ruth Wagoner, recommending that Ruth divorce Porter. Goober says Ruth asked him his opinion, and he advised her, "Oh, I wouldn't pay any attention to

---

*By now, *Billboard* had scrapped its separate listings for airplay, jukebox play, and store sales in favor of a more nebulous consolidated chart based increasingly on airplay and less on record sales.

that. He has women who run after him, but . . . I'm pretty sure Porter hasn't had anything to do with her."

Goober also tells how Porter's bass player-comedian Curly Harris fell in love with a female wrestler, and how Curly, Goober, and Don all shared the same room. Curly called Don "the little monster" with apparent cause Don obtained a photograph of the wrestler, in her professional attire, autographed it for Goober, "I'll remember all the good times we've had," and pasted it on the ceiling over Curly's bed.

"I could write a book that would cause a dozen divorces," Goober says with conviction.

"I used to carry the yellow jackets," Goober says, referring to his responsibility for the Benzedrine. Who knows how many lives Benzedrine has wrecked or claimed and how many musicians' lives it may have saved, traveling those harrowing highways booked by talent agents who were blind or oblivious to the actual distances required.

Goober says, "Sometimes you couldn't see the road, you were so tired. Some of the musicians would get road-happy and want to drive. Don Warden never wanted to take them, he always wanted to be aware of everything. He's a people watcher. When we'd get to a strange town, he'd sit on the square and watch the people."

Red Gale, Porter's rhythm guitar player, laughs and shudders about the road life. Red was in charge of the automobile and the instruments. "Now, I never will forgive Porter and Don for this," Red told me. They gave Red the car and told him to drive it to Edmonton, Canada, while they flew to Nashville to see their wives. Up around Salt Lake City Red got turned around and drove seventy-five miles in the wrong direction. "Those little patches in the road, my mind would tell me, *those are bulls*. And I would be dodging them. Mail boxes would reach out and grab me as I'd go by."

"I miss my days with Porter," says Red. "I don't think we ever had a falling out, but you can't sleep in the car together thirty nights in a row without getting irritated with each other." Red says it was "no fun" fixing a flat tire at thirty-eight degrees below zero in Regina, Canada, with Porter sitting inside the car with the heater on. It took Red and Don about an hour. They could only work a minute or two, taking lug nuts off, before jumping back in the car to warm themselves.

Red says he and Don grew really sick of looking at their boss's Nudie suit. The two of them could only afford two suits apiece, one grey, one blue. "I never will forgive Porter for putting me in those goddam powder blue cowboy boots! And I wasn't a cowboy at all."

Porter, Johnny Cash, and Johnny Horton were all practical jokers, Red testifies. He remembers when a fiddler griped, "When you're on the road, your Val-pak [suit bag] gets heavier every day." So they began slipping a few lead sinkers into his dirty clothes every day. "I don't remember if Porter was there in Duluth, where we turned fifty baby chicks loose from a freight elevator on every floor," says Red. He tells how Johnny Cash would rent an extra room under the name of Joe Quatz, fill it up with hay, then order in dinner for two. "When you opened the door," Red laughs, "all you could see was the top of the mirror and the headboards."

Porter was at the Opry one night, Red recalls, when they hid the bow of one of the fiddlers. There were numerous other fiddle players about, but none would lend him a bow. "Then, when they handed him a bow, they'd put olive oil on it. I remember Porter laughing his butt off at that."

Porter used to travel with the Blind Troubadour, Leon Payne. "We would tell him he was really a German, or a Chinaman, or was black," Red recalls. Porter once roomed with Leon and returned to the room one time to find it in total darkness, but Leon was shaving. Forgetting Leon was blind, Porter asked, "Why don't you turn on the lights? You might cut yourself!"

The so-called Nashville Sound was a-cookin'. Pop flavoring was being stirred into the country brew, sometimes to a sticky-sweet consistency, in order to sell more records. Red Gale was pulled both ways by these musical crosscurrents. He liked to hang out in Printers' Alley, the strip joint and nightclub tourist haven, or in the back room at Tootsie's with guitar players like Hank Garland, who played on some of Porter's records.

Porter himself would chide Red for his up-the-neck, barred chords that Porter called "titlypomps." He wanted Red to play ringing, acoustic, high-lonesome chords in the first position. Porter still wanted the Bill Monroe sound; Red wanted to play like jazz guitarist Barney Kessel.

Porter says Red worried about his guitar playing, his singing, and whether or not his guitar was in tune. Once at the Opry, Red was playing the introduction to "Company's Comin'" when the metal tailpiece of his hollow-body, jazz-style guitar just flew off. "The strings went every which-a-way," says Porter. "It was sort of pitiful, but it was funny. And the people thought it was part of our act. They just tore the house down. It was terrible. One of the other guitar players rushed a guitar out on the stage for Red."

After a year or two at the trailer park, Red moved into a gabled, yellow stone building at 620 Boscobel Street in East Nashville. That was the hillbilly hostelry of Delia (Mrs. Louis K.) Upchurch, known as Mom Upchurch to at least two generations of pickers. Beds cost seven dollars a week, breakfast seventy-five cents, and supper eighty-five cents. She claimed to have harbored around two thousand music men in thirty years, a not incredible number considering her willingness to rent your bed to someone else when you were on the road. Two of Porter's later Wagonmasters, Buck Trent and George McCormick, lived at Mom Upchurch's. Mom didn't allow drinking, so she saved many a sideman from himself. Her alumni included later stars like Carl Smith and Johnny Paycheck, who was known as Donny Young back then.

Mom charged extra for sandwiches and slept by the kitchen with her door ajar. She would wake up if the refrigerator door opened and the light went on. One night Red was trying to manage a cheese sandwich when Mom whapped him on the arm with her yardstick.

Mom Upchurch's will not get a metal historical marker, nor will the Dickerson Road Trailer Park. But if someone had chucked a hand grenade through her door around 1960 and lobbed another into the Dickerson Road park, the Nashville Sound would have been decimated.

Porter often worked the Flame in Minneapolis, a nightclub, but one with a raised stage so no one could dance. It was a "class" nightclub with a horseshoe bar, where most people just came for dinner. Goober remembers the last day of one of their Minneapolis engagements. Red had returned Porter's Cadillac but couldn't explain a dent in the front fender. Then that evening Red was sitting with some customers and wanted Porter to meet them.

"You know I don't go out in the audience in my uniform before I go on stage," Porter said.

"They're right by the door, no one will see you," Red claimed.

Goober laughs, recalling that as Porter was shaking hands, Red knocked over a glass, spilling wine all over Porter's suit jacket. "The only one he had left."

Goober believes Red left the band very soon after this. Red joined another band, then quit the road more or less permanently. "I was flat tired. You can be with a whole bunch of people all the time and still go home and be lonely. And I was scared to death," alluding to musicians he had seen ruined by the road.

Red cherishes many dear memories of the years with Porter, such as the time an aspiring songwriter tried to pitch Porter a song that started off, "Just Molly and me, and the baby makes three," and was titled "My Green Heaven." Red says Porter "just laughed his butt off."

Mae Boren Axton is well known for co-writing "Heartbreak Hotel," Elvis's first million-seller. She was Porter's publicist in the mid 1980s, earning a battle star during a tussle with a tabloid. She first met Porter in the fifties.

Born in Texas but rooted in Oklahoma, Mae was teaching school in Florida and practicing journalism on the side. A New York editor asked her to do a story on "hillbillies" for *Life Today* magazine. What are

Above: *The Flame nightclub, at the corner of Sixteenth and Nicollet, Minneapolis, circa. 1959. Below: On stage at The Flame nightclub in Minneapolis, with sidemen Benny Williams and Little Jack Little plus the house band, circa 1959* [PHOTOS BY JAMES G. ("GOOBER") BUCHANAN].

hillbillies? "They're people who come out of the hills and pick guitar and sing through their noses," she was told.

At Springfield she met Si Siman, who said of Porter, "He's really got talent and I'm going to see that he gets heard." Mae met Porter there, and then repeatedly in Nashville. She found him at once shy and talkative, "the typical American who came from nothing to do something in his own style. People care about him because they know he cares about them. You can tell. He just loves the people when he's on stage.

"For all the rhinestones, all the cutting up, you still think, 'There's someone I *know*.' You think he would do some of the things you'd want to do, but wouldn't. But it's fine if *he* does it.

"But sometimes he's his own worst enemy. He'll say things that are completely honest, but if he just hadn't said 'em, it would be better."

Shadows lay across Porter's marriage even in the 1940s in West Plains, but not until Christmastime 1965 would Porter move out, never to return.

On the road he worked with Patsy Cline, a kind of female Red Foley. At times Patsy could effortlessly hit the pop music bull's-eye with a country song. Porter told Patsy's biographer, Ellis Nassour, how they traveled in Cadillac caravans in the years before the show buses, and that Patsy "liked [his] band and became especially close to them." Patsy was even closer to Porter. "It made a few lonely nights out there on the dismal road more bearable," he says, but they were more comrades than intense lovers.

The Nashville to which Porter had moved his family and musicians was well on its way to becoming Music City, USA.

There's a story that when someone asked Chet Atkins to define the Nashville Sound, he shook his pocketful of change. The truth in that anecdote is profound: Nashville's preeminence as a music capital has more to do with the sound of money than with any music particular to Middle Tennessee.

Nashville was founded by land speculators. The families selected for settlement moved down what is now Gallatin Road around Christmastime in 1779, crossing the frozen Cumberland River on the ice and clambering up the bluffs. They were attracted by the salt lick there, and nearby they built Fort Nashborough. The pioneers were disproportionately Scotch-Irish. The Nashville group came from Watauga, first independent settlement in North America beyond the grasp of British law.

The inventory of the Nashborough settlement listed two fiddles. In the Cumberland settlements vagabond fiddlers like James Gamble (who made his fiddle "walk and talk") were often in demand. Early Nashville newspapers advertised songbooks for sale, probably imported from Philadelphia; and in 1824 *The Western Harmony* hymnal was published at Nashville. Such lore forms a faint link with the later Music Row, and the lady's guitar on display at Andrew Jackson's home, the Hermitage, is another romantic detail.

But more to the point was Nashville's rise as a business center. In 1885 the Methodists published *The Law of Success*, a guide to making money by following the Ten Commandments. And Nashville's self-congratulatory centennial in 1897 created Centennial Park. That same year an insurance company was founded in Alabama—the following year it moved to Nashville and became National Life and Accident. In 1925 it founded WSM, and the "Barn Dance"/Opry as well.

The daughter of Opry founder George D. Hay told Thomas Goldsmith of *The Tennessean* in 1987 that "vested interests" had tried to force her father and Edwin Craig to stop running the Opry, that the *Nashville Banner* attacked it for being "degrading to the cultural image of Nashville."

Understandably, WSM officials hoped to keep country music manageably quaint and folksy and under their thumb. The star-type entertainers were, of course, the hardest to regiment, since they earned more on the road than at the Opry, with its chintzy union-scale pay. Nor did the WSM management sympathize with the entertainers' basic need to wrest a living from the road or they wouldn't have opposed electric guitars, and then drums, for as long as they did. Electric guitars cut through the honky-tonk hubbub on the hardwood floors, while drums gave the dancers a beat they could feel through all the noise. As late as 1959 the Opry fought to keep Stonewall Jackson from using a bass drum when he was performing "Waterloo," which was a hit. And Don Warden's wife, Ann, tells how, when she attended modeling classes in Nashville, "I would not have told them I lived on Dickerson Road in a house trailer and my husband played steel guitar on the Grand Ole Opry for nothin'. In those days, we were looked down on!"

Meanwhile, the Opry continued to decline. In 1958 there were only 144,464 ticket buyers, then 140,710 in 1959, down to 136,520 in 1960. As Chet Hagan writes in his Opry history, the 44 percent fall-off since 1953 reflected the stirrings of rock 'n' roll. Unlike Springfield's KWTO, which thrived on conflicts of interest, Nashville's WSM disdained cashing in when it could have. It seemed positively offended at the thought of office staff wasting time trying to consolidate their country music profits. When they found Opry manager Jim Denny moonlighting as a music publisher, instead of promoting him, they fired him. The flamboyant Denny then started the successful Cedarwood company. And as he slammed the door in leaving—his exit was grade-A theater—he took with him a number of artists to the instantly formed Jim Denny

Artists Bureau, Inc. An early brochure lists just about everyone, including Porter Wagoner. When WSM fired program director Jack Stapp, he hit the sidewalk and formed what is today's largest country music publisher, Tree International.

A 1956 country single for the Maddox Brothers & Rose was "The Death of Rock & Roll." It didn't chart. "Rock and Roll Is Here to Stay" by Danny & the Juniors was a pop hit in 1958 and carried the truer message.

Now in the late fifties, there seemed no hope in sight for country acts like Porter's, who could scarcely get on the country charts and found bookings so hard to come by. Steve Sholes asked Porter to try some rock 'n' roll, but Porter declined. In 1958 Johnny Cash had a pop hit with "Ballad of a Teenage Queen," then decided not to do an encore, pulling back to country.

Meanwhile, the first wave of rock 'n' rollers had more or less left the stage in assorted tragedies and interruptions: Johnny Ace (1954 Russian roulette accident); Carl Perkins (1956 car wreck, broken neck); Chuck Berry (1958 arrest with teenage prostitute, eventual prison); Jerry Lee Lewis (1958 commotion over his possibly illicit marriage to his thirteen-year-old distant cousin); Elvis (merely drafted, 1958); Buddy Holly, Ritchie Valens, Big Bopper (dead in the same 1959 plane crash); and Eddie Cochran (dead in a 1960 car wreck).

Much breath has been spent and ink spilled in deploring what rock 'n' roll did to country music. What rock did *for* country music deserves some space, too. When Elvis cut "Heartbreak Hotel" in the stairwell of the RCA studio on McGavock Street in Nashville, the vibrations took on significant resonance for Chet Atkins (RCA), Owen Bradley (Decca), Don Law (Columbia), and probably Ken Nelson in Los Angeles (Capitol). Elvis was, or had been, country in his music origins, and if he could get such a hearing for his rural voice with black phrasing, country record producers might profit from his example. Elvis was on RCA and would continue to record in Nashville. Imperceptibly at first, rock or pop techniques crept into production, such as backup sweetening added by the Anita Kerr Singers.

And production itself was a new value; no more hits would be cut in radio stations. If the rock 'n' rollers could play tricks with echo chambers and overdubbing, the lesson was not lost on Chet Atkins and his peers on the other labels. Later they would be condemned for dragging country music too far across the center of the road—the Nashville Sound begat the crossover mushiness—but back in the late fifties, they were desperate men fighting for survival. Chet had been fired from too many radio stations, but now Steve Sholes was letting him make all the RCA decisions in Nashville.

The Methodists believed Chet was bringing "bad people" into their McGavock Street building. So on the back of a napkin at the Nashville airport, RCA's chief engineer, Bill Miltentong, drew a picture of what was needed. The napkin drawing became Studio B, where Porter and everyone else cut so many hits. They moved into the new studio on 800 Seventeenth Avenue South in November 1957.

Songwriter and journalist Walter Carter described Studio B for *Country Sounds:*

> The new building took four months to build and cost $39,515. Through the next 20 years, revenue from the records cut there would easily top $100 million. [It] was essentially four cinder-block walls, two stories high, with a flat roof. It had to be an eyesore to the residents of the old neighborhood, which had only recently been rezoned for commercial use.

Much of the equipment was fashioned by engineers Bill Porter and Al Pachucki. Studio B had natural echo, a live sound, and no one used earphones. Al Pachucki was engineer on countless Porter Wagoner sessions, and he said, "The beauty of the room was that everyone could hear everyone the way they should."

Porter modestly reentered *Billboard* for four weeks in 1960 with "The Girl Who Didn't Need Love." It was a number thirty, noteworthy in retrospect for the presence of Dottie West as the anonymous backup singer. He was on the charts only one more week that year, when both sides of a single managed to hit: "Falling Again," number twenty-six, and "Old Log Cabin for Sale," number thirty, which Lorraine had taught him. Lorraine says that side was a hit in Canada for more than a year, something like seventy-five weeks.

The previous year, his single of "The Battle of Little Big Horn" had deservedly failed to hit, being a sorry imitation of "The Battle of New Orleans." In the lyric, General Custer may be leading cavalry troops, but they are bearing antiquated "muskets" instead of trapdoor Springfield rifles and, ludicrously, there are "cannon balls a-flying." (Had Custer actually possessed artillery, laughs western scholar Ted P. Yeatman, then the Indians would have fled to Canada.) Its *rat-a-tat* drumbeat is comical.

An interesting song from this period is "The Legend of the Big Steeple," patterned after "The Three Bells" of the Browns (also on RCA) right down to the bell-like "bom" at intervals. But the song (by Charles Underwood) is a satisfied mind-type commentary on the value of money, versus life and love. A rich man dies one week before his wedding day, and his estate purchases a needed steeple that the church members couldn't have afforded. Skeeter Davis reports that when the song began getting pop airplay in Cleveland, "Porter was almost *nervous* that it might go pop."

Along with a few fiascos, Porter had assembled a distinctive catalogue of recordings through 1960, thirty releases (sixty sides). His sparse accompaniments had progressed from his Drifting Cowboys-style backup sound through his Trio formula into the RCA studio sound abetted by the Anita Kerr Singers. Porter held onto his Hank Williams mournfulness and Bill Monroe exuberance, but you can hear Chet trying to sandpaper him slightly into some Jim Reeves smoothness. The overall integrity of these recordings would serve RCA well in the sixties, when so much of the Porter Wagoner backlog began to saturate the market on countless LPs, often on the budget Camden label, RCA's vehicle for catch-up packagings.

This bulk of uncompromising country recordings, followed by so much more of the same in the sixties, elicited praise from the two leading chroniclers of country music, Bill C. Malone and Charles K. Wolfe. In the 1968 edition of his *Country Music U.S.A.*, Malone calls Porter "one of the most valuable members of the country-music profession, both because of the quality of his singing and because of his commitment to genuine country styles and themes." In his liner notes to *Sixty Years of the Grand Ole Opry*, Wolfe calls Porter "arguably the best honky-tonk singer in modern country music," certainly a surprising judgment, considering Porter's aversion to nightclub work and his avoidance of the let's-get-drunk-type lyrics. But Wolfe is reacting to the soulful Porter Wagoner sound and his popularity on jukeboxes. Through 1982, he had fifty-two records in *Cash Box*, the jukebox hit magazine (exclusive of Porter–Dolly duets) some of which missed *Billboard* entirely.

In summation, Bill C. Malone calls Porter "a hillbilly in a time of stylistic cloudiness" (1985 edition of his book), noting that he didn't fit RCA's country–pop format of the late fifties and early sixties, but they probably kept him around because he was traditional, for contrast. Malone observes that the payoff would be in the late sixties.

Porter began to assert himself in the studio. As reported in *Country Song Roundup*, Chet told Paul Soelberg in 1971 that he and Porter were so shy and introverted ("and I still am") that the two of them had a communication block. He felt Porter placed too much trust in him, that if he had been somebody else, Porter would have felt freer to broach his own ideas. Chet said other artists were similarly hesitant about speaking up, since he'd had a number of hits. Later they might realize they knew more than he did.

That fall Chet had to go to England, so he told Porter to try his own arrangements and hire his own musicians for an upcoming session. On November 23, 1960, Porter recorded "Your Old Love Letters" by

Johnny Bond, the western songwriter and B-movie actor, a song he frequently sings today. It entered *Billboard* March 6, 1961, and reached number ten, Porter's first Top 10 hit in four years. It was on the charts for thirteen weeks. Then on September 21, 1961, he conducted his own session for "Misery Loves Company," written by guitar player Jerry Reed, eventually a recording artist and actor.

"Misery Loves Company" charted in January 1962, and it went to number one. It had been almost six years since his last number one, "A Satisfied Mind."

Such career progress was worth a little money. But as Ruth Wagoner told her husband over and over, "money isn't everything."

"I heard that so many times," Porter remembers. "It really bothered her a lot. But I wasn't doing it just for the money. I don't know if she's ever understood it. It's difficult to explain to someone. There's certain things in life you *have* to do. It's not the money or the ego, or to see if you can be successful. It's a longing inside you . . . you're going to do it."

The Warden family certainly appreciated the money. They got half, and Porter got half, of the royalties generated by the Warden Music copyrights. Don kept these on file in a converted public shower stall down the path from their house trailer.

12

THE BALLAD OF JIMMY DRIFTWOOD

Perhaps the name of Warden Music Company
doesn't ring a bell. But "The Battle
of New Orleans" did . . . it rang
cash drawers all over . . .

—*The Music Reporter*, June 12, 1961

Dolly Parton's immense success owes not a little to the fact that she controls the copyrights on virtually everything she has written since mid 1967. Within weeks of joining "The Porter Wagoner Show," she set up her own publishing company, obviously inspired by the example of Porter and Don's company, Warden Music.* It provided the foundation for Porter's future business success. For years Don ran it from the Dickerson Road Trailer Park.

Dickerson Road today is a study in tawdriness, with adult bookstores and prostitution arrests relieving the monotony of second-hand stores. The trailer park at 1508, however, was (and is) an orderly looking village for people who have chosen to live in large metal containers. Roy Acuff lived up the road in a trailer park in 1939. In 1957 the rent at the Dickerson Road Trailer Park was $7.50 a week, plus utilities. Don and Ann Warden and their son lived at space F–7, and so did Warden Music, a file-folder fantasy for a while. In time they acquired a bigger trailer with a middle bedroom for Don's office.

The trailer park provided a secure place for an entertainer or picker to stash his costumes, demos, and spare instruments while on the road. A married, traveling troubadour could know that his family was in a safe, neighborly environment, even if perhaps he was not. There were sidewalks and ample yard space, and the park's manager was a part-time

---

*Songwriter Sammy Cahn told Joe Smith (*Off the Record: An Oral History of Popular Music*) that Irving Berlin was the only songwriter in the history of American music "who was never demeaned," because he owned 100 percent of every song he ever wrote.

Jimmy Driftwood with his antique, handmade guitar from the nineteenth century [THE PORTER WAGONER SHOW, NUMBER 2, CIRCA 1963].

sheriff's deputy who would don his uniform each evening, strap on his pistol, and patrol.

Residents over the years included Hawkshaw Hawkins; fiddler Chubby Wise; singing star Don Gibson ("Oh, Lonesome Me" and "Blue, Blue Day"); Floyd Tillman, who wrote "Slippin' Around"; colorful Cajun fiddler Doug Kershaw; and comedian Rod Brasfield, who died there. Living there in the 1960s were such members of "The Porter Wagoner Show" as Norma Jean (with her daughter), Mack Magaha, and Buck Trent; and the Porter Wagoner bus was parked there.

As for Warden Music in 1957, it had never had a hit or even anything recorded. Hugh Ashley, of Harrison, Arkansas, had already written for Porter via Si's Earl Barton, and he placed Don in touch with Jimmy Driftwood of Timbo, Arkansas. Born James Morris in 1907, Jimmy was by then the school principal at Snowball, Arkansas, and he was a walking folk song archive. A former teacher, he had been making up songs since the 1930s to sing to his students, not primarily as entertainment but as teaching tools for his American history classes.

His own preference in instruments was not exactly in line with the Nashville Sound or the musicians' union. Jimmy played a bizarre guitar that had been fashioned by his grandfather—the neck from a fence rail, the sides from an ox yoke, and the top and bottom from a bedstead brought from Tennessee.

Over the years Jimmy had become especially frustrated with students who confused historical facts, such as confusing the American Revolution and the War of 1812, just because both were against the British. His wife, Cleda, suggested he clarify the distinction with a song.

So he borrowed the old square dance fiddle tune, "The Eighth of January," named for the date of the Battle of New Orleans, and wrote some new words.

That was in 1936. Now, in 1957 Don Warden was asking for songs, and Jimmy didn't own a tape recorder. So he and Cleda scheduled an appointment with Don at the Clarkston Hotel and headed for Nashville in their beat-up pickup truck.

Walking into the Clarkston with his heirloom, rustic, bedstead guitar, Jimmy was greeted by someone in the lobby, "Oh, a new singer?" Jimmy replied, "No, I write songs. I've come to see Porter Wagoner and Don Warden." The fellow answered, "They've never had anything, and they never will." He telephoned Buddy Killen at Tree Publishing next door and sent Jimmy over to Buddy. Tree was in the Cumberland Lodge Building at 319 Seventh Avenue, part of a now-forgotten, earlier version of Music Row.* Jimmy performed two stanzas of "The Battle of New Orleans" when Buddy halted him. "Son, if that's the kind of stuff you got, you better go home. We couldn't sell one record of that."

Next evening they met Don, and Jimmy presented upwards of a hundred songs. Every three or four tunes, Don would pause and write down its title, logging in twenty-five or so songs. Just after midnight, he began to weary of this one-man, nonstop folk festival. His hand was on the doorknob when Jimmy hesitantly began the first two stanzas of "The Battle of New Orleans," then paused, nervous after his experience with Tree. "That doesn't sound like it ought to be all of it," Don said drolly. Jimmy finished it, and Don said, "That could be a *big* record."

"It's just a history lesson I wrote," Jimmy replied.

"How long you been teaching it?" Don asked.

"Twenty-one years."

Don had them stay over another night to meet Porter and some other Opry stars at the Clarkston. Jimmy sang songs until midnight, and it was then that Porter heard "Tennessee Stud" for the first time. Porter told Don, "If he really wrote these, they're worth nothing but money."**

They took Jimmy down to McGavock Street to meet Chet. Jimmy was carrying his guitar in its customary traveling case, a Dixie Lily flour

---

*This budding music business neighborhood centered around the National Life building at number 301 (WSM studios and offices). Judy Lynn and Marty Robbins had offices in the Cumberland Lodge Building. Down in the Albert Building at number 146 were Carl Smith and Jim Denny with his booking agency and Cedarwood publishing company.

**Porter remembers hearing "The Battle of New Orleans" independently. He was in the coffee shop of the Clarkston when Bill Carlisle told him there was a fellow upstairs with some astonishing songs.

sack. "This probably won't sound as good as one of yours does," Jimmy said to Chet. Jimmy was signed to RCA.

Jimmy contrasts Don Warden with Buddy Killen. "You'd understand it if you've been a hunter. You can get more game out of a lean dog than a fat dog."

Don had known singer Johnny Horton from "The Louisiana Hayride" down in Shreveport, and he pitched him "The Battle of New Orleans." Meanwhile RCA had issued Jimmy's version as a single, and the extra stanzas may have discouraged disc jockeys at first. Then the Federal Communications Commission (FCC) began harassing the record, since Jimmy had rhymed *damn* with Colonel Pakenham, and General Jackson's volunteers gave the British "hell." "You could preach 'damn' or 'hell,' but you couldn't *sing* 'em," says Jimmy. Disc jockey Ralph Emery began playing Jimmy's record on WSM.

Johnny Horton's version of "The Battle of New Orleans" was the first song recorded by Columbia in Owen Bradley's historic quonset hut studio on Sixteenth Avenue South. Don Warden came home from the session and told Ann, "This is going to be really big for us. As soon as this record comes out, it'll pay off this house trailer."

In April 1959 Johnny Horton's record entered *Billboard*'s country charts, staying there twenty-one weeks, ten of them at number one.* It was eighteen weeks on the pop charts, six of these at number one also. Even Jimmy's version, complete with "damn" and "hell" and the surplus verses, had been briefly on the country charts. Very quickly, there were twenty-two versions of the song.

When his first royalty check for "The Battle of New Orleans" arrived, it was for $25,000. Assuming he signed a standard, fifty–fifty contract, that meant Warden Music got as much. There is no telling what the song has earned since, for it's had a million airplays alone.

Next time Jimmy met publisher Buddy Killen of Tree, he remembers that Buddy bent over and said, "Kick me."

"The Battle of New Orleans" won three Grammys: one for Jimmy, one for Johnny Horton, and one for Homer and Jethro's spoof, "The Battle of Kookamonga."

The folk music vogue had been started earlier by the Weavers, Harry Belafonte, and then the Kingston Trio in 1958 with "Tom Dooley." (Tom Dula had been hanged in 1866 for slaying his lover, who had

---

*This could never happen today. Rarely does a song last more than one week at number one, and almost never more than two. Artificial rotation of hits has been the industry equivalent of price-fixing, giving the most number of number one hits to the greatest possible number of artists. In 1992 chart integrity began making a comeback.

infected him with venereal disease.) Jimmy Driftwood rode out this trend, cutting more RCA albums and seeing many more songs recorded by other artists, accruing ever more royalties to Warden Music. "Saga songs" became the fashion, some of them written by Jimmy. Johnny Horton spearheaded this colorful fad, but some of his hits were posthumous. In March 1960 a Texas college student with alcohol in his car, crashed into Johnny's white Cadillac sometime past midnight as Johnny was driving back to Shreveport. Incredibly, Johnny's widow was also the widow of Hank Williams, as she was the hapless girl who'd married Hank in his final, wasting months.

Don and Ann paid off their house trailer, and Warden Music moved out of Ann's livingroom and up in the world. Porter said that Don worked with tireless energy for Warden Music, once traveling through New Orleans to Texas and back, scouting songs, sleeping on the floor of his Volkswagen bus, and taking with him only twenty dollars in expense money.

The two of them drew only token salaries from Warden Music, mostly to cover expenses. Their accountant, Ken Dillard, helped them invest in stocks, such as in a life insurance company, bonds, and eventually in a professional men's credit union. When an "old friend" hit up Porter for a "loan," with a straight face Porter could direct the fellow to the right place! Wisely Porter doesn't carry cash if he can help it— possibly something else he learned not to do from watching Red Foley.

Even when the money was there, he avoided the usual business fiascoes that have sunk so many of his peers, such as fast food franchise flops. When approached with a plan to double his money, Porter would shunt all proposals to Don and Ken, who would review them with some bankers and reject nineteen out of twenty.

Another big hit for Jimmy Driftwood and Warden Music was "Tennessee Stud," a number five hit for Eddy Arnold in 1959. The song opens in 1825 and traces the course of two generations of the family of Jimmy's wife, Cleda. Just like in the song, Cleda's grandfather indeed beat up the father and the brother of the girl he loved back in Tennessee. They did ride off on the horse called the Tennessee Stud. Porter's version of "Tennessee Stud" on his *Me and My Boys* album (1969) displays some brilliant fiddling.

Jimmy Driftwood appeared at the first Newport (Rhode Island) Folk Festival in July 1959 to sing "The Battle of New Orleans." Johnny Horton's hit version wasn't out yet. Porter remembers Jimmy and Don Warden went to New York at about this time so Jimmy could appear on a bill with bluesman Muddy Waters, probably at Newport.

Jimmy's memorable costume featured his broad-brimmed black hat and buckskin coat heavy with fringe. They checked into the Waldorf-Astoria Hotel and, while Don was parking his car, some New Yorkers on the sidewalk began gaping at Jimmy. Don remembers him exclaiming, "There's some of the strangest looking people up here, ain't there?"

Jimmy Driftwood stories are probably inexhaustible. When Jimmy was in New York in September 1959, his idea of welcoming Russian premier Nikita Khrushchev to the United States was to sing his song "The Bear Flew Over the Ocean" outside the United Nations building. Someone had rounded up a large bear for the occasion, and "when I started singing, that bear just sort of hunkered down," Jimmy told me. A picture of the scene made *Life* magazine.

For Porter's television audience, Jimmy once demonstrated another of his arcane musical "instruments," the "mouth bow." He would snap a bow string against his mouth to create a *whon-n-n-ng* effect on the side of his face, like an aboriginal jew's harp. Then Jimmy performed his most famous song with his homemade guitar, with the capo amazingly far up the neck—in the 8th fret—making his G fingering come out sounding in the key of C. Porter even managed to take a turn on Jimmy's guitar, finger-picking no less. Porter said he hoped Chet was watching.

13

"THE PORTER WAGONER SHOW"

His shows were done so well with so much talent.
Certainly the most successful of all the early
television shows, and Porter put it
all together himself.

—Willie Nelson, interview with
Gay Harrah, October 18, 1989

The longest-running country music television show in history was of course "The Porter Wagoner Show." Virtually every star of importance was a guest, from Tex Ritter to black singer Joe Simon. For seven colorful years Dolly Parton was a regular member, then made guest appearances after she officially left. For over half of the program's life-span, around twelve years, the sponsor was the Chattanooga Medicine Company, purveyors of health products to the South since 1879.

Chattanooga approached Noble–Dury advertising agency about a possible country music show in 1960. Auditions were conducted by Elmer Alley and Jane Dowden (Jane Gram today) at 2036 Fifteenth Avenue South. Porter thinks perhaps Webb Pierce, Carl Smith, and the Wilburn Brothers also tried out.

Jane Gram was still working in syndicated television (Opryland's Syndicom) when I interviewed her in 1989. She remembered the auditions ran only fifteen to twenty minutes. About four or five of them reviewed the test tape, and it filled almost everyone with misgivings. Porter was so shy, and they hadn't been able to get him to look at the camera. "Ozark Jubilee" or not, he seemed very inexperienced. "We wondered how we'd get him to do a television show," Jane says. "I remember Porter was so warm and authentic. He was a good salesman, but as I recall he wasn't auditioned as a salesman, just as a performer." One of Jane's colleagues said, "I don't know, I don't know how we'll ever make it go." Jane replied she thought Porter could do it, that he had the ability to communicate. Willis ("Bill") Graham was especially doubtful.

Jane said, "Can I tell you someone else you turned down?"

Bill replied, "Please don't bring up Pat Boone again!" Jane told Chattanooga Medicine Company that she thought Porter had big star potential.

For the audition Porter had used the ever-constant Don Warden, who flew up from a Florida vacation so as not to miss out. Benny Williams had replaced Red Gale on electric rhythm guitar. On fiddle was Little Jack Little.

Porter needed a comedian, so he summoned Speck Rhodes. And for a girl singer Porter brought in Norma Jean Beasler, whom Red Foley used to introduce on the Jubilee as "a little lady with a very plaintive voice." Porter liked her wholesome, pretty-housewife look, though she was in fact single.

Porter told Jack Hurst of *The Tennessean* in 1971, "We started out going into eighteen stations. At that time, I didn't even know what *syndicated* meant."

On the early shows Porter was always nervous, as he worried about how to introduce guests, how to ad-lib commercials, and, especially, how to appear honest. On television any conscious effort at anything usually appears exaggerated. Attempts at looking dignified come across as stiff. Porter scrutinized the playbacks with intense care, noting where he and his band looked like they were having fun or just looked plumb scared. He decided to let his crew-cut grow out, since television makes everything seem more extreme.

They had to make it to the commercials without stopping, so unless a mistake was horrendous they left it in. Since they did their own commercials, initially, sometimes they had to go a full twenty-eight minutes without stopping.* There were times when the show would be shot twice, once with commercials, which they usually did themselves, and once without, for stations who wanted to insert their own.

The shows ran half an hour, with about twenty-two minutes of program before commercials; they usually featured eight songs. Budget for each episode was $700 to $800, and everyone was paid union scale, although as "leader" Porter got double. For years the shows were black and white. Until 1964 they ran twenty-six shows a year, then expanded.

Remembers Jane Gram:

> Porter was always so organized. He was so different from much of what we dealt with in country music. He always came prepared and ready. No delays, he ran it like a business. His punc-

---

*Lawrence Welk said that as the medium improved, they would reshoot him and eliminate his famous verbal gaffes. Then they would decide the original footage, mistakes and all, was more natural and go with that.

tuality was just unfailing. Whether we were having a meeting in an office, he was never tardy for anything and that is just *not* usual. You could set a clock by him when that band left town. He had a great sense of humor and was jolly, but he wanted to get to work. He didn't get on ego trips like some do, with the clock rolling and telling jokes over in the corner. He was working right down to the minute.

Porter hoped to last maybe a year, anything to get some more exposure and consequently more airplay, since he was having hits again. But he had no idea how the show was going to help his draw as a live act. About a year after the show started, he was appearing in Montgomery, Alabama, and then in Dothan, Alabama, when he noticed the crowds were so much bigger in areas where the show was airing than in those where it wasn't, by a ratio of about five to one.

One of the most memorable characters in the cast was Speck Rhodes, "stand-up bumpkin comic" or "black-tooth rube comedian," as he has been called. Speck is a professional leprechaun, with the playful mouth and wistful eyes of the born funnyman.

As early as 1947, Speck and brothers, Slim and Dusty, had been on TV in Memphis. On Porter's road show Speck would play his stand-up bass. On the TV show his additional prop was an old wooden wall telephone with two bells on top. The telephone hooked up Speck with Sadie, his never-seen girl friend whose off-stage task was to frustrate Speck financially, mentally, and sexually.

Sadie even helped sell laxatives. Porter: "What's this I hear about Sadie joining the Women's Ad-Lib Movement?"

"Well, all she said was, she was glad Mother Nature was a woman," Speck answered.

Porter then expounded on how Black Draught made you feel more natural and comfortable while it was doing its job. . . .

"I only had one contract with Porter, the one we signed at the beginning of the TV show. I didn't have to ask for more money but once or twice in twenty years. 'Hee-Haw' wanted me, but I wouldn't go."

Speck Rhodes considers himself a comic actor. There are only two comedians in the Country Music Hall of Fame, Minnie Pearl and Rod Brasfield, but television has painted Speck's image indelibly in the collective memory. The green derby hat, the missing front teeth, the yellow-checked suit, and the high button shoes are scarcely forgettable.

Porter's fiddler was Little Jack Little. By 1959 he had joined Porter's band, leaving in 1964 only to return and play drums in the "Dolly" days. Jack said in 1971, "I don't believe I could work for anyone else. It takes a long time to learn how people think. That way, you'll

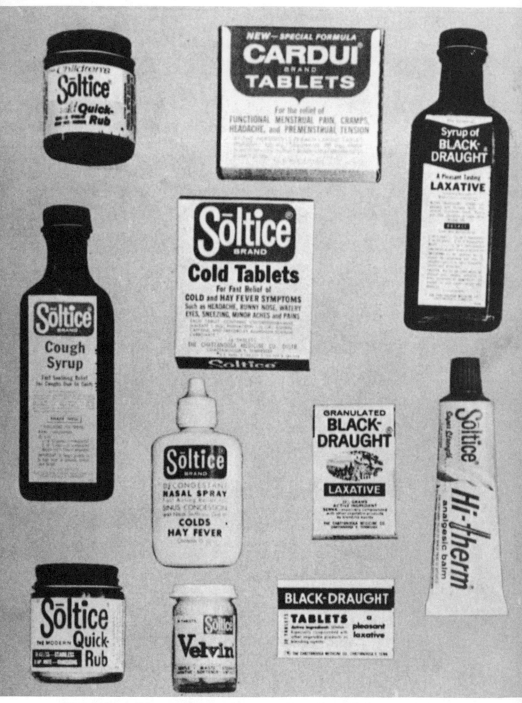

[THE PORTER WAGONER SHOW HITS THE ROAD! *circa* 1965]

almost say the same words they say at the same time, or even before they say it."

A hallmark sound on Porter's records was the twangy lick that goes *DUNH-daah* that anyone would guess is an electric guitar. Wrong. It's the electrified banjo of Buck Trent.

Charles W. Trent was born in Spartanburg, South Carolina, in 1938. He was playing steel guitar at age seven, but the discovery of his grandfather's banjo in the attic permanently sidetracked him. By 1960 he was playing five-string banjo finger-style for Bill Carlisle on the Opry. With competition from Bill Monroe's band and from Lester Flatt and Earl Scruggs, and with the general dearth of work caused by rock 'n' roll, Buck Trent was forced to innovate. He electrified his banjo, joined Porter, and began carrying the banjo even further. Buck liked to tinker, and Porter goaded him on. He invented twisters and other devices to get new and different noises out of the traditional instrument.

Buck told *Music City News*, "My electric banjo is built like a steel guitar, it's totally different from just putting a mike on a banjo." Like a pedal steel guitar, his banjo has a movable bridge that alters the pitch of the strings. It was designed by legendary steel picker and guitar manufacturer Shot Jackson.

Buck inevitably outgrew the format of "The Porter Wagoner Show," going with "Hee-Haw" and recording with Roy Clark. Porter got him on RCA and produced one of his albums. Buck says, "If I ever had to be in military combat, there's no one I would rather serve under than Porter Wagoner."

Buck Trent lived for a time at Mom Upchurch's dormitory for sidemen in East Nashville, and so did George McCormick. George was born in 1933, in Carthage, Tennessee, north of Nashville. He was a protégé of Fred Rose and recorded for MGM records, heavily under the Hank Williams influence. This was his common ground with Porter when they first met in 1953 in Springfield.

George joined Porter's band around 1964 or 1965. He got in on one recording session, singing baritone on a recut of "Eat, Drink and Be Merry." Porter paid George by the day at first, then hired him. "He takes care of his people better than anyone in this town, just about. He made a lot of money, which shows you can pay your people good and still come out. I worked over eight years for him, and I've worked fifteen years for Grandpa Jones."

George says Porter has "given away about two or three fortunes." George played hollow-body electric with an arch-top when he first joined the Wagonmasters. One day Porter presented him with a Gibson Super-400. "They didn't make but about fifteen of them . . . He said, 'If you like it, it's yours.' He'd got it from Shot Jackson, who'd found it in a pawnshop in Roanoke, Virginia, and talked him out of it. He told Shot he would give him some spots on his TV show!"

"People liked the TV show when we made mistakes," reminisces George. "They thought it was funny. We didn't rehearse a lot. We were on the road sometimes 275 to 300 days a year."

Mack Magaha (pronounced mah-GAY-hay) was playing in Elkins, West Virginia, when Porter approached him about joining his show. Porter needed someone to play electric bass, drive the bus, and play a little fiddle—right away, too, since they were taping some TV shows. Mack owed his employers, Don Reno and Red Smiley, two weeks' notice, and Porter said he understood, but added, "Be here as soon as you can."

It was October 1964 when Mack and his wife showed up at the trailer park. Porter was sick and had come off a tour early. He picked up Mack and his wife, Shirley, and took them to a drugstore for dinner. "First time anybody had bought my dinner since I'd been in the music business," says Mack. "He didn't try to impress us at all," adds his wife. "The dinner probably cost $1.50 apiece."

Porter told Mack there wouldn't be much work until after Christmas, but he was paying him $125 a week anyhow. Mack said he'd been working for years for seventy-five dollars a week and was finally up to eighty-five dollars, whereupon Porter replied, "When we work you won't work unless you make at least fifty dollars a day." Mack says, "I couldn't believe this was happening to me. I said to my wife, 'If we can save $3,000, this will be a good move.' First year we saved $8,000."

Mack was born in 1929 near Greenville, South Carolina, in a sharecropper family. In the Korean "conflict," three days before cease-fire on Porkchop Hill, Mack was hit by mortar fire. Both legs were broken. The Red Cross got him a fiddle, and he played in his hospital bed, to the great irritation of a fellow invalid, who complained about "that awful hillbilly music." Mack eventually joined the Don Reno–Red Smiley band.

Speaking of Porter, Mack says, "Mostly he made me feel like I was somebody. Reno and Smiley, I never did get that feeling from them. When Porter and Dolly split up, I was making $250 a day. Other people were going out for fifty dollars a day. I made more money in November and December than I did with Reno and Smiley in the first ten months of the year."

Mack became popular as the "Dancing Fiddle Man" on Porter's road and TV shows. Porter attributes this to his broken legs, saying that Mack never thought he'd use them again, but when he regained their use "he was so damned thrilled and tickled that he would dance. Mack never said nothin' [on the TV show], but the people just loved him, his personality was so good. He came through to the people. You can't fool people, they'll figure your ass out."

Above: *Chattem Drug & Chemical Company, 1715 West 38th Street, Chattanooga, Tennessee. Formerly Chattanooga Medicine Company and sponsor of Porter's TV show* [PHOTO BY AUTHOR]. Below: *Jeannie Seely and Buck Trent, 1967* [COURTESY PORTER WAGONER ENTERPRISES].

Left: *Gilbert* *("Speck")* *Rhodes* [COURTESY PORTER WAGONER ENTERPRISES]. Below: *Porter's son Richard, wife Ruth, and daughters Denise and Debra* [THE PORTER WAGONER SHOW, CIRCA 1962].

Vernon Staggs of the Chattanooga Medicine Company says, "People could identify with Porter. He might murder the king's English, but if he said Cardui would cure you, you'd believe it."

Chattanooga Medicine's most famous product was Black Draught. No matter how you pronounce it, it's good for you, Porter once said, offering *drought* and *drowf* as humorous alternatives. A draught, of course, is a drink of something ("draft"), and at first Red Foley's parents thought he was peddling German dark beer on television! Vernon Staggs, in his company history, traces Black Draught back to the eighteenth century and the British navy. Along with their weekly ration of rum, the sailors were administered a dose of senna, probably in a tea. It offset the sailors' diet of "salt pork, bully beef, and hardtack." By 1840 a commercial version of Black Draught was being marketed by a Tennessee doctor, A. O. Simmons. His son-in-law, M. A. Thedford, took it over, and Thedford's Black Draught became a southern institution. The rural diet of "fat meat, corn bread, hot biscuits, molasses and white gravy clogged the whole system with poisons of constipation," writes Thomas D. Clark in his jovial history of the southern country store, *Pills, Petticoats, and Plows*. The most popular laxative was Black Draught.

After the Civil War, an ex-Union officer who stayed behind in Chattanooga, Z. C. Patten, bought up the rights to Thedford's Black Draught. He also acquired control of McElree's Wine of Cardui, pronounced CAR-joo-eye.

General stores throughout the South sold "Black-Draught for all the Family" and "Wine of Cardui for Women." Oftentimes, the only paint a barn or carriage house might receive was a garish advertisement for the Chattanooga Medicine Company. The method of loading the stores' shelves with the elixirs was a model of free enterprise panache. Extremely popular were the free *Ladies Birthday Almanac* and company-boosting calendars. Imprinted with a store's name, they were distributed each fall on credit. Then, to work off his debt, the merchant would lay in a stock—perhaps an overstock—of the medicines. Whether or not they all sold, next fall came the next wave of almanacs and calendars, with a stream of farm wives clamoring for them. Since they circulated each store's name, the South was inundated with "tens of millions" of them, according to Thomas D. Clark. Black Draught and Cardui (concocted from "semifrontier folk formulas" dating back to the 1830s) became as well known "as sardines and cheese."

Cardui was especially miraculous. One woman gained eighteen pounds in two months, thanks to Cardui, in an age when weight gain was chic and no woman wished to look "sickly." In 7,000 cases of assorted female discomforts, 6,500 cures were proudly reported. Around 1905, Cardui advertised that "What a husband needs is a well-SEXED woman" to share his burdens and pleasures "in a womanly way." Cardui also firmed up the breasts and combated venereal disease, so they claimed.

Company president John A. Patten was a stalwart of the Methodist Episcopal Church, and people in Chattanooga began joking that he was selling a beverage more than a tonic, since Cardui's alcoholic content was 20 percent. In 1905 *Collier's* magazine called Cardui's advertisements "loathsome." Next year, the Pure Food and Drug Act was enacted. By 1914–15 Chattanooga Medicine was being flayed by articles in *Harper's Illustrated Weekly* and in the *Journal of the American Medical Association*. Patten sought relief in court but the remedy killed the patient. In midtrial in Chicago, Patten was stricken with internal pains, was rushed from the courtroom, and died shortly after.

But the company won its three libel cases.

Gradually the alcoholic content of Cardui evaporated, and sales along with it. But the company retrenched and diversified, and in World War II it was the biggest producer of K rations for GIs. By the 1950s there were twenty-six products in the line, and the 1957 sales were $5 million.

But "The Porter Wagoner Show" increased the sales tenfold at least. The very first words heard on the début program of September 14, 1961, were sung by Porter and the band: "Feel fresh and clean inside! Black Draught helps you feel fresh and clean inside!"

The power of Porter's impact was demonstrated when once the company sent out a rather intricate questionnaire to 10,000 viewers, with no more than a 50 percent response anticipated. But when Porter asked people to please fill out the forms, 86 percent of them complied.

Jack Hurst of *The Tennessean* told "an apocryphal story about Porter Wagoner which may or may not be true." Some New York advertising executives were in town for a convention, and one of them wanted to catch a taping of "The Porter Wagoner Show." "You mean you like his singing?" "Hell, no. But man, I've just got to see how he sells all that laxative." Norma Jean says, "We used to joke that we were all *regular* members of the Porter Wagoner Show."

For years the announcer for the show was T. Tommy Cutrer, later a Tennessee state senator. Porter nicknamed him "T" and T. Tommy called Porter "Slick Nickel" or "Slick" for short. Once T. Tommy and Porter were having trouble getting a commercial done. It was requiring several takes. T. Tommy was feeding Porter a teaspoonful of Sōltice cough syrup each time, and these were taking their toll on Porter's digestion. Porter's line was "Boy, that stuff tastes *good*." Don Warden, who often carried a flask, slipped some whiskey into the bottle, and Porter said, "Boy, that's good. That *is* good!" Everyone started laughing. Finally it occurred to them that Coca-Cola would film more realistically than the actual syrup itself (these were the black and white days). But it was too late. Porter had already consumed an entire bottle, and after the final take he rushed to the bathroom and threw up.

*   *   *

Another popular product sold on the TV show was the souvenir book.

There were at least seven of these, and the fans identified with their family-album friendliness, in the best as well as the worst sense of the word. They were jammed full of snapshots taken at live shows, at television tapings, on the road, in the bus, and even at selected members' homes. Sometimes these were mounted twelve to a page. The homey, domestic shots, with wives and children, were typical fan fodder taken in back yards and livingrooms just like any family pictures. Norma Jean, who was single, might pose with her daughter, Roma, in her dressing room at the TV studio or with her parents at their house.

Many of the pictures are too dark, giving the troupe a barbecued, suntanned look, though at times Porter's coloring was authentic, a suntan acquired while fishing. Reg Dunlap, who worked on the show, says they often had to "lighten up Porter a bit" with makeup so he wouldn't clash with his white or pastel Nudie suits. The photos were gleefully unposed. In the latter phase, circa 1968–69, a cut-rate color process was introduced, which might be termed early American Polaroid-primitive, with an unfocused runny look that made everyone seem olive-skinned and Oriental.

Rounding out this print-shop version of "The Porter Wagoner Show" were full-page pictures of as many bottles, packages, and tubes as could be crammed in, looking like a bathroom medicine cabinet with the door flung back, the better to display Velvin Antacid, Sōltice rubbing balm, nasal spray, cold tablets, and the immortal Black Draught and Cardui, in its "New—Special Formula." At the bottom of the page Porter promised that the Chattanooga Medicine Company would send you a sample if you sent them a mere ten cents, and he signed his name to this offer.

The souvenir books cost fifty cents apiece. After the very first offer, Don Warden went to their post office box and there were a few letters with coins inside. Next day, a few more. The day following there were no letters, only pink slips. Don needed help from the postal employees to lug all the bags of mail, huge number two bags that could accommodate all the letters weighted down with coins. They printed 70,000 copies that first year.

At the trailer park, Don rented another shower stall in the wash house and cut a door between Warden Music and the mail room, as they called their expanded office. From a demolished post office they rescued an old rack of wooden pigeonholes, and they set up a large table. Porter took his customary 50 percent off the top and turned over the rest to the troupe.

Mail was assigned on a geographical basis— Shirley Magaha drew

North Carolina as she was from there. Ann Warden says, "I could move to Las Vegas, I learned to roll money so fast. I could tell you what ten dollars worth of quarters were by just holding them."

Ann says she loves "good, dear country people," such as those who mailed in their quarters sewed into cloth on the sewing machine, or perhaps wrapped in foil they had cooked a roast in.

After eight years, the FCC (Federal Communications Commission) noticed Porter was selling souvenir books in excess of the air time allotted for commercials and closed them down.

Besides showcasing every "name" act in country music, Porter's TV program gave a break to many newcomers, such as Waylon Jennings. Porter performed in Waylon's 1967 movie, *Nashville Rebel*. In the "plot," struggling Arlin Grove overcame his rebelliousness enough to merit a spot on the Opry and on "The Porter Wagoner Show."

Stonewall Jackson remembers how much Porter's show helped his records. "Every time I got a record out, every three months, it was like sowing seed—I'd call Don Warden, and that show gave it such a boost." Earlier Stonewall had been a guest on the "Ozark Jubilee" and was so nervous that when Red Foley asked him his middle name, he blurted out, "Wall . . ."

At one point Jeannie Seely replaced Norma Jean on Porter's show. Jeannie was fresh from Los Angeles in 1965, working as a secretary and trying to break in as a singer. Norma was taking time off to get her daughter, Roma, into school, and Jeannie became a guest on the TV show. Then she went on the road. "I have to emphasize the patience Porter must have had with me," she says. Jeannie had too much luggage because she didn't know how to pack and committed the faux pas of curling up in Don Warden's seat at the front of the bus. No one said a word. "The silence was killing me. I thought, *Are they always like this?* So I tried to break the ice. I said, 'Do you know what's brown and full of holes?' Porter said, 'No' and I said, 'Swiss Shit!'"

Jeannie began to fit in to the extent that when Norma came back, they actually did some shows together with Porter. Promoters said it wouldn't work, but it "was a kind of a first," says Jeannie. "Everyone told Porter he was crazy, there wasn't room for two girl singers on one bus."

Then Jeannie did the unforgivable: she had a hit record ("Don't Touch Me") in 1966. This made it necessary for her to leave Porter's show. "You've got to do what's best for your career, 'cause not that many chances come along and when they do, you've got to make the most of them," says Jeannie. "I was being torn apart between Porter and Hank Cochran when I had to leave Porter's show."

*　　*　　*

Don Warden talked Porter into getting a Flex bus. Ann believes only one other entertainer had one, Flatt and Scruggs, with a Martha White flour ad on the side. Don bought one from the marines and drove it back to Nashville. Don welded together the bunks, Capitol City Mattress Company custom-designed the mattresses, and Ann Warden made little curtains and otherwise decorated the interior. "We decorated in green, Norma Jean's favorite color. We had to keep the girl singer happy."

Don installed the power plant on the bus. Even though he knew better, one day he was priming the engine with gasoline from a paper cup when it exploded. George McCormick, who was resting, leapt up yelling, "What happened?" Ann was sweeping up. "There was so much commotion I went screaming up there," she says. "I thought somebody had gotten into a fight, which I couldn't believe, they worked so well together . . . George was laying on Don, with his feet sticking out. Buck was holding the burning cup. Don's hair was burned off, his eyebrows were burned off, skin was hanging off his ears. He pulled down the visor and looked at the mirror and said, 'I've always been so ugly, and *now* look!'"

The third souvenir book, probably 1964, boasts that the TV show was now reaching fifty-eight stations in the United States and Canada. On page one are a number of shots of the Wagoner family, four of them with Ruth, and in each her expression is stoical. In one she is packing a Nudie suit into a suitcase, contemplating the large covered wagon embroidered across the back. On the following page is a portrait of Norma Jean, now on RCA records. Several snapshots of Norma fill the next page, performing, traveling, or tending her infant daughter, Roma, at home.

14

PRETTY MISS NORMA JEAN

I once knew a girl and her story was sad,
She oft-times was courted by the wagoner's lad.
He courted by night and he courted by day—
Now his wagons are loaded and he's going away.

—from "Wagoner's Lad," old folk song

Norma Jean was the all-American girl, and there
hasn't been another entertainer to come along
who was the all-American girl.

—"Hap" Peebles, interview,
September 25, 1989

"**I**f I ever write my life story, I'll call it *Girl Singer*," the lady laughed without bitterness.

She was pouring coffee in her Brentwood kitchen. Brentwood is a gold-plated housing project preferred by music industry stars and executives; the domestic setting fitted Porter's "pretty housewife" characterization of Norma Jean. It was Porter who first called her "Pretty Miss Norma Jean." Friends still tease her, "Hey, Pretty Miss, what're you doin'?"

Norma left Porter's show in 1967. In her television heyday her brown-haired beauty was lit up by a naive freshness. Her smile today communicates more self-awareness. In the mid sixties she projected an innocence that permitted her to deliver feisty, worldly songs in a subdued style, with sometimes veiled meanings. Norma Jean sang complex, female-oriented songs in the days before women's liberation, songs mostly written by men, selected by men, but songs that she made her own.

Norma Jean Beasler was born on a farm near Welliston, Oklahoma, in 1938. She grew up in Oklahoma City, and her aunt taught her guitar.

She was fourteen when she heard Kitty Wells sing "It Wasn't God Who Made Honky Tonk Angels" on the Opry. "I decided then and there that was the greatest voice I had ever heard." There had been other token females in country music—Patsy Montana, Rose Maddox, Texas Ruby, Molly O'Day—but it was Muriel Deason, alias Kitty Wells, who proved a woman's place could be on the jukebox and on the airwaves. Since "It Wasn't God Who Made Honky Tonk Angels" flouted the southern male double standard—where wayward husbands merely "run around" but errant wives "cheat"—Kitty was kept off the Opry. Lines like "Too many times married men think they're still single that has caused many a good girl to go wrong" didn't meet the Opry's hidebound strictures. But since it was a pop hit as well, the Opry relented. After all, unescorted women in beer joints still punched those jukebox buttons that rang up *Cash Box* hits for Opry stars. Women heard themselves in Kitty's songs, and her prim demeanor could reassure anyone. Her ice-hot voice was unforgettable.

With Kitty Wells as her personal beacon light, Norma began touring with western swing bands while still in her teens. The "Ozark Jubilee" turned her down, then changed its mind. Before it folded, she had moved to Nashville, joining Porter's show in 1960. After an unsuccessful try on Columbia records, she signed with RCA in 1963 and joined the Opry that year as well.

One day Porter brought Norma a song, "Let's Go All the Way" (by Dusty Rose) and said, "I know this would be a hit if we did it as a duet, but I want you to have it." But the disc jockeys balked at the suggestive title and erotic-sounding opening, "Oooooohhhh . . . Let's go all the way . . ." Actually the song becomes respectable in the release when the lyric muses about naming a wedding day. Soon it was a favorite with live audiences, and it went to number eleven, on the charts for nineteen weeks, even getting a Grammy nomination. If anyone believed the song was risqué, Norma's wholesome air belied it. She told Walt Trott in a 1987 interview that people probably thought "she doesn't know what she's saying."

"Let Go All the Way" became her identification number. "Back then, we could do a whole career on one song. Your dyed-in-the-wool, lifetime fan remembered and hung with you."

Porter and Norma released only two recorded duets—on live, road albums—and only occasionally sang together on the TV show. Norma says they both have soft voices, in the same register, and that successful singing partners contrast with each other, like Red Foley and Kitty Wells, or Ernest Tubb (or Conway Twitty) and Loretta Lynn.

Norma's nominal producer was Chet Atkins, assisted by Bob Ferguson, who soon took over. But when Norma walked into the studio, she always looked straight at Porter. "Porter is so strong, so opinionated in the studio. But I was doing just exactly what I wanted to do. I thoroughly agreed with Porter." Norma credits Porter with about 75 percent of what's on her RCA records through 1967, from picking songs to arranging them. "He had definite ideas and knew what he wanted. He must have given it a lot of thought."

Once when her hair was up in curlers, Porter called Norma from the studio. Songwriter Harlan Howard had just brought him a hit song, but he thought it would be better for Norma and wanted her at the studio immediately. The lyric was based on the famous gibe at Richard Nixon, titled "I Wouldn't Buy a Used Car from Him." It was her biggest hit to date, going to number eight.

I asked Norma what it was like back when she still had to sing a song all the way through in a recording session. She said, "Oh, we just had to get it right. Once I sang one thirty times, due to various mistakes of the musicians. My second or third take was usually my best one. They were more concerned about the musicians than about me." Today, with multi-track recording, everything can be fixed up. If a singer bungles a lyric or sings off-key, they can re-sing it and be "punched in" at the exact spot, the recording studio equivalent of correcting tape on a typewriter. Engineers can even improve pitch by changing the sound frequency. The song you hear today did not happen all at once in the studio. Norma says there were mistakes on her records—but they're fetching high prices with collectors nonetheless.

In the studio, "Porter was very hard sometimes. He was such a perfectionist." Once Norma left the studio in tears. The song was, fittingly, Liz Anderson's "I Cried All the Way to the Bank," which went to number twenty-one.

The biggest female star after Kitty Wells had been Patsy Cline, who died in 1963, the year Norma went to RCA. Norma flourished as a transition figure in the period before Dolly Parton. Loretta Lynn was supplying considerable punch to women's songs with such pugilistic numbers as "Fist City," the blows to be delivered to the woman messing with her man. In the pop field Nancy Sinatra was promising to tromp all over some man with her boots "made for walking." Norma Jean fits into this context, though with more finesse. She probably benefited from the mid-sixties censorship in country music, when songwriters still contorted themselves to come up with double meanings. Her "Pretty Miss" image also required considerable restraint. "I don't like women's lib songs that much," Norma says, believing her militant "Heaven Help the Working Girl" sounds dated now.

Often she recorded tunes by Vic McAlpin, such as "The Box It Came In." The husband has left, cleaning out virtually every possession, even the wife's wedding dress: only its cardboard box remains. But when she catches up with him, *he'll* end up in a box, one that is lined with satin. A similar song is "The Shirt," which is all the fickle man has left behind. The woman discovers it back in the closet and recalls when "the faint perfume of sweet love filled the night."

The Curly Putman–Don Wayne song, "A Woman's Gotta Make a Stand," is apologetic: the girl has found no happiness running around and

Pretty Miss Norma Jean, 1967 [COURTESY PORTER WAG-ONER ENTERPRISES].

wants to settle down to true love. The defiant "Jackson Ain't a Very Big Town" says the small-town gossips are just jealous because she's going out with the man they used to date. "Your Alibi Called Today" has a wife taking a call from one of her husband's friends, only to realize he's been lying about being out with his buddies. Wives are tempted to cheat, too, at least in "Conscience Keep an Eye on Me," (by Glen Goza and Jack Rhodes), where the wife has trouble telling wrong from right.

Most uproarious is Vic McAlpin's "Don't Let the Doorknob Hit You." The man has lied to the girl about not being married, and "the whole town is asking how low can she get?" She's even picked up the fellow's bad habits of cussing, smoking, and drinking, and it sounds like she can't resist him. Norma recalls Ella Fitzgerald later recorded the song.

✻　　✻　　✻

Norma's highest-charting record was "The Game of Triangles" in 1966. It went to number five. This bizarre record has two other singers, Bobby Bare and Liz Anderson, who play the husband and wife, with Norma cast as the other woman. Husband and wife declare their separate positions, then Norma butts in sweetly with "*my* side." The husband has a traveling job, but heck, no woman can steal a man if he's happy with his wife! The song became an album title, and Norma reprised her home-wrecker role in Vic McAlpin's "One Among the Three of Us" (". . . is always in the way"). On the album's liner notes, songwriter Cy Coben says, "It's only in the field of country music that a song as realistic as 'The Game of Triangles' can find acceptance." This Euclidian adultery singing gimmick apparently didn't catch on: perhaps it was too close to home, considering the fragility of music industry marriages.

With almost a shudder Norma recalls life on the road in the pre-bus days, traveling by car, pulling a trailer, Norma the only woman in the group: nonstop driving on backroads, five or six people jammed together, trying to sleep sitting up, having the luxury of a motel room maybe every other night, arriving "awful-looking, sleepy, dirty." In the phrase of Howard White, who played steel for Cowboy Copas, Hank Snow, and many others, they all knew "every highway out of Nashville."

"It was a way of life," says Norma. "Sleeping in the car. No interstate. Getting there at noon and having to do a two o'clock show. When you've been riding all night in a car, you're not going to feel like getting out there and telling the audience the funniest joke in the world. You had to pretend, I guess."

To illustrate how spaced-out they became from the road, Norma tells how once they arrived at a motel after an arduous drive. She had naturally slipped out of her shoes in the back seat for comfort. Everybody usually did this. Don Warden, who is not a large man, mindlessly thrust his feet into Norma's pretty, red shoes and ambled into the motel to register them all.

Like nearly all name entertainers in the sixties, they were so heavily scheduled and in venues so far apart, extra assistance was needed to keep eyes open and on the road. "Everybody had pills. Now that we know so much about them, I'm surprised we are all alive," says Norma. Another entertainer from those days, Dolores Smiley, who laughs that "girl singers were a necessary evil," also testifies that "most everyone took bennies. You had to make a decision as to whether you wanted to stay awake, take bennies, and not run off the road and get killed."

Norma remembers Doctor Snapp, who kept everyone bright-eyed. Landon B. Snapp II was the genial "diet doctor" of East Nashville who was a kind of pharmaceutical folk hero in the sixties and seventies. He once received a plaque engraved "Special Songwriters' Award for

Helping Co-write More Hits Than Anyone in Nashville." Dr. Snapp, who had a daughter named Ginger, treated excess weight and mental "depression" with the same prescription—Didrex—from his office at 627 Woodland Street. He saw fifty to sixty sufferers a day, and the prescriptions were filled at the aptly named Consumer's Drug Store at 700 Main Street, a short stroll from Mom Upchurch's boardinghouse. Consumer's used a rubber stamp to facilitate refills. A visit to Dr. Snapp cost only five dollars, and, if he happened to be out, you just left the five dollars anyway and picked up a 100-pill prescription to take around the corner. The thundering herd of dieters, some of them observably thin, and depression fighters stampeded into the drugstore, with more than 18,000 prescriptions to be filled in the first six months of 1975. Consumer's rose to the medical occasion and dispensed more than 600,000 Didrexes. Then Cajun fiddler Doug Kershaw blew the whistle on Dr. Snapp, who was soon in court trying to explain that most people had some sort of depression and that musicians especially tended to get "down in the dumps" when not in the limelight. Dr. Snapp, who had been earning $100,000 a year combating the twin maladies of obesity and limelight deficiency, now earned three years in federal prison. He died in 1986.

Norma reiterates, "How we are all alive, I'll never know."

Norma believes Porter's marriage was troubled before she first came on his show. But she says, "I'm not proud of what I did. I'm not taking up for myself. I was as wrong as I could be."

On December 23, 1965, Porter's son, Richard, left for the Army and, ultimately, Vietnam. Porter's divorce complaint of 1986 has him and Ruth separating on December 27, but Richard believes that in fact it was earlier, Christmas Eve. Ruth was at the beauty parlor, and Porter sat down with Debra and Denise and announced he would be moving out. He said it would be better for everyone because he would be happier, that this kind of thing happened in a lot of families. Denise didn't care if it happened in a lot of families. She cried and cried. Ruth and the two girls "had a *great* Christmas, that's the facts," Richard says sardonically.

Porter moved into apartment 104 in the Americana Apartments at 1906 South Street (Chet Atkins Place today), right off Twenty-first Avenue South and close to the Vanderbilt University campus. This spartan little flat was, needless to say, never on the Homes of the Stars tour, and for many years fans would have no inkling of Porter's separation. The severely austere interior of his apartment provided the setting for the cover of his 1966 album, *The Cold, Hard Facts of Life*. In *Dolly Parton: A Photo-Bio*, Otis James calls it "one of the finest country music album covers ever staged"; and in its grainy, B-movie realism, it is. The songs equal the cover and may be the most disturbing collection assembled at one time by a major recording artist in any field, since they deal repeatedly with marital infidelity, murder, and madness.

☀   ☀   ☀

In 1967 Norma conspired with producer Bob Ferguson to record a birthday present in secret for Porter: *Norma Jean Sings Porter Wagoner*. The album contains twelve of Porter's standards like "Your Old Love Letters" and "Company's Comin'." As the liner notes proclaim, "The entire album was recorded without Porter's knowing anything about it, and if you knew Porter you would know what a difficult thing that was to accomplish." Norma explains this further: "Porter was very jealous, and he couldn't get me till late at night. I wouldn't tell him where I'd been. He kept me up all night. We had a really big fight." The next day Chet tried to take Porter golfing, but Porter decided to catch up on work in his second-floor office. Downstairs they recorded the rest of the album . . . then invited him down to hear a "new hit song." Everyone present broke out in "Happy Birthday, Porter," and the tape began rolling, with Norma singing over the studio speakers.

Porter had given Norma Jean an engagement ring, but he would not divorce Ruth. Ruth would not divorce Porter, either. The reasons are complex, only guessable; and it is doubtful either one could explain it satisfactorily to this day. It is certain that neither one would try. First on the list of possible motivations might be Missouri stubbornness, not wanting to admit a failed love. Then, the small-town sense of appearances, since the Howell County values of the 1940s were basically those of the 1840s. Lorraine says Porter told her he wouldn't divorce Ruth so long as his parents lived, and he kept his word.

The business reasons make even more sense. Porter was at the height of his career, with a 1967 hit of "The Cold, Hard Facts of Life" plus two out of his three Grammys for gospel albums with the Blackwood Brothers. A divorce and possible remarriage to the girl singer on his show would hardly have helped sell extra cases of Black Draught or Sōltice. Especially one who had been on his show since 1961 and whose private life remained a mystery to the fans. Porter's strait-laced image had to be rigorously maintained. In 1985 Porter told Glenn Hunter, of the *Journal of Country Music*, that his affair with Norma was so "intense" that parting was inevitable, that he couldn't face divorce and remarriage, and that Norma was putting love in front of business and "I couldn't handle it. With me, business always comes first. Any kind of love affair is much further down the line."

This triangle straight out of a country song was bent to the snapping point. Norma Jean gave Porter back his ring, threw it at him, in fact. It bounced right off. Nonchalantly, he scooped it up, and Norma says he had it reset into a new ring, which he presented to his fishing pal and member of the show, Mel Tillis.

"Does Mel know he ended up wearing your diamond, Norma?"

"No, I don't think so."

Norma went back to Oklahoma City and married country singer Jody Taylor, whom she'd known for many years. Taylor adopted Roma. He owned a furniture store. Eventually she relinquished her Opry membership, being unable to make the required appearances.

She stayed on RCA for several more years. Her two albums in 1968, in the immediate post-Porter period, were particularly gutsy.

In the album *Norma Jean—Body and Soul*, the Lola Jean Dillon song "In the Park after Dark" has two cheaters scheduling their tryst for "six to nine," anticipating by about ten years the Loretta Lynn–Conway Twitty hit "I'm Loving You from 7 till 10." Also on the album is a song Porter recorded as well, "Woman Hungry," by Gene Chrysler, which takes the "meal" metaphor as far as imagination can go. If a man's table at home is not set with "care," he will seek other "fare" at another table. Norma says of it, "Today it probably would seem shocking. But back then, songs were always being taken different ways." Another song on the album probably of personal poignance for Norma was "What Kind of Girl Do You Think I Am?" in which a girl holds out for a wedding ring.

And the album *Love's a Woman's Job* is a kind of psychodrama on vinyl. "You Changed Everything about Me But My Name" is a little heart-stabber by Jeannie Seely and Hank Cochran where self-respect and pride turn to shame. The title song defines a woman's work as taming down a wayward husband. Other songs run a painful gamut: a wife who wants to shoot her husband on sight, a wife who will settle for love from any man since her husband doesn't love her, a wife whose husband drinks up his paycheck, and more. "I wish we had earthy songs like those today," Norma says.

In Oklahoma, Norma Jean raised her stepchildren, ran her own dress shop, and brought up Roma. In 1984 she returned to Nashville and appeared on "Nashville Now" on TNN with, of course, Porter Wagoner. Behind her now were marriage, two divorces, and child-rearing. She was ready to reenter the business and not remain a country music footnote like Bonnie Guitar or Molly Bee, to name two female singers left behind by history. "I was like someone who'd been on Mars for a few years," says Norma. "I didn't know what was happening."

Tom T. Hall wrote the notes to her next album, *Pretty Miss Norma Jean*:

> The musicians in my band (some of them are younger than my clothes) started asking me about Norma Jean . . . I told them about my old songwriting friends who used to call her in the middle of the night to sing songs for her; I told them what I knew. But, what I didn't know was where Norma Jean had been for the past few years.

In the Nashville portion of the "Dolly" show in 1988, Norma Jean was seen on network television sitting with a classical guitar in her lap, talking with Dolly, Jean Shepard, Skeeter Davis, Jeanne Pruett, Minnie Pearl, Jan Howard, Del Wood, and her original heroine, Kitty Wells. When Norma appears on "Nashville Now," she always alludes to Porter's show. "I get work off that show. People remember it who don't know my records."

She still plays her flat-top guitar. Thank goodness, woman entertainers are playing their instruments again instead of merely floating around the stage with their hand-held mikes. Norma remarks, "Roy Acuff always said, 'If you can do something, do it.' And if you're playing with some band, at least you're playing the right chords even if they're not!"

Speaking of her furtive, futile relationship with Porter, she says, "I wouldn't do some things again. I've learned it's better to be a better person."

Norma's home is basic suburban, except for the framed record album covers on the walls and the two acoustic guitars sitting on guitar stands. Like their owner, they're ready to go. Norma plays several dates a month, and in the spring of 1989 she worked one of Porter's shows. She is no longer a girl singer in somebody's troupe. Her successor, Dolly Parton, made the concept obsolete.

Norma has often performed with Buck Trent, and especially with entertainer Georgie Riddle, whom she married in 1990. With poise and good humor, Pretty Miss Norma Jean has made it through.

15

THE PORTER WAGONER SOUND

A song ain't nothin' in the world
but a story just wrote with music to it.

—Hank Williams to Ralph J. Gleason, 1952,
in Ben Fong-Torres, ed.,
The Rolling Stone Reader (1974)

Porter's recording career flourished in direct proportion to the television show, kicked off by "Misery Loves Company" in 1962. The follow-up, "Cold, Dark Waters," by Don Owens, went to number ten in mid 1962 and marked Porter's first real handling of those remorseless, ripped-from-life lyrics that in time became his hallmark. Such somber story-songs were in sharp contrast with the happy-hillbilly personality he projected on the television show.

Down the centuries, ballad singers have served as musical journalists, reporting on local tragedies, from blood feuds and bank robberies to train wrecks and auto crashes. "Cold, Dark Waters" even opens with a reference to journalism, "In tomorrow's newspaper you'll read about me," but that won't be the whole story, "for they'll only say he plunged yesterday to the cold, dark waters below." As he's about to jump at the end of the song, people are closing in and shouting, "Don't let him go!" but he jumps anyway. That will teach the heartless girl a lesson! This little vinyl suicide note has a mournful melody, rather neo–Hank Williams, and it's a sort of classic of its macabre kind.

Fittingly, Porter's next hit was written by ex-journalist Bill Anderson, who would write some chilling story-songs for him later in the decade, including one of his biggest and most notorious. But in early 1963 it was Bill's "I've Enjoyed As Much of This As I Can Stand" that went to number seven for Porter. The narrator bumps into an old love, probably an ex-wife; and though "there's so much more between us than this table," he cannot bear to hear more than a little bit about her latest romance before he wants to leave.

Bill Anderson grew up in Decatur, Georgia, not picking cotton or plowing fields, but working in his dad's insurance agency. Fortunately, upstairs above the office was a radio station that intrigued young Bill. He had already run his own neighborhood newspaper—in college he majored in journalism; later he became a disc jockey. One day somebody at the station exclaimed, "My God! Elvis must be coming to the station!" It was Porter in his big Cadillac with the fins. Earlier Bill had met Porter at Gainesville and invited him to the station, but he didn't figure he'd show up since no one from Nashville ever had. Bill moved to Nashville, writing hits for himself and others to sing.

Finally in 1962 Porter's album career more or less took off.

It had been five years since his début album, A *Satisfied Mind*, which in those struggling years had not sold too well, although it has been repeatedly reissued. On the cover of his next one, A *Slice of Life, Songs Happy 'n' Sad*, he was wearing his first Nudie suit and had a flattop haircut trying to grow out. Songs included the bluegrass standard "Uncle Pen" and two Red Foley standbys, "Tennessee Border" and "Sugarfoot Rag." Also in 1962 appeared *Porter Wagoner and Skeeter Davis Sing Duets*. On the cover there's a painting of Porter in an Ivy League suit, looking like he's escorting Skeeter to a prom, with a big heart suspended in space. Skeeter's higher-pitched voice complements Porter's mellower singing. At the April 1982 Wembley Country Music Festival, Porter and Skeeter were present, and the fans demanded they do a couple of favorites from this album, "The Violet and the Rose" and "Rock-a-Bye Boogie," one of Porter's rare stabs at rock 'n' roll. Perhaps owing to her overseas popularity, the album has been reissued by RCA from of all places, Barbados in the Caribbean.

Also in the sixties, Porter cut three live albums. Ralph Emery recalls that the same night Porter cut one of his live albums, Roger Miller was recording one. Roger ordered in plenty of liquor and food for his live audience, mostly music executives. "So Porter says, 'Keep that booze out of here till I finish recording!'" Ralph remembers. "Roger's album was such a disaster that it was never released. I always thought that was typical of Porter's professionalism."

In early 1963 the West Plains *Quill* headlined, "Porter Wagoner at Father's Bedside." Charlie Wagoner had pneumonia and died that April. Porter's mother, Bertha, would live on in the Oak Street house until her death ten years later.

Production was becoming more and more important. Porter's producer was Bob Ferguson, who had grown up in southern Missouri and had his own hillbilly band in the forties. For the Tennessee Fish and

Game Commission, Bob had produced and mostly written seventy-two films. He also wrote the number one hit for Ferlin Husky, "Wings of a Dove," and produced many of Chet Atkins's records. In addition, Bob was an archaeologist; and in one excavation around Nashville, he found what he identified as a saber-toothed tiger's tooth.

Speaking of Porter, Bob says there are two kinds of recording artists: those you have to produce and those you don't. Porter was always completely prepared, having practiced on the bus, and there were times Bob didn't need to be at the sessions. Producing Porter was often a case of just saying, "I second the motion."

Porter told Paul Soelberg in 1971:

> The rhythm sound is basic. I've never in my life heard a hit record that didn't have a good rhythm sound. For that reason, anything I've been connected with in producing has a strong rhythm, the rich bass, drums, and piano, with the rhythm guitars and their ringing strings.

As the sixties unfolded, Porter's hits wavered between homey, family-type numbers and hard-core blues awash with alcohol.

"Howdy, Neighbor, Howdy," by J. Morris, was in the hyper-friendly, big-grin mode of "Company's Comin'." The song dishes up biscuits, gravy, and country ham along with banjo picking, and went to number nineteen in 1964. "I'm Gonna Feed You Now," by Bob Morris, is about an out-of-work man who finally gets a job and his family can start eating well again. The sing-along chorus sounds like Red Foley; it reached number eleven in 1965.

From the opposite direction came songs like "In the Shadows of the Wine," by Dusty Rose, a number twenty-nine song from 1964, and "Sorrow on the Rocks," by Tony Moon, which went to number five that year in *Billboard* but number one in *Cash Box*. The singer has trembly hands and a wobbly gait, and a sodden self-pity worthy of George Jones: "In this 100-proof condition I ain't in no position to take her back again."

Another Porter Wagoner standard is "I'll Go Down Swinging," by Bill Anderson. Bill pitched it to Porter at his house, and Porter didn't say a word. Finally he told Bill, referring to the RCA mascot, "Next time you hear that song, it'll have a little dog on it." The lyric has the narrator feeding the jukebox in a tavern, trying hard to forget his girlfriend, who is having a "party" with some man at her house. It went to number eleven in 1964.

Porter's momentum with hit records was accelerated by the TV show and by his nonstop touring. In turn, the rise of "The Porter Wagoner Show" paralleled that of Nashville's music industry in the 1960s.

✳   ✳   ✳

Above: *Don Warden, Alfred W. ("Red") Gale, and Porter at the "Grand Ole Opry," 1958* [PHOTO BY LES LEVERETT, COURTESY JAMES G. ("GOOBER") BUCHANAN]. Left: *The song "Itchin' for My Baby" inspired this picture of Porter-as-Elvis. It was the flipside of "A Satisfied Mind" and one magazine's choice as a pick-hit* [COUNTRY AND WESTERN JAMBOREE, JUNE 1955].

In the early sixties songwriters like Hank Cochran, Dallas Frazier, and especially Harlan Howard were making their permanent impression. Even though Porter cut his share of songs from the best writers of this time, he may have missed a few hits because of his aversion to drinking, his lack of time and inclination for hanging around, and his preference for golf and fishing over playing politics at parties. He has never needed "to be seen" around town, and he chooses modest, everyday restaurants when he eats out. Some people have mistaken his shyness and businesslike schedule for aloofness.

Once he complained that he couldn't spend all afternoon having coffee and chatting anymore, not because he had gotten bigger, but because his job had gotten bigger. He once told Ruth White, when she ran his office, that he avoided the Music Row social scene "because everyone's a seller, and no one's a buyer."

Meanwhile, the songwriters' hangout in the sixties was, of course, Tootsie's, the Nashville equivalent of London's Fitzrovia or San Francisco's North Beach, as a literary bohemia. It was at Tootsie's that Willie Nelson tried to sell all rights to "Hello, Walls" to Faron Young for some grocery money. Faron slipped Willie an advance against royalties and taught him to keep his name on his songs instead of selling them outright. Willie's wife worked there, once hurling enough beer glasses in her husband's direction to get arrested, an event that made the evening news.

Lola Scobey reports Willie lying down in the street outside Tootsie's and daring cars to run over him. A better attention-getter was to appear on "The Porter Wagoner Show," and a more pathetic one was when he'd have himself paged at the Nashville airport.

The mass media were finally noticing country music, or at least the money it was starting to earn. Jack Hurst, a veteran Nashville reporter, said the *Nashville Banner* and especially *The Tennessean* in earlier years had "virtually ignored the Opry and its stars except when they got arrested, got drunk, got divorced, got in a fight, or got caught taking a shot at someone." Hurst attributed this in part to the press's historic jealousy of radio, dating from the thirties.

But in 1966 *Saturday Evening Post* published a breakthrough article on Nashville, reporting that "Porter Wagoner, the Thin Man from West Plains, gets $1,400 and up for a show." It quoted Faron Young as saying, "I guess you're going to write another one of those articles about how we're all a bunch of rich idiots. Rhinestones on our clothes and all that."

The author of the article, Charles Portis, who later wrote the novel *True Grit*, tallied up all the recent tragedies: the Patsy Cline plane crash, the car death of Jack Anglin on the way to Patsy's funeral, the Jim Reeves plane crash of 1964, and Roy Acuff's car wreck, which he survived. Portis marveled at how entertainers could spend more than 200 nights a year on the road, "singing their songs, some trash, some gold, about hearts and wrecks and teardrops. They can't talk about those things, so they sing them."

One topic that has always been easier sung about than discussed is life in prison. Songwriter Curly Putman believed that men in prison still had feelings, even if no one cared much what they were. In 1961 Curly sang a one-week hit, "The Prison Song," and also wrote "Jail Birds Can't Fly." But he later wrote probably the most successful prison song of all time, "Green, Green Grass of Home," an immensely popular country as well as pop hit.

On June 7, 1965, Norma Jean recorded "I Wouldn't Buy a Used Car from Him," and on that same session Porter recorded "Green, Green Grass of Home." His was probably the second recorded version, so his idea of reciting one of the verses probably turned it into the monster hit that it became. By 1980 there were over 500 known versions of "Green, Green Grass of Home."

16

THE COLD, HARD SONGS OF LIFE

Country music does fairly well
with death but much better with sin.
But it's best when both are combined.

—*Lilian Roxon's Rock Encyclopedia* (1969)

Curly Putman was a shoe salesman whose company transferred him to Nashville, where he was befriended by Buddy Killen and Roger Miller at Tree Music. Then he was assigned to Memphis, but by 1963 he was back in Nashville writing songs. At some point Curly saw the movie *The Asphalt Jungle* about a criminal in a big city who, despite being a robber, longed to go back home.

"Green, Green Grass of Home" is engagingly conversational. The narrator is getting off a train at the hometown depot for a sentimental reunion with his parents and his sweetheart, Mary. He has been away so long that the boards of the old house are cracked and the paint is peeling. So far, the lyrics and melody are of Stephen Foster quality, fulfilled by a sunny refrain, starting, "They'll all come to meet me . . . " when he'll touch again the green, green grass of home.

Then the narrator awakes and realizes he's been dreaming, that he's in prison. Soon, with the guard and the sad old priest, "arm in arm, we'll walk at daybreak." He doesn't have to say where; in the best ballad tradition, the impending execution is not even mentioned directly. There's no self-pity, only relief that before long "they'll all come to meet me" and lay him beneath the green, green grass of home, below that old oak tree on which he played as a child.

The mood of this song is remindful of the classic American short story, "An Occurrence at Owl Creek Bridge" by Ambrose Bierce. In this story, a Confederate soldier is about to be hanged from an Alabama bridge by the Federals when he escapes, or so you think, and makes it home and into his wife's arms. Then the story pulls you up short. You realize that their tender embrace occurred only in a split-second's fantasy, or out-of-body travel, at the precise moment of death, with the yank of the hangman's noose.

The first recording of "Green, Green Grass of Home" was by an ex-motel manager from Atlanta named Johnny Darrell. Johnny was a guest on Porter's TV show, and Porter wrote liner notes for his first album. Then one day, a short while before their separation, Porter came home and played "Green, Green Grass of Home" for Ruth and Debra in the livingroom. Ruth reacted with "Boy, that's a good song." Soon Porter's version was out and fast eclipsed Johnny Darrell's, attaining number four and being on the charts for nineteen weeks. Astutely, Porter chose to recite the stanza where the prisoner wakes up and sees "four grey walls that surround me." Jerry lee Lewis recorded it Porter's way on an album, and large-voiced British pop singer Tom Jones heard Jerry's album when he was in New York.

In 1967 Tom Jones's version, with recitation, went to number eleven on the U.S. pop charts, number one on the British charts, and was a hit in Ireland, Australia, Holland, and South Africa.

As for Curly Putman, his fame brought him widespread misspelling of his last name as Putnam and permanent speculation that he might have been in prison, which is not the case. As he told *Music City News*, "I just happen to feel for such folks. I wanted to say in a song that a guy in prison is a human being and that no matter how terrible a thing he might have done, his family and friends still love him."

Curly's words and the song—in part—would come true for Porter and for others dear to him in 1976.

On November 4, 1965, Porter recorded "Skid Row Joe." That same month his brother Oscar, an alcoholic, came to grief.

Oscar Wagoner is remembered warmly by Porter's son, Richard. Uncles Oscar and Ed Hall would buy Richard ice cream in West Plains. But Ed Hall drank too much, panicking Lorraine when he was intoxicated. Oscar Wagoner drank too much, also. Married to Ed's sister Eva, Oscar was otherwise a happy, outgoing, hard-working man (since his teens), and to Lorraine was "just as good a brother as Porter was."

Oscar and Eva lived in Garner, Iowa, in a house supplied by the county. Oscar supervised the Hancock County farms, and he played country music in the milk barn because it made the cows more content.

Oscar was good-looking, dressed well, and lived for the weekends when he and Eva could party and dance. Porter says sometimes Oscar needed a drink in the morning, just to get going.

Alcohol may or may not have been involved when one day in November 1965 Oscar was driving at about 100 miles per hour and crashed into a road grader that was parked on the highway. He was not killed but suffered dreadful internal injuries.

On Christmas Eve 1965 Porter moved out of the Berry Road home and never again lived with Ruth, Debra, and Denise. On Christmas Day that most unlikely of characters, "Skid Row Joe," shambled—staggered—onto the *Billboard* charts. Perhaps Porter's morose recording of "Skid Row Joe" kept some people off the highways that New Year's Eve.

Country singer Freddie Hart had written "Skid Row Joe" and sang it to Porter on a whim. Porter jumped on it. Freddie had been a marine in World War II; a bouncer in a nightclub in Phenix City, Alabama; a dishwasher in New York State, and a karate teacher to the Los Angeles police department. Hank Williams once told Freddie Hart, "When you write and sing a song, write and sing it like it was the last one you were ever going to do."

The character of Skid Row Joe gave Porter something to identify with: though Joe was an alcoholic panhandler, he had once been "a real famous singing star." But his children have been taken from him—it was in the newspapers—and now he wants to quit drinking and go home and beg his wife to take him back. And he wants to press his two children to his breast. But the narrator cannot bear to tell ex-singing star Joe that, according to the newspapers, his wife has remarried. He merely wishes Joe a half-hearted, "Good luck, my best to you . . . " Not unexpectedly, Porter elected to recite the most dramatic lines of the song.

"Joe" was in *Billboard* for seventeen weeks, getting up to number three, one notch higher than "Green, Green Grass of Home." Porter was able to watch its climb from a hospital bed, where he had crashed one week after leaving his family. *Cash Box* for January 22 explained this as merely a rest from overwork:

> A "road-weary" Porter Wagoner is recuperating satisfactorily on a strict diet of food and sleep in Nashville's Parkview Hospital, according to his personal agent Larry Moeller. Wagoner entered the hospital under his own willpower Jan. 4 to be hospitalized for approximately ten days prior to beginning his 1966 series of personal appearances. Last year, the Grand Ole Opry artist made more than 230 personal appearances around the United States.

That same day *Billboard* headlined, triumphantly, "Wagoner Resumes"—while acknowledging Porter's recent "physical and nervous exhaustion."

Obviously, "Joe" deserved an encore. So one night down at the Opry, Porter asked Bill Anderson to write a song called "Confessions of a Broken Man." In a couple of days Bill came up with a recitation that asks, just where do you go when you're already on the bottom? Not much choice you've got—either pick yourself up or lie down to *rot*. What a great theme—what a great title—for an album, Porter reasoned.

Almost immediately, on February 8–9, 1966, Porter recorded most of *Confessions of a Broken Man*.

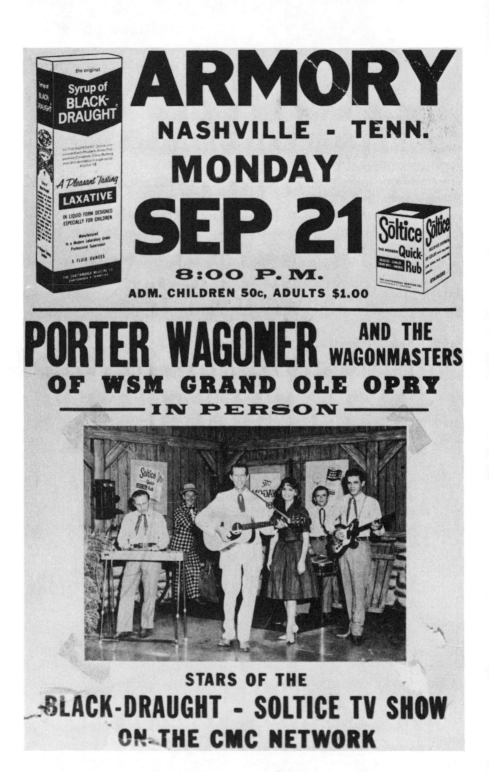

The first track on the album was Hank Williams's sepulchral recitation, "Men with Broken Hearts," about those men who weep, to whom death comes cheap. There's a sob wrenched from his voice on the word *hearts*. Hank had recorded such numbers as by "Luke the Drifter," his more philosophic (and even more melancholic) shadow-self (or psychological "double"). As Luke the Drifter, Hank could shed even more tears into the record grooves than he could as Hank Williams, that renowned jukebox expert on cheating hearts and cold, cold hearts.

Now in 1966 Luke the Drifter had to slide down to make room on his curbside throne for his successor, Skid Row Joe.

Another heart buster from this group is Vic McAlpin's "I Just Came to Smell the Flowers." The drunk seems to be the Will Rogers of funerals—he's never met one he didn't like, and he craves to go to a funeral, any funeral, since there'll be his kind of people there. Crying people. And plenty of flowers; he loves flowers. The inevitable recited passage says he is "too weak to stand, yet not enough man to join the race."

Other similarly inspiring numbers have titles like "How Far Down Can I Go?" and "Thy Burdens Are Greater Than Mine," an epitaph on a tombstone. In three of the cuts on the album, Hank Williams the songwriter is alive, if not in top mental health.

The last number on the album, "My Last Two Tens," is by the incorrigible Vic McAlpin, who wrote "Long, Gone Lonesome Blues" with Hank Williams. It plumbs new nadirs of dejection. The speaker fully expects to be found dead in his car, so he carries a shovel in the trunk to facilitate his own burial. He thoughtfully attaches two ten-dollar bills to the handle, to pay for grave-digging services, and in his pocket is a penny with the Lord's Prayer engraved on it.

Porter had conducted field research for this album by visiting the Skid Rows of Chicago and Minneapolis, dressed in disheveled attire, the better to soak up the seedy atmosphere. Those trips recall Tom T. Hall's penchant for dressing in slouchy clothes and hitting some small towns in quest of good conversations and new song ideas. Porter also was able to study winos firsthand along lower Broadway near the Ryman. The metal gratings on the Ryman's rear entrances were to prevent vagabonds from sleeping on the steps. As Porter would head for the Opry from his car, they might attempt to beg money for a "meal" from him. With his characteristic blend of compassion, thrift, and sense of humor, he arranged with the Opry Corner Cafe at 451 Broadway to feed anyone who ordered a meal and mentioned Porter Wagoner. Every few weeks when he'd go in to settle his bill, he'd find there had been almost no takers.

Porter's secretary from late 1965 to 1981 was Joan McGriff, now Joan Patton. Joan recalls repercussions from "Skid Row Joe." Various sidewalk characters would search out his second floor office in the RCA

[POSTER COURTESY JAMES G. ("GOOBER") BUCHANAN].

building and amble in, usually claiming to be *the* Skid Row Joe. They expected to be compensated since their story had been appropriated for a hit record.

The spring of 1966 was a complicated time for Porter, with Norma Jean off the show attending to Roma. Jeannie Seely was phasing into the show. Porter's hospitalization had been something of a luxury, as well as a necessity, since the TV show was now in eighty markets and his usual idea of a vacation was to tape dozens of half-hour episodes in a few days off the road. In March the fittingly titled *On the Road* live album was released, the cover painting showing him at the driver's seat of his own bus, duck-tail haircut visible, with his face beaming out of the rearview mirror. The backdrop was a road map of the South.

The times were definitely a-changing. Songs like "Nineteenth Nervous Breakdown" by the Rolling Stones were on the pop charts that March, and Johnny Cash was fined $1,000 in El Paso for souvenirs imported from Juarez (668 amphetamines, 475 barbiturates).

Jeannie Seely's "Don't Touch Me" entered *Billboard* on April 16, causing her almost immediate exit from "The Porter Wagoner Show." Certainly April, to invoke T. S. Eliot's phrase, was the cruelest month of the year since on the nineteenth Oscar Wagoner finally succumbed to the torment and shame of a body that no longer functioned after his automobile accident the previous November. *He turned a shotgun on himself.* His funeral was at the State Line Cemetery on the Arkansas border, a few miles from Lark Allen's resting place at Mint Springs, close by Porter's birthplace. Reunited in tears with everyone else, were Mr. and Mrs. Porter Wagoner. Richard came up from Fort Sill; entertainers Speck and Dusty Rhodes were there. Oscar's widow, Eva, moved in with Ed and Lorraine.

In September, Richard Wagoner left Camp Irwin, California, for Vietnam with the Ninth Artillery Division. That month *Confessions of a Broken Man* was released.

On the cover Porter is dressed in clothes that look like discards from a dumpster behind the Goodwill. He's slumped on the back steps of the Ryman next to a trash can, with drooping mouth and vacant, haunted eyes that stare from black-rimmed sockets. Porter's stricken face and the building backdrop are both overcast with a ghastly pale green. The back cover features a black-and-white shot from the same session, Porter huddled in fetal-like withdrawal, his bony body looking like a collapsed house of cards, as if his whole world has caved in. With a bottle of wine at the ready.

Exulted the liner notes:

> This is the album in which Porter shows what a single mo-
> ment of recklessness may lead to. While trodding [*sic*] the solid

ground that is the happy life, only an instant's loss of footing can send a man plunging over the precipice of doom . . . *You possess no other album quite like this one.*

Of the thousands of albums issued each year in all fields, only one can win a Grammy for its cover. The Best Album Package award for 1966 went to Robert Jones and photographer Les Leverett for *Confessions of a Broken Man.*

The November *Country Song Roundup* marveled at how Porter kept regular office hours when in town, and how he strove "to do everything as near to perfection as humanly possible," such as playing golf with a score in the low seventies. "Even when things don't go 'just right,' he makes it a point not to let it show . . . Tall, good-looking, happy Porter is a favorite of country fans everywhere."

Back in the Wagoner household at Berry Road, daughter Debra contemplated the sickly cover of *Confessions of a Broken Man* with a cringe: "I just couldn't believe that was my daddy. He looked like a wino from down behind the Opry." Sometimes when Porter was sick, Ruth and daughter Denise would bring potato soup to his apartment. "I remember we had such a nice, cozy home, everything was so homey," recalls Denise. "And going into that apartment, it was so . . . *apartment,* you know. I'd walk in there, and I felt so sorry for Daddy. It would just kill me. I would walk out and wonder, 'Golly, is *this* life? Is *this* what it is?' And that's a lot for a ten-year-old."

Porter had been touching other bases in the sixties, such as bluegrass and Grammy-worthy gospel.

His *The Blue Grass Story* album (1965) discharged, finally, the debt to Bill and Charlie Monroe incurred back in the thirties and forties.

He recorded *The Grand Ole Gospel* album with the Blackwood Brothers in 1966, the first of three Grammy winners. The liner notes by Mary B. Lynch invoke the pie suppers and the Hall family.

James Blackwood had been born of a sharecropper family in Mississippi, and he and his brothers sang on the radio and traveled about selling songbooks and eventually records. He was a protégé of Victor Stamps, a leader in gospel music publishing. When the Blackwoods moved to Memphis, one of their fans was a local boy who sold Cokes from an ice chest slung from his shoulder, Elvis Presley.

Singing now with the Blackwoods, Porter's baritone held up strong and true on the lead parts. He had learned well—from all those primitive one-track, one mistake-and-you-start-over sessions—how to sing out over the band and be heard.

On *The Grand Ole Gospel* Porter delivers one of his oft-requested recitations, "Trouble in the Amen Corner." It bears the composer credit of Archie Campbell, late star of "Hee-Haw," but Archie only abridged it. It's a popular nineteenth-century poem by Thomas Charles Harbrough, a boy's adventure novelist who died in a county poorhouse in 1924. The lyric narrates the melancholy story of aging Brother Eyre, whose inept singing grates on the ears of the church choir. He's in his late seventies, with cracked voice and bad timing. A delegation of good Christian brethren pays him a visit and advises that his vocal services are no longer in demand. After this ultimatum, they depart and Brother Eyre dies, moving on to a more hospitable musical milieu. Up in heaven there "are no church committees and no fashionable choirs."

Also on the album is "The Family Who Prays (Never Shall Part)," a song to which Porter brought personal understanding. It was written by Ira and Charlie Louvin, whose close-harmony Louvin Brothers duo was enormously influential. No doubt Ira Louvin had expressed himself in the song as well, since in 1961, at a party, his wife hit him over the head with a skillet. Whether or not Ira tried to strangle her with a phone cord, she definitely shot him five times, though not seriously, using only .22-shorts. When Porter and the Blackwoods cut the song, Ira was already dead, having perished the previous year on that hillbilly highway whence so many troubadours have not returned . . . a head-on crash on the way back from a Missouri honky-tonk gig. All six people in both cars were killed, including Ira's latest wife.

In choice of songs to perform, Porter has never relinquished happy hillbilly numbers, and in November 1966 "Old Slew-Foot" charted. It's in his best, family-entertainment vein and is still a favorite on his live shows. Written by Howard Hausey and James Webb, it's the zany saga of an impossible-to-catch bear, which the speaker would like to blast in the rear with buckshot. Its Burl Ives-style innocence was out of step with the complex sixties, and it only went to number forty-eight.

In January 1967 Porter had his biggest song since "Misery Loves Company," exactly five years earlier. "The Cold, Hard Facts of Life" went all the way to number two. Bill Anderson, who wrote it, said, "It's one of my favorite songs of all I've ever written from the crafting standpoint, because it's like a novel condensed into two to three minutes."

The song has one of those cheery melodies that is a counterpoint to the unfolding tragedy, with the title repeated over and over as a refrain. There is no chorus. Pop critics occasionally complain that country melodies don't "match" the words, with happy tunes and grim lyrics. But country writers know the perkier the melody, the more you can get away with. The matter-of-fact beginning—"I got back in town a day before I planned to"—should put any but a naive newcomer to country music on guard, especially considering the narrator's plan to surprise his wife with pink champagne and candlelight. Somehow you don't think that's exactly the surprise she's going to get, since the lyric keeps reiterating that the hero has yet to learn "the cold, hard facts of life."

The hero goes into a liquor store, where a stranger is bragging, "Her husband's out of town and there's a party . . . " The narrator buys his champagne, then leaves the store "two steps behind the stranger."

The stranger is driving in the same direction . . . as we might expect, straight for our hero's driveway. Bill seemingly wastes a line, with the fellow driving inanely around the block until he gets dizzy, but such idle activity only builds tension. After the husband and the stranger drive for the same driveway, songwriter Anderson was simply stuck. As he confesses in his *Whisperin' Bill* autobiography, he just didn't know "how [my] little soap opera was going to end." Bill told me, "It was like painting yourself into a corner. But once you've come through it, you've grown as a writer because you've had to reach down inside somewhere to pull it out."

Bill's idea of pulling out inspiration is to have his hero pull out cold steel. But first his hero notices his bottle of champagne, then drinks "a fifth of courage" and barges right in. The adulterers have terror-stricken faces, and scream "Put away that knife!" (Bill only suggests the violence indirectly.) Immediately we learn our hero is either going to *hell* or will just rot in his *cell*, but either way it's been worth it, since "*who taught who . . . the cold, hard facts of life!*"

The song closes with the backup chorus, the Anita Kerr Singers, singing the "hook" (refrain) one more time. Their chipper Nashville Sound sweetness makes the song all the more jarring. And Buck Trent's banjo gives a final twang like a knife thrust.*

It went to number one in *Cash Box*.

In February the *Soul of a Convict* album was released. The cover has a heavy black border, framing a photograph of Porter sitting in a cell at the Tennessee State Prison. He's wearing 1930s-style prison stripes and a hopelessly forlorn expression. He's clutching an ancient acoustic guitar like it's his only friend left. On the back cover he's singing with some convicts in a cell. Porter's secretary, Joan, remembers him coming back

---

*In his *The Heart of Rock & Soul: The 1001 Greatest Singles Ever Made* (1989), Dave Marsh ranks it at #789, comparing it to Joy Division's "Love Will Tear Us Apart" (#788). Both songs are examples of the Love Song as Suicide Note; each succeeds because the singer, "intoxicated with bitterness," comes to grips with the truth . . . "It centers completely around Wagoner's voice" with the music as a mere accompaniment. Dave says Porter becomes an actor in the drama he's been witnessing. He admits that it's far-fetched, comparing a country classic with "a British trance rock disc from the post-punk dawn"—but the "demented logic" of each song connects them.

from the photo session profoundly depressed by his glimpse of prison life.

The title cut is a morbid recitation about prison conditions (chains, whips, and so forth) written by Eddie Sovine, who was a captive of the Germans in World War II. "The Snakes Crawl at Night," by Fred Burch and Mel Tillis, had been the first release of Charley Pride that previous December on RCA. The song is another cheating-murder ditty, the snakes being the wife and her lover. The husband waits up all night, pistol in hand and "the devil on my shoulder," till they roll in the driveway. In court he gets the death penalty, but not without getting the last word, a chance to sing to the judge about how the snakes crawl at night and "play" after the sun goes down. A happy, bouncy melody puts over the story and its "message."

It was on a night in March 1967, about forty minutes past midnight, that the Viet Cong attacked the Ninth Artillery at Bau Bang, right above Lai Khe. They commenced with mortar fire, then suddenly stopped. Next their infantry charged across a field from a rubber tree forest. Mostly they were cut down by answering U.S. guns.

Porter's son, Richard, manned his artillery piece till dawn. The Americans fired 3,000 rounds that night, and in the morning U.S. aircraft flew twenty-six strikes. There were five Americans killed, fifty-three wounded, and enough Viet Cong killed to make a big pile of bodies. These exuded an increasing pungency in the afternoon sun until a tank, with a huge shovel blade, dug a mass grave.

Richard Wagoner received a commendation for helping the medics, but he emphasizes that this was a unit citation since everyone acted as a team. "Vietnam is a beautiful place, I'd like to go back there," says Richard, but he has no interest in reliving the war nor marching in any parades. For one thing, his uniform stopped fitting him a few years ago.

In May 1967 *The Cold, Hard Facts of Life* album was released. The cover, shot in Porter's apartment, is strictly *cinema vérité*. Each door at the Americana is set into a wall of industrial-looking masonry blocks, providing the ground floor with a cramped, tunnel-like hallway. It's easy to imagine the champagne-primed husband in the song, knife in pocket, stalking down this dim corridor. The cover of the album shows the gloomy dark-gray interior wall of masonry within Porter's pad. On the cheap-looking coffee table sits a half-empty bottle of expensive whiskey. Cuddling on the couch is the cheatin' couple, posed by RCA engineer Roy Shockley and a since-forgotten woman. Roy's hand is flopped onto her midriff, and while his expression is blasé, hers registers mounting panic. Her husband, Porter, has opened the door with his overnight bag in hand, which also holds a cigarette. He has an if-looks-could-kill-mine-probably-will glint in his eyes. The back cover has a two-way effect, showing the back of the lovers' heads, with Porter's hangdog face sagging in resignation as he decides what to do.

The only happy song on the album is "I'll Get Ahead Someday" by Mack Magaha, Porter's fiddler; it was a later Porter-Dolly duet hit. Another song on the album, "Words and Music," by Vance Bullas, has a positive ending. An old man has escaped from an institution where his greedy relatives have imprisoned him to rip off his possessions. The men in the white coats come to drag him back, but a long-lost relative arrives to claim (and rescue) the old man!

"Sleep" by Jack Clement is beautiful and restful, but "A Tragic Romance" by Grandpa Jones certainly *is*. The hero deserts his girl, so she takes up with her own brother, dying thereafter of a broken heart. "Shopworn" by Ted Harris is about a person who feels like a piece of used merchandise.

Dutifully upholding the album's concept of misogyny and murder is "Julie," written by Waylon Jennings. It has a pretty, folky melody with Porter's favorite "flattened 7th" progression (in the key of D, going to the C chord). That July it reached number seventeen for Porter as a single. Julie "liked parties, and clothes that fit tight," and she finally brings home a man to help her pack and clear out. As in "The Snakes Crawl at Night," the woman acts unrealistically careless. Her husband is waiting with his pistol, loaded with "bullets just three . . . one for the stranger . . . for Julie . . . for me." Porter repeats this last line, recitation style.

Songwriter Waylon Jennings had been living with Johnny Cash in an apartment in Madison, north of Nashville, where these unique roommates tried to hide their pills from each other. By 1968 Waylon was touring in a black-painted bus, "The Black Maria," and biographer Albert Cunniff says "even its chrome was painted black."

Waylon's future singing buddy in the 1970s, Willie Nelson, supplied another song for the album, one that could only have been written in the roaring sixties, "I Just Can't Let You Say Goodbye." Already, and amazingly, the song had reached number forty-eight for Willie in 1965, for a merciful two weeks only. Its lilting melody delivers lyrics like "The flesh around your throat is pale, indented by my fingernails," with Porter's closing recitation observing, calmly, that "Death is a friend."

And Bill Anderson wrote the shuddersome "The First Mrs. Jones" on this album. The protagonist tracks a straying wife from Savannah to New Orleans to Atlanta. Then, bolstered by booze, he guns her down in front of witnesses, yet somehow transports her body to the deep woods where he buries her undetected. Tenderly he plants flowers on her grave. Then Porter lapses into one of the most chilling recitations this side of Vincent Price, asking, with a sick chuckle, did his little story scare you? He notices "little beads of perspiration dot your clothes." But he is confident you will come with him peaceably, since "after all . . . you *are* . . . the *second* Mrs. Jones."

One wonders how many of the millions of housewives who have admitted Bill Anderson into their homes, in soap operas and on game shows like "Fandango," are aware of "The First Mrs. Jones."

On July 14 *The Tennessean* reported that, in spite of nationwide rumors to the contrary, Porter Wagoner was alive and playing golf. He had not been shot to death. Nor had Norma Jean been wounded and "critically injured." The article said that "reports of Wagoner's death apparently started June 16 in South Carolina, when someone with a similar name was shot to death in a gunfight . . . 'There have been hundreds of calls from all sorts of places,' said Jack Andrews, Wagoner's agent at Moeller Talent."

Porter's guitar player, George McCormick, says that he once told Don Warden, "Now we guys get along great. So if this show ever breaks up, it'll be over a woman."

Soon after, Porter burst in saying, "I've just hired Dolly Parton to replace Norma Jean!" George and Don looked at each other.

PART THREE

THE YEARS OF DOLLY PARTON

The hour is still, and from afar
Wafted by all that's sweet in night
The tones of some sweet girl's guitar
Are swelling from yon distant height . . .
—William Gilmore Simms, 1833

No coward soul is mine.
—Emily Brontë,
from her last poem, 1846

Dolly Parton began to rival the Parthenon
as a symbol of Nashville.

—Don H. Doyle, professor of history
Vanderbilt University,
to Tom Rogers, *The* (Nashville) *Tennessean*,
October 12, 1985

"I BELIEVE WE HAVE THE RIGHT COMBINATION"

Sometimes you just know . . . sometimes. And that
makes up for all the times you had to guess . . .
All the same things put together made something
different this time. For in the shadows playin'
'round her eyes you see the Harlows and Monroes
and all the deepening shades of tragedy . . .
too much for one young life.

—Fred Foster, liner notes,
Hello, I'm Dolly album, released July 1967.

Norma Jean Exits Porter Wagoner Show to Marry;
Dolly Parton Gets Spot.
—*Music City News* (October 1967)

Nashville had begun to notice Dolly Parton by the spring or summer of 1967, if not earlier.

Dolly had been in town since 1964, and while other people had recorded her songs (usually co-written with her uncle Bill Owens), now she was starting to have hits of her own. She recorded for Fred Foster's aggressive, independent Monument Records. In January her cut of "Dumb Blonde" went to number seventeen. Written by Curly Putman, the line "this dumb blonde's nobody's fool" made a good calling-card for twenty-one-year-old, buxom, bewigged Dolly. Despite having a voluptuous figure, her curves didn't seem tailored for anyone's casting couch; Dolly was determined to excel at songwriting as well. However personally sweet, she was all business. Cowboy cartoonist Max Harrison, a journalist at *Music City News,* had breakfast with Dolly once at the Downtowner restaurant and remembers her eating breakfast with someone different every day. She was always circulating, always pitching songs around town with her uncle Bill Owens. Both were signed to Fred Foster's Combine Music publishing company, and that June Dolly's "I'm in

No Condition" had hit for Hank Williams, Jr., going to number three.

Dolly has said she left songs at Porter's office for Norma Jean, and her "Somethin' Fishy" sounds like a Norma Jean song. It's crammed with infinite shadings of the "fishing" metaphor: the husband is always off fishing, but something other than a large-mouth bass is leaving lipstick on his shirt. Someone close to Porter might have seen Dolly on TV. She'd been a regular guest on the local Eddie Hill TV show, as well as on the Bill Anderson and Wilburn Brothers syndicated shows. Also, she was very visible at a BMI banquet, picking up a songwriter's award with her uncle Bill for "Put It Off Until Tomorrow," which Bill had gotten to Bill Phillips, who had a number six hit of it the previous year. Dolly had sung backup on the record where, as she told Everett Corbin of *Music City News*, "I was more noticeable than anyone had intended because my voice is so odd you can tell who I am even if I'm singing in a group." Dolly had made the record sound like a duet, and Nashville cocked its jaded ear and asked, *Who's that girl?*

Now in mid 1967 Porter was struggling to find a replacement for Norma Jean. He told Glenn Hunter of the *Journal of Country Music* that he personally tried to see things from the fan's point of view. If he hired anyone who looked or sounded like Norma, the typical fan would grumble, "Well, she's good but she ain't no Norma Jean." Porter had screened many female singers, including Connie Smith, Dottie West, and Tammy Wynette, who did a short stint with his show. Too many of these singers had soft, mellow voices, resonant with the slicked-up, smoothed-out Nashville Sound. Dolly was a throwback to centuries-old mountain singing, with a strange voice that her mother attributed to a case of burst tonsils.

Fred Foster at Monument had just issued Dolly's first album in July 1967, and the last words of the liner notes were, "Sometimes you just know, don't you?" Now, with Dolly finally taking off on Fred's label, a call came to set up an appointment.

As Dolly recaptured it in our 1990 interview:

> I used to watch Porter when I was growing up back home, and we'd been watching his show for many years. We were real big fans of Porter's; my dad especially loved him a lot. We always watched the show on Saturdays before I became a part of it.
>
> I think he had seen me on local TV and I had left songs at his office, and then when he called through Fred Foster to come down to have a meeting with him, I thought it was about the songs he had wanted to record of mine for himself and Norma Jean. I took my guitar, and the first one that I sang was called "Everything's Beautiful (In Its Own Way)."
>
> He asked me if I was interested in being part of his show. He said he'd seen me on TV and heard my records and thought I had

the potential to be a big star and of course I couldn't believe I was sittin' there talking to *the* Porter Wagoner, the guy I watched back home doing Black Draught and Sōltice commercials.

Dolly was wearing a discreet white dress, one she would later wear for the cover photo on the very first album she recorded after joining Porter. Her hair was also subdued, and Porter said he needed a girl to dress conservatively for his audiences. As he told Glenn Hunter, "She had exactly the appearance I was looking for—and by that I don't mean her bust size."

Whether or not he envisioned doing duets with her, she was certainly not too tall, standing only five feet to his six feet.

Porter was especially struck by Dolly's song, "Everything's Beautiful (In Its Own Way)," with its bright nature images, such as a fountain flowing from a mountain. The lyric says that even a destructive storm has its certain beauty. "I thought the song said so much about her," Porter told Glenn Hunter. *

He said that when he told Dolly, "I think you're the girl I wanna hire," she let out a squeal and grabbed and hugged his neck. "Oh, gosh, I'm so excited. This is everything I've worked for!" Dolly told me Porter offered her $60,000 a year, an astonishing sum in those days of union scale pay for TV. "It was the most money I had ever heard tell of. And I could not believe it, and I couldn't wait to go home. I went home that very evening, I think, to Sevierville to tell my mom and dad."

Porter has joked that if he'd hired Minnie Pearl or Kitty Wells, gossip still would have started. So he summoned Dolly back to the office with her husband, Carl T. Dean, an asphalt contractor from the Woodbine area of South Nashville. Porter found Carl to be "a quiet, very simple, country person—a very fine man," and he warned him and Dolly that people might suppose he and Dolly were sleeping together if they traveled together. "We all agreed we didn't want that to happen," Porter told Glenn Hunter. "And we all felt sure it wouldn't."

Dolly's first national interview had appeared in *Music City News* that June. In a letter in 1988, Everett Corbin recollected visiting her apartment:

On that night, the first night that I had ever seen her, I was flabbergasted at her enchanting beauty; she was like a breath of

---

*Not to be confused with "Everything Is Beautiful in Its Own Way," copyrighted and recorded in 1971 by Ray Stevens, who produced some of Dolly's Monument sessions. (Dolly's song was later a duet hit with Willie Nelson.)

spring, so young and innocent-looking; so petite and sweet with a natural, unspoiled beauty which in actuality knocked me off my feet. I was simply unprepared to look upon such a captivating young lady; and I was almost fearful to be alone in the room with her, yet realizing that her husband was in the next room.

Everett still has the tape of his interview, and the poised, confident, articulate voice is virtually identical to today's Dolly, but she was a twenty-one-year-old who sounded like a music veteran in her forties. From the unpublished portion:

> They're making a movie right now in town. I've had offers, lots of times, to do some acting—but I don't care to act. I have told 'em I would do a part where I could sing and do a few lines. But I don't really have the desire to get involved in anything I'm not that interested in. But I hope to, and I'm sure I will, do some singin' parts in some movies.
>
> I love folk music and sacred songs. I hope to do a sacred album just as soon as I can. I hope to do a folk album. I write a lot of poetry and stories. Some day I hope to publish a little volume of my poetry. I like to write little children's stories. I'd like to do an album for my own children, or grandchildren.

Asked about family plans, Dolly said:

> We don't have any children as yet and don't have any on the way, but we plan to have some, and we'll probably start having or trying to have a family next summer. But all this booking and everything, I'm just getting started. But I'd like to have four children and I'd like to have six, if we could afford it. If all goes well, and if everybody's healthy and I got the energy to take care of them [laughs]. I'll know after the first one.

Concerning music styles:

> I don't want to be in the rock 'n' roll field. I wouldn't mind at all having a good song that would go pop, but I want to stay basically country because that's what I feel. If that's what you are, that's all you can feel, really.

And as for staying with Fred Foster:

> I'm signing new contracts with Monument now, and I've got one that expires in September, and I'm signing up for three more years. I'll sign it with the writing [songwriting], too, in September, for three more years.

Since this interview was just before Dolly went with Porter, she told Everett she was averaging about twenty road dates a month, thanks to Dub Allbritten's One Nighters, Inc., talent agency. When Dub listed Dolly in *Who's Who in Show Business* (1967–68 edition), he didn't categorize her as "C&W" but kept his and Dolly's options open. He'd made an international star out of Brenda Lee.

Dolly said she was forming a band called Dolly Parton and the Kinfolk, with her uncle Bill on guitar, uncle Louis Owens on bass, cousin Dwight Puckett on bass, and "I play piano and banjo a little, and maybe I'll work up a little routine." Today Bill Owens plays at the Backporch Theater at Dollywood with the Kinfolks band.

Dolly and Carl were living in a modest apartment when Everett interviewed her—here they stayed for several months after she joined Porter's show. City directories place them at 1914 Winthorne Drive, apartment C-25, in the Glengarry Heights apartments. "Carl and I moved into Glengarry apartments," Dolly told me. "I moved there before we got married, about six months before, and he paid for it and I fixed the place up. We got married [May 1966] and that's where we lived till we bought our place in Antioch, Tennessee." (Dolly didn't even own a car, so Ralph Emery used to pick her up at 5:00 A.M. and drive her to his TV show. When she got married, she told Ralph—but not anybody at Monument Records.)

The Glengarry Heights complex is six miles from downtown Nashville near the airport. The "extraordinary views" its brochure advertises include vistas of McDonald's and numerous gas stations. The one-bedroom flat, C-25, that Carl and Dolly rented for about one hundred dollars a month, is identified with the number emblazoned in black electrician's tape. It was humbling to realize that on the other side of the wall had lived a woman who went on to become possibly the world's most photographed female and who by 1981 was earning between $350,000 and $500,000 a week in Las Vegas, according to Leonore Fleischer's *Dolly: Here I Come Again*—who by 1990 had an estimated net worth of fifty million dollars.

Dolly's début with Porter was in Lebanon, Virginia, just 120 miles from where she was raised, probably Friday night, September 1, 1967. As they drove over the mountains in the bus, Porter warned Dolly it would not be easy. The show was at a campground, and the large crowd was expecting Norma Jean. Porter went onstage to tell the audience Norma had been replaced, but he was sure they'd like his new girl singer.

Porter remembers Dolly was nervous, singing "Dumb Blonde" and "Somethin' Fishy" at a higher pitch than usual. He says she talked between songs faster than a machine gun, similar to his own hurried manner in West Plains when he'd mutter, "here's my next song," then rush right into it. The crowd was yelling "Where's Norma Jean?" and "We want Norma Jean!" Porter became angry, went back onstage, and said, "Looky here. Norma Jean's *not* gonna be back on my show. Give this girl a chance, for cryin' out loud!" Dolly came offstage in tears, Porter remembers, and two hours later on the bus she was still crying, eyes and face swollen.

How were they going to do the show next day? Porter worried late into the evening, and finally asked her if she knew any duets. She knew the old 1945 Fred Rose number, "Blue Eyes Crying in the Rain," and they worked it up. "The harmony was a perfect blend," Porter told Craig Baguley in 1989, as reported in *Country Music People*. But they needed an uptempo tune, so he suggested "The Last Thing on My Mind," which had been recorded by the Glaser Brothers but hadn't been a hit. Dolly didn't know it, so she wrote down the words "on a little old piece of paper" in case she forgot them on stage.

Next day things went better, and now Porter and Dolly had at least the right interim combination. He'd go out and introduce her, then break her in by singing duets. No one was going to give Dolly a bad time with Porter alongside her.

The harsh view is that Porter hard-sold her as though she were some new concoction of elixir. The always-understated Don Warden says, "It was not easy for her, for a while." Porter's banjoist, Buck Trent, says, "Dolly Parton cried herself to sleep every night for a year," which may be only a slight overemphasis. On the back of a 1971 album Dolly would say, "It was murder knowin' that everybody was wantin' to see and hear someone else."

Since Dolly had charted two hits with Monument and was getting her and Bill's songs cut all over town—some of them hits—she deserved a new deal from Fred Foster. Her contract was conveniently up, as was her songwriting one with Combine. Fred was reworking her recording deal with more favorable terms. With Monument products now being performed on the Porter Wagoner show—Dolly's TV début featured "Dumb Blonde" and "Somethin' Fishy"—Fred Foster had the big chance of giving Dolly the national exposure he had so long yearned for. He harbored private pop dreams for Dolly that she didn't quite share: "The Porter Wagoner Show" could perhaps be Dolly's bridge to Hollywood. With three million people seeing her every Saturday afternoon, who knows what could be accomplished?

Dolly could not have been luckier than to have signed with Fred Foster back in early 1965, not that she'd had much choice. Fred was a visionary, although sometimes he peered almost too far into her future. It took him almost two years to lower his sights and score his first success with her. He had scored more than a dozen pop hits with Roy Orbison, and Roy was now growing restless on the label. Roy wanted to get into movies. With a yawn, Fred said he didn't own a movie studio.

That portentous spring day in 1965, Billy Graves at Capitol called Fred and recommended Dolly. Ken Nelson at Capitol had just rejected her, as had RCA, and she and her uncle Bill had been door-knocking for about nine months. "There's never a shortage of girl singers," says Fred, but he told Billy to send Dolly and Bill over (Fred's office was at 530 West Main Street in Hendersonville). Dolly sat and sang him four songs, and Fred announced, "Alright, come back tomorrow, and we'll have a contract." Fred says she couldn't believe it. Fred also signed her and her uncle Bill to a Combine Music writing contract, giving them a desperately needed one hundred dollars a week apiece.

Dolly had been in town for almost a year. As all of Dolly's fans know, she moved to Nashville on June 22, 1964, the day after her graduation at the Sevier County High School. From the stage of her baccalaureate ceremony, she'd announced her resolve to move immediately to Music City. The night before leaving she said goodbye over local radio (WSEV). The next morning she left so abruptly that she took along her dirty laundry in a cardboard suitcase, making her Greyhound getaway before someone could obligate her to a graduation party, a summer job, or a date.

When Dolly was ten years old, her mother had signed an agreement with her brother, Bill Owens, that he would manage her until she was eighteen. Dolly was eighteen now, and, just weeks prior to her graduation, Bill, his wife Christina (a month younger than Dolly), and their baby son had moved to Nashville. Dolly was to live with them and baby-sit while Christina worked in a restaurant. They rented a stone house at 1710 Allison Place near the Tennessee State Fairgrounds.

Dolly walked up Wedgewood Avenue to Doc's Launderette at number 762, and threw in her dirty clothes. She stepped out onto the sidewalk to enjoy a soft drink, when a boy driving by—Carl Thomas Dean—waved at her. She waved back. In the next few weeks Carl and Dolly got to know each other sitting on the metal steps plainly visible on the left side of the house. "I didn't live with them very long," Dolly told me. "They broke up, and Bill went on the road."

By early 1965 she was scraping by in an unfurnished apartment within walking distance of Music Row, a second-floor flat at 2050 Bernard Circle in the Colonial Village Apartments. It was also only a few hundred yards from the WSM television studio (and giant antenna) on Fifteenth Avenue South—where Porter's TV show was taped. Dolly's big sister Willadeene feared Dolly would be plagued by "all kinds of sadists and perverts lurking outside her windows," so she brought her a hammer and nails to nail her windows shut. Every creative writer, poets especially, needs those "attic years," or at least months, when nutrition and other niceties take a back seat to creativity. Dolly gave a woman's magazine her "catsup soup" recipe from this period: ketchup, mustard, and relish mixed with hot water from the tap. "To this day, I can't look at a jar of relish without shuddering," Dolly admits.

In her *Shadow of a Song* family history, Willadeene remembers Dolly living in a trailer park. The sisters, Stella and Cassie and Dolly, decorated the trailer for Christmas with a red light, which immediately began attracting men. When Bill and Carl showed up, they wondered what in the world! This was Fulton's Trailer Park down in the gully at 631 Murfreesboro Road, where Bill lived, according to the 1966 and 1967 city directories. Bill was on the road, playing guitar for Carl and Pearl Butler, old friends from Knoxville, when Dolly lived here alone. Down the block at number 605, she waited tables at Dobb's House restaurant. Willadeene describes Bill and Dolly also traveling to far-flung gigs, in these desperate months, in his heaterless car with a blanket across their knees, fortified with a thermos of hot tea.

Fred Foster's advances barely kept them going, although Fred bought Dolly clothes and sank large amounts into her records. Eventually there were twenty-four sides released on albums. If Fred could take a homely kid from the oil fields like Roy Orbison and make him a star, what could he do with this photogenic lass from the Smokies? Most young hopefuls fail, as Fred wrote in his liner notes to Dolly's first album: "[They] find the spotlight shines on stages set too high, and microphones hang deaf-like in studios with no doors." But he was bound to put Dolly over. He had Ray ("Ahab the Arab") Stevens, writer of demented parodies and a gifted musician, produce Dolly, but they came up hitless. She told *Current Biography* (1977) that they thought "it would sound funny for someone who sounded like she was twelve years old to be singing about a marriage that went bad," so they had her sing rockabilly. "But I soon learned that when you ride the fence you just kind of sit there."

Fred was too late or too early for the pop market—the musical sisters of Brenda Lee had come and mostly gone (Sue Thompson, "Sad Movies"; Barbara George, "I Know"; and especially, Lesley Gore, "It's My Party"). Dolly and Uncle Bill wrote a great potential crossover song, "Fuel to the Flame," with minor chords in a gorgeous, complex melody anticipating Dolly's crossover breakthrough in 1977 with "Here You Come Again." "I thought that she was going to be our entrée into the big time," Fred recalled. But Skeeter Davis got the song and the country hit, number eleven in early 1967.

Dolly was becoming very emotional, says Fred, putting her foot down and demanding to cut only country. He told her, "Okay, but I think you're limiting yourself to one field because I think you've got the talent to do anything you want to do." Fred also predicted to her that she would be a movie star. "You're crazy," she told him.

Fred had sunk his money where his mania was—$50,000 into Dolly's buildup. He commissioned Carol Doughty, with the Nashville Children's Theater, to polish up his protégée. Carol lives in Atlanta today and is a drama coach. Reminiscing about Dolly Parton, she says:

> She needed to have some skills as far as stage experience was concerned, such as how to come out on stage and walking. She had a lot of things to learn. Dolly was a very quick study, eager to learn with a very sharp mind, and picked it up very rapidly . . . Coming where she came from, everyone understands each other. And she never lost that [her Smoky Mountain] accent and that's part of her charm, but there needs to be some clarification so people who are not natives to that area will understand what you're saying.

Meanwhile, Chet Atkins remembers saying to Porter, "Who're you going to get to replace Norma Jean?"

"I think I'm going to get Dolly Parton."

What happened next has conflicting versions, but it's a fact that Porter brought in a tape of Dolly's singing and played it for Chet and Harry K. Jenkins, who was in charge overall. The demo was a very sparse performance, just Dolly and guitar. Porter has said Chet and Harry had their reservations, which Chet gently remembers differently. Porter told Glenn Hunter, "Her voice was clear and pure, but it was real skinny, real wiry." He says he shared Chet's supposed reservation, but that "it was no big deal to begin with." In a very low-key discussion they decided to sign Dolly. Porter stressed that he wanted to produce Dolly differently, to work with her intently in the studio, and, most crucially, to introduce her to the public via duets. He offered to make up any losses out of his own royalties, and Chet acknowledges that Porter may have said this. Fiddler Mack Magaha says Porter did the same thing for him, years later, staking his royalties on Mack when *he* recorded for RCA.

But Chet has always chafed about the story that he hated Dolly's singing. Certainly Dolly's voice was not the conventional late-sixties sound, but it was of a sort that Chet must have recognized, a throwback to old-time country music. From East Tennessee himself, Chet had played for Kitty Wells and the Carter Family. Porter's own early fifties voice had been higher, more vehement, in his bluegrass/Hank Williams days. Chet Atkins had no doubts whatever that Porter was going to succeed with Dolly.

For years she would say in interviews that RCA was not signing any more girl singers at the time, that but for Porter's efforts she would not have been signed. Most likely true, but RCA was not in the music business so much as in the money business. A girl with two hits already who was getting TV saturation exposure every week in millions of homes was hardly much of a risk, be it their money or Porter's.

It remained to unload the news on Fred, or rather, to unload Fred. The dumping ground was in the Downtowner restaurant, a popular music business hangout. This particular lunch, which Fred would rather forget, has been chronicled by Alanna Nash in her *Dolly* biography. Bill Owens led the conversation, with Dolly insisting she still wanted to be Fred's friend. When Fred had enjoyed as much of this unappetizing luncheon as he could stand, he headed for the door. Bill attempted to detain him for more conversation but was unsuccessful. "It hit Fred pretty hard," Bill recalls today, and in this the two of them are in agreement.

"Well, I mean, you know that hurt, let's be honest. There's no way out," Fred said in 1990. "I had all the faith in the world in her, I had spent over $50,000. She had agreed to re-sign. I had sent her a new contract with new terms and royalty increases, and she really liked the new contract and said she'd be bringing it in, in a few days."

Dolly had actually cut a new session with Fred, after her contract expired, tantamount to re-signing on her part. "She told me she had to go on RCA in order to sing duets with Porter," Fred continues, and that is certainly true. Fred's lawyers "entered the scene at this moment" and told him he could legally hold Dolly to the label, that he had "a perfect lawsuit."

"No! I don't want anyone with me who doesn't want to be with me," Fred responded. He recalls that Dolly came to him later, saying, "I'm sorry about everything. I made a mistake doing what I did, and I want to make it up to you."

What do you do with stars when they want to move? "I'll tell you what you do," Fred says. "You do what I did with Dolly. Shed a few tears. You hug her neck. Tell her you love her, and 'Good luck.' A friendship's more important than a contract. She has been my friend ever since, and I wouldn't take anything for that. That's more important to me than any amount of records sold. I feel good about what I did. And what I didn't do, I feel better about, actually. I could have muddied the waters for her, but I didn't."

Fred says he has no hard feelings for anyone, that he likes Porter, and if he had been in Porter's place, well . . . As for Bill Owens, initially Fred had thought Bill conspired to lead Dolly away, but he has come to have a high regard for Bill. "We're friends now. He worked his brains out for her! . . . It looks like I was a pretty good prophet. Well, I told her when I signed her, 'I hope you're tough.' She said, 'What do you mean?' I said, 'You are so different that there'll be about as many people hate you as love you.' She said, 'I can stand it, as long as they love me.'"

After a pause, Fred concluded, "I would question whether she really wanted to go . . ."

On September 26, a UPI photo went out across the nation showing Opry star Margie Bowes and former rockabilly Wanda Jackson flanking Norma Jean, who was clutching a cake knife next to her wedding cake. She was marrying country singer Jody Taylor in Oklahoma City.

On October 9, 1967, one day before Dolly's first RCA session, she and Uncle Bill incorporated Owepar, an anagram of their last names, which was their own music publishing company. They might have left their songwriting with Fred Foster, but instincts argued for a clean break and independence. The lawyer making the arrangements also had set up Warden Music around eight years earlier. Since a third signatory was required, Porter's name was added. At this time he owned no shares.

Meanwhile, the plans for a simple welcome-home-Dolly celebration in her hometown of Sevierville, Tennessee, were threatening to escalate. Porter had decided to bring along his whole troupe and turn it into a Dolly Parton Day. And for free!

The show was scheduled for October 7. On the sixth, in the paper Cas Walker's grocery store ran a headline at the top of its food ad: "Welcome, Dolly! Sing some gospel songs while you are here, for Sevier County is truly God's country!!!!" Cas Walker had featured Dolly for many years on his Knoxville television show.

At ten in the morning on the seventh, the entire Wagoner show rolled into Sevierville from Rome, Georgia, in an escorted cavalcade. Mayor Bob Howard presented Dolly with flowers and the key to the city. Then they headed off to Pigeon Forge for a show. Then down to Gatlinburg, the modish tourist haven with its chalets and pseudo-Swiss ambience, for another. Dolly must have sung her songs with relish here; the Parton kids used to hitch-hike to Gatlinburg, only to feel "all them rich snobs" looking down on them for wearing the wrong clothes.

Back at Sevierville at 2:00 P.M., they performed on the courthouse lawn for a crowd of 7,000 people, plus hundreds more from the outlying area. In the first public speech of her life, Dolly said she was "the most honored and excited person in the world." Chet and Bob Ferguson were there, Bob making the surprise announcement: Dolly was on RCA!

Both local papers ran prominent photos of Porter and Dolly, with a two-page spread in the *News-Record*. A few months later her sisters Willadeene and Stella would feel impelled to publish a pamphlet "for the defense" of their parents, to counter "all the misunderstandings" being spread by the gossipers ever since Dolly's day. Titled *Personal Views of*

Dolly Parton's Family, it dramatized their struggles out of poverty. Their daddy had worked twelve-hour days at his regular job, then would come home to his farming chores, dogged by a $5,000 medical bill. Dolly was *not* supporting them in any way—they were a proud and stubborn bunch—and while Dolly was too sweet and nice to answer any of the "false or damaging remarks" in circulation, these sisters had no such reticence: "We strike back with all we've got." Their pamphlet was illustrated with photos of family members, with school annual-style captions listing their skills and interests. It seemed at least half the clan was interested in music . . . playing music . . . singing . . . writing songs. The twenty-page brochure sold for a dollar.

18

"JUST A WILD MOUNTAIN ROSE"

Nearly all mountaineers are singers.
Their untrained voices are of good timbre,
the women's being sweet and high and tremulous,
and their sense of pitch and tone and rhythm
remarkably true.

—Emma Bell Miles, of East Tennessee,
The Spirit of the Mountains (1905)

A s Dolly so often puts it, Sevier County is "in the foothills of the Smokies." She was born just five miles north of the Great Smoky Mountains National Park.

Nature's palette has daubed the Smokies with a year-round rainbow, from the budding hardwoods of spring to the frosted evergreens of winter. The highest mountain in Tennessee, Clingman's Dome has its base in Sevier County, and its lowest slopes are alight with yellow coneflowers whose petals resemble rays of sunlight. The Smokies are scaled by flame azaleas, ranging in hue from red to pale yellow. The entire region was once an inland sea whose receding waters left a vast and lush botanical garden with more than 1,500 species of trees, plants, and flowers, including thirty kinds of orchids.

In the hands of Dolly the songwriter, the Smokies are as gorgeous as a Nudie suit. Her "Will He Be Waiting?" is scented with the sweet mountain laurel, and "God's Coloring Book" is decorated with red and orange flowers that line the mountain streams.

Dolly's lyrics in the Porter period also ached with the tribulations of poverty. Even today the local paper worries about the loss of jobs in the wintertime, since Sevier County has staked its survival so heavily on the tourist traffic to Dollywood and Gatlinburg. Smoky Mountain tourist propaganda depicting happy handicrafters fashioning quilts and carving wood contains a subtext, that of an isolated, hardy people who learned from grinding necessity to make do or do without.

Dolly, who is Scotch-Irish on her father's side and Cherokee on her mother's, was born in a modern-day log cabin on the Little Pigeon

River south of Richardson's Cove and north of Pittman Center. There was an iron foundry at Pigeon Forge, and down the Little Pigeon past the Parton's future cabin site floated barges of iron ore. At Pigeon Forge today tourists can see a water-driven mill, built in 1830, still producing stone-ground flour.

Dolly's most fruitful songwriting period was in the RCA-Porter era, and her lyrics occasionally press the theme of women being abused, or at least subjected to a double standard. In interviews she has complained how, where she grew up, women were held to stricter moral (sexual) standards than men, *by* men.

A half-century before Dolly's birth, and only a mile from the site of the Parton cabin, there dwelled in the 1890s a nest of hillbilly hookers who drew the attention of the masked vigilantes known as White Caps. First they would place on the women's doorsteps birch *withes* (inch-thick sticks). If such sinister, cryptic warnings went unheeded, a late-night visit followed; the women were dragged from their cabins, stripped to the waist, and flogged with birch sticks. Some died of their beatings—witnesses were killed—and the White Caps added robbery to their repertoire, evading conviction by infiltrating juries. All in the name of "whipping out" the wanton women.

Dolly's grandfather, Lloyd Valentine, was a deputy sheriff in this grotesque time. At Knoxville, suspected White Cap Joe Parton was acquitted of murdering a woman, and his attorney was W. A. Parton. That same summer (1895) in Sevier County, one Miss Nancy Parton, with three others, was indicted for "lewdness" (keeping disorderly houses) and "general cussedness"; and this was not her last indictment for "lewdness" (in a raid her male business partner was shot dead).

In an uncanny parallel to Porter's great-grandfather, Lark Allen, Dolly's ancestor Solomon Grooms was also a fiddler who was bush-whacked. Once he was halted by some White Caps; they asked him to play a tune, then blasted him in mid-melody. Grooms's fiddle was handed down to Dolly's colorful uncle, Reverend Jake Owens.

Then a counter mob called the Blue Bills rose up against the White Caps, and the coves and hollers echoed with gunfire. Riding with the Blue Bills were state representative W. A. Parton and Tom Walker, father of Dolly's future television mentor, Cas Walker. Tom Walker drove White Caps from his yard with dynamite while his wife clubbed them with a shotgun; and with W. A. Parton, he escorted the killers of William and Laura Whaley to the Sevierville gallows in 1897. They swung before a crowd of three thousand people.

Sevier County had been hag-ridden by poverty since the Civil War, if not before. Farm prices continued to fall for corn, tobacco, rye, and barley; and farming in the country was always arduous, due to the sloping ground and erosion. People hung on with subsistence farming, living out of their gardens and off their fruit trees.

In 1928 the county ranked seventy-third out of ninety-five Tennessee counties in quality of its farms. As the Depression hit, men hired out to the lumber companies and made moonshine on the side. Local juries were loath to convict the honest whiskey-maker, since home distilling produced a currency universally accepted (the Anglo-Celtic equivalent of Indian wampum).

After thirty years' discussion, the Great Smoky Mountains National Park was designated in 1926. Mountain people were driven from their homes, and both Nashville papers objected to the park; but finally in 1940 President Roosevelt dedicated it officially, and ever since, the tourist-dollar transfusion has pumped economic lifeblood into the area.

But poverty and illiteracy abided. Dolly was the first in her family to finish high school. Her efforts to combat the dropout problem through her Dollywood Foundation are well known. Her own father, Robert Lee Parton, cannot read or write.

Lee Parton married Avie Lee Caroline Owens. Earlier Partons and Owens had also intermarried. In 1978, Dolly tried to explain to a thoroughly perplexed Lawrence Grobel of *Playboy* magazine that this gave her "double first cousins," since her mother's mother's sister had married her father's brother. (*The Encyclopedia of Southern Culture* says Dolly's father is Randy Parton, though Randy is her younger brother.)

The newly married Partons moved into the log cabin on the Little Pigeon River in 1939. It was one large room, with a tiny wash room, and had been built originally as a garage, remembers Sylvia Perryman who lived there with her husband around 1931. Willadeene says it had moss-covered shingles and was set down in a hollow hemmed in by laurel undergrowth and climbing red roses. It's gone today, but it stood behind the main house, which is a caved-in ruin with an ancient chimney of rocks and mud. Just beyond the cabin was the barn where Lee Parton cured his tobacco. Down along the river can still be seen a children's ladder, with short boards nailed up the trunk of a tree overhanging the water. If Dolly didn't clamber up this—she was between three and five when they moved—no doubt Willadeene, David, and Denver did. Crossing the river hangs a rusted cable, remnant of one of the several swinging bridges that once spanned the Little Pigeon.

The Partons seldom had meat on the table, but they raised corn, potatoes, turnips, and beans in their pumpkin patch. When the Little Pigeon rose each spring, the children shuddered, especially when their mother read to them from the Bible about Noah and his ark.

According to all published accounts, Dolly Rebecca Parton was born January 19, 1946. However, when I requested birth verification from Tennessee's Vital Records department, I wrote on the form "Dollie (or Dolly) I need to know *which* spelling," and information came back that Dollie Rebecca Parton was born January 9, 1946. Thus there was a name and date discrepancy.

Dolly was named after her two aunts, as she explained to me, one spelled Dollie, the other Dolly. Her brother Denver has a daughter, Dolly Christina Parton, inspiration of the song "Christina." So as Dolly adds, "There's two authentic Dolly Partons walking around in the world."

In early school records she is Dollie and Dolly in alternate years, Dolly winning out long before graduation. She was Dolly on her first record label in 1959 and on all subsequent ones. But she witnessed a song contract as Dollie Parton in 1961 and was referred to as Dollie in a letter from Tree publishers.

When I later obtained a second birth verification she was now Dolly Rebecca Parton, born January 19, 1946. I was told this reflected the "original," but to the state, this only means the original in its latest form. The document can be amended by affidavit.

Judging from photographs, Dolly's features resemble her mother's, and her coloring, her father's. Dolly has said she has her father's determination and her mother's personality, but her mother was scarcely lacking in determination. Lola Scobey quotes Avie Lee as saying if someone told her she would be killed if she left her house, she would leave anyway: "You've got to face that ghost head-on."

Young Dolly wrote her first song at around age seven, and eventually her lyrics came to reflect the sparkling and enchanting imagery of her childhood. Lola Scobey catalogs such inspirations as butterflies, dime-store jewelry, colored birds, and gleaming quartz turned up by her daddy's plow. When she'd overhear her parents talking about someone's death, it just might turn up in a song, and her mother would wonder where Dolly was getting those morbid topics. She played a broken mandolin strung with some old bass strings, until at age eight she received a Martin guitar from her uncle Bill Owens. Eventually Avie Lee lent the Martin to someone, and it came back with the side bashed in and the neck broken, looking as if someone had jumped up and down on it. By then Dolly was getting local radio and TV spots and reaping understandable peer-group jealousy.

Some of the neighbors feuded with the Partons, and their children would beat up the Parton children every day on the way to school, pelting them with rocks. Lee Parton made a separate path, but still the youngsters were attacked. So he said, "I'm gonna kill somebody if your kids don't stop beatin' my kids up," and with some of Dolly's brothers he went in and "whupped about five grown people in that one family." In retaliation, they started setting their dogs on the Parton kids.

Yet there were no other neighbors to turn to that night in 1955 when Avie Lee almost died. Perpetually pregnant, she was often sick, this time with spinal meningitis and a fatally high temperature. They packed her in ice and fell to praying, while Willadeene alerted the neighbors, who relayed the alarm to town. A funeral home dispatched a vehicle, but Avie Lee recovered. Five months later she lost her baby, Larry Gerold, who was buried in the Caton's Chapel cemetery. A relative at the funeral muttered that the Partons had too many kids anyway. Avie Lee wrote a song about her large brood, "Twelve Little Roses," in which one of the roses is white, for Larry. Larry was to have been Dolly's child to raise. Her own song lyrics are strewn with dead and dying children—"dead baby specials" critic John Morthland calls them. He says Dolly's best songs, from her RCA–Porter period, plumbed the "deep dark mysteries of time, a music of awful deaths and unspeakable human mishaps, of real courage and conviction."

Dolly has made unsettling statements to the press concerning the cold, hard facts of mountain life. Connie Berman, in the *Official Dolly Parton Scrapbook*, quotes her as saying she has seen many strange goings-on and knows where there are many shallow graves in the mountains. To Lawrence Grobel of *Playboy* Dolly admitted that while the kids never learned from their parents where babies came from, their uncles and cousins shared their findings on the topic down in the barn and "as soon as we'd get a chance, we'd try it." Robert K. Oermann from *The Tennessean* asked Dolly about an abused-woman lyric ("What Is It, My Love?"), and she condemned the "macho, redneck attitudes" of her father, her brothers, "and a lot of my people," and said she wouldn't recommend anyone marrying one of her brothers. "Now I love 'em to death, but this song was inspired by my family and how some of 'em treat their women." The stories of Dolly being beaten for having painted her lips with Merthiolate or for making fake eyebrows with burnt matches are stock Parton legends by now, as are all the mentions of the children's bedwetting, from sleeping all crammed together. In her song "Evening Shade," Dolly has a little girl in an orphanage whipped by a matron with a razor strop for wetting her bed, then some other kids get kerosene and wait till the matron is asleep and burn the place down.

The prolific Partons seemed more likely to write than to read. Of course they read the Bible, but the newspapers brought over by Dolly's aunt Estelle Watson from Knoxville were destined for the outhouse. Avie Lee wrote songs and sang the old Anglo-Scottish ballads, with Lee Parton playing banjo. Once she cut an album of sacred songs with daughters Willadeene, Stella, and Cassie. Most of Dolly's siblings wrote songs, four of them recording for major record labels (Stella, Randy, Frieda, and Rachel); and brother Floyd wrote "Rockin' Years," her 1991 smash hit. Avie Lee's father, the Reverend Jake Owens, once had a song cut by Kitty Wells; and her sister Dorothy Jo Hope wrote many songs. Her uncle

Robert Owens, as "John Henry III," had an album, and uncles Louis and Bill wrote numerous songs, Bill especially, who also recorded whenever he could.

Willadeene wrote a mass-market family history and two poetry books, *Denim, Lace and Bandanas,* and *Sounds of My Soul.* Dolly has had published a book of verse, *Just the Way I Am.*

Bill Owens (born 1935) worked construction, sometimes up in Ohio, but played music whenever he could. He says he was concerned that Dolly not lose interest in her music as she grew into her teens. With his eight-year contract on Dolly, Bill was rather an East Tennessee equivalent of Ethel Gumm, who flogged her Gumm Sisters mother-daughter act down the yellow brick road through the portals of Hollywood. The youngest, Frances Gumm, became Judy Garland. Like Judy, Dolly had no choice but to become a star, a child-chattel to her show-biz destiny. Bill went through three marriages chasing the country music rainbow, and he mastered utterly the art of sleeping in his brown 1953 Ford, with its caved-in door that wouldn't open and contrasting blue fender on the driver's side.

Bill got Dolly onto the Cas Walker show, first on radio, then TV. Cas was a millionaire grocer in Knoxville, and Louis Owens thinks it's funny how Cas would slip Bill five dollars in a pinch to make two round trips to Sevier County and back with Dolly, who also got five dollars a show. Cas had first used country music to sell groceries on the radio back in 1929, and, thanks to television, was grossing almost $2 million a month in his stores by 1961. Cas used to throw live turkeys off the roof of his store into the crowd below and once paid a drunk man to be buried alive, as another publicity stunt. For some reason Dolly's teachers didn't think the Cas Walker show was very sophisticated, and some of them didn't like her singing at all.

Cas was obsessed with the White Caps; he published his version as a book in 1937, *White Caps and Blue Bills.* He even tried to interview Bob Catlett, the man suspected of paying for the Whaleys' murder, on his radio show; Bob declined. Cas reissued his book in 1974 in order "to keep history alive." The cover does just that, depicting white-sheeted, rifle-toting neighbors burning a cabin, with the text of their oath printed in red describing what happens to the souls, and especially to the bodies (in graphic detail) of those who testify against the White Caps.

Over the years Cas picked up a flattering number of death threats for his White Caps research. Anyone who has ever remarked upon Dolly Parton's steely resolve might ponder the flamboyant fearlessness of her old television mentor, Cas Walker.

In 1959 Cas phoned Jim Denny to get Dolly a spot on the Opry. There was a difficulty at first because of her age, but Bill Owens prevailed, and she sang "You Gotta Be My Baby," the old George Jones hit.

Above: *Cas Walker, East Tennessee grocery store magnate, country music television pioneer (WIVK Knoxville), and first employer of Dolly Parton. Cas was a member of the Knoxville City Council for thirty years and briefly mayor until recalled.*

[COURTESY DOROTHY GABLE]

Sevier Radio Singer Has New Record

Dolly Parton, 16, Sevier County High School student, who has a five-year contract with a recording firm, has a new record out which reported is selling well.

The recording, "Sure Gonna Hurt" and "The Love You Gave," is the singer's first try in the popular music field.

MISS PARTON

Miss Parton has appeared on radio and television talent shows since she was 10, singing country, western and religious songs. She and her uncle, Billy Earl Owens, guitar player and singer, have a song writers contract with a Nashville company.

She is the daughter of Mr. and Mrs. Robert Lee Parton, of the Catons Chapel Community in

Dolly Parton, summer 1961 promotional picture secured by Dorothy Gable, vice president of the CMA [Warwick Studio, Knoxville, Courtesy Dorothy Gable].

Dolly Parton's signature witnessing a Litton Music Publishers' contract (July 7, 1961) for a song by her uncle Bill Owens, "It Seems Like a Lifetime" [Courtesy Dorothy Gable].

IN WITNESS WHEREOF, the Composers have hereunto set their hands and seals and the Publisher has caused these presents to be signed by its duly authorized officer, the day and year first above written.

WITNESS:

Hollie Parton

_Bill Earl Owens_____L.S.

_____L.S.

WITNESS:

Harold Litton

By _Dorothy Gable_
Litton Music Publishers

She wore a blue silk dress and drew two encores.

The Opry does not confer stardom; it only acknowledges it. By 1961 Bill Owens was calling Dorothy Gable in Knoxville, wanting her to manage Dolly. He'd read in the papers she was vice president of the Country Music Association and had her own publishing company. Dorothy, who had a Connecticut accent and a business-school education, had written country songs that had been recorded. Bill and Dolly dropped by four or five times, once waiting like waifs on the doorstep for Dorothy to come home, and she made them lunch. Dolly and Bill were staying with her aunt and uncle in Knoxville, the Watsons. Other times she stayed with entertainers Carl and Pearl Butler.

Dorothy paid for a photo session and for a recording session at the Sound Album Recording Studio in Maryville. Dorothy still has signed song contracts, including "Dollie" witnessing one of Bill's; copyright forms, August 1961; and canceled checks. But no management contract. Why not? "Because I wanted to see what I could do, first," she explains. "I didn't want to tie them down."

Dorothy also cut an acetate disc of a possible TV music show, featuring Bill and other acts, plus "a singer I think you'll like, as pretty as a doll." She pitched it to Paul Ackerman of *Billboard* in New York.

The CMA was taking off and that April had staged its first big show in Jacksonville, Florida, with an "all-star cast," including Porter, Webb Pierce, Patsy Cline, Faron Young, the Louvins, Mel Tillis, and others. Bill wanted Dorothy to pitch Dolly to her fellow CMA board members, which she explained she certainly couldn't do at a board meeting. The quarterly meeting on August 3, 1961, was at Nashville's Capitol Park Inn. To Dorothy's surprise, as she was leaving, there were Bill and Dolly waiting for her. She made the best of it: nimbly introduced them around, then hailed a cab. She got them to RCA where they were turned down and over to Jim Denny for another rejection.

But farther up Seventh Avenue at Tree, Buddy Killen heard something in her voice he liked. Thanks to Killen, Dolly got on the Ernest Tubb Record Shop "Midnight Jamboree," probably that same weekend.

Buddy wrote Dorothy on September 13: "I would like to get with Dollie and try to find some material for her as soon as possible. Please let me know when she can come to Nashville for a couple of days." Dorothy drove up into the mountains to tell the Partons the news. Then they called her from Aunt Estelle's in Knoxville and announced that Killen had signed Dolly and that Bill would now be managing her. So Dorothy called Killen and pulled out.

Dolly cut five more sides around 1963. They have turned up on various budget labels ever since. They obviously are old demos, and three of them are "dead baby specials," two probably old public domain folk songs; but one of them, "Letter to Heaven," is a song Dolly may have written, since it has a little girl killed by an automobile. Around 1964–65, Dolly recorded many demos for Moss–Rose music publishers. Their snapshot of Dolly wearing nothing but a towel to promote their song "Girl on the Billboard" was suppressed. "Not quite *Playboy* quality," remembers the song's co-writer, Sam Garrett. The Moss–Rose demos are now in New York, so the old Dolly-dubs may one day surface.

Dolly Parton—with a decade of experience including many false starts, failures, and rejections—was now on "The Porter Wagoner Show," with an RCA contract and her own publishing. She was only twenty-one.

19

"THE LAST THING ON MY MIND"

There's a blend there,
and a nostalgia about their duets,
that people will always sense.
It's the sound of an era,
and it was a wonderful era.

—Minnie Pearl, interview, May 17, 1989

The day after Dolly set up her Owepar publishing with Uncle Bill, she went into the studio with Porter. These first sessions—October 10–12, 1967—netted ten songs.

The first release was "The Last Thing on My Mind," written by neo-folksinger Tom Paxton. Its noncountry lyric about the subway rumbling underground is a reminder that it came from Greenwich Village, the milieu of Bob Dylan and Joan Baez, evoking Washington Square and Bleeker Street instead of West Plains or Sevierville. It's a wistful song of parting, with the singer unable to accept the final farewell ("I could have loved you better, I didn't mean to be unkind, you know that was the last thing on my mind"). Images like the steadily growing weeds add to the forlornness, and it makes the perfect elegy for the drawn-out pain of the later Porter–Dolly relationship.

The song opens with a snappy guitar introduction by Wayne Moss in Porter's stock flattened-7th progression (C-B♭-C), which gives the song a bittersweet "signature" when you first hear it. (It took Porter and Wayne Moss an hour to settle on a lick.) More of the same, underneath the melody, gives the song a dolorous, folky feeling. Porter, then Dolly, sing parts and join together on the hook. This set the formula for most of their future duets. The record was released October 31, 1967, entered *Billboard* December 7, stayed seventeen weeks and reached number seven.

Inspired by their first duet chart success, they went back to the studio. Dolly sang solo this time. On December 11, 18, and 20, she cut thirteen sides, one of which, "Just Because I'm a Woman," she had written for Combine. It would be the title cut of her first RCA album and her first hit single for her new label.

Dolly was gradually winning over the road show audiences. Comedian Speck Rhodes remembers, "Dolly came on the show nationally an unknown. 'That squeaky little blond,' some people said. Women nudged their husbands because their husbands would be all eyes, looking at Dolly. But in a year or so, Dolly was accepted as much or more by the women."

For Christmas 1967 Dolly gave Porter a rather large Christmas card, a hand-written poem measuring at least three feet by four feet, titled "A Man Like You." It celebrates Porter as the greatest man of any man Dolly has ever known, that if she ever has a son she hopes he will have Porter's fine qualities (kindness, sincerity, and so forth). The poem should be viewed in context—a twenty-one-year-old girl extolling a forty-year-old country music hero whose show she has watched since childhood and on which she now performs.

Porter had the poem framed and hung it on the wall. It's a good specimen of Dolly's rounded, flowing penmanship. You don't have to be a graphologist to divine an intense, buoyant personality guiding her hand.

In January 1968 their first duo album, *Just Between You and Me*, was released. On the cover Dolly's wig is over half a foot tall, bringing her closer to Porter's height. Their hair, their makeup, their red sweaters are each the same color. "We dressed to match, most of the time," Dolly said under oath in the 1979 lawsuit.

The album establishes the Porter–Dolly formula: trading lines, then singing together. Porter's softer, lower voice undergirds Dolly's higher sound. He is finally doing what he used to do with his sister Lorraine, singing with sibling ease and man–woman contrast. He has often said he and Dolly had "blood harmony," but no one would suspect their voices of being genetically related. Rather, their brother–sister naturalness is in their warmth, their timing, and their instinct for anticipating each other. They pronounced some words differently, so they would have to settle on either the Ozarks' or the Smokies' way of saying the word. Dolly told Paul W. Soelberg that she would usually let Porter end a song, especially if the last syllable were *s* to avoid the sibilant sound. Soelberg observed that while Porter usually sang harmony and Dolly the melody, the effect was the opposite, because of Porter's lower voice. Soelberg felt it was almost like hearing four-part harmony.

Just Between the Two of Us contains three Parton–Owens songs, including their hit, "Put It Off Until Tomorrow." Bill contributes a cheating song, "This Time Has Gotta Be Our Last Time" (no more adultery for this pair, not after this one last session, as they head for the motel). Dolly's own "Mommie, Ain't That Daddy?" caters to Porter's Skid Row, estranged family theme, the ex-husband being reduced to bum status. Even in his castoff clothes he is recognized by his tearful daughter.

On January 31, 1968, they recorded Jerry Chestnut's "Holding On to Nothin'." Porter observes that they sustained some of the syllables for dramatic effect, somewhat in the vein of the catchy cadence of "A Satisfied Mind." Of all their duets, John Morthland found this one to be perhaps "the most dramatic; most urgent, and most sorrowful," prompting him to exclaim, "They made all the other duet teams sound like footnotes."

In February Dolly and Carl bought a large, two-story brick home in Antioch, south of Nashville at 842 Reeves Road. In the May issue of *Country Song Roundup*, Dolly reiterated her desire not to act in movies. As for the tensions between marriage and her career, she said she had a good, understanding husband—that if they had problems, every couple has problems and theirs were only minor ones. In fact, Dolly's husband Carl shunned all contact with the music world, was never seen in public with Dolly; his phobia for publicity exceeded even that of Porter's estranged wife, Ruth. Dolly had told Everett Corbin earlier that even Monument had wanted her to downplay her marriage. It didn't hurt record sales if people could fantasize what they wished about Porter and Dolly. She was on the road more than twenty days a month, spending much of her precious time in Nashville taping TV shows, recording songs, and writing songs, often co-writing with Porter. In his divorce trial of 1986 he would say that his wife had "laughed" at his songwriting efforts, but that Dolly had helped him to write again.

Probably living with Dolly and Carl—having come to town in 1968—was her schoolgirl chum, Judy Ogle. Judy, who served as Owepar secretary after four years in the Air Force, also was born January 19, 1946, which makes her Dolly's astro-twin.

In April Dolly's first RCA album came out, *Just Because I'm a Woman.* The cover photograph shows her standing with hands outstretched, palms up, as if to say "here I am." She's wearing the austere white dress she wore to Porter's office that first day, and its form-hugging fit bespeaks the title of the album literally.

For all the controversy over her alleged shrill voice, Porter and producer Bob Ferguson almost defiantly let Dolly sound like Dolly. The album is almost as spare as a demo in its lack of embellishments, but where necessary to the song, Dolly is permitted to pierce you like an awl. She swoops down into a lower register as the song demands, and there's enough full, open-throated singing to convince anyone that a supple, mature voice like no one else's has arrived.

In the title song, for instance, the backup chorus is allowed to assist Dolly only after she has first sung all the notes unaided. By contrast, many country singers more or less talk their way through the verses, until they reach the chorus or release, where the melody lifts and the backup singers ride in like the U.S. cavalry to rescue them.

Dolly wrote the title song, which throws down the gauntlet and demands equal treatment for women. Why should a man get away with ruining a girl's reputation, then desert her to marry someone with less of a past and leave her in disgrace just because she's a woman? "Baby Sister" on the album pursues this theme, Dolly fishing a sister out of a barroom, hoping that the man who has ruined her will die a thousand times, a thousand ways.* The most arresting track on the album is "The Bridge," which she also wrote. With a spooky, minor-chord folky melody and almost no instrumentation, it tells how a couple used to meet on the bridge until passion overswept them and they headed for the nearest meadow. Now she's back on the bridge, pregnant, ready to hurl herself to the waiting waters below. Jumping out of the song, as it were, in mid-measure, the tune stops with a jolt. You expect to hear more notes and more of Dolly, but you don't. She's gone. Porter had jumped to the cold, dark waters back in 1962. Now it was Dolly's turn.

These kinds of songs were very much of their times, Bobbie Gentry's "Ode to Billie Joe" being the most obvious parallel. But Dolly's lyrics also underscore her calmly insistent, if not very militant, view of female sexuality, namely, that women should enjoy the same freedom as men in life, in love, and especially in songs.

Her own background has been distorted, probably, in the retelling. While she has said her appearance is modeled after "Cinderella, Mother Goose, and the local hooker," and she claims a tight-dresses-and-dirty-jokes image from high school, probably she was restrained and quiet, if not prim. "Just a normal, giggly girl," her guidance counselor, Mrs. Julia Householder, described her in 1988 (*Good Housekeeping*). Dolly didn't have many dates in school. Music drew her more than men did, it would certainly seem. Of course Dolly tells the comical story of how on her senior trip to New York City she and Judy Ogle took in a porno movie—after which a man accosted her, and while Judy was laughing Dolly pulled her pistol and aimed it below the man's belt. The mores of Sevier County seem better captured in a story from the *News-Record*, when the very day before the class trip two adult couples were

---

*Dolly had used the same theme in "The Company You Keep," which she and Uncle Bill had written, a number eight hit for Bill Phillips in 1966, where the singer counsels a younger sister about the bad reputation she's acquiring: "I think you're an angel but folks think that you're cheap." Fred Foster suspects this comes from personal observation.

arrested for "ludeness" [sic] and fined twenty-five dollars each. Dolly wouldn't have lasted long on the Cas Walker show without behaving modestly.

Fully committed to country music, Dolly the songwriter could express the rural woman's yearnings and frustrations with jarring realism. With Loretta Lynn raising hell in her own songs on Decca, it was no time to hold back.

In April 1968, the second of the Porter–Parton duet hits, "Holding On to Nothin'," charted and went to number seven.

Then in May, the next of Porter's temperance-tract albums appeared, *The Bottom of the Bottle*. On the cover a quizzical Porter, in an expensive orange sweater that matches his hair, is peering into a green wine bottle. Inside the bottle is a miniature man. Skid Row Joe, wearing gray rags (Porter in his bum duds), is lecturing his other half, the sober and much larger Porter. It's a brilliant portrayal of alcoholic schizophrenia, of the disreputable drunk that lurks inside of every respectable "problem drinker," such as his late brother Oscar.

The opening cut is "Wino," an Owepar-copyrighted recitation written by Porter and his new songwriting buddy, Dolly Parton. The song would shortly be a B-side of Porter's next single, "Be Proud of Your Man," and one can imagine the shock of a fan turning over this basic country love song to hear the other side. The intro of "Wino" sounds as though it were composed by Spike Jones, the wild, crazed bandleader of the forties. You hear footsteps running down an alley, followed by a garbage can rattling and a cat yowling, then a rustling of bottles and more clanking and more running. A moody jazz beat commences, drums and brushes mostly, relieved by spurts of more running footsteps. In the opening lines of the recitation, Porter talks of progressing "from garbage cans to gutters," admitting he has lost his family and his home. The song asks, has the wino loved and lost, or was he lost and unloved?

Three more of the songs have *wine* in their titles, and the liner notes are signed "Disrespectfully yours, Skid-Row Joe." Joe writes that Porter knows how they feel on Skid Row, and "If I didn't know him better, I'd think he was one of us."

Reflecting on his wino repertoire, Porter said, "I just always had such a soft spot for people like that, because they're so helpless to the fact that they're there. They didn't plan it, they don't know what they done— it's a guy who for some reason in his life made a mistake." As for alcohol, "I tried to like it, but I think seeing this [what happened to Oscar] made me dislike it. I tried to be a social drinker. It would make me sick. There was one kind of wine I got to where I liked it," Porter finished, lamely.

In June 1968, "Be Proud of Your Man," written by L. E. White and Betty Jo White, went to number sixteen for Porter, anticipating

Tammy Wynette's "Stand By Your Man" a few months later. Also in June, Dolly's "Just Because I'm a Woman" charted, going to number seventeen.

Fulfilling Porter's faith in the duet strategy, the Porter–Dolly "We'll Get Ahead Someday" hit the charts the following month, going up to number five. It was a peppy, we'll-overcome-despite-all-our-bills marriage song, by Mack Magaha.

The flip side, and a real sleeper in more ways than one, was "Jeannie's Afraid of the Dark." Through airplay it went to number fifty-one, but it became the most requested of all Porter–Dolly duets. Little Jeannie is afraid of the dark, so she sleeps with her parents. She's doomed by some undiagnosed childhood disease—after she dies her parents place on her grave an "eternal flame." Porter is at his heartbreak best in the recitation. Like Ernest Tubb's "Our Baby's Book," the song is a standard for people who have lost a child.

Dolly remarked in our interview:

> Me and Porter liked to sing those old sad songs, he liked to do recitations, and I liked to sing those pitiful songs, so the more pitiful I could make them, the better we liked them. I always was afraid of the dark when I was little, so that made it easy for me to write that part of the song, and I still don't like being in the dark.

Dolly has told other interviewers about being locked in the coat closet by the children at the Caton's Chapel school and sleeping with the lights on for the rest of her life. And Alanna Nash heard one of Dolly's former teachers suggest that the song was inspired by a real incident, where a little girl cousin of Dolly's was run over outside Dolly's Uncle Jake's House of Prayer church by a man in a truck, who then crashed and killed himself.

Dolly's fear of the dark, along with her many songs about oppressed children and degraded women, at least raises the spectre of child abuse, though whether experienced, witnessed, suspected, feared, or merely understood, is conjectural.

"Jeannie" was in the *Just the Two of Us* album released in October 1968. On the cover both of them have golden hair, brick-colored makeup, and matching lemon-colored raincoats; his shirt and her blouse are of the same green. Even more morbid than "Jeannie" is "The Party" on this album, which only Dolly could have written. A couple likes to party a lot, leaving their children with a baby sitter. The little ones want to go to church on Sundays, but their parents are too partied-out to go. While the parents are at a Saturday night party, drinking, telling dirty jokes, their house burns down. Next day they go to church for a change, and so do their kids, to their own hastily scheduled funeral. Dolly's brighter, carefree side comes out on "I Can," where she and Porter let their imaginations whisk them far away down "the canyons of my mind" in the mood of Bob Lind's "Elusive Butterfly," which Dolly would record many years later.

In the year since Dolly had teamed up with Porter, an incredible marketing pattern had been established: Porter singles, Porter albums as usual, including Camden budget reissues of older songs, gospel material, and Skid Row theme albums; Dolly singles, Dolly albums; and Porter–Dolly singles and albums, all reinforced by syndicated TV and nonstop touring.

There had never been anything like it before, nor would there be again. It was all wound up so tight, it just had to rip apart.

20

"HAVE I TOLD YOU LATELY THAT I LOVE YOU?"

Well, I'm tired and so weary,
but I must go along . . .

—Rev. Thomas A. Dorsey,
"(There'll Be) Peace in the Valley (For Me),"
as recorded by Red Foley

Two men who had meant so much to Porter's career were Steve Sholes and Red Foley.

Steve had signed Porter, Elvis, and countless others to RCA. On April 22, 1968, he was in Nashville on business, driving from the airport, when he suffered a fatal heart attack on the Wharf Avenue Bridge. His car bounced off the guard rails, miraculously missing any other cars. In 1972 Chet Atkins placed Steve Sholes's career in perspective for *Music City News*:

> I think Steve was the first one with any real futuristic vision of what was going to take place here. I came here in 1950. Even then he would tell me how music was going to get closer together; the differences would fade; and it would begin to merge due to TV and mass communications. He was always ahead of everybody else.

Steve Sholes never moved to Nashville, but, trite as it may sound, there was probably no one more beloved in the country music industry.

After the Ozark Jubilee folded, Red Foley moved back to Nashville, but, as Si Siman said in the 1970 *Country Music Who's Who*, "When the Jubilee died, Red did too. After that he really never did work at the business. He played fairs and one-nighters, but he lost some of his enthusiasm to carry on." Johnny Western remembers on one package show when Red received last billing; and even when he had top billing, he had to be put on in the first half of the show, while he was still sober. Watching Bobby Bare get a big applause once, Red sighed, "They used to clap that way for me." Steel player Howard White remembers Red getting booed in Louisville. And songwriter Glenn Sutton tells a story he heard about Red leaving home to get a pizza and not returning for three days. "But when he came home, he was carrying the pizza . . . in the back seat."

Red made repeated headlines in the sixties, and Nashville was obviously wary of having to watch a rerun of the Hank Williams scenario. When a *Tennessean* reporter visited Red in early 1964, Red mused about displaying all his clippings under glass. The reporter (George Barker) wondered at all those IRS tax case clippings, and one about a drug overdose where Red had been rushed to the hospital.

The year 1964 carried many more headlines, including an apartment fire that hospitalized Red and wife Sally. There were at least three arrests, one for driving through nearby Madison at 80 mph, one for protesting a friend's arrest, and one where Sally had him tossed in the drunk tank for the regulation four-hour cooling off period, scarcely making him the only Opry member to have spent four hours thusly.

In the late sixties, the Age of the Beatles, Red Foley was something of an anachronism, dating back to the early thirties and the barn dance days of country radio. Yet he was fighting his way back into prominence, scoring three country hits in 1967, his first in more than a decade.

His last tour was a package show in September 1968. Shortly before the tour, he told his son-in-law, Bentley Cummings, that he never thought he would see his home town of Berea, Kentucky, again. According to his widow, Sally, Red hadn't had a drink in four months; but he was sick, and the doctor wanted him hospitalized. "But you know what they'll say if I cancel," Red told Sally the morning he left.

Red was getting into his car with Sally's son Ken, but three times he came back to the house to tell Sally that he loved her. One of his pet phrases was "have I told you lately that I love you?" after the old Scott Wiseman song that Red had absorbed in his days on WLS in Chicago. Finally Sally told Red that he was starting to scare her, the way he kept telling her that he would always love her.

The tour had two shows scheduled in Fort Wayne, Indiana, on September 19, 1968.

All the entertainers were eating in a restaurant together, but Hank Williams, Jr., remembered that Red wasn't hungry. Jean Shepard and her husband, Benny Burchfield, were there, and since they carried a bottle of Canadian Club in their car, they asked Red if he'd like to join them for a drink (they're teetotalers and born-again Christians today). Red declined, but he paid for their dinner and said, "Tell your children that Red Foley bought you your dinner tonight."

Billy Walker was on the tour, and before the second show Red came to his room, seeming troubled. He unburdened himself to Billy, lamenting all the mistakes he had made in his life. Billy suggested they get down on their knees and pray together, and they did. Billy and Jean both say that on the second show Red sang "Peace in the Valley" better than they'd ever heard him do it. After the show, Red visited Hank, Jr., in his room. He told Hank, Jr., that sooner or later a country entertainer encounters a lot of problems: "You'll have them some day. Your dad had them, and I have them, and you'll have them some day." Then Red said, "I'm dreadful tired now, Hank, I've got to go to bed," which were his last words to anybody.

Red died when he was getting into bed, "apparently of natural causes."

The tour was over, and Sally and her son drove to meet what should have been Red's plane. But when the last plane came in and Red was not aboard, Sally started her car radio to catch some news, but it had stopped working. She called the motel in Indiana, but when she told them who she was, they referred her to the sheriff. So she and her son drove home and she had him call the sheriff. "And that's how I heard. My neighbors came running in, because I let out a scream you could hear for blocks."

Sally remembers seeing Porter at the funeral with tears in his eyes. The Jordanaires sang the song about how there would be peace in the valley some day, and how a man would be changed, changed from the person that he was. In November, Hank, Jr., had a hit with "I Was with Red Foley (The Night He Passed Away)."

The following year Red had his last hit, a re-release of his duet with Kitty Wells, "Have I Told You Lately That I Love You?"

21

ACCIDENTS WILL HAPPEN
(IN CARROLL COUNTY)

Wagoner more then repaid RCA's trust
by recording some of the major hits
of country music, including the
classics "Green, Green Grass of Home"
and "The Carroll County Accident."

—Bill C. Malone, *Country Music, U.S.A.*
(revised edition 1985)

A car-wreck song with images of bloody seats, broken glass, all of it a "tangled mess," is obviously not an Irving Berlin number. As listeners will remember, Mary Ellen Jones drags herself from the twisted metal and lives long enough to testify. Her cover story about why she was riding around with a married man dies along with her; and encased within her lie is a mystery, stashed behind the dashboard.

"The Carroll County Accident" is one more refutation of that silliest of country songwriting rules, Keep it simple. It's as complex as the man who wrote it, not to mention the man who sang it.

It was written by Bob Ferguson, who was taking anthropology courses at Vanderbilt University while working as the major producer of country records at RCA, Chet Atkins having graduated to the desk job he soon wearied of.

As Bob told Dorothy Horstman, author of *Sing Your Heart Out, Country Boy*, he was driving down to Mississippi when he passed a Carroll County sign in Tennessee. Zooming along on the interstate, Bob told himself he'd better slow down or he'd become "the Carroll County accident." Then it hit him: *there* was a song title! When he passed another Carroll County sign in Mississippi, he decided it was an omen. "By the time I completed the trip, the song was practically written. I've since learned there are no fewer than thirteen counties by that name in the United States."

Bob was on his way to a music show being performed for the Choctaw Indians. In our 1990 interview he remembered walking right up to bass man Junior Huskey and declaring, "I wrote a hit." But the song wasn't finished; Bob had the beginning and the end, but no middle. Then one night in Nashville, he finished it and called RCA engineer Bill Vandevoort and said he wanted to put a song down immediately. That same night they opened the studio and went in.

Next morning Bob told Porter, "I wrote a song you might like," and left the tape with Joan. An hour or two later Porter asked, "How soon can we record it?" Porter seems to remember the song wasn't quite finished, that Bob went back and added more.

A couple of days later they recorded it, and two days after that, Porter came in off the road and said, "What do you think of the record?" Bob said nothing. "That's what I think. Why don't we do it again. Buck can come up with a good kickoff on it, better than the other." Bob hastily agreed, "'cause when you get an artist excited over a song, it's like a horse trying to win a race—you go! If the artist isn't excited, you can't make it a hit."

Porter remembers it took three separate takes. "It's a song that has to be exactly in the right groove, with the rhythm to make the song flow properly. The third time I cut it, it came off and I felt like it was a hit and it was." The final session was September 18, 1968.

As with similar story-songs, the opening lines are deceptively tranquil, declaring that "Carroll County" is "kinda square," where the biggest local happening is the county fair, at least until the event everyone calls "the Carroll County accident." The second stanza gets journalistic and brutal. "The wreck was on the highway, just inside the line," and the mood plummets fast. The happily married Walter Browning has been killed in a car crash, and his wedding ring is strangely not on his hand. Out of the mangled mass of metal staggers (or is pulled) the equally respectable Mary Ellen Jones, who unloads a cheater's fairy tale before dying. She says Walter was out on the highway, walking, when he waved her down for a ride.

The narrator is a young boy, and he visits the wreck like everyone else, what a gory mess . . . but he notices something other eyes have missed. Behind the dashboard is tucked a little matchbox held fast by a rubber band. "I thought that was really the neat part of the song," Porter told Alanna Nash in 1981, "because you can picture this kid picking up this matchbox because he knows there's something in it, when he sees the rubber band around it." The little boy drops the matchbox down a well, vowing never to reveal its contents. It was Walter Browning's missing wedding ring, slipped off apparently to accommodate the charms of the late Mary Ellen Jones.

Bob Ferguson says there was a record producer who went to Florida and took off his wedding ring so he could run around. "While it was off his finger, it fell in a gutter on the street and he lost it! And that always stuck in my mind!" In 1968 running around on your wife, ringless, could still cost you your life in a song, though by 1984 Johnny Lee could sing about a whole barroom of people with "disappearing wedding rings" until one irate wife storms in ("You Could've Heard a Heart Break").

Oh yes, "Carroll County Accident" was narrated by Walter Browning's son—and the county has erected a marble monument over his dad. In Carroll County, all's well that ends. As Bob says, "All my songs are moralistic. I don't start out trying to be moralistic, but I listen to them later and I think they are. His own son figured out what was going on. It was entirely a made-up story."

The melody is very simple, but with two modulations (key-changes) getting the song up from C to E, Porter singing four half-steps up the scale at the end. It makes him sound more boyish, fitting perfectly the phase of the song where the kid is realizing what's happened to his dad. There is no chorus, as befits a complicated lyric.

Bob reflects on the song's melody: "My challenge was I had never written a two-chord song, and I had never written a story-song. But all things came together on that song. I'm aiming for a one-chord song, but I ain't got it yet! As for the modulation, well, modulation is an attention-getter. It alerts your audience that here is something ready to happen."

On November 9, 1968, "The Carroll County Accident" entered *Billboard's* charts, staying on for twenty-one weeks and reaching number two. It was Porter's biggest record since "The Cold, Hard Facts of Life," even sneaking onto the pop charts at a low number ninety-two.

Story-songs have a way of coming true in the imaginations of the listeners. Soon Bob was hearing from all the Carroll counties, cards and letters. "Some of them were hair-raising," such as one from Carroll County, Tennessee: "Bob, did you know Governor Browning? His father was named Walter Browning. Did you know that?" Bob's father received an embarrassed phone call from Carroll County, Missouri, where a schoolteacher named Mary Ellen Jones was having to endure Porter Wagoner's big hit record. Ten years later a newspaper in Carroll County, North Carolina, ran a full-page story.

"But I just made it up as I was driving along, and I tried to make it different names, but it always came back to Carroll County 'cause it sings better."

In 1969 the Country Music Association named "The Carroll County Accident" the Song of the Year. That it was published by Warden Music Company, Inc., was no accident.

22

TWO OF A KIND

> I have never in my life seen anybody that would get in
> there and get it better than she would, she always
> done her part in any situation. But she had all these
> dreams and fantasies, and the imagination of a wizard,
> of an Einstein.
>
> —Porter, interview, June 7, 1989

> During that time I had some of the best times and some
> of the worst times of my life. We fought like cats and
> dogs, we disagreed on many, many things, *but* we also
> agreed on many things. And we both are very musical,
> and we both were very sure of what we wanted to do.
> Porter had a pretty hot temper, and mine was not as
> easily stirred up as Porter's but when it did get stirred up
> it was just as hot . . . [laughs] So I think you're right,
> that can add to some of the excitement of writing and
> singing. We had a very passionate relationship in its
> way in that time, and I think that kind of spilled over
> into our singing. We were passionate with our words,
> with our singing, with everything that we did. We're
> both real hot-blooded human beings.
>
> —Dolly, interview, July 3, 1990

I n August 1968 Porter was sitting in his bright blue and yellow bus in Springfield, Missouri, holding forth to a reporter from the Springfield *Daily News* about his grueling itinerary on the highway and in front of the cameras. The occasion was the Ozark Empire State Fair: the attendance of 12,000 was the largest in any of the fair directors' memories.

Porter said they were on the road two hundred days a year, finding time for seventy-eight TV shows as well. "We usually try to stay fourteen shows ahead," and he admitted they shot them quickly, because "I don't like it to look too rehearsed . . . if a few mistakes creep in, I don't think people mind." He might have added, there was little time and less money for retakes.

"Used to be, people thought you were hillbilly and didn't wear shoes if you sang country music. But now I think they have found out it does have poise and class." He attributed this new approval to television and said they were drawing large crowds in the North and East, as well as the West. There had been "a huge turnout" in Los Angeles, and they had just broken all records at the Bluegrass Fair in Lexington, Kentucky: 51,000 people, as opposed to the 34,000 drawn by Al Hirt previously.

Speck Rhodes remembers Porter saying that if he had to choose between television and a recording contract, he'd take the former.

That same year an article about Porter titled "A Satisfied Man" appeared in *Country Song Roundup,* noting that Dolly Parton "brings a new spark to the traditional format." By now the liner notes of the albums were taking on an atmosphere of literary incest. Anyone within grabbing range was pressed into service, and one gets the impression that after a week or two working for Porter or Dolly, you would be writing liner notes. In earlier years Porter's had been written by Don Richardson, Sr., of Jubilee prominence and then by Jane Dowden, who had helped start the TV show. By the late sixties and early seventies, liner notes were written by Porter (for himself, and for Dolly); Dolly (for herself and for Porter); Porter and Dolly (duet album); Bill Turner (TV show announcer); Elmer Alley (TV show director); Paul Soelberg (Porter's publicist); Judy Ogle (Owepar secretary and Dolly's surrogate sister); Shirley Jorjorian (Dolly's future publishing administrator); Joan McGriff (Porter's secretary, on two albums); Denise (Porter's daughter); Bill Owens; Louis Owens (another uncle); Reverend Jake Owens; Bob Ferguson (twice); Tom K. Pick (RCA engineer); Bobby Dyson (session picker); Rex Teal (fishing pal); Mel Tillis (member of the show); the Wagonmasters (six of them on one album); and Dolly's old supporters from East Tennessee radio, Bobby Denton and Skip Trotter. Writers like Jack Hurst, Ed Penney, Ellis Nassour, and Don Cusic also rallied. But more and more, the liner notes themselves made way for mere ads promoting albums by Porter, by Dolly, and especially by Porter and Dolly.

Everyone seemed to notice Dolly's fairy-princess aspirations. In 1973 Speck Rhodes told Peggy Russell of *Music City News* that once on a tour out West, in Albuquerque, they had stopped by a jewelry store. "Now 'most everybody knows that Dolly was raised poor like the rest of us on the show, and she stood there looking in the window and finally she said that someday she was going to have a diamond on every finger. And she does! Lots of diamonds on every finger!"

Booking agent Dolores Smiley remembers that for Dolly it was always "dress up and play," a chance to make up for her lack of clothes and finery when she was young. Dolores, as "girl singer," had technically been in the running for Norma Jean's replacement and remembers Porter's courtesy in calling her personally to tell her Dolly had been selected. At the Minnesota State Fair, Dolores was producing "the first country show they ever had," with Porter, Dolly, the Wagonmasters, and Hank Williams, Jr., in either 1968 or 1969. She was staying at the same hotel as the singers, and Porter was off playing golf; so when she walked into the lobby, a very bored Dolly jumped up, "happy to see any familiar face." Over coffee Dolly told Dolores, "One of these days I'm going to be a really big star. I have written a lot of songs."

Dolores remembers Dolly playing "Coat of Many Colors" for her, a song she had not recorded yet. It was probably too personal a song, being torn from a nightmarish childhood memory of persecution at the hands of other children. She had written it on the road, scribbling the lyrics on dry-cleaning tickets that she had torn from some of Porter's suit bags. Porter later had the tickets framed. Dolly composed the song on her classical guitar, Ann Warden remembers, the hand-painted one that Porter had given her. It is on display at Dollywood today. A portion of the lyric appeared in a 1969 interview in *Country Song Roundup*; it is rare that a song would trickle into print ahead of its recorded version.

Porter's secretary, Joan, remembers that Dolly would write her lyrics on anything at hand, like an old piece of brown paper bag, and bring them to her for typing. Dolly used to confide her dreams to Joan, who likens Dolly's later career to reading a book that she had watched being written. "Everything that Dolly has done has been like turning a page—to see what she said in conversation to me just coming true. She said she wanted her own TV show. And going to Hollywood is another example."

Shirley Jorjorian, who worked at Owepar in 1972–73, remembers Dolly coming in one day with *twelve* songs she'd written the night before and wanting the lyrics typed, so she could immediately demo them at their studio.

And Porter was more and more putting Dolly's career ahead of his own, except that in a sense Dolly's career *was* his own. Both of them were reaping as much as possible from each other. Porter recaptured for me his first conversations with Dolly and her husband:

> "Dolly, I don't want to tie you up for life, but I want to have you with my show for enough years so I will have a building time, to get you to a point where I can maybe make myself some money from you being a part of my show. Because right now, you're not worth a penny to me, I am the complete draw—but what I want to do is build your name to where you contribute to my package and you will be a vital cog in it and you'll pull money through the box office and that's how I'll make money off you."
>
> And she said, "I can guarantee I will stay with you as long as you want me, or let's say, five years, because I would want to do that.

I hope to become a star by then." I said, "Well, that's great thinking and that's exactly what *should* happen."

Throughout the Dolly years and for many years to come, Porter had his own chart records, a fact too often obscured by all the Dolly-dazzle. His next hit after "The Carroll County Accident" was "Big Wind," and it went almost as high, reaching number three in 1969. It's the harrowing story of a hurricane assaulting a farm. The terror turns to horror as the boy's father is killed by the wind. This senseless, impersonal taking of life strikes a new note in Porter's music, reflecting perhaps the mood of 1969. The My Lai massacre had occurred the previous year; that January, floods and mudslides had killed more than one hundred people in southern California. In May, the rock band Creedence Clearwater Revival had had a similar hit with "Bad Moon Rising," about apocalyptic earthquakes, storms, and hurricanes. Now in the summer of 1969, "Big Wind" was on the charts at the same time place names like Chappaquidick, Woodstock, and Rodeo Drive (home of Sharon Tate) were in the national consciousness.

That winter "When You're Hot, You're Hot" reached number twenty-one. It was another Curly Putman song, and it definitely fit the cold weather conditions: there's ice on the woman's lips, and cold wind blows through the marital bedroom.

The Carroll County Accident album was released in February 1969. On the cover Porter has a mean, somewhat crazed expression, and rivulets of sweat furrow his face. He looks as if he's been given some bad news and is about to send some similar tidings to someone in retaliation. On the front of each shoulder of his blue Nudie suit is a red and yellow wagon wheel, circled by rhinestones, and they look like flying saucers with their landing lights on. On the back cover, Porter is slumping with his head down in desolation. Not all the rhinestones in North Hollywood can cheer up this fellow.

The album has peppy numbers like "Rocky Top" by Boudleaux and Felice Bryant and "King of the Cannon County Hills," by Louis M. ("Grandpa") Jones, both of which extol the virtues of moonshine whiskey. In the former, "revenooers" mysteriously disappear; in the latter, hippies with their LSD and pills are condemned. Dolly's "I Live So Fast and Hard" is a picaresque, rambling, rounder type of song, which shows she can write from the male point of view on demand. It displays her graphic eye for detail, by having the narrator sleep in a cardboard box for a crib when he's a baby. Then he's orphaned and picks up more education riding boxcars and sitting in jail. "Black Jack's Bar" by Jimmy Driftwood is a bouncy tavern number, brightened by a sawing fiddle. Its lyric tells what happens to a country singer who messes with another man's wife: the husband comes at him with a knife right there in the beer joint, and the

Right: *Truly, the right combination, 1974* [PHOTO BY LEE LEVERETT]. Below: *Tennessee State Prison, Nashville, 1968. Out-take photo for* Songs of the Prisoner *album cover* [COURTESY PORTER WAGONER ENTERPRISES].

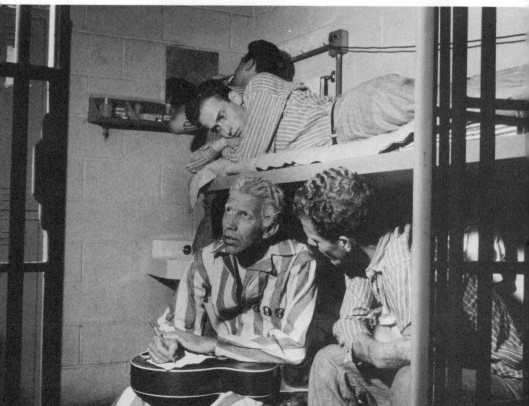

hero clubs him to death with his guitar. Now he's in a prison cell, still playing his guitar and vowing, once he gets out, to slow down a little. And "Banks of the Ohio" is one of Porter's most disturbingly mournful performances. The girl will not marry the narrator, so he plunges a knife into her; her dying words haunt him still. The song was popular with coffeehouse folk singers.

Porter's *Country Feeling* album was a Camden reissue of old material, with Si Siman writing the notes. But the *Me and My Boys* album, issued in August 1969, was an affectionate tribute to the Wagonmasters and Speck. It opens with a recitation, Porter giving each of them a stanza of nostalgic praise, remembering that when Speck joined, the crowds were small and sometimes didn't laugh, that when Buck joined, Porter warned him the money wouldn't be much at first. Little Jack Little was recognized, having rejoined the band around Christmas of 1968, this time as a drummer. (Amusingly, Jack's picture is transposed with George McCormick's on the album's back cover.) One of the arresting cuts on the album is "House of Shame" written by Dolly, in which a mailman visits a nursing home, appalled at how young people put away their parents in such institutions, and how some of the old people in them have never even seen their grandchildren.

One Friday night in 1968 some visitors from California caught a taping of "The Porter Wagoner Show." The portion was being filmed onstage at the Ryman before a regular Opry show. Upstairs in the balcony was Irby Mandrell, ex-California music store proprietor and leader of the Mandrell Family Band, which included his daughter Barbara. Barbara had played steel guitar as a teenager; she was the "Sweetheart of Steel" in Las Vegas. But the Mandrells had closed down their band, and Irby was planning on going into house construction. They were staying in the Dickerson Road Trailer Park next to Buck Trent.

Barbara was struck by Porter's singing partner, Dolly Parton, whose peppy personality inspired her and whose voice reminded her of a fiddle. Dolly was also a guest on the Opry that night. As Barbara acknowledged for the first time publicly in her autobiography, *Get to the Heart: My Story*, it was Dolly's presence that night that goaded her back into the business. She turned to her father and whispered she wanted to start singing again and wanted him to manage her. By 1980 Barbara Mandrell was the Country Music Association's Entertainer of the Year.

Porter and Dolly were onstage at the Ryman on October 18, 1968, for the second annual CMA awards show. It was videotaped for later airing on NBC network television. Porter, sporting a deep suntan and a tuxedo, and Dolly, wearing a formal gown with a petite purse on her wrist, won Vocal Group of the Year. Next to Porter stood Jeannie C.

Riley, who won Single of the Year for her rendition of the very liberated "Harper Valley P.T.A." Jeannie was also wearing a flowing formal dress—one that had been hacked off at the upper thigh level, supplying the network TV audience with plentiful leggy landscape. This mildly shocking miniskirt effect had been the strategy of her maverick producer Shelby Singleton, the better to evoke the miniskirt described in her hit song's lyric (by Tom T. Hall). People thought it was funny, not risqué, which mortified Jeannie in front of tens of millions. She had hoped to come off looking like Marie Antoinette instead of a "Nashville ostrich."

Not in evidence that evening was Dolly's husband, Carl T. Dean. His first and last recorded appearance as a Music Row husband had been the previous year at a BMI banquet. Like Ruth Wagoner, his spouse's world was not for him. In a manner of speaking, Carl became almost the Howard Hughes of country music husbands in his imagined cash-flow, eventually, and in his invisibility.

On New Year's Day of 1969, Dolly Parton became the fifty-fourth member of the Grand Ole Opry. When she joined the Opry, "In the Good Old Days (When Times Were Bad)," which she had written, was still on the charts, reaching number twenty-five. It's in the vein of Loretta Lynn's "Coal Miner's Daughter," providing an unflinching catalog of the images of poverty. Some of them include Dolly's mother taking sick with no money to pay the doctor, her father working till his hands are bloody, the children going to bed hungry and waking to find ice on the floor from snow that blew in through the cracks in the wall.

In 1969 Dolly scored four more *Billboard* hits, three of which she wrote. "Daddy," number forty, was a typically unsettling lyric, about a twenty-three-year-old daughter trying to talk her dad out of running off with a girl younger than herself. She reminds him that if Mother looks older, it's from all those years of working for him. "My Blue Ridge Mountain Boy," number forty-five, pines for the boy she left behind, whose heart she broke and who is now married. Her nostalgia has a strong motivation, since she's become a prostitute in New Orleans. Whores are sweet and caring people, because they have been through a lot, Dolly told Cliff Jahr for *Ladies' Home Journal* during her 1982 publicity push for *The Best Little Whorehouse in Texas* film: "They were people with broken dreams who never had a chance in life or were sexually abused or ignored as children."

In 1969 she had two albums, *In the Good Old Days When Times Were Bad* and *My Blue Ridge Mountain Boy*, both of them containing cover versions of other people's hits. But some original songs crept in as well, such as "Fresh Out of Forgiveness" on the first album, a bluesy, fairly pop song with a pretty melody, written by Uncle Bill and Gene Gill and sounding like a leftover from the Monument period. "Till Death Do Us Part" on the second album is one of her most ruthless lyrics. The girl in the song is going to swallow a bottleful of pills tonight, in order to embarrass her husband and his girlfriend. Perhaps they'll place some flowers in her hand when she's laid out in the funeral chapel.

Probably on the strength of "The Carroll County Accident" award from CMA, Porter was interviewed by *Country Song Roundup* for the February 1969 issue. He said the television show was in eighty-six markets and that 1969 would be the program's ninth season. He personally vouched for Chattanooga's products because he'd been through the laboratories, yet he had turned down some beer and tobacco endorsement offers because he felt it would hurt his image. He also said he had turned down a chance to audition for a network TV show, that he preferred syndicated TV since it allowed him to tour and keep six-to-eight weeks ahead with his TV tapings. His whole show was aimed at the average working person. "I have products to sell that you can't sell to the upper class. They buy everything wholesale; I don't try to do anything for the uptown people."

He held forth on some of his peers. "I think my biggest gripe is people who just don't do good shows. I can't see why anyone would take a business that has been good to them and abuse it. I mean by doing bad shows, going out on the road and getting drunk . . . Fans spend their hard-earned dollars to buy a ticket to see them, and they see nothing but a drunk on stage!"

Porter also said that he had been overbooked to reward promoters who'd made money off the show before and wanted him back. It was hard to say no, sometimes. On March 23, 1969, *The Tennessean* reported: "Porter Wagoner Leaves Hospital," adding that he had just been released after treatment for nervous exhaustion. He went home to rest for a week. In 1970 Porter told Jack Hurst of *The Tennessean* that he had been hospitalized three times. In 1971 Paul Soelberg would make that "several times—because of complete exhaustion and he was placed under strict doctor's orders for absolute rest." Soelberg judged that no human being could shoulder Porter's "relentless workload all the time."

Yet Dolores Smiley could not get Porter to raise his price. He would say, "Well, I'm making good money, and the boys are making good money, and the promoters are making good money, and we're all happy, and there's no sense in charging any more." She still marvels at this: "He's the only artist in my life *bar none* that was caring about the fact that the promoter needed to make money." Dolores has been a talent agent for more than twenty years. "He didn't care if the promoter was getting rich, if he got the money he was promised." She watched other entertainers come along and double their price, but Porter wouldn't.

After a year or so of prodding, Dolores finally got Porter to raise his price about a thousand dollars per show.

✻   ✻   ✻

In the meantime Porter, as well as Dolly, was still being beaten on the radio by the hotter act of Porter Wagoner and Dolly Parton.

Their duet "Yours, Love" by Harlan Howard charted in March 1969, the month he was in the hospital again, and reached number nine. It's an avowal of undying love and, except for the trading-off of lines, is a pretty pop song. In the same mood is "Always, Always," written by Joyce McCord, which reached number sixteen and was driven along by an insistent beat.

The same kind of rhythm propelled "Just Someone I Used to Know" up the charts to number sixteen that fall. It was written by "Cowboy" Jack Clement, a graduate of Sam Phillips's Sun Records in Memphis, where he had produced and written for Johnny Cash. John Lennon once said that *just* was a filler word in songwriting, but it works here: when asked to identify the photograph that each of them carries, they both say "just someone I used to know." It opens with horns, recalling their use in the Johnny Cash–June Carter hit "Ring of Fire" and, earlier, the 1962 pop hit "Lonely Bull" by Herb Alpert & the Tijuana Brass. Porter told Craig Baguley of *Country Music People* in 1989, "It was my idea to use horns on that duet. Chet fell out of his chair and said, 'You're crazy, trying to take horns and put them in country music.'"

Mid October had become Country Music Week in Nashville, with the disc jockey convention by now synchronized with the CMA awards show. Once again in 1969, it was telecast on network TV, and once again Porter and Dolly were nominated for Vocal Group of the Year, but they lost to Johnny Cash and June Carter. Porter had the consolation of "The Carroll County Accident" winning Song of the Year. Dolly netted a Female Vocalist nomination and, for the third straight year, the Wagonmasters were nominated for Instrumental Group of the Year, losing as they would the next four years in a row to Danny Davis and the Nashville Brass. *Music City News* ran a photo of Porter with his arm around Dolly and the caption: "RCA's favorite duet dressed in high fashion. Porter Wagoner in his pink ruffled shirt and Dolly Parton in her white crepe smock and rhinestone full-length gown."

On March 24, 1969, RCA contracted with Porter Wagoner to co-produce with RCA, meaning Bob Ferguson, all sessions on Dolly Parton. It would be several years before Porter would begin receiving credit on the album covers.

It was also in 1969 that Mel Tillis learned that he could stutter on television and be paid for it.

23

MEL TILLIS SPEAKS WITHOUT HESITATION

I think Mel Tillis is a great entertainer
because he picked up a lot of habits from me.

—Porter Wagoner, dust wrapper
of *Stutterin' Boy* by Mel Tillis
with Walter Wager (1984)

Before Mel joined Porter's show, they were already fishing buddies. In his autobiography Mel claims "I taught him how to fish, as a matter of fact." He also says Porter grew jealous over his ability to win football bets. Porter says he cannot remember betting on football. Both agree, however, that when it came to drinking, Mel was more practiced, and the best Porter could manage was a half-hearted attempt at a beer or a glass of wine now and then, mostly then.

Porter often tells the story of Red Sovine and Stonewall Jackson driving to a ball game in Atlanta. In Porter's version, he and the tongue-tied Mel are along:

> Red was driving, and we were all drinkin' beer and throwin' our arms and laughin' and carryin' on. And I was thinking, if some patrolman was to see us, they'd probably lock our ass up, they'd think we're all drunk. I hadn't much more than had that thought, when I seen lights flashing behind us. Red pulled over, and this Georgia state patrolman walked up looking more like Barney Fife [of "Mayberry"] than anyone I've seen. He had that kind of strut, he hit his gun a couple-three times to make sure it was still in the holster and everything.
>
> Well, Red Sovine's real name was Woodrow Wilson Sovine. So the cop asked, "What's your name?" Red said, "Woodrow Wilson." He looked into the back seat and said, "I suppose *you're* George Washington." And Stonewall said, "No, I'm Stonewall Jackson." The patrolman didn't say any more, except "Follow me." Mel's looking over the seat, waving his hands, and after about a mile, he manages to say "We're in *trouble*."
>
> Well, the patrolman took us to the courthouse in Calhoun, Georgia. And this other patrolman sees us, and waves and says, "Porter Wagoner!" Well, I've been introduced by some important

people, but I was never so proud to hear my name in my life. The first patrolman went over and said, "What the hell's going on?" The other one told him we were just some country music singers from Nashville and it would be a waste of paperwork to hold us. The first patrolman said, "Well, I didn't know who they was, they looked like they were crazy coming up the interstate waving their arms."

So they let us go, and nobody said a thing for about ten miles. Then Mel said to me, "Hoss, you're *powerful*."*

Mel Tillis gave his interview at Opryland, sitting in a chair in a trailer owned by The Nashville Network. He was being touched up by the make-up ladies prior to a TV taping. He spoke almost as if rehearsed, as if he'd planned out what to say, and spoke without his stutter, though the muscles of his neck seemed to involuntarily tighten up.

Mel reminisced about seeing Porter live at the Ozark Jubilee when he was in the Air Force. Then he moved to Nashville and began meeting Porter backstage at the Opry. "He was getting bigger and bigger. We got to be good friends when he separated from his wife." Mel got Porter fishing, and Porter became the better fisherman. Mel deplored Porter's dismal little apartment and told him he was too big a star to live there, so Porter moved into apartment 92 at the Versailles Apartments at 3000 Hillsboro Road.

Porter and Mel did their share of fishing at Center Hill Lake with the occasional help of an "old yeller" pill, as Porter recollected in the Tootsie's portion of the "Dolly" TV taping, in a passage that was cut.

According to Porter, one night out at the lake Mel believed that the end of the world was nigh. He told me that Mel is just about fearless, except when it comes to facing darkness. Mel had been nervously counting the falling stars and told Porter there had been six, so far. Porter couldn't have cared less. When it got up to nine falling stars, Mel was plenty spooked and kept prodding Porter, who said, "Hell, I ain't paid no attention to it, I'm fishin'. I didn't come up here to see the weather and count how many stars have fallen."

Then the sky began lighting up like Roman candles, and Mel really got rattled. Porter told me that "way back on the eastern coast, they were doing some kind of experimental stuff, they were shooting in the atmosphere. Well, Mel came unglued. He started throwing stuff out of the boat, his beer and his cigarettes. I said, 'What the hell you doin'?' He said, 'Don't cuss, Chief, *please*, this is the End of Time.' I said, 'No, it ain't no such thing.' And he said, 'Don't cuss, please, we're already in

*This story has different versions, and a rotating cast of characters, though without Stonewall Jackson the story doesn't function. Stonewall maintains an open-door policy on the yarn—so long as he stays in it, he doesn't care who else gets in ("If Porter had a story this good, I'd want to be in it myself").

enough trouble. Don't cuss no more.' I said, 'Hell, I'm not cussin'.' And he said, 'Don't say *hell. This is it!'"

Porter says Mel's chin was trembling so that they headed back to the dock. They noticed an empty boat of one of their friends, Barefoot Jerry, and Porter yelled out his name, and Jerry shouted back, "This is the End of Time, you know." "Well, that clinched it with Mel. When we got back to the dock, he got in his car, and he threw gravel all over the parking lot, heading back to Nashville."

When Porter got home, he called a television station and learned the army (or air force) had been doing some kind of testing. Next morning he called Mel, and had his wife wake him up. "This is the End of Time, my boy" Porter chortled. "What the hell are you still doing here?"*

Mel had already put together a little three-piece band. Once when Porter and he were up at the lake fishing, Porter said, "Tillie, my boy, I'm going to make you a star."

"What do you mean?"

"I'm going to add you to my TV show."

Porter told Alanna Nash in 1981 that he began encouraging Mel to talk onstage (Minnie Pearl also suggested this), since he usually rushed from one song to the next, to avoid stuttering. "Mel, people would love to hear you talk; they won't be making fun of you, they'll be laughing *with* you." Mel began talking. "He seen how they went along with him. It was a natural thing for him to do, it became part of his act." Porter sometimes told audiences that Cardui had cured Mel's stuttering.

Porter cut his share of Mel Tillis songs over the years, but with Dolly on the payroll, Mel hadn't much chance. "I was in competition with Dolly as a songwriter. I had written over six hundred songs before Dolly ever picked up a pencil. I'd pitch him a song, and she'd pitch him three. She wanted him to do her songs, and I wanted him to do my songs, and you know who won. Well, I got bigger, and I gotta thank Porter. When he said he would make me a star, he did it. I don't know if he regretted it or not, but our friendship went to hell."

A point of contention was their fleeting joint ownership of a music publishing company, Sawgrass, its name reflecting Mel's Florida origins. Here's Mel's recollection:

> I had started a publishing company named Sawgrass, and I said we are going to be partners; and I sold him part of it for $5,000. We had a house boat together. I think he kept the house boat, and

*Mel says this happened to himself and the late Shorty Lavender, fiddler and booking agent, not to him and Porter.

somehow he charged me $25,000 to get my half of the publishing company back which I sold last year for $4.5 million. It was all childish. We are buddies, and I wouldn't do anything to hurt him. He's quite a guy, I love him to death, we had our misunderstandings.

And then there's Porter's version:

> He called me to fund the publishing company and I put $25,000 into it to begin with, we'd be half-owners. I go down the first week. He said he needed to rent an office and had the whole damn bottom of a building. Five rooms. We don't even have a song recorded or nothin'—he has three people on the payroll, two song pluggers and a secretary. We have no income at all. I said, "Mel, what the hell are you doin', man? You've got to crawl before you can walk. You're trying to start with a huge front and we don't have a damn cent income. That won't work, man." Well, anyway he got real upset about that and said, "I'll buy your part of the damn company out."

Porter recalled it was a "dead-end street," that the partnership had to be dissolved in its infancy, and that Mel said, "Of all the people I thought would take advantage of me, you're the last one. We're buddies and all this shit, and now you want to rip me off." Mel wanted to buy back his share. Porter said that even though Mel was an asshole, he would gladly co-sign a note for him, since Mel lacked the money.*

The Tillis–Wagoner friendship was further taxed by a fight at Linebaugh's restaurant on lower Broadway. Tom T. Hall describes a colorful, chair-swinging disagreement at Linebaugh's in his autobiographical *Storyteller's Nashville*, at which he was a spectator, albeit a drunk one. But the Friday night brawl Mel reports in his autobiography is probably a different one, with him also claiming to be only a spectator after a little tanking up across the street at Tootsie's. Mel took a stray punch to his throat, while evading arrest by scooting under a table with a friend. He nervously called Porter. Porter recalls the conversation:

> He called me the next morning, 'cause I told him if he ever got in trouble I had a clean show and I didn't want any of my people to be in any of that kind of activity. He said "They had a fight at Linebaugh's, I guess that means I'm fired," and I said, "That certainly does." He said, "There's no point in us not being friends," and I said "Of course not, I love you like a brother but I don't want you being part of my show and you fighting at Linebaugh's at 2 o'clock in the morning."

*Mel completely disputes Porter's version and says he got a $25,000 advance from BMI to back his share.

❊   ❊   ❊

Mel could not do the Opry that Saturday night because for the next three days he could only whisper, the result of the punch in the throat. Sunday morning he went over to the Versailles to face Porter. He recalls:

> I know I got fired at his apartment. He was sitting there in his housecoat eating crackers and milk. And he had a pistol on the table. I said, "You don't need that damned pistol." He said, "You're not the kind of image I want to project on our television show. You went down to Linebaugh's and got drunk and got in a fight." I said, ". . . well, it's your show."*

There remained the issue of the coming tour. Porter said Mel wasn't going. Mel said he was, since his name had been advertised. Well, Porter countered, he wouldn't be permitted to use the Wagonmasters as back-up. Fine, he would put together his own band. Mel remembers getting big applause; they went over well. Soon he was attracting the attention of Glen Campbell, getting onto his "Goodtime Hour" network TV show for great national exposure. So by kicking Mel Tillis off his show, Porter helped kick off his career as an independent act, for which Mel has always been grateful.

But he contracted an immediate allergy to rhinestone suits ("they were going out of style, anyway") and donated his to that future "Mysterious Rhinestone Cowboy," David Allan Coe.

Mel uses the adjective *childish* to describe his and Porter's tensions in 1969, recalling nostalgically, "We've had so many good times together. But I can't tell you the juicy stuff."

The year he left Porter, Mel had already won eighteen BMI awards, having had more than four hundred songs recorded. In 1976 he was voted CMA's Entertainer of the Year, and by 1988 he had charted seventy-six country hit records himself.

At the end of our interview, I told Mel he did not seem to stutter, and he said, "I do stutter, when they turn the camera on me."

---

*Porter says he didn't leave his pistol on the table.

24

TENNESSEE THURSDAY NIGHT

Porter has been at it so long,
everybody in the business
has touched his life.

—Speck Rhodes, interview,
June 19, 1989

I used to kid him about his hometown,
West Plains. I used to say it's no bigger
than Grinder's Switch. We traveled together,
and he's a wonderful storyteller.

—Minnie Pearl, interview, May 17, 1989

"We actually just played poker for fun
and excitement. I really enjoyed that because
there was no hard feelings of any sort. There was
enough stories 'bout the poker games
that would fill a book.

—Porter, interview,
December 13, 1989

Porter has a bottomless fund of stories about the people he has worked with, fished, golfed, and played poker with. And vice versa. The most frequently heard remark while researching this book was, "I could tell you a lot, but nothing you could put in your book." The runner-up was, "Now don't you tell Porter I said that," and a close third was, "Is Porter going to read what you write?"

One of his fondest friends and poker partners was Tex Ritter. Tex was a veteran of more than fifty Western movies, was the singing voice on the *High Noon* soundtrack, and his "Town Hall Party" on network radio and local TV out of Los Angeles (1951–61) was a forerunner to "The

Porter Wagoner Show." Tex moved to Nashville, became president of the CMA, and, more than anyone else, spearheaded the drive to set up the Country Music Hall of Fame.

Porter remembers a tour with Tex when they went to New Jersey. Somebody picked them up in a van, and as they were driving along, Tex asked what kind of backup band was going to be provided. Their host began describing their polka band. "We play all kinds of music, and we play it rather well. We have a *great* accordionist, we have a *great* guitar player, a *great* drummer—" Tex interrupted, "Wait a minute, my boy. There are no great accordionists!"

On November 2, 1973, Tex Ritter was down at the county jail to bail out a band member being held for failure to pay child support when he was stricken by a fatal heart attack. Rushed to Baptist Hospital, he died on arrival.

One of country music's most beloved comics was David ("Stringbean") Akeman, also an accomplished banjoist, a frequent guest on Porter's TV show, and his staunch fishing pal. If they were scheduled to fish, String might call Porter at seven in the morning and pretend *he* was Porter. "String, I don't believe we can go. It's a little too windy and a little too cold this morning. I will check with you later, String," as Porter barely realized what he was hearing.

Porter is proud that String used to prefer riding by car with him ("Porter Wagoner is the safest driver in the world. I'd rather drive with him than anyone") and prouder that String would say, "If all the people were like you, we could throw our locks away."

Stringbean called everyone "Chief."

Once they were scheduled to play at a big picnic at a Catholic monastery in Kentucky. When they arrived, a priest walked up and said, "Are you Mr. Wagoner?" "Yes." "Is Mister Bean with you?" Stringbean rolled down the window, and the priest said, "Mr. Bean, if you're in doubt about any of your material you're going to use—any smutty material or anything that's the least bit shady—please refrain from using it here." String said, "Okay, Chief."

Right after a performance at the Opry in 1973, Stringbean and his wife, Estelle, were murdered by two burglars. Porter and Dolly were among the mourners at the funeral.

The late Marty Robbins was one of Porter's closer pals. He particularly liked one of Porter's songs from the fifties, "Tricks of the Trade," which he loved to accompany with dobro or steel guitar. They played "Tricks of the Trade" together "hundreds of times," usually in the dressing room. In the seventies, when Porter owned Fireside studio with Dolly, Marty often came down, and Porter still has tapes of the two of them singing and jamming.

*   *   *

Porter was often amused by the Raney Family, who performed over WCKY out of Cincinnati, Ohio. He especially thought the name *Zyndell* was funny (Wayne Raney's son), and also how Wayne would say, "Howdy, howdy, howdy" to his partner Lonnie Glosson, who would respond in exactly the same voice, "Howdy, howdy, howdy." (At least when Porter does it the howdies are the same.) Porter tells how he went to work some schoolhouses with Wayne, and how he went back to his house, where he had a little studio. "He'd go into the next room where the equipment was, and say, 'Now I'm going to knock on the wall three times, and then *start!*' Then he came running through the door and started playing the harmonica with us!"

No one seems closer to Porter, at least on television, than "Nashville Now" host Ralph Emery. Sometimes Porter will even host Ralph's show. Ralph has the demeanor and attire of a high school science teacher who might be coaching basketball on the side. His rather staid manner invites respect for country music and adds a certain continuity—more than three decades' worth—and he makes the perfect foil for guests who may be wearing cowboy hats, rhinestones, headbands, or just an expectant smile.

Ralph came to Nashville in October 1957 and in November got a disc jockey job at WSM. He remembers meeting Porter at a dance staged by Roulette Records. "There was an idiot dancing out there with a full drink on his head, and, needless to say, it fell off and crashed on the floor."

Porter says Ralph helped break his hit "I Thought I Heard You Call My Name" that very month (November 1957). It was Ralph who nicknamed Porter "The Thin Man from West Plains," and for every country singer in town, Ralph's "Opry Star Spotlight" all-night disc jockey show was a place to drop by. Ralph remembers Porter and Doyle Wilburn coming by, lonely and needing a place to crash, in no condition for an interview (pills and booze, respectively). And Ralph remembers that when he would squeeze Norma Jean affectionately, she would say, "Porter wouldn't like that . . ."

Ralph watched Porter mature as a television personality. "I think he learned from his tapes and learned by his mistakes, as we all do. And he polished his act as we all do. The secret to winning on television is credibility. If people don't think you're lying to them, they'll believe you." Ralph laments that "there was a time when I couldn't get him to do my radio show. Maybe he thought he was too big for it. I know they were busy, but I could get Dolly. Porter *was* hard to deal with when he hit the top."

Ralph says, "It's too bad Dolly has big boobs" because it distracts you from her singing and especially her songwriting talent." Once Ralph's wife pinned some flowers on Dolly and she said, "Don't burst my balloon." Of the intense Porter–Dolly period, Ralph says, "I think he was a very hard-driving man about their careers. I think there were no committees. Porter ruled until the day Dolly felt like she could have more creative control of her career . . ." I told Ralph that Porter's band members call him "The Chief," and Ralph said, "I can see why."

Ralph tells how Porter once worked a show in Las Vegas with some other country acts, and on the last night as they were lined up for the finale, Porter said, "Folks, I can't speak for all these entertainers up here on stage, but I can tell you one thing. I'll *never* come back to Las Vegas." Ralph says they "literally worked his butt off; he worked more shows in that one week than he ever had in his life."

Porter says when they were traveling they would listen to the Opry on the radio, especially the second set. They called this "the drunk set," since by the second hour the performers had made at least one visit out the back door and down the alley to Tootsie's Orchid Lounge. One of the sponsors was Newport cigarettes, and, coincidentally, Roy Acuff's nickname for Porter was "Port." The Newport advertisement had just come on, and Roy had heard at least the last syllable, "-port," and apparently thought Porter was around someplace. Over the radio Porter could hear Roy asking around for "Port? Port? He's here somewhere . . ." Yet they were several states away, driving down the highway.

Porter used to play cards in the meat market in West Plains during slack times when the boss was gone. And Bob Tubert remembers back in Springfield how they'd play cards down in the furnace room at KWTO, and "the higher-ups upstairs didn't know there were card games going on downstairs." Bob says Porter is good with numbers, "an incredible gambler" who plays his cards intelligently, not emotionally.

Goober Buchanan says Porter told him he had poker winnings that "ran into five figures every year." Once they were rooming together on the road, and Porter said he'd been out all night. "What's-his-name wants to give me *all* his money. We're going to have a game." Next morning Porter came in and said, "He couldn't win at cards so we played craps. And I broke him at craps—he owes me about $1,500."

A passing acquaintance of Porter's in the sixties was David Moran, a liquor store owner today, who back then worked in a store for a man named Mike. Mike was a gambler and would bet on every imaginable sporting event, be it college, amateur, or professional. Porter and Mike were good gambling buddies, and Porter would drop by the store and when Dolly wasn't with him would sometimes chat with David. "I remember him telling about a time he tried Mary Jane [pot] out in L.A. with Roger Miller. He did not like it." On Thursday nights Porter, Mike, booking agent Lucky Moeller, guitarist Grady Martin, and others would meet at a specially rented apartment and play poker. Says David, "If he played with Mike—which he did—it was for some *good* money. Mike did not play cheap. He was a high roller, basically. He played at the thousands level, so you can go from there . . ."

Another of Porter's poker pals was Ernest Tubb, another was Jim Denny, whom Ernest had once wanted to kill or at least scare. Ernest fired three shots from his .357 Magnum in the lobby of the Life and Casualty building after having threatened over the phone he was going to kill someone. Jim Denny stayed upstairs, prudently, while Ernest was taken to jail for a three-hour cool down.

Porter remembers playing poker with Floyd Cramer, the Wilburn Brothers, Ernest, and Grady Martin in the last months of Jim Denny's life. Jim was wasting from cancer, and his wife, Dollie, said, "Why don't you get a game together and come out to our house and play instead of renting a room downtown?" Porter figured this might bring Ernest and Jim back together. He called Jim, asked if he'd mind if he brought Ernest Tubb. "Hell, no. I'd like to win some of his money, in fact." So Porter checked with Ernest, who had the same reaction. "I'd like to win some of his damned money, in fact!" So for several weeks they would play deep into the night until Dollie made them quit.

Lester Flatt, famous bluegrass partner of Earl Scruggs, was another devotée of poker. Lester played his cards close, so when *he* bet, Porter could guess he had a good hand. Porter was one of the few who could beat Lester, because he watched how he played, though admittedly, Lester had beaten Porter often. "He did not know how *I* played, because I played sporadic and different, in different situations," he claims.

One night there was a big game, and pretty soon everyone had dropped out but Porter and Lester. Porter raised him, and Lester raised him back, so Porter knew he wasn't bluffing. "I knew he had a monstrous hand. But I had a big hand as well, and if you've got to call, you've got to call. So I said, 'Well, I know you got me beat probably, but I just got to call. I only got two pair.' And he said, 'Hell, I got aces full.' He had three aces. He reached out to get the money, and I said, 'Whoa, hold it. My two pair . . . are both nines!' I had four nines. He just, well, like he never got over it. It was like someone had just let the air out of him completely."

Lester told Porter, "I won't forget this as long as I live." Every time he'd meet Porter backstage at the Opry, he would just say *"Two Pair!"*

The times and many of the people are gone now. "But our poker playing days, with Ernest and Jim Denny and all them, was really very, very wonderful days. It wasn't the fact of winning or losing, it was the fact of the camaraderie that went on in the games. And things you could talk about up till the next week."

25

"TWO SIDES TO EVERY STORY"

Dolly is like a scientist with her writing.
She is one of the most creative people
I have ever met—and I've met some great ones,
from Hank Williams on.

—Porter, to Paul Soelberg,
"An Indepth Look at Dolly Parton,"
Country Song Roundup (November 1971)

Our relationship was very involved,
but was not exactly as some people
have presented it to be—it might have been
more in some ways and less in others,
but at any rate it was certainly a serious
time in my life, and I think I learned
enough in that seven-year period
to make it in the rest of my career
and in the rest of my life.

—Dolly, interview,
July 3, 1990

In January 1970 Porter's *You Got-ta Have a License* album appeared, with a cover picture of Porter in winter fishing gear, in his boat, hauling a catch of bass out of the water.

The title song went to number forty-one that March. Written by Tommy Collins, it has a happy Cajun beat and Cajun dialect. In the lyric, first a game warden points out the virtues of a fishing license, then a highway patrolman makes the same point about the necessity for a driver's license, then a girl holds out for a marriage license.

Another uptempo song on the album is "Forty Miles from Poplar Bluff" by Frank Dycus and Larry Kingston, the Ozarks classic that Porter still performs, telling how, even in the wintertime, poor folks will survive. Just as long as Daddy has his tobacco and Granny, her snuff.

Perhaps reflecting the season of its release, the album has a mostly wintery mood, with songs like the frigid "When You're Hot, You're Hot." Two especially chilly numbers were written by Dolly. "Roses Out of

Season" is about as frosty as Dolly gets. It's a recitation: a bereaved husband has built his late wife a snowman by her graveside. He stands there, talking by her grave, filling her in on all the latest news. He has a better job, and the pictures from last summer's vacation have finally been developed. Though it's hard to find roses this time of year, he lays some on her grave. He hopes she'll find a way to make him join her. (Dolly told Chet Flippo in *Rolling Stone* that she likes to write songs in cemeteries, they're so quiet and "people are *dying* to get into 'em.") Dolly's "Fairchild" is about a wayward wife. The husband is driving with her in his car, and if she doesn't promise to stay with him, the newspapers will report how they both died in a car wreck!

Then Dolly's aunt Dorothy Jo Hope supplies a Smoky Mountain tragedy, "A Special Prayer Request." A little girl is praying for God to help her mother stop drinking. Daddy has run off. Its companion piece on the record is "A Little Boy's Prayer," written by Jim Owen, another heart-wrenching recitation. A small boy is praying about his Daddy; the mother has just died, and the son fears his father may commit suicide. Porter's tremulous voice sounds like a little boy's or, rather, like the hurt little boy that dwells inside of all big-egoed men. The song closes happily; father and son will make a go of it, without Mama. Porter's daughter Debra was at the session. "There wasn't a dry eye in the studio when he cut that," she recalls.

Back in 1949 Porter worked in a foundry at the Caterpillar Tractor Company in Peoria, Illinois. Now, in early February 1970, he was back in Peoria, featured in the "Shower of Stars" country music package show. He told a reporter from the company newspaper how, when he originally worked in Peoria, almost no one knew he existed, and now when he walked onstage he would be facing three thousand people. "It made me think how lucky I am. I love this life—each show is a new thrill."

On the seventeenth, "The Porter Wagoner Show" appeared at the annual rodeo in San Antonio, Texas. While in town, Porter, Speck, and Dolly visited Brooke General Hospital, especially four orthopedic wards filled mostly with Vietnam veterans. The hospital's press release said of Porter, "He shook hands with every patient he saw and stopped to talk and sign autographs with most of them." Some fast-moving wheelchair patients were heard to remark, "Well, if we can't get all their autographs, we'll settle for Dolly's."

In the May 1970 issue of *Country Song Roundup* Porter reflected at length on the progress of his career. He was glad it had started slowly and had built slowly, because that way "you keep trying harder all the time—it keeps being a big thrill to you." He admitted it had been easier

On stage at the Ryman Auditorium [COURTESY PORTER WAGONER ENTER-PRISES].

when he started, that today a recording artist was expected to be an overnight sensation. If you didn't have a hit record in a year or so, the record company dropped you. Porter was grateful for RCA's patience with him in the fifties and for the "hundreds and hundreds" of people who had helped him over the years.

He said they were now doing seventy-eight TV shows a year, fifty-two of them open-ended (without commercials), and twenty-six with commercials. Some of the shows were done twice—for two markets—indicating how immense his TV workload was. He said his guests were picked by Jane Dowden and Don Warden, sparing him having to say no to a friend or colleague.

In March 1970 Dolly's *The Fairest of Them All* album appeared, with Dolly as a fairy princess admiring herself in the mirror on the cover.

But the first words you hear on the album, "In this mental institution," command your attention in a different way. The song, "Daddy, Come and Get Me," by Dolly, is about a woman who has been committed by her husband who is running around with another woman. The wife is still "crazy" over him but with a broken heart, not a broken mind. She's asking her father to come and get her out of the insane asylum. It would go to number forty as a single.

Dolly wrote or co-wrote nine of the songs on the album, and Bill Owens wrote the tenth. Two of them are typical, ethereal, fluttery Dolly, chasing butterflies and running like a child. In "Just the Way I Am" she may be smiling when you think she should frown; in "But You Once Loved Me Then" the fairyland meadows are forlorn since her lover has left her.

In "Down from Dover," the boy is supposed to come back—"down from Dover"—but it becomes increasingly clear that he's not going to keep his appointment. The girl is pregnant, and, when her baby is born dead, she senses she'll never see the fellow again. With a suitable folk chord progression, it's one of many Dolly Parton songs that might be mistaken for an old English or Scottish ballad. Skeeter Davis says "Down from Dover" is her favorite Dolly song; in 1972 she released probably the first all-Dolly album by another artist, *Skeeter Sings Dolly*.

Another disquieting lyric on the album, even for Dolly, is "Chas." It's narrated by a servant who keeps house for a man named Chas and takes care of his crippled wife and raises their children. In her mind she imagines making love to Chas, but her erotic passion remains a frustrating daydream.

Entering the charts in February 1970 was Dolly's song "Tomorrow Is Forever," a duet written for her and Porter. It went to number nine, another reminder that in *Billboard*, at least, the duo was still hotter than either single act.

That same month their album *Porter Wayne and Dolly Rebecca* was released. The front cover is cutesy-quaint, with an old picture of West Plains Porter in coveralls alongside nine-year-old Dolly's class picture from the Caton's Chapel school. She's wearing her patchwork coat that her mother fashioned from a donated box of corduroy scraps. Always emphasizing the positive, Avie Lee had called it a "coat of many colors" after the coat that Jacob gave Joseph in Genesis 37:3. In the next verse Joseph finds his brothers "hated him and could not speak peaceably to him," out of jealousy. Dolly's classmates weren't jealous, only derisive, shouting "Ragtop! Ragtop!" at Dolly, ripping her buttons. They wanted to see what she had on underneath, which was nothing. Dolly still managed a smile for the class picture. Porter kept the picture in his office as an illustration of Dolly's song about the episode, a song that Dolly had still not recorded.

On the back cover of *Porter Wayne and Dolly Rebecca*, the two of them were no longer "dressed to match." Porter was wearing a giant-lapeled, British-looking, eighteenth-century-style uniform, very much Captain Horatio Hornblower or maybe a refugee from Paul Revere and the Raiders. Dolly was wearing a collar as big as Porter's and appeared ready to lift off the ground, very Star Trek-y, as Lola Scobey observed. *Most* Sonny & Cher-ish.

The album introduces the "funny fight" song concept, where vocal harmonies are counterpointed with verbal *dis*harmonies, as Porter and Dolly swap jabs and jests. The song "Run That By Me One More Time," written by Dolly, has the husband accusing the wife of wasting precious family funds on frivolous shopping sprees. And she says he's blowing their money on wine, and she's not going to believe any more of his lies ("I may be crazy but I ain't that dumb").

A sad but uptempo duet on the album was Dolly's "I'm Wasting Your Time and You're Wasting Mine," one of the parade of songs that predicted their inevitable split-up, caustically observing that the ties-that-bind have now become frayed, loose ends.

Dolly contributed a couple of her morbid songs about children. "Silver Sandals" pities a handicapped girl who trades her crutches for silver sandals, the better with which to ascend the golden stairs to heaven. Porter-as-father drips the usual pathos in his recitation. "Mendy Never Sleeps" is an antihippie tract about a teenage girl who goes without sleep thanks (presumably) to amphetamines. Mendy, whose name alliterates with "many friends" and "miniskirts," catches up on her rest eventually, by dying. The melody suggests the Beatles' "Norwegian Wood."

Thomas Wolfe notwithstanding, you *can* go home again. After a two-and-one-half-year hiatus, the second Dolly Parton Day was scheduled for Saturday, April 25, 1970, in Sevierville, but without Porter and the Wagonmasters. Whatever Willadeene and Stella had been hinting at in their pamphlet—rumors and gossip after Dolly Day back in 1967—it seemed strategic to let her now have her "day" separated wholly from "The Porter Wagoner Show." She even brought a different backup band: famous instrumentalist Pete Drake with his "talking" steel guitar and Mavericks band (D. J. Fontana on drums, ex-drummer for Elvis).

The motive for this latest Dolly Day was to raise money for the Sevier County High School Band Booster Club. Dolly had been a drummer in the band, often sneaking in some songwriting during band practice. The motorcycle police escort and limousine convertible gave the procession a presidential look, especially with Dolly perched high atop the back seat, waving to the mobbed spectators like a First Lady. She was wearing a lime green, scooped-neck dress, with a matching hat with a fluted brim. Her father was at the wheel, with Stella alongside, as they drove down Court Avenue. The whole parade was led—naturally—by the marching band. At one point the traffic backed up for two miles.

Twenty-five hundred people packed the Lon C. Burchfiel school gym for a three-hour show that began at 7:30 P.M. Pete Drake and the Mavericks opened the show.

Then Cas Walker came out and introduced his most famous show business discovery. Dolly was wearing an ivory-colored dress with shiny metal studs and drape-like sleeves; and she had her Grammer flat-top guitar. She did standard numbers from Cas's show, like "Tall Man" (which she didn't write), plus songs from her Monument period. She tossed in a recitation, "Bloody Bones," which managed to combine two or three favorite themes at once. She told how she and her siblings would "fight and scratch," a later song title, when crammed five to a bed, likely to be all awash come morning with all the bed wetting. She told how Mama would scare them into controlling themselves better with tales of ol' Rawhead and Bloody Bones, a centuries-old bogeyman from folklore.

And she sang "Coat of Many Colors," a song popular on the TV show that hadn't been released yet. No doubt she played it in open-C tuning. The song is one more 1960s-style old English ballad. The surface of the lyric is naive, with the little girl proudly wearing her patchwork coat to school. Though the other children laugh, she persists in believing that she is really rich because her mother has sewn love into every stitch. The song ends on a happy note, sincere and unforced, but you sense that the jeers of the other kids have gouged the little girl's heart deeper than she admits to herself.

If poems were still collected in anthologies for the public, "Coat of Many Colors" would be a staple of English-speaking verse. In the nineteenth century it would have been a candidate for Palgrave's *Golden Treasury*. It was Dolly's opening number on Sunday night at 8:00 P.M., September 27, 1987, the first show of her ABC "Dolly" television series.

All the while Bob Ferguson, with engineer Bob Pachucki, was taping the program with special equipment brought down from New

York. The final result was an important document of Dolly the entertainer, A *Real Live Dolly* album. Her voice is mountain-nasal on the high notes, but coming down, expands and opens fully, unlike those country singers who remain pinched in the lower register and tend to go flat.

The Sevier County *News-Record* rhapsodized: "Radiant Dolly Parton Came Home April 25 . . . Her Shirley Temple dimples played effortlessly as the Dresden-like Dolly sang number after number in her slightly tremulous soprano voice."

The ruse had worked. This was not Porter's day. Then suddenly Don Howser introduced him as one of Dolly's "surprises," a pretty good practical joke. Porter had been behind the whole thing!

"I kinda feel like the Fugitive. I've been slipping around trying to keep Dolly from seeing me," he said, telling a convoluted story of being lost in the hollers and wilds of Sevier County. Porter just happened to have along his guitar *and* Speck Rhodes. Speck said Dolly was as pretty as his girlfriend Sadie, and he told how Sadie had been complaining lately about all the two-piece bathing suits now in fashion ("and they weren't very big pieces, lemme tell you"). Sadie had begun preaching the virtues of one-piece bathing suits. "I go along with that, Sadie. Which piece do you think they ought to wear? The top or the bottom?"

After some more gags by Speck, Porter told the audience that in his twenty years in country music, he had never known a finer girl than Dolly.

Then they lit into "Run That By Me One More Time" and another "funny fight" song, "Two Sides to Every Story" (written by Dolly and Uncle Bill). The couple in the song hopes everything can be straightened out by just talking, but with so much bickering and interrupting they clearly need a moderator with a gavel. They also sang that other song inspired by the children at Caton's Chapel school, the ones who'd locked Dolly in the coat closet: "Jeannie's Afraid of the Dark."

At the Sevier County High School, Dolly had never been voted Most or Best anything. In fact, one year several of her teachers had objected to her singing and had kept her out of a school program. In a later song, "Appalachian Memories," an obvious tribute to her uncles, she speaks of them hitching their station wagon to a star and heading to the city in search of gold dust. Now after Dolly Parton Day, the school marching band fund was a couple of thousand dollars richer.

After talking to Roy Horton of Peer International in New York, Porter began combing through the catalogue of Jimmie Rodgers's songs that Roy managed. Roy thought someone should record "Mule Skinner Blues (Blue Yodel No. 8)." Roy said, "If that's not a hit, then there never was one." Porter agreed, but thinking to himself that Dolly could do it.

It had never been a hit for a woman—probably *no* female had ever re-corded it.

Dolly's version was her breakthrough record. Porter takes under-standable pride in this, though his recollections trouble him still. He said it was difficult to keep Dolly "in an area where I knew what was going on." This required "complete control," which is why Dolly was successful from the very start, "almost despite herself, because you would not be-lieve—there would be no way of explaining—the frustration that hap-pened. If I hadn't been a strong-willed person, Dolly would have led me off in a dark dingy road."

Porter recalls that she didn't like the idea of doing the song, but he insisted. "Let's put it down anyway, we've got such a good arrangement on it." He also told her that her career needed excitement, and this would "be a great high" and people would start coming to their shows, eager to see that girl who sang "Mule Skinner Blues."

Bob Ferguson had engineer Roy Shockley go out and buy a whip to crack on the record. Mack Magaha did the whistling.

Dolly, according to Porter, said she didn't want to have to yodel for the rest of her life. "Dolly cried. She said, 'If you think anything of me as a person, you won't release that.' I said, 'Dolly, you're asking me to go against something I'm about. I'm about producing hit records. And pro-moting a girl that's nobody to somebody, that their name will be recog-nized when we get there."

In her 1979 lawsuit deposition, Dolly was asked about not want-ing the song released:

> That *I* didn't want [it] to be released? Are you serious? No sir. That *I* didn't want [it] released? We never discussed whether it would come out. We did it on the recommendation of Buck Trent. A woman never had recorded "Mule Skinner Blues." We thought it was great, how fun it was. Having fun with Porter cracking whips.

As the song opens, it definitely sounds as though Dolly's doing some of her own whistling. Then when she holds the syllable *morn* in "Well, good morn-ing, Captain" for at least five seconds, you really know she's in charge. Her declaration, "I'm a lady mule skinner," was irresist-ible for 1970, especially one who can order around the men in her crew, and if they don't like it they can draw their pay and leave.

When Porter finished the final mix, he knew he had a hit. "You see, you can't go against these things. If you know something and it's what you're looking for, you can't go any other way." The paradoxes are multilayered and delightful: Porter cracking a whip figuratively to make Dolly record a song she didn't want to cut (according to him), whose lyric is a women's lib victory, an ex-waitress butting into a man's job where she cracks her own whip, literally. Dolly had been a waitress a year before joining Porter's show.

"Mule Skinner Blues" was Dolly's first Top 10 hit, a Top 5 in fact, entering *Billboard* in July 1970 and reaching number three. RCA noticed it was getting played on progressive rock FM stations, so it issued publicity claiming that Dolly was making inroads in the youth and underground markets. It was number one in *Record World*, and, as Alanna Nash said in her *Dolly* book, "when the record received a Grammy nomination, it was icing on the cake."

The following month, the duet "Daddy Was an Old-Time Preacher Man" hit the charts, going to number seven. Written by Dolly and her aunt, Dorothy Jo Hope, it was based on her grandfather, Rev. Jake Owens, in whose church Dolly got her start singing. As she said in our interview:

> He was the pastor of our church. He's still living now, he's in a nursing home, and he still preaches to everybody in the home. The family goes up all the time—he holds services there, and I go to see him when I go to Sevierville, and he'll preach to me.

The song was on the *Once More* duet album, also issued in August 1970. On the cover they're wearing matching pink shirt and dress, and pink complexions, gold hair, and, even for them, especially winning, matched smiles. The whole effect is strawberry ice cream all a-slosh with honey.

The album featured Dolly's funny-fight masterpiece, "Fight and Scratch," whose lyrics exemplify art's ability to imitate life. She wastes money on wigs, he wastes money on poker games and fishing. When he's angry, his eyes flash with fire, and if she doesn't like it she can leave! The song was a reunion favorite in 1988–89. Also included was Dolly's "Ragged Angel," whose title gives fair warning. The melody is cheery and childlike, almost like a Christmas carol. Porter sings lullaby-smooth way down below Dolly's sobbing soprano. The exquisite twin vocals permit them to get away with the obligatory infanticide. A little girl named Cindy, whose father is not known and whose mother is seldom home, sleeps on a drafty floor in a blanket, hungry most of the time. Her sole companion is a paper doll (the first song Dolly wrote as a child was about her doll). Things pick up for poor Cindy when Dolly whisks her off to heaven.

Porter's "Jim Johnson" entered *Billboard* in September, staying on the charts nine weeks, attaining number forty-one. It was written by Bill Owens, who had supplied the delicate true love tribute, "Thoughtfulness," for the *Once More* duet album. But "Jim Johnson" is Appalachian Gothic at its most intense. Jim marries a poor widow woman with many kids. He drinks up the money that should have bought the children's clothes and shoes. He even makes them drown some kittens, laughing the while. But when he rapes his thirteen-year-old stepdaughter, he definitely needs to be slowed down, so the speaker in the song, her brother, uses the shotgun. He explains that what he killed was not really a man. "Jim Johnson" did well on jukeboxes.

On the happier side, back in May, had been Porter's *Howdy Neighbor, Howdy* album. On the cover he's wearing a sweater, a big country grin and is extending an outstretched hand. It's an album full of old-timey, positive material, some of it bluegrassy. The liner notes say that country music can be pleasant and cheerful "without sounding too goody-goody." The following month the second of his *Best of . . .* albums was released.

With all these products out there, chances were bright for that October. Porter and Dolly won Best Vocal Duo of the year from the CMA. Other awards had accumulated: *Music City News*, Number One Duet; *Billboard*, Best Duo and Best Duo—Albums; *Record World*, Top Vocal Duo; and *Cash Box*, Most Programmed Vocal Group, meaning jukeboxes.

LaWayne Satterfield interviewed Porter and Dolly for *Music City News*. Porter said Dolly had had to give up a lot to get ahead. Dolly said she saw no end in sight: "I want to keep climbing. Maybe I'm too ambitious, but I like a challenge." Porter condemned those who "hype" their way to the top of the charts or into winning awards. He wanted to earn an award honestly or he didn't want it at all. "I want it to be because I was best, not because someone played politics for it." Dolly told how they watched the expressions on the faces of their audiences to know which songs to do; and Porter said anyone could learn to sing well enough to go onstage, but that entertainers had a magnetism when they went out there that made everyone "notice and respond to what he or she is doing."

Jack Hurst of *The Tennessean* gave Porter one of the longest feature stories of his career to date. Hurst's lead sentence described the standard opening of the television show: "It always begins with a floor shot upward from an oversized cowboy boot as a tall, grinning, genuine good old boy emerges from his dressing room as credits flash on the screen." (Dolly used to call Porter "Old Bigfoot" because of this boot-shot opening.) Jack described how this stock footage was spliced onto the live portion of the show, as suddenly Porter and the Wagonmasters and Dolly would launch into "Howdy, neighbor, howdy . . ." and how the "bright studio lights seem to revel in the rhinestones of his red-and-blue cowboy suit. Left eyebrow arching periodically, he begins to sing in a firm but gentle baritone." Porter reminded Jack of Hank Williams, and he was impressed by Dolly's "made-up country innocence in unbelievably long hair." Jack quoted Porter's style of introducing Dolly on camera. "Now we'd like to get the *purty* member of our show, Miss Dolly Parton, out here."

For one of his simple country boy routines (Jack noted Porter was wearing his "chartreuse shirt with puffed sleeves, a mod red thigh-length vest, dark trousers and subtle black boots"), he reminisced how when he was a boy his dad cut his hair and probably not forty people knew of his existence. He was probably eleven years old before he first went to town. Today when he played West Plains—population 4,026—he drew a crowd of 18,000. Jack guessed Porter was grossing maybe half a million dollars a year! "If I was in it for the money, I guess I'd prob'ly be gettin' ready to retire before long."

Then the hectic pace was addressed in the interview. Porter said his three hospitalizations had not been for personal problems but for exhaustion. "That's not to say I don't have personal problems. Anybody who is a person has personal problems." Porter condemned a recent book that speculated he had been hospitalized either over love problems or friend problems with Mel Tillis. Porter explained how he had rearranged his schedule, with a week off every month for golf and fishing and resting. He owed it to his fans to be rested and to sign autographs after a show instead of leaving like some entertainers did, as if to say, "to hell with you, I'd rather go get me a beer or somethin'."

For those whose lives are already wretched, the holiday season is the worst of all. In November 1970, an old acquaintance shambled back into view with the album *Skid Row Joe—Down in the Alley*. On the cover Porter is standing in his old doorway behind the Ryman, in his ill-fitting cast-off clothes, with hair gone gray, holding his hat in one hand like a kind of flag, signaling for a handout, and a cigarette in the other hand. A decent-looking pedestrian stares back without sympathy.

Dolly contributed a couple of the songs. As she said:

> At that time Porter was doing a lot of songs, he liked that Skid Row kind of stuff, he liked dressing up and wearing makeup, he wanted to do a Skid Row type album. So I wrote those songs specifically for him.

One of hers, "Down in the Alley," is a parody of "Down in the Valley": "Down in the alley, frail bodies tremble in the wind, and the future holds nothing but more wine and more sorrow." Her uptempo "One More Dime" is a panhandler's hustle for ten cents, and it attracted its share of jukebox silver. Although it missed *Billboard*, it had been in *Cash Box* in September before the album was released. Also represented was Uncle Bill. On the "Dolly" show, Dolly joked about how Uncle Bill would call her drunk from Tootsie's, celebrating when they had gotten another song recorded. Bill's contribution here was "The Town Drunk," about a man who can't control his drinking and now it controls him.

Porter wrote his own recitation, "The Silent Kind," about how drunks are taciturn, but how if you could only hear what goes on in their minds you'd hear stories unspeakably sad. The song, like others on the album, alludes to home and family left behind. The whole album underscores Porter's favorite theme of toleration for the seemingly disreputable and luckless souls that frequent life's alleys and gutters. The recitation "I Judged a Man" (by Johnny Mullins, who wrote "Company's Comin' ") is representative, pleading for you not to evaluate a man by the rags he wears.

In 1989 Craig Baguley of *Country Music People* had noted the shift in Porter's material starting in 1965:

> It was about this time that Porter's penchant for relating the tragic life of the wino community and of the darker side of life, both in song and recitation, began to hallmark his performances. Despite the scorn and derision these aspects of Wagoner's music engender among non-appreciative elements—both in country music circles and outside—Porter Wagoner manifests, for me, an unrivalled mastery in this area of country song.

On the lighter side of life there was always Dolly. Already she'd been on Johnny Carson's "Tonight Show" with Porter and "Kraft Music Hall" as well as "Hee Haw." Archie Campbell offered her a permanent spot on "Hee Haw," which she wisely declined.

Sometime in 1970 Porter gave Dolly a contract to sign (the date is blank), and she signed it.

26

"RUN THAT BY ME ONE MORE TIME"

In the end, Dolly accepts Porter's position
as boss and experienced advisor. Much to the dismay
of the rumor-mongers, they have a smooth
working business and personal relationship
without the entanglements of complicated
written arrangements.

—Joshua Castle,
"Dolly Parton, A Total Experience,"
Country Song Roundup (November 1969)

Anyone who's ever charged a Christmas gift, only to learn later it cost more than they budgeted, might identify with Dolly's distress over her music publishing shared with Porter.

Anyone who's ever thought he owned something free and clear, only to be hit with a large bill for it later, might identify with Porter's dismay over the publishing company he shared with Dolly.

And anyone who's ever transferred something precious to a relative, only to experience later regrets, might identify with Bill Owens's frustrations over the same publishing company he started with his niece, then surrendered.

The company was, of course, Owepar. "I don't want to be in Owepar," Bill said on the way out.

In 1967 when they set up Owepar, Dolly and Bill had patterned it after Warden Music. Imitating Porter and Don's stock split, Dolly owned 51 percent of Owepar and Bill 49 percent. But Don Warden was not a songwriter, and by providing endless services to Porter, he certainly had earned his shares. For Dolly and Bill to own shares of each other's songs was something else: they lost sight of their objective, which simply was to publish the songs they wrote or co-wrote.

Then with the same attorney's assistance, on April 3, 1969, Bill gave Dolly all his shares in exchange for royalties on a potential list of forty-three songs, in hope of seeing some of them recorded. Obviously, Dolly could not promise to record any particular songs or any fixed number of songs. It was clear what Bill was giving up, but vague as to what he'd be getting back.

Although Bill wouldn't be writing many more songs with Dolly, he still fancied himself her "manager" of sorts. Dolly told *Music City News* in July 1969 that Bill had "acted as my manager for many years, and I must say that he has done a very good job." That summer Bill began advertising himself as a producer for Circle-B Records at 1012 Seventeenth Avenue South in Nashville. It was housed in one of the converted houses that characterized the flourishing Music Row, one shared by Porter's former booking agent, Lucky Moeller. Across the street was Porter and Dolly's office. Bill said in his ad that he could record and ship a single for five hundred dollars, and he emphasized all of his cuts co-written with Dolly, including twenty versions of "Put It Off Until Tomorrow." His fourth wife, Kathy, was a Circle-B artist, recording Dolly songs, plus wifely duets.

"Bill, like me, is a dreamer," Dolly swore in a 1977 deposition. "He has a new project every day." Bill's attorney countered, "For the record, there's nothing wrong with dreaming, is there?" In her 1979 deposition Dolly regretted that "we were not educated enough as to business to know what to do." But her next remark should be engraved over the gates of Dollywood: "We were just country people with a slight talent tryin' to make the best of it."

Also by 1970, Bill's brother Louis was in and out of town, handling publicity for Dolly Parton Day from her office.

For Christmas 1969, Santa Claus brought Porter 49 percent of Owepar. He said by affidavit in 1979 that nearly all the Owepar songs were written by Dolly, himself, or both of them together. "We are very close to them . . . We did not want to have anyone else be a director of the company because that person would upset our equality, and he would not be close enough to our songs to know how to manage them."

Porter was probably sick of hearing from those around him that he was spending "all" his time on Dolly. Certainly there is no precedent in the history of modern show business for his commitment to her career. Sonny Bono worked as hard on Sonny & Cher, but neither of them had had any experience to speak of when they connected. Porter's investment in Dolly was rather as if Sinatra had picked Barbra Streisand, then whipped her into superstar stature. As with his golf and fishing, with Dolly Porter kept doubling and redoubling his energies. The odds were never that great, and talent has always so little to do with anything. Every time you blinked, there was some new girl singer, half of them singing duets with somebody else. Then there were the impossible-to-equal mainstays like Connie Smith—pretty to listen to and to look at—on

Stock certificate granting Porter his 49 percent of Owepar Publishing Company
[COURTESY THOMAS V. WHITE].

RCA, with seventeen hits, many of them in the Top 5 by 1970, Connie joined the Opry in 1971.

Porter certainly knew in his mind, if not in his heart, that Dolly would leave one day, and he didn't intend to come up short. He says:

> That's where the contract came about. I didn't get a part of her royalties or anything till she left my show. Because I said if you stay with my show five years, and I have built you into a huge money maker, I want to receive something from that. I want to put a lot of energy, thought . . . open a lot of doors, do a lot of things you could never do for yourself, because of my clout in the music business. She said, "That's only fair." So that's how the contract came about.

Dolly's version of the origin of the contract is different. She would say in 1979 that six months after she came on the show she and Porter began having arguments—how to do a song, whether to pull gags onstage (Porter says he vetoed some of Dolly's comedy ideas), and, eventually, how to produce the records, Porter stifling Dolly's more pop impulses.

Dolly said in her deposition, "My father had a very strong will, I was young and hadn't been around that many men, it was just out of fear" that she signed. She did not go over it with a lawyer.

There was no employment contract with Dolly, nor would there be. Porter has the sensible small-town attitude that if you can't trust someone, a contract isn't going to help. So how did Dolly get paid? Her estimated $60,000 a year, to start, was no annual paycheck, but an aggregate from earning $250 to $350 per show while on the road, plus Opry union scale, TV union scale, record royalties and—more and more—songwriting royalties, as both writer and publisher.

Porter told me:

> I knew one day she would leave the show and I wanted to be paid some time for the things I had done for her then. I got nothing at that point from her, not one dime, because she got paid just like I did on the records, she got paid just like I did on the concerts, and the whole thrust of the agreement was, "Someday when you leave my show, I need to be paid for what I'm doing for you now. From 1967 up till the time you leave, I'm getting no money from you, and I'm going to need to be paid sometime for that."

If Porter was getting nothing back from Dolly directly—no manager's percentage, for instance—he wasn't having to pay her profit-shares, either, as he did with band members. Her fee was fixed. He was benefiting from her presence in many ways, from reaping producer royalties on her records and singer royalties as her duet partner to songwriter royalties whenever Dolly cut one of his songs or one of their co-written ones. Naturally, bookings were improving with Dolly on the show. Now he and Dolly were in the publishing business, thanks to her Yuletide generosity of 49 percent of Owepar. Under fire from a lawsuit later, Dolly would say she had done about as much for Porter as he had for her, or she had tried to.

Porter told her at some point, "Somewhere along the line I've got to be paid for this. Let's draw it [the contract] very simple and to the point where we both understand it." The whole topic is still very painful for them. "And to think after that, I would get in a damned lawsuit over it was just ridiculous. Because it spelled out very plainly what it was about," Porter said.

Sometime in 1970 the contract was witnessed by Joan McGriff and signed by Porter and Dolly in his office. Its provisions can be summarized thusly:

1. Dolly gives Porter 49 percent of Owepar stock.
2. As of the date of the agreement, Dolly agrees to pay Porter 15 percent of her record royalties. [This was not done, however, according to both Porter and Dolly.]

3. If Dolly leaves Porter's show, he is to manage her for five years, with a second five-year option which either can dissolve.

    a. Porter as manager shall get 15 percent of Dolly's net income excluding income from her songwriting. To earn this, Porter shall "act as the personal adviser and the business adviser of Dolly Parton and act in her best interest at all times."

    b. This agreement terminates if Porter dies, and no successor will be appointed. Meanwhile, Dolly shall need Porter's written approval on any music career contracts, such as with [examples given] RCA, Top Billing, and with television producers. Porter would collect fees under her contracts for her. He would also have to approve all her contracts.

4. Again [reiterated], Dolly's songwriting is not to be part of this agreement. ["I just had to protect my songs if something happened to Porter. They were always up for grabs. Everybody always wanted my songs; everybody knew there would be something there someday. So I tried to protect them for myself, from the world, as you would your children," Dolly said.]

5. Dolly gets first option to buy Porter's 49 percent of Owepar stock should he want to sell.

6. Porter gets first option on Dolly's 51 percent of Owepar stock.

However restrictive this contract was in places, it was never enforced. Grief-provoking as it became to both signatories, it was a piece of legal Swiss cheese with its laughable loopholes. How could any lawyers, let along judges and juries, determine what would be in Dolly's "best interests," for instance? And to confine a manager only to Dolly's music contracts would let her off the hook regarding movies, books, theme parks, and other enterprises, such as producing other people's records, publishing other people's songs, and producing other people's film and TV projects. Dolly and her manager today have Sandollar Productions for just this eventuality. Other "entertainment and artistic-oriented contracts" would have tied her up tighter.

In fairness to Porter, he was not particularly used to contracts himself, other than homely, standard booking agreements with pals like Hap Peebles, where the handshake and the familiar voice on the telephone are worth all the lawyers in the world. Porter's last manager—other than Don—had been Herb Shucher, briefly, in 1957. He's never really had a manager in the full sense since.

I told Dolly's ebullient attorney from 1979, Stanley M. Chernau, that it all sounded like a bit of conflict of interest. Stan grinned and said that when people say a "manager's" fee, they sometimes really mean a "finder's" fee for having discovered or promoted someone. When RCA producer Bob Ferguson heard that Bill Anderson wanted to manage Connie Smith, he told him, "You discovered this girl up in Cincinnati, and she thinks you're a knight on a white charger, and she always will. And you will always be that to her unless you force her into this management contract." In his autobiography Bill says he tore it up and put the pieces in Connie's hand.

Starting in 1970 Dolly, via Dolly Parton Enterprises, began paying her uncle Bill a $100-a-week salary, "strictly a managing salary, had nothing to do with royalties or songs or anything," Bill testified. It went up to $200 a week until around 1975–76, when it ceased altogether. Bill considered this a justified paycheck for over a decade of time invested in Dolly. Yet in 1977 he affirmed that Porter made all of Dolly's decisions, "told her what to do and what not to do, period." Dolly added that she had been paying Bill "10 percent of everything I made, except my writer's and publishing royalties, until last year [1976]; and loaned Bill many thousands of dollars throughout the years out of my personal accounts." In the 1979 notes of Porter's attorney, Thomas V. White, are references to Christmas loans by Porter to Dolly. At least one is for $20,000 to cover losses by her family in bad business investments.

Then there were the Christmas Cadillacs that so beguiled the press, especially the photographers. Dolly's acerbic answer in 1979 was:

> Porter was always giving me things—things I hardly wanted and could not explain away. But you can hardly refuse Porter without an argument and a fight. But he made me feel, "How do you explain *this?*" He said, "If mature people can't know someone, and buy someone . . . [after all] you're making me money." Such publicity! I always enjoyed the cars and the gifts, though I would have preferred to buy my own.

Dolly even raised the dark question about whether or not she was being charged back for her gifts. The suggestion is unthinkable, since however frugal Porter is personally, he is lavishly generous to people who work for him. Cagey as he is most of the time about business, he always seems to want to know as little as possible about his own or anyone else's finances.

In their joint ownership of Owepar, whenever Porter, Dolly, or Porter and Dolly wrote a song, they each shared publisher royalties above any writer royalties. Then in 1972 they opened a recording studio together, managed by Dolly's uncle, Louis Owens. By the late 1970s there was ample employment available for Porter's, Dolly's, and Bill's lawyers.

Ruth B. White, Porter's office manager for five years, says, "The music business is not a business. Everything is done on emotion." Yes. And undone the very same way.

FROM THE PILLOW ROOM
TO THE RUBBER ROOM

Except for the title tune,
the only interesting songs here
are two by Porter Wagoner.

—Robert Christgau, reviewing Dolly's
Love Is Like a Butterfly album
in *The Village Voice* (1974)

"Some people I was really close to kind of made fun of my writing." Porter was talking to LaWayne Satterfield in 1973, for *Music City News*. Despite having co-written the Carl Smith hit "Trademark," Porter said he developed a "complex" and quit writing songs for about ten years. LaWayne sensed he was speaking "painfully . . . trying to convey the feeling of humiliation, hurt and frustration."

Dolly got him writing songs again, when she'd bring him a song and he'd touch up a line here or there. "Dolly was different from the rest," he explained. "She encouraged me to write and made me believe in myself." Porter would show Dolly a song, and "she shared in my happiness at creating it." Then Dolly, one of the world's great diplomats, would make a suggestion here or there. "She has turned out to be my best critic. She can help without being critical, but she doesn't tear down my confidence."

Porter said if anyone laughs at his songs, he laughs with them and then says, "Let's go down to the bank and have a laugh."

Soon Porter and Dolly were writing songs together, with their Owepar publishing apparatus giving them added dollar-incentive. All of the collaboration credits are legitimate: when Porter or Dolly wrote a song alone in that same period, the songs are credited individually. This is unlike Lennon–McCartney, who used their hyphenated byline as almost a brand name on whatever either of them wrote separately, or Buddy Holly, whose songs were often gratuitously freighted with producer and band member co-credits. Sometimes Dolly would offer Porter half when he made some changes, but he says these were already complete songs: "I don't think making changes merits half a song. The songs that have both of our names on them is no kind of a trade-out, or anything like that. We wrote 'em together and contributed equally."

Their co-writing surfaced on the duet album *Two of a Kind*, released in April 1971. They wrote the first cut on the album, "The Pain of Loving You," which has a strong hook (the title), and a moaning, infectious melody. In our interview, Dolly remembered "'The Pain of Loving You' I wrote with Porter because we liked singing that kind of song, it kind of was how we felt, too, it was like . . . what in the world are we *doin'!*" Dolly recorded "The Pain of Loving You" again for the 1987 multimillion-selling *Trio* album with Linda Ronstadt and Emmylou Harris. Others written by Porter and Dolly on the *Two of a Kind* album included "There'll Be Love" (as long as there's two people in the world), and the title cut, "Two of a Kind," in which they have in common sadness, disappointment, and jealousy but also respect, honor, and admiration.

There now was a market for more positive, striving love songs. The demand was shrinking for dead-baby specials and adultery-immorality plays, with cheaters being punished by hot lead or cold steel or just a car crash. Homeless winos were likewise no longer at home on the charts. The previous month Lynn Anderson, a pretty Dolly competitor with TV background on the Lawrence Welk show, had taken "Rose Garden" to number one, with this affirmative love song even going to number three in pop. Lynn would later tell Joe Edwards of the Associated Press that "Rose Garden" helped to cheer a nation recovering from Vietnam. Lynn could have been speaking about the several spunky, optimistic songs that Porter and/or Dolly wrote for their duets.

Porter often wrote about the lonely side of love, songs that Dolly sometimes recorded. For himself he wrote insanity songs about love literally driving you crazy. He composed a share of philosophical-religious numbers, with recitations, and a few tributes to growing up in the Ozarks.

Almost always his melodies were very singable, slipping the unexpected chord or the interesting rhythm into the country format. Porter the singer made Porter the writer reach most of the time.

Porter's next nine solo hits (1971–73) were all songs that he wrote alone. In August 1971 "Be a Little Quieter" went on the charts, reaching number eleven. Next month it was the opening cut in his *Porter Wagoner Sings His Own* album, the entire mood of which is that of a resurrected Hank Williams, trying to escape from the sixties into the seventies with part of his heart intact.

At first listen, "Be a Little Quieter" sounds like a song about a suburban marriage. She's out in the kitchen, rattling pots and pans, or so the listener thinks, but it's only his memory of her. He asks her memory, won't you be a little quieter? An eerie little song, it went to number eleven in 1971. There are three other songs of desolation, the best of which is "Lonely Comin' Down." Porter was driving home from the Opry one night when the melody and the lyrics came rushing at him. He pulled into a Kroger parking lot and scribbled down the words—then, as soon as he got to his apartment, grabbed his guitar and switched on his tape recorder.

As he told LaWayne Satterfield, " You have to use your imagination a lot. Sometimes when I am alone in the wee hours of morning, I try to imagine how beautiful love is. When I am alone, or lonely, then I can write of the agony of love." In one of his songs the glow from a naked light bulb in the hall intrudes through a crack in the wall, tormenting the speaker; in another the impression of her head left on the pillow, with the scent of her perfume all around, tortures the loser in love.

Another loneliness song is "Albert Erving," showing Porter's compassion for—and identification with—neglected souls. The sharp geographic details evoke the Ozarks. Albert has never known a woman's touch; he has never even held a child. He lives in a squalid house made of logs, with cardboard boxes that chink the cracks to keep out the wind. Albert carves wood, and he has carved the face of a woman whom he names Kathleen, his imaginary lover. It sounds like Skid Row Joe gone to Howell County—or perhaps a Dolly Parton song of pathos set in Missouri.

One of the first of Porter's "positive love songs," as they're called in the trade, is "The Way I See You." It's on Dolly's *Coat of Many Colors* album, released that October. With an exultant, climbing melody, it's a song of the sort Crystal Gayle and Ronnie Milsap would sell on the country market a few years later. Dolly's singing is perfect, and perhaps the fact that Porter sneaked a butterfly into the lyric, on the top of the crescendo, inspired her a bit.

On the same album is Porter's spooky "If I Lose My Mind." A girl is staggering home to mama after an experience with a man—probably a husband. He made her watch him make love with another woman and tried to get her to reciprocate with another man. She says she might have resorted to violence had she remained; she'd rather be in a mental institution than with him.

Dolly also sings "Mystery of the Mystery," with another sumptuous melody, where philosopher Porter says you had best accept the universe and not try to fathom God's ways. You can't ask why life begins, what happens when you die, or where the wind goes: you can only accept it. But the singing is shrill and strident, one of Dolly's rare rotten cuts.

✻   ✻   ✻

In January 1972 appeared the duet album, *The Right Combination / Burning the Midnight Oil.* On the cover are two separate pictures. Porter's is on the left, head in hand, at his apartment, his face at once handsome and anguished. A full ashtray, a box of Kleenex, and what looks to be a Dear John note from the girl fill in the rest. Opposite is a picture of Dolly at her house, sitting pensively by the fireplace in a big wig, holding a picture in her hand. Such lush imagery fueled all the Porter–Dolly gossip, no doubt. Porter says, "In a sense, it's a good thing. Because if they have nothing else to talk about, hell, they'll talk about someone else."

For this album Porter wrote the two title songs and two others. The album opens with his "More Than Words Can Tell," a driving love song with a gospel sound to it. True love can even withstand sadness "like the flaming pits of hell," as the couple bravely grows old together. Then follows "The Right Combination," with its sing-along chorus, "I believe we have the right [pause] com-bination." The song was a hit, and it certainly seemed to be true for the two singers, at least in early 1971. "Burning the Midnight Oil" evokes the picture on the cover: the two live in separate homes, pining for each other and meeting for stolen moments of passion. "The Fog Has Lifted" has a swaying, waltz-time melody, with a couple finding themselves after much doubt and misunderstanding.

Another 1972 duet album was *Together Always*, with five songs by Porter. The album had, inexplicably, two versions of its cover photo. The more common one has the two of them, blond heads touching, with matching red and white outfits. The other one has them out in the woods against some trees. In both versions the picture on the back has them walking hand-in-hand in the same woods, like high school sweethearts, Dolly jutting gigantically as a cheerleader.

Porter wrote five of the songs. "Ten-Four, Over and Out" is his trendy tribute to the C.B. (citizens' band) radio craze, with its all-too-cloying jargon ("I'll be CB-ing you"). A couple of cheating numbers are "Looking Down" (they get no love at home, but the world looks down on their carryings-on), and "You and Me—Her and Him" (with the kind of complexity Norma Jean used to get out of such situations). "Love's All Over" is erotic, with a play on words . . . love is not over with, rather it is "all over us," like the morning dew.

Another very pretty song of Porter's on the album is "Any Place You Want to Go." It has a rolling, folk–pop melody, and Dolly's singing has never been sweeter. The song opens by describing a room with crushed drapes on the wall, a floor carpeted with pillows of all shapes and sizes, mirrors on the ceiling, and candles burning. The couple in the room use their imaginations to go to Lover's Lane (sings Porter), or to the mountain peaks of Spain (Dolly), or even down the Amazon River (both of them).

The song depicts in part one of the rooms at Porter's apartment at the Versailles, known as the "Pillow Room." Nashville writer Marshall Falwell, Jr., remembers Porter telling him it contained 300 pillows, as well as a canopy made from a parachute, which hung down like a sort of tent ("pink or purple, I can't remember which").

Dolly's *Touch Your Woman* album appeared in March 1972—on the cover Dolly is adrift in a sea of pillows—the month after Porter's *What Ain't to Be, Just Might Happen* came out. Porter's title song went on the charts that month, reaching number eight in *Billboard* for fourteen weeks. Porter wrote the song and most of the rest of the album. It's almost certainly country music's first and last insanity "concept album," containing Porter's most notorious song, "The Rubber Room." He said of it:

> That's another [songwriting] situation that was by pure accident. I built this room at my house that had pillows, lights and mirrors and all kinds of things, to not cause illusions but you could imagine you were anywhere. And you could just be there. And one time, I was in this room—I was very tired, I had just come in off the road, I had just gone there to relax. I got a feeling it was like a cell, a room for a person whose mind had just collapsed on them. So I got to writing this song, where here I am in a rubber room [padded cell], I'm running into the walls. They put me in here so I won't hurt myself.

Porter's rubber room is in a building made of stone. The man in the next cell is shouting a woman's name, while the speaker is saying pretty words that he is trying to make rhyme. The melody is in a minor key, with a dirgelike fiddle accompaniment. A chorus sings in stately fashion, as if in a cathedral, while Porter hums with a weird, buzzing-insect sound. On the hook his voice reverberates with excessive, wobbly echo, jarring because he almost never uses much echo: "With his blurry vision of *doom* [echo] in the rubber room." The eerie instrumentation recalls Ennio Morricone's soundtracks for Sergio Leone's Italian Westerns. The song ends with the chorus chanting "Doom, doom, doom . . . "

Porter liked to drop by Berry Road with his guitar and try his latest song on his family. "Deb, what d'you think?" was always a flattering question. But daughter Debra was frightened when her father played her "The Rubber Room."

The day after he wrote it, Porter took it in to Chet, who said, "My God, what a song! That song could be a giant for the right person. It's like an acid rock song." But Porter told Chet he didn't know anyone in that field, so Chet said he ought to do a whole album of similar material. Since Chet was usually noncommittal, "when he *did* talk to you about one of your ideas, it just knocked you out." Porter went home and wrote three more, including "It Comes and Goes," about a man going crazy over a woman. He also wrote "I Need a Friend" from the point of view of a man lashed in a straitjacket. Back in 1968 Porter had released "The Man in the Little White Suit," by Dallas Frazier, about a love-crazed man expecting to be hauled off to an asylum. After Porter had spent a week on his psycho-songs, they were starting to scare *him*. So he told Chet, "I appreciate your idea, but I am *done* writing insanity songs! I wrote my last one just the other night! I can't handle it too damn much more!"

Chet doesn't remember encouraging this sequence of madness songs. "Porter was heavy into prescription medication at that time," Chet writes in a 1992 letter. "I remember thinking 'The Rubber Room' was really weird."

Billboard's Claude Hall welcomed "The Rubber Room," praising Bob Ferguson's production as "one of his richest and most elaborate" and predicting pop as well as country success for the song, if people would just give it a chance.

But "The Rubber Room" missed *Billboard*, though it got into *Cash Box*, so it must have gotten some tavern jukebox play. Sheet music was actually issued for "The Rubber Room," and Porter says an Irish rock band recorded it. Alex Chilton, formerly of The Box Tops, has a hard-rock version, and fans whoop and scream when he does it in concert. In 1980 Robert Bloch, author of *Psycho*, had a short story published called "The Rubber Room."

Of course the *What Ain't to Be, Just Might Happen* album wouldn't have been Porter without some recitations. "I Found a Man" sounds like the return of Skid Row Joe, only more uncanny. The speaker imagines he is helping a homeless man come into church and be saved, then he realizes he has daydreamed it all. There was no one, for the man he helped was really his own lost soul, down deep inside. And "Walter the Weirdo" is another compassionate reading. Waldo is a hermit who lives in a shack by the river, and people suspect (hope) he is a miser. So when he dies, everyone turns out for the reading of his will, craving their share. Waldo was a real weirdo, all right, because he had nothing material to bequeath; so he leaves various philosophical intangibles, such as willing the beauty he has seen to those who do not know God. "That's the way people are," says Porter. "They become interested if they think there might be something in it for them. When I was writing it, I could just picture it, people coming from everywhere, the damnedest crowd you ever seen, people just crowding the courthouse."

"Comes and Goes" is another hallucinatory song. She's there (in his mind), and then she isn't. And "Many Kinds of Love" has the bittersweet message of an "A Satisfied Mind." Porter observes all the kinds of love, from the mother for the baby she is carrying to the poor man loving to work to feed his family to the rich man who lusts after gold.

But it was the title song, "What Ain't to Be, Just Might Happen," that was the hit. It went to number eight, with its happy, bluegrassy melody and witty lyrics. It's quintessential Porter—risking everything for love, laughing at the risk. Once love sent the hero out on the ledge, fourteen stories high, but he has since learned to take things lighter because, after all, "Whatever is to be, will be—what ain't to be, just might happen!"

Porter once hoped to sell a story plot to Alfred Hitchcock. A man goes about murdering people with an icicle, which he sharpens in a pencil sharpener. Though it leaves no trace, to be on the safe side, he disposes of their bodies "by cooking them in some way." The fellow thinks people suspect him. They don't, but he flees anyway, way up north to the Arctic region. He imagines dogs barking and the authorities closing in. He runs and trips and falls. "He was just laying there and looked way up there on top of this big cliff. And he saw this icicle shaking from the rumbling of all those people he thought were chasing him. Well, it did break loose, and he had a heart attack and died. It melted before it got to him; but before he died, just one drop of water hit him—on the heart."

On Dolly's *Touch Your Woman* album are two songs Porter co-wrote with her, plus one he wrote without her, "Loneliness Found Me," with a painfully sad melody. Dolly's voice is at its heart-wrenching best.

That same year, 1972, there appeared *Dolly Parton Sings "My Favorite Songwriter, Porter Wagoner,"* an album whose title inspired a string of snickers down the years.

Though Bob Ferguson is the album's named producer, Porter is probably in control, getting a better take out of Dolly on "Lonely Comin' Down" than he did out of himself on his own songwriter album. His "Do You Hear the Robins Sing?" sounds like a Dolly composition, all alive with butterflies and roses, though putting in a Porter-style jab at people who prefer Astroturf lawns to the real beauties of nature. Dolly delivers a Porter-recitation, "The Bird That Never Flew," about a man who cares for a crippled bird that cannot fly. His "When I Sing for Him" is a gospel song with a forceful melody. She copied out the lyrics with a passion-pink felt tip pen on motel stationery, still in Porter's files.

But the one hit from the album was "Wash Day Blues," which went to number twenty in the fall of 1972. It's an uptempo, comical song about a woman who spends all her time washing clothes, spoofing, perhaps, Porter and Dolly selling Breeze detergent on the TV show.

Porter's own chain of self-written hits continued. "A World Without Music" was a brokenhearted ballad with a strong melody, number fourteen in 1972. "Katy Did" went to number sixteen at the end of the year, a song that Porter still performs. It's the complicated story of two sisters, Liz and Katy ("Liz never knew a man, but Katy did"). "Katy did" is the hook, repeated in different humorous contexts. Roy Shockley says, "I know a lot about 'Katy Did'." I know what Katy *did*," and he says there were two old maid school teachers in Howell County, one more hot-blooded than the other. Porter used to drop by on the way home from school. "What Katy *did*, you understand. That's where he got the inspiration. But you can't print that."

"Lightening the Load" went to number fifty-four in late spring of 1973, a rather standard positive love song. "Wake Up Jacob" followed, reaching number thirty-seven that summer. This amusing saga of a skunk is from Porter's boyhood, the skunk triumphing as skunks have a way of doing.

Then the most unusual song Porter (or almost anyone) ever wrote entered *Billboard* that December. The recitation is titled "George Leroy Chickashea." When the song is mentioned to Debra, she gets chills.

George has white, black, and Indian blood. Consequently, he hates the thought of cotton fields and plantations, as well as Indian reservations. His complex breeding is reflected in his personal armory: he packs a pistol, a switchblade, and a tomahawk, though in the only murder the song reports he uses his bare hands. The song has a predictably happy ending, with George mounting the thirteen steps to the gallows, relieved to be at last released from the torments of his heredity.

The instrumentation has tom-toms, with guttural background vocals chanting, sounding like Hank Williams's "Kaw-liga" (the tribute to the cigar store Indian) crossed with some cult-classic film soundtrack, either horror or Western.

In Porter's office hangs a painting of George Leroy Chickashea. It was used for the cover of the sheet music available for the piano, though hardly in the songs-America-loves-to-sing category.

Porter wrote "George Leroy Chickashea" after seeing the 1971 film *Billy Jack*, where a half-breed Indian back from Vietnam takes his militant stand in Arizona. One night the portrait of George began to form in Porter's imagination. "I couldn't hardly write it as fast as it came. I could picture this guy, he had these really cold, grey eyes. His hair was real coarse. He was just like a guy you would *design* . . . an 'Eight Million Dollar Man.'" Porter commissioned a woman to paint the portrait used on the sheet music. She had to redo the picture for Porter about seven times, until she exactly captured what her patron saw in his mind. "I got to thinking, this guy was so mean, and he didn't *want* to be. He wasn't afraid of nothing. This rattlesnake bites him on the leg, and he just says, 'Now crawl out there and *die*, you bastard!' Those are the type things that are just so real, like I'd seen him in real life."

"George" made it to number forty-three and was in *Cash Box* for seven weeks. It's certainly easier to imagine him on a beer joint jukebox than on the car radio.

*   *   *

"Tore Down" and "Nothing Between" were double hits, the pair charting at number forty-six in late spring of 1974, again, both written by Porter. "Tore Down" is Porter in his fanciful, rounder mode, getting drunk all over town. In rhythm and bluesy excitement, it's close to rock 'n' roll. Lyrically, it's country, George Jones running wild, as it were. The flip side is especially Jonesesque, a sentimental ballad: "Nothing between lost love and lonely, just a few broken vows, and a million old dreams." Porter had finally discussed his marriage publicly, if only in song.

And "Highway Headin' South," which went to number fifteen in 1974, concluded Porter's stretch of nine straight hit records, embracing ten songs, all of which he had written alone. "Highway Headin' South" was written in Montana while he was on a tour and pining for warmer climes. It has his trademark sharp eye for detail ("Montana, you've got five years of my life . . . I'm sick and tired of living like an Eskimo"). The melody humorously drops in the verses, giving the song a twelve-note range.

Porter continued to pour out songs for the duet act.

He wrote the title song of the *We Found It* album, which as a single had gone to number thirty in 1973. His "Satan's River" on the album was at once bluesy and gospel-sounding, Dolly cutting loose in her soulful voice. A particular touching song, "How Close They Must Be," is Porter's portrait of two blind teenagers, holding hands. He and Dolly co-wrote "I've Been Married (As Long As You Have)," a "funny fight" song where they literally kiss and make up—loud-smacking kisses are audible as they trail off in the coda.

The *Love and Music* album, also in 1973, carried several Porter compositions, including the passionate "Love's Out Tonight," adrip with sensuous imagery ("small drops of dew act as nature's perfume"), and the customary strong melody.

Porter 'n' Dolly (1974) had the usual share of Porter songs, but the most successful was a Dolly co-write, "Please Don't Stop Loving Me," which went to number one in late summer. It was the only number one the duet act would have. Ironically, it charted after Dolly had left the road show amid so much tension and hurt.

More and more, in his songwriting Porter had been concentrating on the topic of love, as he tried to steer Dolly toward love as a theme and out of her folksy, Smoky Mountain mode.

His *Ballads of Love* album (1972) was a long leap from the cold, hard facts of cheating and the tribulations of broken men. The pretty blonde on the cover is Porter's daughter Denise, for whom the song "Denise Mayree" was named. The word *love* occurs in five of the ten song titles.

On the *Experience* album (1972), "Barlow Chapin" was one of his tributes to his boyhood. Barlow weighs 220 pounds and can whip any-body in the local high school. After graduation (at least three of Porter's songs tellingly allude to high school graduations), Barlow gets married. After about a year, he's down to less than a hundred pounds, which shows what married love can do to a man. "Darlin' Debra Jean" was inspired by the wedding of Porter's daughter Debra, with himself and Ruth looking on with pride. Getting back to where Porter was emotionally, "He's Alone Again Tonight" is one his numberless songs about solitude and love-inflicted depression.

I'll Keep on Loving You (1973) had one of his best Howell County, happy-memories songs, "Childhood Playground." It's full of details, such as skipping rocks across the water of South Fork Creek and walking fields of new-mown hay. The melody is as bubbly as the lyric.

The Farmer album (1973) is in the same nostalgic vein, and Porter wrote nine of its ten songs, some being tributes to his dad. The "Conver-sation" recitation is sheer wishful thinking, Porter trying to redream his painful past: a farmer is boasting how his farm has put five of his children through college. "County Farm" is about a prisoner, inspired in part, perhaps, by his brother Oscar, who supervised the dairy at the Hancock County Farms in Iowa. And "Moments of Meditation" is a recitation Porter still does on television. It's Porter at his most religious, peacefully accepting, instead of asking why the sky is blue instead of red or why someone like himself is so blessed while somebody else goes hungry. Whoever you are, the song says, it's in "moments of meditation" that you draw closest to God and to Jesus Christ.

Porter showed this contemplative side to LaWayne Satterfield in the songwriting interview. "I think that anyone who writes has to feel the power of God. Let's just say that I know I have a partner who helps me write. I could not write without the help of someone higher than me." He said that sometimes the words would rush out and he would set them down, then call his secretary, Joan, to look them up and tell him what they meant. He found that for Porter writing "is a sort of release for all the things in my mind."

After the interview Porter called LaWayne back and dictated over the phone this verse:

> God must guide the hands that write,
> Of feelings felt so deep inside.
> And God's a part of every line,
> To feel our thoughts with words to rhyme.

Without God's help, the poet's pen
Would be forever silent then.
And words would have no melody,
And music then would cease to be.

So thank you, God, for every word
And every prayer that You have heard.
And may each one that speaks your name
Be blessed like I. Thank you, and Amen.

28

"WE FOUND IT"

It is probably impossible to overstate
the importance of Porter Wagoner's contribution
to Dolly's career in every way.

—Otis James, *Dolly Parton:*
A Photo-Bio (1978)

The hero of Dolly's song "Joshua" sounds like one of Porter's shunned and rejected souls. Joshua is a fearsome recluse who lives in a shack down by the tracks, guarded by a menacing black dog. But the speaker herself comes from an orphans' home, so she sympathizes with the irascible Joshua. She moves into his shack and into his heart. Even the black dog's attitude adjusts accordingly. The country-blues beat (with squawking harmonica) urges the melody along, and Dolly, who feared being typecast as a lady yodeler after "Mule Skinner Blues," yodels her way out of the song, acrobatically.

"Joshua" entered *Billboard* in December 1970 and went to number one and it was number one in *Record World* also. It was her first number one hit. It gave Porter and Dolly a hint of what was to come, since it went to number 108 in pop, "bubbling under" the Top 100 in industry jargon. Earlier in 1970 an anonymous bio sheet claimed Dolly had won "seventeen awards and citations" for her music, and now this number one hit. The following month, January 1971, Porter entered the charts with a song of Dolly's, "The Last One to Touch Me."

In February *Music City News* ran a full-page story by LaWayne Satterfield on "The Porter Wagoner Show." Porter was typically Porter, vaunting his showmanship at the expense of his voice: "I learned a long time ago I couldn't sing very well, so I have tried to make up for my lack of talent by being sincere with everyone. I am thankful I had sense enough to realize where I was lacking—and sense enough to try to overcome it with something else." Jane Dowden of Show-Biz, Inc., was quoted as saying that Porter was "made for the tube. Porter is a person who is made for television, and television is made for him." Dolly joked that "we are all scared to death we'll do something wrong and Porter will fire us."

Satterfield noted Porter's bountiful way with gifts, "huge expensive gifts" for the Wagonmasters and Speck, quoting Porter, "When I come in off the road and go to the bank, I am not stupid enough to think I earned all my money myself." Hence Dolly's 1971 Cadillac El Dorado. "Of course some narrow-minded people might think I have something personal for Dolly, because I give her diamond rings or that Cadillac." LaWayne remarked upon a three-carat diamond given to Dolly on her birthday, "not to mention the other dazzlers she wears on her hands."

Also in February the Porter–Dolly duet "Better Move It on Home" entered the charts, going to number seven. It was written by Ray Griff, prolific Canadian songwriter and himself a recording artist. The record has a strong, bluesy beat. The lyrics might be termed "suburban country": housewife Dolly is fussing at husband Porter, late again. He'd been drinking at a tavern, then fighting the rush hour traffic while she was fuming about dinner getting cold.

In April 1971 Porter was indirectly responsible for a prison riot and a warden being disciplined. It happened in Atlanta, where prison rules demanded that the inmates watch the news. When one prisoner switched "The Porter Wagoner Show" for the news, another one assaulted him. The same two prisoners fought again on Monday, one of them stabbing the other, and a riot broke out. The director of prisons suspended the warden.

Perhaps the initial fight had been over watching Dolly, versus the news. Porter's publicist, Paul Soelberg, sent out a press release from Dolly Parton Enterprises more or less bragging about the prison riot, quoting Jane Dowden that Porter's show had "a devout, almost fanatical following from all social strata." Jane said they drew a lot of mail from prisons, that Porter sang a lot of songs about down-and-out people, and they knew he understood their problems.

Louis Owens was now running Owepar as well as Dolly's burgeoning publicity program. Louis was an early riser, and he and Porter would joke that they'd put in a day's work before anyone else showed up. Louis says he learned the intricacies of music publishing right off the sidewalks of Nashville, that in those days you could run a publishing company out of an envelope.

Louis was especially nervous about "Coat of Many Colors." Every time Dolly did it on TV, they drew more mail than from any other song. Sooner or later some other singer would cut it and beat Dolly out of the hit. In fact, Porter had already recorded "Coat of Many Colors" almost two years earlier, twice, in fact, on April 9 and April 15, 1969.

It could have been a hit for him or for someone else. One of the clichés of Dolly journalism is that she only writes songs that she can sing, that other singers can't sing her songs. But any number of her hits could have been hits if someone else had gotten hold of them first, as Skeeter Davis proved with "Fuel to the Flame."

Soon after Louis's urging, on April 27, 1971, Dolly cut "Coat of Many Colors." Not for several months, however, would it be released by RCA. Like "A Satisfied Mind," it was being maddeningly delayed.

Porter's hit "Charley's Picture" went on the charts in April, a "Porter Wagoner song" if ever there was one. Written by Frank Dycus and Larry Kingston, it's the story of a wino who wears a locket with a mysterious picture inside, "a picture of perfection." On a Sunday morning they find Charley frozen to death and learn for the first time that the picture was of Jesus. The song went to number fifteen.

"Charley's Picture" was included on the *Simple As I Am* album, issued that month. Included, too, was perhaps the most representative of all Porter–Dolly songwriting collaborations, "My Many Hurried Southern Trips." The speaker is a long-distance bus driver, and the melody has an urgent, traveling kind of rhythm. The driver rattles off a series of tiny towns from Porter's part of Missouri, and the chorus says, cryptically, that the passengers have a "reason to ride." There's one of Dolly's inevitable unwed mothers, fleeing in shame to Memphis to deliver her baby in a "home"; there's a prisoner, just released after about fifteen years behind bars; and there's a soldier coming home on leave. The driver closes by calling out more place names, from Dolly's neck of the woods. This charming, touching odyssey runs direct from the Ozarks to the Smokies, without a stop in Nashville.

Increasingly, the hippie or "youth" movement was drawing its occasional inspiration from country music. Back in 1965 Joan Baez had recorded "A Satisfied Mind" (with mandolin), and in 1967 Bob Dylan recorded his first album in Nashville. In 1968 Johnny Cash brought Dylan onto his network television show.

Maybe it was the prison riot that propelled journalist Gene Guerrero to Nashville to interview Porter and Dolly in their little house turned office. His lengthy interview formed a two-part article in *The Great Speckled Bird*, an Atlanta underground, youth-market tabloid.

Gene praised Porter for sticking with country despite the temptations of rock 'n' roll, saying that when you listened to Porter's records "you get the feeling you mean what you say." Gene was impressed with the prison and Skid Row albums. Porter said he had a soft spot for the underdog, repeating his favorite point, that such a man might not be able to help the way he acts. Porter described how he'd seen a wino in Nashville digging through a barrel full of bottles, "like a hungry person would run to a table for a sandwich. It had just a few drops of green gin or something." The man was only around fifty years old, and Porter was struck at how life had tortured him so much.

Gene asked him about songs like "Fightin' Side of Me," Merle Haggard's diatribe that accused Vietnam war protesters of being unpatriotic. Porter's response was startling:

> I can understand why they [young people] wouldn't like a lot of the songs that says those things about them, because I wouldn't either, by God, if they said it about *me*. Not only would I turn the damn thing off, but I would probably do *more* than that. [Merle] Haggard, the guy that recorded the song, is a good friend of mine and a great man, but I don't believe in that kinda song. Even though it's a hit, I don't believe in it. I've had—and I'm not saying this trying to rub some flowers on myself—but I've turned down a lot of songs that I knew were hits because I didn't want to be connected with that thing.

Asked why he thought young people might be turning a little toward country music, Porter said that "the younger generation are people that like to look at life the way it is," and that country music "tells of life the way it is. It tells of heartbreak, of drinking problems, of drug problems, of problems with the law and everything."

Guerrero seemed especially taken with "The Funky Grass Band," by Red Lane and Dottie West, on his *Simple As I Am* album. It's the zany saga of a hillbilly–hippie band, where the dancing fiddle player knocks off the bandleader's toupee with his fiddle bow (Mack Magaha supposedly once caught his bow in Dolly's wig), and where the bandleader stops the bus to relieve himself high in the Ozarks mountains, almost falling down a cliff in the process (which supposedly almost happened to Bill Monroe).

Gene was awed by the duets: "Both have such powerful voices and the same incredible range." Commenting on "The Pain of Loving You," which they co-wrote, he said that "near the first of the song there's a series of high notes that are chilling—the harmony is so good." He especially liked "Curse of the Wild Weed Flower," an antiheroin sermon (written by Dolly and Uncle Louis), with Porter gently inveighing against "blossoms of heartaches and petals of woe." On the record his voice envelops Dolly's as subtly as an echo chamber.

Explaining their duet closeness, Porter said he and Dolly thought alike about songs, that "to have a close harmony you have to be close in different ways . . . The songs mean the same things to Dolly and I. It's sorta like a family can always sing close harmony." Dolly added that she always sang as if she were singing to her family, and not to the TV camera, that she wanted people to look at her and say, "Well, she means what she's saying."

✳   ✳   ✳

Dolly recalled how her voice had perhaps been unsettling to some ears, especially in her Monument period:

> I have a real strange voice. A lot of people it just irritates them to death, 'cause it's piercing. I can understand it, 'cause there's been a lot of people I don't like to hear sing. My voice is real unusual. I sound a lot like a child, I guess. They thought people wouldn't buy me unless I was covered up with music. They wanted to drown out my voice to keep from hurting my feelings, getting embarassed when I heard the record. I'm sure they believed in me, but they thought that was the best thing I could do. So I recorded a type of music I was not familiar with.

Dolly said she didn't write music and couldn't read a note of music, that she only hoped the sheet music was correct because she had no way of knowing. She said words might come to her almost anywhere, that she could write a song in her head, even in a noisy room full of music. Sometimes she even wrote songs in her head while at church, admitting this might not be "very proper."

On social issues, Dolly said a man should rule his household as it says in the Bible, but she resented those people back home who "thought if a woman had ever made a mistake in her life, that she was nothing. A man could go out every week and have any woman he wanted. When he got ready to marry, though, he had to have someone untouched and all this. That just bothered me . . . I know it'll always be that way, 'cause the woman can't do anything—as far as morals."

Asked if being a woman had held her back when she first started out, Dolly said it probably had helped. She could get in to see people better because she was a woman. People probably pegged her for "just a dumb country girl that wouldn't know what was going on and wouldn't suspect anything. But I did." Dolly said all her life she'd almost been able to read people's minds.

The readers of *The Great Speckled Bird* were able to see the first cracks starting to appear in the smiling façade that Porter and Dolly presented to the country music fan press. Dolly said Porter was "great to work with," yet it was not "always smooth sailing," since at times Porter didn't think she knew what she was doing, which led them to "heated arguments." Dolly said Porter was so much like her, so opinionated, that she felt she had to present her ideas and fight for them.

Dolly shocked Gene somewhat by playing him a tape of a rock song she had written, which he thought sounded like Aretha Franklin. Still, she had no intention of recording rock 'n' roll.

As for gossip that inevitably besmirched a woman in a man's music world, Dolly said she had a "lot of things told on me against my morals which are not true. I'm no angel, but if I'd done half the things I've been accused of, I wouldn't be sitting here, I'd be wore out somewhere. I'd be dead." She said she liked to talk to people, that even though she liked women ("'cause I *am* one, my mother was one"), she could talk to men a lot easier when it came to her ideas about music and about business. She might eat supper with a man friend, but not often, because if you talked to a married man, people always thought the worst.

The following month provided another, far greater, opportunity for noncountry exposure. Porter and Dolly went to New York City on a package show produced by Show-Biz, Inc., parent of their TV show and of their booking agency, Top Billing.

On June 3 the two of them were the guests on "The David Frost Show." Then on Friday, June 4, they faced 11,000 people at Madison Square Garden. On the bill with them were Del Reeves, Sonny James, Faron Young, Jim Ed Brown, and their competing duet, Loretta Lynn and Conway Twitty. Porter and Dolly sang "Daddy Was an Old Time Preacher Man," then Porter did "The Carroll County Accident" and "The Last One to Touch Me," followed by Dolly doing "Joshua" and "Mule Skinner Blues," her two pop crossover hits.

Loretta Lynn did "Coal Miner's Daughter," the song she had written about her impoverished childhood in Butcher Holler, Kentucky. "Coat of Many Colors" was three months away from release.

The next night Porter and Dolly played the Opry. Then on Sunday they performed in the Sevierville High School gymnasium for the latest Dolly Parton Day, to raise more scholarship money. Carrying her Grammer guitar, Dolly came onstage, lit into one of her songs, and a huge roar went up.

After the song, RCA executives Bob Ferguson and Wally Cochran presented her with her first gold record. "Just Because I'm a Woman" had sold a million in South Africa. Wally presumably had a straight face when he said "This is the first time a female country artist has received such an award from South Africa."

Porter then delivered perhaps the ultimate Porter Wagoner recitation, a poem he had written. *Music City News* reported the gist of Porter's delivery:

> There's been lots of stories about a love affair between Dolly and me, and I'd be lying to say that I don't love her in many, many ways. But not in the ways the gossiping tongues will lead you to believe.
>
> To me, she's like a sister or daughter I love so well. When they say things about *me*, I don't mind. But when they speak of *her*, I get hot and feel the fires of Hell.

Porter, who had never even begun high school, certainly had delivered a memorable address. In the audience was Dolly's TV boss Cas Walker, who said that in his political experience he had found it generally unwise to issue public denials if you didn't have to.

By now Porter's chief booking agent was Tandy Rice, who ran Top Billing with the help of Dolores Smiley and Andrea Smith. He'd bought the agency from Bill Graham. Tandy had a military background: college at The Citadel and public relations for the Strategic Air Command, and he brought a kind of light-cavalry audacity to Music Row. He still lights up with the esprit de corps of a victorious field marshal when he recalls two of his favorite troops, Porter and Dolly.

He says Porter may be the greatest salesman that ever lived. "For some wacky reason, he can make people jump out of a window with his sales approach." Tandy heard someone say once that he'd rather have his word than a stack of contracts written by Harvard and Vanderbilt lawyers. "I admire forthrightness, people who are not timid, who are not complicated. I don't respect vague, ambiguous, Milquetoast lives . . . Porter was never afraid; he'd say, 'Get it while you can' . . . I remember when he took up fishing, it was just about like putting his finger into an electric socket."

Tandy related how Porter would come in and block off time for the coming year on the calendar. "Now that my time off to write songs and run my business is set, you can fill in all the blanks." He's never seen an entertainer do that before or since.

Then there was Tandy's trip to England with Dolly. Someone brought a fan named Bruce Rutter to meet Dolly, who posed with him for a color picture, which Tandy showed me. Bruce has his bare back to the camera, facing a beaming Dolly. Across his back extends a vast, varicolored butterfly, looking much like a painting by the Pre-Raphaelites in its stained-glass, jeweled effect. It is an exact copy of the gorgeous insect on the cover of Dolly's 1974 album, *Love Is Like a Butterfly*. Dolly autographed Bruce's back and told him that at least he'd have *one* woman with him forever.

Dolly's compulsive affinity for butterflies seemed to connect in Tandy's mind with Porter's own gaudy imagery. It triggered a chain of metaphors as he talked: "Porter the butterfly—Porter the rainbow—Porter the Pied Piper, appealing to the prisms in our mind, the rainbows in our mind, the Cinderella–Yellow Brick Road in all of our minds . . ."

Thinking of the James Thurber story about Walter Mitty, who daydreams about being various heroes, Tandy says, "Porter appeals to the Walter Mitty in them, and it makes them say, 'Go, Porter, Go!'"

Too many of Porter's fellow country singers were either getting drunk in public or acting crude in front of the fans. Porter was sick of how some of them carried on when he traveled with them in package shows. Also, the shows themselves were being priced too high. Late in July 1971, Porter, Tandy, and Don Warden told the press there would be no more package shows for Porter Wagoner. Porter himself explained why he didn't want to be associated with other acts outside of his control: "Whatever happens onstage reflects on us, even if we left the auditorium an hour ago."

Next month in *Billboard*, Bill Williams wrote that "Wagoner was particularly incensed when, at a recent show, another performer exchanged insults with the audience and threw in some abusive language." In fact, some other performer had gotten into a fist fight backstage. Porter was refusing to appear with acts who dressed in slovenly fashion, who insulted the audiences, or got "themselves involved in problems in clubs or alleys."

And Porter told Jack Hurst of *The Tennessean*:

> This is a funny business. You don't necessarily have to serve an apprenticeship; you may have a hit the first time out. You declare yourself a star, and you are one.
>
> When you have your hit, immediately some man calls you and wants you to come see him because he can get you an awful lot more money for every appearance because you've got a hit and you're generally a very marketable commodity.
>
> So you get to thinking to yourself, "Well, Lordy, I must be some kind of superstar and not even know it yet. Let me wash up my Cadillac and get over there and talk to that gentleman." And some of these new boys in the business wind up signing an agreement with a man who starts off by pricing them right out of everybody's consideration.
>
> If he's going to be realistic about it, a singer's going to have to start setting his price according to what he knows his name will draw, rather than what his publicity agent tells him about how good he is, or how great he wishes he was.
>
> [Despite his and Dolly's current string of hits] our price has stayed the same because our act is deliberately priced so the promoter can make money, because if the promoter can't make money, in the end none of us are going to make money.

As for quitting package shows, Porter said he was tired of hitting the same towns all the time. "In Knoxville, they can tell you every line in my face and every line that's going to come out of my mouth before I say it."

Also that summer George McCormick, rhythm guitar player and front-man vocalist, quit the band. Recalls George, "I left. It was getting tedious, I was getting nervous, everybody was getting nervous. Don used to tell Porter, 'You're putting 90 percent of your time into Dolly's career and 10 percent into yours. 'Cause if she makes it and leaves, where's that going to leave you?' But he wouldn't listen at that time."

Dolly had an all-gospel album out, *Golden Streets of Glory.* "The Right Combination" was a duet hit that summer, and actress Goldie Hawn was in Nashville on September 1 to cut Dolly's "My Blue Tears." They used Jack Clement's studio. Goldie's producer, Andy Wickham, was on hand, and Porter suggested he get an "insurance policy" on the tape and recommended Lloyd's of London!

On September 21, 1971, "Coat of Many Colors" was finally released. Concerning the song's subject, Dolly told Red O'Donnell of the *Nashville Banner* that when she was a child, "We were really poor. P–o–r–e! Poor!"

A few days later, on September 27, Porter attended a ribbon cutting in his hometown. Despite a thunderstorm, Mayor Glenn Roe designated a street as Porter Wagoner Boulevard as part of Porter Wagoner Day. The Saturday night show drew 7,000 people, overspilling a 2,000-seat outdoor amphitheater. Si Siman was present, as were Porter's mother, his children, Richard, Debra, and Denise, as well as both his sisters.

Dolly read aloud her "A Man Like You" Christmas poem from 1967. At a couple of points in the evening Porter was overcome with emotion and had to retreat into his bus to gain control. He told the audience, "You must know how touched I am by all this. I don't want to get to talkin' about it too much, or we'll have a cryin' ceremony instead of a singin' show!"

Porter asked everyone to stand and to bow their heads:

> God, thank You for life and for the love of one for another. I pray each one here tonight will understand the feeling I feel, even if I couldn't remember some of the names because it's been such a long time ago. Most of all, thank You for a dream come true and all my people and this greatest day of my life.

If their strategy had been to time "Coat of Many Colors" with Country Music Week in October, the maneuver failed, but it didn't matter. The song didn't enter *Billboard* until the end of the month, but Porter and Dolly won Duo of the Year anyway. It was their third such CMA award and their last. The Wagonmasters won a Top Country Band title from *Music City News,* as they had the year before.

Finally "Coat of Many Colors" hit at the end of the month, and it reached number seven. It is Dolly's favorite song and her most famous song.

The Porter Wagoner Show bus [COURTESY PORTER WAGONER ENTERPRISES].

Back in 1968, *Harper's* magazine had called Porter's bus a "$67,000 marvel" with color TV, carpets, and "a well-appointed bar." Now during Country Music Week, *The Tennessean* covered the latest addition to "The Porter Wagoner Show," the new, $100,000 customized bus. Don Warden had driven it home from the Custom Coach Company in Columbus, Ohio, and his wife, Ann, had decorated it. The article was titled "Wagoner's Wagon Sweetens the Road" and was written by the paper's art and drama critic, Clara Hieronymus:

> Not one inch of space was overlooked in the planning of this carpeted and upholstered rolling condominium. There is a lounge area just beyond the driver's station, with benches cushioned in gold and amber cut velvet and upholstered, like the table top, in real leather. Inset containers keep beverage glasses from spilling; a built-in color TV offers diversion. Or the Wagonmasters may listen instead to stereo tape or stereo radio programs.

Porter's "state room" reminded Clara of the days of Pullman trains, when traveling "was both fun and luxury." She remarked upon his dark blue velour bedspread with a big PW monogram:

> Miss Parton's room, like all the bus interior, is oyster white. Her curtains and coverlet are deep pink, and the mirror above her

tiny washbasin and vanity shelf boasts theater-type makeup lights. A peek into her clothes closet revealed not only a shimmering cloth-of-silver mini-skirted dress and slippers, but a book of Bible stories.

As the only woman in this troupe of traveling troubadours, she has a built-in commode in her private room. The foot of her bed lifts to give access to it, but this is better than having to traipse through the bunk area to the lavatory at the back of the bus.

Clara noted that Don had a state room, set up office-style with typewriter and an intercom. And she marveled at the "incredible feat" of space planning, in laying out the Wagonmasters' room—a cell with *six* bunks, "an absolute minimum of cubic footage. No pot bellies accommodated here!" said Clara.

But she praised the bus for permitting the Wagonmasters to get ready for a show without having to stop anywhere, ready to "step out with complete aplomb, ready to go on."

Truly, with a vehicle like that, the show should be able to roll on forever!

29

LIGHTENING THE LOAD

There are some that look at me with envy
Because I smile a lot, just to hide
The hurt I've brought to those that have loved me,
But couldn't understand me, deep inside.

—Porter, "Late at Night" (1971)

Heading down Franklin Road in South Nashville into the Melrose area, you pass the old Acuff–Rose building on the left. It is vacant now and unmarked. But enough Hank Williams songs came through those doors to generate, even today, hundreds of thousands of dollars in annual royalties. Further down Franklin Road is the bowling alley where Hank used to bowl in his steadier moments, and just a few blocks to the left is where the Wagoners lived for fifteen years on Berry Road.

Farther out Franklin Road are large, expensive homes. High atop a hill on the right sits number 4917, a big white brick home. There's a faintly Moorish aspect to it, from its massive carved door below an octagonal window to its floral wrought-iron trim and the fence made from white decorative bricks. In April 1972 Porter paid $60,000 for the house, which has sold twice since, the last time for $180,000. As late as 1986 the house was pictured in a national magazine's picture book of the stars' homes, the writer joking that it didn't look like you would expect Porter Wagoner's house to look—no rhinestone curtains or flashing purple lights on the lawn.

But Porter never lived in the house. Ruth and Denise did. Richard had moved away, and Debra lived in a dormitory at Belmont College near Music Row, a few blocks from where Dolly struggled in her walk-up garret in 1964.

Porter and Ruth remained separated but not divorced from 1965 to 1986. This strained yet stable arrangement was kept as quiet as possible, even to people in the music business, but especially to the public.

Porter does not enjoy talking about his marriage or his wife. "It wasn't a fact of her having shortcomings at all. If I'd had Marilyn Monroe at home, I would have still gone on the road," he says. They talked about divorce, Porter suggesting Ruth should find herself a good companion for a husband—an eight-to-five type—but she never did. "You can't make decisions for another person," he says. He left home and "for twenty years I paid every bill of hers, she had an unlimited checking account. The only thing that was missing was me. The income was still there, but she didn't have *me*. I was going to be a musician and travel and play and sing." So he bought the Franklin Road home. "That was the only thing I could give her."

Ruth would say, "There's more money, we have a nicer home. But you're not going to be in it. You give us earthly things. But it's not you."

Debra Wagoner was bound close to her father, in part by the music itself. She would sing songs like "I Thought I Heard You Call My Name" in the backyard, or "Your Old Love Letters," since it reminded her of how kids would pass notes back and forth in school. "I don't want it to sound too sugar-coated. There were times I would be lonesome for him. I'd think, 'He's up in Yankeeland with people who don't even know him.' I would call him up and feel better. I don't see how our relationship could be any closer, even if he'd been home every night."

At John Overton High School, Debra was close friends with Debbie Pierce, daughter of singer Webb Pierce. They felt distant from many of the other kids, some of whom would hold their noses and sing as nasally as possible and say, "Your daddy sings that hillbilly stuff." Or they would say, "Your daddy does country music, he don't do nothin' for a living." Debra would retort, "Hey, my daddy comes offstage and you can wring his shirt out, he sweats so much. How many times did your daddy sweat like that?" During what Debra calls "the Dolly era," the questions were mean. Do Porter and Dolly have something going on? "Of course they do, they work day in and day out together." Is he sleeping with Dolly Parton? "Well, what would *you* do?" which backed them up a bit. Is he in love with Dolly? "Everybody's in love with Dolly." And they asked whether Dolly's bustline were the real thing. Unanswered.

Debra says, "Dolly was the big sister I never had."

It was not until the fall of 1971 that Debra remembers getting any respect from other people for what her father did. She and some other students were crowding around the television in the college dormitory, watching the CMA awards show. About half of the students hated country music, but they were watching Debra's father on network TV as he received the vocal duo award with Dolly Parton.

While at college, Debra began to sense Porter felt guilty over having left Ruth. "I felt he was carrying something, a burden or maybe something he maybe should have done." So Debra suggested they have supper together. She told him, "Daddy, I've got something on my heart I've got to talk to you about. I feel as if you're insecure with fatherhood, as if you feel you didn't do enough when we were growing up. Because you and Mama weren't together doesn't mean you weren't a parental figure, that I didn't feel your presence there."

Porter replied, "I guess there has been a guilt there."

Debra told him one of the things you learn in college is that people fall in and out of relationships, in and out of love. "I want you to know there isn't any doubt as to what you've done for me. You did not just walk out and leave us stranded."

The conversation inspired Porter to write "Lightening the Load."

When my shoulders bend to hard labor,
And I work till my back is bowed,
Then your loving hands reach to hold me,
Darling, you always lighten the load.

Debra says once for her birthday Porter said, "Debra, I have a gift to give you that comes from me." He had his guitar with him and sang her the song "Darlin' Debra Jean," which is on the *Experience* album. For her marriage he wrote "Just Beyond the Chapel Door" and told her that anytime she and her husband had a quarrel to stop and play that song.

Dolly Parton was a guest at Debra's wedding. Her car broke down outside of town and she hitchhiked to the church "with a guy who seemingly didn't recognize who she was," according to Melissa York of the *Central Kentucky News-Journal*. "She also sat on the second row and made faces at the groom during the entire wedding."

Debra's younger sister, Denise Kelton, sings back-up and shakes a tambourine for Porter on the Opry. She has no further musical ambitions. Of her dad, she says, "He told me he didn't want me to grow up in the music business. But I got real close to him and even went on the road with him. He became more family oriented."

Earlier it was even harder for Denise than for Debra, being younger. "It was real hard growing up . . . you realize that he's gone, so maybe if I had a choice I would rather have had him home whether he was happy or not, 'cause that's just the way kids think." Other children seemed to judge Denise before they got to know her, saying, "Gosh, her daddy is a country music star, and she's a spoiled brat. She's always had everything she ever wanted. She lives in some gorgeous mansion."

"We lived a very normal life. We weren't rich," Denise said.

When she was twelve years old, Denise began to feel jealousy toward her father's career. "I felt like everyone knew him better than me. I was hardly ever around him. I called him and told him that once." A month before they moved out of the Berry Road house, Denise received a letter written on Holiday Inn stationery from Portland, Oregon. It was postmarked February 11, 1971:

Hi Sugar

Thought I'd write you a few lines and surprise you, as you know I don't like to write letters. I'm sorry I haven't spent more time with you. I know you understand but I love you and want to spend more time with you so you won't grow up not knowing your Daddy. When I get back home, we'll talk more about that. We've had a good tour so far. We've seen a lot of snow out here, but the mountains are beautiful. I've wrote a couple of songs since we left, I told you I wrote one about you. I hope you will like it, its title is "I Believe She Loves Me," and I believe you do. I will close now and get some rest.

I love you very much. Take care of my girl. I'll see you soon.

Your Daddy
Porter

P.S. Tell Debra I love her and will write her next. One letter at a time is about all I can do. Ha ha. That's a Hee Haw.

For Denise, the fall of 1973 was the season of the Great Wagonmaster Rescue That Almost Happened. Earlier she had taken a senior class trip to the Holy Land, which had paused at Athens and then the island of Cyprus. On a boat she met a young man named George Nirgianacis who lived on the isle of Crete. They exchanged addresses. Denise started taking Greek lessons. "We would talk on the phone maybe twice a month, to my mother's total horror." Denise decided to go to Greece to see George. "I was eighteen, I had never been anywhere by myself." She flew to New York with her brother Richard, then by herself to Greece. She stayed about four or five days with George's family.

"One day, all of a sudden, we saw people running up and down the street. We saw tanks! We ran into a store and asked what was going on. War had broken out!" It was a military coup with martial law. "It scared me to death."

Denise was planning to leave next day, but now the airport was closed and the waiting list to make a phone call was so long it took a day and a half to get through to her mother. Because Ruth Wagoner used to fear the children would be kidnapped because Porter was famous, "I told myself I would be so cool and say, 'Everything is fine.' I fell all to pieces and said, 'Mama, I have to come home!" Meanwhile, an upset Ruth had called Don Warden, wondering what they could do. Porter decided Don could fly to Germany, take a train, then rent a car to drive into Greece and find Denise. But it was unnecessary.

Denise left next day, and when she came through customs in New York, there was Don. As she touched down in Nashville, the stewardess said, "You've got to be the last one off the plane." Denise says, "I just looked awful in my cut-off pair of shorts." There was a TV camera, and television reporter Sharon Puckett interviewed her on the Channel 4 news.

✳   ✳   ✳

Right across the street from the Wagoners lived the "Lovesick Blues," in more ways than one. Porter and Ruth had seen Hank Williams perform it at the Ryman in 1949—Porter had cut it on demo-discs for a dollar at Hopper's radio shop—and "Lovesick Blues" had got him out of West Plains via his audition at KWTO in Springfield. Now, right across the road from 4917 Franklin Road, you could see the first few notes of the song in ludicrous wrought iron, on a railing in front of the ranch-style house at number 4916.

Audrey Williams lived there.

The fence "got a lot of attention," says her daughter Lycrecia in her *Still in Love With You* memoir (with Dale Vinicur). Audrey's daughter by her first marriage, she grew up there and knew Hank as her father. Hank and Audrey bought the house in 1949, and when Ruth moved into her home in 1972, Audrey was still hanging on across the way. Rather like Caitlin Thomas, the widow of poet Dylan Thomas, she definitely had "leftover life to kill." Hank still lived with Audrey, ethereally. She confided to a friend that he made love to her in her dreams.

And she tried to cling to the good memories of Hank playing with the kids and tried to banish the bad ones (him brandishing guns and her having an abortion right there in the house) with a succession of lovers, hard drinking, and spiritualism. Her all-girl band, precursor to Porter's "Right Combination" band, was named, unluckily, "The Cold, Cold Hearts," and Audrey's off-pitch singing was disastrous.

One can imagine Ruth's dismay in November 1974 when her neighbor Audrey staged a grandiose yard sale. The press made it a circus; Audrey did her bit by being drunk; and people paid two dollars to saunter through the Hank Williams home. Hank's memorabilia, even his toothbrush, were on display. The city of Oak Hill cracked down on Audrey for running a museum; she defied them for a time. Exactly a year after the yard sale, the Internal Revenue Service closed in. Audrey smuggled out some of her *objets d'art*, and then the Grim Reaper intervened and beat the IRS. Audrey was found dead in the house. Like an unquiet ghost, her house was moved from its foundations, bounced through some bankruptcies, and now rests in peace at the top of Music Row as a tavern.

Later the IRS fell upon Porter Wagoner. Ruth lost *her* house on the hill on Franklin Road in 1982.

Debra's favorite entertainer is not her dad; it's Hank Williams, Jr. She doesn't try to ingratiate herself with Bocephus as Porter's daughter—she keeps her distance and wants to just be his ardent fan. As she told reporter Melissa York, "Stars are to be viewed from afar. Sometimes when you get too close to them, they seem to fall out of the sky."

30

"LIFE RIDES THE TRAIN"

While life rides the train,
time always flies.

—Porter, "Life Rides the Train"
(written 1972), *Highway
Headin' South* (1974)

"Porter Wagoner, Country Music Santa Claus" ran the headline in Red O'Donnell's syndicated Washington *Star* column
in January 1972. "Every performer in show biz should have a boss like
Porter Wagoner. Porter played Super-Santa to pretty Dolly Parton . . . this Christmas with a 1972 'silver blue' Cadillac El Dorado, and
necklace [choker] studded with 38 diamonds that added up to 8¼ car-
ats . . . Dolly didn't forget Porter, either. She gave him a yellow gold ring
[shaped like a belt buckle] decorated with a 1.5 carat sparkler. Color Miss
Dolly 'Zsa Zsa'???"

Owepar Music had also thoughtfully paid to have "engraved in
gold" the name of its top songwriter on the Walkway of the Stars in the
Country Music Hall of Fame and Museum. Dolly and Porter's stars are
next to each other on the blue-grey marble floor.

Audrey Winters of the *Music City News* chimed in: "Buck Trent
got the best deal—he bought Dolly Parton's 1971 El Dorado which only
had 6,000 miles on it. The car was her gift from Porter *last* Christmas."

Dolly biographer Lola Scobey reports that one day Porter came
into Owepar and measured the neck of the lady working there, Maggie
Cavender, later the longtime, long-loved director of the Nashville Songwriters' Association. Porter estimated Maggie's neck to be about the same
size as Dolly's; he wanted that choker to fit exactly right!

The fashion editor at *The Tennessean* in those years, Jacqueline
White, said she once received a phone call from someone identifying
himself as Porter Wagoner. He was seeking some shopping advice. Where
would Jackie suggest he shop for a brassiere (or was it a negligee?) for
someone with large dimensions? She named some stores, then wondered
if she hadn't been hoaxed. "I'm not totally sure it wasn't a prank."

Around Knoxville, according to Lola Scobey, they were saying
that Dolly's husband, Carl, had caught her and Porter in a Georgia motel
room bed and shot them dead. Onstage one evening in 1989 on the

Christmas Day, circa 1970, at the Versailles *Apartments* [COURTESY PORTER WAGONER ENTERPRISES].

General Jackson showboat, Porter said that the newspapers were always exaggerating. "For instance, one time they said my wife caught me and Dolly." Long pause. "And that she shot and killed Dolly, and left me in critical condition." Another pause. "Well, that was all an exaggeration." Final pause. "She only *winged* me. *She missed Dolly entirely!*" Audiences didn't know Porter had moved out on his wife a year and a half before he met Dolly. Norma Jean says that "joke" used to get told on her. In an unpublished 1981 interview, Porter told Alanna Nash his ambition was to live to be ninety-five and be killed by a jealous husband, pause, "in the act." In January of 1990 Porter invited me onstage at the Opry and told a couple of million people that this book would have chapters on him and Dolly "so hot they'll need asbestos covers on the book." On January 14, I wrote to Dolly's manager, Sandy Gallin, that "Good ol' Porter does *not* speak for good ol' Steve in this regard." The letter was not answered.

Sometime in 1972 Skeeter Davis's *Skeeter Sings Dolly* album was released by RCA. "I don't think anyone realized her writing as fast as I did," Skeeter says. "I thought she was a great writer. If I hadn't been selling records then, and making them some money, they wouldn't have let me do it. I felt like her songs were written for me." On "Joshua" Skeeter's voice trails off on the coda with the throwaway line, "That don't sound much like Dolly, does it?"

As one-half of the Davis Sisters, back in 1953, Skeeter had touched the pop charts: she'd had several others that crossed over and no doubt foresaw Dolly's increasing versatility. Skeeter could just imagine what Dolly would be facing soon. Once to reassure her own fans, she'd rather desperately posed for an album cover clutching a pig.

Skeeter did not include "Coat of Many Colors" on that album. That same year another RCA girl singer released it on an album titled *I Guess That Comes from Being Poor*. There's a certain melancholy irony in the fact that it was none other than Norma Jean. For the cover she was posed in front of a shabby old house, and her liner notes laid bare the story of her impoverished upbringing. Still on the label, yet based in Oklahoma raising Roma with husband Jody Taylor, Norma Jean had preceded her replacement, Dolly, with a poverty-oriented "concept" album by almost exactly a year.

Dolly received probably her greatest accolade to date on February 14, 1972, in the agricultural building at the fairgrounds in Eugene, Oregon: a standing ovation for "Coat of Many Colors." Ginny Burdick of the Eugene *Register* reported that each time Porter would start a song he would be interrupted with "thunderous applause," and that Mack Magaha kept stealing the show with his "facile fingers and frenetic bow." The Wagonmasters charmed Ginny with their red shirts and purple suits, red patent leather shoes, and 1950s-style ducktail haircuts.

Porter and Dolly got a standing ovation together for their duets; more applause erupted when Porter hit the first words of "The Carroll County Accident." Ginny seemed impressed with Porter's new songs, two of them written three days earlier: his skunk saga, "Wake Up, Jacob," and his profound "Do You Hear the Robins Sing?"

She asked Porter about country music's detractors. "I think in certain places they *do* look down on country music." He paused. "And I think they should." Porter went on to condemn inept performers who give the business a "bad image . . . you have to do a good job at something for it to be respected."

This was the Northwest tour that inspired Porter to write "Highway Headin' South" on the bus in Montana. But they flew home on a 747 Superjet out of Seattle, itself a noteworthy event. *Music City News* marveled that he had broken his fifteen-year moratorium on air travel, an aversion that has cost him considerable overseas bookings and international recognition throughout his career.

At the end of February, Porter recapitulated the tour for Jack Hurst of *The Tennessean*, admitting that some of the audiences had been lukewarm. "You want to stop halfway through the show, after you've turned cartwheels all the way through 'Company's Comin'" without making a dent, and ask them whether or not they've reached a verdict." But overall the tour proved the show was in great demand and confirmed his vow to boycott package shows. "I want to play to people who came to hear Porter

Wagoner, not Merle Haggard or somebody else. This way I don't waste their time or mine either!"

Then Porter denounced the cheapskate, slipshod standards of the package show bookers when dealing with the media. He said it was hardly news that he had sung "A Satisfied Mind" on the "Ozark Jubilee" fifteen years ago—promoters deserved better than "a manila envelope containing a couple of old pictures and information just about as up to date as that!"

Porter described how his new Information Service (Paul Soelberg) would saturate the market along the route of their tours, ten full weeks of bombardment at measured intervals. First, disc jockeys got Porter albums, Dolly albums, duet albums, then tape-recorded promo-spots of himself and Dolly for their radio stations. Next, special ad copy was sent to the promoters to place in the newspapers. Finally, they mailed detailed bio pieces and specially slanted news stories and photos to all the newspapers. Porter said that no one in the same vicinity would receive identical material; rather, they would each get different photos and write-ups. In at least four cities—Portland, Seattle, Calgary, and Great Falls, Montana—the papers had run two stories each, and these before the show played. In Vancouver, Canada, where the TV show didn't even reach, crowds had to be turned away at the Vancouver Symphony Hall.

Dolly sat down next to Colonel Harlan Sanders, the fried chicken entrepreneur, and traded her success story for his in March 1972. The colonel wore his plantation-white uniform, and the occasion was Lee Giroux's syndicated TV show. Dolly and the colonel made the episode one of the best in the show's history. Without Porter.

LaWayne Satterfield interviewed Dolly in April for *Music City News*, again on her own. She was primly buttoned up, her canyon-like neckline not yet having been introduced in the media marketplace. Overhead, however, towered one of her wigs. Ann Warden says, "Chet wondered, why is she wearing those big wigs? But it turned out she knew what she was doing." Today Dolly claims to have 365 wigs, but says she counts her blessings and not her wigs.

Satterfield called Dolly an "RCA superstar." She told him she wrote songs to "create a whole new world . . . maybe you would call it a way to escape reality." The best time for her songwriting was in the stillness of the early morning when the world lay still asleep, she explained.

Visible tears rose in Dolly's eyes as she relived the searing harassments at Caton's Chapel grade school, from being locked in the coat closet and emerging with a permanent fear of the dark to eating lunch off by herself with her siblings, lest they be laughed at for only having biscuits instead of bread to eat. "I would pretend it wouldn't hurt, but it did." Satterfield judged that Dolly's scholarship fund for Sevierville high school students was her compassionate way of overcoming buried hurts and resentments. Dolly said today she just wanted to be liked by everyone. And that the most important event in her life, other than being born, was being born *again* . . . as a Christian.

The sunny surface that Porter and Dolly exhibited to the world—all a glitter with matching costumes, diamonds, smiles, and matching makeup and peroxide tint, at least for album covers—was just that, a surface. Behind the cosmetic exterior was considerable of what Dolly calls "fight 'n' scratch."

In our interview in 1990 she said:

> Someone made a comment, someone who knew Porter's temper, "Hell, if you can survive Porter Wagoner, you can survive anything." So I kind of believe that in a way. But like I say, on the sweeter side, there were many, many great sides to Porter. He had a big heart. He had a lot of talent. He had a hot temper. He was a great showman, he still is. A great entertainer, I learned a lot from him. I think we agreed on more than we disagreed on. It's just that our disagreements were so severe, that we couldn't put it together.
>
> But Porter had been in the business 20-some-odd years, and I had just started, and I wanted to learn. And I'm not sorry that I did.

Porter in an interview with Paul Soelberg in 1971 spoke with his usual candor:

> I've got an awful temper. I guess I've got one of the worst tempers a person could have. If something really gets to me, it seems like it just tears me all to pieces. I've always been that way, ever since I was a kid. And I know that's not good.

He admitted that sometimes he let things bother him "when they shouldn't," and that he could also be "moody around the band, and really I shouldn't be." Paul added that "frequently he lets little things build up to the danger point, perhaps triggering that temper." Owepar manager Carla Scarborough recalls Porter–Dolly "discussions" you could hear out in the street.

Initially the conflicts were confined to their music. Porter told me in 1989:

> At first after Dolly had been with me a while, everything was very smooth. I made all the decisions, because I was the leader. Then Dolly got to seeing how this worked—with the songs, the record production, and the selling of things and so forth. Then she started offering suggestions, such as "Why don't we do it this-a-way?"

I said, "That's fine to offer suggestions. But don't tell me how to do my business, because I've been doing it longer and know more about it. But feel free to offer your suggestions, always. But don't be mad or insulted if I don't use them. Because I am the screener of those ideas, and don't feel if I don't use them, don't feel embarrassed, or like, 'I'll never give you another idea, because you didn't use the last one!' Don't have that attitude."

After the first year she started bringing me these ideas, a lot of them was completely ridiculous, so far away from the direction I wanted to go. Dolly wanted to be more like Aretha Franklin and scream on songs. Well, I had several discussions with Dolly about her singing. Her voice was high and shrill, that's why. People don't like to be hollered and screamed at when you are telling them a story. It's all right in certain lines, and certain parts, when screaming is necessary. But they don't like to be hollered at, they want something pleasant to listen to. She wanted to go the other direction, and be more like Aretha Franklin. She had her records, she wanted more punch.

She had visions of being a pop star like Roy Orbison. I said, "That is not the direction I will go with you, because first of all, I don't know about over in that field. But I know millions of country fans, and I know what they want and what they like. Them are the people I've got to deal with." I said, "If you want to go pop someday, fine—but if you want to be with my show, I won't allow that because I won't know where we're going. I'm not going out on a blind course, because I'm having success with what I'm doing with country fans."

She went into the studio with her uncle and a couple of other people. And did some demos of some stuff she thought was great. It was just a piece of shit, it was so awful. It was so far out in left field, with echo just booming in every direction."

I commented that Porter has always seemed to use as little echo as possible.

Just a little [echo] to soften it. I went through about 20 microphones at RCA till I found one [an RE-15] that would make her voice tolerable, not to take any of the resonance out of her voice but to cut down that high thing. I finally found one and marked it, and I have it and it has her name on it.

(Porter told Toby Thompson of the *Village Voice* in 1976 that he kept his "Dolly" microphone in a vault.)

And then I started having a few problems with Dolly. She wanted to have her records sound more pop-ish.

Once, morning show host Ralph Emery asked Dolly on television if she might record again with Porter, and she said:

I would if we could come to some sort of agreement, of what we were doing and how we would do it, and if we both had creative control . . . I wouldn't want to go in and do it again with just Porter and get back in the same situation . . .

Ralph: I assume when you made records with him, he had all the creative control, he was the boss?

Dolly: Well, he was the boss, but he didn't have all the creativity, he had control, let's put it that way.

We had some wonderful times, I'll always respect Porter; we went through bad times—we went through seven of the best and seven of the worst years I've ever had in my life. A lot can be said about Porter, uh, both ways . . . I think that we did a lot of good for each other. I will always be grateful for the good things.

Ralph had Porter on a show, and played for him a copy of the above interview with Dolly. Porter responded:

Well, I feel about the same way . . . I think it's true I gave Dolly a big break. I think I contributed a lot to Dolly's career, and she contributed a lot to my career as well. The duets we did I think were great for both of us. The part that Dolly was talking about, about me being the boss—if I was recording with Loretta Lynn, naturally I would not be the boss—if I was recording with Dolly Parton today, naturally I would not be boss. But at that time, I signed the checks, therefore I was boss. . . .

So I don't let people get the wrong idea I'm a bossy type person and that you can't deal with me unless you let me boss you, because I only boss the people that I sign their checks. Because I've recorded with other people that I never bossed around. But when I sign the check and you work for me, I'm gonna tell you what I want.

Mack Magaha says the Glaser Brothers wanted to take Dolly to New York to cut a rock 'n' roll record, and she wanted badly to go with them. So all the way to a show in Raleigh, North Carolina, she and Porter fought about it. She argued, "If people don't like me in the rock 'n' roll field, I can still come back to the country."

He replied, "Why in the hell do you want to leave somebody that's already with you, and then fall back on them if you can't make it?"

Mack says, "I heard that myself. He got real mad about that."

Chuck Glaser believes Dolly probably did more arranging of her recorded songs than is generally acknowledged, since she wrote so many of them and probably heard the arrangements in her head. Arranging is seldom credited separately, being blurred in with producer credit usually. Don Warden says Porter deserves 75 percent of the credit on Norma Jean's records, and "in the Dolly period, 80 percent or probably even more." Engineer Roy Shockley echoes this (Roy worked for Porter at

RCA from 1966 to 1977, then at Porter's studio from 1977 to 1982). "Yes, Dolly had that screaming sound. But the people liked it. Porter kept trying to tune her down. He's fully responsible for Dolly Parton. He put her first, he put her in front from the time I met him. He pushed her out front. He *made* Dolly."

Roy's fellow engineer, Tom Pick, remembers Porter's quest for the ideal microphone. "Every microphone is different. When you record somebody you are trying to get realism out of them. Country music is from the soul, and you try to capture that. You may only get it in one take." Tom remembers Dolly sessions that ran for three hours when they might get three or four good takes of songs down, and many times these were good enough for final takes. Some sessions were so productive they'd maybe have a song in the can to spare, something they could hold back for later. "One session, I think three singles came off that session." Tom says Porter listened to a lot of pop music and was always seeking new drum patterns. He recalls Porter saying that inching toward the pop market was like a baseball pitcher shifting from one pitch to another. "You go pop, then reach for the old rosin bag and have a country single."

Guitar player George McCormick, who escaped from the show just in time, says Porter would hold a song for months, trying to think of new ways to do it. "He used to ask all our opinions on a song . . . Dolly was more pop. It scared us, we were afraid she wouldn't make it. She was writing songs that ought to be recorded now."

Uncle Louis Owens, working at Owepar, felt the same thing:

> RCA, they were just along for the ride. They were not sold on her. She was at least five years ahead of her time. I used to tell her that all the time, "They may not be ready for you, maybe you're over their heads."

Porter's secretary Joan remembers how it became harder and harder to get a song to Porter. Hit writers like Vic McAlpin would leave their tapes in vain. And Porter got more and more intense in the studio, as the pressures to drive Dolly and their duets higher and higher up the charts continued to mount. Musicians might tell Joan, "If you can get me out of the session, don't call me." Joan says, "It was tough, let me tell you. Let me say that much. For the ones closest to them, it was really hard. A lot of it was her creativity trying to overpower his."

Bob Ferguson says:

> We had a wonderful trip in those early years. You listen for ideas, you don't have all the good ideas yourself. Somebody on the fiddle may hit a good lick; you use everybody's ideas. A producer's job was hard in those days . . . Porter became more restrictive in

finding ideas from anybody else, not listening to me, not listening to anybody. He sagged badly. Sometimes we'd wait till he left town to do the final mix.

Once Porter came and said, "No one can hit a lick that I don't tell 'em to hit." And someone got up and said, "You can *have* it, Chief," and left. Now that's not the Nashville spirit. It grew like Topsy, from Dolly's point of view. She couldn't sing songs she wanted to. Though she learned about interpretation [of a song] from Porter, I'm sure.

But it's humanly impossible to hold onto somebody [like Dolly]. Chet tried to talk to him like a brother. But it kept on goin' like a train goin' down hill.

Bob makes it sound like "The Wreck of the Old '97," going downgrade at ninety miles an hour. But it also recalls Porter's own song, "Life Rides the Train," about how some people get permanently off the track and others don't know if life's train is "bound to hell or to heaven on high."

However stressful it may have seemed, the train was still officially on the track in 1972. It was headed uphill, with confidence! A Wagoner family favorite was "Life's Railway to Heaven," which Porter also recorded (so did Norma Jean). It compares life to a mountain railroad. To make that mountain run successful you must keep your hand upon the throttle and a wary eye out for the tunnels, the fills, and the curves (those in the track, that is), "to never falter, never fail . . . your eyes upon the rail."

"OUR LOVE'S THE FIGHTING KIND"

Life at times has been unpleasant,
down the trails where life has led us.

—from "Together Always" by Dolly, number fourteen
hit for Porter and Dolly, 1972

Dolly's measurements were 38–26–36, Red O'Donnell informed America in his syndicated column in September 1972. He also reported the statistic that 90 percent of Dolly's fan letters always asked whether she and Porter were married. Dolly always answered, "Yes, but not to each other." Red asked Dolly why Carl Dean didn't travel with his wife, and Dolly said that the demands of the asphalt business kept him at home, though, in fact, Dean Paving with his dad was going out of business. When were they going to have any children? "I can tell you right now Carl and I are not doing anything to prevent it."

On the radio at that moment was their duet hit "Together Always." Dolly wrote it, though its hopeful title sounds like Porter. In one of his lines, Porter sings that their love will multiply, then be divided, by children. He wrote the flip side, "Love's All Over," his most blatantly sensuous song, with Dolly singing its frankest lines. He admits they used to worry what people thought, they weren't going to hide their love anymore. The album *Together Always* appeared that September, with them hand-in-hand, walking in the woods on the back cover. It included the Pillow Room teleportation trip, "Anyplace You Want to Go," plus two nonlethal songs about children. "Christina" has a pretty melody, and producer Porter gives it a syncopated, soft-rock Eagles beat. Baby Christina is born to a happy couple, and, for a change, a baby in a Dolly Parton song survives. By now Dolly and Carl were raising young Rachel Parton. Reviewing the album, Bill Littleton said in *Country Music*, "Singles from this album could almost be decided on a dart board or by flipping coins—they're all that good."

Back in 1970 ground had been broken for Opryland. On September 6, 1972, Porter, Dolly, and the Wagonmasters became the first country music show to be taped at Opryland USA, the new theme park then under construction. Opryland executive Mike Downs boasted to the press that any tourists who happened to get picked up by the cameras might see themselves later on "The Porter Wagoner Show." The center-piece of the park would be the 4,400-seat Grand Ole Opry House, which opened in 1974.

The move from the Ryman was an urgent necessity. The old tabernacle was a fire trap; there were no personal dressing rooms; toilets had inadequately low water pressure; and there was no air conditioning. To cool the place, metal ducts would have had to be run up the three-foot-thick brick walls, possibly deadening the Ryman's classic acoustics. As Caleb Pirtle III wrote in his history of Opryland, *The Grandest Day*, "The Ryman smelled of sweat and tobacco, booze and popcorn." Former Opry manager Bud Wendell said Opry stars might appear in fine concert halls across the world—but that "the worst place they were ever asked to perform was in their home, the Opry." (His statement is not entirely true; its acoustics have never been matched.)

By 1990 Wendell had become chairman of the Nashville Area Chamber of Commerce. Sitting in his office at Opryland, dressed still like the insurance executive he used to be (at National Life, which owned WSM), Bud said the Ryman was "in the decaying part of town. Standing in the hot lines on a Saturday night, you'd get hit by the panhandlers, and the hookers and the itinerant preachers, and the bootblacks and the hustlers and the pickpockets. There were three or four bars across the street with the occasional shooting. Here we are with a tourist attraction that attracts two to three hundred thousand people a year, and this is how we treat them. There were serious discussions as to whether the Opry would continue. We were *saving* the Opry."

Vic Willis remembers standing outside the Ryman when someone from Channel 5 who didn't recognize him (the Willis Brothers came to the Opry in 1946) asked him, "What do you think about tearing down the Ryman?" Vic said, "Good!" Television news reporter Ruth Ann Leach walked over and Vic added, "Can't heat it in the winter, can't cool it in the summer, men and women have to change clothes with each other, it doesn't hold the people." Roy Acuff said, "You're the only one who agrees with me."

Today, there is no one more identified with the Opry—and by extension, Opryland—than Porter Wagoner, unless it's Roy Acuff. Bud Wendell says Porter once owned the private police department that served Opryland—and that he has been "through the years as supportive of the Opry as anyone on the Opry. Anytime we need him for anything, he's there, he's more than willing."

A month and a half after the Opryland taping, on October 20, 1972, Porter received a tribute luncheon from RCA, commemorating his twentieth year on the label. Kathy Sawyer of *The Tennessean* said that he forgot about "selling songs and laxatives long enough to make an eloquent, if sometimes halting" thank-you speech:

> "I guess this is the first time I've made a speech. I feel half naked up here without my guitar. I didn't realize how that guitar was really a cover up for me."
>
> Blushing to the tips of his sky-blue patent leather pointy-toed boots, the thin blond singer made an emotional statement of gratitude, particularly to "the little blonde lady that I sing with, the finest lady God ever put breath in, Miss Dolly Parton.
>
> "She has meant more to me than anyone in my career," he said. "She's pretty—but I've met a lot of pretty people on the outside, but when you get to know them you find out how ugly they are on the inside. She's not like that.
>
> "For the encouragement she's given me in recording, writing, and so many things, I owe her more than I can ever repay if I'm here another fifty years."

And Porter praised other people, including RCA engineers Roy Shockley and Tom Pick: "because of them, I can't wait to record." (He still relies on Tom Pick for recording sessions.) Then Chet said:

> I've known Porter since he came down here with a crewcut in 1952. Now he's a tycoon. I've seen all that happen, and that's wonderful.
>
> He's a country boy that kinda matured slowly. Just this past year or two he's been writing some of our best songs. He's gonna be one of our great writers. And he's taken up finger-style guitar. No tellin' what's gonna happen from that.

Next, comedian Jethro Burns of Homer and Jethro, the comedy act, stood up to say that Porter was "probably the last guy doing good ol' country music like it was meant to be played . . . the people that are trying to change his style are all out looking for work." Jethro then explained, "Seems like Porter was an ugly kid. He was so ugly he used to tie a porkchop around his neck to get the dog to play with him!"

On an undated "Fact Sheet" from probably 1972, Dolly listed as her "PET PEEVES: People who abuse the country music industry and 'people who don't treat women as equals to men!'"

When Dolly was deposed by Porter's attorney Thomas V. White in 1979, it lasted about eight hours. Porter never knew what Dolly's testimony contained since the case was settled soon after, and he never responded. She said not very long after she signed the 1970 contract, Porter tore it up, or tore up what she thought was the contract. That much had leaked to the newspapers earlier. Needless to say, that was *not* Porter's recollection.

"Did Porter or any member of his band ever hit you?"

"Not intentionally. Once in an anger fit Porter knocked a table over on the bus with his hand. I was unhappy. I didn't really want to go. I really wanted to make it work . . . He's like my dad. I love my dad but I was afraid of him. My father had a very strong will, I was young and hadn't been around that many men . . ."

Dolly mentioned all the torments the Parton kids had endured in school, and how she was probably "quick to defend herself." She said Porter scared her at times, that "he could go for days in a pissy mood, it would tear me all to pieces in a minute, it still does." Porter liked to go to the office when they were off the road, "from daylight to dusk," and expected the same from Dolly. At his worst Porter could tear a picture off the wall, kick the desk, and "You don't know what to think, whether you're going to be next or not!" Dolly said she feared for herself, and even for Porter in light of his brother Oscar's suicide.

"Then he would become extremely kind, and I would think I was over-reacting," Dolly said. "I never said Porter was all bad and I was all good. I must have upset him because he damn sure upset me."

The late Nancy Hurt, who worked for Porter for many years as accountant and then as office manager, earlier worked for Dolly. She was the closest of friends with Dolly's mother, Avie Lee. Nancy once laughed that while she'd never seen Dolly angry, "I've always suspected she's part bobcat."

Dolly's independence and Porter's need to control her were central to their increasing troubles. Porter had expected her to behave like an obedient employee, as *he* had been at Springfield, sopping up advice and direction. When he joined KWTO, as one entertainer among dozens, he already had several years of salaried experience behind him, whereas Dolly had never really worked long on salary anywhere. Her work résumé included brief telephone answering for a sign company in 1964 and waitressing at Dobb's House restaurant on Murfreesboro Road in 1966. For almost a decade before joining Porter, she had been told by her uncles, by Cas Walker, by Fred Foster, and especially by her own dreams, that someday she'd be a big star. So if she acted like a rebellious employee at times, well, she didn't see herself as an employee. On paper at least, she was an independently contracted RCA recording artist, even if also on paper RCA had assigned her to Porter (with Bob Ferguson, implicitly).

Porter, who is always early for appointments, should have checked his watch. The year was 1972, not 1952.

Public sympathy has tilted almost entirely in Dolly's direction. History is usually written by the victors, and Dolly was victorious, and a woman besides. Yet in 1972 she was earning around $80,000 a year; and in his notes, Porter's attorney, Thomas V. White, records a $10,000 Christmas gift to Dolly for 1972. Since joining Porter's show, Dolly had charted thirteen country hits of her own and thirteen duet hits.

Had Dolly stayed with Fred Foster on Monument (and with Combine), she might have ended up just another girl singer, albeit a distinctive one. Porter contributed the impact of the duets, plus constant touring and weekly television, as well as the extra publisher's royalties they shared (mostly from her songs, she would remind Porter's attorney). Other girl singers flitted in and out of the limelight in the late sixties and early seventies, such as Jeannie C. Riley and 1971 Grammy winner Sammi Smith. Sammi says she was supposed to be someone's tax write-off, till she spoiled things by taking "Help Me Make It Through the Night" to number one. Some of the women singers who flourished also utilized the duet tactic, such as Jan Howard, who sang with Bill Anderson on records and on his TV show. Even closer competition was offered by Loretta Lynn and Conway Twitty and by George Jones and Tammy Wynette, who being married (stormily) had much to sing about.

Perhaps Dolly was becoming something of a fixture, like Speck or Mack or Buck, seen year after year every Saturday on television. It almost drove Porter crazy to think that RCA took Dolly for granted, as if she were someone they'd merely acquired wholesale, part of the entire sparkly Porter package. Such frustrations threatened to turn the office, and even the studio, into something resembling the Rubber Room at times. Porter may be a sharp salesman, but it was humiliating to have to constantly resell RCA on Dolly Parton. His grander vision for Dolly's future may not have equaled her own in all its details (such as her desire to have a Porterless future as soon as possible), but he was way ahead of everybody else. As for the various confrontations behind closed corporate doors, Chet Atkins says in his droll fashion, "He's *never* boring."

Chet told *Country Music People* in 1991, "We used to sit around all the time saying, 'When is Dolly going to be number one? She's the greatest damn thing in the industry.' Same thing with Willie [Nelson, whom RCA dropped]."

But women singers didn't sell that many country records. Women bought most of the records, and, especially in the country field, were not particularly interested in singers of their own sex, however much they might identify with a faithful if hurting Tammy Wynette or with a scrappy Loretta Lynn. Women make stars out of men. Female acts sell 12 percent of the records, journalist Bob Oermann of *The Tennessean* reported with considerable dismay in 1991.

Of course Dolly's blend of naïve voluptuousness, childlike beauty, and heart-wrenching lyrics was no real threat to the average housewife, however much her husband might pause to appreciate Dolly while trying to find that Saturday afternoon football game on television.

But Dolly wasn't all that successful even within country music. Her biggest hits were mostly still to come, and her Female Vocalist of the Year award was three years off. Tammy Wynette, passed over by Porter as Norma Jean's replacement, had married George Jones and had already won Female Vocalist of the Year three years running (1968–70). And Loretta Lynn had managed to win Entertainer of the Year that same fall (1972), pushing women ahead a little bit, being the first female to win it. Meanwhile, even the Porter–Dolly duet act was not going to win any more awards, although in baseball terms, they outscored their nearest competitors 3–2 in *Billboard* hits.* The duo image naturally blurred their respective identities. Porter the duet partner especially over-shadowed Porter the solo act. Dolly certainly was sick of reading that she was "Porter Wagoner's singing partner," though this information was sinking further and further down in the news columns.

The solution was to intensify everyone's efforts. If RCA would only wake up, they all might elevate Dolly to the top of country music, then slide her across into pop. If or *when* Dolly left, at least Porter would have a percentage payback of her earnings to reward him for all his efforts (except that Dolly says she thought the contract was torn up). Anyway, Porter obviously needed to work harder. He would have to spend more time selecting, arranging, sometimes writing songs for Dolly. He would have to spend more hours in the studio tinkering with the sound. He would have to spend more time telling RCA to spend more time promot-ing Dolly Parton. The TV show tapings and the road show touring (100,000 miles a year) would have to be squeezed in there somehow.

And if there was any time left, Porter Wagoner the singer should not forget to keep making records. After all, there were plenty of good songs in the Owepar catalogue. Even Porter Wagoner the solo singer had a spot on "The Porter Wagoner Show."

Years later, in an unaired segment of the "Dolly" show, Porter mentioned taking "old yellers" to keep awake while fishing. Then Johnny Russell said he stayed out of Tootsie's because he wasn't into drinking, pills, or chasing women. Everyone looked at him askance. Chet told me that he had about eleven artists on drugs in the early 1970s, and Bob Ferguson laments the role of "yellow jackets" in the studio. One of Porter's fishing pals from the seventies, Rick ("Rabbit") Hibbett, says one of their fishing friends who used to care for people's boats died of an amphetamine overdose. And Rabbit remembers hearing Porter and Dolly at Porter's trailer at Kentucky Lake near Paris, Tennessee, in probably 1972, arguing noisily.

*Porter and Dolly, twenty-one; Loretta and Conway, fourteen; George and Tammy, thirteen; Jim Ed Brown and Helen Cornelius, thirteen (*Joel Whitburn's Top Country Singles 1944–1988*).

Dolly has often likened their relationship to a marriage—a business marriage. And what do troubled couples do, sometimes unwisely, to stave off divorce? They have a baby, never thinking of the risk of a broken home, child support, or lawyers' fees.

Already the two of them owned considerable community property, but they now added more. If Owepar had been a kind of corporate stepchild Porter had adopted, then Fireside Studio became his and Dolly's firstborn business baby. Ground for Fireside was broken in December 1972, behind the building at 813 Eighteenth Avenue South, on Music Row.

Earlier in 1972 they had purchased the house next door, the former Starday building. This converted house would now serve both Porter's and Dolly's separate "enterprises" plus Owepar, and even an ASCAP publishing firm, Silver Dagger. Jack Hurst of *The Tennessean* judged that they needed all this space thanks to Dolly's songs being recorded by Merle Haggard, Conway Twitty, Skeeter Davis, Nat Stuckey, and pop artists Goldie Hawn and Nancy Sinatra with Lee Hazelwood. They reportedly paid around $35,000 in cash for the building, while announcing plans to build a studio next door for around $100,000.

Out in front of 813 a large wagon wheel was half sunk in the lawn.

When work started next door, assorted Partons and Owenses rallied for duty. Dolly's entire career at times resembles a vast WPA-style work project for her kinfolk. The asphalt parking lot to the rear was naturally poured by Dolly's husband, Carl T. Dean of Dean Paving. Fireside would be a "separate" business and would rent from Owepar. Owepar's secretary-treasurer, Louis Owens, would own 40 percent of Fireside, while Porter and Dolly each owned only 30 percent. In time, Louis's 40 percent would become permanently mislaid in the complex paperwork. At least in the ledger book, to paraphrase their hit "Holding On to Nothin'," Porter and Dolly were definitely holding on to *somethin'*.

Porter-free interviews with the press were now a conspicuous Dolly trend, or perhaps goal. The journalists tended to report another trend, that of Porter dropping by before they were finished. In December 1972, Jerry Bailey interviewed Dolly for *Country Music* magazine. Jerry was captivated by her four-inch high heels, her mountainous mounds of blond wig, and her tight-fitting blue pants "revealing curves reminiscent of Marilyn Monroe," plus seven rings on her fingers. When Porter poked in, Dolly asked him what she was getting for Christmas. In what became an oft-quoted exchange, he promised her "another chance" for Christmas. But, said Dolly, that's what she got last Christmas. No, she'd gotten more than that—she'd received a Cadillac and a diamond necklace *and* another chance.

The December *Music City News* ran a picture of the smiling

couple haloed by their luminous, matching pale hair. Porter had a pen in his hand. A little early perhaps, they were receiving their Christmas gift from RCA, "another chance" to be sure—"a new long-term contract." Presenting it was Rocco Laginestra, RCA president, joined by Chet Atkins and Bob Ferguson, all smiles, though they probably sensed by now they were not indispensable any longer. Standing by was Chet's assistant, Jerry Bradley. Jerry's rising executive star was not going to be hitched to Wagoner any longer than was necessary.

The contract, dated December 1, 1972, required that Dolly cut twenty-five sides (songs) per year for the next five years. As an inducement, she got a little Christmas office party gift, so to speak: $35,000, "non refundable," meaning it wasn't an advance against royalties but a free-and-clear little something for her Christmas stocking. Of course the 125 sides would all be produced by Porter, who also picked up 4 to 5 percent royalties for his labors.

That Christmas the number one song in pop music was "I Am Woman" by Helen Reddy. Its assertive message of female independence rankled a lot of disc jockeys, though they admitted their wives just loved it.

Soon after Christmas, Michael Willard heralded Dolly's "success story" in his syndicated column, based on her holiday gifts from Porter— "a royal blue Cadillac with a powder blue interior. He also threw in a set of diamond earrings."

32

"I WILL ALWAYS LOVE YOU"

"I hope life treats you kind . . . "
—Dolly, "I Will Always
Love You," number one hit,
1974 and 1982

"Dolly, nobody gives a shit about 'Mama's Old Black Kettle,' or 'Daddy's Working Boots.' *Who cares?*" Porter was saying back in 1973, referring to two of her Smoky Mountain tributes. Songs which he himself had recorded.

"Sing something people can connect with. Love. *Love!* They are all familiar with it. They don't care about working boots. No matter what the hell your dad done in his boots, the people don't care, they are not familiar with it, they know nothing about it. You've got to write *love songs* if you're going to be successful. You write me some love songs that we can record, and then we'll be in business, because people know about that."

"I'll write you a love song."

"Please do."

Now Porter had to compete with the Dolly he had been producing and promoting. This Dolly was the darling of the critics; her "Tennessee Mountain Home" had gone to number thirteen early in 1973, a song that made Bob Powel of *Country Music People* "almost smell the hay and taste the grits cooking for breakfast" and a record which Charles K. Wolfe praised for its banjo (Buck Trent) and harmonica (Charlie McCoy) in his notes to the Time-Life Books album.

Simultaneously, John Denver's "Rocky Mountain High," also on RCA, was high on the pop charts. Both songs have impeccably crisp production, and the precise, crystalline clarity on Denver's records—you can hear the guitar picks strike the strings—resembles the kind of perfection Porter was always seeking. The *Rocky Mountain High* album was already out when Dolly's *Tennessee Mountain Home* appeared that March. But in the world of John Denver, people rarely worked, except perhaps to hitchhike to Colorado and clamber up a peak to enjoy the view. In Dolly's album, besides songs about Avie Lee's cooking kettle and Daddy's boots, was a slower, moodier version of "In the Good Old Days (When Times Were Bad)." Dolly includes a tearful recitation, "The Letter," reading an actual homesick letter from Nashville in 1964: "Don't you worry about me gettin' in trouble, 'cause I'll be good."

Bob Oermann, in *Country Sounds*, would call it Dolly's "most outstanding solo album to date." John Morthland praised its "mountain soul" while admitting the nostalgia was starting to cloy. Robert Christgau of the *Village Voice* agreed that while the title song was a masterpiece, overall the "pastoral nostalgia, while always charming, is sometimes a little too pat."

The album became famous for the paintless house on the cover, complete with metal washing machine on the porch. This was the Parton's Locust Ridge home, but when Dolly purchased it and restored it, the media in 1990 began calling it her birthplace, which it is not. The liner notes distinguish it from the log cabin, including a painting of the latter to make it doubly clear.

But all this Smoky Mountain squalor no longer captivated the housewives or the disc jockeys. A female singer needs to be identified with grown-up romantic passions. The solo career of Tammy Wynette was far eclipsing Dolly's, at least on the charts, however popular Dolly might be on TV. Tammy brought her own personal marital scars to her singing, audible in her pang-in-the-throat vocal style, as she mixed fidelity with pain in hit after hit. By 1973 she'd scored twelve number ones (with more to come), plus a number one duet hit. Tammy didn't wallow, lyrically, in the Mississippi cotton fields where she'd toiled as a child. Her canny producer, Billy Sherrill, relied almost wholly on proven, professional songwriters. Porter and Dolly were recording almost nothing but their own or her kinfolk's songs, so they couldn't blame RCA for everything.

When Dolly brought in "I Will Always Love You," Porter exclaimed, "Wow, that's the most commercial song. You give me that, and you can have all the others, all you've ever written. I'm talking about making a career, making money—I'm not talking about what I like. I love your 'Daddy's Working Boots' and 'Mama's Old Black Kettle.' But I'm talking about building your career. Give me this song. It will make you more famous, and more money, and that, after all, is what we're after. Getting more people in through the box office. Where I can make some dollars off of you. That song will make you money as long as you live, 'cause as long as people live, they're going to be loving, they're going to love each other. Because when they don't, they're gone!

"Can you imagine this guy dating this girl? They're at the drive-in, listening to the radio, and what're they going to want to hear? 'Mama's

Old Black Kettle'? Shit no, they don't care about 'Mama's Old Black Kettle,' they're thinking about love. Can you picture this guy holding this girl in his arms, and 'I Will Always Love You' comes on? If that don't send this guy in love with her, the son of a bitch is *gone!*"

The more Porter would brag on Dolly, the harder she'd work. Soon she had brought him more than twenty songs about love. On her 1975 album *Dolly* she wrote, "I love to write songs, and love is one of my favorite subjects to write about." In her back cover portrait, her expression is mistily erotic, and her metal-studded red pantsuit enwraps her tightly enough to corner the I-will-always-love-you vote from the red-blooded male electorate. Flaring outward in four directions behind her are metallic-looking, golden ribbony rays of pseudo-sunlight: Dolly as art deco butterfly.

Porter says when he first fell in love his favorite song was "When My Blue Moon Turns to Gold Again." He adds, "If you'll just look at the business you're in, you can see what they like of what you do." He illustrates with an anecdote about doing a spiritual recitation at a show in Ponchatoula, Louisiana, when a woman unzipped her purse and got out a handkerchief. "It just killed me, because I knew the song meant so much to her." He figures these recitations may remind some women of their late husband or some other loved one. "Those are the kind of things you must do in your writing and your performing for the people you must sell to."

The lilting melody of "I Will Always Love You" certainly would drive a couple tighter into each other's arms. But the passionate message is mostly in the title, which also is the chorus. The verses are in the ironic, farewell vein. Dolly sings that if she stays she will only be in the way. In her 1979 deposition Dolly said of the song, "I was leaving, and I wanted to say something, and for the *good* things." She said it was not a love song in the man-woman sense.

"I Will Always Love You" went to number one twice on the country charts (1974 and 1982), though lyrically and melodically it's virtually a pop song. Dolly always closed her television show (1987–88) with a dreamy-eyed rendition of it; often she signs letters and Christmas cards with "I will always love you."

Onstage at Dollywood with Porter on April 29, 1989, she said what she has often said before, that she wrote it for him. The lyric proclaims that all she's taking with her are bittersweet memories: "We both know that I'm not what you need."

33

"WE'LL GET AHEAD SOMEDAY"

Porter Wagoner is a legend like Hank Williams.
People in restaurants and taverns
tell stories about Porter Wagoner.

—Stella Parton, interview,
February 8, 1989

When Patty Loveless joined the Grand Ole Opry on June 11, 1988, she became its sixty-fourth member. Porter officially welcomed her onstage with a bouquet of roses. Patty was only thirty-one, but she'd been coming to Nashville since the summer of 1971, when she was fourteen. She and her brother Roger had gotten their first encouragement at Porter's office.

Patty and Roger Ramey were from Pikeville, Kentucky. Their father was a coal miner and a fan of Porter's TV show. Patty and Roger used to practice Porter and Dolly numbers, as well as Loretta Lynn–Ernest Tubb songs. In Louisville someone started calling them "The Singin', Swingin' Rameys."

Patty was immensely inspired by watching Dolly on television, especially when she would talk about songwriting. "When I went to Nashville," Patty remembered in an interview, "I had a few songs under my belt." About thirty in fact. At Porter's office, he seemed impressed with her singing and invited them to a TV taping that very evening. Patty remembers Porter picking up their motel tab for a few more days. "I couldn't have anybody in my family treat me any better." Porter even paid for their bus trips, as they came back to Nashville repeatedly. "I used to feel guilty about it, but he seemed to enjoy our company." Out at Center Hill Lake they would pass weekends together "just sitting around and singing."

Sometimes they'd check into a hotel, call Porter, and he'd invite them over to the Versailles. "Dolly would end up meeting us over there. I remember 'My Blue Tears' was out, and I started singing the lyrics and she'd start singing the backup, the harmony part." Patty was always excited being around them.

Porter taught her a lot about singing, about vocal dynamics, "things vocally I use to this day." She liked to sing loud, and he would show her on "The Pain of Loving You" how to sing softly on the verses, then to cut loose on the chorus. He'd strum along on his guitar. "When he spoke, I would listen, I would feel it was something of importance and it wasn't just a bunch of bull. He was a very serious man when it came to music."

Porter began introducing Patty and Roger to people in the music industry, and they began finding their way. In 1973 the Wilburn Brothers hired her to replace Loretta Lynn. Patty won them over with her rendition of Dolly's hit, "Mule Skinner Blues." She married the Wilburn's drummer, named Lovelace, but she adopted the stage name Loveless to avoid confusion with film performer Linda Lovelace. Acknowledging Dolly's impact upon her career, she told Bruce Honick of *Nashville!* magazine: "She was more like a sister, and had this warmth about her that I just dearly loved."

Patty told Carolyn Hollaran, author of *Our Brightest Stars in Country Music*, that Porter's mother had experienced a premonition about Porter dying in a plane crash. "His mother called and told him not to take a trip on a plane. He listened—canceled his trip—and the plane that was to carry him crashed."

The Fireside Recording Studio officially opened in March 1973, with Porter, Dolly, Louis Owens, and Ralph Emery hosting the festivities. Jack Logan was the manager. At one point in the mid seventies, the secretary at Fireside was one of Dolly's sisters, Stella Parton.

As a little girl, Stella had wanted to be a nun. The Partons weren't Catholic, advised her mother, so maybe she could be a missionary. After she left home, her less-than-divine destination for most of a year was a place called Hillbilly Heaven, in Lorton, Virginia, where Stella played country music.

In 1972 her missionary zeal resurfaced somewhat, when she appeared in a picture with Dolly and Uncle Louis in *Music City News*, launching her gospel group, Stella Carroll and the Gospel Carrolls. Stella gravitated to desk duties at Fireside, taking her salary not in cash but in studio time, and with her first eighty dollars' worth, cut a six-hour session on sixteen-track. Gradually she assembled her first album, *Stella (And the Gospel Carrolls)* on Inspiration Records but from the Fireside address, the disc itself stuffed into an RCA sleeve. Porter also produced an RCA session of Stella that was never released.

Once Dolly was sick, and Stella filled in for a few road shows. She was rather startled at the intense décor of the interior of Porter's bus. At

Welcome to Patty Loveless, sixty-fourth member of the "Grand Ole Opry," June 11, 1988 [COURTESY ROGER RAMEY].

the end of the tour, Stella recalls with embarrassment how she got off the bus with all the band members present. And there was Dolly to meet her hollering: "Hey Stella, you didn't pee in my bunk, now did you?"

When Dolly yanked free from Porter in 1974 and formed the Traveling Family Band, Stella refrained from joining, clutching onto her independent identity. Her own string of chart records followed.

Stella says that if she had a music business problem she could take it to Porter for advice. He wouldn't tell her what he thought she wanted to hear; he would tell her what he really believed.

34

"THE NIGHT PORTER WAGONER CAME TO TOWN"

O n January 22, 1973, George Foreman knocked down heavy-
weight champion Joe Frazier six times in the first two rounds.
The fight was telecast from Kingston, Jamaica. But not everyone caught
the fight, at least according to this song recorded many years later by
T. C. Brown:

THE NIGHT PORTER WAGONER CAME TO TOWN
By Bobby Braddock and Charlie Williams

Richard Nixon was still president,
Coke and Pepsi sold for fifteen cents,
I was still in love with Mavis Brown
The night that Porter Wagoner came to town.

Foreman knocked out Frazier on TV,
That was one big event we didn't see,
'Cause no one stayed at home for miles around
The night that Porter Wagoner came to town.

Momma ironed my shirt and Daddy let me take the truck,
I drove on out to Grapevine and picked old Mavis up,
We hit the county line for one quick round,
The night that Porter Wagoner came to town.

A thousand people sweltered in the gym,
Then I heard someone whisper, "Hey, that's him"—
That's when the crowd let out this deafening sound
The night that Porter Wagoner came to town.

On and on and on it went—
Speck Rhodes and Mack Magaha and Buck Trent
(And how did they get Dolly in that gown?)—
The night that Porter Wagoner came to town.

Aunt Essie had her picture made with Porter by the bus,
She said he was down to earth, just like one of us,
Then Mavis said, "Why don't we hang around,
It ain't often Porter Wagoner comes to town."

Porter signed his autograph on Beulah Risner's fan,
Then Mavis got acquainted with the Wagonmaster band;
The effect on all our lives was quite profound
The night that Porter Wagoner came to town.

35

"THEY DREADED TO SEE ME COMING . . . " (THE RCA EXPERIENCE)

Office intrigues will anger him.
He simply can't stand people keeping
secrets from him. He must know
everything that's going on.

—"The Leo Boss,"
Linda Goodman's Sun Signs (1968)

When a man sees things
and hears sounds that's not there,
he's headed for the Rubber Room.

—Porter, "The Rubber Room,"
a number forty-three *Cash Box* hit (1971)

"**F**ans Ask Dolly's Marital Status," ran a Greeneville, Tennessee, *Sun* headline in January 1973. Reporter Darrell Rowlett called her "country music's most discussed songstress" whose good looks overshadowed her "strong, high-pitched voice" and songwriting talent. Physically Dolly was "top-heavy." Other journalists were calling her "Diamond Dolly," said Darrell, thanks to Porter's annual generosity. He was like "a helpful older brother and benefactor."

Thus began 1973, the year when Dolly emerged more and more as a conspicuously independent entity, separate from "The Porter Wagoner Show." That year RCA, with a Missouri mule kick in the head from Porter, would rouse from its sluggish stupor, blink, and notice as if for the first time . . . Dolly Parton.

Her broad smile illuminated the cover of *Country Music* magazine that March, with a milestone interview by Jerry Bailey. She praised Porter and Uncle Louis for making Owepar a success, and said all the time away from her husband only made their days together the more precious. In a sidebar to the interview, Dave Hickey praised her song "I'm

Doing This for Your Sake," where a mother gives up a child for adoption. Dolly took old clichés and slapped them "on the bottom," he said, giving them new life. Dave said pop songs are sung *to* the audience, whereas country songs are sung *for* the audience; and he defended Dolly's subject matter, "suicide, adultery, madness, drugs, betrayal, illegitimacy, incestuous desire, and worst of all (in the pop music land of plenty) poverty."

Porter became the butt of reporter Ken Woodford's Dolly-centered joshing that May in the Charleston *Daily Mail*, when they played Charleston, West Virginia: "Poor Porter (that's Porter Wagoner who bosses the show that carries his name) is rarely mentioned in the [fan mail] questions, and no one seems to care what his waist, hips, and chest measurements are." The writer also added, "Oh yes, that feller Porter what's-his-name will be there too, and if you can think of something to ask him, I'll bet he'd appreciate it."

And it must have been Dolly who fascinated West Coast promoter Bob Eubanks. *The Tennessean* on May 8 headlined "Wagoner Troupe Signs $1 Million Show Deal." Tandy Rice had signed a hundred-show contract with Eubanks for 1974. Bob was the popular host of ABC-TV's "The Newlywed Game" who somewhere found the time to promote concerts on the side. He was seen in Nashville frequently, often around Porter's office.

Even as Dolly was contemplating uprooting herself professionally, she was sinking deeper domestic roots in Middle Tennessee soil. In the spring of 1973 she and Carl began building a house on a rolling hill in fashionably rural Brentwood. It is on Crockett Road between Wilson Pike and Concord Road, and many people have noticed how the locale evokes the atmosphere of Sevier County. Dolly's imposing twenty-three-room mansion, with its six columns and red roof, was surrounded in 1973 by seventy acres.

The house cost a reported $60,000 to build, and construction was supervised by Dot Watson, Dolly's uncle from Knoxville. Pitching in, of course was the Parton–Owens work gang with Carl Dean—all of them warmed up by the recent stint at Fireside. One of Watson's relatives, Jenella Justus, who runs a general store about a mile from Dolly's birthplace site, remembers Dolly's music room. The wallpaper was a-swarm with butterflies, and the fireplace was fashioned partly with logs from the birthplace cabin on Pittman Center Road. Dolly's big country kitchen had an electrified replica of an old wood stove. The bottom of her swimming pool was decorated with her butterfly symbol.

Such a big house afforded Dolly more wall space for her ever expanding hoard of plaques and award certificates. In 1989 she would spend $16,000 on a two-room closet to house her wigs, costumes, and seventy-five pairs of boots. The Brentwood headquarters would also shelter her precious song files, including more than one hundred removed from Owepar abruptly, to Porter's consternation. In time the Dollywood museum would absorb the overflow of her relics and spangled duds.

All the attention lavished on Dolly was embarrassing to Porter, but not because it tended to minimize him. It was embarrassing that everyone but RCA seemed to sense Dolly was ready to break out big. He had at least two confrontations with RCA during 1973. Porter's difficulties with RCA came in the wake of similar conflicts with other recording artists, such as Waylon Jennings, who disliked getting "Dear Artist" form letters from New York.

Porter says that if he went to New York, and told RCA, "I'm Porter Wagoner," they would not recognize his name. But if he said, "I'm Artist number 7012," they would say, "Oh. Artist number 7012. How *are* you!"

In 1973 Ernest Tubb released a song, "The Texas Troubadour," where he complained that people in New York thought he was "too country." The people on the New York sidewalks seemed in too much of a hurry, with hearts as cold as the concrete that they walk on. Porter wrote it.

In the 1930s and 1940s RCA had been the biggest record company. Gradually they lost out to Columbia, where Mitch Miller outguessed the market, from Frankie Laine to his Sing-a-Long syndrome in the sixties. But Mitch Miller hated rock 'n' roll, so RCA could feel a certain supremacy in the fact they had Elvis. Still, in the country market there was nowhere to go but up. Since Chet Atkins had played on everyone's sessions, he had developed an ear for songs, as when he began getting hits out of Don Gibson, Jim Reeves, Bobby Bare—and more authority out of Steve Sholes.

But the Nashville Sound chumminess of the 1960s at times masked a certain slothfulness. When Floyd Cramer had the hit single "Last Date" in 1961, RCA had taken thirteen months to get out the follow-up album. Jerry Bradley told a New York interviewer in 1977 that Lawrence Welk, of all people, beat them with his own hit album featuring "Last Date."

Chet came in playing guitar and went out the same way. His only regrets were probably the time he wasted pushing an executive's pencil when he could have been running a session or asking Bob Ferguson how the last one had gone. He told Patrick Carr of *Country Music* magazine in 1991, "Then the company got a big personnel department, and they'd write every year and say, 'What are your goals for 1968? What are your expectations for this employee and that employee?' and all that bullshit." Soon the world's most famous guitar player was reading English grammar texts so he could sound more like an executive and less like an East Tennessee high school dropout.

Certainly Chet needed an ambitious assistant like Jerry Bradley. Not being a musician, Jerry had a certain objectivity, and studios fascinated him. He had helped his dad, Owen Bradley, build the Mount Juliet "Bradley's Barn" operation. Wondering if RCA could sell more records, Jerry teamed with maverick Tompall Glaser, who assembled old tracks by Waylon, Willie, Tompall, and Waylon's wife, Jessi Colter, into the *Wanted: The Outlaws* album. It became the first platinum (million-selling) album in country music. Jerry Bradley was no longer just Owen Bradley's kid.

That was in 1976. But back in 1973 Dolly hadn't even had one gold album (500,000 sales). Johnny Cash and Charley Pride had had several. Loretta and even newcomer Donna Fargo had had two. Dolly had been around for almost a decade on major labels, and her old friends at Monument had scored a gold album in late 1973 with Kris Kristofferson, who was seen as more of a writer than a singer. Kris's producer, Fred Foster, had predicted movie success for Dolly. While she was still selling medicine show products, Kris was now in the movies. Porter couldn't even get Dolly a speaking part on a CMA awards show ceremony the following year. Couldn't Dolly just hand somebody an award and be a "co-presenter"? No. Her wigs were too big for network TV for one thing. Journalist Bill Littleton couldn't even get Porter and Dolly a featured spot in a series of radio specials—he was told they had the old-fashioned, spangled image that modern country music was trying to progress beyond.

Perhaps symptomatic of changes and losses, Chet Atkins lost eighteen inches of his intestine to the surgeon's knife in 1973. That same year he was inducted into the Hall of Fame. Chet would joke that he hung on with RCA for the hospitalization insurance. As late as 1977 he was still some sort of vice president, a title by then as redundant as all those Best Instrumentalist plaques he had on his wall.

Just as Chet needed the help of Jerry Bradley, so did Jerry need the help of Joe Galante. RCA assigned Joe to the Nashville office in 1973. By 1981 he had Jerry's job, helping Jerry to consider other options in 1982; and by 1990 Joe Galante was president of RCA. Joe had earned his promotion by championing such high-profit country acts as the Judds, Alabama, and Clint Black.

In 1987 Joe Edwards of the Associated Press learned that Joe Galante's first exposure to Nashville country music had been through a recording of Porter's. Joe Edwards found Joe Galante to be an "unlikely choice" to be running RCA's country division, since he grew up in New York City "and has little musical background." Galante had a business administration degree from Fordham University and worked only two years as a budget analyst for RCA before being officially planted in Nashville, at the age of twenty-three. In 1973 when he learned he was being transferred to Nashville, as "manager of administration," someone sent him a sample record. A Porter Wagoner record.

"I had no idea what it was about. I couldn't relate to it at all," Galante recalled.

"Nobody likes a hot shot" is an old saying. Recording artists, their managers, other executives, many of them complained to Chet about Joe. In his fatherly way Chet told him that maybe people just didn't understand him, but probably they understood Joe Galante all too well. Joe, unreformed budget analyst to this day, had a pesky curiosity about which country acts weren't selling records. His hotel room doors began attracting anonymous notes of the "get out of town" variety.

Bob Ferguson says the goal was to get rid of all the acts that he and Chet had developed, such as Hank Snow. However, Hank inconveniently had a number one hit in 1974.

Jerry and Joe were trying to drag a sixties record company toward the eighties, quite against its will at times.

Joe Galante refused repeated attempts to interview him for this book, saying that since he had not been involved with Porter, there would be no interview, and that Jerry Bradley was the person to talk to. Jerry Bradley also refused to be interviewed, not wishing "to open *that* can of worms."

"I didn't want to get crossways with Porter or Dolly," Chet Atkins said in 1990. He was in London, talking to Craig Baguley of *Country Music People*. "That was right when I was moving out [in 1973], and I knew Dolly wanted to see Jerry Bradley privately one day. Porter heard about it and came in from the lake to protect his interests, and that was hairy for a while."

Porter was off on a two-day fishing break, so Dolly's coast should have been clear. Maybe somebody tipped him off. As he drove back from Center Hill Lake, perhaps he was singing "The Cold, Hard Facts of Life" with its line "I got back in town a day before I planned to." Dolly's car was outside Porter Wagoner Enterprises, but no Dolly inside. Porter steamed over to RCA.

He barged in "behind closed doors" and, according to his attorney Tom White's notes, Jerry Bradley "was very upset . . . very touchy. Dolly started crying and said she didn't want to get in the middle of a dispute."

Dolly got the hell out.

"Bradley, you're a snake in the grass, and I think you're trying to deal directly with Dolly and keep me out of it," Porter shouted.

Porter called Chet down from upstairs, and "apparently Porter blasted Bradley pretty good with Chet there. Chet and Porter then went to lunch, and apparently Chet said he basically agreed with Porter but that Porter should have been more diplomatic with Bradley. "Since that time, Bradley has been very friendly to Porter," White says, "but I think it's very clearly understood between the two of them that there's no love lost."

Later Attorney Tom White asked Dolly who could bear witness to the duress she felt she was under. She replied, "Jerry Bradley, Joe Galante, and Mel Ilberman, vice president of RCA in New York." Dolly gave an example of an occasion. She said Porter had told her RCA would drop her if she left his show, but she wanted to hear this from them. She "was a grown woman" who felt she had some rights.

> I went to RCA one morning, one of the mornings I usually would have been in Porter's office just doing nothing, just being there, whatever. So I went up there, and walked to RCA and just to talk, see what was going on, and see whether they were not interested in me.
> And we were just sitting there having a conversation. Porter comes through the door, didn't even stop at the secretary's desk—the door was latched, he didn't even knock. He comes storming through the door and throws the door open and says, "What the g.d. hell's going on here?" And everybody looked, like, "What's the big deal? We're only talking to a person that got out of her cage for a minute."

So Jerry Bradley and Joe Galante, if need be, will be glad to testify to *that* or come forward, to tell you of that particular instance.

Porter told me in 1989:

> You know, the thing that was so insulting was the fact that they were trying to slip around my back to do something. I told them at the meeting, "I'm an adult, you don't have to slip around behind my back. You tell me what you want to do and I'll help you do it."
> I don't like people to try to ease around me because I can understand what it is, regardless of what it is.
> She didn't have any contract to stay with me. I wanted her to leave my show and get another producer to produce her pop. Because that's the direction she wanted to go. I was not qualified to produce pop records, and I told her that and I told Bradley that at the meeting we was talking about.

Porter believes he was resented partly because of his holding too much power within the RCA structure.

What other country singer had producer control over three acts? Matter-of-factly, Porter was paid to do what Willie and Waylon would have paid to do: run his own sessions. This seemingly lopsided authority granted to Porter by contract must have appalled Jerry, son of Owen Bradley. Jerry harbored his own yen to be a producer, and he became a successful one. And no doubt Joe Galante wondered who let "The Rubber Room" out as a single.

In September 1973 Dolly's *Bubbling Over* album was released.

The back cover fairly bubbles over with a cornucopia of Porter-produced Parton product. Twenty album covers are reproduced in miniature, looking like postage stamps mounted in an album—ten duets, ten solos, entailing two hundred sides generating plentiful cash flow to Owepar. Dolly's face twenty times on album covers helped fix her image in the public consciousness, with Andy Warhol-like repetition. (Warhol, who always wore an outlandish wig himself, came dressed as Dolly to a "drag party" at Studio 54 in 1978.) Then in an ad-insert in *Country Music* magazine (March 1974) there were seventeen Porter Wagoner albums for sale. Even if some of the latter were destined for deletion, by anybody's count—allowing for some duplications via "best of" repackagings—there were three hundred-plus sides available by Porter and/or Dolly on RCA. Fred Foster was hawking a Dolly double album of twenty-four cuts for those who needed more.

The television show never quit either. It was seen in around 4.5 million homes, with many times that in paid subscribers. Though some might sneer at such syndicated shows, the prime time network TV country shows had flared and fizzled: Roger Miller, Glen Campbell, and Johnny Cash. Porter outlasted them all by staying within his limits and not watering it down as prime time country shows are wont to do.

Porter was asked to help out one show with flagging ratings, and he said, "I'm not going to get on a sinking ship when I wasn't on it when it left the shore."

In a 1955 article "The Voices of RCA Victor" in *Country Song Roundup,* Steve Sholes said benignly that "the unaffected simple personalities in the country business outweigh the others to a very great extent. Temperamental? Sometimes. Easily upset? On occasion. But disagreeable? Hardly ever."

Of his encounters with RCA, Porter says, "They dreaded to see me coming because I was different from any of the other people they had dealt with, because I was not afraid of them, Bradley or none of the people with RCA. Because I knew I was right, because when you're right, the fear is gone."

In the fall of 1973 the RCA executives came down from New York to enjoy the festivities of Country Music Week. This was probably when Porter made one of several sales presentations on how to better sell the products in his line. Joan slipped the special ball into her typewriter and typed up his thoughts. Porter, who could give the Boy Scouts lessons in being prepared, headed off to meet the RCA executives.

36

THE SALES PITCH (1973)*

The 3 acts that I represent are . . .
Dolly Parton
Porter and Dolly
and Porter Wagoner

These are 3 completely separate and different recording acts. And must be treated as such. Each as individual acts. Each act should be as much an individual as, for instance, Nat Stuckey, Kenny Price and Waylon Jennings. There is no reason why a Porter Wagoner record or a Dolly Parton record should not be promoted simply because Porter and Dolly have out a duet.

Dolly Parton is 26 years old [27] and just at the beginning of the heart of her recording career. Her stage presence is perfect. She communicates with the audience unbelievably. Both men, women and children . . . young and old alike, are Dolly Parton fans. She received from the last 40 concerts played, 34 standing ovations. This is completely unheard of by any other female entertainer in any branch of show business.

Dolly's performance on records is equally as exciting as her in-person concerts. The only difference is Dolly's records must speak for themselves or they don't get spoken for. What Dolly must have is the RCA sales and promotion team speaking for them. RCA sales and promotion has absolutely let the most talented country girl singer the label has ever signed just ease along gaining whatever popularity that happens to come her way whether it be from Porter and Dolly duets, TV exposure or whatever.

While Decca Records promotes Loretta Lynn to the #1 spot over and over again. Columbia Records creates so much excitement for Lynn Anderson records she had to become a #1 girl singer. Tammy Wynette comes from nowhere and in 2 years' time with extensive promotion created in her behalf, became the #1 girl singer. Donna Fargo, a school teacher a year and a half ago, now has

---

*Reproduced *verbatim,* but for paragraphing and some spelling improvements. Porter overuses the phrase "#1," though there are other charts than *Billboard's.*

a good bid for the #1 spot. She had one #1 record and received more recognition than Dolly Parton has received for all her #1s combined.*

Gentlemen, this is ridiculous. These are not accidents that these girls became #1. They are #1 because of hard work in fields of sales and promotion, creating excitement, letting everyone know there is a new super star on the horizon. Jeanne Pruett, a local housewife with a house full of children, passes Dolly Parton on the way to the #1 spot. Everyone everywhere knows of her #1 record. Gentlemen, I doubt if there's anyone in this room that can name the Dolly Parton records that have been #1. I think it is time we do something about this. There's many people in Nashville that don't know that Dolly Parton even had a #1 record.

Dolly Parton is seen by 23 million people every week on TV [closer to 4 million viewers, as opposed to subscribers]. Every week RCA Victor is mentioned alongside of Dolly. There has not been one single show she has done with me on TV that she did not do either an album cut or a single and it was mentioned as such. Dolly is by far the most popular Country girl singer on TV. There is not anyone even close to her in that category. It is not just her beauty that makes her more popular every week on TV, it is also her singing. There are many, many more reasons that make people want to buy Dolly Parton records. First and most important, she is the most exciting female that you have in your catalogue. To mention a few other reasons, they see Dolly in person on 120 concerts per year, averaging 3000 people-plus per concert. She is seen 20 times a year on stage at the Grand Ole Opry [and heard on radio].

She is constantly working on new dimensions to further her record career. Network exposure such as the "Today" show, the Rowan and Martin special, the Burt Reynolds special to be seen in November, the Jack Paar Show.

I think it is high time that RCA gets excited about Dolly Parton and do something about it. As of now, when Dolly Parton has a new release there is no more excitement than if Vernon Oxford had a new release. Dolly is a young, vigorous talent, let's make a super star while we have all the other things going for us. Then we can play golf, go to cocktail parties, while the harvest from our work is rolling in from a well-established record seller.

It is hard for me to believe that RCA, the largest recording company in the world, does not have a girl singer in the top 5 nominees this year for the network CMA show seen coast to coast

*Joel Whitburn's Top Country and Western Records 1972–1973 (1974) lists the Top 30 artists: Tammy Wynette is number five, Lynn Anderson is number seven, Donna Fargo is number eight, Connie Smith is number twenty-one, Tanya Tucker is number twenty-four, Loretta Lynn is number twenty-six. Dolly is not on this list at all.

on TV. Neither does RCA have a Best Record nominee in the top 5 nor does it have a Best Album nominee. We do not have a best male vocalist in the top 5 nominees of the year. Don't you think there is a message in that alone?

Our sales and promotion department at this time reminds me of a football player that ran the ball so slow they gave him a penalty for delay of game while he was running toward the goal line.

I would like to point out some of the enthusiasm that I have shown for Dolly Parton . . . Porter and Dolly . . . and Porter Wagoner. Since January 1 of this year I have spent 505 hours in the recording studio. This includes recording, over-dubbing, remixing, in quad, stereo, mono, over 100 sides . . . to furnish you with the very finest product not only to the best of my ability, but in constant conference with Chet, Bob Ferguson, and Jerry Bradley, in regard to the best move to make to sell records and improve quality of product. This is not to mention the many, many hours that go into it before I reach the studio. Our demo sessions that I pay for myself, done in my own studio, getting the product in its best form to record here at RCA.

You can imagine, after all of these hours of hard work plus a heavy road schedule and TV schedule, then see the product you have worked so hard on, die in the hands of someone that does not show enough interest!

The duets are naturally much easier to sell because of both Dolly and my name being attached to them, but first and most important is Dolly Parton records individually. Unless Dolly receives the recognition she must have individually by the company, we must quit recording duets. The reason for the duets to begin with was a plus for your catalogue, an extra sales vehicle for you. But Dolly and I neither one of us must be known first as a duet. We must be known first as individual artists. Once this is done, not only will it increase sales on Dolly Parton and Porter Wagoner records individually, but will also add a plus to our extra vehicle, the duets.

We need 6 months to a year extensive promotion by the company for Dolly Parton. Taking every means to establish her in the industry good and solid, where she will be of much more value to everyone concerned. Once we get her good momentum, we're set.

I feel one of the ways the company can really help in this area is by taking first things first. For instance, coming off of a #1 record, you know the next release is certainly going to be a good seller, so I think what happens in this case, we move on to something else when we should stay and promote the follow-up release even more, because this gets the sales momentum much higher. If we fail to promote the follow-up record, the artist loses momentum—then we're right back where we started and have to come up with a hit to gain the momentum back. So once we get the ball rolling, we need extensive promotion on our big records, then the momentum is there. I'm not asking the company to do this extensive promotion alone. I'm prepared to participate in the cost, the creation of ads, a complete catalogue promotion or whatever needs to be done in the field to get the job done.

Also, Dolly will be available to make tapes, promos, TV appearances and any other areas needed, but we must have your help. At this time we have three of the best new singles ever recorded by Dolly. They not only can go in the Country field, but easily in other directions as well. I have prepared excerpts from 9 new singles. I will continue to furnish you with a product you can be proud to connect your name with. Together we can make a girl singer for RCA that will not only win awards, but will also be a consistent record seller for many, many years.

As for the other artist that I represent which is me . . . I'll make some records for you so damn good you can't help but promote them. In fact, some of them you would like to sell door to door.

"ARE YOU GOING AWAY WITH NO WORD OF FAREWELL?"

It's a sad situation, I must say,
When someone wants to leave as bad
as you want them to stay.

—Dolly,
"When Someone Wants to Leave"
(recorded 1973)

Porter:
(jokingly with Dolly in the WSM dressing room):
"You're a smart ass!"
Dolly:
"Well, I've never seen yours
do anything intelligent."

—Bill Turner, interview,
December 6, 1989

"**F**easting their eyes on Dolly Parton was really an 'eye opener' for the disc jockeys at the RCA breakfast," ran the picture caption in *Music City News* in November 1973. Dolly was onstage singing, joking with Johnny Russell, and dedicating her piece of the show to Porter, "sitting somewhere in the audience," as she put it.

"Porter Pushes Dolly's Bandwagon" was a December headline in *The Tennessean*. Dolly Parton might be as visible as the Smoky Mountains themselves, wrote Jerry Bailey, but her own record company was fairly blind to the contours of her talent. "The fellows from New York had no idea there was any problem," said Porter. "They only saw the annual royalty checks, and from that they judged we must be well satisfied."

Porter had told RCA that maybe the duet act was cheating Dolly of individual acclaim. Dolly hadn't been nominated for any CMA awards. "I guess it was because she was too close to me," he says. He had offered personally to kick in expense money to help RCA market Dolly. "Wagoner decided on a campaign of public exposure for Miss Parton— without himself." Dolly was going to be on the Dinah Shore, Dean Martin, and Mike Douglas shows.

"Seeing more of Dolly, however, will not necessarily mean seeing less of Porter," Jerry said gamely. Porter now had an "exclusive booking arrangement" with Bob Eubanks's Concert Express Company, which the previous year had gotten Merle Haggard into the White House to perform at First Lady Pat Nixon's birthday party. Porter confessed to hearing a lot of bitching from promoter-friends. "They felt they helped me all along, and I owed them something," then he condemned those of them who rented "the cheapest building in town with no atmosphere at all. From the appearance they could just as well be having a rodeo or a roller skating contest there." Porter said with Eubanks he'd be getting away from the cobwebbed dressing rooms where you sat on rude board seats. "After all, these ain't the overall and button-down shoe days. The concert hall should look like somebody important is performing there instead of just some hillbilly."

Porter the producer hoped he was having a "progressive" effect on Dolly's records. Jerry acknowledged that while Dolly wanted to be called country, she wouldn't mind some of that pop airplay. Her recent singles "Joshua" and "Jolene" meant that a Tennessee mountain voice could compete with "the soulful tones of Roberta Flack or the breathy expressions of Helen Reddy."

Dolly was photographed cuddled inside Porter's curving arm, beaming, her big wig tilted against his cheek, like a couple of high school seniors at the prom or in the back of the school bus.

Bill Turner, director of the TV show, admits he underestimated Dolly. With awe and pleasant surprise he watched her prove him wrong. He had pegged her for just another girl singer. She sang as she was told, spoke only when she was told. "None of us knew when she arrived how smart she was or how determined she was. She was just the same with the average fan as with the biggest star. Always the same person, just Dolly." For the first two or three years she relied totally on Porter. "There was a transition on his show when Porter was in charge . . . and then he wasn't."

Bill must have loved and understood them perfectly. Once for a gift he gave them each a matching pair of Derringer pistols. Porter's were blue, Dolly's silver—the "Ladysmith" model. They had four consecutive serial numbers.

Porter lost Dolly to another woman. Her name was Jolene, and the song of that name was now on the charts; it went to number one. "Jolene" was Dolly's second number one, but it went to number sixty on the pop charts; her other number one, "Joshua," had reached a low number 108 in pop. "Jolene" was pulling Dolly out of whatever rural rut she'd been mired in, with "I Will Always Love You" soon to carry her further.

A girl in a Girl Scout uniform who looked only twelve years old had approached Porter at a concert, handing him a picture of herself inscribed "Love, Jolene." What a pretty name! Dolly likes "name" songs, having recorded songs titled for siblings Stella, Cassie, Frieda, Bobby, Randy, and Willadeene (unreleased). She was taken with Jolene's fair complexion and green eyes. Dolly stuck the picture in a drawer.

She only remembered Jolene months later, while practicing a new lick on her guitar, "that funny little sound—that little lick they play on the intro," she says. It's a folkie hammering-on, in a minor key, one she would almost duplicate later on her big hit "The Bargain Store."

As she strummed, Dolly began singing "Jolene, Jolene," her voice climbing up. The mellifluous "Jolene, Jolene" is repeated four times. Each time it's higher, bouncing up the scale like a ball bounding up a stairs; almost like "Over the Rainbow," the song jumps an octave right at the start. It has the effect of a chorus—the song is all chorus—and opening with a chorus is something of a pop device. The minor-chord melody has an antique "Greensleeves" feel to it.

In the lyric, Dolly pleads plaintively to Jolene not to steal away her husband, even though Jolene's the prettier woman. The tone is soft and tender—contrasting with Loretta Lynn's angry, cutting "You Ain't Woman Enough." Such restraint helped "Jolene" reach a wider audience. Dolly had Jolene's picture enlarged and framed.*

"Jolene" was recorded twice, June 12 and 14, 1973, with "I Will Always Love You" cut in between. Discussing the released version, John Morthland said Dolly's voice "swoops and soars almost as a counter-melody to the lines played on acoustic guitar," while praising Porter for using only a few instruments on the session.

Significantly, New Wave singer Patti Smith, herself a published poet (Rimbaud and Bob Dylan influences), recorded "Jolene."

Another indicator of Dolly's pop potential was "Bubbling Over," recorded that same day and the title song of her next album. "Bubbling Over" has a late-fifties record hop beat—Dolly finally *is* Brenda Lee. "Bubbling Over" was to have been a single, but "Jolene" won. Shut your

---

*Dolly's aunt, Dale Parton, reports an alleged episode of Dolly-as-Loretta, going to fist city as it were (interview by Shelby Loosch, *Globe*, 1991). Supposedly Jolene was really a "cute red head" bank teller, and Dolly confronted Jolene about her interest in her husband, Carl, and Jolene "reached right over the counter and tore off Dolly's wig in front of everyone!"

eyes with "Bubbling Over" playing, and picture Dolly bopping out on the gym floor in her bobby sox.

Porter should have been euphoric. With "Jolene" such a smash, with RCA finally cooperating, and with that hundred-city tour ahead for him and Dolly and the boys in 1974, the horizon was alight with a halo glow.

But just a few days after the Jerry Bailey interview, he was speeding through the night by car to West Plains. His mother was dying. The cop who stopped Porter didn't believe him and hit him with an on-the-spot fine. When the policeman later read about his mother's death (December 13, 1973), he mailed Porter back his money.

At the funeral home, amidst all the floral wreaths and baskets, Porter placed a guitar case all bedecked with blue flowers. His mother had bought Pug (Porter) that first National guitar with his rabbit-trapping earnings.

The day of his mother's death, "George Leroy Chickashea," Porter's recitation about the weird, mixed breed strangler with a pistol, tomahawk, and switchblade entered *Billboard*. A few days later Skeeter Davis was kicked off the Opry (for eighteen months) for having denounced the Nashville police over the air—they'd arrested some proselytizing young Christians in a shopping center. Then the day after Christmas Dolly recorded "When Someone Wants to Leave," about how one person doesn't care at all and the other cares too much.

Dolly was still talking in terms of Porter as late as January 19, at least to the press. She told visiting English journalist Tony Byworth that if Porter could overcome his phobia of flying, they'd like to perform in Britain.

The final discussion about her future took place one night in a motel in Tulsa, in February 1974. Tom Rutledge, later a guitarist for both Porter and Dolly, heard about it secondhand and told Alanna Nash: "The band said you could hear them all over the motel." Mack Magaha confirms that it was definitely hard to sleep that night, and that next morning the two of them came to breakfast coolly wearing dark glasses and announced calmly that Dolly would be forming her own band once they fulfilled about two months more of show dates.

"Porter felt I was ready to go out on my own, which is a very unselfish decision on his part," Dolly said in their press conference of February 19. They traded lines like a well-orchestrated duet with lyrics by Don Warden. "Dolly is now a superstar in every way. She's well prepared to go on her own. I am very happy that I helped Dolly in preparing for this day." *Music City News* reported a few days later that Porter would still act as Dolly's "advisor" and manage her business affairs. "Porter and I will continue to be the best of friends."

George Leroy Chickashea [COURTESY PORTER WAGONER ENTERPRISES].

In her 1979 deposition Dolly would complain about the conflicting versions of her departure: (1) that she quit; (2) that Porter fired her; or (3) that it had been a joint decision. Prior to leaving there had been "a huge argument that was frightening to me," she said.

"I was sorry we parted on the terms we did," Dolly said in 1990, "although I felt that I tried in every way to get Porter to go with me to all the places I wanted to go. I felt Porter wanted to be part of it as long as I did it under his total direction, and I felt I couldn't grow like that. So we disagreed, and I'm not sorry for the choices I made."

They were still together in April when "I Will Always Love You" entered *Billboard*. It went to number one. Roy Shockley remembers Dolly crying while she sang it at the session, and he realized it would not be long before she left. The flip side was "Lonely Comin' Down," written by Porter, about waking up in a strange place, seeing a strange face in the mirror as you realize someone is finally gone. Robert Christgau of *Village Voice* said the song proved Dolly should sometimes sing other people's songs. John Morthland in *Best of Country Music* was awed at how delicately and imperceptibly she shifted into a vibrato on the record, and added, "the mournful fiddle that hovers over this song without ever controlling it is another masterful touch from Porter." The verses sink down low and blue, but the release builds up Orbison-style. Then it returns to the desolation, way down low. It would have been a good song for Conway Twitty.

The new Opry House at Opryland was perfect for television. A major TV special was aired on April 26 on NBC, hosted by Johnny Cash. The producer was Joseph Cates, a veteran of Broadway and twice an Emmy-winner. As Chet Hagan noted in his history of the Grand Ole Opry, this marked the last network appearance of Porter and Dolly . . . until 1988, that is.

Various dates and places have been given as being the "last" Porter–Dolly live appearance. A clipping at the Country Music Foundation library from the Salina (Kansas) *Journal* has Porter and Dolly singing their "final duet in Salina" on April 20, 1974. But it's not clear if that's their last show nationwide or just in Salina. Another story from the Des Moines *Register* for May 26 announced they would both appear June 7 at the Veterans' Auditorium. Yet in attorney Tom White's legal notes, their last road date together is (somewhere) on June 9, 1974, after an Opry spot of June 4.

Porter wrote a song called "Last Chance for Happiness" that asks whether a woman could walk away and "let the swirling water take my life?" He cannot survive without her love. He wrote another, "Falling Water River," named after one of the tributaries of Center Hill Lake. After being rejected by a girl, the singer will jump into Falling Water River and leave a note by the bank "for all the folks at home."

Engineer Roy Shockley says, "I remember on a Monday morning he came in and said, 'Dolly has left me, and I'm going to Center Hill Lake for fishing.' And I know he stayed six weeks. Chet and Bob was so concerned about it that Tom Pick and I went up. We thought Porter might go over the edge."

38

"THE SUN DON'T SHINE ON THE SAME DOG EVERY DAY"

I've had my share of rain, loneliness and pain . . .
The dog or the sun, one will move, every time.

—Porter, "The Sun Don't Shine on
the Same Dog Every Day" (1973)

"I don't plan to hire a well-known established star for my show. I will hire a girl that I can help develop her talents and help her make a name in country music with pride and dignity as Dolly has," Porter said at the famous break-up press conference in February 1974.

Reportedly, between 3,000 and 4,000 audition tapes swamped his office. He narrowed these to eighteen, interviewing each of the hopefuls. Barbara Steakley, a twenty-eight-year-old Nashville keypunch operator, had submitted a photo and two single 45 records of songs she had written. She was more interested in songwriting, but had toured Vietnam twice, once with Roy Acuff. She had dressed demurely for the troops because Roy hadn't wanted a "leg show."

Barbara had been born on a farm halfway between Nashville and Knoxville. She was a tall, pretty yet homey blonde, statuesque, utterly un-Dollyish. She met Dolly at a TV taping, and Dolly said, "Don't let this go any further, but you're my pick. You're real, and believe me I can tell the difference." Porter still wasn't sure until he tested Barbara in the studio. He shortened her name to Barbara Lea.

"She is quiet, and I needed someone like her so I can do all the talking," Porter joked at a press conference that July. They wouldn't be singing duets together, he said. He and Dolly still would, in the studio. Porter went on to say he had worked "day and night" on Dolly's career, it had been so hard at first getting people to accept her, "even as talented as she is." He had put all his thoughts into her career and it had really drained him. He said he met with RCA several times, that once the president of the company had flown to Nashville in the RCA plane, that "several times" he had laid his career on the line for Dolly. "The last two years I worked 10 percent on my own career and 90 percent on Dolly. So I kept asking myself the question, What the hell you doing this for, man? You're crazy."

On the road there was no opposition to Porter's choice. Barbara said, "I don't remember audiences ever being ugly or hollering for Dolly. I was so scared at first, they must have felt sorry for me. I never thought I was that good, but I never got any negative audience reaction. Porter . . . helped *all* the time."

One thing had not changed: the grind. "I might have been home two days a week, Porter was constantly doing something. And if we had two days off, we'd go into the studio, or be taping for television, or doing the Opry, or cutting spots for radio stations . . . we kept busy all the time," she said.

Barbara stopped caring—or knowing always—what state they were in. Once they were in Alabama, and she thought they were in Georgia. She'd just encored and was heading to take a drink of water when Porter said, "If you think you're still in Georgia, these people will think you're drinking more than water." Her face went "blood red" as Porter smoothed it over. "He's just one of the best emcees there's ever been. He and Roy Acuff are the best, they keep the show moving, they talk to the audience."

Porter produced all of Barbara's sessions. "He knew what he wanted," she said, "and he wanted to hear it." Sometimes he would rise up out of his chair and start out in the studio. Everyone would get very quiet. "He was real good for me, 'cause I was very nervous. And I would say, 'I'm real nervous right now,' and he'd say, 'Then let's walk,' and he'd put his arm around me and we would walk around the studio."

Barbara continued, "I've seen Porter nervous [on stage], and I've heard people pretty high up in the business say you'd better hope you never get over those butterflies."

For *Music City News* she and Porter posed to celebrate her signing of an RCA contract and the release of her first single, "Ain't Love Grand." Between them, smiling a broad, benevolent grin, was Jerry Bradley.

Back in 1967 in the wake of her two Monument hits for Fred Foster, Dolly had planned to create Dolly Parton and the Kinfolks when Porter intervened. In 1974 she formed the Traveling Family Band. Porter recalls that Dolly said, "What I want to do now is have a family band. I want my family to play on the road, we'll cook on the road, we'll have a great time."

Porter told her, "Dolly, that won't work. I wish it would for you. In my years of country music, I've worked with families and just brothers. They get along like cats and dogs. You won't get along."

She replied, "Well, we're close."

Porter says, "One of the things that really bothered Dolly was she'd never talk about her family to me because I'm too honest. I would always tell her straight: 'If they're my folks, your folks, it don't make a damn who they are. I like them. I love my people, I loved my brother Oscar, but he couldn't sing worth a shit. If it had been up to Dolly and her family in the beginning, she would never have been successful. Her family are good people, but you've got to go that extra mile to be successful. You've got to have the drive to get your ass out there and do whatever's necessary to make it happen. I made it happen because I wouldn't turn her loose until it did."

"It's kind of like the movie *Patton*. 'Start another war? I'm a having a *great* time.' It's that type of thing."

The front man for the Family Band was brother Randy Parton, playing bass, who'd done the same job for Jean Shepard. Porter would briefly produce Randy for RCA, and later in the 1980s Randy had five chart records. Cousin Dwight Puckett was on drums, cousin Sidney Spiva on steel guitar. "I didn't use my kinfolks because they were kinfolks, I used them because I thought they were the best I could find," Dolly had told Jerry Bailey.

Their début date was August 11 at the Ponderosa Park in Salem, Ohio, booked by Tandy Rice's Top Billing. Dolly was now managed by Bob Eubanks. On August 25 she opened for Merle Haggard, and Cynthia Kirk of the *Hollywood Reporter* said that her Family Band members "need a great deal of work to be worthy of all the applause she kept urging the audience to give them." However, when Ronnie Milsap played the Felt Forum in New York that September, Bobby Bare was on the show and so was Dolly, billed as the "Marilyn Monroe of Country Music" with two brothers, two sisters, and a cousin. "The sibling harmonies were unbelievably powerful," remembers Ronnie.

Porter says your own relatives aren't going to take you as seriously as musicians you've picked for their playing skills. It's hard to picture Dolly, who so needs to be liked, hinting that a sibling could improve some stage presence or that an uncle or cousin should master that special instrumental lick that makes the song come alive. Family band members aren't likely to develop into industry veterans like George McCormick, Mack Magaha, or Buck Trent (road musicians who can play on hit record sessions); nor are they likely to be motivated by surprise gifts of horseshoe diamond rings or fishing or golf gear.

She had to have her own bus. "I am using a color scheme of blue and green throughout," she told LaWayne Satterfield. "And in my room, baby pink." In one report, the bus itself was pink, and Dolly buses then and since have flashed a butterfly logo.

Attempting to maintain a bus and road band was of course dangerously expensive. Dolly's starting price for a show was probably $3,000 since it was $3,500 on a July 1975 contract; and it's all too easy to achieve stardom and bankruptcy at the same time. Her cash flow and road managing problems seemed to mount simultaneously with the increased demand for her show. And her business interests were correspondingly expanding; besides Owepar and Fireside, owned with Porter, she had started up Velvet Apple and Song Yard music publishers, locating them in a Brentwood shopping center, as far from Music Row as possible and nearer her home.

Though the Traveling Family Band experience became something of an "I told you so" for Porter, it was still the best—really the only—choice Dolly had. At age twenty-eight she was like a teenager leaving home for the first time, and she needed desperately something Porter could not provide: permission to flounder and occasionally fail. There's no other way to learn than to make all those "road" mistakes that no doubt the Porter Wagoner Trio had made in the fifties. From making bus repairs to gauging distances properly on a road map, from ferreting out disc jockeys in their sometimes remote locations to insisting that promoters pay up, from fixing sound equipment to coping with poor acoustics in dingy halls and raucous nightclubs, Murphy's Law—whatever *can* go wrong *will* go wrong—was likely written for, if not by, a road manager.

The way for Dolly to make more money was to stretch farther toward the pop market, placing even more strain on her Family Band. This crossover direction catered to the industry drift at the moment and was anticipated at every turn by Porter in the studio within his country format.

Such was "Love Is Like a Butterfly," which went to number one in the late summer of 1974. The lyrics lack the poetic tension of some of Dolly's better songs, but lines like "multi-colored moods of love" sing delightfully. Porter says he didn't deliberately push the production on the song more toward pop, the song itself just pulled him that way. Years later John Morthland said the melody was too happy, while praising simultaneously Porter's pop tendencies, as well as his restraint. Had the song been cut in Los Angeles, John says Dolly's producers would have loaded it up with strings, horns, and too many backup voices. Porter's 1974 treatment is in the vein of Olivia Newton-John who, like John Denver, was crossing over from pop to country and making Nashville highly nervous and jealous. "Love Is Like a Butterfly" went to number 105 on the pop charts.

Now that Dolly had left Porter's show, her performance on the charts was all the more extraordinary (three number ones in a row). Without much personal contact except in the studio, now they could channel more time into singing, songwriting, and producing, instead of bogging down in defensive (and offensive) debates.

In January 1975 "The Bargain Store" entered *Billboard*, going to number one. In it Dolly says her life is "like unto" a bargain or thrift store and, though the goods may be secondhand, if you browse around, you may find something you like. Some of the disc jockeys bridled at such seeming suggestiveness. In 1977 Dolly told Chet Flippo of *Rolling Stone:*

> When I said the bargain store is open, come inside, I just meant my *life* is open—come into my life—so I wasn't even thinkin' of it as a dirty thing. I just felt at that time I had probably been kicked around some. Not by my husband—he is the *best* person that ever lived. But you know, me and Porter, we just kind of said things, hurt each other's feelings and, you know, trampled around on territory that was real sensitive, cut each other about songs. It's just—I felt black and blue and I just wanted to heal back up and mend myself back together and get on with my life.

In 1975 Dolly's "The Seeker" went to number two and number 105 in pop. She wrote it in her music room, all in a rush, in about ten minutes. "It's a sinner's song, and it was really inspired. I looked at Judy [Ogle], and she had chills over her too."

Porter remembers Dolly bringing in the song in three-quarter time. Waltz time is good for emphasizing a lyric, but in some songs can be draggy. He says one night he bolted out of bed with the song running through his head, grabbed his guitar, and out came "The Seeker" in four-four time. It's recorded that way, with a driving gospel beat.

The lyric is thoughtful and disturbing. The speaker is a poor, sinful creature ("there is no one weaker than I am") who has fallen by the wayside, like an empty and useless vessel, badly in need of a rescue. She craves someone to pick her up and guide her, though whether God or merely some compassionate person, she leaves vague. Dolly told Chet Flippo she was a "vanilla sinner—too bad to be good and too good to be bad. Because it wouldn't be all that hard to be good, but I just don't know that I want to be. I think I won't have no fun if I'm too good." Dolly said some of her friends had been born again, "So I wrote that out of a heavy heart. Because I am certainly not a Christian. I will try some of anything, I mean I will."

Back in 1974 Olivia Newton-John won Female Vocalist of the Year from the CMA. She also had nominations for Entertainer of the Year, for Single of the Year, and Album of the Year. Born in England but raised in Australia, she had gravely affronted Nashville by assaulting the top of both the pop and country charts simultaneously.

Immediately, Porter, Dolly, and around fifty others were summoned to the home of George Jones and his wife, Tammy Wynette. They formed ACE, or Association of Country Entertainers, with Dolly on the membership screening committee and Porter among the eight vice presidents. Bill Anderson served as chairman and as human lightning rod for the media static.

ACE issued a tortured press release claiming to be mad at no award-winner in particular, but stressing that they felt nominees in the future should be presently employed in the country music field, quickly adding that none of them would object if any of their records crossed over to pop, while insisting they would concentrate on the country charts, make no mistake!

At issue then, and since, was the CMA's lust for prime-time viewers of its annual, televised awards show. This has often required weighting the cast with semicountry, or even noncountry, acts who possess more name recognition in the surveys run by the New York advertising agencies. Porter condemns this pandering to the prime-time market: "Operate from a position of strength, not weakness. Make them come to you." Even if it means a show that has to be aired on Saturday afternoon? "Hell, yes."

Singer and author Jan Howard says of the gold stars that honor famous entertainers outside the Hall of Fame, "They cost a thousand dollars each. The first six are 'mine'—I traveled from Miami to Los Angeles to Detroit to raise money for the CMA at my own expense. I have never even been a presenter at a CMA award show. You have people on there that can't even talk, have no stage presence whatever."

The ACE delegate to the CMA was Charley Pride. Porter says, "The kind of representation we was getting was zero. He was very popular, he was making all kinds of money, his career was flourishing. How could he go in and complain? He's a black guy, the first one in the history of the business to be a superstar, he's raking in money from every direction. He was our representative—how's he going to complain? They would laugh at him."

So they asked Porter to represent them at a CMA meeting in San Antonio. Porter can't recall "what all transpired, but I know I was not very popular at the time." Porter says he doesn't like "flowering" things up but prefers to tell people exactly how he sees things.

At one meeting, Vic Willis told members they'd better stop worrying about Olivia Newton-John and worry about themselves. When he asked for a show of hands to the question, "How many of you have a recording contract?" not many hands went up. Vic told them they'd better work on getting records played, that when Billy Walker or Jean Shepard went to a town the radio stations wouldn't have their records, "they didn't even know who they were."

Vic remembers asking Jo Walker, executive director of the CMA, whether Frank Sinatra could be nominated if he received enough votes. She replied, "If he's nominated, he'll be accepted." Vic says, "That tells you a lot."

Porter was contemptuous of ACE's whining about the past, calling the group "a bunch of people complaining about how they've been mistreated down the line." He would tell them, "We can meet here and hash out old problems, and say, 'Five years ago I shoulda been given this award,' and all you're doin' is pissin' in the wind. Who cares what should have happened!"

As soon as everyone had enjoyed as much of ACE as they could stand, it became a memory, and a repressed one at that.

The pop world that so tempted and terrified Nashville lay galaxies away from Music Row, and Music Row seemed farther and farther away from Opryland on the other side of town. In his song "Are You Sure Hank Done It This Way?" Waylon Jennings declared that rhinestone suits and big shiny cars were passé, that the industry needed a change. Caught in the middle was Porter, one foot on the Opry stage, the other kicking the corporate desk at RCA trying to make them push Dolly ever more popward. This dichotomy fascinated Dave Hickey, whose "The Last Great Hillbilly" profile was the cover story of *Country Music* in May 1975. Dave contrasted Porter the entertainer—swapping gags with Speck Rhodes concerning miniskirts, laxatives, and outhouses—with Porter the producer—expounding on electronics at his "neo-Arabian" office at Fireside. Porter told Hickey he'd gone through more than two dozen microphones for Barbara Lea and upwards of a "thousand" board settings. He flashed a notebook replete with board-settings for every singer and musician that he used on a session, so that no time would be wasted testing sound levels beforehand. He possessed thirty unreleased singles of Dolly and played ten for Dave, who found the songs to be top quality and the production "as daring and original as production can get while still sounding country."

Dave theorized that Porter's shyness and lack of education had steered him away from the Nashville social scene and down into his recording studio lair, where he could be in full control. Dave blamed the abruptness or taciturnity he might sometimes exhibit on his insecurity and, under the rhinestones, feelings of inferiority. These were the post-hippie years of college-oriented "cowboys" with double first names like Billy Ray and southern accents as calculated as the angle of their hat brims. Headquarters for some of the most talented was the Glaser Brothers' office at 916 Nineteenth Avenue South ("Hillbilly Central"), with pinball games for recreation.

A block away, and at least a generation away, slumped Porter Wagoner over his mixing console at Fireside.

Sometime that September Porter called Don Warden at home and asked him to come down to the office. "I intend to cut 'way back on my dates. I may take a year or more off. You're welcome to stay with me, but I think it would be a good move to go with Dolly." Don says that even at that time, Porter was much bigger than Dolly, that it was no easy decision, and if Porter had asked him to stay he would have. "Dolly could have just been in the ranks of another girl singer. I felt she might be a big star but I was not sure." Three times Don said, "It was not an easy thing to do."

Don was the best gift Porter ever gave Dolly, and as Porter said at his September 29 press conference, "the most qualified of anyone I know in the music business." Dolly badly needed a road manager and a business manager. "Without Don Warden she might have ended up like Dottie West," says Roy Shockley of the late singer whose bankruptcy and tax plight dug her early grave.

After the 1975 CMA awards meeting, Porter came into the Owepar office and told Carla Scarborough, "Charlie Rich ought to give lessons in how to ruin a career in five minutes." Charlie had been Vocalist of the Year in 1973, Entertainer of the Year in 1974, and the night before had presented the 1975 Entertainer of the Year award. Or rather, had started to. Seeing that it was John Denver, he whipped out his cigarette lighter and set the paper ablaze.

At least the Female Vocalist of the Year was—finally—Dolly Parton. "I just hope that everybody thinks I deserve it," she was quoted as saying by Elizabeth A. Harris of UPI. "I hope nobody thinks I got it because of what happened last year," referring obliquely to the Olivia Newton-John commotion.

More and more, Dolly was traveling that highway headin' west. Out in Los Angeles in 1975 she met Linda Ronstadt and Emmylou Harris. Linda was a graduate of the sixties, and both girls, Emmylou especially, were veering toward country music. Both released Dolly songs on albums in 1975.

When Dolly got back from Los Angeles, she told Porter that she wanted at least some producer credit on her releases in the future.

On January 22, 1976, Red O'Donnell broke the news in the *Nashville Banner*: "Porter Wagoner, after twenty-five years, is quitting the 'grind' of personal appearances." He quoted him as saying, "I just don't have enough time and energy to tour anymore. I spent about 500 hours in recording studios last year. I want to become more active in that field . . . I'm not selling my blue sequin outfits. I'll need them for TV."

Porter asked Joyce Triplett over at RCA to make some changes on their record label credits. All future releases by Dolly, Porter and Dolly, and even Randy Parton should bear the following: "Produced and Arranged by Porter & Dolly" with their last names omitted. The same day they talked (April 2, 1976) Joyce fired off a memo to New York.

On April 13 Porter made another of his presentations to the RCA management.

39

THE SALES PITCH (1976)*

Meeting April 13, 1976, with Mel [Ilberman] and RCA Exec's.

First of all, I have no doubts, Mel, in your beliefs in Dolly or me. You've shown me that several ways by making adjustments in our favor at contract negotiation. But there's a break-down somewhere along the way in <u>sales</u>, <u>promotion</u>, and <u>getting anything done at RCA</u>. Can you believe that this company has been billing me for <u>over a year</u> for studio time on a Randy Parton session which I sold to this company—<u>studio time included</u>. I've taken this problem to <u>Joe</u>, <u>Jerry</u>, and <u>Mr.</u> [Ed] <u>Hines</u>. I've called the manager in Indianapolis, still I get the damn bill every month. <u>What</u> is going on in this company?? There are songs that show on the books, <u>unreleased masters</u>, that have already been out in albums, some in singles.

Concerning my records, my latest single was released <u>last September</u>. My next single is scheduled four to five weeks after Dolly's next single according to Joe, which means I will have out a single in the middle or later part of <u>June</u>. Don't you think <u>10 months</u> is <u>just a little long between release dates on singles</u>?? Why should my records suffer and my release dates be shuffled around simply because I produce Dolly Parton's records? Dolly is no more part of my records than Skeeter Davis or Danny Davis. Incidentally, my release last September was treated with as much excitement as if I were a brand new artist strictly on speculation. <u>This must change!</u>

Concerning Dolly's records, there must be something, <u>I mean must be something</u>, done about Dolly's records in the <u>underground markets</u>. This is the area where we can sell more Dolly Parton albums than all the other fields combined. The kids of the underground nature are really into Dolly in a big way. They love her

---

*Again, reproduced exactly from the original with no word omissions or changes. The many underlinings, and in one case double-underlinings, are in the original.

333

records. They attend her concerts. But her albums are not at their stores. Their stores are the ones with the psychedelic windows. You know, the ones that look like someone threw buckets of paint on them. Dolly's albums can not be found at these stores. They're up the street at the big nice record shop with the clear glass window and a beautiful display inside where you'll find the Best of Floyd Cramer, the Best of Perry Como, etc. But back in those little psychedelic places are where people like Linda Ronstadt, Emmylou Harris, Papa John [Creach] and so forth sells millions and millions of albums. I believe Dolly's should be in these stores. Why aren't they? Why have [we] not ran any kind of ad or even a "thank you" in Rolling Stone magazine for doing a 2 page spread on Dolly Parton mentioning four of the biggest names in rock music claiming Dolly as their idol? Rolling Stone, the largest circulation of its kind in the world, why have we not done something in the way of promotion with them?? Rolling Stone, People, and the Village [Voice] magazine from New York and approximately 7 other leading underground papers have done in-depth articles on Dolly, so the promotion is already done for us.

But we must have product in the stores, the underground stores before they can buy. Dolly is very unhappy about this situation and she has a right to be. Kids on every concert ask her why her albums are not in the record store?? Dolly says they are and they are, but not in their record store. We must get them in these stores. They won't go [to] the other store up the street with the shiny bright windows and the best of's in stock. That's squaresville to these kids or they think of it as Pop & Mom's store.

(Insert Medley)

[Porter intersperses some recent Dolly cuts on tape]

In the March issue of Record World the story . . . a full page and a quarter . . . titled "For RCA Artist, the Time is Now," I failed to find Dolly's name included anywhere in this article, which I think is embarrassing to Dolly as well as myself. Plus the 2 full page RCA record ad with no mention of Dolly and the only act in this ad that is equivalent to Dolly in drawing power or stature in progressive music is Waylon Jennings. I can't believe this could happen if we are all sold on Dolly. This is not directed toward Jerry individually, this is just one of many such things that has happened with RCA lately. If we are going to promote this girl to super stardom we have got to make different plans to the ones we have had to this point. We must re-group, forget what has happened, forget personal feelings, get everything together, start it all together, then if she does not become a super star we can say we tried in every area available to us. And that's all she or I would ever ask from anyone.

40

A DAY LATE
AND A DOLLY SHORT

Understand that *high velocity change*
is a constant in the music business.

—Jesse Burt and Bob Ferguson,
So You Want to Be in Music! (1970)

With each passing month, Porter and Dolly snuggled closer and closer together in the cash drawer. *Billboard* headlined in February 1976: "Nashville Publishers Adopt Global Outlook"—with Gerry Wood reporting: "As Dolly Parton's worldwide stature grows, the publishing company she owns with Porter Wagoner, Owepar Publishing, has added a foreign division headed by Carla Scarborough."

Carla said that Dolly had had songs cut in England (by Olivia Newton-John, Billy Connolly, and the American Percy Sledge), plus ten songs cut in Germany, Ireland, Sweden, and Australia by other singers. In Australia Dolly had earned a gold record for "Jolene," and was the writer of two Top 10 songs in South Africa. Carla said many publishers were missing out on their foreign profits, and probably had monies piling up overseas if they would but look for them (51 percent of record sales were outside the United States).

Later that year *Billboard* would reveal that Owepar had earned $100,000 in the past year from foreign publishing alone—Carla said they were selling songbooks in Australia, South Africa, and Holland.

In late spring of 1976 Dolly went to New York without telling Porter, with Judy Ogle probably riding shotgun. Dolly's appointment was at the RCA building with vice president Mel Ilberman, who had signed her 1972 contract, and with company president Ken Glancey. When he had worked for CBS, Glancey had been introduced by president Goddard Lieberson at a banquet as "that rare combination, a practically unknown combination, I would say—a charming, cultured, witty man, an astute businessman . . . and a gentile," according to Frederic Dannen's *Hit Men: Power Brokers and Fast Money Inside the Music Business.*

In 1989 Mel Ilberman remembered, faintly, that Dolly wanted out from under all Nashville control. Dolly told reporter Sally Duncan that after meeting with RCA, she found them behind her 100 percent. Years later Jerry Bradley would reminisce for Tom Roland in *Billboard Book of Number One Country Hits:* "Dolly knew exactly what she wanted to be. She sat right on my couch one day and said, 'When you son-of-a-bitches learn how to sell a female Elton John with long hair and big boobs that dresses like a freak, then we'll make some money.'"

Jerry Bradley hoped to strike some sort of rapprochement between the warring factions, so into the midst of the Porter–Dolly tug-of-war he thrust attorney John Lentz as a neutral mediator. John was not with RCA. His father, Judge Ned Lentz, had sprung young Brenda Lee from her Springfield cage in 1957 and in the early seventies had heard the Wilburn Brothers' suit against the fleeing Loretta Lynn, an escaped girl singer with a twenty-year contract.

Porter, Dolly, John, and Jerry met in Jerry's office. John says, "We came up with what I thought was a very fair proposal for both sides, and unfortunately Porter would not accept it, and as a consequence they later did battle. RCA was trying to bend over backwards to make everybody happy, Porter and Dolly. I think more than anything, Porter felt, rightly or wrongly, that he was instrumental in Dolly's success and wanted not to be shut out of her continuing success." John was coping with Porter's rights to produce Dolly, and his vehement desire to get their last duet album released. John says, "We never got down to putting it to paper because the deal blew up. We left the meeting; I thought we had a deal. And then later, after everyone thought about it, I think Porter felt it wasn't rich enough. That's when the deal fell apart." John isn't sure, but he thinks the collapsed deal may have included some other work Porter wanted released. "The bottom line was, the meeting bore no fruit. At the time we thought it did, but later it evaporated. And as a consequence you know what happened."

I prodded John, saying, "The oversimplified version is, they're stopping an album that can make Porter some money. But I'm sure it was more complex than that."

"It was more complex than that. RCA was trying to gently nudge that deal through, and they really weren't taking sides. In fact, Bradley was walking on eggs trying to mollify both Dolly and Porter. I think he was being fair, trying to accommodate them and stretch things. But the problems were just too big. The rift was too wide to be crossed." Pause. "They were very cordial at the meeting.

"Basically, Dolly just wanted to go her own way, and Porter said, 'Look, I've got these agreements, and I helped build you and make you and I want to reap some of the rewards.' She wasn't really holding out on the album. She just wanted to be, well, free."

But what about Jerry Bradley?

"Jerry is a pretty private person and not one to go for the limelight. He's not a typical Music Row kind of guy who wears the credentials brightly. He's not showoffy."

Was Joe Galante around?

"He was in and around, but he was on the periphery. Jerry was in the middle."

Smack dab.

Porter's attorney, Tom White, asked Dolly in 1979 about the blocking of the album (called, ultimately, *Porter & Dolly*, in 1980). Dolly said: "We were driving each other crazy. Somebody had to make a decision. To move. RCA decided not to release the duet album. It would just bring us back together—to stir us up again would have been disaster. It wasn't my decision, but I was happy it didn't throw us back together."

Chris Chase came to Nashville from New York to interview Dolly, and the story ran in the *New York Times Magazine* in May 1976. The article featured a beaming picture of her and Porter in the studio. Porter's songwriting was now *Times*worthy since a snatch of "Highway Headin' South" was quoted, except it was attributed to Dolly, who had also recorded and co-published it. She said, "I have diamonds for all of my fingers, all gifts from Porter except my wedding ring." She confessed it used to distress her when people misconstrued all the presents, making it sound like he was "my lover, my sugar daddy. But time takes care of things like that, and my husband always knew. If your husband don't know who you love . . . " Chris said Dolly's voice trailed off, then resumed. "Because of my songs, Porter makes money. Because of Porter, I make money."

But how to fire Porter as producer? Bob Ferguson says Dolly took him aside and said, "It's going to take a while to untangle it all and get loose. I respect you, and I want you to know what's going on. I know you and Porter are from the same place," meaning southeastern Missouri.

"Dolly, when I have an artist, the artist is an artist on their own . . . Okay, you gotta do what you gotta do," he promised.

In 1977 Porter told Mike Kosser of *Country Style* that "all of this changeover came to me secondhand." The following year he told John Morthland of *Country Music* that "the entire move was done behind my back between her and RCA, and that's a very discolorful way to do a person." In her *Dolly* biography, Alanna Nash quotes Charlene Bray at Top Billing as being in support of Porter. Obviously Dolly told Porter at some point, though it easily could have been after RCA did. Certainly when they talked, it was already a fait accompli.

Over the years, Porter has repeatedly said that in meeting after meeting with RCA, he offered to step aside if need be and help Dolly find a pop producer. Maybe no one believed him.

Alanna Nash also recounts the version where Dolly fired Porter in the office, with Don Warden in the next room on stand-by alert. Needlessly, since Porter was so devastated he plumb forgot to lose his temper.

On June 29, 1976, a telegram from Beverly Hills, California, arrived at Owepar: "Please give Judy Ogle all contracts of all Dolly Parton songs that are not copyrighted as of this date. Thank you, Dolly Parton." Owepar employee Ann Kosloff followed orders.

Ann recalls her stint at Owepar as the most enjoyable in her seventeen years in show business. She was never bossed around and had complete authority to function, but she says at times she had difficulty serving the company's interests and not being partial to either Porter or Dolly. Once Porter had a song plugger working Dolly's song "To Daddy," then they were told to take it off the market because Emmylou Harris was going to cut it, assuring a hit record of the song. Porter was upset, and Ann realized she was working for two chiefs.

As for removing contracts and tapes, Dolly said in her 1979 deposition:

> I wanted the tape boxes, and Porter and me were having such severe problems. Those were my only copies, they were done on my tapes at my house on my machines, written on my paper with my pencils. I brought them to protect them, out of anger . . . not even knowing if the building would be standing there the next day, due to some of the arguments we had. I think there were 122, not all songs, some were work tapes and they did not belong to Owepar.

Neither Porter nor Dolly was exclusively signed to Owepar, they were not even staff writers for their own company—they had forgotten to hire themselves. They were mere stockholders and officers.

On July 1 the *Nashville Banner* announced that Dolly had signed with Katz–Gallin–Cleary, a Los Angeles management firm, which also handled Mac Davis and that old ACE nemesis from Melbourne, Olivia Newton-John. Dolly's new manager was Sandy Gallin, born in New York City in 1940, with a bachelor's degree in communication arts from Boston University. He had started in the mailroom of GAC talent agency (ICM today) and ended in a vice president's chair. Mike Kosser, after interviewing Porter, wrote that Katz–Gallin–Cleary "promptly told RCA that all the Porter and Dolly duets still in the can should stay in the can because it would hurt Dolly's career to be associated with Porter Wagoner. This is hard stuff for a proud man to take."

When Dolly was making her countryward U-turn in 1989, promoting the *White Limozeen* album, she told Patrick Carr of *Country Music*:

> I got run out of town because I couldn't make a living with songs like "Coat of Many Colors" and all that other stuff I really loved.
> Take my manager, Sandy Gallin . . . Country music has just never excited him. He's never understood it, or had any respect for it . . . It's not just Sandy who has no feel for country music, either. It's also a lot of the other people who are involved with me.

Obviously Top Billing could no longer handle Dolly, and eventually she told that to Tandy Rice. Dolly's departure was widely criticized at the time, and some resentments still simmer. Nashville has never been noted for much management or promotion acumen, and its most audacious manager, Col. Tom Parker, has always seemed like an outsider despite maintaining a Nashville headquarters for more than forty years.

Sandy Gallin was the best thing since Porter to happen to Dolly. They are now completing their second harmonious decade together, which is something of a record, at least in the pop music world where noisy fallings-out after a couple of years are almost the norm. In fact, if Porter had had someone marketing Porter Wagoner with the same imagination and gusto with which he flogged Dolly, his own star would twinkle higher in the heavens today.

In 1989 and 1991 I attempted to interview Sandy Gallin, leaving many messages and writing two letters. One of his representatives informed me that Sandy had no real place in a Porter Wagoner biography since he had no involvement whatever with Nashville. Sandy Gallin was Dolly Parton's manager during at least three years of her financial-legal enmeshment with Porter, including two lawsuits.

The Porter–Dolly scenario has been compared to the film *A Star Is Born*, preferably the 1954 version with Judy Garland outshining mentor James Mason. The song "The Gal That Got Away" from that movie would be a good song for Porter to record should he ever go pop. But as songwriter Arlie Duff writes in his *Y'all Come* autobiography ("Y'all Come" is one of Porter's standards), "Porter . . . just remember, it's better to have loved and lost than to have had no publishing company at all."

No tears for Porter. He simply worked, or overworked, himself out of a job, though admittedly he let them dismiss him before his contract had run out. He yielded like a man. Neither Porter nor Dolly ever employed legal counsel in their dealings with RCA or with each other at the time of parting. 'Twas the last thing on their minds.

Dolly certainly left in style. Porter got hit after hit out of her, though he certainly had a sharp songwriter supplying the material. After "Washday Blues" (1972), which he wrote, Dolly's next ten hits until Porter relinquished his grasp were written by her favorite songwriter.

Her strongest period on the charts was after she left Porter's road show but before she left his production control: seven hits, all but one in the Top 10 and three of them number one, with one number two and one number three.

After "The Seeker" came "We Used To," which went to number nine in 1975, "Hey, Lucky Lady" (number nineteen), then "All I Can Do," which entered the charts the same month Dolly went with Katz-Gallin-Cleary and rose to number three. In the same period there were three more duets in the Top 10, two more duet albums, and six more Dolly albums. "Say Forever You'll Be Mine" was number one in *Cash Box*.

Writing in *Country Sounds*, Bob Oermann saw *Jolene* (1974) as a transitional, maturation album, from starlet to star. It contained a beginner's song, "It Must Be You," by child prodigy Blaise Tosti at age twelve in 1969. His mother, Lucia, had been a makeup artist on Porter's TV show. Critic Tony Byworth called *Love Is Like a Butterfly* (1974) a "hell of an album"; Robert Christgau of the *Village Voice* praised Porter's writing— "Highway Headin' South" and "If I Cross Your Mind"—while saying Dolly "repeats herself (and apes others) nicely enough."

The 1975 album *The Bargain Store* includes her retort to all the gossip: "He Would Know"—if she cheated on her husband he would *know*. In *Dolly: A Photo-Bio*, Otis James called the album's production "flawless" and wondered why Dolly would forsake Porter's direction as a producer. He praised "the pacing and balance of the songs, to the details that make even the less exciting songs worth listening to—the terrific guitar break on 'The Only Hand You'll Ever Need to Hold' to subtle filling by the backup vocalists [The Nashville Edition] on Porter's tune, 'Love to Remember.'"

Best of Dolly Parton appeared in 1975 (not to be confused with the longer-titled *The Best of Dolly Parton* in 1970), with Porter getting retroactive producer-arranger credit. It went gold in 1978 (500,000 copies). It's the third Dolly album to include Porter's "Lonely Comin' Down" and also contains his "When I Sing for Him" gospel masterpiece. The album had a Daisy Mae-style poster tucked inside.

Porter's last album on her behalf was *All I Can Do*, recorded March 1–4, 1976. (On March 1, Dolly cut "To Daddy," which she never released and which went to number three for Emmylou Harris in 1978, another refutation of the Dolly-can-only-write-for-Dolly canard.) Another rejoinder to all the ribald rumors is "Shattered Image." As a little girl, Dolly would look at her reflection in the still waters of a creek, then throw in a rock to shatter the image, she recalls. Well, people are throwing rocks at her today: "we all do things we don't want told." But stay out of Dolly's closet if your own is full of trash. Well, Dolly's closet was full of cash at the moment (about $100,000 a year), so some notoriety was inevitable. Best track on the album may have been Emmylou Harris's "Boulder to Birmingham"—*Stereo Review* praised the "mountain grace" in Dolly's very moving rendition, while finding some of her singing otherwise "too tired or rushed," rating the album: "Performance: Less than she can do." Alanna Nash found most of Dolly's lyrics and melodies on the album "mindlessly perky" and Dolly the singer to be on automatic pilot.

Toby Thompson, in town for a major feature article for *The Village Voice*, attended one of the sessions and noticed Dolly was road-weary. A fatigued Porter was artfully coaxing another take out of a tired Dolly. She reminded Toby of some Nashville housewife in her "flowered shirt-waist, chocolate bellbottoms, four-inch heels," though he sensed her sensuality probably disconcerted the country market ("heap of blonde hair . . . inflated torso"). Porter seemed to fascinate Toby equally, with "oyster-shaped bags drooped below the infamous pompadour," his caricature appearance (silver belt buckle, tailored jeans, fancy boots, "suede pipe Nudie blouse") contrasting with his magisterial perfectionism. His amiable grin and cheerful dialogue seemed to mask an attention to detail more befitting a pop or rock producer. Porter seemed a combination coach, medicine man, and psychologist as he sweet-talked Dolly into re-singing something. In the dimmed lights of the studio he floated like a lost, solitary figure cloaked in the shadows behind the plate glass partition, his lanky frame swaying to the rhythm of the music. He'd been working on the album twenty-one days.

"I sometimes think I'm too particular, but to me a record's like a monument," Porter told Toby. "Important that it's done right."

In his ironically titled book, *So You Want to Be in Music!*, Bob Ferguson described how methodically Porter prepared for an album, from selecting the writer of the liner notes to selecting the cover design, from conferring in advance on which songs to use to picking the pickers beforehand. Bob writes, "Nothing is hit-or-miss about a Porter Wagoner album. Stars like him are in the business of making hits. Working in a meticulously planned recording session is a privilege, indeed."

Dolly told Tom Roland, author of *Billboard Book of Number One Country Hits*, that she relied on Bob Ferguson "more than Porter even knew or would have wanted me to. Porter did a great job on the records. Porter was more aggressive than Bob, but Bob had a lot of creative control. He was great at keeping order in the studio, which often got out of order because of Porter's temper with the musicians." Dolly says Bob kept things in perspective, had many creative ideas—more than he ever was credited with—yet makes it sound like he needed a gavel during some of the sessions. She asked Bob to be at her first post-Porter session. "Bob Ferguson was a good country producer," Chet told me. "Ferguson would let people have their way if they knew what they wanted." Bob told Paul Soelberg that Dolly's "input is good, and she isn't domineering. And in recording nobody can afford to be domineering. That can destroy a session."

As for Porter the martinet, the pressures had mounted partly because costs had risen (vinyl derives from oil and the energy crisis was one more excuse for raising record prices). By the mid-seventies, the competition was intense.

Mike Kosser quoted one of the later Wagonmasters, Ronnie Blackwell, in *Country Style* (1977): "Porter treats his sidemen great—most stars treat 'em like they're not there"; and songwriter Rory Bourke: "Just watching him in the studio, you get the feeling he's a warm, caring person who genuinely cares for people—not just the ones who can help him." But his story contained the first of Porter's doldrums interviews, where he complained of having worked 568 hours in RCA studios two years before (paid hours) and 95 percent of them on duet or Dolly records. "But I haven't seen Dolly in almost a year! Why can't she just be my friend? I don't expect anything from her. But someone you've worked with that long, you'd like for them to say hello to you." Kosser observed "real pain on the man's face as he talks, seated in this fantastic studio he has just rebuilt—Porter and Dolly's studio."

In her 1977 deposition, Dolly was asked, "Do you get along with Mr. Wagoner at present?"

"I'm sure we do," she replied. "I ain't seen him in a year. How can you *not* get along? I've been on the road solid for eight months."

In 1978 Porter told John Morthland of *Country Music* that if he hadn't produced all those hits for Dolly and for the duet act, "I would have been in serious trouble . . . I would probably be in the nuthouse somewhere, trying to figure out what I had done wrong."

Dolly has justly complained that too much talk about Porter in the studio makes it sound like maybe she couldn't sing. The live television tapes, the Grand Ole Opry reference discs, the *Real Live Dolly* album refute that emphatically. There are people who can't sing or can't sing well, for whom the producer functions as an electronic makeup artist or plastic surgeon. If they're off key, their intonation can be adjusted or masked with instruments (the high, sharpish sound of the steel guitar is a good antidote to flat singing), or with backup singers. Producing Dolly, Porter labored in quite the opposite direction, striving for as natural a voice as possible, bringing Dolly as intimately to the listener's ear as in a live show. It took him years to get their records more and more live sounding, with less and less echo. Echo itself is an instrument and can be used brilliantly. Dolly obviously enjoyed romping with it in her pop period. But it's lazy. The producer has less to worry about, less to prepare for. Contrast both cuts of "I Will Always Love You"—both went to number one, but the second one sounds artificial. Echoing Dolly on a slow song especially (it's fine on rock 'n' roll) is like dumping a keg of store brand ketchup on filet mignon or varnishing an heirloom portrait just because company's comin'. Dolly reverts to Porter-quality naturalness on the *Trio* album where she and her female buddies were largely in control (producer was George Massenburg), a project that was a decade in the dreaming. Her 1991 number one hit, "Silver and Gold," was also unalloyed Dolly.

In 1981 John Morthland (*Best of Country Music*) wrote, "I wish there was someone with comparable restraint working around her today. Yes, Porter Wagoner held her back in some ways, but once she was free of him she wasted no time in overcompensating grotesquely in the opposite direction."

In his *Hit Men* saga of pop music practices, Frederic Dannen refers to the "Stalinization" process, where record company executives who are now out of fashion become systematically eliminated from memory and from all mention.

To an extent, this happened to Porter. His name was decreasingly mentioned, even in detailed descriptions of Dolly's career, or carefully minimized. It might be acknowledged that Dolly sang with Porter, but not that they had twenty-one duet hits and fourteen duet albums. Often Dolly is reported to have "left Porter" in 1974, but in fact he was producing her well into 1976. Dolly's "seven years" with Porter is closer to nine (eight and a half), in the studio at least. This period of 1967–76 yielded twenty-three chart records and nineteen albums of Dolly as a solo artist. She also received eight Grammy nominations and four more with Porter, though admittedly she won no Grammys until later.

The heavy cross-pollination of Dolly's and Porter's songwriting is likewise mostly ignored, at least in the casual mass market publications. Some of this is the nature of show business: The future is the news, not the past. Some of it is an Orwellian rewrite of history.

Facts that didn't serve the interests of publicity were often transposed or suppressed. Sometimes it was implied that Dolly went on Porter's TV show after signing with RCA; a 1980 RCA bio has her immediately signing with Katz-Gallin in 1974 after leaving Porter's show instead of in 1976; the duets are almost always omitted; and, needless to say, Fred Foster and Monument Records are not names likely to be read in promo handouts.

By contrast, Dolly herself seems to deal out credit equitably when not badgered into a corner by a lawsuit or a tabloid attack. There's glowing Wagoner wall space at her Dollywood museum, for instance. However, the poster "Dolly's Dream" by Lew Stamm sold at Dollywood shows a young Dolly playing an oversize guitar with dreamlike pictures overhead of Sylvester Stallone, Burt Reynolds, Jane Fonda, Lily Tomlin, and Queen Elizabeth, each with Dolly. Porter's daughter Debra owns the poster. "He's not in it. I have it framed. I know those aren't all of Dolly's dreams."

But the most enduring myth is that Porter was unaware of the pop scene. Common sense would say that any entertainer who travels on the road is going to be more aware of much that an executive, however educated, may not understand in his plush office reading *Billboard*. Porter, it seems, is too often presented as a hick who held Dolly back, a charge to which he replies:

> That's bothered me more than any fuckin' thing about the split up between Dolly and me. I did know what was going on at all times. I know what the hell's going on out there. I knew the type of people we were selling to. Like the little record shops with the psychedelic windows. That took a lot out of me, mentally, to make those things happen and get a company to really get in there and get it for Dolly. It was always an uphill fight. I think Dolly would be the first to tell you that. You have to be in touch with what you're doing in this business, and who you're dealing with or what you're going for, or you just fall by the wayside. I tried to tell them how to market her, and where to take things, but they didn't know *what* the hell was going on!

In a later interview Porter condemned record company executives who only read "prepared stuff" written for the media. They don't see "the honesty coming from the people out there as to what's happening." Porter would tell RCA, "Hell, I'm dealing with these people, so I'm out there, so I *know* what they're thinking." Finally after much goading, RCA decided "to put megabucks behind Dolly." Porter had been telling Mel Ilberman that this would do it, that enough money would cross Dolly over into the pop market. "That's exactly what happened," he says. "Because they were prepared at that time to put megabucks into her career, so there's no way she could have missed."

One published rumor has Porter being apprehended out in Brentwood near Dolly's home with his pistol. (Shades of Jerry Lee Lewis outside Graceland demanding to see Elvis.) Checking with the police, I was referred to the Williamson County Sheriff's office. Nothing under Wagoner, Porter, or Waggoner, Porter. "Say, that's not the country singer, is it?" Well, yes. "I think we *do* have something on George Jones . . ."

Down on Music Row, at RCA, the wrecking ball was in full swing.

In his book *So You Want to Be in Music!*, written with Jesse Burt, Bob Ferguson said in his list of "Things to Watch" that number one was guarding yourself against exhaustion, since in the record business, "long hours, fast work under high pressure, and constant excitement are hazards." Bob was something of a sixties producer whose style was informal and courteous. "At RCA we had an open-door policy. We just wanted the best songs to have hits, the only thing we had to do was have hit records," Bob said in 1990. "Joe Galante was very rude. Chet said, 'They won't listen to me anymore.' I think that's the saddest words I ever heard. It was the crash of the company and its reputation. Jerry Reed said, 'It ain't no family no more.' I had fifty-one artists overall. They were trying to get rid of my artists, one by one."

Chet had written the foreword to Bob's *So You Want to Be in Music!*, and Bob and Chet could have written the sequel. Bob had left for the Indian territory, settling down with his beloved Choctaws. Chet escaped to the safety of the concert stage and said in 1989, "I hired Jerry Bradley and turned everything over to him. Jerry tended to want to get rid of all the artists I had brought along, and that's normal. People want to get credit for what *they've* done."

Maybe RCA was pulling out of the country business. It looked that way to some when Jerry Bradley closed Studio B in 1976. Studio B was a money loser, with more and more acts cutting sessions where (and how) they wanted, then bringing their masters to the company. Porter, with his ever-improving Fireside studio, was swimming in this trend.

By 1978 Jerry was telling Patrick Thomas of *Advantage* magazine that RCA's country sales were five times what they'd been in 1975.

Porter still had his television show and plenty of chances to glitter at Opryland, plus a new fantastic studio where he could produce *all* sorts of music. At least he felt secure on the label that had dropped Nat Stuckey and which Dottie West had "left."

41

"WILL THERE BE NOT A TRACE LEFT BEHIND . . . ?"

If you're going to move,
you gotta move while you can.
—Dolly, under oath, 1979

Porter's daughter Debra says Dolly "always took us under her wing." "She was very tasteful in all her dealings with us."

Dolly told Debra, "No matter where I'm entertaining you're always welcome."

During the breakup period, "she called, wanted to talk, wanted to be sure I understood. She felt it was necessary," Debra recalls.

Sometime in the summer of 1974 Dolly sent a handwritten letter to Debra and her husband, Mike Loy:

Dear Debra & Mike,

I just wanted to write you a note and say thank you for coming to my first show with my own band. I should have told you before now how much it meant to me but I've always been *behind* on everything.

I hope we can always be friends because I have come to love all of you in a very special way. I hope nothing that ever happened between Porter and me will ever affect our friendship. Porter is a wonderful man with many great qualities, he has done so much for me and I will do everything I can to repay him through the years. There are many ways I can help him like he has helped me and I will never miss a chance to do whatever I can for him. I am very grateful to Porter, we have had our troubles but we have forgiven each other of all the hurt we have caused each other. We have agreed to be great friends and I plan to keep my end of the deal— we both have our faults but so does everyone. I just wanted to tell you myself that Porter and I have worked our problems out. Thank God for letting things work out so well for both of us. Porter seems to be much happier now and so am I. I hope God will be on my side, Porter's side and your side. Sometimes it's easier to write down what you feel than it is to say it, but I wanted to let you know

that your friendship means a great deal to me and I hope I don't
ever do anything to disappoint you.

Please be my friend—you are always welcome wherever I
am—

May God bless you
Your friend Always

Love

Dolly

P.S. Why didn't you come back to see me? Did I do something
wrong? If so, I hope you will forgive me. I was nervous the day you
came over. I may have done something to hurt your feelings. If so,
I didn't mean to. Please accept my apology.

Sometime in the summer of 1976 a pink envelope was delivered
to Porter. Inside on the pink letterhead of Dolly Parton Enterprises was
the following handwritten letter:

Porter,

Show-Biz said they couldn't pay the $11,000 bill you sent
from Fireside, so I told them to send a bill to me for what they
thought it would have cost at another studio had they been able to
work without technical problems and with studio musicians and
they said this $4,500 was all they could pay. I can't pay the rest
either. I really wish I could but I wouldn't ask you to if it was
turned around. Please try and understand that I am only trying to
be fair with everybody. I don't want to offend you or anyone else. I
just want to be happy and I honestly want you to be happy too. I
know this whole thing is hard to understand but someday I hope
you can see my reasons for making all these changes.

I think you are very talented, you've done great things in
the past for me and for other people and I know you will continue
to do great things in the future. I never doubted you as much as I
had started to doubt myself. I just needed to make changes—I
wasn't happy—and I want so bad to be. I love you and respect you
for what you have done. I wanted to tell you all my feelings but I
couldn't without crying and I know you hate that. I can't even
write them down. So I will just say I'm sorry if I've hurt you more
than I had to. I just didn't know any other way out. We will both
be better off.

I know you know me better than anyone and I know you are
sure there is more to the story than I will ever be able to tell but the
ending is still the same. Please try to be happy. I hope I will be.
May God bless both of us and whatever the future holds—

As always

Dolly.

Dolly also left this souvenir. Joan typed it, of course.

```
TO PORTER WAGONER,
NOW THAT OUR TIES TOGETHER WITH R C A HAVE BEEN CUT,
BECAUSE OF MY APPRECIATION AND RESPECT FOR YOU, FOR
ALL THE THINGS YOU HAVE DONE FOR ME IN THE PAST
AND FOR HELPING ME MORE THAN ANY PERSON,TO HELP ME
BECOME SUCCESSFUL, I AGREE TO CONTINUE TO PAY YOU
15% (fifteen per cent) OF GROSS INCOME ON MY R C A
RECORD ROYALTIES FOR THE DURATION OF THE CONTRACT
NEGOCIATED BY YOU.
```

Dolly Parton
Aug. 26, 1976

Dolly had told several people that she would do whatever she had to do, pay whatever she had to pay, to get free. The most severe interpretation against her would be that she had used Porter and had used him up. But a Parton partisan might say that Dolly was no longer locked in the coat closet, that the lights were turned on now. She could sleep with them on for the rest of her life.

Porter did not need more bad news. But on October 25, 1976, his onetime protégé and nephew, Charley Hall, had his photo on the front page of the Fort Worth *Star-Telegram*. Blood was running down his face, and his hands were cuffed behind his back as the police led him away after an incredible confrontation involving dozens of police cars.

Charley and his gang had been robbing people at gunpoint over a five-state area. They had just captured a mobile home with four hostages inside and were hurtling through Fort Worth in a twenty-five-mile chase. They had hoped to get to a helicopter and escape to Mexico. Instead, they almost crashed a police barricade. They came out shooting with their M-1s and M-16s (they had a twenty-five-piece arsenal), exchanging volleys with the law. One officer said, "It looked like a fire fight in Vietnam."

They wounded one policeman.

Charley got forty-five years, and almost every month his parents, Lorraine and Ed, made the bus trip to Texas. Broken by grief, Ed Hall died.

Porter's secretary, Joan, remembers typing many letters on Charley's behalf from Porter to the Texas officials. In 1979 Charley's brother Jerry died in a car crash. Finally, in 1984 Charley was paroled to his mother in Springfield.

Before he went astray, Charley had tried to become a country singer. Porter produced sessions for him, even had him on his TV show; Charley still owns Porter's very first Nudie suit, which Porter gave to him. Lorraine says prescription drugs and honky-tonk hoodlum companions led him astray and she hopes a baring of Charley's story will help someone, somewhere. He is bedfast today; Porter visits him when he's in Springfield.

In the month following Charley's spectacular collision with authority, November 1976, Porter's "When Lea Jane Sang" entered *Billboard*. It was mistitled; it's "When Lea Jane Would Sing" on the lead sheet. Porter wrote it, and it has the sort of highly singable folky melody that he does so well, somewhat in the mode of John Denver's "Back Home Again." There are two versions, and the hit rendition appeared on an RCA album only in England. Another take, without backup singers, came out on an obscure budget album.

The backup voices are the Lea Jane Singers. The voice of Lea Jane Berinati stands out, rather like Dolly's did on the Bill Phillips record that first brought her notice, prompting the listener to wonder, who's that girl singing? so emotional is the performance. Lea Jane had written in a ninth grade term paper of her career plan to come to Nashville; eventually Porter recruited her and her group to sing on his and Dolly's records, and for the TV show. Lea Jane remembers being so broken up by hearing Porter do "Trouble in the Amen Corner" that she feared she couldn't regain her own composure in time to sing her part on the show. Nashville's backup singing was rather bland at times, Lea Jane felt, and she wanted to bring more feeling to her work. "A record can be perfect and no one may buy it if it lacks the feeling," she says.

But the lyric of "When Lea Jane Sang" was not about her. Porter just liked the sound of her name; it sang well. It starts out happy, about a couple united by love and music. Then the mood changes:

> Our search for fame took Lea Jane and me to bigger places;
> Our simple life we traded for new friends,
> And it wasn't long until her song took on a different
>   meaning . . .
> Our love grew thin and hurt moved in to each song she would
>   sing.

It's easy to imagine how two singers could have traded lines back and forth, as their love is sundered by the woman's search for success without him. It would have made a fine duet.

PART FOUR

THE LAST GREAT HILLBILLY

I've been through a lot of hell in my lifetime in the
music business, but it's worth it two times over. I've
been through poverty, love, jilt and hate at one time or
another, but I still love the music business, and feel
it's been great to me. When I leave this business, it will
be with my hands folded, lying in a box. What I stand
for may not be right for everybody else, but it's right
for me.

—Porter, to Terry Manley,
Des Moines *Register*, October 27, 1979

I depend a lot on Porter to carry this thing on when
Roy and Bill and Hank and some of us are gone.
Porter will be one of the people who fall
into line in succession, of the people
who mean so much to the Opry.

—Minnie Pearl, interview,
May 17, 1989

He's not afraid to get on that bus and ride
with that band a thousand miles if they have to.
There's so few of those left.

—Don Fowler, booking agent,
interview, July 18, 1990

42

BACK TO THE LAKE

When the show split, Porter retired.
He had a lot of heartache;
it really hurt him.

—Don Fowler, interview,
July 18, 1990

"**I** never fished much until I moved to Nashville. I had never learned to cast with a rod and reel," Porter told Kelly Delaney in 1983 for *Country Song Roundup*.

As a boy in Missouri he had occasionally gone fishing when the fields were too wet for working. They would cut some willow fish poles, dig some worms, and fish for freshwater bream ("brim" in Missouri). His 1970 hit "You Got-ta Have a License" evokes all this: two brothers fishing with willow poles, with worms, minnows, and sourdough for bait until the game warden descends and makes them throw back their catch.

Porter's fishing haven for twenty years was Center Hill Lake, a man-made lake about seventy miles east of Nashville in DeKalb County. Porter found its beauty enchanting, with its cliffs hundreds of feet high and dramatic plunging waterfalls. The tranquil beauty of the scene was a soothing balm to a spirit often smarting from the slings and arrows of Music Row. Porter has often said that the closer he gets to nature, the closer he feels to God, and he likes to quote an old saying: God doesn't count the days that you fish against your lifespan.

At first he discovered that fishing was as much work as golf. He'd hung up his golf bag out of frustration at taking the game too seriously; now he was coming home exhausted from trying to catch a bass every time. One senses that Porter's fishing forays were more like safaris or military operations until finally it dawned on him that fishing was supposed to be fun.

Soon after Center Hill Lake was formed, it became the number one nighttime fishing hole in the Nashville area. Anglers would troll at the mouths of the creeks at night, with their large lures and pork rind, then Doll flies, when these came into fashion. "I love it then, when you hear the whippoorwills and hoot owls calling, and the lake is so calm it looks like a huge mirror," he told Kelly Delaney.

Somebody once asked Tony Bean, a well-known Tennessee fisherman, "How do you find Porter Wagoner out on the lake?" He answered, "Go out there late at night and find the darkest spot of the lake you can find, and yell, 'Hey, Porter!' and somebody'll say, 'Yeah?' That's where he'll be."

Porter started out by following the local custom of hooking his flies with a lizard ("mud eels" from Indiana) or with pork rind. Then he went to plastic worms, and his tackle box looked like his stage costumes, a festival of color—spotted, checked, or speckled plastic worms. His favorite worm color was the favorite color of his Nudie suits, purple (or violet), an especially enticing color down in the clear waters of the lake. The plastic worm approach was the most relaxing way to fish. He'd throw his baited line up on the shore first, then slowly drag it out into the water. "To my way of thinking, fish are pretty smart," he told Delaney. "They know something just didn't fall out of the sky. They know it ain't rainin' worms." Porter figures the fish ought to see the worm coming from the bank, where they're used to seeing their food come from.

"Porter fishes with that artificial worm," says Little Jimmy Dickens, Opry star and Hall of Fame member. "He's taught me how to work it, leave it lay, then retrieve it."

First Porter throws his sinker (an egg sinker) up onto the bank. It slides down the line to the first rock or drop-off. Then the worm comes following. Next, he maneuvers his line to another drop-off, and the worm follows still. This will lure the smallmouth bass where they wouldn't hit a big sinker plunging toward the bottom.

One night Porter peeked out the window of his fifty-eight-foot houseboat and there were skin divers in the moonlight. A song began coming to him about a convict in a cell, in a prison beside a lake. He just followed the song where it led him; it became "The Divers Are Out Tonight." He says, "I think some songwriters will tailor things so much, they don't leave their minds open to come what will. I had no idea the song would take those turns."

"The Divers Are Out Tonight" is a kind of aquatic version of "Folsom Prison Blues" with an O. Henry-type surprise ending. The divers are recovering a strongbox from a bank robbery, and the prisoner is doing five years for that very robbery, one he didn't commit. With a mournful heart he watches the divers dividing the money, knowing the prison warden will not believe him if he tries to tell what really happened.

With a note of bleak resignation the song ends:

They say no one can swim Big Sandy,
With its swirling undercurrent and rough tide,
But if I could just get through the bars on this window
I'd try the Big Sandy tonight.

Another song written at Center Hill was "Mystery Mountain." Porter was fishing from a bluff when suddenly, about a hundred yards away, a huge landslide began rumbling down into the water. "It was the most unbelievable sound I ever heard in my life, big rocks hitting the water and trees falling—when that land moved, the trees crashed too. It was an awesome sound." Porter headed back to his houseboat, rushed inside, and began thinking of tales his father had told him about going over to his grandfather John's farm and of the big bluff that lay between. John Wagoner was the one who dodged wild panthers in his early days in Howell County. Mystery Mountain is guarded by panthers, along with some support troops like rattlesnakes and wild boars. The speaker is determined to brave the heights of Mystery Mountain, but then a panther screams and he panics. He runs back down the slopes; Mystery Mountain can keep its mystery.

Most uncanny of all was "Indian Creek," written when Porter was in his 17.5-foot bass boat with the triple hull, about twenty miles from his houseboat, up Indian Creek. A storm arose, and he went up a long slough and into a little pocket where he could escape the wind. He pulled a poncho over his head and finally hooked up his boat where it wouldn't be blown up on the bank.

Lightning was stabbing the sky over the hills of Indian Creek, like fireworks going off. "There was a lot of magic happening," Porter recalls. In the noise of the thunder Porter could hear Indians chanting and dancing on the bank. The lyrics came tumbling out of his imagination. Then he seized a pen and a piece of brown paper from one of the lockers and began trying to write in the rain. "It was fading, hell, you could hardly make out what it was after it was wrote down."

He felt he could almost make out one of the Indians, a chief named Tonya. Then "the storm blew on through and the clouds gave way." Back in Nashville Porter played "Indian Creek" for Bob Ferguson. "How'd you know about Chief Tonya?" asked Bob. He opened a book and showed Porter a picture of a real Indian chief.

"That's some of the things that happen when you are writing songs. It's very, very strange," Porter mused.

Porter rushed to the Wagoner home and rapped on the door in the dark. Debra wondered who it could be and with some caution turned on the light. "Daddy, what are you *doing* here?"

"Deb, I've written a song . . ."

INDIAN CREEK

Way down yonder at Indian Creek,
The braves still dance when the tom-toms beat,
And their bonfires light the sky like flaming gold;
When the moon has passed and it's dark as pitch,
You can hear the strangest stories ever told.

Though they moved away long, long ago,
Through the hills and the hollers they still echo;
The mournful sounds of their retreat
Still echo in the hills of Indian Creek.

One night in the sand on the banks of a branch
I saw Chief Tonya do his famous war dance,
Wah hah wah ho yo,
With his feathers all colors and his strings of beads,
Dancing on the banks of Indian Creek.

When the moon is full and the clouds give way,
The creek lights up just as bright as day.
Sometimes the water gets crimson red,
From the battles they fought and the blood they shed,
When they lived on the banks of Indian Creek . . .
When they lived on the banks of Indian Creek . . .

One of Porter's recent fishing buddies is his guitar player, L. D. ("Rick") Wayne. One night out at Center Hill, under a full moon, Porter turned to L. D. and said, "You know what, I have shared the stage of the Grand Ole Opry with Roy Acuff, and I've sung duets with Dolly Parton, and I've been in a movie with Clint Eastwood, but none of those thrills measures at all, compared to sitting on this long, skinny point in this beautiful moonlight, throwin' for smallmouth bass. You just can't beat that."

A touching Porter Wagoner fishing story concerns the last request of his pal "Cedar Stump." Cedar had asked to be cremated and his ashes scattered over Center Hill Lake. When he died, Porter kept the promise, making the rounds in his boat, dropping the ashes around each of Cedar's personal fishing spots.

Porter no longer fishes at Center Hill Lake. He keeps his Sumerset houseboat, with maroon stripe down the side and maroon carpet, tied up in a fifty-foot slip at Four Corners Marina at J. Percy Priest Lake. The lake is a 14,000-acre reservoir formed by a dam built by the U.S. Army Corps of Engineers on Stone's River. It lies within Davidson County (Metropolitan Nashville), and Porter's houseboat neighbors include gospel and pop singer Amy Grant and her songwriter-guitarist husband, Gary Chapman.

More than fifty mounted bass used to decorate the walls of Porter's office, including one smallmouth bass weighing close to ten pounds. But for more than fifteen years he has been releasing his catches back into the water, after perhaps detaining the fish briefly for a photograph. These are sent off to a craftsman who can make a plastic replica that would fool anybody.

In spite of having designed the eighteen-foot Nighthawk with side-mounted lights for the Winner Boat Company, Porter doesn't enter fishing competitions. However, in 1988 he sponsored his own celebrity fish-in, with Ricky Skaggs and Lee Greenwood among the contestants and Judy Rodman one of the winners, the prize money going to charity. He goes to fishing contests only to watch. He feels an entertainer might steal some limelight from the real fishermen, the real pros.

43

DOWN BY THE FIRESIDE

Certainly nobody but Porter could have
designed this studio, which strikes the eye much
like one of his dazzling rhinestone costumes.

—John Morthland, "The Last of the
Hillbillies Speaks His Mind,"
Country Music, July 1978

If you don't progress in your work,
then you're dead. I don't see any newspaper
stories reading like Will Rogers wrote 'em.

—Porter to Bill Hance,
Nashville Banner, March 23, 1979

When Porter left the road in 1975, RCA began staggering his releases about a year apart, killing all their chances. By 1975 he was finished as a top singles artist. In 1974 he'd had three chart records, the second and third having reached the Top 20. But "Indian Creek" received no push, and "When Lea Jane Sang" was delayed for around a year.

The momentum was lost, so when the very moving "I Haven't Learned a Thing" appeared in 1977, it only went to number seventy-six. Considering who was on it, it should have done better: it was a duet with Merle Haggard as "guest vocalist." The lyric is a kind of "Lost Highway" meets "Skid Row Joe": a preacher's boy makes the mistake of learning guitar and playing in nightclubs, and before he turns thirty his hands are so shaky he "can barely make the chords." His latest audience is a group of Skid Row mission inmates. The lyric, by Sonny Throckmorton, recalls Merle's own "Mama Tried," and Merle's voice trails miles behind Porter's, deliberately behind the beat and sometimes singing different words. The shambling vocal effect works, and it's probably unique.

Merle was so struck by the laid-back ambience of Fireside, where they cut the song, that he did two albums of his own there. He'd sit in the rocking chair by the Fireside fireplace, picking and singing, with the sidemen gathering around like in a jam session. In gratitude, Porter presented Merle with a string of Center Hill Lake bass.

"I Haven't Learned a Thing" was on his best album in a long time, simply titled *Porter* (1977). *Country Music* magazine named it "Album of the Month," Ed Ward praising "the quiet, understated subtlety of Porter's approach" and comparing the "loping" gait of some of the tracks to Don Williams's subdued style. "Porter's whole presentation breathes years of experience," Ward wrote.

Porter the producer was now in full control of Porter the singer, who in the terminal Dolly days had occasionally sounded weary. He was again back on top of his vocals, refreshed and true. An especially moving cut was "The Arizona Whiz" by Max D. Barnes. A rock star fails to show up at a college concert, so an old blues harmonica player, "The Arizona Whiz," fills in. He sings of "matrimony, broads and booze, love and war," and he closes with a gospel song. None of the spellbound students leaves while he is performing. Porter recites a throwaway line that says it all: "I heard they paid him twenty dollars." Also on the album is "Ruby Jones" (by Ritchie Adams and Mark Barkan), reassuring his loyal fans that the cold, hard facts of life are alive and well. The song is set in 1964 in Vietnam. Ruby Jones patriotically services servicemen in her tent, until one of her patrons is suddenly distracted from her charms by a burst of Viet Cong gunfire. The altruistic Ruby throws her body in front of his, taking "the bullet that had my name." He misses Ruby to this day.

Most of the album was cut at Fireside. It had started as a mere demo studio, advancing to a custom studio (for vanity or subsidized recordings), progressing finally to a studio capable of providing masters acceptable to major labels. Porter retooled it in 1977, having admitted in an interview it wasn't yet up to RCA standards, no doubt smarting under its occasional malfunction. Fireside went from sixteen to twenty-four tracks, and in 1979 Porter announced forty-eight track capability.

Some of Fireside's popularity owed to its Porter-style atmosphere. On opening day in 1973 *Music City News* had attempted to describe it:

> Designed with the idea of relaxation and comfort for the musicians and workers, Fireside features a rustic interior surrounded by natural rocks and cypress paneling. Fixtures include an antique wagon wheel [with] hanging light pieces with built-in adjustable mood lights, and restored antique pieces from the historic, recently razed Brass Rail Restaurant in Nashville's famed Printers' Alley.

Porter sold Fireside years ago, and it's changed hands a few more times. Gone today is the original orange carpeting, but otherwise it's mostly the same inside, with the wedge-shaped control room with green felt-covered roof. Overhead extend large timber cross-beams, giving the interior a spacious, barn-like look. The electric fireplace reinforces Porter's zodiac "fire" motif (Leo is a fire sign).

Porter's manager in 1978 was Brooke Newell, wife of noted guitarist Fred Newell, a familiar musician on The Nashville Network today. Brooke remembers that Porter's engineers would ritualistically sprinkle glitter dust on the carpets before each session. He kept frosty Cokes on hand and all the favorite brands of cigarettes, free for his musicians, plus lots of candy, especially to sate his own sweet tooth. Porter also liked to drag everyone to eat at a greasy spoon restaurant nearby, thoughtfully keeping plenty of antacid Rolaids under the console back at the studio.

An inside metal staircase used to lead up to the mixing room; it's a small clothing store today, reached only by an outside metal staircase. The walls of the room are still lined with orchid-colored crushed velour. Roy Shockley remembers it supposedly cost five thousand dollars to do the walls. The mixing room was also a Pillow Room ("there must have been a thousand pillows," laughs Roy); and a hydraulic lift elevated the mixing console up and down, so you could stand up and mix, or lie down and work from the pillows. Roy says he once spent a night in the Pillow Room. "Pillows and owls. He had owls everywhere. And a lot of neon." The Pillow Room was reputed to be Porter's upstairs pleasure dome. Visiting the room in 1978, John Morthland of *Country Music* likened it to a "disco in Bombay," with "revolving, reflecting glass balls overhead, colored lights blinking around the dark room, and a few shrine-like objects sitting on the ledges."

I asked a former employee if the Pillow Room was used for trysts. "Trysts?" she repeated. "Yes. Trysts. Yes." Or so she had heard.*

John Morthland also noted Fireside's separate piano room, to prevent sound leakage from other instruments. There also was a vocal room, with sand poured into the walls, plus a drum room with slanted walls and ceiling. Porter believed Nashville lagged behind other cities "in terms of drum sound" since drums need "room to breathe" and they should sound "deep and bright." Each instrument and voice had its special microphone and special sound level. Redundantly, John marveled how Porter left nothing to chance; this was how he did everything.

But Michael Kosser pierced behind the Fireside façade when he interviewed Porter in the throes of his Dolly-dejection (*Country Rhythms*, 1977):

> A long look at the tall thin man today reveals a wealthy but
> very unhappy man who has spent the last few months as a hermit

---

*By now Porter was living at 6105 Hickory Valley Road, complete with Jacuzzi (a wall had been torn out to accommodate it) and Pillow Room with a lavender-dyed parachute suspended from the ceiling for an Oriental, tent-like effect.

quietly puttering about his studio. His puttering has produced one of the most beautiful studios ever to hit Nashville, and chances are it will make him even richer—but happy? Maybe not.

Keyboardist Mike Lawler was one of Porter's apprentices in the 1970s. Wanting very much to break into session work, he hung around all he could, sometimes playing for free. When he least expected it, Porter might sneak up behind him in the studio and slip a new hundred-dollar bill into his pocket. Porter also might inquire about Mike's house note and keep him from falling behind. Mike is almost embarrassed to call Porter his father figure, but he says without Porter, he might never have made that nigh-impossible transition from road musician to studio-quality player. Mike later was good enough for the Allman Brothers, and he credits Porter with his rise in the music business. (Porter told Mike how once at a RCA convention in a hotel, he accidentally walked in on Elvis—the King—kneeling in fealty to a famous movie queen.)

Fred Newell and his wife have their own stories about Porter's generosity. Once Fred's home tape recorder stopped working, so he threw it angrily at the wall. Brooke mentioned this in passing to Porter, who called Fred to the studio on a Saturday morning. Fred drove in from the country, figuring he'd have to redo a guitar part on a recording. Porter presented him with a new machine and said, "You're going to need this next week for doing charts." Once when Fred wanted to buy some discarded speakers, Porter simply ordered Roy Shockley and Tom Pick to transport them to Fred's car, while firmly demanding, "Where are your car keys?"

Brooke showed me a bracelet Porter had given her. She'd been on the job a couple of weeks when Porter's girlfriend called her up, "cussing me out for letting someone in his dressing room at the Opry he'd said he didn't want in." Brooke told Porter she probably wasn't cut out for the job of managing him, but next week he invited her into Hal Durham's office at the Opry, shut the door, and gave her the bracelet. "If anytime things aren't going right, you look at that, and that tells you how *I* feel about the job you're doing."

When Porter learned that Fred didn't even own a revolver and all the other musicians did, Brooke says, "Next thing we knew Porter presented Fred with a pistol. There was real tight security, so Porter would always go out with his hand on his pistol in his pocket or in his belt because there was a lot of crime in the Music Row area."*

*By 1989, a *Tennessean* article by Sheila Wissner and Robert K. Oermann, headlined "Music Row Becoming Murder Row," listed four murders in the years 1985–89 alone. In one of these an attorney was shot to death in the basement of Porter's old apartment building, the Americana; an architect was killed in his

Porter had sunk a half-million dollars into Fireside. This was a definite advance over the Hopper radio shop days in West Plains, with the dollar-demos on acetate, or the Cliff Thomas garage by the loading dock with its concrete walls and two-track machine, Cliff waiting for the street traffic outside to subside.

By the early eighties, with country music growing so very complex and artificial, it was fashionable in some quarters to pine for the good old days of monaural records. Many of the undoctored classics from the forties and fifties could have easily upstaged much of the muddled "contemporary country" then in vogue.

Porter knows how bad some of the old recordings were. They lost much of the natural timbre of the human voice, plus the "live" sound of the instruments. Both were absorbed, or distorted, by wretched acoustics and simply not transmitted to the primitive tape. He laments the tinny sound on some of his own early RCA releases. While the typical late seventies producer was trying to add to, or alter, the natural sound of the voice and instruments, Porter was striving to preserve, or recapture, the original sound.

After years of club or concert work, a singer often sings too loud for the delicately adjusted equipment. Rather than make the artist sing softer, Porter would set the sound levels to where the singer could relax and perform as if onstage. A recording artist needs to forget about being in a studio and concentrate on the meaning of the song. In 1975 Porter told Dave Hickey of *Country Music* that on his and Dolly's later recordings there was less reverberation and less limitation on the voices. "On the newer records, the singing isn't so perfect, but it's much more real. It's the accidents and irregularities that let you know there's a person there singing to you."

He says the only reason to hide a voice in the arrangement is if the singer can't sing. "Country fans like to hear the vocal in its purest form. They like to hear all the vocal." Porter believes the key to big hit records, the real standards, is that the vocal is out front with the personality of the singer coming clear so "you can hear them breathe."

Porter told Glenn Hunter in 1983 that he wanted the instruments to sound like themselves, that an instrument played with feeling sounds

---

office; a symphony violinist was killed; and most sinister, a *Cash Box* employee in charge of the weekly hit charts was shot to death in the street. He was discovered by songwriter Candy Parton (distant Dolly kin), and Johnny Cash and Kris Kristofferson heard the shots and came running from their *Highwayman II* recording session. In 1990 a young Atlantic recording artist, Tracy Lawrence, was shot four times rescuing his girlfriend from a robbery attempt near the Hall of Fame.

like a human heart beating, that the one thing the electronics wizards have yet to invent is a machine with that heartbeat feeling you get with an acoustic or steel guitar.

Porter especially objects to the absence today of recognizable intros or signature lines on records. "It's almost like they use the same intro for every damn thing anymore." His session pickers knew he wanted something original and always strove to come up with something different. "They knew I didn't want any old shit they'd played the day before for Bradley, and played for Chet the day before that." Fred Newell says he learned a lot about the electric rhythm guitar when playing for Porter: "He wasn't real big on the old Nashville ring-a-ling acoustic rhythm, he wanted something a little more aggressive, with a little more drive. Even on ballads Porter wanted them to be tender, but not run-of-the-mill like they were done somewhere else." Newell was Porter's music director on the later TV shows and played with him on the Opry for three and one-half years.

Barbara Lea was replaced by Linda Carol Moore for the TV show. Linda had studied music at Belmont College and by 1990 was in New York pursuing a theatrical career. She calls Porter "fearless when it came to experimenting with a type of music that was in contrast to his traditional country style. He always accepted the challenge of the unfamiliar. And he would always arrive at a formula that would work in the studio. He had the true admiration of his contemporaries . . . Nashville at that time was on the eve of change. The boundaries of traditional country and country/pop were questionable. Porter saw the expanding horizons in country music as an opportunity to grow."

Porter's lack of education was part of the secret to his success, he told John Morthland: "God gave me a lot of common sense; a person that don't have a big education watches stuff that's going on around him and learns more than a person that feels they learned it all out of a university. I didn't learn electronics at school; they didn't teach it there. We was trying to get the lamp wick trimmed to burn the coal oil lamp."

Sometime in the late seventies Porter made one of his greatest recordings, "The Fiery Death of Willie Boudine." Almost no one has heard it, however, since it only appeared on some obscure budget albums as "Willie Bodine." David Allen Coe also released the song.

It was written by Jay Bolotin, legendary singer–songwriter conspicuous for his austere, spooky black and white clothes. "He looked like the kind of guy who could put a spell on you," remembers Porter. Jay was also a graphic artist, educated at the prestigious Rhode Island School of Design. Merle Haggard was producing him down at Fireside. "In a desperate attempt to describe him to a friend," wrote songwriter-poet Bill Ede in the *Louisville Music News* in 1990, "I called him a combination

Linda Carol Moore, featured singer on "The Porter Wagoner Show" (TV) 1976–79 [COURTESY LINDA CAROL MOORE].

of Leonard Cohen, Richie Havens, and Chet Atkins."

Willie Boudine is the antihero of a long, unraveling saga of madness and salvation in the Kentucky coal fields. Jay Bolotin brought him to life in his traveling show, "The Hidden Boy," performed on Nashville's Vanderbilt campus in 1990. In the theater lobby hung his one-man art show of poems and woodcuts, in black and white as stark as his costume, with the words and the art interwoven and interdependent, William Blake-style. His lyrics have the impact of Loretta Lynn revised by Poe; his pictures are as unsettling as Doré or Bosch.

The recording of "Willie Boudine" by Porter is one of the strongest rockabilly singles that never was. The song is a kind of "Wreck on the Highway" meeting "The Ballad of Thunder Road." Porter's version opens with a salvo of slashingly chilling acoustic guitar licks. The first words are six o'clock news-brutal, but delivered with drawn out pain like a ballad, punctuated with Porter-style pauses: "Somebody died on the highway . . . the beer and the gasoline burn . . . there's a black flume of smoke over Eastern Kentucky . . . and who there among you will cry-y-y . . . about the fiery death of Willie Boudine!!!" The rest of the melody is frenetically exciting, the lyrics tracing Willie's career as a "practicing soldier of crime," robbing grocery stores in lieu of working in the mines, once throwing up all over the floor in midstickup. He spends his loot on his car and on pictures of Jesus and dies in a high-speed flight from the law. The thrilling chord changes throughout the song jerk to a halt at the end, with a synthesizer chord played in a different key by Mike Lawler. Porter repeats the mournful opening, "Somebody died on the highway . . ."

The record resonates with the fate of Porter's nephews: Charley Hall and his motorized guerrilla shootout in Fort Worth and Jerry Hall and his automotive death in Missouri.

Jay Bolotin played guitar on the session. He hadn't joined the union—didn't want to—so when he shook hands with Porter for the last time, a couple of crisp hundred dollar bills ended up in his palm.

"Porter's going disco!" Music Row murmured in disbelief in 1978. A disco demo by a band called Down and Dirty was making the rounds. In actuality, they were some Porter-pickers incognito. And into his own most requested songs he had been sneaking a disco beat, explaining somewhat defensively that all the rumors were just exaggerations; he was merely updating his rhythm ideas. (Bill Anderson was another defector toward disco.) In his compulsive quest to stay current, Porter had his engineers tape him the latest radio hits, and he would listen to them while driving to and from the studio each day. Roy Shockley chuckles, "When he got into disco, we'd a-like to lost him there. He went wild on that disco!"

Before Porter sold Fireside, a metal plaque was posted listing 115 entertainers who had recorded there, including Chet Atkins, Ernest Tubb, Mickey Gilley, Floyd Cramer, Con Hunley, Marty Robbins, Leona Williams, Isaac Peyton Sweat, Hank Cochran, Betty Jean Robinson, The Chuck Wagon Gang, The Nashville Brass, Mel Tillis, Bobby Bare, Vernon Oxford, Paul Richey, Shel Silverstein, Jim Ed Brown, Little David Wilkins, Jerry Foster, Bill Rice, Paul Craft, Bobby Borchers, Connie Eaton, Jay Bolotin, Bob Luman, Johnny Bush, Philomena Begley, Tony Alamo, Mack Vickery, Hank Locklin, Jerry Reed, Merle Haggard, Mack Magaha, George Riddle, Sharon Vaughn, Sunday Sharpe, Rory Bourke, Gary Buck, Tommy Overstreet.

Dolly once called Fireside "the studio our songs built," and the plentiful Owepar royalties had constructed, then mightily improved, the famous facility. Everyone believed that the thriving Fireside studio would eventually pay Owepar back and become self-supporting. At the rate Porter was recording, this seemed likely. But the hole in Owepar's pocket, through which so many coins trickled down by the Fireside, simply had to be sewed up.

*   *   *

Carla Scarborough, Owepar manager, wrote to Dolly at Christmastime 1977:

> First we weeded out all the non-productive hangers on [names deleted] and their friends who were using this company for their own ends. Then we completely separated Owepar's and Fireside's finances—Now, Fireside pays rent, they pay their own utility bills, their insurance, their Coca Cola's, their maintenance. It hasn't been easy, but we've attacked these problems one at a time and been able to attain our objective.
>
> The next thing on the agenda is the money Fireside owes Owepar [details] . . . After the first of the year, Owepar will be housed in the 811 building—This will give us the space we need, plus additional separation. Nancy [Hurt] is an excellent employee, very loyal, intelligent and industrious . . . I feel good about the company, I know it is being run economically and efficiently, and no one here is taking advantage of Owepar—except in the area we discussed—which is out of my hands.
>
> Our foreign revenue is almost equal with our domestic royalties, of which I am very proud. Would you believe they called me from Tree Publishing last week and made an appointment to come over and discuss foreign publishing. They want to find out how we do it. I do wish you could arrange some international tours, especially in Japan and Germany.

Dolly, of course, owned half of Fireside, Uncle Louis's controlling share having evaporated in the Porter–Dolly hot spell. Yet she complained that she could not book sessions there unless Porter was the engineer or it was otherwise convenient. "He goes there to do everything he wants to do for his pleasure or his business. I've never had this luxury," Dolly said in the lawsuit, ostensibly quoting Porter, "Ain't nobody books any g–d–sessions in this g–d–studio except me."

In 1977 Dolly and Carl moved temporarily to Nashville from Brentwood, Dolly thinking the water there was making her sick. They rented the Tudor-style house at 3717 Woodmont Boulevard with no fanfare (Judy Ogle lived with them), living almost secretively, according to the next-door neighbor. Often their lights were on all night, but soon enough the tour buses were halting for a gander at Dolly's new digs.

In 1978 Bill Hance of the *Nashville Banner* called Porter's office about Dolly's husband, Carl. Bill wanted to know why Carl wouldn't consent to an interview. Porter's secretary, Joan, exclaimed, "I don't know why Carl won't talk. Dolly's talking more now than ever." Hal Durham at the Opry remembered that Carl used to drive Dolly to the Opry, but waited in his car for her and didn't come in to see her perform. Hance circumvented the padlocked gate at the Brentwood farm and banged on the door of Carl and Dolly Dean's house. Carl answered the door, but he refused any formal interview, though genially offering, "We'll go to some beer joint, sit down and talk all day. But not for print." Concerning all the worldwide media interest in Dolly, Carl sniffed, "To hell with all that other stuff." When Bill protested that his boss didn't want him to get only an off-the-record interview, Carl shrugged, "I'm sorry, but I don't sign your paychecks, you know."

Hanging around Porter, keyboardist Mike Lawler often fell to reminiscing about his days on the road with soul singer James Brown. Mike had badly wanted to play for Brown and on a fluke was permitted to fill in, playing with Brown for two years, touring, and playing on many sessions. Four times Brown fired Mike for "stupid reasons," rehiring him each time "for equally stupid reasons." Then James was scheduled to tour Tunisia, and Mike quit, fearing that he might be fired a fifth time and end up stranded in North Africa.

So he began phasing into studio work in Nashville, especially at Fireside. Porter made "a big deal" about Mike being the first to use a synthesizer on the Opry. He seemed especially fascinated by Mike's talk about James Brown. One day early in 1979 Porter asked him if he thought James should be invited to perform at the Opry.

Mike managed a brave "Yeah-h-h-h-h . . . "

44

THE NIGHT JAMES BROWN CAME TO TOWN

James Brown appeared at the Opry House
and set off a spark that flashed
from Nashville around the globe.

—"Ramblin' Rhodes" [Don Rhodes],
column, February 3, 1980

I thought we would get worldwide press coverage,
which we did. I felt like it would cause a lot
of excitement on the Opry, which it did.
I felt like there would be some resentment of it,
which there was. But weighing all that,
I felt like it was a great night for the Opry.

—Porter to Glenn Hunter, 1983

Porter first saw James Brown in the late fifties or early sixties at a show in Newark, New Jersey. Topping the bill were Fats Domino, Little Richard, Chuck Berry, and James. It was on a Saturday night, and since Porter was playing in the same theater the next day, he caught the performance.

"I seen the whole show, it was a great show," he recalls. "When the band came out and started the introduction of James Brown, it was one of the most exciting things I had seen in my lifetime. The band kept getting the music hotter and hotter, and the beat was so dynamic it was unbelievable. When they finally introduced James, it was like a storm hit the building—a deafening roar of people standing, with spontaneous screaming and hollering." Never in his life had he seen such a show-man—doing acrobatics, tossing the mike from one hand to the other, dancing, sweat pouring off him. "It laid heavy on my mind what a showman he is," says Porter. Afterwards he went up and introduced himself.

James would soar, whirl, sail through the air, splaying his legs in a

367

Left to right: Mike Lawler, James Brown, Porter, April 1979 [PHOTO BY DON PUTNAM, COURTESY PORTER WAGONER ENTERPRISES].

"contortionist's split," according to Geoffrey Stokes in *Rock of Ages,* the *Rolling Stone* rock history. He would rise "as if pulled by unseen strings," then slump to his knees "begging for love." He might pound a few chords on the piano, then collapse at the foot of the mike stand. James told Don Waller of the *L.A. Weekly* that you should make people tired because that's what they pay for. Sounding just like Porter on the subject of costumes, James said audiences didn't want to see performers who look like somebody off the street, which is why his band members wore uniforms. "I'm not gonna look in the audience and see *my* uniforms. You're gonna have to look at the stage to catch the show, 'cause nobody's gonna look like *me* in the audience. That's what it's about." James became famous for his repeated donning of colored capes, thrown upon him at measured intervals by a band member.

Eight or nine years later, Porter met James again at an airport in Atlanta. James remembered him; they talked some more. Another time Porter saw him at a theater in Nashville, under a hair dryer, drying off the sweat to keep from catching pneumonia. At one such encounter Porter said, "You ought to come to the Grand Ole Opry."

"I'd love to," Brown replied. "You just invite me and I'll come."

Four or five more years passed, and he began thinking, why shouldn't James come? "The Grand Ole Opry is made up of entertainment, not necessarily marvelous singers but entertainers. That's what the show is built on, it has some comedy, it has some singing."

So he told Bud Wendell and Hal Durham, "I think we could get worldwide attention, and once in a while that's helpful. Even if it's Coca-Cola, or even if it's the Grand Ole Opry. It's like Old Man River, you can keep rolling along but it's nice to have a shot in the arm once in a while to make something exciting happen."

I asked Bud Wendell, "Were you braced for James to do noncountry material? His soul-'n'-sweat routine?"

"We probably knew that was what he was going to do. That would not be an untypical situation, for an artist to come on and do what it is that his audience knows him for."

"So you took your risk?"

"Yeah."

Brown's first hit, "Please, Please, Please," had been broken over WLAC radio in Nashville in 1955. "WLAC was all we ever listened to," James wrote in his autobiography (with Bruce Tucker). The 50,000-watt station reached many states, and three of its white disc jockeys, Gene Nobles, John R. Richbourg, and Hoss Allen, sounded black. Their ghetto-lingo double entendres went right past their employers' ears while tickling those of blacks and white college kids.*

"Please, Please, Please" proved James could croon (these were the Sam Cooke years), but he became famous for staccato blues bleating, with his band blasting one chord over and over. Although James had later recorded in Nashville, that was hardly reassuring: "Hot Pants" as well as "Sex Machine." James had supported the war in Vietnam; but this was 1979. The very thought of him sweating out there on the hallowed Opry stage was sending some of Porter's peers into a cold sweat. Or a hot rage.

Porter's idea of "crossover" (from R&B to C&W) was certainly achieving its goal of attracting publicity. "It will be a historic night," he told the press. "There's never been a soul singer on the Opry before," though booking agent Dolores Smiley remembers Little Ruby Falls and O. B. McClinton had appeared earlier on the Opry.

The James Brown announcement came two weeks after Porter's disco début—and last bow—at Nashville's Exit/In. The Exit/In at Elliston Place was one of the nation's premier listening rooms. Somewhat on the order of Los Angeles's Troubadour, it was a showcase for folk, jazz, blues, outlaw country—anything but Opry-brand hillbilly.

The unlikely occasion for Porter's splash was a benefit for the Progressive Music Association, "a group that seeks to promote pop music

---

*Nobles drank on the job—and WLAC had an "audition room" where country singers and girl guests were clandestinely taped—and the jocks also monitored performances at the Noel Hotel across the street with binoculars. See Wes Smith's dee-jay history, *The Pied Pipers of Rock 'n' Roll* (1989).

in Nashville," wrote Laura Eipper for *The Tennessean*, "a cause dear to Porter's heart." The standing-room-only crowd for the night of Wednesday, January 31, was a sell-out. But was Porter selling out?

His five-piece band, Mighty High, with Fred Newell on electric guitar and Mike Lawler on synthesizer, looked the part. They wore skin-tight jeans, dark glasses, and sang songs about "jailbait and gigolos" as "blinding colored lights" pulsated.

Back in the dressing room, Porter chatted with Jay Bolotin, who was wearing his "regulation black and whites." Jay marveled at Porter's cutaway purple jacket and huge belt buckle. "If you pay this much for a belt, you ought to be able to see it," he told Jay. When he hit the stage, the spotlight lit up his "purple rhinestone-studded suit outlining wagons and wagonwheels," wrote Bill Hance in the *Nashville Banner*. And he was waving "a small white rhinestone-covered Western hat to the cheering audience."

Jay joined him for a line-trading duet of "Willie Boudine," and even cult hero J. J. Cale, whose "Cocaine" was an Eric Clapton hit, got onstage. Porter's own repertoire, however, was strictly hoary standards like "Ole Slew-Foot" bolstered by disco syncopations, just a little faster (Porter threw in some disco dance steps). He told Bill Hance he didn't want to become "history . . . "I don't want to sell antiques. I want to sell today's merchandise." And he told Laura Eipper, "I guess a lot of people will think I've lost my mind . . . Country is actually pretty close to disco or rock. Hell, you can sing 'Y'all Come' to disco."

Porter drew waves of resounding cheers from a hard-to-please audience of music industry personnel, although one person was quoted in more than one report: "Who's Porter Wagoner trying to fool? You can tell he's still country by listening to him. Besides, he's still got those wagon wheels on his pants. This is what we in the trade call keeping up with the Partons."

In February, along with Paul Revere-style warnings that James Brown was coming, intermittent stories about Porter versus Dolly appeared in the press. One story on February 13 (unattributed) was headlined: "Porter Battles with Dolly Parton." It trotted out his lowest-ebb interview from the previous fall, one with Carolyn Lawrence of WSM-TV (winning the rotten timing award as Dolly had just won CMA's Entertainer of the Year):

> To me, Dolly Parton is the kind of person I would never trust with anything of mine. Regardless of what it was or who it was—I mean her family, her own blood—she would turn her back on [them] to help herself.
>
> She couldn't stay. I let her go. Dolly didn't quit me, I gave

her notice in Tulsa, Oklahoma, that she needed to get her own band together because I wasn't going to travel and have a girl I had to fight with on the road with us.

I'm not bitter because Dolly left my show in any sense . . . I was just disappointed to find out that she's not made of what I thought she was. Like the *Playboy* thing [interview]. Do you think Kitty Wells would do that? Dolly wants to do everything possible for her. She's living in a fairyland . . .

Dolly punched back, telling Laura Eipper for *The Tennessean*:

It had nothing to do with Porter or his capabilities. It's just that I wanted to do different things than he wanted. I mean, what are you going to do, waste your youth? Wait until you're old and then regret never trying? I would rather try everything, and when I'm old regret a few things I did than regret not doing anything.

They were seven of the best years and seven of the worst years of my life. I mean, we didn't get along that well. We disagreed because we were both so stubborn and set in our ways, both extremely creative.

That was not a very easy parting. Porter was upset at me pretty bad, and from things I read is still pretty bitter at me, but I certainly had my reasons and he certainly knows what they were—I don't care what he says, he knows why I left.

Dolly told Laura that Porter still profited from her. He still earned money from Owepar. "He still makes a percentage of my record royalties for another period of time, through a contract he negotiated for me in the past. I could have stopped a lot of that stuff if I had wanted to," she added. "But you never hear that side. You only hear what a bitter, vicious person somebody is." Dolly didn't seem to know Porter was not receiving those record royalty percentages any longer; her management had cut him off.

"They may not be kissing any longer," concluded Laura, "but they sure are telling!"

In a similar story on February 25, Joe Edwards of the Associated Press asked Porter about the previous fall's rancorous remarks. "Everything I've been quoted as saying was true. I won't retract anything. The truth hurts people. I came down hard on her because it was true."

Was Porter bitter? "Not at all."

Joe liked the new *Porter Wagoner Today* album: "Wagoner is now singing 'soft' country music that's more melodic and more orchestrated." Porter said that Roy Acuff, Ernest Tubb, and Hank Snow had "chosen to be part of country music history, and I admire them for that," but that he aimed to keep up with the times. The cover photo showed record buyers what they'd missed by not catching the Exit/In spectacle: Porter with purple clothes a-glitter, thanks to a special "star" camera filter creating a blinding reflection effect, clutching a hand-held mike Las Vegas-style, more like Tom Jones or Charlie Rich. But the songs were almost defiantly traditional, such as the murder folk classic, "Banks of the Ohio," if updated slightly. Rich Kienzle in *Country Music* praised his use of the synthesizer, but otherwise judged the album to be more conservative than 90 percent of Nashville's current product, and he meant that as a compliment . . . the album just might be Porter's "finest hour."

Porter's most infamous hour, to date, was close at hand. James Brown was scheduled for Saturday night, March 10, at the Opry House. On March 6 the Memphis *Press-Scimitar* ran the headline across the top of the front page: "Invitation To Soul Singer James Brown Brings Disharmony To Grand Ole Opry," with a UPI story underneath displaying a smiling picture of Porter. The story dipped heavily into Bill Hance's *Nashville Banner* report of the day before (March 5).

"I could throw up," said piano player Del Wood in the most eloquent of the Opry outbursts. "It's not an antiblack issue, don't get us wrong, it's not racial." She went on to praise DeFord Bailey, O. B. McClinton, and Charley Pride. Since her own piano style was strongly ragtime (Del was the only female country act to have a Top 10 instrumental hit), she was no doubt sincere. "The next thing you know, they'll be doing the strip out there!"

Jean Shepard was Jean Shepard: "The Grand Ole Opry is supposed to be a mainstay in country music—and it's fighting for its life. What's he going to sing, 'Papa's Got a Brand New Bag'?" She condemned the Opry management and said Opry fans weren't going to enjoy tuning in and getting James Brown. "And you can't tell me rock 'n' rollers are going to wait six hours to hear James Brown. It's a slap in the face to those people who drive thousands of miles to see the Opry and have to be subjected to James Brown. If Mr. Brown's on the first show, I'll appear on the second. If he's on both, I won't appear at all."

Justin Tubb said, "I don't understand it. None of us do . . . If it was Ray Charles, I'd be waiting to hug him when he came off the stage," recalling Ray's albums of country songs. Ben Smathers of the Smoky Mountain Cloggers square dance act said George D. Hay would be turning over in his grave. Of Opry stars, only Skeeter Davis spoke publicly in Porter's defense.

Opry damage-controller Jerry Strobel tried to remind everyone that numerous other unexpected visitors had graced the Opry stage: Perry Como, President Nixon (yo-yoing with Roy Acuff in the midst of Watergate), Senator Robert C. Byrd (a fiddler himself), Paul McCartney, Carol Channing, Ann-Margret, even President Carter's daughter, Amy. He didn't mention *opera* star Helen Traubel, who'd been booed when little

Jimmy Dickens brought her onstage back in the fifties.

Bill Hance in the *Nashville Banner* recalled some other Opry frictions from the past: Ernest Tubb defending his use of electric guitars, Bob Wills hiding his drummer behind the stage curtain, and Hank Williams being forced to substitute the word *milk* for "beer" in "My Bucket's Got a Hole in It."

The name of DeFord Bailey kept coming up. When George D. Hay first called the WSM Barn Dance "The Grand Ole Opry" over the air in 1927, it was right after a harmonica solo by DeFord, a crippled black elevator operator at the National Life building. When Hay had first heard him play, he threw his famous wooden steamboat whistle up in the air with glee, and soon dubbed him the "Harmonica Wizard." For a while Hay featured Bailey more than any other Opry act and personally looked out for his welfare. On the road, his fellow Opry members also invariably looked out for him in the face of demeaning discrimination: sometimes he had to be smuggled into hotels disguised as a valet or bellhop, and often had to eat in the kitchen or out in the automobile (where he often had to sleep). Roy Acuff, Bill Monroe, and especially the Delmore brothers were his steadfast allies on the road. Roy especially liked to use him in his own shows when he was getting started, DeFord was such a draw.

He played his harmonica with a megaphone attached; he was famous for his fast-moving train songs, and for a time recorded for RCA.

But George D. Hay persuaded him *not* to enter a harmonica contest in Detroit for fear he'd win first prize—a Lincoln automobile—and disconcert the white folks in Nashville. DeFord felt he was held back from really being a flamboyant entertainer, since it would never do for a black to be too sensational. "Like some members of his race, and other races, DeFord was lazy," said Hay in his Opry history that was reprinted down the years. Hay said he gave him a year to learn some new songs, then fired him in 1941. "I knowed it waz comin', Judge, I knowed it waz comin'," he said, according to Hay. DeFord forgave him, believing WSM to be the real culprit (unaware, probably, that Hay had once published a book of anti-Negro "jokes" called *Howdy Judge* in 1926). Most of his songs were ASCAP, and WSM's switch to BMI songs probably was the real cause.

DeFord still made token Opry appearances, Bill Monroe paying him out of his own pocket, and in 1974 he was welcomed onstage at the Opry House for his own seventy-fifth birthday party. In 1978 he spurned a spot in an Opry network TV special ("No, I don't want to work with 'em again," he told producer Chet Hagan). He eked out a living shining shoes at the corner of Twelfth and Edgehill, and journalists could get a spitshine out of him, but little else. "I wasn't getting but four or five dollars a night," he told Paul Hemphill (*The Nashville Sound: Bright*

Lights and Country Music), "and they kept me standing in the back."

DeFord died in 1982, and Opry comrades like Roy Acuff, Bill Monroe, and Herman Crook dedicated a monument to him in 1983. Roy said DeFord should be in the Hall of Fame.

To a great extent, black entertainers were expected to be subservient, and—especially—sexless. Lena Horne was neither, so she was cut from a 1946 film by censors in Memphis and Knoxville. Yet black and white cultural relations were complex, as the case of Jamup and Honey shows. Jamup and Honey were the Opry's blackface comedy act of the 1930s and 1940s. Latterday critics are prone to cringe at blackface humor as "racist," yet about half of Jamup and Honey's fans were black. Chet Hagan reports that when the Opry toured, blacks would show up to see them, causing dismay among the owners of segregated theaters.

In 1966 RCA launched Charley Pride, country music's first (and, to date, only) major black performer. Nervously, they held back any photos of him until he'd scored some hits. No one seemed to care about Charley Pride's pigmentation, however. He had sixty-four chart records through 1988.

In 1975 Porter (and Bobby Dyson) wrote "Guitar Brown," a tribute to the three-piece combo he had listened to as a child outside of West Plains . . .

> *Good country music and a little bit of rock.*
> *Not enough to hurt it, just a beat that's hot;*
> *It's always crowded, folks come around*
> *To hear Larry on the drums, Good Jelly on the bass, and Guitar*
> *Brown.*

James Brown would later tell Ramblin' Rhodes that he identified with Porter's story about pretending he was on the Opry while he was plowing behind the mules, then hearing someone laughing behind his back. "I can relate to that. My own daddy told me I'd never make it by singing. My own daddy told me that." Back in Augusta James had listened to, and liked, Lefty Frizzell, Little Jimmy Dickens, and Cowboy Copas over the radio. "Country music is really just the white man's blues," he said.

As James's arrival at the Opry neared, some of the dissidents organized a boycott, keyboard man Mike Lawler remembers. Backstage hospitality is part of the Opry, but apparently the place was going to look empty.

Quickly Bud Wendell began offering backstage passes to anyone who wanted to see James Brown. Like an electric jolt, the message galvanized Nashville's subterranean rock community, and Mike Lawler believes around three hundred people showed up to crowd the wings of the stage and witness James Brown *live* at the Grand Ole Opry.

Mike was on keyboard, Fred Newell on guitar, and R. E. Hardeway (also from Porter's band) on drums. Fred remembers Jimmy Nolan was there from James's band and Charles Sherrell ("Sweet Charles") the singer. The Opry got in some lukewarm licks by banning James's horn section.

When James came out, he threw back his head and screamed, "*I feel . . . good!!!*"

Then he launched into a polite string of songs: "Your Cheatin' Heart," "Georgia," and "Tennessee Waltz." Finally James Brown delivered, unleashing a five-song soul set that included "Papa's Got a Brand New Bag." Bill Hance said he "writhed and sweated through the performance," conceding that what he did, he did very well. Twice James left the stage, twice returning in a different colored cape draped on his drenched shoulders by his "valet."

He did his famous splits and microphone tosses from hand to hand, having polished both skills down at Fireside earlier, as if he needed any practice.

"I wish I could go out there and speak my mind, but I won't," someone overhead Roy Acuff muttering. A black lady even called in from Natchez to complain about what she was hearing over her radio. Michael Kosser remembered later (in *Country Music '88*) that James received what most Opry acts receive: polite applause. Phylis Martin in *Country Music* agreed: "None the less, Brown, in the end, won over the people whose opinion really counted: the Opry audience members themselves." He got an encore, as Porter would remind people later. Still, Michael Kosser wrote that when Roy Acuff recaptured the stage, "the greater part of 4,400 people must have felt that Moses had arrived to deliver them from the Egyptians."

Dolores Smiley says, "I drove to the Opry and heard James Brown over the car radio, and when I got there it was abuzz in the backstage area. I purposely went late. It sounded terrible on the radio. When I went backstage, everyone was outraged and upset. I thought it was funny."

There was a press party afterward at the Opryland Hotel, and Porter posed with his arm around James. Brooke Newell was quoted in *Country Music*, "It's a mutual admiration between the two." Of the Opry cast outcry, Brooke says, "I think a lot of it was, he was a black artist, and the second part, they thought he was going to be a wild man and they didn't want any part of it. They thought it was some kind of sacrilegious experience to have a black soul singer."

It was reported that James had broken all records by performing thirty minutes, but Porter said it was only seventeen minutes. He had the tape to prove it.

A few days later Bill Hance shook his head in print: "People have been sitting and wondering lately about Porter Wagoner. They can't understand some of the things he's done." He quoted Porter:

> I admit there was tension in the air that night when I introduced him. I could feel it. But I think he did something for the Grand Ole Opry that five of the biggest and best country artists couldn't have done. He focused attention on the Opry stage from all over the world. It's hard to get that done.
>
> The fact the man is the greatest in his field makes him worthy to be there or anyplace else in the world, in my opinion.
>
> But I'll admit, his being here was maybe like me playing the Metropolitan Opera in New York. Why, those people would look through their opera glasses at me and probably chew 'em up.

Porter says there were people there from Italy, Japan, and other countries, just to see James Brown, and that one by one his colleagues apologized for their original remarks.

James himself told Ramblin' Rhodes that "they treated me like I was a prodigal son. They treated me so nice I felt guilty. I felt I got as much praise as a white man who goes into a black church and puts $100 in the collection plate." James was proud that actor John Ritter, star of "Three's Company," had heard him over the car radio, turned around, and headed for the Opry House. James said he was a fan of John's late father, Tex Ritter. Rhodes noted that James had cut a disco version of Bill Anderson's "Still."

The following September, Stevie Wonder performed at the Opry singing Charlie Rich's hit "Behind Closed Doors" and received good applause. James himself played at the Opry House (not an Opry show) on March 26, 1985, as part of a black music tribute to WLAC disc jockey John R. Richbourg.

When Porter got back to the lake after James Brown, one of his rustic fishing pals, a fellow with some teeth missing, said, "Between the nigger and the blonde, you sure got yourself a lot of publicity lately." On March 21, 1979—eleven days after hosting James Brown on the Opry—Porter sued Dolly Parton Dean for three million dollars.

"FIGHT AND SCRATCH, FIGHT AND SCRATCH"

I want to know what I may take with me.
I don't want to be accused of stealing . . .
Please will you tell me what
belongs to me and what doesn't?

—Liza Doolittle to
Professor Henry Higgins,
Act IV of Shaw's *Pygmalion* (1914)

"Like I say, I only write songs,
I'm not a lawyer."

—Dolly, under oath,
September 29, 1977

The opening act for the Porter–Dolly lawsuit duet was the Bill Owens action of 1977, which dragged on until nearly 1979.

Bill sued Porter and Dolly, and he also sued their publishing company, Owepar. Bill had founded Owepar in 1967 with Dolly, then had given her his 49 percent share in 1969 by written agreement. The stock transfer had carried with it a vague obligation or hope that some of Bill's songs would get cut. This was the same 49 percent of Owepar Dolly had given Porter for Christmas. These stock shares that Dolly had slipped under Porter's tree had a long string attached, and Bill was yanking hard.

He alleged that she had breached their 1969 agreement, and he demanded back all of the stock she had given to Porter. He asked for all publisher royalties due him, plus $150,000 punitive damages and "treble damages against plaintiff Wagoner" for having induced Dolly to break their agreement in the first place. Tennessee statute 47-15-113 awards "treble damages" to punish outsiders who meddle in someone's contract.

Louis Owens says he could have sued, too, over his lost share of Fireside, but he wouldn't do that over a mere studio. "A studio is just a machine for making music," Louis says, "Like a guitar." But songs and publishing rights, now that's entirely different.

377

"Me and Bill don't have a fight between us," said Dolly in her deposition. "I want Bill to have what is due Bill. I would rather lose money myself than cheat Bill out of something we owe him."

But the "owe" in Owepar had become a sick pun. Exactly what Owepar owed Bill Owens became increasingly harder to discover as the "discovery" process of depositions wore on. Dolly, Porter, Bill, Louis, Ann Kosloff—with each of their depositions the picture became more blurry. Year after year, Bill had come by Dolly's house pitching song after song. In all, he had eight recorded. Dolly admitted that sometimes she would bump one of her own in lieu of one of Bill's, while emphasizing that she and Porter wanted the best no matter who wrote it. Porter's judgment always won out. "You can't always do a song you don't believe in," Dolly said. "I don't like to have prisoners on albums. I don't want to record a song that I'm going to have to fight for, so that I can never enjoy listening back to it. It's as simple as that."

Dolly characterized herself as an "employee" and said that Porter had "an air of authority about him which would make country people like me and Bill and Louis a little uneasy, which is actually a compliment to Porter in some ways." Her assessment of the case was profound: "Everything was verbal, which was ignorance, now it's showing up . . . With people as close as me and Porter have been, that's why we wind up in messes like we are in now, without things in writing, and verbal agreements and half-answered questions and half-answered an-swers." When Dolly was reminded that she had acted as chairman and that Bill had acted as secretary at Owepar's only board meeting (1967), she retorted, "We both acted like fools."

Owepar had been set up by the same attorney who incorporated Warden Music in 1959, and who drafted Bill's stock transfer in 1969. Someone else formalized the 1970 Porter–Dolly contract of 1970, which gave Porter the stock that had formerly been Bill's and obligated, or tried to obligate, Dolly after she left Porter. In the late sixties there were few lawyers in Nashville specializing in the music business, and documents that might hold up in any other field have a tendency to blow up in the parties' faces in show business. Bill, Dolly, and Porter had acted in good faith, but there were now two legal time bombs ticking at the feet of these three honest people.

Porter had never seen the Dolly–Bill "agreement," as it was called, which didn't seem very specific or enforceable. He and Dolly had both sincerely believed they owed Bill something substantial. In May of 1975 they'd paid him $28,000 so he could pay off his farm in White Chapel, Tennessee. The check had been signed by Louis Owens, an Owepar employee. The discussion leading up to this had been quite lengthy, Dolly recollected: "By talking in circles, like most of my relatives do—me, for one—and with all the deep discussions that Porter always got into, I'm sure we were there at least two hours."

As it turned out, they had only acquired eight songs from Bill's separate company, Kimtam, which was named for his children Kim and Tammy, the intended beneficiaries. When Bill noticed he hadn't been receiving any payments from Owepar for songs recorded (or contracted) since 1972, he asked Ann Kosloff and she found nothing owing. He complained to Dolly and she advised him to get a lawyer, so he did. His attorney wrote her a letter that went unanswered. "I knew Bill was going to sue me, I mean, you know he said he was."

Asked what percentage of Owepar she owned, Dolly said, "It makes no difference whether it was fifty-one or all, I ain't seen none of it yet."

In her 1979 deposition, in Porter's lawsuit, Dolly would say, "We were so unorganized at Owepar from the beginning, none of us actually knew what was going on. We did not fulfill an agreement, honestly, with Uncle Bill. We had never given him a fair shake. We were not educated enough as to business to know what to do."

The depositions had their lighter moments. After giving her last name as Dean, Dolly was asked if, professionally, she was known as Dolly Parton. "Dolly Parton, right." As for her "principal occupation," she couldn't really narrow it down. "I'm a writer, singer, entertainer, publisher." Was her mother alive? "Yes, very much alive." Bill was asked what street he lived on. "I live in the country, there ain't no street." Porter, when asked how many times had he not asked Bill to leave the studio, said, "I don't believe I would advise anybody to get rid of their family." And had Bill received any special favors from anyone in Dolly's family? "I eat supper at my sister's [Dolly's mother] house one night, if that's a favor."

Bill revealed the existence of his management contract on Dolly through her mother, from when she was ten until eighteen. "We were both stuck in the Smoky Mountains," said Dolly, "and looking for a dream." But her attorney and Porter's seemed startled to learn Bill had been receiving a "managing" salary from 1970 to 1976 of $100, then $200 a week, plus (according to Dolly) "10 percent of everything I made, except my writer's and publishing royalties, until last year; and loaned Bill many thousands of dollars throughout the years, out of my personal accounts, which has nothing to do with all this."

Bill's attorney confirmed that such payouts had nothing to do with Owepar; rather, they were Bill's retroactive recompense for his years and miles of chauffeuring Dolly to the Cas Walker show and to Nashville. "See, I've managed Dolly, took her to radio stations and stuff, since she was nine years old, and she's lived with me over eight years of her life [summers in Knoxville with the Watsons]. I guess she felt obligated to do some of my songs," Bill explained, "other than the fact they were good songs."

Bill admitted never having asked Porter for any monies due. Asked why he waited so long to sue, he spoke of the pain of suing his own niece. The defense attorneys were perplexed that Bill could draw a "managing" salary, and yet complain that he couldn't get near Dolly because of the all-possessive Porter.

The Owepar ledger for 1975, 1976, and 1977 was tantalizing. Many dozens of songwriters were listed, some with no monies earned, and numerous others with the phrase, "unrecouped advances" beside their entries. One well-known songwriter had not earned his $21,934.64, for instance. The "total advances unrecouped" came to $59,857.65. In all, a certain folksy, homey, country store atmosphere hung over the Owepar books, conjuring up images of barrels full of, not crackers, but money—to be scooped out across the counter to the hard-toiling song-writers in their periods of hard times. Ann Kosloff estimated she wrote 150 to 200 checks every six months to the twenty-five to thirty writers active at any one time. Songwriters on the whole had legitimately earned $63,202.04, $69,202.04, and $118,023.02 in the three-year period. Owepar itself, as publisher, had earned $126,404.08, $138,814.14, and $236,046.04.

Owepar's most successful songwriter was, of course, Dolly, earn-ing $40,452.32, $57,109.36, and $102,655.43, with 199 songs in the catalogue. Songwriter Porter was on the decline, earning $19,771.23, $9,061.91, and $10,790.97 with 134 songs including thirteen Dolly co-writes. Dolly's subsequent attorneys would tally Owepar's totals most differently.

However sapped Owepar may have been by its perpetual propping-up of Fireside, it was definitely on the upswing, even if much of its capital was pumped in by Dolly's songs worldwide (England, Ireland, Scandinavia, France, Germany, Holland, South Africa, Australia, Japan). As Bill said, ruefully, "They built a hundred-thousand-dollar studio with Owepar money, bought two, three buildings with Owepar money."

Trial was scheduled for January 1979. Then Bill settled, healthily. Porter paid five-sixths and Dolly one-sixth.

In late 1976 Porter's attorney, John Nelley, began writing letters to Dolly's Los Angeles management. By April 1978 he was unburdening himself in a letter to Stanley M. Chernau, Dolly's Nashville attorney. Nelley and Chernau had recently shared the Bill Owens experience, and, in fact, still represented the two factions of Owepar.

Nelley said all he could get out of Los Angeles was a couple of phone calls, that he sent them "great multitudes" of papers, some of which they lost; so he duplicated them and mailed them again. He said the Los Angeles folks were friendly on the phone, but it was starting to remind him of working with the federal government: "Everyone in the federal government is friendly and will talk to you, but trying to get anything out of them is almost impossible." Nelley said Porter wanted this resolved, that he knew Dolly did too; but "the fact that the people in Los Angeles are dragging their feet might kill this deal and it's going to be very difficult to resolve."

Under pressure from the Bill Owens lawsuit, Owepar began holding board meetings on paper. The "Annual Meeting of the Board of Directors" was held November 25, 1977. Dolly Parton Dean chaired the meeting; Porter W. Wagoner served as secretary. Someone nominated Dean for president and Wagoner for secretary and treasurer, then nominations closed "and the same were unanimously elected." The only business conducted was the awarding of a $300-a-week salary to secretary–treasurer Wagoner, plus a $3,500 bonus, and a bonus in the same amount to the new president. The president's lawyer, Stan Chernau, became Owepar's registered agent. Two days later the directors met again and voted themselves $200 expenses for each Owepar meeting they attended. Porter's travel costs would have been slight, since he had only to walk from 813 to 811 Eighteenth Avenue South.

In January 1978 Dolly's Los Angeles attorney, Peter Hoffman, began broaching the idea of liquidating Owepar by buying Porter out. Dolly wanted to own and control her songs, and only her songs, no one else's. Porter could have Fireside. This move, seemingly in the right direction, was premature: it ducked the issue of Dolly's agreements with Porter, especially the 1970 one that hopelessly tangled Owepar with Porter's lien on Dolly's future earnings. In May, Hoffman tried to dissolve both Owepar and Fireside, valuing them together at $306,000, exclusive of Dolly's song catalogue, which he priced at $700,000. Hoffman's letterhead bore the names of sixty-five attorneys; and he spelled Porter's name "Mr. Waggoner." His attempt failed, and by 1979 they had learned how to spell Wagoner in Los Angeles.

Then in June, Owepar's two-person board convened again. They decided that monies paid to officers, employees, and songwriters should be reviewed from time to time, especially songwriters "contributing substantial royalties to the corporation." Then corporation officer Wagoner was voted a $20,000 bonus, as was songwriter Dolly Parton Dean.

A minutes book for Owepar board meetings was now being prudently maintained.

The November meeting also assigned officers Dean and Wagoner to represent Owepar on the Fireside board of directors (Fireside Sounds, Inc., as it was known to the lawyers).

*   *   *

By 1979 Porter had enlisted Nashville trial attorney, Thomas V. White, to help John Nelley. White believed the 1970 contract was simple enough, that had it involved anyone but such celebrities, there would have been no difficulty in enforcing it. White says he knew Dolly wanted to do right by Porter, although the definition of *right* was certainly in flux. By ignoring almost two years' patient communication from Porter's representatives, Dolly's management had invited the lawsuit, White believed.

Dolly's new managers must have cringed when they finally read over the 1970 contract, shuddering at its lucidly clear clauses. No doubt their own counsel told them not to worry, that it was one big conflict of interest that wouldn't withstand scrutiny. But Dolly had kept concealed from them the very existence of her other obligation with Porter, the 1976 promise to pay. Asked later by Tom White if her manager had known she was signing that promise, she replied, "Of course not. They would not have allowed it. To me this was a personal matter."* This indicates she had signed it after going with Katz-Gallin-Cleary. News of the Bill Owens lawsuit, based on yet another preexisting piece of paper (from 1969), must have been another jolt. And the Owepar–Fireside morass was one more reminder of why Dolly had wanted out of Nashville. From any standpoint, she was carrying considerable baggage when she touched down in Los Angeles. Sandy Gallin should have put her legal luggage on a better set of scales and checked his new client in more carefully. With Dolly such a hot property, someone should have done a title search.

It was also rather naïve (or callous) of Katz-Gallin-Cleary to think Porter would tolerate indefinitely the squelching of that last duet album. Dolly's Nashville attorney, Stan Chernau, should have been directed to deal with Porter, as he had with Bill Owens. Dolly smarts under the memory of the lawsuit still, as does Porter. She told me:

> Porter gave me my first really big break, and I still hope as the years go by that I will be able to do things to pay Porter. I feel I have done many things already, but they're not the kind of things I would care to go into. He might. But even still, with the lawsuit and him suing me for a million dollars, that hurt me pretty bad. I felt at the time it was mostly done out of spite, and I would have paid him anyway had I owed him money. But like I say, a lot of bad things happened between us, but I guess that often happens when you're trying to break off a partnership and a relationship of long standing.

Engineer Roy Shockley remembers that Porter showed him Dolly's contract and said he learned in West Plains you don't sue somebody when they don't have money, you wait till they do. In her deposition Dolly accused both Bill and Porter of waiting until her net worth had increased sufficiently. But soon after Dolly left, John Nelley had begun his futile letter writing and phoning, which dragged on for nearly two years. Tom White insists that Porter did not want to file the suit until he, White, convinced him nothing else would get Dolly's management's attention. Porter went back to the lake, thought it over, then reluctantly gave him the go-ahead.

The timing couldn't have been worse, considering his fraying connections with RCA. The year 1979 was one of record industry recession, symbolized by the disco fiasco. By the late 1970s companies were boasting of records that had "shipped platinum," or sold a million, but on the basis of wholesale orders only. Vast quantities of returns might deluge the record company warehouse later. Such losses were redistributed throughout the roster of acts, forcing country acts sometimes to pay for some of the megamistakes made on the pop market.*

Meanwhile Nashville was indulging its own "urban cowboy" fad delusions.

On March 2, 1979, Porter dropped by his office and casually told his manager, Brooke Newell, that he would be on the evening news (Channel 4) with reporter Lonnie Lardner. Porter had promised Lardner a lawsuit exclusive, and, as Newell discovered, he had promised some other reporters as well. She had her apologizing cut out for her. When Porter went on the evening news, Newell, John Nelley, and Tom White were "absolutely horrified . . . we were just flipping out . . . What is he doing there? Then it was funny," she recalls. Porter was sitting at the news desk, and at the show's conclusion turned to Lardner and said, "Now will you run away with me?"

Next morning's *Tennessean* ran the headline "Porter Plans To Wrap Dolly In Flashiest Suit Yet" across the top of the front page. A 1973 picture had been sliced in half, with Dolly on the left side of the page smiling in Porter's direction and Porter on the far right smiling back. This photo formula was used again and again as the lawsuit wore on, as a kind of parody of the duet album covers, a sit-com grand ole soap opry. Reporter Laura Eipper, alluding to disco and James Brown, said Porter "has been the subject of several controversies recently." Newell remembers, "The tabloids were all over town trying to scrape up some dirt."

Jerry Flowers of RCA's Artist Relations was concerned about how two of the label's artists were now relating. (Four days before the suit was filed, Porter's single, "I Want to Walk You Home," had entered *Billboard*, and John Nelley had thanked RCA by letter for its enthusiastic promotion.) So why hadn't RCA been warned of the lawsuit? "Frankly, it's none of your business," Newell told Jerry Flowers.

"This really concerns us, it's really a lot of our business," Flowers retorted.

---

*With all the tape piracies, there was an industry joke about how you could "ship gold . . . and get back platinum returns . . ."

Then Newell said, "I'm sorry, this is business, it's Porter's business." She reflects, "You don't tell somebody in advance there's going to be a lawsuit, you just let it happen." Her husband, Fred, echoes this sentiment: "People don't understand business is business."

The complaint filed March 21 accused Dolly of not paying Porter's 15 percent of her record royalties after leaving his producer control in 1976, while admitting the fascinating fact that she had been doing so in the family band phase, 1974 to 1976. She or "her agents" were accused of blocking both the duet album and "at least ten duet singles," causing both Owepar and Porter to lose money. She was accused of looting Owepar of 130 songs with which to start up Velvet Apple and Song Yard, while also plotting to stack Owepar's board with Parton allies to outvote Porter. Worst of all, she had supposedly talked him into leaving the road to spend more time on her records in the studio, then had resisted his later kind request to manage her career.

Porter demanded 15 percent of her net income from June 1974 through June 1979; plus an additional 15 percent of her record royalties since she'd stopped paying him; plus two million dollars for lost income from Dolly's recording and touring. Another round-number demand was for one million dollars in lost producer and "other" income from Dolly. Porter also asked that the duet album and ten duet single sides be released, that Dolly return those 130 songs "removed" from Owepar (not mentioning they were her songs), and that Owepar be shut down and its assets split between Dolly and Porter, 51 percent to 49 percent.

"We have no comment," Sandy Gallin told *The Tennessean*. Brooke Newell joined him in this.

Once Porter's suit was filed, Laura Eipper's follow-up story in *The Tennessean* was headlined "Porter Bears No Ill Will But Sees Long Bout With Dolly," and quoted Porter: "It's not a personal thing. There's no bitterness or anger involved in any way. I'd hoped we could reach a settlement before now, but this is a last resort." Attorney Stan Chernau (for Dolly) branded Porter's suit a "hodgepodge," speculating that he must have an ego problem about her soaring career. He told *Record World* there was nothing to settle, that he wondered which legal theories Porter would follow "since he has given three diametrically opposed statements" about Dolly's leaving.

In May, Dolly accidentally boarded an airplane with Porter also on board. He didn't see her, and she swapped seats with someone in tourist class. A female reporter was on board and, after Porter disembarked, told her, "It's okay, Dolly, the coast is clear." *Nashville Banner* writer Red O'Donnell called it "a once-in-a-flighttime happening" in a story headlined "Dolly, Porter Fly United (Somewhat)."

Since Dolly had not yet responded to the suit, in June Tom White tried to win the case by default, telling the *Nashville Banner*, "This is not

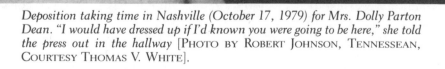

Deposition taking time in Nashville (October 17, 1979) for Mrs. Dolly Parton Dean. "I would have dressed up if I'd known you were going to be here," she told the press out in the hallway [PHOTO BY ROBERT JOHNSON, TENNESSEAN, COURTESY THOMAS V. WHITE].

being done for publicity." Two hours before deadline Dolly responded, accusing Fireside of not paying its rent since August 1978 and of being run for Porter's "own pleasure and benefit." She denied they were "deadlocked" in their corporate affairs, as Porter had alleged, yet proposed to resign her seat on Owepar's board and substitute Stan Chernau and her piano player-arranger, Greg Perry. Porter immediately asserted by affidavit that he and Dolly could not "get along in directing the company" and accused her of trying "to railroad" her own ideas through at Owepar, and to "distribute to herself out of the corporation the songs she wants."

Then Tom White tried—and failed—to win an injunction against Dolly to prevent her from expanding the Owepar board. On an almost daily basis the journalists, acting as war correspondents, filed their dispatches from the front. In the month of June alone, many legal missiles were fired until finally on June 27 *The Tennessean* exclaimed: "Dolly's Directors Control Board." Tom White suddenly decided that Owepar's board makeup wasn't so important after all; it was really the company's assets that were at issue.

Dolly's new board promised to investigate Fireside's finances forthwith.

White began flailing Chernau for not answering many of his interrogatories (written questions), and Chernau told *People* magazine, "I think some of them are frivolous." Chancellor Robert S. Brandt gave Chernau a week to answer the questions, which were supposedly four months overdue. Chernau claimed he thought he and White had an understanding about the deadline.

Chancellor Robert Brandt eventually slapped Stan Chernau with a $250 fine on June 29, a fine he had to pay Tom White since Dolly had dodged deadlines, if not headlines, by being on the road. That same day, Dolly answered Porter's questions, posed by Tom White, in writing, including the amusing opinion that you couldn't really "move" a song out of an office or anywhere else (referring to the Judy Ogle pillage of 130 tape boxes) because a song is an intangible right. Whoever thought of that 'un, *purty good!* The inventory of the song heist included some fetching titles: "Blackmail," "Child I Gave Away," "Failure to Communicate," "A Gallows for the Morning," "Mixture of Love and Hate," and numerous songs about the pangs of breaking up.

Next day the headline blared: "Dolly Claims Porter Tore Up Contract." Chernau admitted his client had slipped through town but was bound for Los Angeles and "a tour of the Orient." He asked why Dolly would have signed the short-form 1976 promise-to-pay if the 1970 contract had not been voided.

Meanwhile, Porter was at Center Hill Lake until August.

"Dolly Says Coercion Involved In Contract" was the July 6 *Tennessean* headline, the story alleging "duress" and "mental intimidation."

Kirk Loggins quoted Tom White as saying that anyone who knows Dolly's "capabilities" wouldn't think she could be pressured into anything. He asked why it had taken them one hundred days to come up with the "duress" defense. "The instrument in question is not a complicated legal document. It's a relatively simple contract," White went on. "I can't imagine anyone with any degree of intelligence couldn't understand the terms."

And if it *had* been signed under duress, White asked, why had it taken Dolly four years to leave Porter's show?

But if the contract was so good, Chernau asked, why had it taken Porter three years to sue?

Chernau further objected that the contract lacked some of a contract's standard elements; perhaps it wasn't really a contract. It lacked "consideration" (as in, "In consideration for . . . ")—that is, Porter's services-to-be-rendered weren't specified very clearly. It lacked a fixed period of time in the matter of the 15 percent of record royalties. As Dolly would say in her deposition, "Would a person be expected to pay 15 percent *forever?*" Chernau harped on perceived conflicts of interest, such as a manager insisting he produce the records when another producer might be in the client's better interests. He accused Porter of violating a Depression era, New Deal reform law, the Securities Exchange Act of 1934, with its "anti-fraud rule."

The Tennessean headline of August 11 hooted "Could Face Jail, Dolly Warned." Opposite Dolly's stock smiling picture on the right-hand side of the page was one, not of Porter, but of Chancellor Brandt looking back at her with a judicially stern expression. "The discovery orders of this court will be complied with even if it means a contempt citation and the commitment of the defendant to jail," said Brandt, "citing the failure of defendants in some other music industry lawsuits" to meet deadlines.

In an unattributed column "That's Entertainment," Chernau netted his own headline: "Dolly Parton's Lawyer Sings The Country Blues. Nashville attorney Stanley Chernau's life is turning into a country-western song. 'I've grown old and weary. I can't go home. My kids want to hit me 'cause I look so bad,' he moans." Speaking of Chancellor Brandt, he said: "It goes all over the goddam world that he's going to send Dolly Parton to jail." Even *The National Law Review* ("Will Dolly Be Singing in the Slammer?") quoted Chernau, who said jestingly, "Somebody asked me if Dolly Parton is going to jail. I said she will if she doesn't get a different lawyer."

Chernau's hands had been tied, since he had been unable to supply Dolly's tax returns which White had been demanding. Her Los Angeles lawyers had been witholding them. Chancellor Brandt said, "I have heard Dolly Parton is a very honest person . . . but we have a place across the street [the jail] for people who don't comply with the court."

White had finally stumbled onto something Dolly's management didn't want revealed—now he had the leverage he needed! (Later, teaching a class in litigation at Vanderbilt, Brandt would cite this episode as an example of how the right discovery question can win a case.)

Sandy Gallin's Los Angeles attorney, Peter Hoffman, was in Nashville on August 22; but he, Chernau, and White could reach no settlement agreement In September, Tom requested copies of every contract Dolly had signed with anyone, from Fred Foster forward.

White says the case became much less amicable, once the "duress" and "coercion" assertions were introduced and that he pleaded that these defenses be withdrawn, to make his own efforts less forceful. They weren't.

Dolly's last recording session on Porter's behalf was held October 17, 1979, not at Fireside, but on the twenty-first floor of the First American Center, in Tom White's office. Dolly talked, not sang, filling up five cassettes. White was gentle and polite as he proceeded, but the questions grew increasingly pointed as the deposition progressed. Some were excruciating, a women's lib nightmare.

She conceded she certainly owed Porter some sort of "15 percent," though of what and for how long she was much less sure. "Yes, I felt an obligation. But how do you ever know how much you owe . . . ?"

Dolly belabored how hectic it had been with Porter; yes, he had given her much good advice on her career, though by the years 1974–1976 "most of it was arguments so it was hard to tell which of it was advice." Asked how she had convinced Porter she didn't want his advice anymore, she said, "There are some things a man can't communicate to another man that the other gender of the species can do." As for standing up for herself, namely her song rights, "I wasn't like a mouse at all these things." Dolly observed drily that after she joined Porter's show, his booking price had risen but her pay had not. However, through royalties, her income was up to $100,000 in 1974, when she left. "He made a lot of money during the time I was with him. I would like to take pride in thinking I contributed. In my own mind, it was pretty well equal. I have worked hard in his behalf." She said she always tried to make the best of things, "otherwise I would probably have jumped in the river."

Dolly also said she had done "a lot of praying and fasting" before leaving Porter, and that it was up to her and God, that other people can't play God, that "God cannot be people but has to be the God I grew up with."

She was much less persuasive when trying to explain why her management had stonewalled Porter for so long. She really didn't know, having turned it all over to them.

Tom White says he thought Dolly's deposition would lead to a settlement within thirty days, and he was right. So the greatest Porter Wagoner show of all—a public trial—was never held.

White says that dissolving the Porter–Dolly empire was like dismantling some large corporation such as General Motors. I weighed the evidence in the case myself—on the postage scale in Tom's office—I can testify that the papers of evidence alone came to twenty-three and one-half pounds, and this figure doesn't include many dozens of pages of Dolly contracts, tracing her post-Porter ascent from $4,500 a night to $37,000 a night.

White and Chernau rolled up their sleeves and plunged their legal hands into the murky depths of Owepar–Fireside. Together they both represented both companies, reflecting their clients' joint ownership. In her deposition, Dolly called Owepar "confused," and she was corrected by her counsel: "Her statement that things were confused is an understatement."*

Porter's settlement figure was most respectable, and White exacted ten ringside seats at Dolly's Las Vegas opening night for himself. Dolly got all her songs back, into the waiting arms of Velvet Apple and Song Yard publishing companies; Porter kept his songs and Fireside. And while he may have lost most of his remaining support at RCA, he gained a pack of new enthusiasts for his career—fans of a sort—down at Nashville's Federal Building, in the offices of the Internal Revenue Service.

The lawsuit was still a demoralizing topic for Porter in 1990: "One of the things that was so heartbreaking is having to sue for something already owed to you that you have earned and have agreed to, and to have to bring a lawsuit to get that to happen."

He added, kindly, "One of the things I think was uncomfortable for Dolly was her personal feelings toward me, not business—but any time you get a lot of personal feelings involved in something, it really gets muddy and heartbreaking to both parties. I think she maybe felt she wouldn't be capable of handling it because of the personal feelings in it, which was probably true."

On the *Heartbreaker* album (1979) Dolly says in "Nickels and Dimes" (written with brother Floyd) that while she no longer sings on the street corner for coins, now that she's hit the big time she knows she still

---

*In 1980 Dolly paid $50,000 for a church building in Nashville for her Aunt Dorothy Jo to preach in; later it was converted to a house, and her father, then one of her brothers, lived there. The utilities, the cable TV, the taxes, the title, and the city directory listing have been under a wide assortment of names. Some of the bills are paid in Los Angeles. One of her former employees says maybe Dolly had wanted initially to keep it secret from her management. "Dolly was always buying things . . . "

owes some nickels and dimes. Dolly played a pseudo-dumb blonde secretary in the 1980 film *Nine to Five*, who, with her co-workers, uses rat poison and rope to improve communications with her male boss. On her *Burlap & Satin* album (1983), in "Appalachian Memories," she says life is a mill, she's been through the mill; but at least she hangs on to her creativity. And in "A Gamble Either Way," the teenage hitchhiker finds that when you ride for free, sometimes you pay the highest price.

Once the ink on the settlement was dry, Porter headed down to Fireside, scrubbed off the instrumental tracks on ten duet sides, and overdubbed some new ones. Finally *Porter & Dolly* could be released. The album cover was black, and the two of them wore white, united by two separate photographers. Dolly floated ethereally in a diaphanous gown. Porter was at his Buffalo Bill best, his suit lit up by the customary embroidery. Dolly's portrait was by Ed Caraeff; Porter's was by Hope Powell, former photographer for Porter and Dolly.

No Porter–Dolly album would be complete without a song like "Little David's Harp." Little David is born on Christmas Day, takes up harp playing, dies on his seventh birthday. When it comes to certain instruments such as the harp, David finds you *can* take it with you.

One of the cuts, "If You Go, I'll Follow," a co-write but no longer a co-publish, went to number twelve in 1980. But "Making Plans" (by Johnny Russell and Voni Morrison) went to number two. The vintage heartbreak harmonies and lyrics (making plans to forget versus making plans to be lonesome) were still in style.

"SUDDENLY IT HAPPENED, I LOST EVERY DIME"

Well, it's hard to keep my hands on my woman,
With Uncle Sam's hands in my pants,
And if I can't afford the music,
How the hell am I gonna dance?

—Phil Thomas, Ronny, Gladys and Don Scaife,
"Me and the I.R.S.," number thirty-three
hit for Johnny Paycheck, 1978.

He had a silverplated bus and a million country fans,
Now there's just a few of us, and he drives a little van.

—Bobby Braddock, "Would You Catch a Falling Star?"
number six hit for John Anderson, 1982.

"**A**re you ready for the country?" Waylon Jennings asked defiantly in a song. Porter's new manager, Brooke Newell, was fresh from the "Outlaw Festival" business with Waylon, Jessi Colter, and Tompall Glaser. Newell quickly had to ask herself, *Are you ready for Porter Wagoner?* Her chipper press release pledged to help Porter "grow to full potential in the many professional areas he's so active in." Within weeks she found these to include disco, James Brown, and suing Dolly.

At least her client's new single "I Want to Walk You Home," by Mac Gayden, was getting good response. *Cash Box* said of it, "Flavored with a light disco beat coupled with great production by Porter, this tune deserves serious attention in all markets." It went to number thirty-four in *Billboard*.

Its follow-up, "Everything I've Always Wanted," represented the faintest of Tin Pan Alley flirtations. The song had been sung by Ethel Merman and Red Buttons for the animated movie *Rudolph and Frosty: Christmas in July*, scheduled for July 1979 release. The composer of the song and the soundtrack was Johnny Marks, who'd written "Rudolph the Red-Nosed Reindeer." Johnny came to Nashville and posed with Porter at Fireside for a press picture. The song was progressive country (with the wistful C major 7th to D minor chord riff); it went to number thirty-eight in the midst of the Parton lawsuit bombardment.

Despite the explosive headlines, the record gave Newell some positive publicity to exploit, so she managed to coax Porter back into some limited touring. She even got him off the ground, into airplanes. Porter had sold his bus to Willie Nelson who said it reeked of Dolly's perfume, giving him fantasies, until his band ripped out the staterooms and toilet and made a lounge. So Newell nudged Porter into Lear jets, and he took along trusty Speck, plus her husband, Fred, and Dave Kirby (electric guitars), Bobby Dyson (bass), Stu Basore (steel), and Jerry Carrigan (drums). Once when the pilot showed off some harrowing aerial acrobatics, he got an earful from Porter when they reached the ground.

Newell noticed that in spite of Porter's long exile from the road, his show was in as much demand as ever; there had been no falling off, and she could book him as often as he would let her. This wasn't often enough. Porter's finances were increasingly chaotic, yet he didn't want to tour as much as he needed to. Nor was flying always the best way to go. After one air-lifted engagement, all Porter made was seventy-five cents, laughs Carla Scarborough.

In the early seventies several people, more or less simultaneously, decided it would be a good idea to lure the fans to Nashville for their own week of seeing the stars and dropping loads of money in the process. (Fans weren't really welcome during Country Music Week in October, with all the boozy parties and award-giving, itself an outgrowth of the disc jockey convention.) Porter was among the first to suggest Fan Fair, and the CMA staged the first one in 1972. The main Fan Fair ritual has the stars imprisoning themselves in booths and smiling and signing autographs hour after hot hour.

In 1979, at Opryland on June 4–6, Fan Fair fans could catch Porter doing marathon tapings of his television show. Three more days of taping the following week accomplished twenty-six shows in six days of tapings. His guests included the Kendalls, Joe Sun (whose "Old Flames Can't Hold a Candle to You" became a hit for Dolly in 1980), Jim Ed Brown and Helen Cornelius, Mickey Gilley, Johnny Russell, Cristy Lane, Don King, Billie Jo Spears, David Houston, Jimmy C. Newman, Razzy Bailey, and Ronnie McDowell. The tapings were at Opryland's quaintly titled theaters: Flipside, Gaslight, Folk, Showboat, and Theater-by-the-Lake.

However, with headlines like "Wagoner's Attorneys Seek Parton Default" enlivening the end of Fan Fair week and a crescendo of bad press rising a couple of weeks later, such as "Dolly Claims Porter Mismanaged Studio," it is easy to see why Mack Magaha says the lawsuit hurt Porter with the Opry.

It also must have hurt him with RCA. Yet despite his retirement from the road, broken only slightly by the jetting around in 1979, Porter continued to have moderate chart success: two hits in 1978 (one Top 40), three in 1979 (two top 40). A double album, *The Best of Porter Wagoner*, had been marketed on television in 1978, a mixture of old and new cuts of old songs. And *Porter Wagoner Today* was being well received in 1979.

In October 1977, Louis Couttolenc of RCA in New York and Chet Atkins, who was still a vice president, presented Porter with a twenty-five-year award plaque. Porter's 1972 contract had expired in 1977, and according to Tom White's notes, Porter was re-signed by New York over Nashville's objections, since he still owed money on a $60,000 advance received in 1975.

John Morthland in his *Best of Country Music* imagined some RCA accountant scowling at Porter's name in the ledger book and saying, "This hillbilly crap's gotta go."

John Nelley couldn't interest RCA in twenty gospel sides, so he and Porter issued *When I Sing for Him* as a double-sided album on their own P & J label.

Out of the pop garden, with all its thorns, Porter deftly plucked a rose.

"The Rose" was the title song of the 1980 film with Bette Midler, based on Janis Joplin's self-destructive lifestyle. Written by Amanda McBroom, with an Orbisonlike melody that resolves on a low note, the song makes the rose a symbol of love. The rose survives the winter to bud and bloom in the spring. Whether love is a river drowning the frail reed, or a razor that slashes deep, or maybe a never-sated hunger, love—even the pursuit of love—is the best we have. "The Rose" instills the courage to love again, even after heartbreak.

Porter recorded it, packing a lifetime of gains and losses into his singing.

He told Patrick Carr of *Country Music:*

> Look, I have just cut, sung and produced the best damn country single of my life, and it's going to be a real test. I'd love to record more, but only if I can do what the people want to hear. "The Rose" will be a good barometer of that. I had a single out last year, "Everything I've Always Wanted," and I thought that was a great song, but the lawsuit was going on at the time, and RCA didn't get behind the record because they didn't know how the lawsuit was gonna turn out. Now, all that stuff's settled, so it's just RCA and me. I hope the company gets behind "The Rose," but I just don't know if they will.

To Patrick's question, "And if they don't?" he replied:

> I really don't know. If it isn't a hit, I'll feel that RCA really isn't for me. If they can't sell *this*—or if they don't want to—I don't feel that I could make a product that they *would* sell.

Meanwhile "The Rose" had gone to number three in pop with Bette Midler's version and won a Golden Globe Best Original Song award. So any major country artist's record of it would have been a hit, probably a Top 10 or Top 20. The lawsuit's publicity would have helped because the lyrics, with all their pain and hope, would have offered the Porter–Dolly voyeurs plenty of emotions they could read into every line. With the duet album out and "Making Plans" at number two, "The Rose" would have been a complement, cutting Porter loose from Dolly and marking him as a strong singles artist once more, with a bold, new record. In conjunction with the film, it would have been impossible for Porter's "The Rose" not to have bloomed.

But Porter had underestimated RCA. He feared they would not promote "The Rose." Instead, they simply refused to release it. With him threatening to pick up record sales momentum again, by means of a modern-sounding, guaranteed hit, maybe he was forcing their hand. Or maybe they just didn't hear the record's potential. But blocking "The Rose" was RCA's long-sought final solution to the Porter Wagoner problem. It would have been a massive country hit, maybe crossed over, and it would have guaranteed a healthy payback of Porter's advances.

Instead, RCA delivered the coup de grace, dropping him in early 1981, as he was finishing his twenty-eighth year on the label. Thus was "The Rose" laid on the grave of Porter Wagoner's recording career, a career whose royalties had once been staked as collateral in the event a new girl singer named Dolly Parton lost them money.

Joe Galante would tell William E. Greer in 1987 in *Advantage*, a now-defunct business magazine in Nashville, that when he came to Nashville he "found people you could sit down and talk to, who actually had the time to sit down and talk with you." Around 1978 Hank Snow and his accountants found the time to sit down and talk with RCA. Jerry Bradley was still in charge; Joe Galante handled the marketing. Hank's sleuths were only allowed by law to go back ten years, but they found $425,700 owed their client from 1966–76. Hank estimated that perhaps he had lost two to three million dollars more in his earlier, hit-filled years. Like a low-income debtor, RCA worked out a repayment plan with Hank, in installments over fifteen years with interest, then dropped him in 1980, his forty-fourth year. In 1987 Hank told Bob Oermann of *The Tennessean*, "I'll always believe that audit had something to do with it." Hank said tourists at the Opry would come up and ask, "Why can't we buy your records anymore?" As of 1992, Hank Snow sings as well as he did in 1952.

As for Porter, he felt he'd been bushwhacked, and he lit out after them. But he could hardly afford the powder and ball. Although he still owed his attorney for his last lawsuit, his counsel began researching New York contract law to see what they could hang on RCA. Joan and Porter were told to list all the sins of omission at RCA–Nashville those past few years. The cast of witnesses, and especially the soundtrack, for this charade can well be imagined. But the lawsuit fantasy faded and fizzled. Frederic Dannen in *Hit Men* quoted an attorney as saying: "Do you think lawyers fail to understand that artists come and go, but RCA is forever?"

Brooke Newell had escaped while the vamoosing was good. She wearied of Porter's checks ricocheting at the bank and of staving off hungry musicians looking for their pay after the television tapings. Newell says Porter thought his word was good, that no musician should think he wouldn't be paid by Porter Wagoner. In her mental memory album are graven the sad words, *I tried to warn Porter.*

At least he had some big chips in his winnings, as a result of the lawsuit against Dolly. So he purchased part of an orange grove in Texas. But two heads are not always better than one, especially when they are attached to the bodies of entertainers going into business together. Porter and some colleagues entered a consortium and, like lemmings, stampeded off the precipice. They had financial "advisors." Money allocated to maintain the grove never reached the proper hands in Texas, and the trees died. The Internal Revenue Service took aerial photos of the "investment."

The IRS said Porter owed $489,000. Carla Scarborough, who was now managing Porter Wagoner Enterprises and possibly Porter, began shuffling houses, humans, dogs, and horses, selling off the Hickory Valley Drive house and Ruth's home on Franklin Road. Ruth was moved into a more modest home where she lives today.

One day Porter told Scarborough of his triumph at a store in elitish Green Hills. All Porter wanted was a cheap razor and a package of blades. The price was close to ten dollars, so he walked out. He found the same item at Kroger for around half that, bought it, and went back to the Green Hills store. He found the manager and asked him why the razor and blades cost so much. Well, there's storage and there's transportation, and more storage and overhead, the manager explained. Porter flashed his Kroger purchase and said, "Then why don't you buy them over at Kroger's and just mark 'em up?" Says Scarborough, "Here we are, trying to figure out how to pay the IRS hundreds of thousands of dollars, and Porter's out trying to save money on razor blades!"

Dolly has always tactfully described the lawsuit to the press as merely her opportunity to "buy back" her song rights; Porter still had his Owepar catalogue. Needing some fast cash, Scarborough elected to garage-sale his song publishing, vindicating Bill Owens's prophetic "I don't want to be in Owepar" remark of 1969. The best customer for these old, familiar goods was, of course, Dolly. Today she owns the bulk of Porter Wagoner songs.

✻   ✻   ✻

Journalists continued to be fascinated by Porter, even if privately they pegged him for a kind of hillbilly Heathcliff haunted by Dolly (playing Cathy) in the storm outside the windowpanes of memory. They would listen intently as he explained how to work a plastic worm so as to fool the bass or how to keep the guitar sounds from leaking onto the vocal tracks down at Fireside. Porter didn't talk down to writers, with good ole boy evasive rhetoric like, "Well, son, you jus' gotta be in the studio to know what I mean." Instead, he seemed to enjoy explaining modern-day recording techniques fully and precisely.

Porter had even produced a soul music album for black singer Joe Simon, and with about the opposite amount of fanfare as the James Brown stunt had received.

In February 1981 Dick Wolff of the *Nashville Banner* reported that Porter and engineers Tom Pick and Mike Shockley had applied for a patent for a unique mixing room shaped like a bullet "to avoid any sound traps." The oval room measured twenty-five by ten feet and rested on "an estimated twenty-three tons of sand." The sand was for soundproofing. One end of the room was squared off, a "sound buffer," and the speakers were at the other end, on a sand-filled platform. The sound was propelled by the curving walls toward the squared end of the room. "No matter where you go in the room, you get exactly the same sound," said Roy, who explained that traditional mixing rooms permitted sound to rebound off corners and walls.

The womblike walls were fashioned of hand-cut wood, each piece having been soaked and laboriously bent by hand to the proper curvature, then hand fitted. "It was pretty expensive," admitted Porter. "It's very pure sound, almost unbelievable. God gave us the voice box, which is the basic element of sound. We just copied that basic design."

The patent for the three inventors was denied, and today the mixing room is a lounge with chairs and sofas. Sitting there you feel like Jonah in the belly of the whale.

In November 1981, Alanna Nash interviewed Porter for her "Brenda Lee's Country Profile" syndicated radio show. Earlier he had refused to talk to her while she was writing her *Dolly* biography, possibly for legal reasons. She found a happier fellow than she had seen in years and observed that he almost looked younger. Later in the interview she artfully asked his opinion on plastic surgery. He said a breast lift for a woman, or a face lift for anyone, was fine if it made them feel better. Dolly had given a similarly equivocal answer to Barbara Walters in 1977.

Alanna was enthusiastic that he was back on the road, since he had multiplied his ten to twelve dates a year at least by ten. In effect, the IRS had booted Porter out of the Pillow Room and onto the hillbilly highway—he needed desperately to work. Porter told her how happy he was to be touring again with a new show: Mack Magaha still on fiddle, Bruce Osbon on guitar, R. E. Hardeway on drums, Mike Pearson on keyboard, Dennis Bottoms on five-string banjo, and Larry Moore on bass ("a very energetic man"). "I had standing ovations for 75 percent of the shows, something I never got before. For the first time in a long time, I'm excited about my career."

When Alanna asked him about "The Rose," he said they were shopping the master. When she asked him about leaving RCA, he said it had made him pretty sad.

Beverley Keys of K.E.Y. Records mentioned in 1980 that she'd been to the movies to see *The Rose* and spotted Skeeter Davis in the audience, crying at Bette Midler's stingingly authentic portrayal of Janis Joplin. Skeeter got the song "The Rose" out on a small label, but it was not a major-label country hit until 1983. Conway Twitty had been at Porter's session and had been awed by the complex imagery and enchanted by the bittersweet message. He recorded it as a recitation as the latest in his long string of number one records.

Porter's "The Rose" ended up on the aptly titled *One for the Road* album that he issued himself. It was a "road" album, the kind stars sell out of their buses to fans. In Porter's case, out of his van, beginning in 1981.

Porter Wagoner reduced to *van* status? More than one person has refused to believe this. But Porter, whose positive thinking makes Norman Vincent Peale sound pessimistic, seemed ecstatically proud about driving around in a van. He reaped the predictable press pictures by sitting inside his new Ger-Win van at the factory in Bristol, Virginia. Porter bought two Ger-Wins, in fact.

Leaning back in the company president's chair, he said, "I want to take my show to some of the small, rural areas." Porter also said he'd been presented with some movie scripts, but only plotless ones for low-budget films. He wanted to be in a good movie like *Urban Cowboy* or *Coal Miner's Daughter*.

The image of a washed-up has-been was belied, at least, by Porter's buoyance. "Happiness and excitement go together," he had told Alanna Nash. "I'm going around grinning, and people wonder what's wrong."

He certainly had a big grin on in March 1982, under a tall white cowboy hat, with matching white suit, when he posed for the press. He was presenting a huge replica of a skeleton key, at least four feet long, to some investors from Oklahoma. They, too, wore cowboy hats, and one of them wore a fringed buckskin jacket. They were now the proud possessors of Fireside Sounds, Inc.

✽   ✽   ✽

He would have even more time for the road without Fireside, and without the TV show as well. Chattanooga Medicine had left the show in 1973, pulling out of its rustic market after almost a century and developing a New York-style woman's product called Pamprin, up-staging its old folk remedies, Cardui and Black Draught. New sponsors stepped in, but by the late seventies the show was in the doldrums. Brooke Newell says that too many people with only slight talent had been given spots on the show, while big name guests no longer needed "The Porter Wagoner Show." Regardless, the pop country music of the late 1970s made the show particularly irrelevant. The show straggled into its twentieth year (1981), then died.

Bill Turner, its former producer, says, "We had network TV competing, network variety shows. Other shows got the big names; we paid [union] scale. That's all we ever paid. We had our own 'Pop Goes the Country' and 'Nashville on the Road' in competition. But I think Saturday afternoon sports and 'Solid Gold Weekend' [pop music show] had more to do with it than anything."

Its successor, "Porter Wagoner at Opryland," lasted one season (1984) on The Nashville Network. But TNN, as it's called, began bringing back the feeling of the old syndicated shows like Porter's, most notably on "Nashville Now."

His show survived a while in reruns. Then in 1989 Willie Nelson, one of his old guests from the sixties (when Willie wore short hair and a sports coat), purchased all "The Porter Wagoner Show" tapes for his own projected "Cowboy" cable network. To close the deal Willie dropped by Porter's office near Donelson, and the two old friends hugged each other in the parking lot.

Porter's comeback was orchestrated by the IRS, the same folks who'd kept Red Foley on the road and who'd harried James Brown into touring Africa and Japan to pay his $4.5 million tax bill. Sure, the IRS was still hounding Dottie West when she died, causing them image problems, but nobody's perfect. They got Willie Nelson off the golf course by seizing his golf course and back into the grooves selling his memories in a television album.

Thanks to the IRS, Porter's "falling star" was in fact skyrocketing back up, if at a slightly lower trajectory. The years 1982–83 netted an almost tiresome barrage of favorable publicity, such as a story by Joe Edwards of the Associated Press headlined, "Glow Returns: Wagoner's Back After Breather and He's Hot."

In late 1981 he had filled in for Johnny Cash at a concert in New York and he finally made it to England in 1982, debuting at the Silk Cut Festival at Wembley. Alan Cackett of *Country Music People* was one of several British Porter-watchers who had paid closer attention to his actual music than most stateside writers, praising how he handled lost love and loneliness (in "Watching" and "This Late Love of Mine") and noting recent songs like the underrated "When Lea Jane Sang." Cackett acknowledged Porter's production of Dolly's first crossover hits, as well as his own songwriting: "He dabbled in the problems of madness in a convincing and compelling way."

In July 1982 Porter, Minnie Pearl, and Roy Acuff did a guest spot in federal court in Kansas City. They were testifying that "Opry" only meant Grand Ole Opry, that a country music show up in the Ozarks shouldn't be allowed to use the name.

A lone sour note was struck in July 1982, in, of all places, West Plains. Porter was playing a show at the Heart of the Ozarks Fair. He gave an interview to the *Quill*—but not to his old airwaves alma mater, KWPM. As late as 1989, Bob Neathery, KWPM's founder, said some people were still peeved with Porter over this and even introduced a motion at city council to change the name of Porter Wagoner Boulevard to something more prosaic. Bob talked them out of it.

Otherwise, Porter's "positive" publicity continued to swell. In 1982 he appeared at the World's Fair in Knoxville. Onstage at the Opry, Bud Wendell presented him with a fish-shaped tray, inscribed to "Porter Wagoner, The Grand Ole Opry's Kingfish, 1957–1982." Then, in a nightclub in Elk City, Oklahoma, a fan tried to buy his cowboy hat. "It's not for sale," he said, but when the fan offered one thousand dollars, Porter shot back, "It's yours."

Tom Carter of the Tulsa *World* tried to place the old Porter of the television show into new perspective:

> He'd put you to giggles with songs so corny that "Hee Haw" seemed sophisticated. He'd put you at peace with recitations so melodramatic, a soap opera was legitimate theater. He'd put you through a gamut of moods by never putting you on.

Carter called him a "sapling with human limbs . . . gangly hybrid of Liberace and Ichabod Crane." He speculated as to whether Porter combed or chiseled his hair into place, concluding that if he was a spectacle, he was a genuine spectacle. Porter acknowledged to Carter that maybe the recent crossover fad was a good thing because it broadened the market. "He knows he isn't the greatest singer alive," Tom said, "and as someone pointed out, makes up in nerve what he lacks in talent."

Even a freelance photographer from New York visiting Nashville for a rock 'n' roll magazine told the *Nashville Banner* that Porter was one of Nashville's more surprising sights. "He looked more like Porter than I had expected. His hair was yellower, curlier. His suit was purple. If more Americans saw Porter Wagoner, Dolly Parton would not look so exaggerated."

*   *   *

In Los Angeles in 1982, Porter hunted up maverick record producer Tom ("Snuff") Garrett, who had literally made it from the sidewalks of L.A. to producing people like Frank Sinatra. He was familiar with Porter Wagoner, and it took him about ten minutes to decide he wanted to produce him, too. He got Porter a deal with Viva, a Warner Brothers label. Snuff had already brought David Frizzell and Shelly West to the attention of Clint Eastwood; their duet, "It Wasn't God Who Made Oklahoma," ended up in the Eastwood movie, *Any Which Way You Can*. Likewise, Snuff got Porter a song—and also a part—in *Honkytonk Man* starring Clint Eastwood.

The film was based on Clancy Carlile's novel set during the Depression. Clint plays Red Stovall, a songwriting California ne'er-do-well who sets out on a trip to the Grand Ole Opry to try his musical luck. The Dust Bowl mood of hard traveling is strictly Steinbeck, Woody Guthrie, and Merle Haggard in its grainy realism. Red sings in seedy roadhouses along the way and eventually the Ryman looms in sight.

As Red waits to audition, he hears another would-be singer try and fail. It's a singer named Dusty, played by Porter, and the song that doesn't get it is "Turn the Pencil Over," written by DeWayne Blackwell. Red passes his audition and spends his last days in Nashville singing and dying of tuberculosis. Like Jimmie Rodgers, he makes his final recordings with hemorrhaging lungs. Marty Robbins is also in the movie; so is fiddler Johnny Gimble.

Norman Mailer compared *Honkytonk Man* to *The Last Picture Show*, calling it "one of the saddest movies seen in a long time, yet, on reflection, terrific."

Snuff produced the soundtrack, and Viva released "Turn the Pencil Over" before the movie was shown. It went to number fifty-three, and *Billboard* said, "Wagoner's back on the major label scene with this thoroughly effective domestic tearjerker. The production is appropriately stark, and Wagoner's voice is moving, sure, and to the point."

"Turn the Pencil Over" is in lonesome waltz time, and you can hear the acoustic guitar. The lyric is one that all too many entertainers could have sung with feeling, since it wrings out the hurt a broken home causes the children. This time, however, the husband is the homebody, as he watches his kids draw pictures. Johnny has drawn a picture of their house, with Mommy and Daddy visible; but Christy says, "Turn the pencil over" and erase the sun from the sky. Mommy's gone again.

The follow-up was "This Cowboy's Hat," by Jake Brooks, which went to number thirty-five and was on the charts fourteen weeks. It's mostly a recitation, but with a minor-chord release in the middle, which Porter sings. One critic placed it with "Blue Suede Shoes," considering its hands-off! message. In a diner, some motorcycle gang members jeer at a

Porter Wagoner and Clint ("Honkytonk Man") Eastwood, 1982 [COURTESY PORTER WAGONER ENTERPRISES].

fellow's cowboy hat. It is as special to him as their leather jackets are to them, he explains. The hat belonged to his late father, and its rattlesnake hatband was fashioned by his brother who died in Vietnam. The feather stuck in the band came from an Indian friend killed by a hit-and-run motorist, and the hat pin came from a girlfriend who is not likely to return. Snuff produced it, as he did the 1983 album *Viva Porter Wagoner.*

In January 1983 Porter's finances came to light publicly for the first time. Red O'Donnell told *Nashville Banner* readers that he had owed the IRS $400,000. A letter had been sent to the Grand Ole Opry seeking help in "locating Porter Wagoner" and Hal Durham opened it. The unsigned form letter even contained Porter's Eighteenth Avenue business address. Porter told the *Banner* that he'd been performing at the Opry for twenty-five years, was in his office almost daily when not touring, and was listed in the phone book. "After all, I'm not the invisible man," he said. He added that he planned to turn himself in and see what they wanted. "Maybe they want to give some of the almost half-million bucks I paid them back to me."

Wearing his cactus-and-cowboy hat uniform, he then pulled out both his pants pockets for photographer Les Leverett. The caption of the picture published in the paper was "Porter Wagoner: Out of Pocket."

✻   ✻   ✻

The first part of Dolly's 1984 film *Rhinestone* is set in the Lone Star Café in New York City. Porter played the Lone Star in March of 1983. Writing in the *New York Times*, Jon Pareles guessed that maybe the city made Porter nervous, judging that he only found himself when he sang his string of hits, while acknowledging his "calm, conversational baritone" and noticing the contrast between his basic "hearth and home values" with the actions of the "murderous husband" in "The Cold, Hard Facts of Life." An almost opposite review appeared in *Cash Box* by Jim Bessman:

> His soft-spoken, weathered story-tellin' baritone still conveys simple, straightforward, honest emotion—exactly what real country music is supposed to be, and he does it better than almost anyone. And he comes armed with some of the finest country songs in the last couple decades, many of which were sung here.

Jim was impressed at Porter's thank-you after every song—punctuated with a doff of his cowboy hat—and with Mack Magaha's manic enthusiasm and cut-up antics alongside.

Carla Scarborough believed that Porter worked very well with women, that this might become a "theme" in his career. He had told Alanna Nash that he aimed to surround himself with women employees. Ironically, this was while the women who worked in his office were trying to decipher what the boys had done with the money.

With more than one hundred dates a year, Porter was thinking of new ideas for his band. The revived Wagonmasters had gotten him back into the limelight, but he was still reaching for a competitive edge in his act. Vic Willis (of the Willis Brothers) had been using Wanda Vick and some of her woman friends as musicians on Ernest Tubb Record Shop shows. Wanda's steel guitarist friend, Lisa Spears had heard Porter was considering an all-girl band, so Wanda got in touch with him.

Vic told Porter that when your hit records stop happening, you've got to come up with something else. "These girls will make you *look* good and make you *sound* good."

THE ALL-GIRL BAND—
"THE RIGHT COMBINATION"

This is not a thing we're trying,
it's something we're *doing*!

—Porter to Vernell Hackett,
Country News (April, 1984)

There was more said about us
than you'd probably ever want to hear.
Everyone was real supportive of us,
but they were waiting for us
to go out there and fall on our faces, too.
They were waiting for it *not* to work.

—Becky Hinson, interview,
September 9, 1989

It was late 1983 when Wanda Vick and Porter first met. He said if she'd put a band together, he's rent a rehearsal hall for their audition.

Base player Becky Hinson remembers at the first audition Porter was his typically businesslike, polite self. "I think it took him a while to sell him on the deal. We met for lunch, we met several more times."

Porter told Vernell Hackett of the *Country News* that the band was a real challenge and he was going to have to guard himself against getting upset over trifles. He acknowledged being a real nit-picker. By now he had another bus, and he showed Hackett his typed list of road rules, such as: keep your personal objects out of the aisles; keep your clothes in your own storage space; don't pack more than you need for any one trip, and so forth.

Vernell Hackett wrote that Porter ordered some more subdued costumes for himself, to go with the girls' outfits. The band was to wear tuxedo-cut jackets in gold, black, magenta, or other colors, and pants with a designer-jean appearance but in various colors and fabrics. Their boots would be "feminine-looking, with a chain trim across the front."

Certainly an "all-girl band" (today we would call it an all-woman band) was a cute, catchy idea. But making it sound more than a publicity stunt or a flashy but fleeting fling, like his disco excursion, would take some dedicated doing. Porter would have to sell the women as musicians, not just as sexy props.

Becky remembers, "There were a lot of times when he'd get mad and we'd get mad in rehearsals. But it worked."

Porter had plenty to work with.

Wanda was the most versatile of the group, playing fiddle, electric guitar, dobro, mandolin, and banjo. She was from Alabama and had a music business degree from Nashville's Belmont College, now Belmont University. Nancy Given was a cum laude graduate from the University of South Carolina, in jazz and commercial music. She played drums. Lisa Spears of Lawrence, Kansas, was the steel guitar player. And Glenda Kniphfer—a childhood friend of Wanda's—played old-style bluegrass acoustic guitar, with Carter-lick rhythm, as well as lead. Glenda also picked some banjo and mandolin.

Then there was Becky Hinson from Indiana by way of Montana, a bass player and singer, who figured, "I'll try anything once, as long as it's good," and Patti Clements, keyboardist from Arlington, Virginia, with a degree from the Manhattan School of Music.

They had an almost tedious list of credits—winning this or that local talent contest or regional instrumentalist championship. Wanda had played in Lynn Anderson's band for three years. Becky's husband played steel guitar for John Conlee's band; Lisa had been working in Little David Wilkins's band; Nancy had played with the Motown act, the Temptations; Patti had composed "An Afternoon at Cheekwood," a piano piece she performed with the Nashville City Ballet, and so on.

By contrast, when Porter was starting out, the contest had been to perform well enough to impress some girl at the pie supper, to stay awake at the wheel, and to hope they paid you enough at the schoolhouse to buy some gasoline and maybe some hamburgers.

Soon they were at Porter's office, borrowing record albums, delving into his files of lyric sheets, getting into his music and getting it down.

He told Trish Walker from *Country Music People*, "These girls truly inspire me. We have been rehearsing for four weeks and under any other circumstances, I would have been bored out of my mind. After twenty-five years in the business [thirty-three starting with KWTO], there's not much I can get excited about. But if I have got something great to show to the people, it inspires me to do it. I am so proud of these girls and I want to show them off to the world."

Their début was on the Opry. Then on Valentine's Day 1984, they appeared before millions on "Nashville Now" over The Nashville Network (TNN). "There are a lot of truly talented female musicians out there," said Porter. "It's just that nobody has ever tapped this source before."

The inevitable name-the-band contest ignited more publicity, with 12,000 names floating in, like Porter Wagoner & the Rhinestones. But the winner was *The Right Combination*, the title of the 1971 duet he had written. It was submitted by Nelle Poe Yandell from Mountain View, Arkansas; she won a trip to Nashville and an onstage welcome at the Opry from Porter. Nelle was one of the original Poe Sisters, a country duo that had accompanied Ernest Tubb to Carnegie Hall in 1947. Other, less publicizable names could be heard behind the girls' backs, such as Porter and his Wagon Tongues and Porter and his Six-Pack of Slits.

Jan Howard remembers the hubbub over the girl band. "There was a lot of talk when he changed bands, but I thought it was fantastic—now that's *thinking*, that's show business, and they're all darned good musicians. People thought it was a show-biz move, and it might have been, but it was a good move. I respect people for using their intelligence."

Certainly this all-girl band was a history-making assemblage, at least in country music.

Lisa, the steel guitar player, had come to town to join a girl group called Nashville Satin, but such groups had always been rare to nonexistent. Back in 1969–70, Audrey Williams's the Cold, Cold Hearts hadn't exactly set the woods on fire (the versatile Audrey singing both flat and sharp). But Ann Jones and her Western Sweethearts, a six-piece band from California, had scored some minor success around 1950. The four-piece Coon Creek Girls had been a popular act on the "Renfro Valley Barn Dance" in the 1930s and 1940s. Earlier, in 1923 two women, Samantha Bumgarner and Eva Davis, had been among the first string-band musicians to record, playing fiddle and banjo duets for Columbia records.

Women, too, were more likely than men to transmit the old folk songs from generation to generation, as Don Cusic points out in his biography of Reba McEntire (Porter's sister Lorraine and Dolly's mother, Avie Lee, are two examples). But commercial performing was strictly for the men, especially in the South. Charlie Seeman explained in *Country: The Music and the Musicians*, "The morals of any woman who dared to pick up an instrument and climb on a stage were considered questionable at best."

But in the Northeast (New York and Boston) there were at least seventeen "lady orchestras" or ensembles in the years 1871 to 1898. However, when a woman couldn't make a gig, a man might have to fill in for her dressed as a woman. A popular vaudeville group was the Fadettes, who performed six thousand concerts from 1890 to 1920, and their leader, Caroline Nichols, played ten instruments. According to Judith Tick (in *Women Making Music: The Western Art Tradition*), as part of the show Nichols would feign an onstage tantrum, haughtily dismiss her band, then carry on alone.

In the *Atlantic Monthly* in 1894 Edith Brower asked, "Is the Musical Idea Masculine?" Her answer was yes, but for the interesting reason that men were more emotional than women. Boy babies cried as loud as girl babies, Edith noticed, and she dismissed alleged female emotionalism as mere "nervous excitability." Women, being calmer and more thoughtful, were less suited for music! A more conventional male opinion was voiced in 1904 in *Musical Standard*: "Women cannot possibly play brass instruments and look pretty, and *why* should they spoil their looks?"

But other than as novelties, women instrumentalists were usually discouraged from competing with men until after World War I. Gradually they became accepted, or at least tolerated, in classical symphonies.

Of course, Porter was much less interested in his band's gender than in its overall impact. The strategy was vintage Wagoner. First, stun the audiences and the media with visual flash, then follow up with musicianship. Admittedly, some of the promo pictures had a Charlie's Angels, Oriental potentate look, the women wearing shiny suits and adoring expressions, fanning out around Porter like spokes on the Wagoner wheel with Porter at the hub. As he had done with his side musicians of yore, Porter onstage flaunted their performances as individuals, giving them as much of the spotlight as they could stand.

The rejuvenation was profound, with Porter feeding off the vibrations, pulling as much extra energy as possible from the band, avoiding the phony "star" role where an artist is supported by robot side pickers. The Opry was, of course, their hometown bandstand, making Porter's portion a refreshing relief from the acts that cruised by with the Opry staff band on automatic pilot.

"Don't misunderstand," insisted Bob Oermann in *The Tennessean*, "this is *not* some novelty act that the master showman has come up with. These women can play the fire out of their instruments." Porter told Trish Walker of *Country Music People* that they'd be going to England for the Peterborough Festival in August 1984, then to Scotland for three dates and Ireland for four more. He said that British audiences didn't like hype; they had minds of their own "and don't care how many times they are told something is great or wonderful or has sold millions. If they don't like it, they don't like it."

But on September 6, 1984, Ernest Tubb died of emphysema. The family was there—his wife, Olene, sons, and granddaughter Capri— with Porter. "He was unconscious. He just quit breathing. He took a breath and that was all," Porter told Red O'Donnell for the *Banner*. "He

The Right Combination. Back row: Lisa Spears (steel guitar), Glenda Kniphfer (acoustic rhythm guitar), Patti Clements (keyboards), Becky Hinson (bass); front: Wanda Vick (fiddle, banjo), Nancy Given (drums).

was a wonderful man. He probably helped more people in country music than any one person."

Outside the room were singers Jack Greene and Jeannie Seely, themselves duet favorites like Porter and Dolly. Jack was a graduate of Ernest's Texas Troubadour band. Like Porter, Tubb had launched various solo careers. He had joined the Opry in 1943, had sung duets with Red Foley (maintaining a long-running pseudo-feud for laughs). By 1991 Ernest's granddaughter Capri Chambliss was managing Porter's office.

In November, Porter and the Right Combination toured Canada on a goodwill tour, as ambassadors from the Opry and Opryland. Porter was plugging his "Porter Wagoner at Opryland" TV show and told Sandy Neese of *The Tennessean* that "every time I mention Canada from the stage of the Grand Ole Opry, I get a tremendous reception." At a nightclub in Hanover, during a local TV taping, a reporter had handed him a guitar, which he passed to Glenda, and they went right into "An Old Log Cabin for Sale" and "A Satisfied Mind," and the crowd responded with big applause.

Glenda's father had been a musician, and she had grown up in a family band. "Someday you won't be a little girl anymore, and you'll need to be a good player, not just a novelty act," her daddy would tell her. Glenda owns about fifteen guitars. Her road guitar was a white-enameled Takaminie with a pickup, though she says, "You miss the wood sound with a pickup." Glenda eventually recorded her own album, *Flatpickin' Favorites*, which Porter produced at Fireside, even though he no longer owned it; it appeared on the prestigious Flying Fish folk label in 1987. Names like Bill Monroe, Vassar Clements, and Jesse McReynolds light up the credits; Nancy Given played drums.

A double album, *Porter Wagoner at His Best*, was released in early 1985 on the independent CBO label for marketing on television. Actually it was two single albums, in separate packages, but titled as one and sold together. The girls backed Porter on this collection of mostly Porter standards, though a cover of Hank Williams's "I'm So Lonesome I Could Cry" was included. He delivered a memorably forlorn version.

Porter returned to a major label with the MCA/Dot *Porter Wagoner* album in 1986. His pal and guitarist, Fred Newell, produced it. Lost on the album is one of the best cuts of his career, "Love Paid It All." Porter wrote it as a tribute to somebody's lifelong, happy marriage; his had legally ended, finally, that same year. Melody lines like "love is how we're born," then, spoken lines like "love is *why* we're born" stamp it with the Wagoner, heart-wrung hallmark. Thomas Goldsmith called it "tender, melodic"; and even before she joined the band, the song impressed Glenda when she heard Porter do it on the Opry.

The all-girl band continued to attract national attention and good reviews. Carla Scarborough admitted to Bruce Honick of the *National Examiner* in 1985 that "it started out being a gimmick, to help Porter's career, but every woman in the band is a professional who is good enough to work for anybody in the business. Porter often says the best man for any job is a woman."

The first big bump in the road occurred *on* the road in 1987.

One Sunday night Porter's office manager, Ruth B. White, took a call from Wanda Vick. She had just gotten back from a tour. She said she hadn't liked the way the bus driver was driving, so the other girls elected her to broach this with Porter. She told him she would drive herself to future dates—or even fly—but that she was "under conviction" not to ride the bus anymore. Porter offered to fly her home, right then, if she wished. She called him "Hitler," and immediately the bus was detouring to the nearest airport.

Wanda aspired to run her own band anyway. Soon Nancy Given joined her, and they formed the nucleus of the all-girl act Wild Rose. In time they had a major label and hit records. As with Buck Trent, who wearied of being a Wagonmaster and progressed to "Hee-Haw" network TV opposite Roy Clark, now Porter had helped two more musicians gain exposure and experience, and eventually freedom to expand.

Porter's leadership in career development, planned and unplanned, may well be his greatest talent.

Replacing Wanda, at least on fiddle, was Kathy Kuhn from Indiana. When she was sixteen years old, she had come to Opryland on vacation, where she had met Mack Magaha and banjoist Mike Barnett, who were "the ones who really inspired me. One of my main goals was to work at Opryland. I went backstage after one of the shows and played with Mack, and he encouraged me. Four years later I got a job there, and I worked five years in the bluegrass show."

Kathy spoke of how Porter gets excited onstage with the band. "He does it for a reason. The audiences love it, and so many entertainers don't do that. He gets the band involved and the audience involved. You have to learn to be an entertainer, or else you'll just be a picker."

The women gradually thinned from the ranks, sometimes replaced by men. Patti Clements was in the group at least five years. In all that time she said Porter never lost his temper with her playing, though he had good reason a time or two. She says he was too hard on himself, on his own singing. The women also felt he had a phenomenally acute ear for hearing whether an instrument was out of tune or not.

Becky Hinson remained longer, demonstrating an aggressive stage presence, whanging on her solid-body bass and singing empathetic duet vocals with Porter. Her contribution to "A Satisfied Mind" (taking Don Warden's old tenor part) brought something new to the song. Becky embraced the transition from an all-girl band to a mixed band. "I got tired of being around a bunch of giggly girls after a while. I wanted not to be branded as a girl bass player."

With imagination, courage, patience, and occasional impatience, Porter had made Nashville—and country music generally—more receptive to all-woman bands, and to just plain musicians who happened to be women.

BEHIND (CLOSED)
OPRY DOORS

Longtime Opry Members May Get Boot
—front-page headline,
Nashville Banner,
April 18, 1985

Back in December 1964, the headline "Opry Drops 12 Top Stars" in boldface running across eight columns on the front page of the paper understandably created a sensation in Nashville. The twelve were either being fired for missing the requisite number of Opry dates, twenty-six a year, or for failing to pay the Opry's booking agency its 5 percent kickback, shakedown fee when they booked themselves independently of the WSM "talent service." As Chet Hagan reported in his *Grand Ole Opry* history, the Opry stated that "nobody is mad at anybody," while noticing with embarrassment that it had tried to fire Chet Atkins but found it had never hired him! Opry members like the "Queen of Country Music," Kitty Wells, departed, whether fired or quitting in protest remaining one of country music's unsolved mysteries.

Many older Opry cast members were similarly incensed when, on April 18, 1985, the *Nashville Banner* named ten acts allegedly marked for dismissal. WSM had been ensnarled in intense contract negotiations with the musicians' union, talks that both sides insisted were "friendly" until the story broke. Next day WSM conceded that some acts were going to be bumped into "senior status," and would have fewer spots per year.

In a letter to the *Banner,* freelance writer Ralph H. Compton complained, "These contract 'negotiations' which would drop a dozen traditional artists from the Opry remind me of the old adage of feeding one's friends to an alligator in the hope it will eat him last."

The timing was crucial. On April 13 the Opry had aired its first regular (weekly) television show on TNN, thirty years and two months since the début of the Ozark Jubilee in 1955. And on the eighteenth *The Tennessean* announced that the Opry's sixtieth birthday would be celebrated that fall over network TV, Dolly Parton to be in attendance.

410

On April 21 Dennis Washburn of the Birmingham, Alabama, *News* did a feature story, "Grand Ole Opry Is Now Regular Saturday Feature," highlighted by an interview with Porter. "One of the hottest news items in country music last year was when Wagoner changed his band," Washburn wrote. "We're not trying to produce a slick TV show," he quoted Porter as saying. "This is an honest show with country people singing their songs and doing their thing—not in a polished, schooled way. It's people in their natural habitat." Porter said he tried to be at the Opry at least thirty Saturdays a year because "there's a feeling about being on the Opry stage that no other stage gives."

As for the older acts threatened by cutbacks, there was grumbling about age discrimination and ingratitude, about having forsaken lucrative road dates to keep Opry membership, and so on.

A locker room meeting was held May 8—Roy Acuff, Ernie Ashworth, Bill Carlisle, the Four Guys, Jack Greene, Jan Howard, Lonzo and Oscar, Jimmy C. Newman, Ray Pillow, Del Reeves, Benny Burchfield (Jean Shepard's husband), Jeannie Seely, Connie Smith, Justin Tubb, Billy Walker, Charlie Walker, Teddy Wilburn, Vic Willis, Del Wood in attendance—with coach Wagoner trying to reinstill some esprit de corps into the team:

> The reason for this meeting is to see what we can do for the Grand Ole Opry, not what the Grand Ole Opry can do for us. The reason I have called this meeting is because of my love for the Grand Ole Opry and for you.
>
> I love to work with each one of you people in this room. I would rather work with you than anyone else.
>
> You will have a chance to speak later in the meeting and discuss whatever you want to discuss. Every one of you will have a chance.
>
> What we need to talk about is making ourselves more valuable to the Opry.
>
> I can imagine how humiliated each one of you were that your names appeared in the newspaper [some of those present were not in the news story]. Let me assure you, that article was *not* authorized by the Grand Ole Opry management. The phasing out of [an] artist is something we need to discuss deeply—anyone that would be phased out—would be purely because they can't contribute—and there is not a person in this room that can't contribute more to the Opry than you are doing.
>
> I have seen each one of you in your heyday—and you were *great*—you can be even *greater* today.
>
> The Opry is built on entertainment, not on hit records. At the beginning of the Opry and during its first years of growth, they didn't know what a hit record was. But they knew how to sing songs that people loved and how to entertain people.

There's too much emphasis on hit records. Let's place our emphasis on entertaining.

As an example—one of the highest paid entertainers is Wayne Newton. He has never had a hit in his career [actually four, 1963–80]. There was a girl on my show a few weeks ago at the Opry who has had several number one records, but she did not know how to entertain the Opry audience.

The Opry is being monitored more closely now than ever before, seeing who's entertaining and who's not . . . the reason for this is, fans write the Opry and say they didn't enjoy it. The exposure we have in front of thousands of fans means we have to entertain them—or be phased out.

If you don't work on your career, you and you alone are responsible. You have complete control of your career.

Talent . . . talent consists of dedication, determination, drive, and ambition. Those are the things that make up talent. We have age and experience on our side. We need to take advantage of it. We know how to entertain—so let's do it.

We need to have a look of pride and experience when we come onstage. Roy Acuff, for instance, looks as proud today when he walks on the stage of the Opry as he did when I first saw him at the old Ryman. We need to all have that look.

Choosing material and wardrobe . . . We need to pick songs that will please the audience and draw applause. In choosing material for the earlier shows—it needs to be uplifting to set the pace for the rest of the evening. Choice of material at this time can either liven up the crowd or put them to sleep . . . Our dress should be clean—whatever we are wearing should look clean.

One of the reasons we must work harder now than ever before is during the past two years we lost two legends off the Opry, Ernest Tubb and Marty Robbins. We must pick up the slack as though we were doing a show somewhere and two of our headliners did not show up.

When we have new acts on the Opry visiting us, singing their hits, we need to make them feel welcome. These young people look to us for an example. They have great respect for us. They need to leave there respecting us even more. Remember—because of our age and experience we have a great influence over these new artists.

We need to help each other more—help each other to get applause. We don't compete with each other. We should be proud of each other—we are all a part of the show.

Enthusiasm creates energy. We need lots of energy, confidence, and new pride in the Grand Ole Opry.

The day after the meeting, a copy of Porter's speech was sent to Bud Wendell with a cover letter.

MUSIC CITY, U.S.A.

Within the next three years WSM
estimates that it could invest up to $50 million
in actual production, marketing and broadcasting
of its own network-quality music shows.

—Kip Kirby, "Music Is Central to WSM
Cable Thrust," *Billboard*, March, 28, 1981

There might be people on the Opry who do
a better job than me, but no one tries harder
or considers it more important.

—Porter to Neil Pond, "Porter Wagoner:
A Simple Man in Fancy Clothes,"
Country America, June 1990

"This could be Nashville's epitaph: Here lies what once was known as the capital of country music," wrote Everett J. Corbin in the opening sentence of his book, *Storm Over Nashville: A Case Against Modern Country Music*, published back in 1980. Corbin had given Dolly that first major interview in 1967.

Certainly the early eighties was one of the worst periods for traditional country music. The shutdown of "The Porter Wagoner Show" in 1981 seemed to fit right in with the general malaise. Older acts were being dropped, even as the industry flung more and more money into the fickle winds of "crossover." In 1983 an executive was telling *Music Row* magazine that the year 1982 had "stunk" in terms of profit. Also in 1983 RCA dropped Razzy Bailey, even though he'd had five number ones in a row in 1980–82, one more reminder of how little airplay now actually correlated with record sales.

The disc jockeys expressed themselves by failing to show up for Country Music Week in 1984. Those who did were angered that none of the record labels were throwing their customary wild parties in the hotels; *The Tennessean* reported that some "said they were disgusted and not ever coming back." At the top of the article was a photo of Porter holding a large knife, pointing in the direction of Roy Acuff's chest. Porter was in his cactus clothes, guffawing, while Lorrie Morgan fed Roy a large piece of birthday cake. The Opry was celebrating its fifty-ninth anniversary, and festivities that year centered more on the Opry than on the record industry. Porter at least knew where *his* priorities were.

By 1985, in *Music Row* John Lomax III bemoaned the current scene for being "a mess, a vast wilderness of clichéd ballads performed by modestly talented singers fronting grandiose production befitting Bach or Beethoven." John said it was all a Tower of Babel, that the noise was itself drowned out by the larger roar of voices declaring, "It's not *my* fault."

Meanwhile Porter was enjoying renewed demand on the road with his all-girl band. The bookers could sell Porter easily, thanks to the nearly twenty-one years of his TV show. After the short-lived "Porter Wagoner at Opryland," he continued to inject himself into television. By 1992 he was certainly the most recognizable country music entertainer on cable TV. With typical, quotable candor, he had told reporter Carolyn Hillard in 1984 that people liked his recitations so much, "I guess you could say I'm better at talking than I am at singing."

In the late 1970s Opryland Productions began toying with the idea of a cable network. Tom Griscom set it in motion, with Elmer Alley directing the programming and David Hall establishing the network. Alley had started with WSM–TV in 1950 and had been the director of "The Porter Wagoner Show." Hall had started as a janitor at WSM, then with an electrical engineering degree from Vanderbilt had taken over Opryland's lights and sound system before it opened in 1971. In October 1982, at a Beer and Ballyhoo gala in New York City to celebrate the inauguration of TNN, it was announced that three million subscribers had already signed. TNN went on the air on March 7, 1983.

Within months it was sold, along with the entire Opryland empire, to Oklahoma communications magnate Edward L. Gaylord. The Gaylord business dynasty was based in Dallas and included a broadcasting station in Oklahoma City and the *Daily Oklahoman*, founded in 1903 (a "mad dog conservative" paper, according to Chris Bell and Jim Ridley in *Nashville Scene*). Gaylord told Bill Fletcher of the *Nashville Banner* in 1983, after buying Opryland, "We don't want the Commie population of a decadent area like New York," but as was his habit, Gaylord kept his politics out of TNN and let the local staff rule with virtual autonomy. Thus TNN maintained an unbroken link with WSM's past.

By 1986 TNN was drawing 4,000 unsolicited letters a month and answering them all. By 1991 it could claim 53 million subscribers, or around one American in five; by rough guess, that would be around five million watching at any one time, greater coverage than the old "Porter Wagoner Show." TNN goes into just over half the households in the nation.

*　　*　　*

The saturation-expansion of TNN was simultaneous to the revival of traditional country music. At the CMA awards show in 1986, Reba McEntire and George Strait declined a chance to sing a pop medley with Lionel Richie, someone's idea of a ratings booster. By now RCA's Joe Galante had an acoustic guitar tilted against the wall in his office, and not as a mere prop. Besides the Judds, he presently had K. T. Oslin, the hardest-hitting deliverer of women's problems lyrics since Loretta, Tammy, Dolly, or Tanya. And she wrote her own songs.

This wave of New Traditionalists was soon followed by a rush of boys in big hats, some of them with big biceps to match. Some of the new women singers styled themselves folk singers, and most sought to influence the production of their records. On television, at least, such newer and more traditional acts provided a friendly complement to Porter Wagoner, even if none of them had been born when he and Lorraine had first sung "Leaf of Love" over KWPM in 1947.

Porter has become a staple guest on "Crook and Chase," and especially on "Nashville Now" hosted by Ralph Emery (whom *Cable Guide* has called the "most popular man in cable television"). On "Nashville Now" Porter invariably opens and closes the show with a song and uses his own band. On "Country Standard Time" he's been a host with Carol Lee Cooper, showing newly marketed videos of songs snipped from old programs like Porter's own show, preceded by nostalgic chatter about entertainers from 'way back when.

His best showcase is obviously "Grand Ole Opry Live," when one of his half-hour Opry portions is telecast. In the entire world of entertainment, there are few emcees as skilled or as convincing when welcoming other people onto their stage.

Once on "Nashville Now" he said, "Minnie Pearl just had a baby." Then the camera showed a *horse* named Minnie Pearl in her stall at Opryland, with her newborn colt. The foal is named Red *Foley*. A worse gag is Porter's true story of fighting the cold weather while riding a horse in a parade. He found that long underwear was too bulky to fit under his rhinestone suit, that the only garment that would work was a lady's girdle. He bought one. Then he realized it would be a long while in the parade without a break, so he made a stop at the latrine down in Tootsies. Porter tells, with relish, how an adjacent wino looked up, in shock to see him coping with his girdle!*

Not just his zany humor has shown up on television. Once in 1991, he was about to distribute some Porter Wagoner T-shirts to the

---

*In his *Don't Bend Over in the Garden, Granny, You Know Them Taters Got Eyes*, Lewis Grizzard offers a list of people he doubts have ever had sex, along with hypothetical reasons. Porter heads the list, because of the difficulty he must have in getting out of his costume.

television studio audience. But when one of his band members threw one of the shirts instead of walking it over, and missed, millions got a split-second glimpse of his temper, replaced almost as quickly with the old smile.

It's certainly fitting that a television personality like Porter had as a grandfather, on his mother's side, a traveling preacher who was also an itinerant photographer. And considering his many public appearances on horseback, it's fitting that his other grandfather rode flamboyantly into West Plains astride a black stallion, and that his great-grandfather was a Howell County horse breeder who was shot out of the saddle.

In April 1990 he led an Easter parade through Opryland, riding one of the park's quarter horses named Porter. Following were "costumed characters, a marching band, park guests and the Easter Bunny," reported *The Tennessean*'s Thomas Goldsmith. Soon after, Porter, with various Opryland mounted police, was up in Louisville riding in the Pegasus Parade, an offshoot of the Kentucky Derby. "Louisville is also expecting crowds of about 250,000 for its parade," continued Goldsmith, "which will feature sixteen major floats, twenty-three marching bands, five of those big helium balloon characters—and Porter Wagoner in all his sequined splendor."*

His horse-loving friend at Opryland is Danny Eldridge, with the imposing title of Loss Prevention Department, Special Functions and Mounted Supervisor. Opryland uses its mounted police for opening day ceremonies, and their favorite rider is Porter. "We put him on horseback from time to time and lead him out," says Eldridge. He and Eldridge and other riders will go wherever a parade beckons, since it's always good publicity for the park.

Neil Pond of *Country America* reported that of his three Tennessee walking horses, Ebony is the oldest but Rex is the gentlest and the one he prefers for parades. "I'm proud of my horses and my home," Porter said.

In the Nashville Palace house band at Opryland was Rick ("L. D.") Wayne, an exciting electric lead guitar player and sometime vocalist. Porter used to drop by the Palace and found L. D. to be a fellow bass fisherman. After a night's hard picking, at two in the morning the

---

*That same spring Porter was grand marshal of the Fiesta River Parade in San Antonio, seen by another quarter of a million people as he floated down the San Antonio River, which runs through downtown San Antonio past the city's Riverwalk. "In this parade, you really *are* on a float," Porter told Goldsmith. "I'm practicing my 'parade wave,' and I'm selecting clothes with the shiniest rhinestones."

two of them would head out for some nocturnal angling at Percy Priest Lake. Eventually L. D. joined the Right Combination, phasing in on road dates while Glenda stayed anchored in the more acoustic sound for the Opry.

L. D. was born in Augusta, Georgia, came to Nashville in 1973 when he was eighteen, and played two-and-one-half years with Tom T. Hall as one of the Storytellers band. Porter has taken him into the studio and cut an album-quality master. Once L. D. was with him when a boat company approached with an offer of a free boat for an endorsement; Porter's fast-draw reply was, "I won't take one unless L. D. gets one."

Like virtually everyone who has ever played for Porter, L. D. differentiates live performing from mere musicianship: "When you get out there, you're not making records, you're entertaining."

Ed Chambliss, who joined the Right Combination around December 1986, is from Nashville and says, "I started playing dives around town when I was fifteen. I went on the road when I was eighteen." He's played with Mel Street, Jim Ed Brown, Billy ("Crash") Craddock, and by 1976 was doing studio work with Porter, becoming a Wagonmaster briefly in the winter of 1981–82, in Porter's van phase.

Ed's wife, Capri, now runs Porter's office, having started out handling Porter's fan mail and tape and album sales. Speaking of Porter, Ed says, "Those ears are some of the finest—they don't miss a trick on any kind of music. Tricks like slowing down the tape for a drum track, then speeding it up for the next one, and it swells up the previous sound. He was one of the first, if not the first, to put a small mike on the inside of a flat-top guitar [in the studio]."

The oldest member of the band is Hank Corwin, on steel guitar. Hank was a Porter Wagoner fan in the fifties in his home state of New York. He worked clubs around New Jersey and remembers meeting Porter at the Paris ballroom in Newark. Hank graduated from New York's Juilliard School of Music, served in the navy, then in 1966 headed for Nashville.

In 1971 he gave an acerbic interview to *Country Song Roundup*. Hank said that most musicians would break their backs for the artists but not vice versa; that most musicians were exploited, and when they spoke up at all, they were silenced or fired; that entertainers wanted the best pickers possible, but not to the point of paying for them; that in Nashville there existed "a pseudo caste system" with the musician "at the bottom of the society."

He paused to say that a few entertainers were considerate, such as Porter, "but they are in the minority."*

---

*In his *Man in Black* autobiography, Johnny Cash says Merle Haggard is an entertainer who always credits his sidemen, that doing so makes the star look bigger.

To burn his remaining bridges, Hank said, "If you take notice, almost all the records produced in Nashville sound alike," blaming the closed-shop session system. "One musician can only come up with so many ideas. It's a shame."

Hank said in 1989 that if it weren't for a chance to play for Porter, he probably wouldn't be working the road because he was at the point in his career where he could pick whom he played for. "Porter's always been the kind of man that will take a hold of his own destiny. A lot of these young stars, they have one hit record and get a bus and a six-piece band, and all this overhead. Then two years later they wonder where all their money went. It's like being an athlete—you only got so many years of a recording career."

I caught Porter and the Right Combination at the Nashville Palace one sultry July evening in 1989. He didn't work the nightclub as other entertainers of his stature might have: the audience wasn't kept perpetually waiting for the "big star" to arrive. Instead, the first set started early and after the band had warmed up the audience, he was onstage repeatedly, introducing his pickers. As ever, each had numerous chances to shine: an acoustic demonstration from Glenda, very hot licks from L. D., and so forth.

The band cut loose with more and more electricity. People kept streaming in, and Porter wrapped the longish sets around the mood of the crowd. The only trouble was there were too many people and not enough time. The overflow of latecomers after midnight had missed the show, so he came back and threw out a fourth, unscheduled set. It was not your routine pattern of forty minutes of the jukebox, followed by twenty-minute sets of the singer and band.

Nevertheless, he was in his office at eight the next morning for one of our interviews. I said, "I can tell my kids I saw the Porter Wagoner Blues Band play rock 'n' roll last night." I kidded him that he didn't know how to work a tavern: "You're supposed to show up at 11:30, run through your hits, and be gone by 12:15!"

Porter laughed. "I think some stars just want to see how much punishment they can make the audience take. One year Webb Pierce just took his bass player, and they flew around the country playing with house bands. Next year nobody wanted him back."

Another Opryland USA venue is the *General Jackson*, a four-deck paddlewheel showboat that plies the Cumberland River. Its Victorian Theater can seat 620 diners and accommodate 1,000 spectators for a show. Working the after-dinner crowd one June evening, Porter complained about some insects flying about—you could see them, the room was open-air—and suddenly with a gulp and a choke, he appeared to have swallowed one. He turned it into a joke, and I marveled. Weeks later I told Speck Rhodes, who said I'd swallowed a *very* old gag.

Another time at Opryland, he demonstrated how he can function even when shorn of his music. The occasion was a show titled "And the Winner Is" in the 1,100-seat American Music Theater, one March afternoon in 1988. He was introducing eighteen Opryland singers who performed a medley of fifty different award-winning songs from all fields (Grammy, Tony, Emmy, Oscar, Dove, CMA). He was wearing a conservative midnight blue suit, relieved by some quiet rhinestones embedded in the fabric. At one point he asked everyone to stand up and stretch, then suggested they put their hands together and practice clapping. He deadpanned, "Thanks very much for the standing ovation." Remembering Porter on shows, Vic Willis says, "You'd think he was introducing Jesus, he was so slick. He would make a good used-car salesman. No, a good used-car sales manager. He would have kept the guys selling . . . Here, let me show you how to sell."

In many other ways, Porter is an Opry icon, and a useful one for advertising purposes. He may loom up on a billboard with other entertainers, touting Opryland beside a freeway. He may decorate the covers of sundry tourist guides or brochures on the newsstands. Or he may light the 135-foot-tall Opryland Christmas tree, where 110,000 light bulbs compete with his rhinestones and the light bulbs win.

In a long-forgotten novel called *Fortitude* by Hugh Walpole, the naïve hero gradually learns that the meaning of life is courage. Throughout the story he is intrigued by a statue of a brave horseman whose face he can never quite see. It is blurred by the wind and the rain. In his mind he calls the statue *The Rider*. After winning—then losing—worldly success, he sees the storm finally clear. For the first time he can see the face of *The Rider*. The statue's face is *his* face. Having weathered everything, *he* has become *The Rider!*

Similarly, Porter has become one of his own Opry heroes, such as thrilled his ears over the weak radio reception in Howell County. Exactly when he felt he belonged on the Opry is not clear. He was insecure at first; Jan Howard, who came to Nashville in 1960, felt he was distant and aloof. She says that today "Porter seems more human, he's friendlier." Others echo Jan, finding him mellow and relaxed, having been so for many years. Jan says she was scheduled for a trail drive in Montana and told Porter, "I've got to ride a stupid horse, and I'm scared to death of horses. I've got jeans and boots and a hat and all that stuff, but I don't have the courage." Porter offered to break Jan in by letting her ride his own horses.

A note to Porter from Mel McDaniel could probably speak for many artists: "Dear Porter, You are always damn good to me when we work the Opry & I just wanted you to know how much I appreciate your kindness. Take Care—Your fan & friend, ol' Mel."

Jeannie Seely says, "In the later years, Porter has been such a strong, strong ally and friend on the Opry. He's so good when he introduces me, and he trains you to tell him something extra, so he'll have something extra to say. He and Ernest Tubb trained me."

In a sense, he is best viewed from behind from the Opry stage, back in the wings, behind the curtains. Seeing the back of his head and his silver-on-blue costume, his hand waving over his head, whipping the audience up to the pitch he knows it wants to reach, you see the lesson being taught that many country singers will never learn. The CMA title "Entertainer of the Year," for instance, doesn't itself measure entertaining ability, but throws in *record sales* as part of the qualifications as well as "overall contribution to the Country Music image," whatever that means. Some current hot acts will learn more about entertaining when they cool off and the hillbilly highway gets more rocky under the wheels of their buses, if they hang onto their buses. Sexy cover photos doth not an entertainer make—though, past a point, neither do old songs and older jokes, something the creative new breed could teach their Opry elders.

Jean Shepard says, "The minute they kicked off a song by Porter, you knew who it was. Today, I have to listen close to tell who's who. He knows exactly what he's going out on that stage for, to entertain people. That's show business; he's always dressed the part."

But some country acts barely look as though they're in show business. There are country singers who dress like sidemen in some out-of-date band; some dress like Ralph Emery, or even Bud Wendell. Porter dresses like an emcee for a revue in Las Vegas. Backstage in the lounge of the Opry can be seen performers who, like Porter, don't look like bank managers, such as Little Jimmy Dickens in red suit and colossal cowboy hat. Or Wilma Lee Cooper, in a bright square-dance-style dress, dwarfed by her big J-200 Gibson. Or Hank Snow, still Nudie-suited after all these years, with the Napoleonically erect carriage that earned him the nickname "The Little General." Or the Riders in the Sky in their garish cowpoke gear like some loony parody of the singing movie cowboys of the thirties. Or Skeeter Davis, in a fey fairyland costume with giant, jutting shoulder pads, looking like an escaped munchkin from the Land of Oz, hurling candy from a sack into the audience on Valentine's Day.

There are fans who might not buy a new Porter Wagoner album, but they still want to be photographed with him. As he told Debi Moen for *Performance* magazine in 1989, "You have to build that rapport, because if they don't pay you—buying tickets—you're *gone!*"

THE DOLLYWOOD
FOUNDATION

We're inevitable.
Don't you feel it?
—John Gilbert to Greta Garbo,
in *Queen Christina* (1934)

Pigeon Forge, Tenn. (AP)—*Porter Wagoner*
will join *Dolly Parton* in concert for the first time in
more than ten years, a spokesman for
Parton's theme park Dollywood [Dan Rohman]
said yesterday . . . Parton's split with Wagoner
in 1976 was marked by public bickering over
their business partnership.
—*The Tennessean*, March 25, 1989

"**W**agoner, Parton To Team Up Again" was the nationwide wire service headline.

The occasion? The grand opening of the fourth annual season of Dollywood, Dolly's theme park at Pigeon Forge in the Smokies. She once compared herself to the girl next door, "If you happen to live next door to an amusement park." Already Dollywood was drawing over a million visitors a year, since it combined craft shops and rides with a menu of basic country acts at its Celebrity Theater (CMA's "Theater of the Year" by 1990).

The pretext for a Porter–Dolly reunion was a benefit to aid the Dollywood Foundation, which she had established in 1988 to combat the 40 percent high school dropout rate in Sevier County.* She had initiated

---

*In 1990 Dolly told a thousand educators at the National Dropout Conference at Nashville (across from the Ryman at the Convention Center) that "Coat of Many Colors" was a true story—and how the Parton children wet their beds, and "if you go to school smelling like pee and people laugh at you, some kids just think,

the Buddies program similar to alcohol and drug rehabilitation strategies in which pairs of students support each other to remain in school. The payoff is a thousand-dollar "fellowship" if a twosome graduates.

Porter and Dolly were scheduled for four shows on Saturday and Sunday, April 29 and 30. At the Dolly Parton Celebrity Theater all 1,739 seats sold out at once. Seats were twenty dollars each, and "premium" seats went for between twenty-five and one hundred dollars. Porter and the Right Combination opened each show, with Wanda and Kathy, plus Hank Corwin on steel guitar, "L. D." Wayne and Fred Newell on guitars, Ed Chambliss on drums.

At the first show, they began with "Ole Slew Foot" to a partly screaming audience. The Dollywood customers gave a larger-than-usual laugh to Porter's stock Opry joke about how if you place a snapshot of him in your corncrib, the rats will bring back corn they stole seven years ago. This was followed by a trusty road joke about how he couldn't get any sleep because the maid kept beating on his motel room door all morning. "I didn't let her out till about noon." After telling an anecdote about overhearing a couple in the restaurant discussing him behind his back (the wife saying he looks "gorgeous" on TNN, the husband saying he looks like he's eighty years old), Porter paused to milk the laugh. "Take your time, folks," he said, "I'll wait on you." Once during the show he turned his back to the audience and walked away as if in a fit of pique, halted, then turned slowly with a widening grin as the audience delivered.

When entertainers do a string of their greatest hits, they often cut them short, medley fashion. Porter did "A Satisfied Mind," "The Cold, Hard Facts of Life," and "Green, Green Grass of Home" as if they were brand-new songs, his band playing delicately, with studio-session care. When he got to the recitation about waking up inside those four gray walls, his voice had that quality of bewildered surprise—as if he were groping for the words—when the character suddenly realizes he's back in prison, doomed to die, and soon.

Then he gave a speech praising Dolly for helping poor kids to stay in school, as Dolly herself came bustling out on stage. She threw Porter a wry look and quipped, "It looks like I never went anywhere." Over whoops and screams, Porter lit into Tom Paxton's timeless line, "It's a lesson too late for the learning, made of sand, made of sand." And when Dolly sang, "I've got reasons a-plenty for going," she broke out laughing. After the song, she reminisced about cutting the *Real Live Dolly* album with Porter at Sevier-

(Continued from page 421)

piss on it, and just drop out." Dolly said if Governor Ned Ray McWherter didn't do something about education, they might have to shoot him or at least roll his front yard in toilet paper. "I like him very much—he's a big-hearted, big-mouthed guy."

ville nineteen years earlier, when she instigated her first scholarship fund for local students. Next, Porter introduced "Fight and Scratch" as "coming so natural to you and I." When they went into "Holding On to Nothin'," the crowd's outburst was louder than ever. After he sang "I'm so tired of holding on to nothin'," Dolly laughed, "Well, that's our relationship!" But she was mournfully serious on lines like "We've squeezed the life from every dream, but still go right on bluffin'." More spontaneous cheers went up when she hit the lyric "God only knows how long, how hard we've tried!" There was another uproar from the crowd at hearing the first words of "Just Someone I Used to Know." And whistling and clapping along in time accompanied "Daddy Was an Old-Time Preacher Man." At one point Porter said, "You folks can clap. That's what they *usually* do."

Then Dolly followed with her set, backed by her Mighty Fine Band, doing songs from her new *White Limozeen* album ("Why'd You Come in Here Lookin' Like That?" would go to number one). She hoped people would buy the new record, because "it takes a lot of money to look this cheap." When she introduced a heart-wrenched version of "I Will Always Love You," she credited Porter with inspiring it.

Journalist Edward Morris covered the concert for two trade publications. For *Billboard:*

> It wasn't exactly the reunion of the Beatles, but to country fans it was just as significant: Porter Wagoner and Dolly Parton singing songs and swapping gibes again on the same stage . . . It was by no means a descent into nostalgia. "Looks like I never went anywhere," Parton observed as she watched the slim and sartorially resplendent Wagoner take command of their set.
>
> Indeed, there was as much friskiness, mischief and raw emotion in the new pairing as there was in the old. Wagoner is the only singing partner Parton has ever had who is as glittering, self-assured, and viper-quick with comebacks as she is. Besides sparkling brightly together, Wagoner and Parton sounded as good as they did when they were the Country Music Assn.'s duet darlings in the early '70s.

For *International Musician:*

> There they were—wisecracking Porter Wagoner and effervescent Dolly Parton—bobbing and weaving and gibing at each other on stage and looking as blondly outrageous as they did ages ago, when they were the true Prince and Princess of Nashville.
>
> They were magnificent. Their voices were superb, and their songs utterly believable. Neither seemed to have aged a day.

Porter and Dolly had finally broken even. The following spring he would tell Stuart Tomlinson in the Portland *Oregonian* that "the bitterness between them dissolved on stage with the fans' reactions."

51

A SATISFIED MIND

I would like to be remembered as being
an honest man, and a man that has
put something back in an industry
that he has taken a lot out of.

—Porter to Jimmy Lancaster,
Southwestern Missourian, 1987

I t's been forty years since Porter left West Plains in the fall of 1951 and headed for Springfield. He traded the cramped quarters of his parents' home for the solitude of a rented room, right down the street from radio station KWTO. He probably walked to work.

Porter could walk to work today if he had to. He lives in a digni-fied brick house on Pennington Bend Road, a few miles from the Opry House. The home is spacious but not ostentatious, more like the abode of a retired businessman than a "Home of the Stars" photo opportunity. His son Richard, who works at Opryland, lives in an apartment down-stairs. The boat trailer at the beginning of the driveway and the two small stone lions flanking the concrete parking space are the sole indications that it's Porter's place.

Circling your way around Pennington Bend Road on your way to the Wagoners', you feel like you're on an island in the Chesapeake Bay or maybe in New England. The water-locked community inhabits a penin-sula girdled on three sides by the Cumberland River. The isolation knits the neighbors together like they're villagers secluded from Nashville and sequestered behind Opryland, almost severed from the present (with the twentieth century hurtling past on Briley Parkway, which bisects the Bend). The original pioneer, Graves Pennington, arrived in 1780. A number of illegal stills flourished on Pennington Bend, one of them on the Forkhum property that abuts Porter's lot today (the still's ditch lies under Briley Parkway). Another still was sheltered on Crab Island (owned today by Opryland), where the whiskey runners could float their wares down to Nashville. Rather an ironic heritage, considering the Bend's most famous resident has recorded so many anti-drinking sermons in songs and recitations.

424

When Neil Pond visited Porter's home for a *Country America* interview in 1990, he was introduced to the horses and golden retrievers. "I've never really developed a taste for fancy things," Porter said. "I've always felt the simple things in life are probably the ones that mean the most and last the longest." Down at the Opry House, Porter opened Locker 84 and offered some further evidence of his simplification program: *silver* boots with studded toes and wagon wheels and cactuses that could go with any costume. "I got tired of having to buy a new pair of colored boots to match every outfit."

If Porter were all that simple, however, he would still be cutting meat. His first employer in West Plains, Ted Pernick, says if Porter had stayed with butchering, he could be earning two hundred dollars a week today. Maybe even three hundred a week!

How, then, to sum up the career, and especially the character, of this most fascinating American entertainer?

The proximity of Porter's home to Opryland makes its own silent statement. It vindicates his Howell County daydream of sharing the same stage with Roy Acuff and his more desperate West Plains ambition to somehow, someplace, become a full-time entertainer. For forty years Porter has enjoyed steady employment with two radio stations—KWTO, then WSM—and their television creations, the "Ozark Jubilee" and TNN (with only two to three months off in 1956–57 when he made the switch). Even his twenty-eight-year ride with RCA was instigated by KWTO and reinforced by his WSM–Opry membership. His twenty-year service with Show-Biz, Inc., for the TV show is a further tribute to his loyalty and longevity. He still books through Show-Biz's old offshoot agency, Top Billing.

Porter's allegiance to the Opry is especially the reflex of a corporation man ("You can't criticize WSM, Steve, they've done *everything* for me!"). Though exceptions to his famous costumes may prove the rule, on at least four album covers in the sixties he was wearing Ivy League suits, not Nudie gear. It's not hard to picture him working for WSM's founder, National Life and Accident, selling insurance policies. The secret to salesmanship is not so much fast talking as sincere talking. And making *all* your calls. Porter would have made ten out of ten of his sales calls, and thrown in a couple of more to up his odds. Above all else, he's a law of averages player, as his methodical marketing of Dolly proved.

His Opry stature, resembling that of a senior executive, takes on special relevance in the 1990s.

Thanks to Garth Brooks and others, country music has finally pushed past pop and rock to become the first choice of radio listeners and record buyers. Yet Brooks, Clint Black, and Lorrie Morgan, to name some newer acts, seem especially proud of their Opry membership. The spotlight illuminating them inevitably falls on the blue or purple suit of probably the Opry's most enthusiastic member, with his silver boots and matching hair.

Such a commitment to the Opry might seem ironic in the wake of the Branson tumult of 1991. Branson, Missouri, is an Ozarks tourist resort with a smaller permanent population than West Plains. Numerous "name" entertainers have migrated there, opening their own theaters and giving Nashville a kick in the head from the Missouri mule called competition. While he's the most famous entertainer to come from the Ozarks, he told local journalist Jimmy Lancaster in 1987 that he had no intention of moving there. *

Porter and Nashville gambled on each other in the winter of 1956, and both of them won. By 1991, the year *Forbes* and *Fortune* magazines ranked Nashville in the top ten cities, Porter had certainly become one of the city's most visible citizens. Who else would you expect to lead the thirty-ninth annual Christmas parade through the streets on horseback before an estimated 100,000 onlookers? "I've always loved parades," he told Carrie Ferguson of *The Tennessean*. "They bring out the child in us all." A few days later, Porter put on a special show at the Opryland Hotel for executives of the American Bus Association, underscoring the statistic that Nashville draws over 50,000 bus trips every year bearing over two million tourists.

The music generated by Nashville attracts international interest as well, such as Tree International's sale of its copyrights (including "Green, Green Grass of Home") to Sony in 1989 for $50 million. Craig Baguley, editor of the United Kingdom's *Country Music People*, visits Nashville twice a year. He collects all of Porter's records, considering him the most representative of all traditional country singers, though admitting he prefers George Jones on ballads. And Richard Weize, pony-tailed and blue-jeaned entrepreneur of Bear Family Records of Hamburg, Germany, is reissuing all of Porter's recordings from 1952 through 1962 in a prestigious boxed set of compact discs.

---

*The music barns of Branson are like modern-day schoolhouses, and it's all like one big pie supper. In 1960, the year the Ozark Jubilee died, a family music group called the Mabe Brothers began performing at Silver Dollar City near Branson. They called themselves the Baldknobbers, after the White Cap-style vigilantes (three of whom were hanged at Ozark, Missouri, in 1889). Earlier they had been the Blansit Trio at (where else?) KWTO. Sometimes the attendance was no more than fifty, and when audiences fell below twelve, the Baldknobbers would cancel. It's probably all Si Siman's fault. Had he never gone into KWTO with his Popsicle cart in 1933, the "Ozark Jubilee"—and conceivably Branson—would never have happened. As for Silver Dollar City, it established an outpost in the Smokies that became Dollywood.

Recently Father John Heffernan, chaplain of the Canadian Country Music Association, was in town to visit the Opry. My wife drove him to the airport while he taped an impromptu interview with me. He wanted to see T-o-o-o-otsie's, as he pronounced it, with a very long *o*, and Music Row. He asked me to sum up Porter, and I told him, "Well, he tries to tell the truth in a song. He's sung songs other people wouldn't have sung, like 'The Cold, Hard Facts of Life.' He had several albums about alcoholism, not glorifying it but pitying it. He's tried to get down deeper and closer to where people feel in a song, both in things he's written and in things he's wanted to record. He's paid some heavy personal prices by almost being married to the business. I can't think of another entertainer who's thrown himself more into the business than Porter. I think he's one of those people who'd be playing for free. I think he'd *pay* to play if he had to."

In many ways he has.

Back in February 1966, Porter had been in the hospital, in the wake of his Christmastime parting from his family. "Skid Row Joe" was on the charts.

It was exactly twenty years later, February 1986, that he decided he wanted a divorce. Ruth White and his accountant Nancy Hurt could not dissuade him. He was already paying his wife $1,300 a month, so why fix it if it ain't broke? But Porter was adamant. Soon Ruth Wagoner herself was calling Porter Wagoner Enterprises, asking the women to pick her out an attorney. Why wasn't Ruth referred to the Yellow Pages or to the bar association? Because Porter instructed Nancy, most emphatically, to get Ruth the very best attorney possible!

Ruth filed for divorce in March 1986, citing "irreconcilable differences," an understatement since they had maintained different addresses for just over twenty years. Porter figured that a divorce was mere paperwork, a legal severing that would obligate him, cheerfully, to keep up the $1,300 a month. Ruth's attorney thought in terms a mite grander.

Even after his IRS-induced financial crash-diet, Porter's portfolio weighed in at between $700,000 and $900,000. He drew songwriter royalties from Dolly's Velvet Apple company and publisher royalties from Warden Music for tunes like "The Battle of New Orleans" and "The Carroll County Accident." He owned a $50,000 houseboat and two $4,000 bass boats, a $14,000 house trailer, and over half a million dollars in real estate, including twenty-seven lots in Sumner County north of Nashville. His nightly gross on the road was $5,000, and he was working steadily, with his compulsive Opry dates (often four per weekend) and television spots providing plentiful petty cash for plastic worms and other necessities. In three months he and the girl band had sold a thousand cassettes, and RCA still paid residuals.

But it cost money being a star. The England–Ireland tour of 1984 had grossed $27,000, with $12,150 after expenses, still pretty good for five days' work. For "Porter Wagoner at Opryland" he had spent $13,553.77 on costumes.

The trial that October was about as pleasant as such events usually are. The Wagoner children were tugged in two directions, briefly. Although Porter's guitar player-girlfriend Glenda had not entered his life until he'd been separated from Ruth for eighteen years, Ruth's attorney summoned Glenda to the witness stand for atmospheric effect. She wore an expensive beige suit and a worried mien. *The Tennessean* reported Porter's wounded testimony, about how back in the fifties, when he came home from shows with fans' lipstick on his collar (sounds like the Connie Francis song), Ruth's "jealousy nearly ruined his career." Porter said she disparaged his songwriting, destroying his self-confidence. Only years later did he overcome his writer's block, thanks to Dolly.

Presiding was Judge Muriel Robinson, noted locally for her photogenic face, gold hair, and adroitness in domestic relations cases. (Judge Robinson later married Porter's friend Tandy Rice.) The judge ruled that Porter could keep on paying the $1,300 a month alimony, but he would have to cough up $175,000 as well, $100,000 in the next ninety days. He could hang on to his real estate, his boats and vehicles, his famous wardrobe, and anything else connected with his career. Ruth could keep her house, her 1979 Cadillac, her jewelry, and her furs.

But since Porter never divorced (or annulled his marriage to) Velma Johnson, perhaps he shelled out this $175,000 needlessly. Based on the documents—and lack thereof—it would seem he has only been married once and divorced once, but involving two different women, rather like Chet Atkins, who was fired by the Opry that had forgotten to hire him.

In actuality, Porter was real estate rich and cash poor. So to meet the divorce settlement, he sold off his office building at 811 Eighteenth Avenue South. The wagon wheel sunk in the ground was uprooted like its owner. In early 1988 Porter moved into an anonymous looking office deep in an industrial park complex atop a hill halfway between Nashville and Opryland. Nancy Hurt ran the office, Ruth White having moved on. In this obscure location Porter could store his trove of master tapes from Fireside and his large closetful of costumes, as well as display all his memorabilia. In the lobby he hung up a gold album he had produced, *Best of Dolly Parton,* across from his Grammy statuettes. In his office he kept a dog, a large white ceramic RCA pooch, Nipper, as he was called. The walls of the hallway and other rooms were papered with countless awards from BMI, CMA, trade publications for the television show, and more. Dozens of framed album covers looked down from the walls, and since so many were from the duets, the mood in spots was rather wall-to-wall Dolly.

Porter's listening room, with tape decks and video player—and a priceless library of selected tapes from the TV show—was upholstered with a scattering of comfy pillows. Porter bought these in one day and strewed them neatly about. He also set up a number of fancy lights, which could switch over to different colors. A lighting store was having a going-out-of-business sale, so he asked one of the clerks how much the lamps priced at around sixty to seventy dollars were going for. She suggested he offer the other clerk about ten dollars for them, meaning ten dollars apiece, but Porter offered ten dollars total for several lamps, and the clerk capitulated. Soon he was back at the office bragging to Nancy about the deal he'd gotten.

Once Nancy caught Porter trying to steal his own bus. It may say "Porter Wagoner" over the windshield, but it strictly belongs to Porter Wagoner Enterprises. Porter the fisherman wanted to take it on an expedition with his fishing pals. Nancy said no: it's for business only. The fisherman won, and Nancy fretted over how to enter this in her books.

On August 21, 1990, *Nashville Banner* reporter Rob Moritz encountered Porter outside night court. He had just sworn two warrants, charging Glenda Kniphfer with criminal trespassing and vandalism. "It's no big deal," Porter told Rob. "If it was, I would tell you." Traffic Lieutenant Glenn Yates said, "It was an old acquaintance that he knew her from the past." Rob's story next afternoon began: "Woman's Truck Breaks Porter Wagoner's Gate. Flashy country music star Porter Wagoner may be singing his hit 'I've Enjoyed As Much Of This As I Can Stand' after a woman crashed through the gate of his Nashville home Tuesday night . . . Kniphfer allegedly 'broke down the security fence' in front of Wagoner's home on Airline Drive [wrong address] with a red Mazda pickup truck, the warrants stated."

Glenda had lit out running, and that girl got clean away!

And the day after that, Bob Oermann in his column reminded readers that Glenda was a Flying Fish Records recording artist (as Glenda Faye) and "sometime member" of Porter's band. Interviewing Porter at the Nugget Casino in Sparks, Nevada, for the tabloid *Star* that November, Roger Hitts asked him about the episode. Porter's philosophic answer was, "I've had a lot of affairs. Love and romance are big factors in anyone's life. It's been a major part of my life, and I hope it always will. I'm out there looking."

But that's not the whole of the story. Earlier, Glenda had conferred with ex-band member Wanda Vick, than reinvaded Pennington Bend Road with a convoy of six police cars. She refused to press charges ("I didn't want to do anything to hurt Porter"), only wishing to recapture her clothes, her guitars, and especially her Labrador retriever Lucy. "I lived with Porter seven years," says Glenda, "and I only want to remember all the good times, especially all the fishing trips."

* * *

In January 1991 country singer Johnny Paycheck was released from prison, where he'd spent a two-year sabbatical after a bar room shooting. Johnny had fired a "warning shot" at a fellow during a discussion about deer meat and had inadvertently grazed his scalp. Johnny had tried to apologize but was arrested at his trailer. Now, in May 1991 the Associated Press was announcing that Johnny would be in a movie, *Paradise Park*, set in a trailer park up in West Virginia.

With Porter Wagoner.

Somebody once said Porter would make a great football or baseball announcer. After filming *Honkytonk Man*, he told reporter Joe Edwards, rather wistfully, that he'd like to play a gambler or a sheriff in a movie. There was something of both in his role in *Paradise Park*. He was playing the governor of West Virginia.

The film was produced by West Virginia movie maker Danny Boyd, who has horror movie credits for *Chillers* and *Strangest Dreams: The Invasion of the Space Preachers*, "cult classics" reportedly. Obviously, those fantasy films were good preparation for *Paradise Park*, whose action occupies one day at a West Virginia trailer park where, according to the Associated Press, "God is scheduled to appear and grant each resident a wish." The plot line is a series of dreams in the minds of the characters.

God's dropping-in on the trailer park residents coincides with the arrival that same day of the governor of West Virginia, politicking at the park. Actor Wagoner already had the hand-shaking part of his role down pat.

Discussing the movie, Bob Oermann identified Johnny Paycheck and Porter as "the two country stars with, shall we say, less-than-matinee-idol looks," while promising they would be doing a soundtrack album together.

Onstage Porter gives as much of himself as possible to the audience, but once out of the limelight he shuns utterly the "seen-about-town" image cultivated by so many celebrities. Porter could not care less about being in the social columns. He hangs out with his family, his musicians, and his fellow fishermen. But one thing he takes with him from the stage is his storytelling.

After an Opry date, he'll change out of his spangles, don tailored jeans and tailored denim shirt, and hunker down on the floor of his dressing room. He'll regale his band members with story after story about Opry stars from many yesteryears ago.

Porter says Uncle Dave Macon would carry his own ham with him and would ask the restaurant to cook him a slice of his own ham along with the eggs. He tells a famous story about Uncle Dave on a

Opryland horse named Porter with his namesake. Others are named Miss Minnie, Roy, ET, Big John (for Johnny Russell), Little Jim, Hank (for Hank Snow), and Travis (for Randy) [PHOTO BY DONNIE BEAUCHAMP].

perilous trek through the Rockies. Looking down from the dizzying heights, Uncle Dave started loudly praying, "Lord, if I survive *this*, I'll quit drinking *forever.*" When they finally got down from the mountains and were out on the salt flats, the other musicians could hear Uncle Dave popping the cork from his flask. "Uncle Dave," they chided, "we heard you tell the Lord you were going to quit drinking if you got down safely."

"Oh, the Lord knows I was just kidding."

Cowboy Copas was on Porter's first TV show, and Porter remembers that on the road Cope, as he was called, would always order last in the restaurants. For a spell, it seemed every time they stopped, the restaurant would be out of whatever Cope would order. He would order a plate lunch—they had just run out. Or he'd order right off the menu, and the waitress said she was out of that. Finally they stopped and Cope saw some lemon meringue pie in a plastic case hanging over the counter. "Give me a piece of that yaller pie in that cage," he said. "I can see you ain't gonna run out of that 'cause I can *see* it."

And Porter brings back to life Lazy Jim Day, who died in 1959. Lazy Jim had been a janitor and radio station manager, and he played a couple of instruments. He was proud of his "The Singing News" routines. As an Opry comic, he would resurrect old jokes as pseudo-news stories, preceded always by the word *headline*, which he would shout. Millions of Opry listeners would see imaginary headlines in their minds.

Porter demonstrates: "Headline . . . Man Leaves Home to Go to Store for a Loaf of Bread and Hasn't Returned after Ten Years." Pause. "Now what should his wife *do?*" Longer pause. "Honey, you'd better eat without him."

When Porter finishes laughing, a tinge of melancholy overcasts his face. He shakes his head. "The trouble with the music business today is there are no characters like that anymore."

The Porter Wagoner the public is likely to recognize might be eating in a family-priced restaurant and signing autographs, such as at the Bonanza Restaurant in Jackson, Ohio, in November 1990. Porter told Randy Heath of the Jackson *Journal Herald*, "The music hasn't changed, but the promotion has. Randy Travis, Clint Black, sound just like twenty years ago." Porter was playing two shows at the high school auditorium; and if the schoolhouses are bigger than those he started playing in (one-room), Porter said, "I like smaller towns a lot better, they are excited to see you . . . It's the kind of town I would always play in if I could."

Randy noted that he was playing 110 road dates a year.

"I love it on the road. It's the best part of the whole business."

The Porter Wagoner to leave in the reader's mind is a tall, scrawny fellow with disarrayed hair held down, barely, by a baseball cap and wearing a jump suit. The scene is the parking lot on an isolated hill above

Elm Hill Pike, close to Donelson, Tennessee, outside Porter Wagoner Enterprises around twilight of a sultry summer's evening. Loading guitars and suitcases into his bus, he's laughing with his band members like a Scoutmaster hitting the trail with his troop. Bound for somewhere out in America.

That bus, like its predecessors, may be the best home Porter has ever known. Those buses have cost him more than he could ever deduct for the IRS. Popular music in general costs more than we, the customers, ever pay for it. When dreams come true in show business, it's often with a vengeance.

But Porter, who likes a bargain when he goes shopping, would say he's gotten a good deal from the music world and from the fans. And from life.

His brother Glenn Lee Wagoner would be proud of him, if perplexed at some of the details. Red Foley would applaud and forgive any of the dark corners. Proud, too, would be Porter's great-grandfather Larkin Allen, the two-pistoled, pie supper fiddler who raised horses and hell around Howell County in the nineteenth century.

Howell County, Missouri. In the Ozarks.

How many times have you heard someone say,
"If I had his money, I would do things my way."
But little they know that it's so hard to find,
One rich man in ten with a satisfied mind.

Once I was winning in fortune and fame,
Everything that I dreamed for to get a start in life's game,
But suddenly it happened, I lost every dime,
But I'm richer by far with a satisfied mind.

Money can't buy back your youth when you're old,
Or a friend when you're lonely, or a love that's grown cold;
The wealthiest person is a pauper at times,
Compared to the man with a satisfied mind.

When life has ended, my time has run out,
My friends and my loved ones, I'll leave, there's no doubt;
But one thing for certain, when it comes my time,
I'll leave this old world with a satisfied mind.

APPENDIXES

INTERVIEWS

Special thanks to: Urel Albert; Bill Anderson; anonymous (re: Larkin Allen murder); anonymous (re: Carl T. Dean); Hugh Ashley; Chet Atkins; Mae Boren Axton; Glenn W. Ball; Archie Bassham; Tom Bassham; Brian Bisney; Evelyn Bland; Elsie (Eldringhoff) Bohrer; Jay Bolotin; Dale Bradford; Lola (Wagoner) Brant; Nova Bratcher; Travis Bray; Brenda Lee; Gwendolyn Brotherton; James ("Goober") Buchanan; Roma (Beasler) Campbell; George Carpozi, Jr.; Merilee Cartwright; Marshall Cawvey; Ed Chambliss; Kenneth Chapin; Pat Chapin; Berniece (Holloway) Chapman; Stanley M. Chernau; Mrs. Nudie Cohen; Biff Collie; Ralph H. Compton; Hank Corwin; Manuel Cuevas; Betty (Foley) Cummings; T. Tommy Cutrer; Skeeter Davis; Little Jimmy Dickens; Kay Diselbis; Carol Doughty; Jimmy Driftwood; Louis Dunn; Danny Eldridge; Ralph Emery; Don Evans; Mrs. Loyd Evans; Reg Dunlap; Audie ("Buster") Fellows; Bob Ferguson; Eula Fite; Sally Foley; Fred Foster; Don Fowler; Dorothy Gable; Alfred W. ("Red") Gale; Sam Garrett ("Hank Mills"); Chuck Glaser; Gene Goforth; Lucile and Orbie Goodwin; Jane (Dowden) Gram; Earl ("Red") Hall; Judge Frank Hall; Lloyd Hall; Lorraine (Wagoner) Hall; Mr. and Mrs. Hardin; Lola (Holloway) Harris; Max Harrison; Dr. Perry Harris; Herschel ("Speedy") Haworth; Rick Hibbett; Ernest Hickle; Becky Hinson; Don Hoglen; Burl Holloway; Euel Holloway; Harold Dee Holloway; Norman Holloway; Velma (Johnson) Holzkamper; Jan Howard; Gene Hudson; Nancy Hurt; Mel Ilberman; Stonewall Jackson; Shirley Jorjorian; Denise (Wagoner) Kelton; Eulis Kenslow; Jimmy ("The Flying Cowboy") Kish; Glenda Kniphfer ("Glenda Faye"); Ann Kosloff; Kathy Kuhn; Mike Lawler; Barbara (Steakley) Lea; John Lentz; Little Jack Little; Bobby Lord; Patty Loveless; Debra (Wagoner) Loy; Windy Luttrell; George McCormick; Sybil McDonald; Mack and Shirley Magaha; Alice Maguffee; John B. Mehaffey; L. D. Money; Harold Morrison; Kenneth Moss; Johnny Mullins; Murray Nash; Brooke Newell; Fred Newell; Norma Jean; Bruce Osbon; Bill Owens; Louis Owens; Dolly Parton; Stella Parton; Joan (McGriff) Patton; Tom Paxton; Minnie Pearl; Harry ("Hap") Peebles; Sylvia Perryman; Virgil Phillips; Tom Pick; Fred Rains; Tandy Rice; Don Richardson; Bill Ring; Don Russell; Lola Satterfield; Carla Scarborough; Jeannie Seely; Jean Shepard; Roy Shockley; Si Siman; Mrs. Ray Simmons; Dolores Smiley; Carl Smith; Vernon Staggs; Pete Stamper; Mort Thomasson; Mel Tillis; Charles W. ("Buck") Trent; Bob Tubert; Bill Turner; Leroy Van Dyke; Leroy Vaughan; Wanda Vick; Porter Wagoner; Richard Wagoner; Billy Walker; Cas Walker; Gary Walker; Ann Warden; Don Warden; E. W. ("Bud") Wendell; Howard White; Jacqueline White; Ruth B. White; Thomas V. White; Vic Willis; Slim Wilson; Bessie Yadon.

SOURCES

Many published sources are clearly identified in the text. Others are cited in the chapter notes, but they represent but a fraction of the actual research. Interview sources are listed on pages 000–000.

CHAPTER NOTES

Introduction: [B. Wendell:] Lola Scobey, *Dolly, Daughter of the South* (1977); Nancy Anderson, "Country's Porter Wagoner Back on the Road Again," *Tennessean Showcase*, May 29, 1983; Pat Nolan, "Her Ex-Partner Reveals: Why Dolly Is Going Down the Tubes," *Globe*, January 19, 1988; Jack E. Custer, "Thomas Green Ryman," *Waterways Journal*, January 27, 1979; March 8, 1979.

Chapter 1: Dorotha Reavis, "Howell County History: 1839–1866," *West Plains Gazette*, Spring–Summer, 1978; "Howell Countians in the Civil War," *West Plains Gazette*, Winter, 1980; Alice Carey Risley, "Pioneer Days in West Plains and Howell County," *Missouri Historical Review*, July, 1929; Elmo Ingenthron, *Borderland Rebellion* (1980); Duane Meyer, *The Heritage of Missouri: A History* (1963); Orin E. Dunlap, Jr., *Dunlap's Radio & Television Almanac* (1951); State of Missouri, Certificate of Birth 37240, Porter Wayne Wagoner.

Chapter 2: Terry Fuhrman Hampton, "The History of West Plains," *West Plains Gazette*, Winter, 1987; [*Rural Radio:*] Bob Pinson, Paul Kingsbury, "Word From Home," *Country: The Music and the Musicians* (1988).

Chapter 3: Elizabeth Schlappi, *Roy Acuff, etc.* (1978); *Graduation Exercises of the Howell County Rural Schools*, May 2, 1942.

Chapter 4: [W.P.A.] *Missouri: A Guide to the "Show Me" State* (1941); Sharp County, Arkansas, Certificate of Marriage, Porter Wagoner, Miss Velma Johnson, April 29, 1944; Howell County, Missouri, Marriage License, Porter Wayne Wagoner, Ruth Olive Williams, January 25, 1946; Peggy Russell, "Speck Rhodes Spells C-O-M-I-C for Country," *Music City News*, October, 1973; Edward Morris, "Speck Rhodes Keeps 'Em Laughing," *Country Music*, July, 1977; Michael Cochran, "Say Hello to the Real Speck Rhodes, etc.," *West Plains Gazette*, January 2, 1981; Ralph H. Compton, "Speck Rhodes: Fifty Years an Entertainer," *Rhinestone Rooster*, Fall, 1982.

Chapter 5: "Bob Neathery: Missouri's Radio Pioneer," *West Plains Gazette*, March 4, 1982; Colin Escott, with Martin Hawkins, *Good Rockin' Tonight, etc.* (1991); Jack Hurst, "Opry's Porter Wagoner: Pride of a Rhinestone Wall Street," *Tennessean Showcase*, October 11, 1970; "Porter Wagoner: In His Own Words," *West Plains Gazette*, Fall, 1980; Sherlu Walpole, "Joe Fite: Trail Blazing Bus Driver," *Springfield!* Magazine, August 9, 1985.

Chapter 6: Paul W. Soelberg, "The Porter Wagoner Story," *Country Song Roundup* 2, February, March, 1972; Gaylon H. Watson, "A History of KWTO, Springfield," master's thesis, University of Missouri (June, 1964); Lester E. Cox Papers, Historical Manuscripts Collection; University of Missouri; Wayne Glenn, "Transcribed Music of the 1930 Ozarks," *Ozark Mountaineer*, December, 1975, and "A History of KWTO," two-hour audio tape (1975; expanded, 1976); Chet Atkins, with Bill Neely, *Country Gentleman* (1974); [Chet Atkins:] *The Guitar Player Book* (1979); Sherlu Walpole, "Music Man Si Siman," *Springfield!* Magazine, May, June, July, 1985; Gene Guerro, "Porter Wagoner and Dolly Parton," *The Great Speckled Bird*, May 17, 1971 and May 25, 1971; [disc jockey convention:] "Madness, Mayhem, and Music," *Billboard* ("The World of Country Music," section two), October 28, 1967; [Jimmie Helms:] Everett J. Corbin, *Storm Over Nashville, etc.* (1980); John W. Rumble, "The Emergence of Nashville As a Recording Center, etc.," *Journal of Country Music*, December, 1978, and "Fred Rose and the Development of the Nashville Music Industry, 1942–1954," Ph.D. thesis (history), Vanderbilt University (1980); Debi Moen, "Porter!," *Performance*, November, 1989.

Chapter 7: Charles Stamper, *The National Life Story, etc.* (1968); "Red Foley Announces His Marriage to Sally Sweet," *The* (Nashville) *Tennessean*, December 17, 1952; Chet Hagen, *Grand Ole Opry* (1989); "Foley to Stay on Opry, But Ends Contract," *The* (Nashville) *Tennessean*, April 21, 1953; John Seigenthaler, "Foley, Cast Take Park by Storm," *The* (Nashville) *Tennessean*, July 20, 1953; Dirk Vellenga, with Mick Farren, *Elvis and the Colonel* (1988); Craig T. and Peter G. Norback, eds., *TV Guide Almanac* (1980); [Foley's pop hits:] *Joel Whitburn's Pop Memories, 1890–1954, etc.* (1986); Jim Ellison, "Slim Wilson: Country Before It Was Cool," *Springfield!* Magazine, November, 1984; Howard Tutle, "Ozark Folk Tunes and Comedy Make Springfield a TV Center," Kansas City, Missouri, *Star*, January 29, 1956; Dickson Terry, "Hillbilly Music Center," St. Louis *Post-Dispatch*, February 5, 1956; Tim Brooks and Earle Marsh, *The Complete Directory of Prime Time Network TV Shows, 1946–Present* (rev. ed., 1981); Reta Spears-Stewart, "The Ozark Jubilee Saga," *Springfield!* Magazine, April, 1991 into 1992 (part eight, November, 1991: Porter Wagoner, Brenda Lee).

Chapter 8: "The Red Hayes Story," *Country Music People* (U.K.), July, 1972; [Hayes:] Dorothy Horstman, *Sing Your Heart Out, Country Boy* (1975; rev. ed., 1986); *News-Leader* story in *Porter Wagoner Fan Club Journal* (1983).

Chapter 9: S. J. Diamond, *People*, November 25, 1976; "California Youth Trend: Country and Western," *Fashion World*, February 13, 1969; Martin Kasindorf, "'Battling Nudie': Gotta See Him to Believe Him," Bloomington, Indiana, *Sunday Herald*, December 5, 1971; Susan Witty, "Nudie's Fabulous Follies, etc.," *Country Music*, January, 1973; Mae Boren Axton, Country Singers as I Know 'Em (1973); "Nudie, Daring Designer of Cowboy Clothes," *Country Fever*, Summer, 1980; Judy Raphael, "Cuevas Tailors for the New Urban Cowboy," *Los Angeles Life Daily News*, May 9, 1985; Tanya Indiana, "All Duded Up," *New York Press*, November 18, 1988.

Chapter 10: Robert K. Oermann, "Nashville Is 'Music City' for a Reason," *Music City News*, May, 1983; Albert Goldman, *Elvis* (1981); "If Jesus Came. . .," *Time*, March 26, 1956; "They Love Mountain Music," *Time*, May 7, 1957; "Hillbilly TV Show Hits Big Time," *Business Week*, March 10, 1956; "Court Denies Injunction in Brenda Lee's Case," *Music Reporter*, August 31, 1957; Arline Chandler, "Brenda Lee: My Best to My Friends," *Springfield!* Magazine, March, 1988; George Barker, "Grand Slam for Brenda Lee," *Tennessean* Magazine, August 25, 1957; "Foley Appeals Claim Tax Underpaid $252,143," *Nashville Banner*, April 4, 1959; "Foley to Undergo Psychiatric Test," *Nashville Banner*, September 10, 1960; "Red Foley on Country Music Comeback," Kansas City, Missouri, *Star*, July 2, 1961.

Chapter 11: Harry Shapiro, *Waiting for the Man: The Story of Drugs and Popular Music* (1988); Otto Kitsinger, "Leon Payne," *The Leadsheet* [Nashville Songwriters Association International], Vol. IV (1989); [Mom Upchurch:] Howard White and Ruth White, *Every Highway Out of Nashville* (1990); Ellis Nassour, *Patsy Cline* (1981; rev. ed., 1985); Harriette Simpson Arnow, *Seedtime on the Cumberland* (1960); Don H. Doyle, *New Men, New Cities, New South: Atlanta, Nashville, etc.*, (1990); Thomas Goldsmith,

"Opry Spotlight: Would Opry Founder Like Show Today?" *The Tennessean*, March 13, 1987; Arnold Shaw, *The Rockin' 50s, etc.* (1974); Walter Carter, "Landmarks: Studio B, etc.," *Country Rhythms*, December, 1986.

Chapter 12: Nelle Phelan, "Jimmy Driftwood, etc.," *Country Music*, July, 1976; Don Rice, "Teacher, Historian, Balladeer," *Best Years*, Winter, 1981; Hugh T. Wilson, "The Jimmy Driftwood Story," *International Country Music*, January and February, 1989; Dale Vinicur, booklet for *Jimmy Driftwood: Americana*, compact disc boxed set (1990); Michael LeVine, *Johnny Horton—Your Singing Fisherman* (1982).

Chapter 13: Neika Brewer, "The Show Biz TV Story," and Gene Goforth, "Country Music TV Syndication," both in *Country Music Who's Who 1972*; John Scott Colley, "The Sound Seen: Country Music on Television," *Journal of Country Music*, Fall–Winter, 1974; [John W. Rumble and Ronnie Pugh] "Television's Role in Country Music," *CMA Close Up*, January, February, March, May, June, August, and October, 1988; January and February, 1989; Paul Soelberg, interview with Little Jack Little [transcript], August 17, 1971; "Buck Trent, the Five-String General," *Country Song Roundup*, November 1969; LaWayne Satterfield, "Buck's Dancing Fingers," *Music City News*, December, 1972; "MGM Proudly Presents George McCormick," *Hillbilly and Cowboy Hit Parade*, Winter, 1957–58; Robert C. Bicknell, "Cardui: The Story of a Nostrum," *Harper's Weekly*, October 23, 1915 and "Black Draught: The Story of Another Nostrum," *Harper's Weekly*, November 30, 1915; Stewart H. Holbrook, "Favorites of the South," *The Golden Age of Quackery* (1959); Vernon L. Staggs, "Chattem, Inc." [typescript] (1989).

Chapter 14: Porter Wagoner, with Glenn Hunter, "Hello, Dolly," *Journal of Country Music*, Vol. X, No. 1 (1985); Walt Trott, "Norma Jean, etc.," *Country Sounds*, January 1987; David Fox, "600,000 Pills Ordered for Snapp?" *The Tennessean*, January 18, 1977, and "Snapp: Issued Didrex Legitimately," *The Tennessean*, January 21, 1977; Marsha Vende Berg, "Witness: Patients Left Fee for Pills," *Nashville Banner*, January 18, 1977, and "Jury Convicts Snapp of 23 Diet Pill Counts," *Nashville Banner*, January 22, 1977.

Chapter 16: "Curly Putman," *Country Songs and Stars*, July 1967; Kent McNeel and Mark Luther, "Curly Putman," *Songwriters with a Touch of Gold* (1976); Irwin Stambler and Grelun Landon, "Freddy Hart," *Encyclopedia of Folk, Country, and Western Music* (1984); [Oscar Wagoner:] Clerk of the Court, Docket 4, page 59, Hancock County, Iowa; James Blackwood, with Dan Martin, *The James Blackwood Story* (1975); Howard Miller, *The Louvin Brothers* (1986); Albert Cunniff, *Waylon Jennings* (1985).

Chapter 17: Everett Corbin, "Dolly Parton 'No Dumb Blonde'," *Music City News*, September, 1967; Ralph Emery with Tom Carter, *Memories: The Autobiography of Ralph Emery* (1991); Ellis Amburn, *Dark Star: The Roy Orbison Story* (1990).

Chapter 18: Jerome Doolittle, *The Southern Appalachians* (1975); Laura Thornborough, *The Great Smoky Mountains* (1937; rev. enlarged ed., 1942); Wilma Dykeman, *The French Broad* (1955); C. Bradford Pierce, *Great Smokies* (1990); Michael Frome, *Strangers in High Places: The Story of the Great Smoky Mountains* (1960; rev. ed., 1980); Beverly Parton Bowen, *The Parton Genealogy, 1806–1975* (1975); Willard Yarbrough, "Sevier County White Caps Brought Disgrace in 1890s," Knoxville *News-Sentinel*, September 22, 1968; Cas Walker, *White Caps and Blue Bills* (1974); *The Gentle Winds of Change: A History of Sevier County, Tennessee, 1900–1930* (1989); Lawrence Grobel, "Playboy Interview: Dolly Parton," *Playboy*, November, 1976; Application for Verification of Fact of Birth, April 6, 1990 and August 20, 1991; Robert K. Oermann, "Dolly Rides Back into Country 'Limozeen'," *The Tennessean*, July 8, 1989.

Chapter 19: John Morthland, *The Best of Country Music* (1984); Nancy Anderson, "Dolly Parton: A Hometown Report," *Good Housekeeping*, February, 1988.

Chapter 20: "Sholes' Death Leaves Void in Music Industry," *Music City News*,

May, 1968; John Pugh, "Chet and RCA Helped to Create Nashville Sound," *Music City News*, March, 1972; George Barker, "A Travelling Man's Gotta Zigzag," *The Tennessean Magazine*, February 2, 1964.

Chapter 21: George Barker, "A Little Bit of Choctaw," *The Tennessean Magazine*, March 1, 1964; Tom Ingram, "He's a Pro in Two Fields," *The Tennessean*, October 15, 1971.

Chapter 22: "Second Mark Falls at Fair," *Springfield News Leader*, August 10, 1968; "Porter Wagoner: A Satisfied Man," *Country Song Roundup*, May, 1968; Joshua Castle, "Dolly Parton: A Total Experience," *Country Song Roundup*, November, 1969; Jeannie C. Riley, *From Harper Valley to the Mountain Top* (1978); Cliff John, "Golly, Dolly!" *Ladies' Home Journal*, July, 1982.

Chapter 23: [David Allen Coe:] Alanna Nash, *Behind Closed Doors, etc.* (1988).

Chapter 25: "Porter Wagoner Recalls Days in Peoria," *Caterpillar Folks*, March 20, 1970; "The Girl From East Tennessee: Dolly Parton," *The Nashville Sound*, April 14, 1970; "Oh, You Beautiful Doll," *Cash Box*, May 9, 1970; LaWayne Satterfield, "Comments from the Country's Top Duet: Porter Wagoner and Dolly Parton," *Music City News*, November 1970.

Chapter 27: LaWayne Satterfield, "'I Write from Inspiration,' Says Porter," *Music City News*, February 1973; ["Rose Garden":] Tom Roland, *Number One Country Hits* (1991); Robert Bloch, "The Rubber Room," in Charles L. Grant, ed., *The Dodd, Mead Gallery of Horror* (1983).

Chapter 28: Audrey Winters, "11,000 Cheer Country Music in Madison Square Garden," *Music City News*, July, 1971; "Dolly Parton Day Huge Success in Hometown," *Music City News*, July, 1971; Bill Williams, "Porter Wagoner Show to Solo in Smaller Markets," *Billboard*, August 28, 1971; Jack Hurst, "Slump Slows Music Tempo," *The Tennessean*, August 30, 1971; LaWayne Satterfield, "The Wagonmaster Honored with Porter Wagoner Day," *Music City News*, October, 1971; Judy Hogg, "Dolly and Porter Blend Voices to Win Acclaim," Beaumont, Texas, *Enterprise*, October 13, 1971; [Hieronymous:] *The Tennessean*, October 10, 1971.

Chapter 29: *Country Music Stars and Their Homes* (1986).

Chapter 30: Red O'Donnell, "Fancy Yule Gifts for Country Stars," Dallas *Morning News*, January 1, 1972; Ginny Burdick, "'Down Home' Music Brings Eugene Fans to Their Feet," Eugene, Oregon, *Register-Guard*, February 15, 1962; Jack Hurst, "Porter Wagoner Says New Publicity Program Works," *Nashville Tennessean*, February 29, 1972; "Dolly Parton Tapes TV Success Story," *Music City News*, March, 1972; LaWayne Satterfield, "The Many Faces of Dolly Parton Reveal Love, Compassion," *Music City News*, May, 1972; Toby Thompson, "Dolly Parton Is Such Sweet Sorrow," *Village Voice*, April 19, 1976.

Chapter 31: Red O'Donnell, "Nashville Sound: Dolly Parton's Answer," Houston *Post*, September 3, 1972; "Porter's Show Is Taped at Opryland USA," *Music City News*, October 1972; Kathy Sawyer, "'Naked' Porter Begins 21st Year with RCA," *The Tennessean*, October 21, 1972; Craig Baguley, "Interview: Chet Atkins, etc.," *Country Music People*, February, 1991; Bill Hance, "Porter Wagoner to Build New Recording Studio," *Nashville Banner*, December 16, 1972; Jerry Bailey, "Dolly Parton Wants to Glitter as a Musician," *Country Music*, February, 1973; Michael Willard, "Dolly's Story One of Sweet Success," Knoxville *News-Sentinel*, February 23, 1973.

Chapter 32: Bob Powel, "Dolly Parton," *Country Music People*, November, 1985; Robert K. Oermann, "Dolly Parton: Here She Comes Again," *Country Sounds*, May, 1987.

Chapter 33: Bruce Honick, "The 'Real' Patty Loveless," *Nashville!*, October, 1989; "Porter, Dolly Open Fireside Studio," *Music City News*, April, 1973.

Chapter 34: Darrell Rowlett, "Inside Country Music: Fans Ask Dolly Parton's

Marital Status," Greenville, Tennessee, *Sun*, January 24, 1973; Rex Woodford, "Other Than Songs, What About Dolly?" Charleston, West Virginia, *Daily Mail*, May 15, 1973.

Chapter 35: [Jerry Bradley:] Wayne Robbins, "Record Producer Enjoys Autonomy," *Tulsa Daily World*, February 27, 1977; Patrick Carr, "Chet Atkins: 'I Just Want to Play'," *Country Music*, January 2, 1991; Bill Littleton, record review, *Country Music*, December 1972; Robert Windeler, "Bio: Chet Atkins Helped Country Music Move Uptown—And Now He Regrets It," *People Weekly*, November 16, 1974; Bob Colacello, *Holy Terror: Andy Warhol Close Up* (1970).

Chapter 37: Jerry Bailey, "Porter Pushes Dolly's Bandwagon," *Tennessean Showcase*, December 2, 1973; LaWayne Satterfield, "Dolly Parton Talks about the Birth of 'Jolene'," *Music City News*, January, 1974, and "Dolly Splits from Porter," *Music City News* March, 1974; Robert Christgau, *Rock Albums of the '70s, etc.* (1981).

Chapter 38: Jerry Bailey, "Porter Goes to Bat for Barbara Lea," *The Tennessean*, July 11, 1974; Cynthia Kirk, "Concert Reviews: Merle Haggard, Dolly Parton," *Hollywood Reporter*, August 27, 1974; Ronnie Milsap, with Tom Carter, *Almost Like a Song* (1990); LaWayne Satterfield, "Dolly Parton Keeps Smiling and Bubbling Over," *Music City News*, June, 1974; Dave Hickey, "Dolly Triumphant, Dolly the Star," *Country Music*, July, 1974; Bill Dick, interview with Blaise Tosti (unpublished); Lee Rector, "Association of Country Entertainers Established for Many Reasons," *Music City News*, December, 1974.

Chapter 40: Gerry Wood, "Nashville Publishers Adopt Global Outlook," *Billboard*, February 21, 1976; Chris Chase, "The Country Girl," *New York Times Magazine*, May 7, 1976; Patrick Carr, "Dolly Parton: Hungry for the Real Thing," *Country Music*, September–October, 1989; *Stereo Review*, January 1977; Mike Kosser, "Wagoner 'Hurt' by Loss of Dolly," *Country Rhythms*, April, 1977; [Grammy nominations:] Lori Schue, *Dolly Parton: Highlights from Hometown to Hollywood* (1990); Patrick Thomas, "*Advantage* Interviews: Jerry Bradley," *Advantage*, October, 1978.

Chapter 41: Judy Hedy, "Lea Jane Berinati," *Country Song Roundup*, December, 1977.

Chapter 42: Kelly Delaney, "On Their Own Time: Outdoors with Porter Wagoner . . . Gone Fishing," *Country Song Roundup*, November, 1983; *Larry Munson's Fishing Guide to Tennessee Waters* (1965).

Chapter 43: Ed Ward, "Album of the Month," *Country Music*, February, 1978; "Porter, Dolly, Open Fireside Studio," *Music City News*, April, 1973; John Morthland, "The Last of the Hillbillies Speaks His Mind," *Country Music*, July, 1978; Dave Hickey, "Porter: The Last Great Hillbilly," *Country Music*, May, 1975; Glenn Hunter, unpublished interview, 1983; Bill Ede, "Jay Bolotin Has Been 'The Hidden Boy'," *Louisville Music News*, April, 1990; Bill Hance, "Dolly's Mystery Man Opts for Quiet Life," *Nashville Banner*, March 2, 1978, and "He's the Same Porter But with a Disco Beat," *Nashville Banner*, February 1, 1979; Laura Eipper, "Porter Wows 'Em—But Is It Disco?" *The Tennessean*, February 2, 1979, and "Porter's Bitterest Remarks Turn Dolly's Happiest Hour Sour," *The Tennessean*, October 12, 1978; Bill Hance, "Opry Discord Has a Familiar Note," *Nashville Banner*, March 9, 1979, and "'Soul' Spot Angers Opry Regulars," *Nashville Banner*, March 10, 1970; David C. Morton, with Charles K. Wolfe, *DeFord Bailey, etc.* (1991); Phyllis Martin, "Porter Wagoner Catches Disco Fever, Takes James Brown to the Grand Old Opry, and Sues Dolly Parton," *Country Music*, May, 1979; Bill Hance, "Wax Fax: Porter Attuned to Changing Times," *Nashville Banner*, March 23, 1979; Ramblin' Rhodes, "Opry a Highlight for James Brown," Augusta, Georgia, *Herald*, February 3, 1980.

Chapter 45: Complaints filed in Chancery Court, Davidson County, Tennessee: No. 77-500-I, Bill Earl Owens vs. Dolly Parton, Owepar Publishing Company, and Porter Wagoner, March 24, 1977; No. 79-478-III, Porter Wagoner and Owepar Publishing Company, vs. Dolly Parton Dean, et al., March 13, 1979; Laura Eipper, "Porter Bears

No Ill Will But Sees Long Bout with Dolly," *The Tennessean*, March 23, 1979; Bill Hance, "Wagoner's Attorneys Seek Parton Default," *Nashville Banner*, June 9, 1979; Mike Pigott, "Dolly Charges Porter Mismanaged Studio," *Nashville Banner*, June 18, 1979; "Will Dolly Be Singing in the Slammer?" *National Law Review*, August 27, 1979; Kirk Loggins, "Dolly, Porter Agree to Settlement," *The Tennessean*, November 15, 1979.

Chapter 46: "Wagoner Names New Business Manager," *Top Billing Gazette*, February, 1979; "Porter Wagoner to Tape 26 Shows," *Nashville Banner, June ?, 1979*; Robert K. Oermann, "Hank Snow Offers a Word to the Wise," *The Tennessean*, June 4, 1987; Dick Wolff, "Trio's Idea Sounds Good," *Nashville Banner*, February 24, 1981; Larry E. Williams, "Bristol My Kind of People: Wagoner," South Bend, Indiana, *Tribune*, December 6, 1981; [studio sale:] *The Tennessean*, March 27, 1982; Alan Cackett, "The Country Stalwart Who Created Fresh Impetus in the 70s," *Country Music People*, April, 1982; " 'Opry' Means Only One Thing, Country Stars Testify," *The Tennessean*, July 4, 1982; Tom Carter, "Porter Wagoner, Country Music Prophet Who Never Strayed," *Tulsa World*, August 8, 1982; Boris Zmijewsky and Lee Pfeiffer, *The Films of Clint Eastwood* (1988); Red O'Donnell, "Porter Has a Laugh at Taxing Experience," *Nashville Banner*, January 13, 1983; Jim Bessman, "Talent on Stage," *Cash Box*, April 1, 1983.

Chapter 47: Trisha Walker, "Porter Wagoner," *Country Music People*, August, 1984; Edith Brower, "Is the Musical Idea Masculine?" *Atlantic Monthly*, March, 1894; Red O'Donnell, "Opry's Ernest Tubb Dies of Emphysema," *Nashville Banner*, September 6, 1984; Sandy Neese, "Opry Spotlight: Porter Wagoner Wows 'Em on Canadian Goodwill Tour," *The Tennessean*, November 2, 1984; Bruce Honick, "The One-Man All Women Band," *National Examiner*, March 12, 1985; Robert K. Oermann, reviews, *Music Row*, April, 1984 and (undated) 1986; Thomas Goldsmith, "Porter Wagoner Keeps All the Bases Covered," *The Tennessean*, March 20, 1986.

Chapter 48: Ralph H. Compton, "Opry Traditionalists Out," Nashville *Banner*, April 29, 1985.

Chapter 49: Carter Moody, "The Black and the Red Ink—Facts, Figures, and Comments—Nashville Studios," *Music Row*, April, 1983; Robert K. Oermann, "DJs No Longer the Focus of Music Week Limelight," *The Tennessean*, October 14, 1984; John Lomax III, "Trouble in Paradise," *Music Row*, August, 1985; Diane Bartley, "Viacom Brings Broadway to Nashville," *The Tennessean*, October 21, 1982; Greg Bailey, "Hall Says TNN Is a Driving Force, etc.," *Nashville Banner*, June 17, 1985; Chris Bell and Jim Ridley, 'Can Hee-Haw Be Saved?" *Nashville Scene*, October 3, 1991; Joe Edwards, "RCA's Head Does Everything But 'Sweep Up'," *Nashville Banner*, June 26, 1987; Thomas Goldsmith, "Porter to Saddle His Namesake," *The Tennessean*, April 13, 1990; "A Sideman Tells His Story: Story on Hank Corwin," *Country Song Roundup*, June, 1971.

Chapter 50: Kathleen Windsor, "Dolly Warns Governor to Deliver on Education," *Nashville Banner*, March 28, 1990; Sheila Wissner, "From Humiliation Comes Inspiration," *The Tennessean*, March 28, 1990; Edward Morris, "Country: Porter, Dolly Stage Reunion," *Billboard*, May 13, 1989, and "Country Ramblings," *International Musician*, June, 1989.

Chapter 51: Jeanette C. Rudy, *A Bend in the Cumberland* (1991); Carrie Ferguson, "It's Chistmastime on Broadway," *The Tennessean*, December 1, 1991; Complaint for Divorce, Ruth Olive Williams vs. Porter Wayne Wagoner, Davidson County, Tennessee, March 11, 1966, Docket No. 860713—Final Decree, December 8, 1986, No. 860-713; Kirk Loggins, "Wagoner's Marriage Dissolved," November 27, 1986; Roger Hitts, "I Turned Dolly Parton into a Winner—and Made a Loser Out of Me," *Star*, March 12, 1991; Robert K. Oermann, "Country Stars to Co-Star in Upcoming Film Project," *The Tennessean*, May 27, 1991; [Lazy Jim Day:] Linnell Gentry, *A History and Encyclopedia of Country, Western, and Gospel Music* (rev. ed., 1969).

DISCOGRAPHY

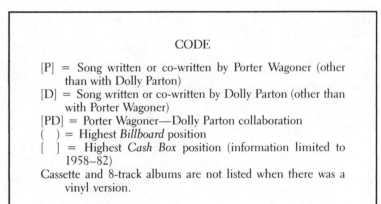

CODE

[P] = Song written or co-written by Porter Wagoner (other than with Dolly Parton)
[D] = Song written or co-written by Dolly Parton (other than with Porter Wagoner)
[PD] = Porter Wagoner—Dolly Parton collaboration
( ) = Highest *Billboard* position
[ ] = Highest *Cash Box* position (information limited to 1958–82)
Cassette and 8-track albums are not listed when there was a vinyl version.

I. RCA SINGLES
[Prefix 20 signifies 78 rpm; 47 signifies 45 rpm]

A. Solo Singles

Settin' the Woods on Fire/Headin' for a Weddin' [P], 20-4996, *1952*
I Can't Live With You (I Can't Live Without You)/Takin' Chances, 20/47-5086, *1953*
Don't Play That Sing/That's It [P], 20/47-5215, *1953*
Trademark [P]/A Beggar For Your Love, 20/47-5330, *1953*
Bringing Home the Bacon/An Angel Made of Ice, 20/47-5430, *1953*
Dig That Crazy Moon! [P]/The Flame of Love, 20/47-5527, *1953*
Trinidad [P]/Bad News Travels Fast, 20/47-5631, *1954*
Love At First Sight [P]/Be Glad You Ain't Me [P], 20/47-5754, *1954*
Company's Comin' (7)/Tricks of the Trade, 20/47-5848, *1954*
Hey, Maw/How Quick, 20/47-6030, *1955*
A Satisfied Mind (1)/Itchin' for My Baby [P], 20/47-6105, *1955*
Eat, Drink and Be Merry (Tomorrow You'll Cry) (3)/Let's Squiggle, 20/47-6289, *1955*

442

What Would You Do (If Jesus Came to Your House)? (8)/How Can You Refuse Him Now?, 20/47-6421, 1956
Uncle Pen (14)/How I've Tried, 20/47-6494, 1956
Tryin' to Forget the Blues (11)/I've Known You From Somewhere, 20/47-6598, 1956
A Good Time Was Had by All/Seeing Her Only Reminded Me of You, 20/47-6697, 1956
I'm Day Dreamin' Tonight/I Should Be with You, 20/47-6803, 1957
Good Mornin', Neighbor/Who Will He Be? 20/47-6844, 1957 [withdrawn February 27, 1957, according to Richard Weize, Bear Family Records]
I Thought I Heard You Call My Name (11)/Pay Day, 20/47-6964, 1957
Doll Face/Your Love [P], 20/47-7073, 1957
As Long As I'm Dreaming/Turn It Over in Your Mind, 20/47-7158, 1958
Heaven's Just a Prayer Away/Tomorrow We'll Retire, 20/47-7199, 1958
Tell Her Lies and Feed Her Candy/Haven't You Heard? [25], 47- 7279, 1958
Dear Lonesome [26]/Just Before Dawn, 47/7374, 1958
Me and Fred and Joe and Bill (29)/Out of Sight, Out of Mind, 47-7457, 1959
I'm Gonna Sing/I Thought of God, 47-7532, 1959
Our Song of Love/The Battle of Little Big Horn, 47-7568, 1959
The Girl Who Didn't Need Love [includes Dottie West vocal] (26) [30]/Your Kind of People, 47-7638, 1959
Legend of the Big Steeple [21]/Wakin' Up the Crowd, 47-7708, 1960
Falling Again (26) [39]/An Old Log Cabin for Sale (30), 47-7770, 1960
Your Old Love Letters (10) [7]/Heartbreak Affair, 47-7837, 1961
Everything She Touches Gets the Blues [43]/Sugarfoot Rag, 47-7901, 1961
Misery Loves Company (1) [1]/I Cried Again, 47-7967, 1961
Cold, Dark Waters (10) [11]/Ain't It Awful, 47-8026, 1962
I've Enjoyed As Much of This As I Can Stand (7) [3]/One Way Ticket to the Blues, 47-8105, 1962
My Baby's Not Here (In Town Tonight) (20) [15]/In the Shadows of the Wine (29) [9], 47-8178, 1962
Find Out/Howdy, Neighbor, Howdy (19) [7], 47-8257, 1963
The Life of the Party/Sorrow on the Rocks (5) [1], 47-8338, 1964
I'll Go Down Swinging (11) [4]/Country Music Has Gone to Town, 47-8432, 1964
I'm Gonna Feed You Now (21) [17]/The Bride's Bouquet, 47-8524, 1965
Green, Green Grass of Home (4) [7]/Dooley, 47-8622, 1965
Skid Row Joe (3) [4]/Love Your Neighbor, 47-8723, 1965
I Just Came to Smell the Flowers (21) [27]/I'm a Long Way from Home, 47-8800, 1966
I Dreamed I Saw America on Her Knees/When I Reach That City [with the Blackwood Brothers], 47-8882, 1966
Ole Slew Foot (48)/Let Me In, 47-8977, 1966
The Cold, Hard Facts of Life (2) [1]/You Can't Make a Heel Toe the Mark, 47-9067, 1967
Julie (15) [8]/Try Being Lonely, 47-9243, 1967
Woman Hungry (24) [15]/Out of the Silence [D], 47-9379, 1967
Be Proud of Your Man (16) [19]/Wino [PD],47-9530, 1968
The Carroll County Accident (2) [1] (No. 92 in pop)/Sorrow Overtakes the Wine, 47-9651, 1968
Big Wind (3) [6]/Tennessee Stud, 74-0168, 1969
When You're Hot, You're Hot (21) [14]/The Answer Is Love [D], 74-0267, 1969
You Got-ta Have a License (41) [31]/Fairchild [D], 47-9802, 1970
Little Boy's Prayer (43) [25]/Roses Out of Season [D], 47-9811, 1970
Jim Johnson (41) [30]/One More Dime [D], 47-9895, 1970
The Last One to Touch Me [D] (18) [13]/The Alley [D], 9939, 1971
Charley's Picture (15) [10] (No. 116 in pop)/Simple As I Am [D], 47-9979, 1971
Be a Little Quieter [P] (11) [9]/Watching [P], 48-1007, 1971

The Rubber Room [P] [43]/The Late Love of Mine [P], 74-0581, 1971
What Ain't to Be, Just Might Happen [P] (8) [6]/Little Bird [D], 74-0648, 1972
A World Without Music [P] (14) [14]/Denise Mayree [P], 74-0753, 1972
Katy Did [P] (16) [9]/Darlin' Debra Jean [P], 74-0820, 1972
Lightening the Load [P] (54) [43]/Tomorrow Is Forever [D], APBO-0923, 1973
Wake Up, Jacob [P] (37) [42]/Stella, Dear Sweet Stella [D], APBO-0013, 1973
George Leroy Chickashea [P] (43) [51]/Cassie [D], APBO-0187, 1973
Tore Down [P] (46) [67]/Nothing Between [P], APBO-0233, 1974
Highway Headin' South [P] (15) [29]/Freida [D], APBO-0328, 1974
Carolina Moonshiner [D] (19) [26]/Not a Cloud in the Sky [P], PB-10124, 1974
Just for the Lonely Ones [P] [65]/It's My Time (To Say I Love You) [P], PB-10281, 1975
Indian Creek [P] (96)/Thank You for the Happiness [P], PB-10411, 1975
When Lea Jane Sang [P] (66) [60]/Storm of Love [P], PB-10803, 1976
I Haven't Learned a Thing [with "guest vocalist" Merle Haggard] (76) [54]/Hand Me
    Down My Walking Cane, PB-10974, 1977
Mountain Music [D] (64) [58]/A Natural Wonder [P], PB-11186, 1978
I'm Going to Feed 'Em Now [P] (31)/Ole Slew Foot (31), PB-11411, 1978 [both sides a
    reissue]
I Want to Walk You Home (34)/Old Love Letters, PB-11491, 1979
Everything I've Always Wanted (32) [34]/No Bed of Roses, PB-11671, 1979
Hold on Tight [P] (64) [57]/Someone Just Like You, PB-11771, 1979
Is It Only 'Cause You're Lonely? [P] (84)/When She Was Mine, PB-11998, 1980

Gold Standard Series Reissues

What Would You Do (If Jesus Came to Your House)?/How Can You Refuse Him Now?
    447-0416.
A Satisfied Mind/Eat, Drink and Be Merry, 447-0417
Sorrow on the Rocks/Misery Loves Country, 447-0714
Green, Green Grass of Home/The Cold, Hard Facts of Life, 447-0786
The Carroll County Accident/When You're Hot, You're Hot, 447-0846
The Rubber Room [P]/Be a Little Quieter [P], 447-0932
What Ain't to Be, Just Might Happen [P]/A World Without Music [P], 447-0947

B. Duet Singles with Dolly Parton

The Last Thing on My Mind (7) [7]/Love Is Worth Living [D], 9369, 1967
Holding On to Nothin' (7) [7]/Just Between You and Me, 47-9490, 1968
We'll Get Ahead Someday (5) [9]/Jeannie's Afraid of the Dark [D] (51) [55], 47-9577,
    1968
Yours, Love (9) [10]/Malena [D], 74-0104, 1969
Always, Always (16) [9]/No Reason to Hurry Home [D], 74-0172, 1969
Just Someone I Used to Know (5) [3]/My Hands Are Tied, 74-0247, 1969
Tomorrow Is Forever [D] (9) [10]/Mendy Never Sleeps [D], 47-9799, 1970
Daddy Was an Old Time Preacher Man [D] (7) [7]/A Good Understanding [D], 9875,
    1970
Better Move It on Home (7) [6]/Two of a Kind [PD], 9958, 1970
The Right Combination [P] (14) [11] (No. 106 in pop)/The Pain of Loving You [PD],
    47-9994, 1971
Burning the Midnight Oil [P] (11) [5]/More Than Words Can Tell [P], 74-0565, 1971
Lost Forever in Your Kiss [D] (9) [5]/The Fog Has Lifted [P], 0675, 1972
Together Always [D] (14) [8]/Love's All Over [P], 74-0773, 1972

We Found It [D] (30) [20]/Love Have Mercy on Us [D], 74-0893, *1973*
If Teardrops Were Pennies (3) [3]/Come to Me [D], 74-0981, *1973*
Here Comes the Freedom Train/All Aboard [P] [Porter solo], [no number], *1973* [Recorded at RCA for the American Freedom Train Foundation]
Please Don't Stop Loving Me [PD] (1) [2]/Sounds of Nature [PD], PB-10010, *1974*
Say Forever You'll Be Mine [D] (5) [1]/How Can I Help You Forgive Me? [P], PB-10328, *1975*
Is Forever Longer Than Always? (8) [9]/If You Say I Can, PB-10652, *1976*
Making Plans (2) [3]/Beneath the Sweet Magnolia Tree [D], PB-11983, *1980*
If You Go, I'll Follow You [PD] (12) [11]/Hide Me Away [D], PB-12119, *1980*

Gold Standard Series Reissues

Just Someone I Used to Know/Daddy Was an Old Time Preacher Man [D], 447-0860
Holding On to Nothin'/Just Between You and Me, 447-0899
We'll Get Ahead Someday/Jeannie's Afraid of the Dark [D], 447-0900
The Right Combination [P]/Burning the Midnight Oil [P], 447-0923
Lost Forever In Your Kiss [D]/Together Always [D], 447-0952
Please Don't Stop Loving Me [PD]/Sounds of Nature [PD], GB-10506
Say Forever You'll Be Mine [D]/How Can I Help You Forgive Me? [P], GB-10675

II. NON-RCA SINGLES

I'm So Lonesome I Could Cry, [Fireside] SO-17149, *1981* [disc jockey sample "with Jimmy Sturr & His Orchestra"]
Ole Slew Foot (one side only), [Fireside] SO-17273, *1981* ["Porter Wagoner and the Wagon Masters"]
Turn the Pencil Over (52) [52]/Johnny Gimble and the Texas Moonlight Waltz, [Viva] 7-29875, 1982
That Was Then, This Is Now/Bottom of the Fifth [P], [Viva] 7-29596, 1983
This Cowboy's Hat, (35)/She Don't Have a License to Drive Me Up The Wall, [Viva] 7-29772, 1983
Johnny's Christmas Tree/Happy Birthday, Jesus [P], CBO 144, 1984
I'm Alive and Well/Dixie Breakdown, [Fireside] SO-17521 [color pictorial sleeve: "Porter Wagoner and his All Girl Band"], 1984

III. RCA (AND CAMDEN) ALBUMS
[LPM = monaural; LPS = stereo; CAL = Camden monaural; CAS = Camden stereo]

A. Solo Albums (including live road-show albums)

Satisfied Mind (1956), LPM-1358. *Side One*: A Satisfied Mind; My Bonfire; Ivory Tower; Company's Comin'; Born to Lose. *Side Two*: Midnight; That's It [P]; I Guess I'm Crazy; I'm Stepping Out Tonight; Living in the Past; Tricks of the Trade. [Reissues: Japanese, RPL-2048 (1985); Stetson, HAT-3064 (1988)]
A Slice of Life—Songs Happy 'n' Sad (1962), LPM/LSP-2447. Produced by Chet Atkins and Anita Kerr. *Side One*: Uncle Pen; One Way Ticket to the Blues; My Name Is Mud; I Thought I Heard You Calling My Name; Tennessee Border; I Went Out of My Way. *Side Two*: Sugarfoot Rag; Cryin' Loud; Misery Loves Company; I Gotta Find Someone (Who Loves Like I Do); Take Good Care of Her; I Wonder Where You Are Tonight.

Porter Wagoner and Skeeter Davis Sing Duets (1962), LPM/LSP-2529. Produced by Chet Atkins. *Side One*: Rock-a-Bye Boogie; Have I Told You Lately That I Love You?; Above and Beyond; Heaven Help Me; A Little Bitty Tear; Sorrow's Tearing Down the House (That Happiness Built). *Side Two*: Gonna Find Me a Bluebird; Violet and a Rose; There's Always One (Who Loves a Lot); We Could; My Greatest Weakness; Anymore. [Reissue: RCA Barbados (1984)]

The Porter Wagoner Show (1963), LPM/LSP-2650. Produced by Chet Atkins. *Side One*: Company's Comin'; I've Enjoyed As Much of This As I Can Stand; Silver Threads and Golden Needles (Norma Jean); I'll Take a Chance on Loving You (Porter and Norma); What Would You Do (If Jesus Came to Your House)?; Bill Bailey (instrumental). *Side Two*: Tell Her Lies and Feed Her Candy; Medley: Poor Old Hardluck Joe (Curly Harris); A Satisfied Mind; I Want to Live Again (Norma Jean); It Keeps Right on A-Hurtin' (Norma Jean); The Family Bible.

A Satisfied Mind (1963), CAL-769(e). *Side One*: A Satisfied Mind; Born to Lose; I Can't Live With You (I Can't Live Without You); Ivory Tower; Settin' the Woods on Fire; I'm Stepping Out Tonight. *Side Two*: Company's Comin'; I Like Girls; Your Love [P]; As Long As I'm Dreaming; Midnight; Eat, Drink and Be Merry (Tomorrow You'll Cry). [CAS-769 (1966)]

Y'All Come (1963), LPM/LSP-2706. Produced by Chet Atkins. *Side One*: Y'All Come; I Wanna Go Home; Crying My Heart Out Over You; Company's Comin'; Don't Let Me Cross Over; Angel Band. *Side Two* Come On In; Pick Me Up on Your Way Down; Shutters and Boards; Bad News Travels Fast; There's a Rainbow in Every Teardrop; Be Careful of Stones That You Throw.

3 Country Gentlemen [Hank Locklin, Hank Snow, Porter Wagoner], LPM/LSP-2723. Produced by Anita Kerr. False True Lovers; They Listened While You Said Goodbye; Keepers of the Key; Eat, Drink, and Be Merry.

Porter Wagoner in Person (1964), LPM/LSP-2840. Produced by Chet Atkins. *Side One*: Howdy, Neighbor, Howdy; Misery Loves Company; Head over Heels in Love with You (Norma Jean); I Didn't Mean It (Norma Jean); Foggy Mountain Top; Sweet Fern (Speck Rhodes); medley; Sally Goodin' (Jack Little instrumental). *Side Two*: Come On In; My Baby's Not Here (In Town Tonight); Talk Back Trembling Lips (Norma Jean); Private Little World; Comedy (Speck Rhodes); Find Out; An Old Log Cabin for Sale; John Henry (Jack Little instrumental).

The Blue Grass Story (1965), LPM/LSP-2960. Produced by Chet Atkins and Bob Ferguson. *Side One*: Country Music Has Gone to Town; Blue Moon of Kentucky; Will You Be Lovin' Another Man; Little Cabin Home in the Hills; Uncle Pen; I'll Meet You in Church Sunday Morning. *Side Two*: Howdy, Neighbor, Howdy; Before I Met You; Cotton Fields; I Wonder How the Old Folks Are at Home; Head Over Heels in Love With You. [Reissue: Stetson, HAT-3133 (1989)]

An Old Log Cabin For Sale (1965), CAS-861(e). *Side One*: An Old Log Cabin For Sale; Dear Lonesome; Your Love [P]; Hey, Maw!; Our Song of Love. *Side Two*: Everything She Touches Gets the Blues; The Battle of Little Big Horn; Tomorrow We'll Retire; Let's Squiggle; Me and Fred and Joe and Bill.

The Thin Man from West Plains (1965), LPM/LSP-3389. Produced by Chet Atkins. *Side One*: Another Day, Another Dollar; Lovin' Lies; I'm Gonna Feed You Now; My Friends Are Gonna Be Strangers; Tomorrow We'll Retire; Sorrow on the Rocks. *Side Two*: My Baby Turns the Lights on Uptown; The Bride's Bouquet; Dim Lights, Thick Smoke and Loud Music; I Couldn't Care Less; Memories from the Past; I'll Go Down Swinging. [Reissue: Stetson, HAT-3099 (1989)]

"Your Old Love Letters" and Other Country Hits (1966), CAL-942/CAS-942(e). *Side One*: Your Old Love Letters; Tryin' to Forget the Blues; Pay Day; I Should Be With You; Heartbreak Affair. *Side Two*: Out of Sight Out of Mind; Seeing Her Only Reminded

Me of You; Tell Her Lies and Feed Her Candy; Bad News Travels Fast; Haven't You
Heard?

The Grand Ole Gospel [with the Blackwood Brothers Quartet] (1966), LPM/LSP-3488.
Produced by Chet Atkins. *Side One*: When I Reach That City; Hide Me, Rock of
Ages; The Family Who Prays (Never Shall Part); My Last Two Tens; If We Never
Meet Again; Good Mornin' Neighbor. *Side Two*: Trouble in the Amen Corner;
There's a Higher Power; I See A Bridge; I'm Using My Bible for a Road Map; House
of Gold; Wait a Little Longer, Please, Jesus.

On the Road—The Porter Wagoner Show (1966), LPM/LSP-3509. Produced by Chet
Atkins. *Side One*: One Way Ticket to the Blues; I Wouldn't Buy a Used Car from
Him (Norma Jean); A Violet and a Rose (Porter and Norma); Turkey in the Straw
(Mack Magaha and Buck Trent instrumental); The Little Shirt Mother Made For Me
(Speck Rhodes); Old Camp Meeting; Where the Old Red River Flows (George
McCormick); Sally Goodin'(Mack Magaha and Buck Trent instrumental). *Side Two*:
Country Music Has Gone to Town; medley; Let's Go All the Way (Norma Jean);
Camptown Races (George McCormick); Don't Ever Take No For An Answer (Speck
Rhodes); Green, Green Grass of Home; Katy Hill (Mack Magaha and Buck Trent
instrumental).

The Best of Porter Wagoner (1966), LSP-3560(e). *Side One*: Y'All Come; Sorrow on the
Rocks; Misery Loves Company; I've Enjoyed As Much of This As I Can Stand;
Green, Green Grass of Home; Company's Comin'. *Side Two*: A Satisfied Mind;
Dooley; I Thought I Heard You Call My Name; Uncle Pen; Skid Row Joe; I'll Go
Down Swinging.

Confessions of a Broken Man (1966), LPM/LSP-3593. Produced by Bob Ferguson and
Chet Atkins. *Side One*: Men with Broken Hearts; I Just Came to Smell the Flowers;
May You Never Be Alone; Skid Row Joe; Take Me Back Home and Try Me One
More Time; How Far Down Can I Go? *Side Two*: I'm a Long Way from Home;
Confessions of a Broken Man; My Tears Are Overdue; I've Been Down That Road
Before; Thy Burdens Are Greater Than Mine; My Last Two Tens.

I'm Day Dreamin' Tonight (1967), CAL-2116/CAS-2116(e). *Side One*: I'm Day Dreamin'
Tonight; Living in the Past; Be Glad You Ain't Me [P]; Cold, Dark Waters; Your Kind
of People. *Side Two*: Trademark [P]; That's It [P]; Bringing Home the Bacon; Takin'
Chances; Dig That Crazy Moon! [P].

Soul of a Convict and Other Great Prison Songs (1967), LPM/LSP-3683. Produced by Bob
Ferguson. *Side One*: Boston Jail; The Convict and the Rose; I Relived My Life Today;
I'm Just Here to Get My Baby Out of Jail; Let Me In; The Big River Train. *Side Two*:
The Snakes Crawl at Night; They're All Going Home But One; Folsom Prison Blues;
Soul of a Convict; Green, Green Grass of Home; I Heard That Lonesome Whistle.

The Cold, Hard Facts of Life (1967), LSP/LPM-3797. Produced by Bob Ferguson. *Side
One*: The First Mrs. Jones; Words and Music; The Cold, Hard Facts of Life; Sleep;
Hundred Dollar Funeral; If I Could Only Start Over. *Side Two*: Tragic Romance; Try
Being Lonely; I'll Get Ahead Some Day; I Just Can't Let You Say Goodbye; Shop-
worn; Julie.

More Grand Ole Gospel [with the Blackwood Brothers Quartet] (1967), LPM/LSP-3855.
Produced by Bob Ferguson. *Side One*: Where No One Stands Alone; Rank Strangers;
You're Not Home Yet; Lord, Let Me Build a Cabin in Glory; There'd Be No Need
for a Heaven; Where the Soul Never Dies. *Side Two*: Beautiful Wings; God Walks
These Hills With Me; Day of Wrath; God's Wonderful Way; I'll Fly Away; Thirty
Pieces of Silver.

Green, Green Grass of Home (1967), CAL/CAS-2191. *Side One*: Green, Green Grass of
Home; Ole Slew-Foot; Eat, Drink and Be Merry (Tomorrow You'll Cry); Stranger's
Story; False True Lover. *Side Two*: You Can't Make a Heel Toe the Mark; The Man in

the Little White Suit; The Keeper of the Key; They Listened While You Said Goodbye; I Dreamed I Saw America on Her Knees.

The Bottom of the Bottle (1968), LPM/LSP-3968. Produced by Bob Ferguson. *Side One*: Wino [PD]; Daddy and the Wine; Swinging Doors; The Bottom of the Bottle; In the Shadows of the Wine; She Burnt the Little Roadside Tavern Down. *Side Two*: The Bottle Let Me Down; One Dime for the Wine; Wine; Turn the Juke Box Up; I Threw Away the Rose; Bottle, Bottle.

Porter Wagoner and the Blackwood Brothers Quartet in Gospel Country (1968), LSP-4034. Produced by Bob Ferguson. *Side One*: I'm Going That Way; Lord, I'm Coming Home; Pastor's on Vacation; Canaan's Land; Dreaming of a Little Cabin; If Jesus Came to Your House. *Side Two*: I'll Meet You in Church Sunday Morning; Mama's Bible; The Finer Taste of Man; The Wings of a Dove; Suppertime; From the Cradle to the Grave.

The Carroll County Accident (1969), LSP-4116. Produced by Bob Ferguson. *Side One*: The World Needs a Washin'; Banks of the Ohio; Sing Me Back Home; Barefoot Nellie; Sorrow Overtakes the Wine; Black Jack's Bar. *Side Two*: The Carroll County Accident; Rocky Top; Your Mother's Eyes; King of the Cannon County Hills; I Lived So Fast and Hard [D]; Fallen Leaves.

Country Feeling (1969), CAS-2321. *Side One*: Country Music Has Gone to Town; Blue Moon of Kentucky; Wakin' Up the Crowd; Legend of the Big Steeple; Will You Be Lovin' Another Man? *Side Two*: Head Over Heals in Love with You; Falling Again; Doll Face; Just Before Dawn; Little Cabin Home in the Hills.

Eddy Arnold, Bobby Bare, Don Gibson, Hank Snow, Porter Wagoner Sing Popular Songs (1969), CAS-2333. Cotton Fields; Uncle Pen.

Me and My Boys (1969), LSP-4181. Produced by Bob Ferguson. *Side One*: My Boys[P]; Tennessee Stud; Big Wind; What I'd Give to Hear a Baby Cry; Through This World of Mine; Peace on Earth Begins Today. *Side Two*: My Ramblin' Boy; A Picture from Life's Other Side; Shuckin' Corn; House of Shame[D]; He's a Go Getter [D]; I Couldn't Wait Forever [D].

You Got-ta Have a License (1970), LSP-4286. Produced by Bob Ferguson. *Side One*: When You're Hot, You're Hot; The Way He Said Your Name; Roses Out of Season [D]; Southern Bound; Fairchild [D]; My Special Prayer Request. *Side Two*: You Got-ta Have a License; Stranger's Story; Forty Miles from Poplar Bluff; Little Boy's Prayer; Walk On, Fool.

Howdy, Neighbor, Howdy (1970), CAS-2409. Produced by Bob Ferguson. *Side One*: Howdy, Neighbor, Howdy; I Wonder How the Old Folks Are at Home; Blue Moon of Kentucky; Cotton Fields; A Gathering in the Sky. *Side Two*: Country Music Has Gone to Town; Head Over Heels in Love with You; Before I Met You; Little Cabin Home in the Hills.

The Best of Porter Wagoner, Volume II (1970), LSP-4321. Produced by Bob Ferguson. *Side One*: The Cold, Hard Facts of Life; Big Wind; Little Boy's Prayer; I Couldn't Wait Forever; Men with Broken Hearts; Ole Slew-Foot. *Side Two*: The Carroll County Accident; You Got-ta Have a License; When You're Hot, You're Hot; Banks of the Ohio; Pastor's Absent on Vacation. [Reissued as *The Best of Porter Wagoner* in the United Kingdom by BMG-RCA, LSA-3006, 1974.]

Skid Row Joe—Down in the Alley (1970), CAS-4386. Produced by Bob Ferguson. *Side One*: Here's a Toast to Mama; Sidewalks of Chicago; The Silent Kind [P]; The Alley[D]; The Town Drunk. *Side Two*: Mama; Bottle of Wine; One More Dime [D]; I Judged a Man; When I Drink My Wine [D].

Simple As I Am (1971), CAS-4508. Produced by Bob Ferguson. *Side One*: The Funky Grass Band; That's How I Learn to Love; My Many Hurried Southern Trips [PD]; Jim Johnson; The Answer Is Love [D]. *Side Two*: Charley's Picture, The Last One to

Touch Me [D]; Simple As I Am [D]; The Fire's Still Burning [D]; Malinda [D].

Porter Wagoner Country (1971), Camden 2478. *Side One*: Out of the Silence (Came a Song) [D]; Be Proud of Your Man; I Guess I'm Crazy; I Haven't Seen Mary in Years; I've Enjoyed as Much of This As I Can Stand. *Side Two*: I Went Out of My Way; I Gotta Find Someone (Who Loves Like I Do); I'll Meet You in Church Sunday Morning; Tricks of the Trade; I Wonder Where You Are Tonight.

Porter Wagoner Sings His Own (1971), LSP-4586. Produced by Bob Ferguson. *Side One*: Be a Little Quieter [P]; Watching [P]; Albert Erving [P]; The Agony of Waiting [P], Late at Night [P]. *Side Two*: The Late Love of Mine [P]; Lonely Comin' Down [P]; The Way I See You [P]; Brother Harold Dee [P]; How High Is the Mountain [P].

Blue Moon of Kentucky (1971), CXS-9010 [Camden]. *Side One*: Blue Moon of Kentucky; Country Music Has Gone to Town; An Old Log Cabin for Sale; I Wonder How the Old Folks Are at Home; Little Cabin Home in the Hills. *Side Two*: Green, Green Grass of Home; Born to Lose; Ivory Tower; A Satisfied Mind. *Side Three*: Company's Comin'; Howdy, Neighbor, Howdy; Eat, Drink and Be Merry (Tomorrow You'll Cry); Heartbreak Affair; Your Old Love Letters. *Side Four*: The Battle of Little Big Horn; The Man in the Little White Suit; Bringing Home the Bacon; I'm Day Dreamin' Tonight. [Reissue: Camden/Picknick, same number, 1975.]

What Ain't to Be, Just Might Happen (1972), LSP-4661. Produced by Bob Ferguson. *Side One*: What Ain't to Be, Just Might Happen[P]; Waldo the Weirdo [P]; The Rubber Room [P]; If I Lose My Mind [P]; Comes and Goes [P]. *Side Two*: I Found a Man [P]; More Than Words Can Tell [P]; Little Bird [D]; Sitting in the Shade [D]; Many Kinds of Love [P].

Ballads of Love (1972), LSP-4734. Produced by Bob Ferguson. *Side One*: Ballad of Love [P]; Love, You're So Beautiful Tonight [P]; Denise Mayree [P]; Look What Love Has Done to Me [PD]; The Hands of Love [P]. *Side Two*: Love's Melody [P]; Love's All Over [P]; With You [D]; With You [D]; How Close They Must Be [P]; Together You and I [D].

Experience (1972), LP-4810. Produced by Bob Ferguson. *Side One*: Katy Did [P]; Like You Were Years Ago [P]; Barlow Chapin [P]; Where Does Love Go [P]; With You [D]. *Side Two*: A World Without Music [P]; I've Got Work to Do [D]; Darlin' Debra Jean [P]; I'd Leave It All to Be with You [P]; He's Alone Again Tonight [P].

The Silent Kind (1973), CAS-2588. Produced by Bob Ferguson. *Side One*: The Silent Kind [P]; Roses Out of Season [D]; Uncle Pen; Fairchild [D]; Y'All Come. *Side Two*: One More Dime [D]; The Cold, Hard Facts of Life; Malinda [D]; House of Shame [D].

I'll Keep on Lovin' You (1973), APL1-0142. Produced by Bob Ferguson. *Side One*: Lightening the Load [P]; Keep on Loving You[P]; Stella, Dear Sweet Stella [D]; The Truth or a Lie [D]; Treat Her Kind [P]. *Side Two*: Childhood Playground [P]; Jasper County Law [D]; Can You Tell Me [P]; Talkin' to Myself [D]; Through the Eyes of a Blind Man [P].

The Farmer (1973), APL1-0346. Produced by Bob Ferguson. *Side One*: Conversation [P]; The Farmer [P]; Daddy's Working Boots [D]; My Dad[P]; Moments of Meditation [P]. *Side Two*: Wake Up, Jacob [P]; The County Farm [P]; The Sun Don't Shine (On the Same Dog Every Day) [P]; Country Bo-Bo [P]; Bones [P].

Tore Down (1974), APL1-0496. Produced by Bob Ferguson. *Side One*: Tore Down [P]; The Finish Line [P]; Nothing Between [P]; Cassie [D]; Graduation Day [P]. *Side Two*: Old Black Kettle [D]; George Leroy Chickashea [P]; Somewhere in the Night [P]; I See Love [P]; Happy Faces [P].

Highway Headin' South (1974), APL1-0713. Produced by Bob Ferguson. *Side One*: Life Rides the Train [P]; Freida [D]; Highway Headin' South [P]; Lonelyville [P]; Last Chance for Happiness [P]. *Side Two*: Not a Cloud in the Sky [P]; Holding Lonely

Hands [P]; An Old Memory Gets in My Eye; Lonely Without You [P]; I'll Start Tomorrow [P].

Sing Some Love Songs, Porter Wagoner (1975), APL1-1056. Produced by Porter Wagoner. *Side One*: Just for the Lonely Ones [P]; The Late Love of Mine [P]; She's Everywhere [P]; The Last One to Touch Me [D]; Something to Reach For [D]. *Side Two*: Love with Feeling [P]; This Night [P]; Love to Remember [P]; If I Cross Your Mind [P]; She Left Me Love [P].

Porter (1977), APL1-2432. Produced and arranged by Porter Wagoner. *Side One*: Don't This Road Look Rough and Rocky; Hand Me Down My Walking Cane; Childhood Playground [P]; The Funky Grass Band; Walking in That California Sunshine. *Side Two*: I Haven't Learned a Thing [with Merle Haggard]; The Arizona Whiz; Ruby Jones; Crumbs from Another Man's Table; Old Log Cabin for Sale.

Blue Moon of Kentucky (1977), ACL-7046 [Camden/Pickwick]. *Side One*: Blue Moon of Kentucky; An Old Log Cabin for Sale; I Wonder How the Old Folks Are at Home; The Battle of Little Big Horn. *Side Two*: I'm Day Dreamin' Tonight; Green, Green Grass of Home; Born to Lose; A Satisfied Mind; I've Enjoyed As Much of This As I Can Stand.

The Best of Porter Wagoner (1978), DVL-2-0354 ["RCA Special Products" for I & M Teleproducts]. *Side One*: Highway Headin' South [P]; Misery Loves Company; Cold, Dark Waters; Katy Did [P]; Your Old Love Letters; The Cold, Hard Facts of Life. *Side Two*: The Carroll County Accident; Eat, Drink and Be Merry (Tomorrow You'll Cry); Big Wind; Be a Little Quieter [P]; Charley's Picture. *Side Three*: A Satisfied Mind; Sorrow on the Rocks; Green, Green Grass of Home; I'll Go Down Swinging; What Would You Do (If Jesus Came to Your House)? *Side Four*: I've Enjoyed As Much of This As I Can Stand; The Last One to Touch Me [D]; A World Without Music [P]; Be Proud of Your Man; What Ain't to Be, Just Might Happen [P].

Porter Wagoner Today (1979), AHL1-3210. Produced and arranged by Porter Wagoner. *Side One*: I'm Gonna Feed 'Em Now; Ole Slew Foot; I'm Gonna Act Right; Tennessee Saturday Night; High Country. *Side Two*: Banks of the Ohio; I Couldn't Care Less; I Guess I'm Crazy (For Loving You); Your Old Love Letters; All I Need. [United Kingdom release: RCA-BMG, PL-13210.)

Collector's Series: Porter Wagoner (1985), AHL1-7000. *Side One*: The Carroll County Accident; The Last One to Touch Me [D]; Misery Loves Company; Try Being Lonely; You Got-ta Have a License; Highway Headin' South [P]; Rocky Top. *Side Two*: Your Old Love Letters; A Natural Wonder [P]; Hand Me Down My Walking Cane; What Ain't to Be, Just Might Happen [P]; Ole Slew Foot; Carolina Moonshiner [D].

B. Duet Albums with Dolly Parton

Just Between You and Me (1968), LPM/LSP-3926. Produced by Bob Ferguson. *Side One*: Because One of Us Is Wrong [D]; The Last Thing on My Mind; Love Is Worth Living [D]; Just Between You and Me; Mommie, Ain't That Daddy [D]; Four O Thirty Three. *Side Two*: Sorrow's Tearing Down the House (That Happiness Once Built); This Time Has Gotta Be Our Last Time; Before I Met You; Home Is Where the Hurt Is; Two Sides to Every Story [D]; Put It Off Until Tomorrow [D].

Just the Two of Us (1968), LSP-4039. Produced by Bob Ferguson. *Side One*: Closer by the Hour; I Washed My Face in the Morning Dew; Jeannie's Afraid of the Dark [D]; Holding On to Nothin'; Slip Away; The Dark End of the Street. *Side Two*: Just the Two of Us; Afraid to Love Again; We'll Get Ahead Someday; Somewhere Between; The Party [D]; I Can [D].

Always, Always (1969), LSP-4186. Produced by Bob Ferguson. *Side One*: Milwaukee, Here I Come; Yours, Love; I Don't Believe You've Met My Baby; Malena [D]; The

House Where Love Lives; Why Don't You Haul Off and Love Me? *Side Two*: Always, Always; There Never Was a Time; Good As Gold; My Hands Are Tied [D]; No Reason to Hurry Home [D]; Anything's Better Than Nothing.

Porter Wayne and Dolly Rebecca (1970), LSP-4305. Produced by Bob Ferguson. *Side One*: Forty Miles from Poplar Bluff; Tomorrow Is Forever [D]; Just Someone I Used to Know; Each Season Changes You; We Can't Let This Happen to Us; Mendy Never Sleeps [D]. *Side Two*: Silver Sandals [D]; No Love Left; It Might As Well Be Me [D]; Run That by Me One More Time [D]; I'm Wasting Your Time and You're Wasting Mine [D].

Once More (1970), LSP-4388. Produced by Bob Ferguson. *Side One*: Daddy Was an Old Time Preacher Man [D]; I Know You're Married But I Love You Still; Thoughtfulness; Fight and Scratch [D]; Before Our Weakness Gets Too Strong. *Side Two*: Once More; One Day at a Time; Ragged Angel [D]; A Good Understanding [D]; Let's Live for Tonight.

Two of a Kind (1971), LSP-4490. Produced by Bob Ferguson. *Side One*: Oh, The Pain of Loving You [PD]; Possum Holler; Is It Real? [D]; The Flame [D]; The Fighting Kind [D]. *Side Two*: Two of a Kind [PD]; All I Need Is You; Curse of the Wild Weed Flower [D]; Today, Tomorrow and Forever; There'll Be Love [PD].

The Best of Porter Wagoner & Dolly Parton (1971), LSP-4556. Produced by Bob Ferguson. *Side One*: Just Someone I Used to Know; Daddy Was an Old Time Preacher Man [D]; Tomorrow Is Forever [D]; Jeannie's Afraid of the Dark [D]; The Last Thing on My Mind. *Side Two*: The Pain of Loving You [PD]; Better Move It on Home; Holding On to Nothin'; Run That by Me One More Time [D]; We'll Get Ahead Someday.

The Right Combination—Burning the Midnight Oil (1972), LSP-4628. Produced by Bob Ferguson. *Side One*: More Than Words Can Tell [P]; The Right Combination [P]; I've Been This Way Too Long [D]; In Each Love Some Pain Must Fall [D]; Her and the Car and the Mobile Home. *Side Two*: Burning the Midnight Oil[P]; Somewhere Along the Way [D]; On and On; Through Thick and Thin; The Fog Has Lifted [P].

Together Always (1972), LSP-4761. Produced by Bob Ferguson. *Side One*: Together Always [D]; Love's All Over [P]; Christina [D]; Poor Folks Town [D]. *Side Two*: Ten Four-Over and Out [P]; Lost Forever in your Kiss [D]; Anyplace You Want to Go [P]; Looking Down [P]; You and Me—Her and Him [P].

We Found It (1973), LSP-4841. *Side One*: Love City [P]; Between us [D]; We Found It [P]; Satan's River [P]; I've Been Married (Just As Long As You Have) [PD]. *Side Two*: I Am Always Waiting [D]; Sweet Rachel Ann [D]; That's When Love Will Mean the Most [P]; Love Have Mercy on Us [D]; How Close They Must Be [P].

Love and Music (1973), APL1-0248. Produced by Bob Ferguson. *Side One*: If Teardrops Were Pennies; Sounds of Night [P]; Laugh the Years Away; You [D]; Wasting Love [P]. *Side Two*: Come to Me [D]; Love Is Out Tonight [P]; In the Presence of You [P]; I Get Lonesome by Myself [D]; There'll Always Be Music [D].

Porter 'n' Dolly (1974), APL1-0646 [reissued as APL1-4251]. Produced by Bob Ferguson. *Side One*: Please Don't Stop Loving Me [PD]; The Fire That Keeps You Warm [D]; Too Far Gone [D]; We'd Have to Be Crazy [D]; The Power of Love [P]. *Side Two*: Sixteen Years [P]; Together You and I [D]; Without You [D]; Two [D]; Sounds of Nature [P].

Say Forever You'll Be Mine (1975) APL1-1116. Arranged and produced by Porter Wagoner. *Side One*: Say Forever You'll Be Mine [D]; Something to Reach For [D]; Again [P]; Our Love; The Beginning [D]. *Side Two*: I Have No Right to Care [D]; If You Were Mine; Love to See Us Through; How Can I Help You Forgive Me? [P]; Life Rides the Train [P].

Porter & Dolly (1980), APL1-3700. Produced and arranged by Porter Wagoner. *Side One*: Making Plans; If You Go, I'll Follow You [PD]; Hide Me Away [D]; Someone Just

Like You; Little David's Harp [D]. *Side Two*: Beneath the Sweet Magnolia Tree [D]; Touching Memories [P]; Daddy Did His Best; If You Say I Can [D]; Singing on the Mountain [P].

Sweet Harmony (1982), PDL2-1013. ["RCA Special Products" for Pair Records, Inc.] *Side One*: Together Always [D]; Love's All Over [P]; Christina [D]; Poor Folks Town [D]. *Side Two*: Ten Four–Over and Out [P]; Lost Forever in Your Kiss [D]; Looking Down [P]. *Side Three*: Forty Miles from Poplar Bluff; Tomorrow Is Forever [D]; Just Someone I Used to Know; Each Season Changes You. *Side Four*: Silver Sandals [D]; No Love Left; It Might As Well Be Me [D]; Run That by Me One More Time [D].

C. Extended Play Albums (45 rpm)

Satisfied Mind (1957), EPA-937. *Side One*: A Satisfied Mind; I Like Girls. *Side Two*: Living in the Past; Midnight.

Company's Comin' (1957), EPA-938. *Side One*: Company's Comin'; Born to Lose. *Side Two*: I'm Stepping Out Tonight; I Guess I'm Crazy.

The Blue Grass Story (1965), VLP-2960. *Side One*: Uncle Pen; Blue Moon of Kentucky; Will You Be Lovin' Another Man? *Side Two*: Howdy, Neighbor, Howdy; Cotton Fields; Head Over Heals in Love with You.

The Thin Man from West Plains (1965), VLP-3389. *Side One*: My Baby Turns the Lights on Uptown; Dim Lights, Thick Smoke and Loud Music; I'll Go Down Swinging. *Side Two*: My Friends Are Gonna Be Strangers; Lovin' Lies; Sorrow on the Rocks.

D. Overseas Albums (solo and duet): Partial List.

A Little Slice of Life (1963), RCX-7157 [Canada]. *Side One*: Uncle Pen; I Went Out of My Way; Tennessee Border. *Side Two*: Sugarfoot Rag; I Wonder Where You Are Tonight; Misery Loves Company.

Y'All Come (1963), RCA-7158 [United Kingdom]. *Side One*: Y'All Come; Don't Let Me Cross Over; Company's Comin'. *Side Two*: Come On In; In the Shadows of the Wine; Pick Me Up on Your Way Down.

Porter Wagoner in Person (1964), LPM/LSP-2840 [Germany]. [Fewer songs than the U.S. album of the same number.]

Most Requested (1975), VPL 1-7041 [Australia] [Porter Wagoner and Dolly Parton]. *Side One*: Little Boy's Prayer [Porter solo]; Jeannie's Afraid of the Dark [D] [Dolly solo]; Love Is Like a Butterfly [D] [Dolly solo]; Jolene [D] [Dolly solo]; The Party [D] [duet]; Silver Sandals [D] [Dolly solo]; Charley's Picture [Porter solo]. *Side Two*: Brother Harold Dee [P] [Dolly solo]; Waldo the Weirdo [P] [Porter solo]; Coat of Many Colors [D] [Dolly solo]; Just the Two of Us [duet]; Pastor's Absent on Vacation [Porter solo]; House of Shame [D] [Porter solo]; The Cold, Hard Facts of Life [Porter solo].

The Hits of Porter 'n' Dolly (1976), KEL-1-8095 [Canada]. *Side One*: Better Move It on Home; Just Someone I Used to Know; If Teardrops Were Pennies; Tomorrow Is Forever [D]; We Found It [P]; Yours, Love; Burning the Midnight Oil [P]; Please Don't Stop Loving Me [PD]. *Side Two*: Daddy Was an Old Time Preacher Man [D]; Say Forever You'll Be Mine [D]; The Right Combination [P]; Lost Forever in Your Kiss [D]; How Can I (Help You Forgive Me)? [P]; Always, Always. [United Kingdom release: BMG-RCA, PL-42193, 1977.]

The Hits of Porter Wagoner (1976), KEL-1-8094 [Canada]. *Side One*: Carolina Moonshiner [D]; Tore Down [P]; Nothing Between [P]; What Ain't to Be, Just Might Happen [P]; Katy Did [P]; Be a Little Quieter [P]; A World Without Music [P]; Indian Creek [P]. *Side Two*: Highway Headin' South [P]; Charley's Picture; Wake Up, Jacob [P]; Just for the Lonely Ones [P]; The Last One to Touch Me [D]; Lightening the

Load [P]; George Leroy Chickashea [P]. [Probable United Kingdom Release: BMG-RCA, 42182, 1978.]

20 of the Best (1982), BMG-RCA International INTS-5197 [United Kingdom]. *Side One*: A Satisfied Mind; Your Old Love Letters; The Carroll County Accident; Eat, Drink and Be Merry (Tomorrow You'll Cry); I'll Go Down Swinging; Company's Comin'; Big Wind. *Side Two*: Green, Green Grass of Home; Everything I've Always Wanted; I Just Came to Smell the Flowers; Misery Loves Company; What Ain't to Be Just Might Happen [P]; I've Enjoyed As Much of This As I Can Stand; When Lea Jane Sang [P]; Sorrow on the Rocks; The Cold, Hard Facts of Life. [Reissued 1984: NL-89094.]

IV: NON-RCA ALBUMS (Domestic and Overseas): Partial List

When I Sing for Him (1979), [P & J Productions] 79-1. Produced by Porter Wagoner. *Side One*: Life's Railway to Heaven; Old Camp Meeting; Peace in the Valley; Satan's River [P]; Where the Roses Never Fade. *Side Two*: I Thought of God; I Found a Man [P]; Heaven on My Mind; Just a Rose Will Do; The Bird That Never Flew [P]. *Side Three*: Where Would John Baptize Jesus?; What Would You Do (If Jesus Came to Your House)?; Singing on the Mountain [P]; Satan Gets the Gold [P]; City on the Hill. *Side Four*: Swing Low, Sweet Chariot; Rank Strangers; Trouble in the Amen Corner; When I Sing for Him [P]; Lord, Build Me a Cabin in Glory. [Reissue: Tudor, MHM-100502.]

Porter Wagoner's Greatest (1981), [Tudor Records] MHM-100302. Produced by Porter Wagoner. *Side One*: A Satisfied Mind; Misery Loves Company; Sorrow on the Rocks; Green, Green Grass of Home; Skid Row Joe. *Side Two*: The Cold, Hard Facts of Life; Big Wind; Carroll County Accident; Eat, Drink and Be Merry (Tomorrow You'll Cry); What Would You Do (If Jesus Came to Your House)? [All new versions.]

Not a Cloud in the Sky (1981), [Kaola] KOT-15111 [8-track]. Produced by Porter Wagoner. Slipping Away [P]; Silence in the Wind [P]; Memory Garden [P]; Natural Wonder [P]; Not a Cloud in the Sky [P]; I'll Start Tomorrow [P]; Raining Blues at Midnight [P]; Love with Feeling [P]; Katy Did [P].

A Fool Like Me (1981), [Kaola] KOC-15114 [cassette]. Produced by Porter Wagoner. *Side One*: Willie Bodine; Every Day's Just Like Sunday [P]; Hold on Tight [P]; A Fool Like Me; I'm Looking for Someone to Love. *Side Two*: Happy Birthday, Jesus [P]; Girl with the Blue Velvet Band [P]; Country Bo-Bo [P]; Bones [P]; Enough to Make a Grown Man Cry.

One for the Road (1982), [Fire Records] SO-17055. Produced by Porter Wagoner. *Side One*: The Rose; I'm So Lonesome I Could Cry; Is Anybody Going to San Antone?; Your Lying Blue Eyes; Touching Memories [P]. *Side Two*: You're the One Lesson [P]; Coat of Many Colors [D]; Dooley; You Never Said a Word [P]; When the One You Love Says I Love You [P].

Down Home Country (1982), [Accord] SN-7179. Produced by Porter Wagoner. *Side One*: Angel Band; Baby Linda [P]; Crumbs from Another Man's Table; Can You Tell Me? [P]; When the One You Love Says I Love You [P]. *Side Two*: Devil's Alley [P]; I Can't Be Your Man [P]; I See Love [P]; I Know I'm Gonna Be Loved Tonight; He Really Must Have Loved You [P].

Porter Wagoner (1982), [Country Fidelity] CFX-201. Produced by Porter Wagoner. *Side One*: Country Bobo [P]; Willie Bodine; Enough to Make a Grown Man Cry; Happy Birthday, Jesus [P]; I'm Looking for Someone to Love. *Side Two*: Girl with the Blue Velvet Band [P]; Every Day's Just Like Sunday [P]; Hold on Tight [P]; A Fool Like Me; Bones [P].

The Early Years (ca. 1982), [Music Masters, Ltd.] MM-GS-1027 ("Collector's Series" produced by Porter Wagoner). Produced by Porter Wagoner. *Side One*: I'm Looking for Someone to Love; Girl with the Blue Velvet Band [P]; Every Day's Just Like Sunday [P]; Hold on Tight [P]; A Fool Like Me. *Side Two*: Bones [P]; Country Bobo [P]; Willie Bodine; Enough to Make a Grown Man Cry; Happy Birthday, Jesus [P]. [None of these is an "early" cut.]

Porter Wagoner Special: The Early Years (ca. 1982), [Music Masters, Ltd.] MM-GS-107 ("Collector's Series"). Produced by Porter Wagoner. *Side One*: Katy Did [P]; Memory Garden [P]; Natural Wonder [P]; Treat Her Kind [P]; When Lea Jane Would Sing [P]. *Side Two*: Until the Wind Stops Blowing [P]; The Divers Are Out Tonight [P]; Love with a Feeling [P]; Slipping Away [P]; Silence in the Wind [P]. [Same cover picture but different color than MM-GS-1027; no "early" cuts.]

Natural Wonder (1982), [Heritage Sound Recording Distributors], HSRD-782. *Side One*: My Friend; Natural Wonder [P]; I'll Start Tomorrow [P]; Love With a Feeling [P]; Not A Cloud in the Sky [P]. *Side Two*: Love Shine [P]; Keep on Loving You [P]; It Can Happen Overnight [P]; If You Go, I'll Follow You [P]; Life Rides the Train [P].

A Good Time Was Had By All (ca. 1982), ARTL Country Series [United Kingdom], PM-30006. *Side One*: A Good Time Was Had By All; I Thought I Heard You Call My Name; I've Known You From Somewhere; Good Mornin', Neighbor; I'm Gonna Sing; Who Will He Be? *Side Two*: A Beggar For Your Love; Turn It Over In Your Mind; How Can You Refuse Him Now?; What Would You Do If Jesus Came to Your House?

"Porter's Hits" (ca. 1982), [Romulus Records] A-1843. Produced by Porter Wagoner. *Side One*: Enough to Make a Grown Man Cry; Willie Bodine; Raining Blues at Midnight [P]; When the One You Love Says I Love You [P]; Touching Memories [P]. *Side Two*: When Lea Jane Would Sing [P]; Slipping Away [P]; Memory Garden [P]; Not a Cloud in the Sky [P]; Happy Birthday, Jesus [P].

Soundtrack from the Clint Eastwood Film, Honkytonk Man (1982), [Warner Brothers: Viva] 1-23739. Turn the Pencil Over.

Porter Wagoner "At His Best" (1983), [CBO Records, two discs with different numbers and separate covers, but with the same title and marketed together; accompanied by The Right Combination] CBO-1012. Produced by Porter Wagoner. *Side One*: Green, Green Grass of Home; Ole Slew Foot; Skid Row Joe; I Thought I Heard You Call My Name; Katy Did [P]. *Side Two*: Carroll County Accident; I've Enjoyed As Much of This As I Can Stand; Pick Me Up on Your Way Down; Trouble in the Amen Corner; I'm So Lonesome I Could Cry. CBO-1013. *Side One*: He Stopped Loving Her Today; If You're Going to Do Me Wrong (Do It Right); The Cold, Hard Facts of Life; Your Old Love Letters; A Satisfied Mind. *Side Two*: The Rose; Crying My Heart Out over You; Have I Told You Lately That I Love You?; Misery Loves Company; Is Anybody Goin' to San Antone? [Also on Premier Records, PPD-2005.]

Viva Porter Wagoner (1983), [Warner Brothers: Viva] 1-23783. Produced by Snuff Garrett. *Side One*: This Cowboy's Hat; That Was Then, This Is Now; I Thought I Heard You Call My Name; Living in the Shadows; Heaven, Hell or Macon. *Side Two*: We Can't Stop; Green, Green Grass of Home; His and Hers; Misery Loves Company; Bottom of the Fifth [P].

Porter Wagoner—Country Memories (1983), [SP Records and Tapes] SP-1324 (cassette). Produced by Porter Wagoner. *Side One*: Misery Loves Company; A Satisfied Mind; Eat, Drink and Be Merry; Skid Row; *Side Two*: Green, Green Grass of Home; Carroll County Accident; The Cold, Hard Facts of Life; Big Wind. (A *Country Memories* was released on K-Tel Goldmasters, GM-0215, in Europe in 1984).

Love Shine (1984), [Astan] LP 20115 (German) [USA cassette. Q40115]. *Side One*: Love Shine [P]; "Keep on Loving You" [P]; It Can Happen Overnight [P]; If You Go, I'll

Follow You [P]; Life Rides the Train [P]. *Side Two*: Love Paid It All [P]; Somewhere in the Night [P]; That's When Love Will Mean the Most [P]; Storm of Love [P]; Nothing Between [P].

Porter Wagoner and the Right Combination, (ca. 1984), [no label] R-C-1077 (cassette). Produced by Porter Wagoner. *Side One*: [songs by the band]; Porter singing "A Good Love Died Tonight" and "What a Memory We'd Make." *Side Two*: Katy Did; Green, Green Grass of Home; Carroll County Accident; Trouble in the Amen Corner.

Porter Wagoner (1986), [MCA-Dot Records] MCA-39053. Produced by Fred Newell. *Side One*: One More Time; Love Paid It All [P]; Sugarfoot Rag; For a Good Time, Call Naomi; Louisiana Saturday Night. *Side Two*: The Same Way You Came In; Sorrow on the Rocks; What a Memory We'd Make; Satan Wore Satin; Uncle Pen. [Reissue, cassette, as Sorrow on the Rocks, MCA-20551]

Heartwarming Songs (1990), [Hollywood] HCD-419 (compact disc and cassette). Angel Band; Baby Linda [P]; Crumbs from Another Man's Table; Can You Tell Me? [P]; When the One You Love Says I Love You [P]; Devil's Alley [P]; I Can't Be Your Man [P]; I See Love [P]; I Know I'm Going to Be Loved Tonight; He Really Must Have Loved You.

My Very Best (1990), [no label] PW-1990 (cassette). Produced by Porter Wagoner. *Side One*: The Farmer and the Lord; Supper Time; Skid Row Joe; Be Careful of the Stones You Throw; Trouble in the Amen Corner. *Side Two*: Let's Talk About Love; Moments of Meditation [P]; I Found a Man [P]; If Jesus Came to Your House; The Bird That Never Flew [P].

Porter's Pure Gold (1991), [no label] PW-1991 (cassette). Produced by Porter Wagoner. *Side One*: Carroll County Accident; Green, Green Grass of Home; A Satisfied Mind; The Cold, Hard Facts of Life; I've Enjoyed As Much of This As I Can Stand. *Side Two*: Mother Church [P]; Misery Loves Company; This Cowboy's Hat; The Last One to Touch Me [P].

V. PRODUCER CREDITS ON ALBUMS (excluding Porter, Dolly, Porter–Dolly albums): Partial List of Published Credits Only.

Buck Trent: *Sounds of Now and Beyond* (1972), [RCA] LSP-4705. Produced with Bob Ferguson.

Mack Magaha: *The Dancing Fiddle Man* (1974), [Special Products] Fire-1813; *Mack Magaha Plays Bluegrass Country at Opryland* (1979), [Fireside Studio] SO-15033; *Bluegrass Country Show "Live at Opryland"* (1980), [Fireside Studio] SO-16424 (with Porter as "special guest").

Tony Alamo: *Love Songs for Sue—And You* (ca. 1976), [Alamo Records] 2233. (Porter sings a duet with Tony Alamo on *Mister D.J.* (1977), [Alamo Records] SA-253419.)

Philomena Begley: *Fireside Country—Philomena Begley* (1977), [Top Spin Records (United Kingdom)], TSLP-113.

Howard Lips: *American Hamburger Way* (1978), [Phoenix Records] PXR-136.

Opryland Singers: *Country Music USA* (ca. 1980), [Opryland Records] OP-1002, 63-song medley; *Opryland Presents Country Music USA* (1981), [Opryland Records] OP-1007, 1981 cast album: 62-song medley.

Opryland Gospel Quartet: *Opryland Presents The Opryland Gospel Quartet in Concert* (1981), [Opryland Records] OP-1006.

Joe Simon: *Glad You Came My Way* (1981), [Posse Records] POS-100002.

Melissa Kay: *Porter Wagoner Presents Melissa Kay* (1986), [Reed Records] PRU-1117. Produced with Hank Corwin. (Porter sings on three of the songs.)

Glenda Faye: *"Flatpickin' Favorites"* (1987), [Flying Fish Records] 432. (With introduction by Porter.)

Sources

Alan Fearby, "The Porter Wagoner Story [with discography], *Country News and Views* [United Kingdom], July, October 1967; Von Hauke Strübing and Kurt Rokitta, "Diskografisches," *Country Corner* [Germany], Number 54, May 1977; Number 55, July 1977; Jerry Osborne, *Country Music Buyers-Sellers Reference Book and Price Guide* (1984); George Albert and Frank Hoffman, *The Cash Box Country Singles Chart 1958–1982* (1984); Charles Garrod, ed., *RCA Victor Record Listings 20-1500–20-7300* (1986); Robert K. Oermann, "Dolly Parton: Here She Comes Again" [with discography], *Country Sounds* (May 1987); *Joel Whitburn's Top Country Singles 1944–1988* (1989); Kenneth L. Stewart, unpublished Porter Wagoner discography (1989); Tony Byworth, ed., *Music Master Country Music Catalogue* (1991); Richard Weize, "Porter Wagoner—The Discography" [1952–62 session history] (1992). Special thanks to Hugh Ashley, Craig Baguley, Reimar Binge, Jerry Osborne, Ronnie Pugh, Kenneth L. Stewart, Dale Vinicur, Richard Weize.

ACKNOWLEDGMENTS

The following folks generously provided information, documentation, or otherwise assisted in valuable ways: Linda Anderson (*Ozark Mountain Country Review Magazine*); Beckey Badgett (Fireside Recording Studio); J. Baley; Mario Balma; Jerry Barney; Mike Battiato; Terry Beard; Annette J. Bently (Ralph Foster Museum, The School of the Ozarks); Vicky Bergfeld; Laurel Boeckman (State Historical Society of Missouri); Becky Bowling (Red Wagon Antiques); Joe Butler; Anita Jones Caldwell; A. W. ("Red") Caldwell; Allen Case; Robert Chapin; Harold Cochran; Russ Cochran (*West Plains Gazette*); Dan Cooper (The Great Escape); Everett J. Corbin; Ina Crag; Gary William Crawford; Clyde Foley Cummings; Richard Davis; Earl Dighton; Ernestine Doss (secretary to Howell County Treasurer); Bill Ede; Eunice Eledge (Dollywood Ambassadors); Bob Ensign (Bob's Record Rack, Ozark, Missouri); Anita Evangelista; Marshall L. Falwell, Jr.; Betsy Fisher (Area Resource Center, Metropolitan Nashville Public Library); Randy Fox; Robert C. Glazier (*Springfield! Magazine*); Michael Glenn (Springfield-Green County Library District); Wayne Glenn (Meyer Communications, Inc.); Theresa Hambrick (Tennessee State Library and Archives); Jean Griffith; Stacy Harris; Larry Haschemeyer; Denise C. Jackson; Dave Jeffries (State Historical Society of Missouri); Loudilla Johnson (*Music City News*); Janella Justus; Edward King; Otto Kitsinger; Donna Kolby; Lonnie Lynne LaCour; Jimmy Lancaster; Zela Lawhorn; Debbi Logue (Grand Ole Opry); Fran Lovell (Chancery Court, Nashville); Farrell McCartney; D. A. Majors (Red Wagon Antiques); Frank L. Martin, III (*West Plains Daily Quill*); Angela Meyer (*West Plains Gazette*); Jim Miller (*Country Music, U.S.A.*); Roy Miller (Kand-D Land, Inc.); Bernadette Moore (BMG-RCA, archives); Herman Moore; Terry Morrow (*Mountain Press*, Sevierville); Alanna Nash; Ellis Nassour; Richard Ochoa; Genella Olker (Tennessee State Library and Archives); Mike Payne; Ed Penny; Jon Peterson (Earthquake Records); Jon Philibert (*Country Music People*); Bob Phillips; Gail Pollock (Independent Producer Corporation); Ronnie Pugh (Country Music Foundation Library and Media Center); Buddy Ragan (The Nashville Network); Roger Ramey; Lois Rasmussen; Don Richardson; Earl Richardson; J. W. Riely (Florsheim Shoe Co., West Plains); Bob Robison; Bob Rowland; Elizabeth Schlappi; Al Sherman (Alshire Records); Scott Siman; Millie Sloan; G. Bernard Smith (Howell County Public Schools); Billy Smith (One-Nighters); Doug Smith; Terry S. Smith; Fae Sotham (*Missouri Historical Review*); Reta Spears-Stewart; Kenneth L. Stewart; Darl and Becky Stockum; Jake Stokes; Glenn Sutton; Jeff Tamarkian (*Goldmine*); Rico Tee; Nona Thomas; Laurel Thompson (KWPM); Elizabeth Uhlig (University of Missouri); J. Matthew Van Ryn (BMG-RCA); Dale Vinicur; Jean Wagoner; Ruth Wagoner; Maggie Ward (Fireside Recording Studio); Donna Waskoviak (Sevier County

Schools); Tansy and Dow Wallace; Richard Weize (Bear Family Records); Liz Whitfield; Rick Williams; Charles K. Wolfe; Lorna Wuyts; Ted P. Yeatman; Shirley Younts; Lou Ziegler (*Springfield News-Leader*).

Thanks to the staff of the West Plains, Missouri, library, and to the staffs of the *Nashville Banner* and *The* (Nashville) *Tennessean* libraries; to these publications for running notices and letters: *The New York Times Book Review* ("Author's Query"), *CMA Close-Up, Country Song Roundup, Goldmine*, and *Music City News*; and to my wife, Anne, and daughter, Mary Rose—and Ruth B. White and Lorraine Hall—for reading the manuscript in whole or in part.

Gratitude, as well, to copyeditors Alice Ewing and Nicki Pendleton, for saving me from myself, and especially to the never-impatient Ron Pitkin of Rutledge Hill Press. Verily, the Right Combination!

Permission to utilize copyrighted material is hereby gratefully acknowledged:

"Just Someone I Used to Know," by Jack Clement. Copyright © 1969, Songs of Polygram International, Inc., and Glad Music Co. All Rights Reserved. Used by permission.

"Diamonds and Rust," by Joan Baez. Copyright © 1975, Chandos Music (ASCAP). All Rights Reserved. Used by permission.

"My Boys," by Porter Wagoner. Copyright © 1969, Warden Music, Inc. (BMI). All Rights Reserved. Used by permission.

"Company's Comin'," by Johnny Mullins. Copyright © 1954 Sebanine Music, Inc. All rights administered by Warner-Tamerlane Publishing Corp. All Rights Reserved. Used by permission.

"(There'll Be) Peace in the Valley (For Me)," by Thomas A. Dorsey. Copyright © 1939, Unichappell Music, Inc. All Rights Reserved. Used by permission.

By Porter Wagoner: "The Rubber Room," © 1971; "Late at Night," © 1971; "The Divers Are Out Tonight," © 1972; "Childhood Playground," © 1973; "My Dad," © 1973; "Lightening the Load," © 1973; "Life Rides the Train," © 1973; "The Sun Don't Shine on the Same Dog Every Day," © 1973; "Guitar Brown," © 1973; "When Lea Jane Sang," © 1976. All songs copyright © by Velvet Apple Music (BMI). All Rights Reserved. Used by permission.

By Dolly Parton: "Together Always," © 1972; "I Will Always Love You," © 1973; "When Someone Wants to Leave," © 1974. All songs copyright © by Velvet Apple Music (BMI). All Rights Reserved. Used by permission.

"The Night That Porter Wagoner Came to Town," by Bobby Braddock and Charlie Williams. Copyright © 1985, Sony-Tree Publishing Co., Inc. and Careers-BMG Music Publishers, Inc. All Rights Reserved. International Copyright Secured. Used by permission of the Publisher.

"Would You Catch a Falling Star?," by Bobby Braddock. Copyright © 1981, Sony-Tree Publishing Co., Inc. and Careers-BMG Music Publishers, Inc. All Rights Reserved. International Copyright Secured. Used by permission of the Publisher.

"Me and the I.R.S.," by Don Scaife, Gladys Scaife, Ronny Scaife, and Phil Thomas. Copyright © 1978, Songs of Polygram International, Inc., Partner Music and Algee Music Corp. All Rights Reserved. Used by permission.

"A Satisfied Mind," by Red Hays and Jack Rhodes. Copyright © 1955, Fort Knox Music, Inc., and Trio Music Co., Inc. Copyright renewed. Used by permission. All Rights Reserved.

"Parton, Wagoner, Stage Reunion," by Edward Morris, May 13, 1989 *Billboard*, © 1989, BPI Communications, used with permission from *Billboard*.

Photograph page 368, © 1992 by Don Putnam.